Sewing Success?

Sewing Success?

Employment, Wages, and Poverty following the End of the Multi-fibre Arrangement

Editors
Gladys Lopez-Acevedo
Raymond Robertson

THE WORLD BANK
Washington, D.C.

1 2 3 4 15 14 13 12

This volume is a product of the staff of The World Bank with external contributions. The findings, interpretations, and conclusions expressed in this volume do not necessarily reflect the views of The World Bank, its Board of Executive Directors, or the governments they represent.

The World Bank does not guarantee the accuracy of the data included in this work. The boundaries, colors, denominations, and other information shown on any map in this work do not imply any judgment on the part of The World Bank concerning the legal status of any territory or the endorsement or acceptance of such boundaries.

ISBN (paper): 978-0-8213-8778-8
ISBN (electronic): 978-0-8213-8973-7
DOI: 10.1596/978-0-8213-8778-8

Cover photo: © Corbis.
Cover design: Naylor Design.

Library of Congress Cataloging-in-Publication Data
Sewing success? : employment, wages and poverty following the end of the multi-fibre arrangement / editors, Gladys Lopez Acevedo, Raymond Robertson.
   p. cm. — (Directions in development)
   Includes bibliographical references.
   ISBN 978-0-8213-8778-8 (alk. paper) — ISBN 978-0-8213-8973-7
1. Textile industry—Developing countries. 2. Import quotas—Developing countries. 3. Developing countries—Economic conditions. I. Lopez Acevedo, Gladys. II. Robertson, Raymond, 1969-
   HD9868.D44S49 2012
   331.7'6770091724—dc23
                                                                    2011045979

Contents

Boxes

Figures

Tables

Acknowledgments

This book was cofunded by the Poverty Reduction and Economic Management Central Unit Network and the research grant RF-P126215-RESE-BBRSB from the World Bank's Research Committee for a global study, "Employment, Wages, and Poverty following the End of the Multifibre Arrangement." The objective of the book was to assess the effect of the post-Multi-fibre Arrangement (MFA) changes in employment and wages—two key determinants of poverty—so that policy makers can maximize the poverty-reducing potential of the post-MFA economic environment. The book covered analysis in nine developing countries. The countries included represent South Asia (Bangladesh, India, Pakistan, and Sri Lanka), Southeast Asia (Cambodia and Vietnam), Latin America and the Caribbean (Honduras and Mexico), and North Africa (Morocco).

The research team was led by Gladys Lopez-Acevedo (Task Team Leader and Senior Economist, Poverty Reduction and Equity Department, [PRMPR]) and Raymond Robertson (Professor, Macalester College; Consultant, PRMPR) under the guidance of Jaime Saavedra (Director, Poverty Reduction and Equity Unit, PRMPR). Members of the team and tasks were as follows: Raymond Robertson wrote chapters 1 and 2 (introduction and framework); Cornelia Staritz (Austrian Research Foundation for International Development [ÖFSE]; Consultant, PRMPR and International Trade Department [PRMTR]) and Stacey Frederick (Center on Globalization, Governance and Competitiveness [CGGC], Duke University; Consultant, PRMPR) wrote chapter 3; Ana Luisa Gouvea Abras (Consultant, PRMPR) wrote chapter 4 on Bangladesh, India, Pakistan, and Vietnam; Elisa Gamberoni (Economist, Gender and Development Department [PRMGE]) wrote chapter 5 on Honduras, Mexico, and Morocco; Yevgeniya Savchenko (Consultant, PRMPR) wrote chapter 6 on Cambodia and Sri Lanka; and Gladys Lopez-Acevedo and Yevgeniya Savchenko wrote chapter 7 (conclusions). Cornelia Staritz (ÖFSE; Consultant, PRMPR and PRMTR) and Stacey Frederick (CGGC, Duke University; Consultant, PRMPR) wrote the nine background global value chain country case studies. The team is grateful to Christopher Humphrey (Consultant, PRMPR) for providing feedback on organization, content, and editing of the chapters and to Michael Alwan for formatting and editing the book. We would like to acknowledge analytical inputs provided by Hong Tan (Consultant, PRMPR), Monica Tinajero (Consultant, PRMPR), Kalpana Mehra (Consultant, PRMPR), and Jimerson Asencio (Consultant, PRMPR). The study would not have been possible without the assistance of and input from local partner institutions and governments. In particular, we gratefully acknowledge the National Statistical Office of Mexico (Instituto Nacional de Estadística y Geografía; INEGI), Abigail Durán, and Adriana Ramirez.

We would like to thank colleagues for their insightful suggestions, in particular Gary S. Fields (Professor, Cornell University), Jose Cuesta (Senior Economist, PRMPR), Sanjay Kathuria (Lead Economist, South Asia Economy Policy and Poverty Sector Unit [SASEP]), Md. Abul Basher (Economist, SASEP, Dhaka Office), Carlos Sobrado (Senior Economist, Poverty Reduction and Equity Unit East Asia and Pacific [PRMEAP]), Julian Latimer Clarke (Trade Economist, East Asia Poverty Reduction and Economic Management Sector Department [EASPR]), Rinku Murgai (Senior Economist, SASEP), and Ulrich Bartsch (SASEP). We are grateful to colleagues from the World Bank for their comments at various stages in the process of developing the concept note and the drafts and presentations of the book. We are grateful to all of them, in particular Jose Guilherme Reis (Lead Economist, Trade Unit, PRMTR), Pierella Paci (Sector Manager, Gender Unit, PRMGE), Gabriela Inchauste (Senior Economist, PRMPR), Hassan Zamman (Lead Economist, PRMPR), Maria Laura Sanchez Puertas (Economist, Social Protection), Reema Nayar (Lead Economist, SAS), Reena Badiani (Young Professional, East Asia and Pacific [EAP]), Andrew Mason (Lead Economist, East Asia Poverty Reduction and Economic Management Sector Department

[EASPR]), Louise Fox (Lead Economist, Africa Public Sector Reform and Capacity Department [AFTPR]), Paolo Verme (Senior Economist, Social and Economic Development Group [MNSED]), Maurice Kugler (Senior Economist, Latin America and Caribbean Poverty Gender and Equity Group [LCSPP]), and Ambar Narayan (Senior Economist, PRMPR). The research also benefited from presentations of draft papers at Bank workshops in January, April, and May 2011. We gratefully acknowledge the insightful comments and suggestions of participants at these workshops.

About the Authors

Gladys Lopez-Acevedo is a Senior Economist in the World Bank Poverty Reduction and Equity Unit. Her research interests include poverty, labor markets, and evaluation. She is a fellow in the International Initiative for Impact Evaluation and has published extensively in the areas of poverty, labor markets, and evaluation in academic and policy journals. Prior to joining the Bank, she served as Senior Adviser to the Vice Minister of Finance and as Director in the Economic Deregulation Unit in the Government in Mexico. She was an Associate Professor at the Instituto Tecnologico Autonomo de Mexico (ITAM). She holds a B.A. in Economics from ITAM and a Ph.D. in Economics from the University of Virginia.

Raymond Robertson is Professor of Economics at Macalester College. His research has been published in the *American Economic Review*, the *Review of Economics and Statistics*, the *Journal of International Economics*, and others. He is a nonresident fellow at the Center for Global Development, a member of the State Department's Advisory Committee on International Economic Policy (ACIEP), and a member of the U.S. Department of Labor National Advisory Committee for Labor Provisions of Free Trade Agreements. He received his Ph.D. from the University of Texas after spending a year in Mexico as a Fulbright Scholar.

Stacey Frederick is a research scientist at Duke University's Center on Globalization, Governance and Competitiveness (CGGC). She received her B.S. degree in Textile Management and her Ph.D. in Textile Technology Management at North Carolina State University. The core of her research agenda revolves around using value chain analysis to explore a variety of topics. Within the textile and apparel industry, her work began with local economic development projects to enhance the competitiveness of the U.S. textile industry. Recently, she has expanded her research to identifying economic and social upgrading opportunities in the global apparel industry.

Elisa Gamberoni is an Economist in the Gender and Development Unit at the World Bank. Prior to assuming this post, she was Policy Officer in the World Bank Geneva Office, where she focused on issues related to international trade and labor markets. Prior to joining the World Bank, she was research assistant for the Swiss National Center of Competence and Research. She obtained her Ph.D. in International Relations (with the specialization in International Economics) from the Graduate Institute of International and Development Studies (HEID) in 2009; she holds an M.A. in International Relations from HEID.

Ana Luisa Gouvea Abras is a Consultant at the World Bank. Before joining the World Bank, she completed her Ph.D. in Economics at the University of Maryland College Park, where she worked as research assistant in applied macroeconomics and labor topics. Before moving to the United States, she worked as a Consultant for the Secretariat of Economic Monitoring at the Ministry of Planning in Brazil. She obtained B.A. and M.A. degrees in Brazil from the Universidade Federal de Minas Gerais and the University of Sao Paulo, respectively.

Yevgeniya Savchenko is a Consultant in the Poverty Reduction and Equity Unit at the World Bank. She works on issues related to skills development, labor markets, and trade. Prior to joining the group, she worked on skills development, labor markets, and competitiveness issues in the South Asia Region, the Europe and Central Asia Region, and the World Bank Institute. She holds an M.S. in Economics from the University of Illinois at Urbana-Champaign (UIUC) and is a Ph.D. Candidate in Economics at Georgetown University in Washington, DC.

Cornelia Staritz is an Economist and works at the Austrian Research Foundation for International Development (ÖFSE) in Vienna. She received her M.A's in Economics and Commerce at the Vienna University of Economics and Business and her Ph.D. in Economics at the New School for Social Research in New York. She worked previously at the Vienna University of Economics and Business and at the International Trade Department of the World Bank. Her research and teaching focus on economic development, international macroeconomics, international trade, global value chains, and economic and social upgrading in the context of global value chains.

Abbreviations

ACFTA	ASEAN-China Free Trade Agreement
ACP	African, Caribbean, and the Pacific
AFL-CIO	American Federation of Labor and Congress of Industrial Organizations
AFTPR	Africa Public Sector Reform and Capacity
AGOA	Africa Growth and Opportunity Act
ASEAN	Association of South East Asian Nations
ASI	Annual Survey of Industries
ATC	Agreement on Textiles and Clothing
BGMEA	Bangladesh Garment Manufacturers and Exporters Association
BIMSTEC	Bay of Bengal Initiative for Multi-Sectoral Economic Cooperation
BOI	Board of Investors
CAFTA	Central American Free Trade Agreement
CASDEC	Cambodia Skills Development Center
CBI	Caribbean Basin Initiative
CBTPA	U.S.-Caribbean Basin Trade Partnership Act
CEE	Central and Eastern European
CGTC	Cambodia Garment Training Center
CMEA	Council for Mutual Economic Assistance

CMI	Census of Manufacturing Industries
CMT	cut-make-trim
CSES	Cambodia Socio-Economic Survey
CSO	Central Statistical Organization
DOT	Bangladesh Department of Textiles
DR-CAFTA	Dominican Republic–Central America Free Trade Agreement
EAC	East African Community
EAP	East Asia and Pacific
EASPR	East Asia Poverty Reduction and Economic Management Sector Department
EBA	Everything but Arms
ECOWAS	Economic Community of West African States
EDI	Electronic Data Interchange
EIA	Mexico Annual Industry Survey (Encuesta Industrial Annual)
EIM	Monthly Industrial Survey (Encuesta Industrial Mensual)
ENEU	National Survey of Urban Employment (Encuesta Nacional de Empleo Urbano)
EPAs	economic partnership agreements
EPHPM	Encuesta Permanente de Hogares de Propósitos Múltiples
EPZs	export processing zones
EU-15	the 15 member states of the European Union (EU) as of December 31, 2003, before the new member states joined the EU: Austria, Belgium, Denmark, Finland, France, Germany, Greece, Ireland, Italy, Luxembourg, the Netherlands, Portugal, Spain, Sweden, and the United Kingdom
FDI	foreign direct investment
FIAS	Foreign Investment Advisory Services
FIP	Factory Improvement Program
FOB	free on board
FTA	free trade agreement
GALs	guaranteed access levels
GATT	General Agreement on Tariffs and Trade
GCEC	Greater Colombo Economic Commission
GDP	gross domestic product
GMAC	Garment Manufacturers' Association in Cambodia

GSP	Generalized System of Preferences
GTZ	German Technical Corporation
GVCs	global value chains
HHI	Herfindahl-Hirschman Index
HIES	Household Income and Expenditure Survey
HS	Harmonized Commodity Description and Coding System
HTS	Harmonized Tariff Schedule of the United States
IFC	International Finance Corporation
IIWD	inter-industry wage differential
ILBFTA	Indo–Sri Lanka Bilateral Free Trade Agreement
ILO	International Labour Organization
IMMEX	Maquiladora Manufacturing and Export Services (Industria Manufacturera, Maquiladora y de Servicios de Exportación)
INEGI	National Statistical Office (Instituto Nacional de Estadística y Geografía)
IPC	Instituto Politécnico Centroamericano
ISES	India Socio-Economic Surveys
JAAF	Joint Apparel Association Forum
LCSPP	Latin America and Caribbean Poverty Gender and Equity Group
L/C	letters of credit
LDCs	least developed countries
LFS	labor force survey
LICs	low-income countries
MENA-4	Tunisia, Morocco, Arab Republic of Egypt, and Jordan
MFA	Multi-fibre Arrangement
MFA/ATC	Multi-fibre Arrangement/Agreement on Textiles and Clothing
MFN	most favored nation
MNSED	Middle East and North Africa Social and Economic Development Group
MMF	man-made fibers
NAFTA	North American Free Trade Agreement
NCC	National Coordination Council
NDP	National Development Plan
NGO	nongovernmental organization
NIEs	newly industrialized economies
NSSO	National Sample Survey Organization

OBM	original brand manufacturing
ODM	original design manufacturing
OEM	original equipment manufacturing
OPT	Outward Processing Trade
PITEX	Temporary Importation Program to Produce Articles for Exportation (*Programa de Importación Temporal para Producir Artículos de Exportación*)
PMAP	Post-MFA Action Program
PPP	purchasing power parity
PRMEAP	Poverty Reduction and Equity Unit East Asia and Pacific
PRMGE	Gender and Development Department
PRMPR	Poverty Reduction and Equity Department
PRMTR	International Trade Department
PSLM	Pakistan Social and Living Standards Measurement
ROO	rules of origin
SAARC	South Asian Association for Regional Cooperation
SADC	Southern African Development Community
SAFTA	South Asian Free Trade Agreement
SAPTA	South Asian Preferential Trading Agreement
SAR	special administrative region
SAS	South Asia Sector
SASEP	South Asia Economy Policy and Poverty Sector Unit
SLAEA	Sri Lanka Apparel Exporters Association
SMEs	small and medium enterprises
SMI	Survey of Manufacturing Industries
SOEs	state-owned enterprises
SSA	Sub-Saharan African
T&G	textile and garment
TCF	third country fabric
TSUS	Tariff Schedules of the United States
TUFS	Technology Upgradation Fund Scheme
UN Comtrade	United Nations Commodity Trade Statistics Database
UNDP	United Nations Development Programme
USAID	United States Agency for International Development
USAS	United Students against Sweatshops
USITC	U.S. International Trade Commission
VHLSS	Vietnam Household Living Standards Survey

WMS	Welfare Monitoring Survey
WRAP	Worldwide Responsible Accredited Production
WRC	Worker Rights Consortium
WTO	World Trade Organization

Dollar amounts are in U.S. dollars unless otherwise specified.

Overview

Gladys Lopez-Acevedo and Raymond Robertson

The global textile and apparel sector is critically important as an early phase in industrialization for many developing countries and as a provider of employment opportunities to thousands of low-income workers, many of them women. At the same time, the sector has been strongly shaped by international trade policy and regulations, notably the Multi-fibre Arrangement (MFA) and the Agreement on Textiles and Clothing (ATC). The end of the MFA/ATC on January 1, 2005, was expected to have a major impact on the apparel sector and apparel workers in many developing countries, and in turn on the prospects for future employment, wages, and poverty reduction.

The goal of this book is to explore how the lifting of the MFA/ATC quotas has affected nine countries—Bangladesh, Cambodia, Honduras, India, Mexico, Morocco, Pakistan, Sri Lanka, and Vietnam—with the broader aim of better understanding the links between globalization and poverty in the developing world. Analyzing how employment, wage premiums, and the structure of the apparel industry have changed after the MFA/ATC can generate important lessons for policy makers for economic development and poverty reduction.

The end of the MFA was followed by rising apparel exports, falling prices, and a reallocation of production and employment between countries. Since China was expected to be, and certainly was, a clear winner in the post-MFA world, much of the world's attention has been focused on that country. But the story of what happened in the rest of the developing countries in terms of exports, wages, and employment has yet to be told. One main objective of this book is to take a first step in telling that story by focusing on some of the other leading apparel producers.

This book uses in-depth country case studies as the broad methodological approach. In-depth country studies are important because countries are idiosyncratic: differences in regulatory context, history, location, trade relationships, and policies shape both the apparel sector and how the apparel sector changed after the end of the MFA. In-depth country studies place broader empirical work in context and strengthen the conclusions.

The countries in this book were chosen because they represent the diversity of global apparel production, including differences across regions, income levels, trade relationships, and policies. The countries occupy different places in the global value chain that now characterizes apparel production. Not surprisingly, the countries studied in this book represent the diversity of post-MFA experiences. While some large Asian apparel exporter countries managed to increase production, apparel exports and employment fell in other countries. Apparel employment rose in Bangladesh, India, Pakistan, and Vietnam between 2004 and 2008. In Honduras, Mexico, Morocco, and Sri Lanka, however, apparel employment fell. Some of the change in employment is explained by upward movement through the apparel value chain, as in Sri Lanka. Other countries remained suppliers of low-end products with almost no involvement in the other stages of production.

This book highlights four key findings.

The first is that employment and export patterns after the MFA/ATC did not necessarily match predictions. This book shows that only about a third of the variation in cross-country changes in exports is explained by wage differences. While wage differences explain some of the production shifts, domestic policies targeting the apparel sector, ownership type, and functional upgrading of the industry also played an important role. Countries that gained the most—including Bangladesh, India, Pakistan, and Vietnam—implemented proactive policies specific to the apparel industry. This finding points to the importance of performing in-depth country studies to describe factors that help explain the changes in wages and employment that occurred after the end of the MFA.

Second, changes in exports are usually, but not always, good indicators of what happens to wages and employment. This fact is especially important for policy because it shows that simply using exports as a metric of "success" in terms of helping the poor is not sufficient. While rising apparel exports correlated with rising wages and employment in the large Asian countries, rising exports coincided with falling employment in Sri Lanka. In some cases, rising global competition (and the resulting fall in employment) may provide the impetus to shift toward higher-valued production and services. For example, Mexico had falling apparel exports and employment but seems to have been able to absorb these workers into other industries. But when countries are not at the point where shifting into higher-valued goods and services is possible, rising competition can generate real losses. This seems to be the case in Honduras, where falling apparel exports correlated with falling wages and employment. The implication is that facilitating the movement into higher-value economic areas in the face of rising global competition is important.

Third, this book identifies the specific ways that changes in the global apparel market affected worker earnings, thus helping to explain impacts on poverty. This book finds that wage premiums change in predictable ways: rising in most countries that proactively adapted to the MFA phaseout and expanded their market shares, and falling in countries that failed to respond in a timely fashion to the changing environment. This finding means that not only are employment opportunities generally lost when exports contract and gained when exports expand, but one of the most important features that made these "good" jobs—the wage premiums—also fall or rise. This change represents a double impact for workers in developing countries.

Fourth, in terms of policies, the countries that had larger increases in apparel exports were those that promoted apparel sector upgrading; those that did not promote upgrading had smaller increases or even falling exports. Although this finding may imply that upgrading facilitates competitiveness, upgrading does not always correspond to increases in employment or wages. In some cases, the opposite might be true (as in Sri Lanka, where upgrading coincided with employment decline, particularly for women). Apparel industries in other countries (such as Bangladesh and Cambodia) were able to expand employment while staying at lower levels of the value chain. In Honduras, where neither proactive upgrading nor workforce development programs were present, increased competition and subsequent production shifts represented real losses to workers. Having a vision for the evolution of the textile and apparel sector that incorporates developing worker skills is important. A further notable finding is that in an industry driven by reputation-sensitive buyers in importing countries, concern for labor conditions and worker treatment may be not only a labor rights issue but also a competitive advantage, as the case of Cambodia suggests.

This book takes an important step toward understanding how workers fared after an important policy change—the end of the MFA/ATC—and as such does not claim to be definitive. Addressing some of the limitations of this book would generate valuable extensions of the current work. For example, this book describes how apparel workers fared after the end of the MFA, but it does not claim to identify strong causal relationships. More accurate identification of causal relationships would require pooling much more data across countries than are currently available. Pooling such data would be a natural and valuable extension. Second, the welfare analysis in this book is mainly focused on wages and employment. Studying worker flows into and out of the apparel sector would increase our understanding of some of the important welfare effects of policy reforms, as well as reveal important lessons about the underlying dynamics of labor markets in developing countries. Third, the financial crisis of 2009 was a severe disruption to global trade. The crisis was occurring while research for this book was under way, and therefore this book does not include any of the potentially long-run effects of the crisis. Understanding which effects of the crisis were permanent or transitory, especially with regards to global value chains, would help policy makers design appropriate safety nets to catch workers who might otherwise slip through the cracks in the increasingly global economic order.

PART 1

Employment, Wages, and Poverty after the End of the MFA

CHAPTER 1

Introduction

Raymond Robertson

Reducing poverty in developing countries is a critical goal of policy makers and international development institutions. Understanding the links between globalization (especially policies shaping globalization) and poverty is a cornerstone of effective policy. The goal of this book is to take the first step toward understanding how a major policy change—the end of the Multi-fibre Arrangement (MFA)—affected poverty by describing the evolution of two key determinants of poverty—employment and wages—in nine developing countries. Describing how each country reacted to the change in policy and the subsequent changes in employment and wages provides important lessons for policy makers seeking to maximize the poverty-reducing potential of the post-MFA economic environment.

Academics and analysts may disagree about some of the drivers of poverty alleviation, but growth—defined as a sustained increase in gross domestic product (GDP) per capita—is unquestionably one of the "necessary" conditions. Few if any countries manage to reduce poverty without

The author of this chapter is grateful for comments provided by Gladys Lopez-Acevedo, Ana Luisa Gouvea Abras, Yevgeniya Savchenko, and Cornelia Staritz. The poverty tables (1.3a and 1.3b) were compiled by Ana Luisa Gouvea Abras.

growth. The link between globalization and growth is hotly debated. Frankel and Romer (1999), Noguer and Siscart (2005), and others have found that engagement in the global economy is correlated with, and probably leads to, higher national per capita income. One reason that engagement in the global economy is important is that firms that are engaged in the global economy through exports and foreign direct investment (FDI) are more likely to innovate (Alvarez and Robertson 2004), pay higher wages (Lipsey and Sjoholm 2004; Oladi, Gilbert, and Beladi 2011), and increase labor demand.

But growth alone is not enough. GDP per capita increases when employment or wages increase. Poverty falls if employment or wages increase for the people at the lower end of the income distribution. This is why Loayza and Raddatz (2006) suggest that the *composition* of growth matters for poverty reduction. They find that countries that experience growth in labor-intensive sectors are more likely to reduce poverty. Labor-intensive sectors not only provide employment, but also often hire workers from the lower end of the wage distribution.

Apparel as a Key Sector

Apparel is perhaps the most prominent labor-intensive globalized sector in many developing countries. Not surprisingly, therefore, apparel production has been the source of much controversy. Critics of apparel production in developing countries point out (correctly) that total earnings are often below average and that working conditions are often quite poor, with higher-than-average hours and poor conditions in factories.

Average wages are low in apparel, but one reason for this is that apparel workers come from the bottom of the wage distribution within the domestic labor market—predominantly young, less educated women. Robertson et al. (2009) compile five country studies that compare globalization, wages, and working conditions across industries and find that, controlling for age, education, and the fact that women are paid less than other workers throughout the economy, apparel workers earn a sector-specific premium over the economywide average. Furthermore, they find that working conditions are better in globally engaged industries. In other words, apparel jobs are often "good" jobs, relative to domestic alternatives. These wage premiums directly contribute to poverty reduction. De Hoyos, Bussolo, and Núñez (2008) focus on Honduras and find that poverty would have been 1.5 percentage points higher had the assembly sector (*maquilas*), which is heavily concentrated in apparel and textiles, not existed.

Yamagata (2006) finds a similar result for Cambodia: prior to the end of the quota system, entry-level workers in Cambodia's apparel factories earned wages well above the poverty line.

The relatively high concentration of women is another reason apparel is an important sector when considering the link between globalization and poverty.[1] The focus on women and women's wages is especially important given that increasing female income improves survival rates for girls (Qian 2008). Furthermore, paid employment opportunities for women are particularly important for poverty reduction because, all else being equal, women are more likely to be poor than men. When women work, fertility rates fall and their talent contributes to GDP, generating efficiency gains and higher per capita growth rates. These effects are widely recognized and help explain why the third and fifth United Nations Millennium Development Goals[2] involve improving the status of women.

The fact that apparel offers employment opportunities for lower-wage workers provides a link between apparel and poverty at the individual ("micro") level. But there is a link at the "macro" level as well. When a country begins to engage in the global economy, one of the first steps often involves an expansion of the apparel sector. Great Britain, Japan, the United States, and other counties all had an "apparel phase" of their development. Apparel often acts as a gateway into manufacturing for countries and workers whose alternatives might be in agriculture, the informal sector, or low-productivity service work.

This sector is an important first step to industrialization for developing countries for several reasons. First, start-up costs are relatively low. Firms can open with relatively small capital investments (sewing machines) and relatively low training costs. The production is relatively simple and material costs can be low. These low start-up costs encourage entry. Second, there are clear links with the domestic and global economy in the apparel sector. Nearly 70 percent of apparel exports come from low-income countries. The industry is characterized by value chains that involve international division of stages of production (Gereffi and Frederick 2010; Staritz 2011). In the language of economics, the production is internationally fragmented. Third, the fragmentation of production creates opportunities for moving up the value chain. Countries can enter at the simplest stages and gain experience that helps them move into more complicated processes farther up the value chain. These higher stages usually involve more skill and capital, and they may be associated with higher productivity and higher wages.

The Importance of the MFA/ATC

Few industries have been as affected by global regulations as the apparel industry. The MFA was implemented in 1974 by industrial countries outside the normal rules of the General Agreement on Tariffs and Trade (GATT). The goal was to help industrial countries adjust to the rising production capacity of the developing countries. Under this arrangement, textile and clothing quotas were negotiated bilaterally. On January 1, 1995, the MFA was replaced by the Agreement on Textiles and Clothing (ATC), which brought the MFA under the rules of the World Trade Organization (WTO).[3] As a transitional instrument, the ATC established a time frame to eliminate quotas and integrate clothing and textiles into the 1994 rules of the GATT.

The MFA restricted trade, but it also created opportunities for countries that might not otherwise have developed their apparel sector. In an important paper, Evans and Harrigan (2005) document how the MFA quotas shifted U.S. apparel imports away from Asia toward Mexico and the Caribbean. The MFA preferences of the European Union (EU) for Bangladesh created the incentive to develop the apparel industry there, thus laying the foundation for future increases in apparel production. For other countries, such as China, the limits created the incentive to establish production in other developing countries that were not filling their quotas. In this way, the MFA had very significant effects on the pattern of global apparel production.

Removing these quotas through the ATC had important welfare effects in importing countries (Harrigan and Barrows 2009) and meant that global apparel production could be allocated according to market incentives rather than regulation. Most people consider labor costs to be the most important market incentive, but there are many other relevant factors. For example, access to markets, distance, ease of establishing a factory, infrastructure (such as the cost of electricity or access to water), and government regulation can all affect global production patterns once the system of quotas has ended.

Choosing the Focus Countries

One of the clear winners in the post-MFA environment is China. China's significant export growth in apparel and other sectors has perhaps diverted attention away from other apparel producers. This book seeks to fill that gap by focusing on important apparel producers that have received relatively less attention and yet may exhibit important lessons for policy makers. The cross-country analyses in the following chapters give an overview of the structure, development, and upgrading experiences of the apparel industries after the MFA and assess the impact of the MFA phaseout on employment and wages in nine developing countries. The countries included represent South Asia (Bangladesh, India, Pakistan, and Sri Lanka); Southeast Asia (Cambodia and Vietnam); Latin America and the Caribbean (Honduras and Mexico); and North Africa (Morocco).

The choice of these countries followed four criteria. The book was the significance of apparel in the overall economy. We selected countries in which apparel exports account for an important share of total merchandise exports and apparel production employment accounts for a significant share of formal sector employment. In most countries, this employment also involved a high share of female employment.

The second criterion was regional coverage. The book covers important apparel producer countries from all regions. There is an evident focus on Asia, which is justified by the region being the main "winner" after the MFA with regard to apparel export market share, but at the same time showing quite distinct interactions of policy, exports, and employment.

The third criterion was position in the global value chain. To be able to draw broader conclusions, the book focuses on countries that have different positions within the global apparel industry. Three dimensions are particularly important: the functions performed (simple assembly, full production but not design, or design with manufacturing); the extent of backward links; and ownership structure (local versus foreign ownership).

Finally, as a matter of practicality, we also had to consider data availability. The book uses household survey and enterprise or establishment survey data to assess the implications of the MFA phaseout for countries, firms, and workers. Such an analysis requires surveys over a certain time period. The data are analyzed using a comparable methodology in order to facilitate comparisons across countries, and therefore the data had to be roughly comparable as well.

Despite the fact that the nine countries are all considered "developing," they showed considerable variation in export change after the end of the MFA/ATC. Honduras and Mexico both experienced a decline in total apparel exports after the MFA. Five other countries—Bangladesh, India, Morocco, Pakistan, and Sri Lanka—experienced growing apparel exports, but less than might be expected on the basis of GDP per capita (or wages) alone. The remaining two countries—Cambodia and Vietnam—experienced higher-than-expected growth in their apparel exports. To identify some of the possible reasons exports expanded in some countries and fell in others, one must examine the structure of the apparel industry both globally and within each of the study countries.

The Link between Apparel and Poverty (Motivating the Choice of Variables)

The main focus of this book is to examine how apparel exports, wages, and employment changed after the MFA/ATC, with a particular focus on workers in poverty. The apparel sector has traditionally been one of the first steps for countries making the transition from agriculture to manufacturing (especially for women). Therefore, the sector's evolution has important ramifications for the entire economy and a country's potential to develop and reduce poverty.

Cross-country comparisons indicate that the apparel industry offers opportunities for individuals to improve their working conditions and gain higher returns from their education. On average, apparel workers have more education than do agricultural workers but levels similar to those of workers in the rest of the economy (table 1.1) (although within apparel, women tend to have less education than men). Apparel wages usually lie above the wages for agricultural jobs and are comparable to those in the service sector (table 1.2). The evidence thus suggests that moving from agriculture into apparel jobs is a channel for social upgrading.

Moreover, the apparel sector seems to be associated with lower poverty than other low-skilled sectors (table 1.2; tables 1.3a and 1.3b). The

Table 1.1   Years of Education by Sector

Country	Year	Average years of education (All workers)	Average years of education of female workers		
			Apparel	Agriculture	Services (sales)
Bangladesh	2009	4.4	5.4	1.0	2.8
Cambodia	2008	6.1	5.8	4.6	6.2
Honduras	2007	6.9	7.4	4.7	7.2
India	2007	5.9	5.8	2.3	5.2
Pakistan	2008	5.0	3.6	0.7	4.3
Sri Lanka	2008	8.8	10.2	7.4	9.2
Vietnam	2008	8.7	8.7	7.6	8.4

Source: Household and labor force surveys, several years.
Note: Samples restricted to persons 10–69 years old.

Table 1.2   Average Log Wages by Sector

Country	Year	All sectors	Apparel	Agriculture	Services (sales)
Bangladesh	2009	7.9	9.3	5.4	8.9
Cambodia	2008	12.5	12.5	11.7	12.5
Honduras	2007	8.0	8.3	7.1	8.1
India	2007	6.4	6.4	5.9	6.5
Pakistan	2008	10.8	10.6	10.5	10.7
Sri Lanka	2008	8.9	8.9	8.7	8.9
Vietnam	2008	7.4	7.0	6.8	7.2

Source: Household and labor force surveys, several years.
Note: Log wage values are in domestic currency and therefore are only comparable within countries.

Table 1.3a   Percentage of Working Poor by Sector

Country	Year	All sectors	Apparel	Agriculture	Services (sales)
Bangladesh	2000	43	27	63	33
	2005	37	35	29	57
Cambodia	2004	34	10	43	35
	2007	23	8	31	32
Honduras	2003	12	2	27	8
	2007	15	2	37	10
India	2005	26	23	28	31
Pakistan	2002	20	21	34	30
	2005	13	5	23	6
Sri Lanka	2002	9	8	10	9
	2007	4	2	5	4

Source: Household and labor force surveys, several years.
Note: Percentages of workers within each sector who earn less than the established national poverty threshold. Samples restricted to persons 10–69 years old.

Table 1.3b   Poverty Rates by Sector

Percent, using PPP measure

Country	Year	National poverty rate	Apparel	Agriculture	Services (sales)
Bangladesh	2000	58	39	72	37
	2005	50	45	43	57
Cambodia	2004	40	32	74	61
	2007	28	25	55	48
Honduras	2003	18	6	27	8
	2007	23	3	43	12
India	2005	42	49	63	60
Pakistan	2002	36	36	58	49
	2005	23	17	44	14
Sri Lanka	2002	14	16	24	20
	2007	7	11	21	17

Source: Household and labor force surveys, several years.
Note: Percentages are the share of workers within each sector that earn less than $1 (purchasing power parity, PPP) per day. Samples restricted to persons 10–69 years old.

14   Sewing Success?

share of apparel workers below the poverty threshold (measured in two different ways—$1 a day or working poor) gives an idea of the relative position of apparel in terms of poverty. Apparel workers enjoy relatively good labor earnings compared to workers in agriculture or even in services. The difference in average wages between these sectors suggests that an expanding apparel sector is likely to move workers out of poverty by creating opportunities for workers to leave services or agriculture. Conversely, if a decline in exports is followed by relocation of workers from apparel into other labor-intensive sectors such as agriculture, those workers are at risk of falling into poverty.

The apparel sector is also an important source of economic opportunity for women. The female share of workers in apparel is substantial. Apart from Bangladesh, India, and Pakistan, women constitute at least two-thirds of overall employment in apparel. Women still make up higher shares of employment within apparel (compared to other sectors) in countries with low female labor force participation in the rest of the economy, such as Bangladesh and Pakistan. Hence, understanding the way the apparel industry evolves has significant implications for the development of women and for poverty reduction because of the high impact of women's wage-earning opportunities.

Structure of the Book

One goal of the book is to use the best available data to generate relevant stylized facts on how prospects for workers may have changed after the end of the MFA/ATC. To provide structure for the empirical analysis, chapter 2 lays out a theoretical foundation for the empirical methodology applied in chapters 4–6. Chapter 2 shows how the MFA phaseout should affect both employment and wages and how the short-run and long-run wage effects will differ. The framework motivates the focus on employment and wages and describes an approach to decompose wages and thereby identify the components of wages that are important in lifting workers from poverty. The chapter also provides an overview of the data sources used in chapters 4–6.

Chapter 3 describes the complexity of modern apparel production, with a particular focus on global value chains. Each of the study countries has a unique place in global apparel production, and the production structure in each country has reacted differently to changes brought about by the end of the MFA/ATC. One of the key lessons from chapter 3 is that changes within the apparel sector involve various degrees of upgrading, defined as moving up the value chain. The governments of some countries were more active than others in developing proactive policies to facilitate and encourage upgrading in the apparel industry, and these policies largely correspond with evidence of successful upgrading. Understanding changes within the industry is critical for understanding the subsequent changes in exports and the effects on workers.

Chapters 4–6 analyze household, labor force, firm-level, and industry data for the nine study countries. Chapter 4 focuses on the "large" Asian countries (Bangladesh, India, Pakistan, and Vietnam). The large apparel workforce is in some cases a function of country size and history of apparel production (Bangladesh and India), but it is also a function of rapid recent growth of the apparel sector (Vietnam). Chapter 5 examines countries that faced serious challenges with the MFA phaseout (Honduras, Mexico, and Morocco). These countries were largely focused on a single market, prior to the end of the MFA/ATC. The market focus was primarily the result of proximity—Latin American countries focused on the U.S. market, and Morocco focused on Europe. Chapter 6 considers smaller Asian countries (Cambodia and Sri Lanka). These two are similar in that they both managed to increase exports, but they took very different approaches in terms of policy. Chapter 7 concludes and presents directions for future work.

Finally, part 2 provides an analysis of the development of the apparel industries and policies in the context of the MFA phaseout in the nine case study countries examined in this book. The focus is therefore not specifically on employment and wages but more generally on the structure of the apparel industries in these countries. The nine chapters in part 2 are structured in the same way. The first part discusses the development of the apparel industry with a focus on developments related to the MFA phaseout and how the industry has fared post-MFA. The second part gives an overview of the structure of the apparel industry ordered along the different dimensions of upgrading identified in part 1. The third part discusses trade regulations with a focus on preferential market access toward the main end markets, particularly of the United States and the EU-15, and regional markets as well as proactive polices in the context of the MFA phaseout.

Notes

1. Several recent papers have focused on the gender dimensions of globalization, including Rendall (2010); Aguayo-Tellez, Airola, and Juhn (2010); Oostendorp (2009); Özler (2000, 2001); and Sauré and Zoabi (2009).

2. The United Nations established eight Millennium Development Goals for 2015. The third promotes gender equality and female empowerment, while the fifth focuses on maternal care.

3. In this book, we will use the MFA and the MFA/ATC interchangeably.

References

Aguayo-Tellez, Ernesto, Jim Airola, and Chinhui Juhn. 2010. "Did Trade Liberalization Help Women? The Case of Mexico in the 1990s." Working Paper 16195, National Bureau of Economic Research, Cambridge, MA.

Alvarez, Roberto, and Raymond Robertson. 2004. "Exposure to Foreign Markets and Firm-Level Innovation: Evidence from Chile and Mexico." *Journal of International Trade and Economic Development* 13 (1): 57–87.

de Hoyos, Rafael, Marizio Bussolo, and Oscar Núñez. 2008. "Can Maquila Booms Reduce Poverty? Evidence from Honduras." Policy Research Working Paper 4789, World Bank, Washington, DC.

Evans, Carolyn, and James Harrigan. 2005. "Tight Clothing. How the MFA Affects Asian Apparel Exports." In *International Trade in East Asia, NBER–East Asia Seminar on Economics, Volume 14*, ed. Takatoshi Ito and Andrew K. Rose, 367–90. Chicago: University of Chicago Press.

Frankel, Jeffrey A., and Paul Romer. 1999. "Does Trade Cause Growth?" *American Economic Review* 89 (3): 379–99.

Gereffi, Gary, and Stacy Frederick. 2010. "The Global Apparel Value Chain, Trade, and the Crisis." Policy Research Working Paper 5281, World Bank, Washington, DC.

Harrigan, James, and Geoffrey Barrows. 2009. "Testing the Theory of Trade Policy: Evidence from the Abrupt End of the Multifiber Arrangement." *The Review of Economics and Statistics* 91 (2): 282–94.

Lipsey, Robert E., and Fredrik Sjoholm. 2004. "Foreign Direct Investment, Education, and Wages in Indonesian Manufacturing." *Journal of Development Economics* 73 (1): 415–22.

Loayza, Norman, and Claudio Raddatz. 2006. "The Composition of Growth Matters for Poverty Alleviation." Policy Research Working Paper 4077, World Bank, Washington, DC.

Noguer, Marta, and Marc Siscart. 2005. "Trade Raises Income: A Precise and Robust Result." *Journal of International Economics* 65 (2): 447–60.

Oladi, Reza, John Gilbert, and Hamid Beladi. 2011. "Foreign Direct Investment, Non-traded Goods, and Real Wages." *Pacific Economic Review* 16 (1): 36–41.

Oostendorp, Remco H. 2009. "Globalization and the Gender Wage Gap." *World Bank Economic Review* 23 (1): 141–61.

Özler, Şule. 2000. "Export Orientation and Female Share of Employment: Evidence from Turkey." *World Development* 28 (7): 1239–48.

———. 2001. "Export Led Industrialization and Gender Differences in Job Creation and Destruction: Micro Evidence from the Turkish Manufacturing Sector." Working Paper 116, Economic Research Forum, Cairo.

Qian, Nancy. 2008. "Missing Women and the Price of Tea in China: The Effect of Sex-Specific Earnings on Sex Imbalance." *Quarterly Journal of Economics* 123 (3): 1251–85.

Rendall, Michelle. 2010. "Brain versus Brawn: The Realization of Women's Comparative Advantage." Working Paper 306, Center for Institutions, Policy and Culture in the Development Process, Department of Economics, University of Zurich.

Robertson, Raymond, Drusilla Brown, Gaëlle Pierre, and Laura Sanchez-Puerta, eds. 2009. *Globalization, Wages, and the Quality of Jobs: Five Country Studies.* Washington, DC: World Bank.

Sauré, Philip, and Hosny Zoabi. 2009. "Effects of Trade on Female Labor Force Participation." Working Paper 2009–12, Swiss National Bank, Geneva.

Staritz, Cornelia. 2011. "Making the Cut? Low-Income Countries and the Global Clothing Value Chain in a Post-Quota and Post-Crisis World." World Bank study, World Bank, Washington, DC.

Yamagata, Tatsufumi. 2006. "The Garment Industry in Cambodia: Its Role in Poverty Reduction through Export-Oriented Development." Discussion Paper 62, Institute of Developing Economies, JETRO, Chiba.

CHAPTER 2

Theoretical Foundation and Empirical Approach

Raymond Robertson

This chapter has three main goals. The first is to illustrate how changes in trade policy generally, and the Multi-fibre Arrangement/Agreement on Textiles and Clothing (MFA/ATC) specifically, work their way through the economy to affect workers. This discussion identifies the key variables that will be the focus of the empirical analysis. The second goal is to describe the empirical approach that will be used in the cross-country chapters to generate the stylized facts that describe how workers have fared after the end of the MFA/ATC. The empirical approach combines a comprehensive overview of the industry (chapter 3) and quantitative analysis (chapters 4–6). The final goal is to describe the data used in chapters 4–6.

Modeling Global Apparel Production Decisions

The structure of modern apparel production is increasingly separated into stages that are then completed in different countries. Design may take place in Milan, textile weaving in Japan, and finally cutting and assembly

The author of this chapter is grateful for comments provided by Gladys Lopez-Acevedo and Cornelia Staritz. The data description (table 2.1) was provided by Yevgeniya Savchenko.

in labor-abundant countries. This structure, commonly known as a "value chain," is largely driven by buyers (large consumer-oriented corporations) who seek to maximize profits by allocating their purchases, and therefore production, across apparel-producing countries. These purchases are counted as exports from apparel-producing countries in official statistics.

Given the importance of buyers in global production chains, one way to begin thinking about changes in global apparel production is to start with a representative buyer's goal of maximizing profits. Buyers know their consumers, and we assume that they have a predetermined quantity they wish to produce based on current market conditions. These market conditions can be described with a downward-sloping demand function by which buyers can increase the quantity they sell only by dropping prices. Buyers then decide where this quantity will be produced.

To illustrate the buyer's problem more formally, we begin with a simple profit maximization problem. For the sake of simplicity, we assume that buyers are selling a homogeneous good (of constant quality, but we can relax this standard later) at a price that is determined in the final goods market (and therefore does not depend on where the product is produced). In the first stage, buyers will pick an optimal quantity to sell on the basis of average production costs and current market conditions. Once they have decided how much they want to sell, the next question they face is where to source this production.

In this case, we model this decision as a choice between apparel-producing countries. Country differences translate into differences in production costs. As long as marginal costs are increasing in each country (which is not a very strong assumption, especially if the marginal cost includes risk), it will make sense for buyers to distribute production across many countries. Buyers will pick the production quantity for each country i, q_i, that solves

$$\max \quad \pi = P(Q)q_i - C_i(w,x,q_i). \tag{2.1}$$

In this equation, $P(Q)$ represents the market price (that is here presented as a decreasing function of the sum of production in all source countries $Q = \Sigma q_i$), and $C_i(w,x,q_i)$ represents a cost function. Costs are a function of wages, since apparel is universally considered to be a labor-intensive good, and other factors, x (such as electricity, regulation, shipping, risk, and other factors). Costs are also a function of q_i to capture the possibility of rising marginal costs as production increases.

Buyers evaluate this equation for each country and for the set of all possible countries. When solving across all possible countries, the solution to this problem specifies that the optimal production in a given country, i, q_i^*, is a function of the costs in country i, costs in the other countries, and global demand (represented with the variable d).

$$q_i^* = f(c_i, c_{\sim i}, d),\qquad(2.2)$$

An increase in costs in a given country reduces the production in that country. Likewise, an increase in the costs in other countries, all else being equal, increases the production in country i. An increase in global demand, holding all else constant, increases production in each country.

The MFA was a system of quotas that restricted the amount of imports from a given country. In this framework, a quota could be modeled as an upper bound on exports from country $i, \bar{q}_i$, and in the lower-cost countries, $q_i^* > \bar{q}_i$. In addition to the obvious effect of restricting q_i, this framework also shows that the quota would shift production into other countries with potentially higher costs. That is, for a given total production quantity Q, limiting production from one country would necessarily cause production in other countries to increase. The resulting pattern of production would be inefficient, since actual quantities would differ from optimal quantities.

Changes in Global Apparel Exports after the MFA/ATC

This model suggests that the end of the MFA would have three effects. First, overall production would increase due to the more efficient allocation of production across countries. Second, the increase in supply would be accompanied by a drop in global apparel prices, as producers facing a downward-sloping demand curve P(Q) would have to drop prices to sell more. Third, and possibly most important for this study, the end of the MFA/ATC would allow buyers to shift production to where they consider it to be optimal. Specifically, production would increase in countries for which $q_i^* > q_i$ and fall in countries that had enjoyed the "overflow" of demand due to the quota system. In this model, low-wage countries would export more and high-wage countries would export less because apparel is very labor intensive.

As this model suggests, global production did increase after the MFA ended. The worldwide value of total apparel trade increased from $193.7 billion in 2000 to $335.9 billion in 2008.[1] The total value of apparel exports grew 30.0 percent between 2000 and 2004, and a further 33.5 percent between 2004 and 2008. In addition, there was a noticeable drop in the unit values of apparel, a common proxy for prices, in the United States and Europe.

The model's third prediction also matches the data. The rising global apparel trade and falling unit values were accompanied by a significant shift across countries during 2000–2009; see, in particular, Brambilla, Khandelwal, and Schott (2007) and Gereffi and Frederick (2010).This shift was only partially driven by wage concerns, as can be seen by comparing apparel wages with the change in apparel exports before and after the end of the MFA/ATC (figure 2.1).[2] The clear nonlinear relationship between these two variables suggests that wages were an important consideration when shifting apparel production—low- and high-wage countries tended to increase exports, while exports tended to fall in the

Figure 2.1   Log Change in Global Apparel Exports and Log Apparel Wages

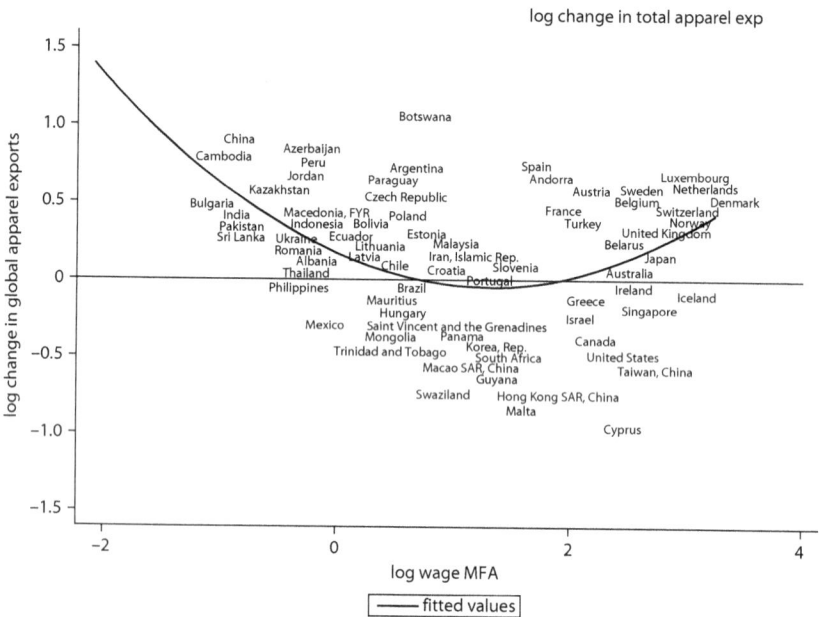

Sources: United Nations Commodity Trade Statistics Database (UN Comtrade). Wage data from Labor Statistics (LABORSTA) database (http://laborsta.ilo.org/).

Note: Size of economy name is proportional to the MFA period world exports. Fitted values of log change in total exports are calculated using quadratic prediction. Apparel export data taken from UN Comtrade show a significant amount of heterogeneity over time. The data are often incomplete, so to maximize the number of economies for which data are available, we take the average of 2000–04 to represent the MFA/ATC period and the average over 2005–08 to represent the post-MFA/ATC period. Data for years after 2008 are available in the UN Comtrade database, but 2009 and 2010, the most recent years available at the time of writing, were strongly affected by the global financial crisis. MFA/ATC = Micro-fibre Arrangement/Agreement on Textiles and Clothing.

middle-wage countries. Wages, however, were definitely not the only factor. In fact, only about 30 percent of the variation in the change in exports after the MFA/ATC is explained by wages. China is a case in point. Many countries with comparable wages (as recorded in the Labor Statistics [LABORSTA] database) had much smaller increases—and many even had decreases—in apparel exports. Evidently, factors besides wages explain the other 70 percent of the variation in the change in exports. For example, if there are sunk costs to exporting, economies of scale, or learning by doing, as have been documented in the literature (Das, Roberts, and Tybout 2007), the fact that the MFA allowed countries to start exporting creates the possibility that experience with exporting apparel may have changed the initial conditions that might have otherwise made apparel production less likely (or even impossible). These possibilities mean that the changes in apparel exports across countries after the MFA are not inevitable. That is, it is possible that some countries benefiting from the MFA quotas (because they did not have the conditions to begin exporting apparel without quota access) retained their exports after the end of the MFA.

Regression techniques can help identify the relative importance of some of these other factors (table 2.1). As indicated in figure 2.1, the square of initial wages shows a quadratic relationship with the change in apparel exports. This relationship goes away when the sample is restricted to just the low-wage countries in table 2.1, columns 3 and 4.[3] Interestingly, whether a country has a free trade agreement (FTA) with the United States has a large and negative correlation with change in apparel exports. One possible explanation for this fact is that the data are cross-sectional. That is, the comparison group does not include the same countries without an FTA. The negative coefficient might be explained at least in part if the United States entered into FTAs with countries that were to fare poorly after the end of the MFA/ATC. In fact, part of the motivation for entering into the Central American Free Trade Agreement (CAFTA) was the fear of losing quotas and the resulting competition from China.

To consider the possibility that some of the additional variation in the change in exports was due to business conditions, we added 13 variables from the Doing Business surveys that included electricity (procedures and time to connect), contracts (procedures and time to enforce), register property, and start a business.[4] The only variable that was consistently significant across various specifications was the time to build a warehouse. Surprisingly, this variable consistently emerged with a small positive coefficient. The bigger point of these results is not that warehouse

Table 2.1 Determinants of Change in Apparel Exports, before versus after the MFA/ATC

	(1)	(2)	(3)	(4)
	Main	FTA	WB	All
Log initial wage MFA	−0.275	−0.254	−0.107	−0.104
	(0.052)**	(0.052)**	(0.044)*	(0.044)*
Log initial wage MFA squared	0.103	0.091	0.043	0.033
	(0.031)**	(0.031)**	(0.032)	(0.033)
FTA		−0.362		−0.176
		(0.179)*		(0.156)
Time required to build a warehouse (days)			0.002	0.001
			(0.000)**	(0.000)**
Expected years of schooling, female			−0.145	−0.143
			(0.031)**	(0.031)**
Fertility rate, total (births per woman)			−0.179	−0.138
			(0.080)*	(0.087)
Literacy rate, youth female (% of females ages 15–24)			0.013	0.015
			(0.006)*	(0.006)*
Constant	0.203	0.251	0.687	0.470
	(0.072)**	(0.074)**	(0.723)	(0.746)
R-squared	0.26	0.30	0.72	0.73
Number of observations	83	83	49	49

Sources: United Nations Commodity Trade Statistics Database (UN Comtrade) (exports), International Labour Organization (ILO) Labor Statistics (LABORSTA) database (wages), Doing Business Indicators, and World Bank Development Indicators.

Note: All regressions performed with ordinary least squares (OLS). The dependent variable is the difference between the average apparel exports to the world over the 2000–04 period and the average apparel exports to the world in 2005–08. All regressions are weighted by the average apparel exports to the world over the 2000–04 period. The FTA variable is a dummy variable equal to 1 for countries with a free trade agreement with the United States. "Time required to build a warehouse (days)" is averaged across all available years in the World Development Indicators Doing Business variables. Other Doing Business Indicators were included in other regressions but had limited, if any, effects on the change in apparel exports. These variables included electricity (procedures and time to connect), contracts (procedures and time to enforce), register property, and start a business. FTA = free trade agreement; WB = World Bank; MFA/ATC = Multi-fibre Arrangement/Agreement on Textiles and Clothing.

** - significant at 5 percent level, *- significant at 10 percent level.

construction time is significant, but that the other 12 variables are not. The resulting implication is that cross-country regressions of business conditions do not take us very far in understanding the changes in apparel exports after the end of the MFA.

Another set of variables that might affect the change in exports relates to conditions faced by female workers. Do, Levchenko, and Raddatz (2011) suggest that the change in exports of female-intensive goods is directly affected by the a priori status of women. To explore this possibility, we tested three variables from the World Development Indicators database: years of schooling for women, fertility rate, and literacy among women aged 15–24. Higher rates of female schooling are correlated with smaller increases in a nation's apparel exports. This is consistent with the argument that countries with less educated women are more attractive for apparel production because wages are lower and more education may not be sufficiently helpful in the production of basic apparel. Fertility's effect on apparel exports is relatively large and negative. Female literacy has a statistically significant positive effect. Overall, these results are surprisingly consistent with the individual-level demographics of apparel workers: young, less educated (but literate), single women.

As the model predicts, there has been a significant reallocation across countries. These changes seem to be correlated with not only wages but with worker characteristics as well. The goal of this book is to describe how workers have fared after the end of the MFA/ATC. The next step, therefore, is to extend the framework to illustrate how these changes might affect workers.

From Quotas to Workers

For better or worse, worker welfare is fundamentally affected by labor markets. Labor markets are characterized by labor supply and labor demand. One of our guiding assumptions is that the reallocation of production across countries will affect country-specific labor markets mainly by affecting labor demand. Ending the MFA could potentially affect labor supply as well, but probably only in the long run. Labor demand is a *derived demand* in the sense that it is derived from production decisions (Hamermesh 1993). The changes resulting from the end of the MFA are clearly the result of production decisions at the firm level, making labor demand the natural link between quotas and workers.

To illustrate how labor demand links quotas and workers, we now move from modeling the buyers' decisions to modeling the hiring decisions of an individual apparel-producing firm. In its simplest neoclassical form, the demand for labor is derived from a representative firm's own profit maximization decisions. Assuming q_i (the same q_i described above) is produced with labor (L) and other factors (K), individual firms will maximize profits by minimizing costs. Firms minimize costs by choosing the optimal level of L and K based on factor prices (wages and, if K represents capital, rental rates). In this model, wages (and rental rates) are assumed to be determined by the relevant countrywide factor market and therefore are generally assumed to be exogenous for individual firms. In other words, wages here are assumed to be determined in *general equilibrium*. We relax this assumption later in this chapter, but for the time being, we assume that the firm takes wages (and rental rates) as given and that the firm solves

$$\min_{K,L} C(w,r) \, subject \, to \, q_i = F(K,L). \tag{2.3}$$

The per-output demand for labor is derived by taking the derivative of the cost function with respect to the wage.

$$\frac{dC(w,r)}{dw} = L^*(w,r) \tag{2.4}$$

The resulting unit labor demand is a positive function of the price of capital, and a negative function of the wage rate. Total labor demand, l, is equal to the unit labor demand times output.[5]

$$l_i = q_i L^*(w,r) \tag{2.5}$$

Holding labor supply constant, the changes in labor demand drive the ultimate effects on workers. While ideally we would measure the changes in worker welfare, welfare is difficult to measure. We can, however, measure income and some other nonincome dimensions of working conditions. Our focus on income is a reasonable one because we are focusing on changes that occur in the labor market, and income is perhaps one of if not the first dimension workers are concerned about when evaluating their labor market experience.

Empirical Strategy

In the framework, income is equal to the time spent working (in terms of hours, weeks, or months) times the wage rate w. When focusing on a group of workers, such as apparel workers or workers in poverty, income can be defined as the product of employment (l), hours (h), and wages (w), or

$$income = y = lhw. \tag{2.6}$$

The change in income can therefore be decomposed into changes in each component, as in

$$\% \ \Delta y = \% \ \Delta l + \% \ \Delta h + \% \ \Delta w. \qquad (2.7)$$

This equation provides a simple framework for our analysis of labor markets because it suggests that the change in income that results from the end of the MFA can be decomposed into three parts that can be analyzed empirically. Changes in employment (% Δl) capture changes *between* apparel and other sectors that are driven directly by changes in labor demand. The changes in hours (% Δh) represents changes *within* the apparel sector. Hours are certainly important, but there are also many other changes within sectors that might affect workers. We therefore use h to represent hours as well as other within-industry changes.[6] Changes in wages (% Δw) represent changes in wage levels, and we broaden this concept to include changes in working conditions. Working conditions are often considered to be a form of worker compensation. We discuss each component below in turn.

Changes in Employment (% Δl)

The first step in understanding the employment effects of the end of the MFA/ATC is to analyze changes in employment in the apparel sector within each country (relative to other sectors). The simple framework above shows that an increase in the relative demand for apparel exports should induce a shift in employment toward apparel. In other words, holding technology (broadly defined) constant, there should be a positive relationship between changes in apparel exports and changes in apparel employment (which, with high-frequency data, can be estimated directly) relative to other sectors within the economy because labor demand is derived from production.

Sector-specific employment is preferred to economywide employment measures, like the unemployment rate. Helpman, Itskhoki, and Redding (2010), one study in a growing recent literature on trade and labor market frictions, show that the predictions of trade liberalization (or a trade shock) on unemployment are ambiguous. Since unemployment is generally driven by economywide factors, such as business cycles, historically, globalization has received relatively little weight. In particular, apparel is a significant employer of women in many countries but may not constitute an unusually high share of overall employment. As a result, focusing on the overall employment impact (such as the unemployment rate) of the MFA might not be as productive as focusing on the apparel industry directly.

The shift between sectors in employment is especially relevant for women (and therefore poverty). If the relatively high-wage[7] apparel sector expands, it might create opportunities for women to leave the low-wage sectors of agriculture or domestic service. The reverse is also true. One might also use the relative skill intensity of different sectors to get an idea of the effects on overall demand for skill within the economy.

Changes within Apparel (% Δh)

The framework described illustrates the most basic "horizontal" relationship between quotas and workers, but the "value chain" structure of apparel production creates the potential for a "vertical" response by firms. In fact, given the complexity of within-industry dynamics, a straightforward positive correlation between apparel exports and apparel employment is probably not likely. Recent advances in both theory and within-industry empirics—starting with Melitz (2003) and including Davidson, Matusz, and Shevchenko (2008); Dix-Carneiro (2010); Felbermayr, Prat, and Schmerer (2011); and others—suggest that a complete picture of the effects on workers should also include an analysis of changes within industries.

To classify these various outcomes, consider figure 2.2. The horizontal axis represents employment, with increasing (decreasing) employment represented by areas to the right (left) of the vertical axis as described earlier. Upgrading, such as adopting more capital-intensive techniques, producing higher-valued products, or developing "upstream" production of source materials (such as textiles) domestically, is represented along the vertical axis. Values below the horizontal axis represent downgrading (for example, moving down the value chain). This rubric creates four areas. Some countries may manage to both upgrade and increase employment and therefore land in area A (for example, Bangladesh, India, and Vietnam). In contrast, other countries may end up in area C (for example, Honduras and Mexico) after the end of the MFA, representing lack of upgrading and a loss of employment. Perhaps the most interesting areas are B and D. Area B (for example, Morocco and Sri Lanka) represents economies that upgrade but experience falling apparel employment. Economies in this category may be the most likely to be those making the transition out of apparel and into higher-valued

Figure 2.2   Employment Effects

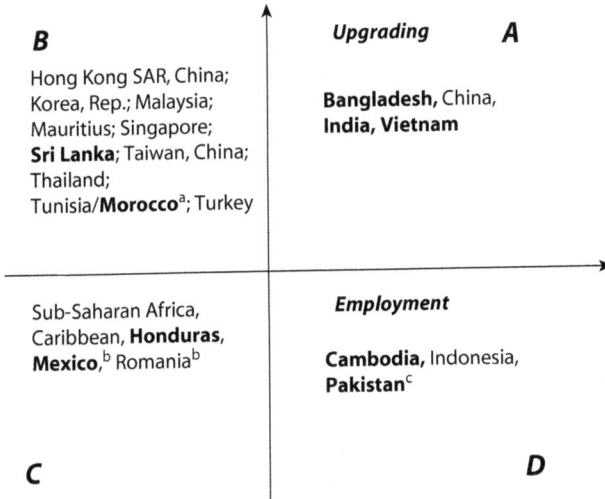

Source: Authors' estimation.
a. Upgrading not as substantial as in other cases.
b. No upgrading within apparel and textile sectors but upgrading to other sectors.
c. Upgrading more substantial than in other cases.

goods (such as electronics). In contrast, countries that successfully specialize in the most labor-intensive parts of the value chain would fall in area D (for example, Cambodia and Pakistan). The chapters that follow implicitly and explicitly apply this rubric in their analyses of changes in employment after the MFA.

The first step toward applying this rubric is identifying where individual countries fit into the global value chain by describing the stages of apparel that are produced within each country. Since apparel is characterized by value chain production, the production structure within a country has a potentially tremendous effect on the ultimate employment effects. Gereffi and Frederick (2010) and chapter 3 discuss the main stages of functional upgrading in the apparel value chain. Data on each country's stage in functional upgrading from assembly to original brand manufacturing should be combined with data on the changes in apparel exports after the end of the MFA, because the different stages may involve different employment patterns. For example, the textile sector generally employs more men than the apparel sector. A shift in domestic production toward textiles as a result of the end of the MFA could have significant implications for employment of men and women. Hence, understanding the changes in the overall production structure within each country is critical for a full understanding of changes in employment and poverty. Recent theory focuses on within-sector heterogeneity, which creates more nuanced results than those predicted by the standard neo-classical trade models. An observed increase in skill intensity within an industry could be due to the relatively high survival (or entry) of skill-intensive firms or due to individual firms becoming more skill intensive. It is therefore useful to distinguish changes that occur within industries (between firms within a given sector) and those that occur within firms.

Within-Industry Composition

The insights of Melitz (2003) suggest that within-sector heterogeneity plays a critical role in the effects of trade liberalization. Some apparel firms may be better managed or implement innovative strategies not available to other firms. The differences between firms within a given sector lead to changes in the composition of the sector. For example, Melitz (2003), Bernard et al. (2007), and others have suggested that exporting firms are very different from nonexporters. Changes in export opportunities within a given sector may therefore affect exporters differently than nonexporters, changing the composition of the sector. Coşar, Guner, and Tybout (2010), for example, identify the importance of the composition of firms within particular industries when tariffs fell in Colombia.

For the purposes of this book, the female share and skill (education) share of employment within the sector are particularly important. These shares reveal within-industry changes that should corroborate the descriptive value chain analysis described above. For example, if there is significant within-industry skill upgrading because of moving up the value chain, it might be because the end of the MFA created opportunities for relatively skill-intensive export firms, raising the overall employment of skilled workers within the sector. If demand is shifting away from less skilled workers, and these are the workers more likely to be associated with poverty, then poverty may increase even as exports rise.

Within-Firm Composition

Gereffi and Frederick (2010) and chapter 3 suggest that the twin shocks of the end of the MFA and the global financial crisis produced changes within sectors that may also have induced firm-level changes.[8] If firms are moving up the value chain, they may become more capital intensive and therefore shed workers, which may increase output per worker. Movement up the value chain for a particular firm is correlated with an increase in skilled worker employment and may be negatively related to the female employment share. Analyzing these changes with firm-level data, when available, provides a very comprehensive picture of the effects of the end of the MFA on employment.

Changes in Wages (% Δw)

When deriving labor demand above, we assumed that wages were taken as given by the firm and that there was, in essence, a single wage for a given worker that was determined by labor supply and labor demand. In practice, an individual's wage is affected by many factors. Some factors might be considered *specific* to one's industry or firm: experience, firm- or industry-specific human capital (including social capital), and match quality. Returns to specific characteristics might be negotiated between workers and firm owners (which might, for example, be divided according to a Nash bargaining solution). Other factors might be called *general* characteristics, such as gender, age, and education, that command returns based on marketwide forces.

There has been a recent surge in literature focusing on *within-sector* wage inequality (Helpman, Itskhoki, and Redding 2010) that is based on heterogeneous firms within sectors. These papers take advantage of the advances in labor market frictions found in search models and produce predictions that complement the between-factor inequality predictions of neoclassical trade models. They tend to focus on within-factor inequality that results, for example, from differences in match quality or ex ante unobserved productivity. In particular, Helpman, Itskhoki, and Redding (2010) suggest that within-factor inequality can overwhelm between-factor changes in inequality following trade liberalization. The Helpman, Itskhoki, and Redding (2010) model also suggests that the change in inequality depends on the degree of trade prior to the shock. While the outcome is the same when all firms export as when no firms export, the change in inequality after a trade shock depends on the share of exporting firms prior to the shock, and therefore inequality could rise or fall after the trade shock. It is not surprising that there is a significant debate about the effects of trade on both wage levels and wage inequality.

Returns to general characteristics match the derivation of labor demand above in the sense that they are exogenous to the firm. Changes to general characteristics are determined by economywide markets (in general equilibrium). One example of a general wage characteristic is the male-female wage differential. The general component of women's wages will be affected by globalization if globalization results in a sufficiently large change in the demand for women workers. Since apparel is a significant employer of women (and is generally women's gateway to manufacturing employment in developing countries), it is possible that the end of the MFA would have general equilibrium effects in a country in which the apparel sector was a significant employer of women.

Globalization affects general and specific characteristics differently; therefore, to be comprehensive, an analysis of wages requires both a theory that explains these different effects and an empirical approach that can separately identify them. Separately identifying the different effects is at the heart of the large literature that focuses on wage inequality, as inequality per se involves identifying wages of different groups (such as gender, education, industry, or other characteristics).

Empirically, the first step in this kind of wage analysis is to decompose the wages into their component parts. It is extremely common in labor economics to decompose wages into component parts using a Mincerian wage equation. The Mincerian equation used regresses log of wage for worker k at period t on a set of worker characteristics such as years of education (edu_{kt}), gender (dummy variable gen_{kt} that equals to one if the worker is female), age_{kt}, age_{kt}^2, j industry (ind_{jkt}) and i occupational ($occup_{ikt}$) dummies, hours (h_{kt}) worked, and a remaining match-specific component captured in the residual term ε_{kt}.

$$\log(wage_{kt}) = \beta_0 + \beta_1 gen_{kt} + \beta_2 age_{kt} + \beta_3 age_{kt}^2$$
$$+ \beta_4 edu_{kt} + \beta_5 h_{kt} + \sum_i \delta_j ind_{jkt} \qquad (2.8)$$
$$+ \sum_i \lambda_i occup_{ikt} + \varepsilon_{kt}$$

The analysis in chapters 4–6 includes estimating equation (2.8) separately for each country and year of survey data. Each chapter corrects for the possibility of selection bias coming from censoring of female wages using the two-step Heckman approach. Participation is defined as having positive wage value, and the variables used in the selection correction equation are gender, age, age squared, years of education, and a series of dummies for marital status. The analysis proceeds by comparing changes in the returns to general characteristics and specific characteristics with globalization measures, such as ending the MFA or more specific variables such as industry prices.

In several cases, it is possible to construct country-specific measures of working conditions. Several variables are potentially related to conditions: employment status, injury at work, child labor, overtime, ratio of in-kind over cash pay, and ratio of benefits over cash pay. Conditions are considered favorable to the worker if he or she (i) is paid as a regular employee with fixed wages, (ii) is not under the age of 14, (iii) reports no work-related injuries, (iv) works no more than 40 hours a week (or less than six days a week), (v) has a low ratio of in-kind over cash work, and (vi) has a high ratio of benefits over cash pay.[9]

To empirically analyze working conditions, dummy variables equal to one for each good condition are averaged across all conditions for each worker. The regression exercise in equation (2.9) has as dependent variable average work condition (wc_{kt}) of individual k in period t as a function of (i) years of education (edu_{kt}); gender (dummy variable $female_{kt}$ that equals to one if the worker is female); age_{kt}; age_{kt}^2; j industry (ind_{jkt}) and i occupational $(occup_{ikt})$ dummies; and p marital status dummies $(married_{pkt})$;(ii) policy dummies and interactions trend, MFA, MFA_{female}; and (iii) a remaining match-specific component captured in the residual term ω_{kt}.

$$wc_{kt} = \gamma + \theta_1 female_{kt} + \sum_p \alpha_p married_{pkt}$$

$$+ \theta_2 age_{kt} + \theta_3 age_{kt}^2 + \theta_4 edu_{kt} + \sum_j \vartheta_j ind_{jkt} \qquad (2.9)$$

$$+ \sum_i \mu_i occup_{ikt} + \beta time + \Phi MFA + \psi MFA_{female} + \omega_{kt}$$

The data are divided into two periods: period one corresponds to survey years before 2005, and period two corresponds to survey years 2005 and onward. The terms of interest are the effect of the MFA phasing out on working conditions of textile and garment workers (time variable equal to one if year is 2005 or later, MFA dummy that equals one for workers in textile and garment industry for 2005 and later years) and the effect of the MFA phasing out on working conditions of female textile and apparel workers $(MFA_{female}$ dummy equal to the interaction of the MFA dummy with the gender dummy). Since the definitions of the dependent variable are not homogeneous across countries, the analysis also includes as a robustness check one working condition at a time in a probit regression instead of the average wc_{kt} for each worker.

Trade theory suggests there should be a positive relationship between output prices and industry-specific wage differentials in the short run. Specifically, the relationship between output prices and industry-specific wage premiums should be proportional to the degree of short-run specificity of workers. Since it is generally accepted that workers are more mobile in the medium-to-long run, it is reasonable to expect that the relationship between prices and industry-specific wages is strongest in the short run.

In the longer run, the price shock to a given industry will spread through the rest of the economy and general equilibrium effects might become apparent. Therefore, in the longer run, the industry-specific price change will be positively correlated with the relative wage of the factor intensively used in that industry. One way to examine this correlation is to examine the change in apparel prices and the relative wage of women in the economy.

Data

One goal of this book is to bring together the best available data to identify the changes described earlier in this chapter. The data used in the book come from multiple sources. Trade data come from the United Nations Commodity Trade Statistics Database (UN Comtrade), the United States International Trade Commission (USITC) database, and the Eurostat database. We also used the World Bank Development Indicators, the Doing Business Indicators, and national statistical agencies. Four types of surveys were used to carry out analysis for different countries depending on the availability of the data: enterprise surveys, industry surveys, household surveys, and labor force surveys. In Morocco, we based our analysis on International Labour Organization (ILO) labor data and employment data from Rossi (2010) due to the lack of availability of standardized surveys. Table 2.2 summarizes the sources of the data used in this work.

Enterprise Surveys

We used the World Bank Enterprise Surveys for Honduras and Pakistan. The surveys are conducted by the World Bank at the firm level and are a representative sample of an economy's private sector. The Honduran Enterprise Survey is a panel of 216 firms collected in 2003 and 2006. The Pakistan Enterprise Survey is a panel of 402 firms conducted in 2002 and 2007. The surveys cover a broad range of business environment topics, including access to finance, corruption, infrastructure, crime, competition, and performance.

Table 2.2   Data Sources

Country	Survey type	Year	Survey description
Bangladesh	Household	2000, 2005	Household Income and Expenditure Survey (HIES)
	Household	2009	Welfare Monitoring Survey (WMS)
	Labor Force	2002, 2005	Labor force survey (LFS)
	Industry	1995–96, 2001–02, 2005–06	Census of Manufacturing Industries (CMI)—1995–96, 2001–02; Survey of Manufacturing Industries (SMI)—2005–06
Cambodia	Household	1996, 1999, 2004, 2007, 2008, 2009	Cambodia Socio-Economic Survey (CSES)
Honduras	Household	2001, 2003, 2005, 2007	Encuesta Permanente de Hogares de Propósitos Múltiples (EPHPM)
	Enterprise	2003, 2006	World Bank Enterprise Survey, panel
India	Household	1999, 2004, 2005, 2007	National Sample Survey Organization (NSSO): India Socio-Economic Surveys (ISES)
	Industry	1989/90, 1994/95, 2000/01, 2005/06 fiscal years	Annual Survey of Industries (ASI)—formal sector; National Sample Survey (NSS)—informal sector
Mexico	Labor Force	2003, 2007	National Survey of Urban Employment (Encuesta Nacional de Empleo Urbano, ENEU)
	Enterprise	2003–08	Annual Industry Survey (Encuesta Industrial Annual, EIA), panel
Morocco			International Labour Organization (ILO) data, Rossi 2010
Pakistan	Household	2005–06, 2007–08	Pakistan Social and Living Standards Measurement (PSLM) survey
	Labor Force	2001, 2003, 2008	Labor force survey (LFS)
	Enterprise	2002, 2007	World Bank Enterprise Survey, panel
Sri Lanka	Household	2002, 2006	Household Income and Expenditure Survey (HIES)
	Labor Force	2002, 2008	Labor force survey (LFS)
	Industry	1993, 1998, 2007	Annual Survey of Manufacturing
Vietnam	Household	2002, 2004, 2006, 2008	Vietnam Household Living Standards Survey (VHLSS)
	Industry	2000, 2008	Vietnam Industrial Survey

Source: Authors.

Industry Surveys

Industry surveys are typically collected by the national statistical offices at the establishment or firm level. They usually contain information on measures of firm performance such as sales, gross value of production, cost of inputs, employment, total compensation, and other variables.

The Mexico Annual Industry Survey (Encuesta Industrial Annual, EIA) is collected by Mexico´s National Statistical Office (Instituto Nacional de Estadística y Geografía, INEGI). We used the linked panel of establishments over the 2003–08 period. The sample size varies from 6,400 to 7,100 establishments. The EIA is highly representative of the manufacturing. Micro establishments with less than 15 workers and those that belong to the *maquila* sector are excluded from the sample. Additional information on production and nonproduction workers was elicited by matching EIA with the Monthly Industrial Survey (Encuesta Industrial Mensual, EIM).

The manufacturing sector data for Bangladesh comes from the Bangladesh Bureau of Statistics and comprises establishment-level cross-sectional data for three points in time: the 1995–96 and 2001–02 Census of Manufacturing Industries (CMI), and the 2005–06 representative Survey of Manufacturing Industries (SMI). The number of observations varies from 4,716 to 6,174. The CMI/SMI covers all manufacturing establishments with 10 or more workers, though some respondents in the sampling frame of the 1995–96 and 2001–02 CMI reported employment figures of less than 10 workers. For consistency over time, establishments with less than 10 workers in the 1995–96 and 2001–02 CMI were dropped to make the data comparable to the 2005–06 SMI, which did not include such micro establishments.

The manufacturing sector data for India consist of four cross-sections of establishment-level data—fiscal years 1989/90, 1994/95, 2000/01, and 2005/06—on the formal and informal sector collected by the government of India. The surveys are enumerated by different government agencies. The Central Statistical Organization (CSO) covers the formal sector—establishments with more than 10 workers (20 workers if not using power) registered under the Factories Act—and it surveys the formal sector every year through the Annual Survey of Industries (ASI). The informal sector is surveyed periodically by the National Sample Survey Organization (NSSO) through the National Sample Survey (NSS), with a sampling universe of all manufacturing establishments not covered under the Factories Act. Due to the large sample, the establishment-level data were aggregated into cells by three-digit industry, state, seven employment-size categories spanning the formal and informal sector, and new entrant and incumbent status by year.

The Sri Lanka manufacturing sector data are provided by the National Statistics Office in summary (cell data) format by industry, firm size, and provincial location due to confidentiality restrictions. The data cover three years—1993, 1998, and 2007 (the latest published survey available)—and come from the Annual Survey of Manufacturing. The Vietnam Industrial Survey is conducted by the General Statistics Office of Vietnam. We used the 2000 and 2008 panel of 448 firms.

Household Surveys

Household surveys are cross-sectional population representative surveys conducted by the national statistical offices on a periodic basis. The surveys elicit detailed information about household variables and individual characteristics of household members. The following variables are included in the analysis: wage, education, age, marital status, gender, location, industry, occupation, some working conditions, and hours worked.

The Bangladesh household surveys were conducted by the Bangladesh Bureau of Statistics. The Household Income and Expenditure Survey (HIES) was collected in 2000 and 2005 and covered 7,440 and 10,080 households, respectively. The Welfare Monitoring Survey (WMS) was collected in 2009 and covered 14,000 households. The Cambodia Socio-Economic Survey (CSES) was collected by the National Institute of Statistics. The data in this book include the 1996, 1999, 2004, 2007, 2008, and 2009 surveys, which contain roughly 12,000 households each. The Honduran household surveys (Encuesta Permanente de Hogares de Propósitos Múltiples, EPHPM) were carried out by the Honduran Institute of Statistics. This book uses the 2001, 2003, 2005, and 2007 surveys, which cover roughly 21,000 households each. The India Socio-Economic Surveys (ISES) were conducted by the National Sample Survey Office. The ISES 1999, 2004, 2005, and 2007, which cover on average 60,000 households each, are used in this book.

The Pakistan Social and Living Standards Measurement (PSLM) survey was conducted by the Pakistan Federal Bureau of Statistics. We used two rounds—2005–06 and 2007–08. The PSLM surveys are conducted at the district level by covering approximately 77,000 households and at the provincial level by covering approximately 16,000 households at alternate years. The Sri Lanka HIESs were carried out by the Sri Lankan Department of Census and Statistics. We used 2002 and 2006 HIESs, which cover about 22,000 households each. The Vietnam Household Living Standards Survey (VHLSS) was collected by the General Statistics Office of Vietnam. We used four rounds of VHLSS—2002, 2004, 2006, and 2008; each survey contains around 45,000 households.

Labor Force Surveys

The labor force survey (LFS) is a standard household-based survey of work-related statistics.[10] LFSs are typically cross-sectional, nationally representative surveys collected at the individual level that contain detailed information about work-related activities (for example, employment status, occupation, industry, and wages); household characteristics (for example, size and location); and individual demographic characteristics such as age, gender, education, and others. The LFSs are typically carried out by the national statistical offices.

The Bangladesh LFS was collected by the Bangladesh Bureau of Statistics. We used 2002 and 2005 Bangladesh LFSs that covered approximately 140,000 and 110,000 individuals, respectively. The Mexican analogue is the National Survey of Urban Employment (Encuesta Nacional de Empleo Urbano, ENEU) collected by INEGI. Quarterly data for 2003 and 2007 cover around 300,000 individuals each quarter. In Sri Lanka, the LFS is conducted quarterly by the Department of Census and Statistics. We used annual data for 2002 and 2008 covering around 60,000 individuals each. The Pakistani LFS is carried out by the Federal Bureau of Statistics. We used three years of surveys—2001, 2003, and 2008; each has a sample size of around 120,000 individuals.

Notes

1. Source: United Nations Commodity Trade Statistics Database (UN Comtrade). See chapter 3, table 3.5 for more detail.
2. Apparel wages are the log of the dollar value of hourly apparel wage (or closest approximation) available in the International Labour Organization's (ILO's) Labor Statistics (LABORSTA) database. See http://laborsta.ilo.org/. Domestic currency wages are converted to dollars using the same-period nominal exchange rate.
3. The restriction to low-wage countries here occurs because of data availability.
4. Including these variables reduced the number of available observations because they cover fewer countries than trade and gross domestic product (GDP) per capita data.
5. This fact implies, ceteris paribus, that total labor demand is a positive function of output prices.
6. The term h here is therefore related to the L term.
7. The apparel sector is a relatively high-wage sector compared to other low-skilled, labor-intensive sectors such as agriculture and basic services.

8. One example of a relevant empirical approach is Verhoogen (2008).

9. Actual variables used in estimation for each country depend on the data availability. Refer to specific chapters for exact definitions of working conditions for each country.

10. This is the ILO definition.

References

Bernard, Andrew B., J. Bradford Jensen, Stephen J. Redding, Peter K. Schott. 2007. "Firms in International Trade." *Journal of Economic Perspectives* 21 (3): 105–30.

Brambilla, Irene, Amit Khandelwal, and Peter Schott. 2007. "China's Experience under the Multifiber Arrangement (MFA) and the Agreement on Textiles and Clothing (ATC)." Working Paper 13346, National Bureau of Economic Research, Cambridge, MA.

Coşar, A. Kerem, Nezih Guner, and James R. Tybout. 2010. "Firm Dynamics, Job Turnover, and Wage Distributions in an Open Economy." Working Paper 16326, September, National Bureau of Economic Research, Cambridge, MA.

Das, Sanghamitra, Mark J. Roberts, and James R. Tybout. 2007. "Market Entry Costs, Producer Heterogeneity, and Export Dynamics." *Econometrica* 75 (3): 837–73.

Davidson, Carl, Steven Matusz, and Andrei Shevchenko. 2008. "Globalization and Firm-Level Adjustment with Imperfect Labor Markets." *Journal of International Economics* 75 (2): 295–309.

Dix-Carneiro, Rafael. 2010. "Trade Liberalization and Labor Market Dynamics." Working Paper 212, Center for Economic Policy Studies, Princeton University, Princeton, NJ.

Do, Quy-Toan, Andrei A. Levchenko, and Claudio Raddatz. 2011. "Engendering Trade." Background paper for the *World Development Report* 2012 on Gender Equality and Development, World Bank, Washington, DC.

Felbermayr, Gabriel, Julien Prat, and Hans-Jörg Schmerer. 2011. "Globalization and Labor Market Outcomes: Wage Bargaining, Search Frictions, and Firm Heterogeneity." *Journal of Economic Theory* 146 (1): 39–73.

Gereffi, Gary, and Stacey Frederick. 2010. "The Global Apparel Value Chain, Trade and the Crisis: Challenges and Opportunities for Developing Countries." Policy Research Working Paper 5281, World Bank, Washington, DC.

Hamermesh, Daniel. 1993. *Labor Demand*. Princeton, NJ: Princeton University Press.

Helpman, Elhanan, Oleg Itskhoki, and Stephen Redding. 2010. "Inequality and Unemployment in a Global Economy." *Econometrica* 78 (4): 1239–83.

Melitz, Marc J. 2003. "The Impact of Trade on Intra-industry Reallocations and Aggregate Industry Productivity." *Econometrica* 71 (6): 1695–725.

Rossi, Arianna. 2010. "Economic and Social Upgrading in Global Production Networks: The Case of the Garment Industry in Morocco." Unpublished dissertation, University of Sussex, U.K.

Verhoogen, Eric A. 2008. "Trade, Quality Upgrading, and Wage Inequality in the Mexican Manufacturing Sector." *Quarterly Journal of Economics* 123 (2): 489–530.

CHAPTER 3

Developments in the Global Apparel Industry after the MFA Phaseout

Stacey Frederick and Cornelia Staritz

Introduction

At the end of 2004, the most significant change in the recent history of global apparel trade took place with the phaseout of Multi-fibre Arrangement (MFA) quotas. Global apparel trade had been governed by a system of quantitative restrictions for more than 40 years. The phaseout of the quotas had crucial implications for the structure of the global apparel industry and for trade, production, and employment patterns across the world. Competition and price pressures have intensified, and global buyers have modified sourcing policies that had been previously driven by quotas. Apparel industries around the world prepared for the MFA phaseout by adapting strategies and increasing investments to enhance capacities and capabilities. However, there were large differences in how active different countries and firms were in preparing themselves for increased competition and buyers' changing sourcing policies post-MFA.

The authors of this chapter are grateful for comments provided by Gladys Lopez-Acevedo, Raymond Robertson, and Yevgeniya Savchenko.

The analysis in this chapter finds that the global apparel industry experienced important reallocations of production and employment between countries and within countries post-MFA. Cost competitiveness, particularly in labor costs, and preferential market access have remained major factors in explaining how suppliers have fared in the new environment of global apparel trade after 2004. However, the development of supplier countries and firms has also been crucially determined by their upgrading efforts and the existence of proactive policies by the private and public sector alike to support such efforts. Upgrading is broadly defined as moving to higher-value activities in global value chains (GVCs). Upgrading efforts—particularly with regard to increasing functional capabilities in the apparel industry, establishing backward linkages to important input industries such as textiles, producing more sophisticated products, and diversifying end markets—are crucial in understanding how different suppliers have fared post-MFA. Cost competitiveness and preferential market access alone seem to be not enough to place countries among the "winners."

This chapter aims to (i) give an overview of the structure of the global apparel industry, (ii) assess global dynamics in the apparel industry in the context of the MFA phaseout, and (iii) discuss the role of different supplier countries and how they have been affected by the MFA phaseout. The rest of this chapter comprises five parts. The first part provides an overview of the structure of the global apparel industry by describing the apparel GVC and its main actors. The second part discusses the regulatory environment of global apparel trade, in particular the MFA, its phaseout, and preferential market access. The third part analyzes implications of the MFA phaseout and how different supplier countries and firms have fared post-MFA. The fourth part provides a short overview of the development and structure of the apparel industries in the nine case study countries. The fifth part concludes.

Structure of the Apparel Industry

The apparel industry has traditionally played a central role in the industrial and socioeconomic development process of low-income countries (LICs). In most developed countries of today and newly industrialized economies (NIEs), the apparel (and textile) industry was central in the industrialization process (Dickerson 1999). Given its low entry barriers (low fixed costs and relatively simple technology) and its labor-intensive nature, the industry absorbed large numbers of unskilled, mostly female workers and provided upgrading opportunities into higher value-added activities within and across sectors. For women, the industry is often the largest employer after agriculture, and in many developing countries, it has been one of the few avenues to paid and formal employment for women.

The apparel industry is one of the largest export sectors in the world and has become increasingly globalized. The industry has expanded rapidly since the early 1970s, and many developing countries have been integrated into apparel exporting, which has provided employment for tens of millions of workers (Gereffi and Frederick 2010). In 2008, global apparel exports accounted for $336 billion, making apparel one of the most traded manufactured products. Developing countries have accounted for a rising share of these exports, and the apparel industry constituted the first manufacturing sector where exports became dominated by developing countries. In the mid-1960s, developing countries accounted for around 25 percent of worldwide apparel exports, a share that had risen to above 70 percent by 2000 (Morris 2006). For most LICs, apparel exports are by far the largest manufacturing export. For instance, the apparel industry in 2008 accounted for 71 percent of total merchandise exports in Bangladesh, 85 percent in Cambodia, 49 percent in Honduras, and 41 percent in Sri Lanka (table 3.1).

Table 3.1   Apparel's Share of Total Merchandise Exports, 1990, 2000, 2004, and 2008

percent

Country/region/economy	1990	2000	2004	2008
World average	3.2	3.1	2.9	2.3
Haiti	—	76.9	71.2	86.0
Cambodia	—	69.8	70.8	84.8
Bangladesh	38.5	79.3	74.2[a]	71.1
Lesotho	—	73.1	46.1	69.2
Macao SAR, China	65.6	72.8	69.4	52.7
Honduras	7.7	68.0	35.8	48.6
El Salvador	31.6	56.9	63.2	43.0
Madagascar	—	37.4	69.7	42.6
Sri Lanka	32.2	51.8	48.0	40.9
Mauritius	51.9	60.9	46.9	36.0
Pakistan	18.1	23.8	22.6	19.2
Morocco	16.9	32.3	30.9	16.6
Vietnam	—	12.6	15.5	14.3
India	14.1	14.1	10.5	6.1
Mexico	1.4	5.2	3.8	1.7

Source: World Trade Organization International Trade Statistics: 2001, 2005, and 2009.
Note: Data represent given year or the nearest year with reported information. Haiti through Mauritius are the top 10 economies listed for 2008. — = data not available.
a. 2005 data for Bangladesh are reported because 2004 data are a significant outlier (54.5) that is not consistent with national data sources.

As in many other sectors, the apparel industry is organized in GVCs where production of components and assembly into final products are carried out via interfirm networks on a global scale. To simplify analysis, activities can be separated into the apparel supply chain and the apparel value chain. The supply chain focuses on the physical transformation and transportation of raw materials through final products, and the value chain focuses on activities that add economic value to products at each stage but are not necessarily manufacturing or logistics related. Together, these make up the GVC for apparel.

Apparel Supply Chain

The apparel supply chain can be roughly divided into four stages that are intertwined with the textile industry (figure 3.1): (i) raw material supply, including natural fibers (such as cotton and wool) and man-made fibers (MMF) (such as polyester, nylon, and acrylic); (ii) yarn and fabric production and finishing (textile industry); (iii) apparel production; and (iv) distribution and sales channels at the wholesale and retail levels. Natural and synthetic fibers are produced from raw materials such as cotton, wool, silk, flax, and chemicals. These fibers are spun into yarn that is used to produce woven or knitted greige fabric. The fabrics are then finished, dyed or printed, and cut into pieces to produce apparel, home furnishings, and industrial and technical textile products. The apparel industry is a significant consumer of textile products that are sewed to make final apparel articles.

A large part of apparel production—which includes cutting, sewing, and finishing activities—remains labor intensive, has low start-up and fixed costs, and requires simple technology. These characteristics have encouraged the move to low-cost locations, mainly in developing countries. In contrast, textile (yarn and fabric) production is more capital and scale intensive, demands higher worker skills, and has partly remained in developed countries or shifted toward middle-income countries. Some economies are important apparel *and* textile exporters, such as China; the EU-15 (including intra-EU trade); Hong Kong SAR, China; India; and Turkey (table 3.2).[1] Japan, the Republic of Korea, Pakistan, and the United States are important textile exporters, while Bangladesh, Indonesia, Mexico, Tunisia, and Vietnam are major apparel exporters. It becomes clear from this comparison that LICs have higher representation in the apparel industry. An important exception is Pakistan, which exports made-up textiles such as bedding and home textiles.

Figure 3.1 Apparel Supply and Value Chain

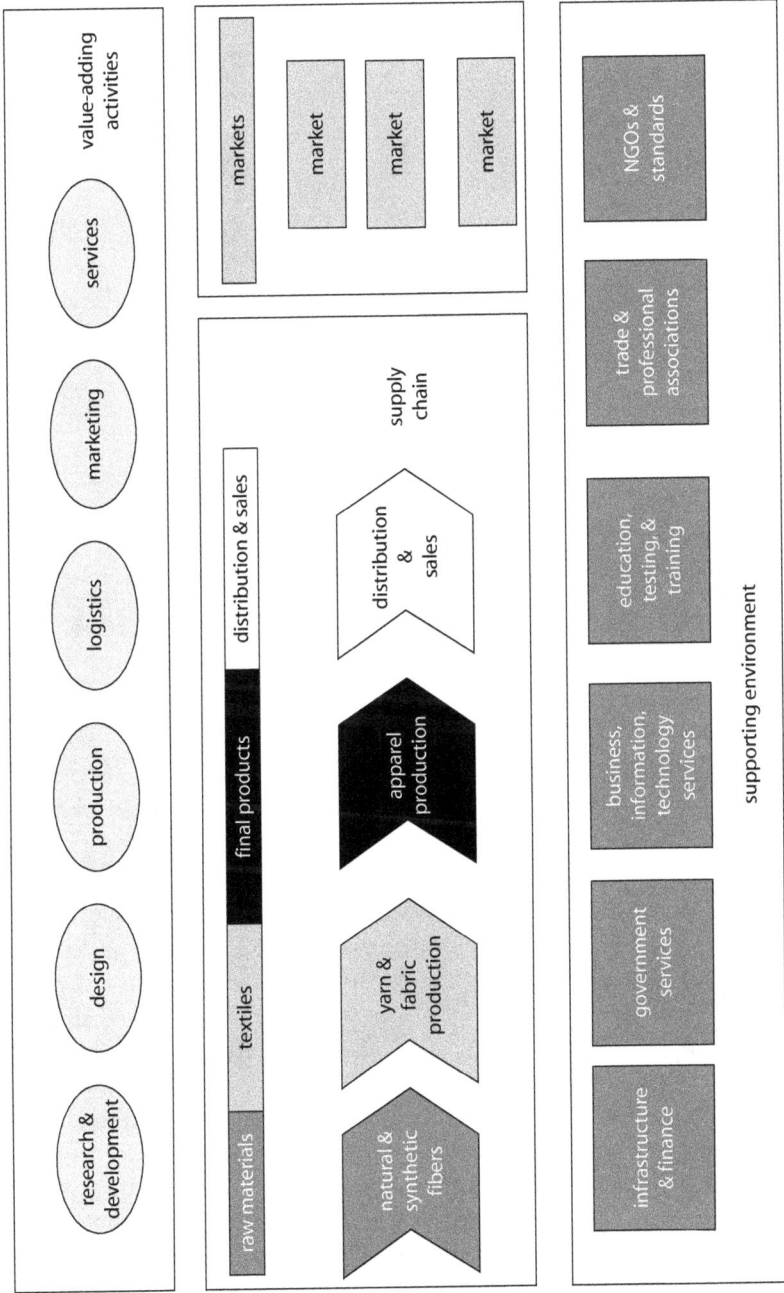

value-adding activities

research & development | design | production | logistics | marketing | services

markets

market

market

market

raw materials | textiles | final products | distribution & sales

supply chain

natural & synthetic fibers → yarn & fabric production → apparel production → distribution & sales

supporting environment

infrastructure & finance | government services | business, information, technology services | education, testing, & training | trade & professional associations | NGOs & standards

Source: Frederick 2010.
Note: NGO = nongovernmental organization.

Table 3.2   Top 10 Apparel and Textile Exporters to World by 2008 Values

Country/region/ economy	Apparel exporters		Country/region/ economy	Textile exporters	
	Value ($, million)	Share (%)		Value ($, million)	Share (%)
World	335,878		World	222,134	
China	130,394	38.8	EU-15	64,254	28.9
EU-15	60,076	17.9	China	52,969	23.8
Turkey	15,769	4.7	United States	11,690	5.3
Bangladesh	13,464	4.0	India	10,430	4.7
India	12,210	3.6	Other Asia, nes[a]	9,475	4.3
Vietnam	9,541	2.8	Korea, Rep.	9,167	4.1
Indonesia	7,630	2.3	Turkey	7,906	3.6
Hong Kong SAR, China	5,107	1.5	Japan	7,180	3.2
Mexico	4,634	1.4	Pakistan	6,825	3.1
Tunisia	4,489	1.3	Hong Kong SAR, China	3,806	1.7
Top 10 share		78.4	Top 10 share		82.7

Source: United Nations Commodity Trade Statistics Database (UN Comtrade); apparel exporters: Harmonized Commodity Description and Coding System (HS) 1992: Codes 61 and 62; textile exporters: Standard International Trade Classification (SITC) 65, Rev. 3. Retrieved 4/3/2011.

Note: Exports represented by world aggregate imports from all countries. EU-15 = the 15 member states of the European Union (EU) as of December 31, 2003, before the new member states joined the EU: Austria, Belgium, Denmark, Finland, France, Germany, Greece, Ireland, Italy, Luxembourg, the Netherlands, Portugal, Spain, Sweden, and the United Kingdom.

a. nes = not elsewhere specified; essentially refers to Taiwan, China.

Within the apparel industry, the two segments—woven and knitted apparel—each account for around half of total apparel exports. The top three traded woven apparel products include men's and boys' cotton trousers and shorts, women's and girls' cotton trousers and shorts, and men's and boys' cotton shirts, which together account for 30 percent of total woven apparel exports. The top three traded knitted apparel products include cotton pullovers and cardigans, cotton T-shirts and singlets, and MMF pullovers and cardigans, together accounting for 40 percent of total knitted apparel exports.

The supply chains of these two types of apparel are quite distinct—they use different types of yarn, fabric, machinery, and manufacturing technology, and they differ with regard to vertical integration due to different capital intensities in the fabric production stage. Woven apparel is made from woven fabric that is cut into pieces and sewed together by apparel manufacturers. In most cases, the apparel assembly stage is not in the same factory as the fabric weaving mill. Backward integration into weaving, dyeing, and finishing is generally capital intensive and uses more energy than apparel assembly processes. Labor-intensive handlooms exist to make woven fabrics, but handloom fabrics are mostly used for home textiles or traditional apparel rather than ready-made apparel for export markets.

Knitted apparel can be made from a variety of knitted fabric types, or the final product can essentially be knitted from yarn into an apparel product without a distinct fabric production stage. Countries often move into knitted fabric production prior to woven fabric production because a knitting machine is generally less expensive and uses less energy than a weaving machine. Furthermore, products that use flat knit fabrics (sweaters, pullovers, dresses, suits, trim, and so forth) can be made with hand knitting or semiautomatic flatbed knitting machines that are labor intensive, and they are often found in developing countries with large, low-wage labor pools despite more advanced electronic versions. Thus, knit apparel lead times have declined faster as more countries have invested in backward linkages.

Apparel Value Chain and Lead Firms

In addition to the tangible, manufacturing-related steps in the textile-apparel supply chain, a series of "intangible" activities also adds economic value to apparel products. The apparel value chain consists of seven main value-adding activities: product development, design, textile sourcing, apparel manufacturing, distribution, branding, and retail. These activities are controlled by a combination of lead firms and apparel manufacturers.

Apparel represents a classic example of a buyer-driven value chain. GVCs can be differentiated into producer- and buyer-driven chains.[2] Buyer-driven value chains (which are common in labor-intensive consumer goods industries such as apparel, footwear, toys, and consumer electronics) are characterized by decentralized, globally dispersed production networks and coordinated by lead firms that control activities that add value to apparel products (such as design and branding), but they often outsource all or most of the manufacturing process to a global network of suppliers (Gereffi 1994, 1999; Gereffi and Memedovic 2003). In the context of heightened global competition at the supplier level, rents derive less from relatively standardized and commodified production-related activities that are globally available, and more from activities that differentiate the product in the eyes of the consumer. These activities are protected by higher entry barriers and are the core competencies of lead firms, typically large global retailers, and brand owners.

Four main types of lead firms can be indentified in the apparel value chain: mass merchant retailers, specialty retailers, brand marketers, and brand manufacturers (figure 3.2). In the case of brand marketers and brand manufacturers, the lead firm is also the firm recognized as the apparel "manufacturer." Brand manufacturers (such as VF, Hanesbrands, Fruit of the Loom, and Levi's) own apparel manufacturing plants, coordinate textile sourcing, and control marketing and branding activities in the chain. Their production networks are often set up in countries with reciprocal trade agreements. Brand marketers, on the other hand, control the branding and marketing functions, but they do not own manufacturing facilities. These "manufacturers without factories" include firms such as Nike, Polo, and Liz Claiborne. From the consumer's perspective, there is no difference between apparel manufacturers and marketers. Both categories develop brands that are sold at discount or department stores or through specialty retail outlets owned by the manufacturer or marketer. In the 1970s and 1980s, the brand manufacturer category was much more significant, but it has been on the decline over the past two decades as manufacturers have also started outsourcing production-related activities to focus on higher-value segments of the chain (Frederick 2010).

Retailers are involved with the branding and marketing of product lines developed for and sold only via their retail locations. These products are often referred to as private label. Discount and department store retailers (such as Wal-Mart, Target, JC Penney, Marks & Spencer, and Tesco) are separated from specialty stores (such as Gap, Limited, H&M, Mango, and New Look) because the latter only sell apparel-related merchandise and all of the products sold in the store are private labels. Mass merchants sell a diverse array of products representing their own private labels as well as national brands in the same store. Similar to apparel marketers, retailers do not own manufacturing facilities. Retailers either work directly with an apparel manufacturer or with a sourcing agent who coordinates the supply chain. The retailers' strengths are in marketing and branding, and they tend to have relatively limited knowledge of how to make the products they are procuring. Thus, retailers prefer suppliers (or agents) capable of bundling and selling the entire range of manufacturing and logistics activities. Over the past decade, the importance of national brands has declined significantly as private label merchandise has expanded (Frederick 2010).

Figure 3.2 Types of Lead Firms in Apparel Global Value Chains

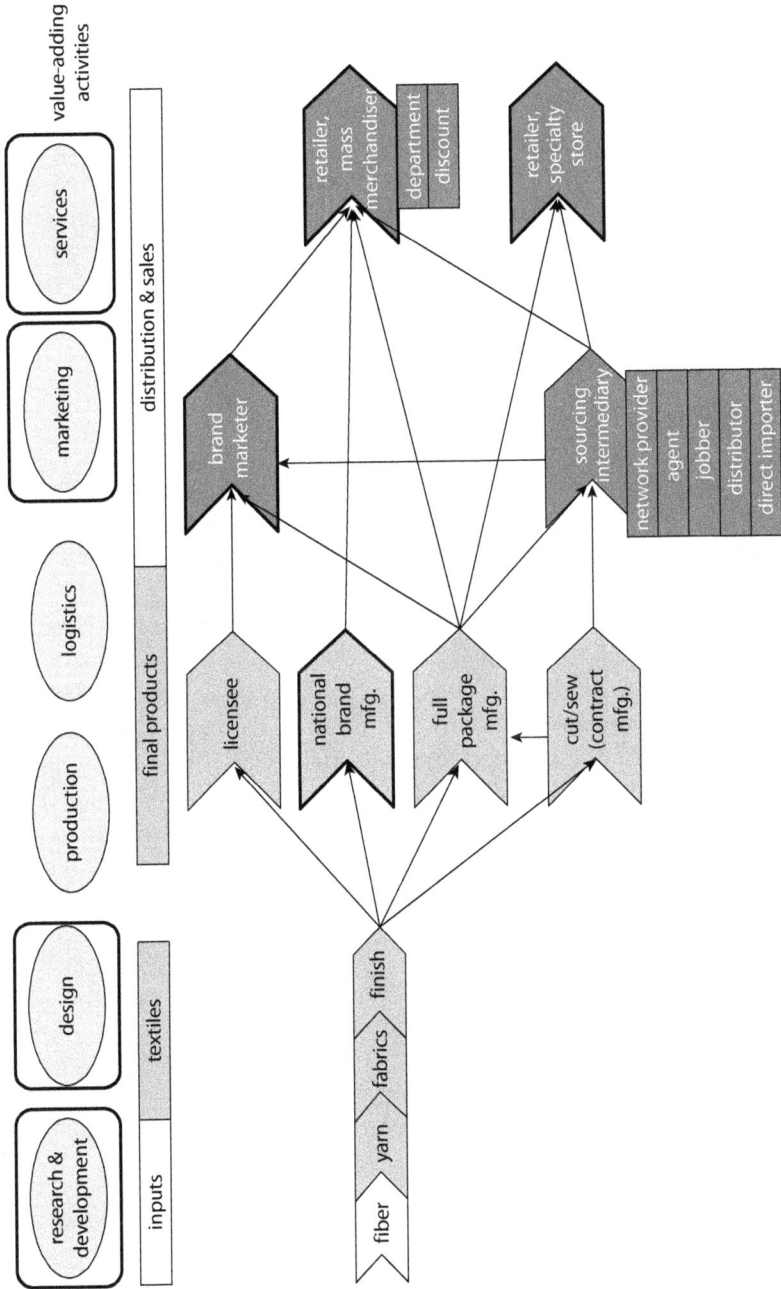

Source: Frederick 2010.
Note: mfg. = manufacturing.

49

Types of Suppliers and Upgrading

Apparel manufacturing is highly competitive and is becoming more consolidated. Developing countries are in constant competition for foreign investments and contracts with lead firms, leaving many suppliers with little leverage in the chain. Given this intense competition and the commodity nature of manufacturing activities, upgrading strategies are extremely important for suppliers to survive and improve their positions in GVCs. Upgrading is broadly defined as moving to higher-value activities in GVCs to increase the benefits (for example, security, profits, skill, and technology or knowledge transfer) from participating in global production (Bair and Gereffi 2003). Supplier countries and firms can pursue several strategies to upgrade in the apparel value chain (Gereffi et al. 2001; Humphrey and Schmitz 2002; Gereffi, Humphrey, and Sturgeon 2005; Frederick 2010):

- *Functional upgrading:* Increasing the range of functions or changing the mix of activities to higher-value tasks; for example, moving beyond direct production-related activities to input sourcing, logistics and distribution, product development, design, and branding.
- *Supply chain upgrading:* Establishing backward manufacturing linkages within the supply chain, in particular to the textile industry.
- *Channel upgrading:* Diversifying to new buyers or new geographic or product markets (particularly important in the context of stagnating demand in traditional export markets such as the United States and the EU-15 and increasing demand in fast-growing emerging markets).
- *Product upgrading:* Shifting to more sophisticated products with higher unit prices.
- *Process upgrading:* Reorganizing the production system or introducing new technologies to gain efficiency.

These upgrading strategies have an important role in explaining how different supplier countries have fared post-MFA, and they are related in several ways. Functional upgrading is of particular importance, and the other upgrading strategies can be viewed as "steps along the way" to achieve functional upgrading. The functional upgrading trajectory also represents the main categories of apparel suppliers (Gereffi and Frederick 2010):

- *Assembly and cut-make-trim (CMT):* The apparel manufacturer is responsible for sewing the apparel and may be responsible for cutting the fabric and providing simple trim (buttons, zippers, and so forth). The buyer provides product specifications and the fabric. The apparel factory is paid a processing fee rather than a price for the product.

- *Original equipment manufacturing (OEM) and free on board (FOB):* The apparel manufacturer purchases (or produces) the textile inputs and provides all production services, finishing, and packaging for delivery to the retail outlet. The buyer provides the design and often specifies textile suppliers. FOB[3] is used in the industry to describe this type of manufacturer, as well as full package.
  - ○ *OEM with domestic textile capabilities:* The shift from CMT to OEM is often associated with the development of a domestic textile industry. The addition of textile mills is an important step in supply chain upgrading. An industry for knitted textiles often develops before woven textiles due to differences in capital intensity.
- *Original design manufacturing (ODM):* The apparel supplier is involved in the design and product development process, including the approval of samples and the selection, purchase, and production of required materials. The apparel supplier is also responsible for coordinating all OEM activities.
- *Original brand manufacturing (OBM):* The apparel supplier is responsible for branding and marketing the final products. The apparel firm may do these activities on a contract basis on behalf of the buyer, or it can mark the transition from apparel supplier to a lead firm, typically in domestic or regional markets.

Apparel-producing countries are often categorized by the functional capabilities of the majority of apparel manufacturing firms within the country, despite important variations and the existence of firms providing broader functions (table 3.3). Caribbean and Sub-Saharan African (SSA) countries as well as Cambodia are typically limited to CMT capabilities, usually focusing on low-cost volume products. An increasing share of apparel manufacturers in Bangladesh, Indonesia, Mexico, and Vietnam fall into the OEM category, which makes up the bulk of apparel manufacturers. China, India, and Turkey have OEM and ODM apparel exporters but also OBM capabilities in their home markets. Full-package service-providing countries coordinate supply chain and value-adding activities such as design, and they invest or contract out manufacturing to other countries (Frederick and Gereffi 2011).

Table 3.3   Functional Capabilities and Country Examples

Functional categories	Capabilities	Country/region/economy examples
CMT (assembly)	Marginal supplier; low-cost volume production	Cambodia Caribbean and Honduras Sub-Saharan Africa (with the exception of Mauritius)
FOB (OEM): full-package provider	Preferred supplier; scale economies in volume production	Bangladesh Indonesia Pakistan Vietnam
	Niche supplier; specialize in specific product areas	Mexico Morocco Sri Lanka
ODM: full package with design	Strategic supplier; high-value, complex products or volume for exports; brand development (OBM) for domestic market	China India Turkey
Global lead firm	Global brand owners; marketing and retailing	EU-15 Japan United States
Full-package service provider	Coordinate supply chain and OEM or ODM activities; contract out manufacturing or invest in production in foreign countries	Hong Kong SAR, China; Korea, Rep.; Taiwan, China (1980); Malaysia, Singapore (1995); Thailand (2010)

Source: Authors.
Note: CMT = cut-make-trim; FOB = free on board; OEM = original equipment manufacturing; ODM = original design manufacturing; EU-15 = the 15 member states of the European Union (EU) as of December 31, 2003, before the new member states joined the EU: Austria, Belgium, Denmark, Finland, France, Germany, Greece, Ireland, Italy, Luxembourg, the Netherlands, Portugal, Spain, Sweden, and the United Kingdom.

Regulatory Context

Besides the crucial importance of organizational dynamics, institutional and regulatory factors decisively influence global production and employment patterns and upgrading prospects in apparel GVCs. The apparel industry has been one of the most trade-regulated manufacturing activities in the global economy. Until 2005, global apparel (and textile) trade had been governed by a system of quantitative restrictions for more than 40 years under the MFA, which was signed in 1974 and was predated by the Short-Term Cotton Agreement (1961) and then the Long-Term Cotton Agreement. The MFA crucially shaped production, trade, and employment patterns in the global apparel industry. Its objective was to protect the major import markets (Canada, Europe,

United States) by imposing quotas on the volume of imports to allow those countries to restructure their sectors before opening up to competition. The quota restrictions, however, led to the spread of production to an increasing number of countries and gave many developing countries a way to establish an apparel industry. Seventy-three countries were subject to quotas by Canada, the EU, and the United States, but most countries with quota restraints did not use their full quota. Thus, when manufacturers (mostly from Hong Kong SAR, China; Japan; Republic of Korea; Taiwan, China; and later, China) reached quota limits in their home economies, they searched for producer countries with underutilized quotas or for countries with no quota to set up apparel plants there or source from existing apparel firms. In particular, producers from Hong Kong SAR, China; Taiwan, China; and, to a lesser extent, Korea spread their operations to other Asian economies and, especially in the 1990s, also to Latin America and the Caribbean and SSA countries (Gereffi 1999). Many of these countries previously had no important apparel exporting industry and thus initially faced no quota restrictions under the MFA.

During the Uruguay Round of negotiations, signatories of the General Agreement on Trade and Tariffs (GATT) decided to bring apparel (and textile) trade under the newly founded World Trade Organization (WTO). The Agreement on Textiles and Clothing (ATC) was signed in 1994 and called for phasing out the MFA by the end of 2004 and, hence, all quotas on apparel and textile trade between WTO members. Although the quota phaseout had been planned as a gradual process spanning four phases and 10 years, importing countries backloaded the removal of quotas, and the majority of quotas on quota-constrained products were only removed at the end of 2004 (Kaplinsky and Morris 2006). While 2005 was supposed to mark the end of the quota system, the major importing markets of Europe and the United States, as well as some middle-income countries (Argentina, Brazil, South Africa, and Turkey), introduced a number of temporary restrictions on imports from China under the Safeguard Agreement negotiated as part of China's WTO accession from 2005 until the end of 2008. For most products, however, the quotas agreed upon were much larger and had higher growth rates than those previously applied under the ATC.

While quotas were eliminated to a large extent in 2005 and totally in 2009, tariffs still play a central role in global apparel trade, particularly in developed countries and in those developing countries that have important textile and apparel industries as well as large end markets (for example, China, India, and South Africa). Average most favored nation (MFN) tariffs on imports of textiles are 6.7 percent for the EU and 7.5 percent for the United States, and for apparel, 11.5 percent and 11.4 percent, respectively. However, these tariffs vary considerably for different product categories. In the United States, tariffs on apparel products vary between 0 and 32 percent, with duties on cotton products ranging on average between 13 and 17 percent and duties on synthetic products ranging on average between 25 and 32 percent. In the EU, tariffs on apparel products vary between 0 and 12 percent; there are no systematic differences between cotton-based and synthetic products These tariffs exceed the average of manufactured products, which is typically around 3 percent.

Since apparel exports face some of the highest tariffs on manufactured goods, preferential market access has a substantial impact on global production and trade patterns. Major preferential market access schemes can be divided into two types of agreements (table 3.4):

- **Regional and bilateral trade agreements:** Developed countries, in particular the EU, Japan, and the United States, have negotiated regional trade agreements[4] to further regional production networks. Developing countries have also increasingly negotiated regional trade agreements.[5] However, negotiations and implementation have been slow, and textile and apparel products are often found on negative lists. In addition to regional agreements, countries have increasingly negotiated bilateral trade agreements, with the EU and the United States being most active in this regard. These bilateral agreements cover apparel products to different extents.

- **Generalized System of Preferences (GSP):** Twenty-seven developed countries have provided tariff preferences to over 100 beneficiary countries through the GSP. However, tariffs for apparel products are only marginally reduced in the standard EU and U.S. GSP. Within the GSP, some countries have negotiated preferential access for lower-income countries, such as with the Everything but Arms (EBA) and the GSP+ initiatives by the EU[6] and the Africa Growth and Opportunity Act (AGOA) by the United States.[7] Canada and Japan have also improved preferential market access for least developed countries (LDCs) in their GSP in the early 2000s. Preferential market access in these agreements is governed by more or less restrictive rules of origin (ROO), which have a crucial impact on outcomes.

Table 3.4   Summary of Major Preferential Market Access Schemes

Granting Country	Program and start date	Benefit	Rules of origin	Beneficiary countries
EU	GSP (1971)	20% MFN duty reduction	Double transformation	GSP-eligible countries not covered by other agreements
EU	Euro-Mediterranean Partnership (1995)	Depends on specific bilateral agreements	Double transformation	Mediterranean countries: Algeria; Egypt, Arab Rep.; Israel; Jordan; Lebanon; Morocco; Palestinian Authority; Syria; Tunisia; Turkey
EU	GSP-EBA (2001)	Duty- and quota-free	Double transformation[a]	LDCs
EU	GSP+ (2005)	Duty-free	Double transformation	Vulnerable developing countries; conditional on implementation of core human rights, good governance, and protection of the environment conventions
EU	EPAs (2008–09)	Duty-free	Single transformation	ACP countries that signed an (interim) EPA
United States	GSP (1976)	Duty-free	Does not include textile and apparel	GSP-eligible countries
United States	NAFTA (1994)	Duty- and quota-free	NAFTA yarn-forward	Canada, Mexico
United States	AGOA (2000)	Duty- and quota-free	AGOA/United States yarn-forward for most products; assembly only for lesser developed countries	Selected Sub-Saharan African countries
United States	DR-CAFTA (2006)	Duty-free	DR-CAFTA/United States yarn-forward with some exceptions	Central America (except Panama) and Dominican Republic
Japan	GSP (1971)	Rates vary from duty-free to 50% of MFN rate	Triple transformation[b]; several of the product lines have ceilings open for utilization by all preference-receiving countries on an equal footing	LDCs
Canada	GSP (2003)	Duty-free	Allow use of fabrics from Canadian GSP beneficiary countries	LDCs

Source: Authors.

Note: GSP = Generalized System of Preferences; GSP+ = GSP that offers preferential market access to vulnerable developing countries; MFN = most favored nation; EBA = Everything but Arms; LDCs = least developed countries; EPA = economic partnership agreement; ACP = African, Caribbean, and the Pacific; NAFTA = North American Free Trade Agreement; yarn-forward = yarn should be produced in NAFTA country; AGOA = Africa Growth and Opportunity Act; DR-CAFTA = Dominican Republic–Central America Free Trade Agreement.

a. The European Union (EU) revised its rules of origin (ROO) from double to single transformation for LDCs, which came into effect on January 1, 2011.

b. Bangladesh has enjoyed double transformation ROO for knit products—Harmonized Commodity Description and Coding System (HS) 61—since April 2011.

Implications of the MFA Phaseout

At the end of 2004, the most significant change in the recent history of global apparel trade took place. To a large extent in 2005 and totally by 2009, countries could no longer impose quotas on apparel imports, and global buyers became free to source apparel in any amount from any country, subject only to tariffs. Important shifts in the competitive dynamics and sourcing policies of buyers have taken place, with crucial implications for trade, production, and employment patterns in the global apparel industry.

Shifts in Competitive Dynamics and Sourcing Policies

Under the MFA, the sourcing policies of buyers were strongly determined by access to quotas. As quotas phased out, other considerations began to dominate sourcing policies, a change that had important implications for the competitive dynamics in the global apparel industry. The most important shifts are described below (Gereffi and Frederick 2010; Frederick and Gereffi 2011; Staritz 2011).

Cost competitiveness: Cost competitiveness has increased post-MFA because of overcapacity and declining apparel prices. Under the MFA, many countries established apparel industries to use their nonexisting or excess quotas, leading to overcapacity in global supply after the quota phaseout that heightened cost competition. Further, quotas added an additional indirect cost to the price of apparel exports from quota-constrained countries (such as China). Due to the scarcity of quota, exporters had to "purchase" the right to use part of a country's allocation, thus adding an additional indirect cost to the final price. The average unit values of apparel imports (used to represent the price apparel producers get for their exports) in the EU-15 and the United States fell after China entered the WTO in 2001, reflecting a global increase in apparel supply (figures 3.3 and 3.4). Also, after 2004, unit values declined in the U.S. market due to overcapacity and increased competition in the post-MFA context. In the EU-15 market, unit values stagnated in 2005 but increased in 2006 and 2007 and only fell in 2008.

Consolidation of supply base: Buyers have had a greater choice after the MFA phaseout, and sourcing decisions have focused on the most competitive suppliers who offer consistent quality, reliable delivery, large-scale production, flexibility, and competitive prices. Thus, manufacturing requirements have increased and become more sophisticated. Buyers have also been striving toward more cost-effective forms of supply chain

Figure 3.3   Average Unit Values of U.S. Apparel Imports, 1995–2008

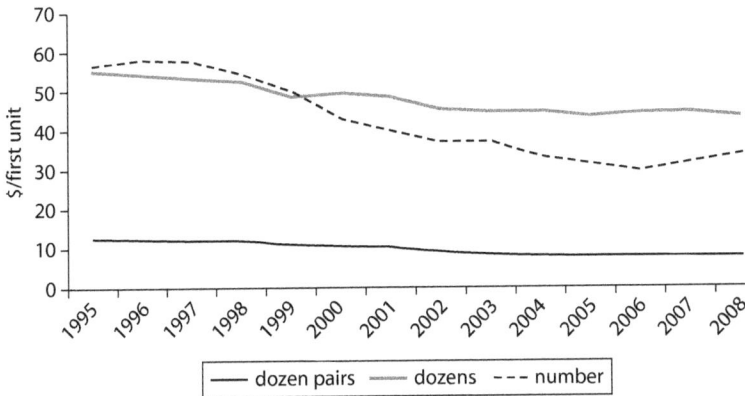

Source: United States International Trade Commission (USITC).
Note: Apparel represented by Harmonized Commodity Description and Coding System (HS) Codes 61 and 62.
U.S. General Customs Value; unit values represent customs value, first unit of quantity by quantity types.

Figure 3.4   Average Unit Values of EU-15 Apparel Imports, 1995–2008

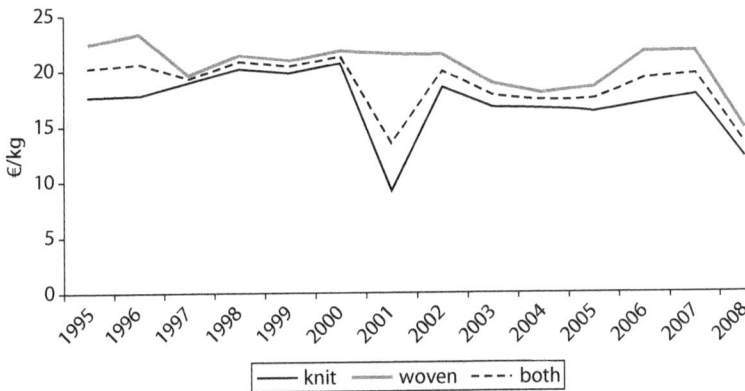

Source: Eurostat.
Note: Apparel represented by Harmonized Commodity Description and Coding System (HS) Codes 61 (knit), 62
(woven), and 61+ 62 (both). Dip in 2001 is because of the quantities for Bangladesh. The dip is attributable to
two six-digit HS Codes: 610711 (M&B Knit Cotton Underwear) and 610821 (W&G Knit Cotton Underwear). EU-15 =
the 15 member states of the European Union (EU) as of December 31, 2003, before the new member states
joined the EU: Austria, Belgium, Denmark, Finland, France, Germany, Greece, Ireland, Italy, Luxembourg,
the Netherlands, Portugal, Spain, Sweden, and the United Kingdom.

management and to reduce the complexity of their supply chains; hence
they tend to focus on large and more capable preferred suppliers, with
whom they develop strategic partnerships. This trend has led to a consolidation of the supply base, reducing the number of supplier countries
and firms within countries.

Nonmanufacturing capabilities: Buyers have also increased the functions they demand from suppliers. Besides manufacturing capabilities, buyers desire nonmanufacturing capabilities such as input sourcing and financing on the supplier's account, product development and design, inventory management and stock holding, and logistics and financing (that is, invoicing on a 60- or 90-day basis) capabilities. The objective of buyers to concentrate on their core competencies and reduce the complexity of their supply chains has spurred the shift from CMT to full-package suppliers. This shift has increased entry barriers into apparel exporting; firms without broader capabilities (besides manufacturing)— and, in particular, without sourcing capabilities—face challenges in the global apparel industry post-MFA.

Importance of time factors: Lead times and production flexibility were already crucial sourcing decisions in the MFA/ATC environment because of the shift to lean retailing and just-in-time delivery, where buyers defray the inventory risks associated with supplying apparel to fast-changing, volatile markets by replenishing items on their shelves in very short cycles and minimizing inventories (Abernathy, Volpe, and Weil 2006). Lean retailing was made possible by developments in information technology (for example, bar coding and point-of-sale scanning, electronic data interchange, and automated distribution centers) and is a response to stagnant apparel demand since the early 1980s as well as to rapidly changing consumer preferences. Post-MFA, the importance of lead time and flexibility has been reinforced because of buyers' quest to shorten product life cycles and increase the number of seasons (sometimes known as "fast fashion").

Labor and environment compliance: Compliance with labor and environmental standards has increased in importance in buyers' sourcing decisions post-MFA in response to pressure from corporate social responsibility campaigns by nongovernmental organizations (NGOs) and compliance-conscious consumers. Labor and environmental compliance has emerged as an important issue because of the labor intensity of the apparel industry and the environmental impact of the textile industry (for example, high energy use and wastewater output). Buyers take compliance seriously, and most have developed codes of conduct that include labor and environmental standards and conduct regular audits. Compliance with buyers' labor and environmental standards is generally a minimum criterion for entering and remaining in their supply chain.

Physical and bureaucratic infrastructure: Besides firm-specific sourcing criteria, country-specific factors are central in buyers' sourcing decisions.

Trade agreements and preferential market access still have a crucial role in global apparel trade, as discussed above. Good and reliable physical and bureaucratic infrastructure has become more crucial to remaining competitive in the global apparel industry in the context of increasing cost competitiveness, declining lead times, and higher demands from buyers. Key factors are the quality of transport, logistics, and customs infrastructure and services and the reliable access to energy, particularly for more capital-intensive textile production. In addition, access to low-cost finance is central when firms develop from CMT to full-package suppliers, as they have to be able to finance inputs and production and offer credit lines to buyers.

Export Patterns Post-MFA

The MFA phaseout and the related shifts in competitive dynamics and buyers' sourcing polices have had crucial implications for apparel export patterns. There are "winners" and "losers" at the country level, but also among different types of firms and workers within countries.

Total exports: China significantly increased its export share in the context of the MFA phaseout (from 28.3 percent in 2004 to 38.8 percent in 2008) and is by far the largest exporter of apparel (table 3.5). Bangladesh, Cambodia, India, Indonesia, and Vietnam also increased their exports more than the world average (figure 3.5). Collectively, the top 15 export economies increased their market share from 77.4 percent to 84.6 percent from 2004 to 2008.[8]

Exports to the United States: The EU-15 and the United States are by far the largest apparel-importing markets, accounting for 67.3 percent of global apparel imports in 2008. Developing countries' apparel exports are strongly concentrated in those two markets. In the U.S. market, China increased its import share from 10.5 percent in 2000 to 32.8 percent in 2008 (table 3.6). Vietnam, the second-largest exporter to the United States, increased its market share from 3.7 percent in 2004 to 7.0 percent in 2008. Other "winners" in the U.S. market include Bangladesh, Cambodia, and India. Mexico was still the number three exporter country in 2008, but its import share declined dramatically from 14.6 percent in 2000 to 5.6 percent in 2008. The import share of the Dominican Republic–Central America Free Trade Agreement (DR-CAFTA)—which includes Costa Rica, the Dominican Republic, El Salvador, Guatemala, Honduras, and Nicaragua—also fell, from 15.3 percent in 2000 to 10.5 percent in 2008. According to USITC, SSA countries increased their import share in the U.S. market from 1.3 percent to 2.6 percent between

Table 3.5 Top 15 Apparel-Exporting Economies, 1995, 2000, 2004, 2005, and 2008

Country/region/economy	Value ($, million)					Market share (%)				
	1995	2000	2004	2005	2008	1995	2000	2004	2005	2008
World	152,532	193,669	251,656	268,417	335,878					
China	32,868	48,019	71,137	89,829	130,394	21.5	24.8	28.3	33.5	38.8
EU-15	37,857	33,983	46,643	47,757	60,076	24.8	17.5	18.5	17.8	17.9
Turkey	5,261	6,710	12,397	12,922	15,769	3.4	3.5	4.9	4.8	4.7
Bangladesh	2,544	4,862	7,945	8,026	13,464	1.7	2.5	3.2	3.0	4.0
India	4,233	5,131	7,298	9,468	12,210	2.8	2.6	2.9	3.5	3.6
Vietnam	831	1,595	4,408	4,737	9,541	0.5	0.8	1.8	1.8	2.8
Indonesia	3,255	4,675	5,286	5,673	7,630	2.1	2.4	2.1	2.1	2.3
Hong Kong SAR, China	10,463	10,144	9,313	8,495	5,107	6.9	5.2	3.7	3.2	1.5
Mexico	2,871	8,924	7,285	6,683	4,634	1.9	4.6	2.9	2.5	1.4
Tunisia	2,400	2,645	3,590	3,476	4,489	1.6	1.4	1.4	1.3	1.3
Morocco	2,250	2,444	3,476	3,326	4,463	1.5	1.3	1.4	1.2	1.3
Romania	n.a.	2,737	5,369	5,172	4,216	n.a	1.4	2.1	1.9	1.3
Thailand	2,706	3,672	3,968	3,860	4,200	1.8	1.9	1.6	1.4	1.3
Cambodia	63	1,214	2,434	2,696	4,043	0.0	0.6	1.0	1.0	1.2
Sri Lanka	1,680	2,518	2,973	3,082	3,809	1.1	1.3	1.2	1.1	1.1
United States	4,402	5,157	3,173	3,681	n.a.	2.9	2.7	1.3	1.4	n.a.
Korea, Rep.	4,423	4,692	3,546	n.a.	n.a.	2.9	2.4	1.4	n.a.	n.a.
Other Asia, nes[a]	2,998	3,059	n.a.	n.a.	n.a.	2.0	1.6	n.a.	n.a.	n.a.
Philippines	n.a.	2,599	n.a.	n.a.	n.a.	n.a.	1.3	n.a.	n.a.	n.a.
Poland	2,306	n.a.	n.a.	n.a.	n.a.	1.5	n.a.	n.a.	n.a.	n.a.
Top 15 share	**120,835**	**147,009**	**194,836**	**216,186**	**284,044**	**79.2**	**75.9**	**77.4**	**80.5**	**84.6**
Pakistan	1,279	1,731	2,665	2,673	3,504	0.8	0.9	1.1	1.0	1.0
Honduras	970	2,524	2,926	2,897	3,035	0.6	1.3	1.2	1.1	0.9

Source: United Nations Commodity Trade Statistics Database (UN Comtrade).

Note: Apparel represented by Harmonized Commodity Description and Coding System (HS) 61 and 62; top 15 by year; n.a. = not applicable (indicates economy not in top 15 in given year). Countries highlighted in gray are the nine country case studies. Retrieved 4/3/2011.

a. nes = not elsewhere specified; essentially refers to Taiwan, China.

Figure 3.5   Percentage Change in Apparel Exports between 2004 and 2008, Top 15 and Case Study Countries and Selected Economies

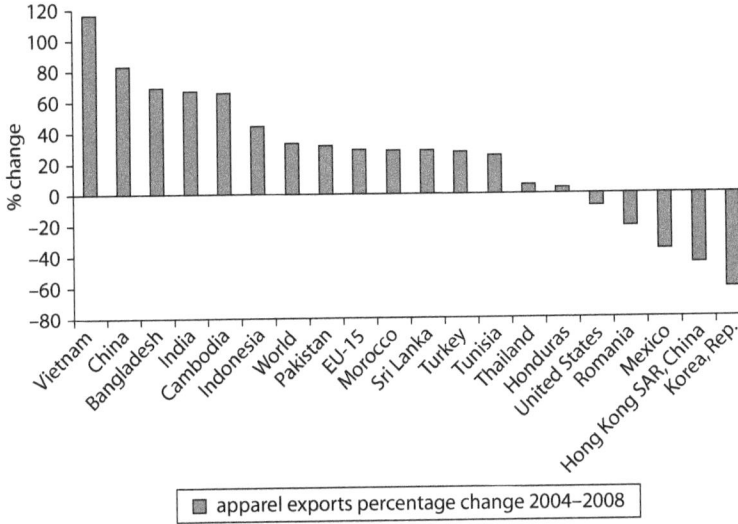

apparel exports percentage change 2004–2008

Source: United Nations Commodity Trade Statistics Database (UN Comtrade).
Note: Apparel represented by Harmonized Commodity Description and Coding System (HS) 1992: Codes 61 and 62; includes top 15 countries in both 2004 and 2008 (Korea, Rep., and United States are not in top 15 in 2008). Retrieved 4/3/2011. EU-15 = the 15 member states of the European Union (EU) as of December 31, 2003, before the new member states joined the EU: Austria, Belgium, Denmark, Finland, France, Germany, Greece, Ireland, Italy, Luxembourg, the Netherlands, Portugal, Spain, Sweden, and the United Kingdom.

2000 and 2004, an increase that was driven by AGOA, but from 2005 onward they lost market share. Collectively, the top 15 exporters decreased their share in U.S. imports from 75.4 percent in 1995 to 69.7 percent in 2004, but then increased to 82.2 percent by 2008.

Exports to the EU-15: In the EU-15 market, intra–EU-15 trade accounts for the largest import share, which, however, decreased from 43.4 percent in 1995 to 37.4 percent in 2008 (table 3.7). China is the second-largest importer and increased its import share from 7.0 percent in 1995 to 23.4 percent in 2008. Turkey, the third-largest importer, increased its share from 6.3 percent to 8.8 percent from 1995 to 2004, but then lost export share in the context of the MFA phaseout, as did Tunisia, Morocco, and Romania. Generally, the import share of regional supplier countries from Greater Europe, including Turkey as well as Central and Eastern European (CEE) and North African countries, fell, from 27.3 percent in 2004 to 21.3 percent in 2008. Bangladesh and India increased their market shares after the MFA. The share in EU-15 imports

Table 3.6 Top 15 U.S. Apparel Importer Economies, 1995, 2000, 2004, 2005, and 2008

Country/region/ economy	Customs value ($, million)					Market share (%)				
	1995	2000	2004	2005	2008	1995	2000	2004	2005	2008
Total	**36,103**	**59,206**	**66,869**	**70,807**	**73,102**					
China	4,653	6,202	10,721	16,808	24,000	12.9	10.5	16.0	23.7	32.8
Vietnam	n.a.	n.a.	2,506	2,665	5,151	n.a.	n.a.	3.7	3.8	7.0
Mexico	2,779	8,618	6,845	6,230	4,129	7.7	14.6	10.2	8.8	5.6
Indonesia	1,189	2,060	2,402	2,882	4,035	3.3	3.5	3.6	4.1	5.5
Bangladesh	997	1,942	1,872	2,268	3,355	2.8	3.3	2.8	3.2	4.6
India	1,163	1,852	2,277	3,058	3,122	3.2	3.1	3.4	4.3	4.3
Honduras	932	2,416	2,743	2,685	2,675	2.6	4.1	4.1	3.8	3.7
Cambodia	n.a.	n.a.	n.a.	1,702	2,371	n.a.	n.a.	n.a.	2.4	3.2
EU-15	1,740	2,245	2,289	2,171	2,065	4.8	3.8	3.4	3.1	2.8
Thailand	1,042	1,841	1,822	1,833	1,696	2.9	3.1	2.7	2.6	2.3

Hong Kong SAR, China	4,261	4,492	3,879	3,523	1,559	11.8	7.6	5.8	5.0	2.1
El Salvador	n.a.	1,602	1,720	n.a.	1,533	n.a.	2.7	2.6	n.a.	2.1
Pakistan	n.a.	n.a.	n.a.	n.a.	1,508	n.a.	n.a.	n.a.	n.a.	2.1
Sri Lanka	919	n.a.	n.a.	1,653	1,490	2.5	n.a.	n.a.	2.3	2.0
Guatemala	n.a.	n.a.	1,947	1,817	1,388	n.a.	n.a.	2.9	2.6	1.9
Philippines	1,489	1,876	1,765	1,821	n.a.	4.1	3.2	2.6	2.6	n.a.
Dominican Republic	1,698	2,390	2,036	1,831	n.a.	4.7	4.0	3.0	2.6	n.a.
Korea, Rep.	1,661	2,263	1,808	n.a.	n.a.	4.6	3.8	2.7	n.a.	n.a.
Taiwan, China	1,917	1,951	n.a.	n.a.	n.a.	5.3	3.3	n.a.	n.a.	n.a.
Canada	774	1,745	n.a.	n.a.	n.a.	2.1	2.9	n.a.	n.a.	n.a.
Top 15 share	**27,214**	**43,495**	**46,632**	**52,947**	**60,077**	**75.4**	**73.5**	**69.7**	**74.8**	**82.2**
DR-CAFTA	4,725	9,059	9,559	9,150	7,668	13.1	15.3	14.3	12.9	10.5

Source: U.S. International Trade Commission (USITC).

Note: Apparel represented by Harmonized Commodity Description and Coding System (HS) Codes 61 and 62; top 15 by year. DR-CAFTA = Dominican Republic–Central America Free Trade Agreement, n.a. = not applicable (indicates economy not in the top 15 in given year). EU-15 = the 15 member states of the European Union (EU) as of December 31, 2003, before the new member states joined the EU: Austria, Belgium, Denmark, Finland, France, Germany, Greece, Ireland, Italy, Luxembourg, the Netherlands, Portugal, Spain, Sweden, and the United Kingdom.

Table 3.7 Top 15 EU-15 Apparel Importer Economies, 1995, 2000, 2004, 2005, and 2008

	Customs value (€, million)					Market share (%)				
	1995	2000	2004	2005	2008	1995	2000	2004	2005	2008
World	**50.377**	**78.117**	**85.393**	**90.366**	**103.758**					
EU-15	21.838	30.513	32.642	34.093	38.812	43.3	39.1	38.2	37.7	37.4
China	3.542	7.450	11.038	16.420	24.330	7.0	9.5	12.9	18.2	23.4
Turkey	3.189	5.322	7.520	7.857	7.612	6.3	6.8	8.8	8.7	7.3
Bangladesh	0.967	2.567	3.689	3.509	4.667	1.9	3.3	4.3	3.9	4.5
India	1.588	2.005	2.434	3.201	3.826	3.2	2.6	2.9	3.5	3.7
Tunisia	1.729	2.567	2.586	2.454	2.580	3.4	3.3	3.0	2.7	2.5
Morocco	1.631	2.356	2.417	2.262	2.386	3.2	3.0	2.8	2.5	2.3
Romania	0.972	2.558	3.679	3.450	2.349	1.9	3.3	4.3	3.8	2.3
Poland	1.604	1.826	1.153	0.998	1.421	3.2	2.3	1.4	1.1	1.4
Vietnam	n.a.	n.a.	n.a.	n.a.	1.201	n.a.	n.a.	n.a.	n.a.	1.2
Sri Lanka	n.a.	0.831	0.806	0.795	1.113	n.a.	1.1	0.9	0.9	1.1

Indonesia	0.908	1.800	1.320	1.188	1.114	1.8	2.3	1.5	1.3	1.1
Bulgaria	n.a.	n.a.	1.046	1.072	1.127	n.a.	n.a.	1.2	1.2	1.1
Pakistan	n.a.	n.a.	0.906	0.770	0.865	n.a.	n.a.	1.1	0.9	0.8
Thailand	0.546	0.911	0.868	0.770	n.a.	1.1	1.2	1.0	0.9	n.a.
Hong Kong SAR, China	2.547	3.104	1.923	1.682	0.826	5.1	4.0	2.3	1.9	0.8
Hungary	0.729	1.001	n.a.	n.a.	n.a.	1.4	1.3	n.a.	n.a.	n.a.
Korea, Rep.	n.a.	0.891	n.a.	n.a.	n.a.	n.a.	1.1	n.a.	n.a.	n.a.
Mauritius	0.448	n.a.	n.a.	n.a.	n.a.	0.9	n.a.	n.a.	n.a.	n.a.
United States	0.443	n.a.	n.a.	n.a.	n.a.	0.9	n.a.	n.a.	n.a.	n.a.
Top 15 share	**42.683**	**65.703**	**74.026**	**80.520**	**94.229**	**84.7**	**84.1**	**86.7**	**89.1**	**90.8**
Greater Europe[a]	12.746	20.599	23.330	22.603	22.136	25.3	26.4	27.3	25.0	21.3

Source: Eurostat.

Note: Apparel represents Harmonized Commodity Description and Coding System (HS) Codes 61 and 62; world value represents the sum of EU-15 intra and extra trade, n.a. = not applicable (indicates country not in the top 15 in given year). EU-15 = the 15 member states of the European Union (EU) as of December 31, 2003, before the new member states joined the EU: Austria, Belgium, Denmark, Finland, France, Germany, Greece, Ireland, Italy, Luxembourg, the Netherlands, Portugal, Spain, Sweden, and the United Kingdom.

a. Greater Europe includes Turkey, Central and Eastern Europe (Romania; Poland; Bulgaria; Czech Republic; Hungary; Slovak Republic; Slovenia; Estonia; Latvia; Lithuania; Macedonia, FYR; Croatia; Serbia; Montenegro; Albania; Bosnia and Herzegovina; Moldova; Ukraine; Belarus; and the Russian Federation), and MENA-4 (Tunisia; Morocco; Egypt, Arab Rep; and Jordan).

of the top 15 exporters remained stable at around 85.0 percent between 1995 and 2004, but then increased to 90.8 percent by 2008.

Post-MFA consolidation: The top 15 exporters decreased their share in total (global) apparel exports as well as exports to the United States and the EU-15 between 2000 and 2004, but increased their share post-MFA between 2004 and 2008. Clearly, the MFA phaseout has led to a consolidation of exporter countries. Consolidation of sourcing countries can be also measured by a modified version of the Herfindahl-Hirschman index (HHI), which is calculated by taking the total sum of the squared market shares of all countries exporting apparel, as follows:

$$HHI_j = \sum (S_{ij})^2 \cdot 10,000$$

where S_i is the share of country i expressed as a percentage of total world exports of product j. A decline reflects a decrease in "concentration" or, more accurately, a greater degree of spatial dispersion of export sourcing in that sector (Milberg and Winkler 2010).[9] In the United States and the EU-15, the HHI remained quite stable until 2004 but then increased considerably, in particular in 2005 in the context of the MFA phaseout (figure 3.6). The United States shows a higher concentration of apparel imports, which can be largely explained by including the individual EU-15 countries for EU-15 imports and not the EU-15 as a group in the HHI calculation.

Country classification: Based on export data, it can be concluded that within the top 15 global apparel exporter countries, low-cost Asian apparel exporter countries such as Bangladesh, China, India, and Vietnam and, to a lesser extent, Cambodia and Indonesia have increased their export shares in the context of the MFA phaseout. In contrast, the market shares of higher-cost Asian apparel exporter countries such as Hong Kong SAR, China; Korea; Malaysia; the Philippines; Taiwan, China; and Thailand have declined. Regional suppliers such as Caribbean, Central American, and Mexican suppliers to the United States and North African and CEE suppliers to the EU-15, as well as SSA countries and several LICs in other regions, have lost export shares (Frederick and Gereffi 2011; Staritz 2011). The export performance of the main apparel-exporting countries post-MFA can be categorized as follows:

Increasing or steady global market share

- **China:** China has been the clear winner in global apparel exporting in the past 15 years. Between 1995 and 2008, China's share of global

Figure 3.6   Herfindahl-Hirschman Index (HHI) for Apparel Imports to the United States and the EU-15

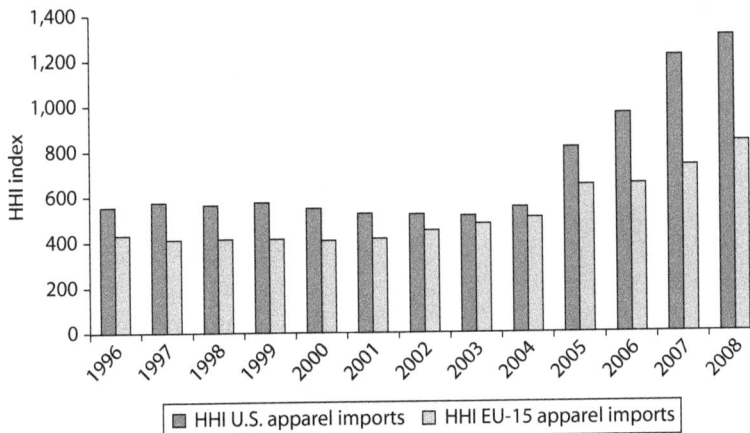

Sources: U.S. International Trade Commission (USITC); Eurostat; Staritz 2011.
Note: Apparel represented by Harmonized Commodity Description and Coding System (HS) Codes 61 and 62.
EU-15 = the 15 member states of the European Union (EU) as of December 31, 2003, before the new member states joined the EU: Austria, Belgium, Denmark, Finland, France, Germany, Greece, Ireland, Italy, Luxembourg, the Netherlands, Portugal, Spain, Sweden, and the United Kingdom.

apparel exports increased from 22 percent to 39 percent, representing an increase in value from $32.9 billion to $130.4 billion.

- *Growth suppliers:* Bangladesh, Cambodia, India, Indonesia, Pakistan, Sri Lanka, and Vietnam have increased global market share since the early 1990s *and* post-MFA.
- *Steady suppliers:* The EU-15, Morocco, Tunisia, and Turkey increased export values until 2008 and have maintained relatively stable global market shares through the quota phaseout.

Decreasing global market share

- *Decline with quota phaseout:* Canada, DR-CAFTA (Honduras), Mexico, Poland, Romania, Thailand, and the United States experienced declines during the MFA/ATC quota phaseout and after the MFA.
- *Past-prime suppliers:* Hong Kong SAR, China; Korea; the Philippines; and Taiwan, China, were once leading apparel exporters, but their global market shares have decreased since the early 1990s.

Global economic crisis. The impact of the phaseout of the China safeguards at the end of 2008 has to be assessed together with the global economic crisis that started in 2008 but evolved particularly in 2009. The global economic crisis has had important direct and indirect impacts on the apparel industry. Direct impacts include the downturn in global demand, which has led to reduced demand for apparel exports in major import markets such as the EU, Japan, and the United States; declining prices; and the reduction of trade finance, which has made it difficult for suppliers to finance exports (Staritz 2011). Total U.S. apparel imports declined by 3.3 percent in 2008 and by 12.0 percent in 2009; in the EU-15, apparel exports increased slightly by 1.5 percent in 2008 and decreased by 5.2 percent in 2009. Estimates for job losses attributable to the global economic crisis in different developing countries include 75,000 in Cambodia, 10 million in China, 1 million in India, 100,000 in Indonesia, 80,000 in Mexico, 200,000 in Pakistan, and 30,000 in Vietnam (Forstater 2010, cited in Gereffi and Frederick 2010). The crisis has also accelerated changes in the sourcing policies of global buyers, in particular the trend toward consolidation with regard to supplier countries and firms, as buyers used the reduction in orders to focus sourcing on their strategic and most capable suppliers. Another critical impact of the crisis might be a change in import structures. Although the EU and U.S. markets will remain the major import markets—at least for some time—emerging markets will gain in importance in the postcrisis world (Cattaneo, Gereffi, and Staritz 2010; Staritz, Gereffi, and Cattaneo 2011). The Economic Intelligence Unit estimates apparel retail demand for selected countries for the period 2008 to 2013. The fastest growth in the period is estimated for Brazil, China, Eastern Europe (including the Russian Federation), India, and Turkey (EIU 2008, cited in Textiles Intelligence 2009). With regard to world exports and import shares in the EU-15 and the United States, country trends after the MFA have generally continued and even accelerated after the phaseout of the China safeguards and during the global economic crisis.

Firm-Level Dynamics Post-MFA

Developments have also diverged within countries as different types of firms and workers have been affected differently post-MFA. Larger and more capable firms that provide broader functions have been "winners," in contrast to smaller firms focusing on dependent assembly activities. Worker skills and "social upgrading" have also increased in importance. The following developments are particularly important regarding firms and workers (Frederick and Gereffi 2011; Staritz 2011).

Concentration at the firm level: In most countries, larger firms have been better able to withstand the changing competitive dynamics and

sourcing policies of buyers brought about by the MFA phaseout; firm closures and employment losses have concentrated in medium and particularly small firms. Thus, in the majority of countries, a consolidation process
has been under way, with larger firms increasing production and employment shares at the expense of smaller firms or acquiring smaller firms.

Shift from CMT to OEM: Supplier consolidation and increasing
requirements with regard to manufacturing and nonmanufacturing capabilities have spurred the shift from CMT to full-package suppliers. In the
context of heightened entry barriers into apparel exporting, firms without broader capabilities (besides manufacturing) and in particular without sourcing capabilities face challenges in the global apparel industry
post-MFA. Assembly firms have faced the most difficulties, while firms
providing broader capabilities have been better prepared to face the post-
MFA changes.

Importance of skills: The apparel industry requires a large share of
unskilled and semiskilled workers, but the importance of skills has
increased for general line operators and particularly for supervisors, technical positions, and managers. Lack of skilled workers is one of the major
constraints to competitiveness and upgrading of the apparel industry in
many developing countries. This deficiency also dampens overall employment opportunities, as few skilled workers can have large employment
effects on unskilled and semiskilled workers. Increasing requirements
from buyers have increased the demand for relatively skilled workers and
high labor productivity. Skills upgrading and workforce development
initiatives have become crucial strategies post-MFA.

Social upgrading: With increasing buyer requirements and the prevalence of codes of conduct as well as increasing social unrest related to low
wages in the apparel industry in many developing countries, an export
strategy solely based on low wages does not seem to be a sustainable post-
MFA strategy. Low labor cost is a crucial competitive factor, but it has to
be matched with other factors. Social upgrading—defined as improvement
in the position of workers as reflected in decent working conditions—and
the interactions between economic and social upgrading have also become
important (Barrientos, Gereffi, and Rossi 2008).

Gender implications: Female employment intensity is generally very
high in the apparel industry compared to other manufacturing sectors,
reaching on average around 80 percent. However, there are differences in
female worker intensity in different segments of the industry, with the
textile industry being generally dominated by men, along with certain
segments and production processes of the apparel industry. Intensified

competition can lead to a higher demand for women, as they often accept lower wages and poorer working conditions compared to men. However, the increasing importance of skills and upgrading to more skill- and technology-intensive production processes and to broader capabilities, including backward linkages into textiles, may reduce demand for female workers, as women are often less skilled and are concentrated in low value-added jobs such as sewing.

Main Factors Explaining Post-MFA Developments

In light of the increasing demands by global buyers for high levels of manufacturing and nonmanufacturing capabilities, short lead times, production flexibility, and labor and environmental compliance, cost competitiveness and preferential market access seem not to be enough to remain competitive in the post-MFA apparel industry. Although cost competitiveness, particularly labor costs, and preferential market access have remained major competitiveness factors after 2004 and several LIC apparel exporters (such as Cambodia) have extended or stabilized market shares based on these factors, cost competitiveness and preferential market access are not the whole story.

Most countries' apparel sectors that increased market shares post-MFA have upgraded their industries to meet buyers' increasing requirements in terms of service reliability, quality, production flexibility, lead times, compliance, and broader nonmanufacturing capabilities. This upgrading was often supported by proactive policies driven by the private and public sectors. Countries such as Bangladesh, India, Sri Lanka, and Vietnam have been particularly active in developing industry strategies and upgrading along several dimensions. Other countries, such as Cambodia, Honduras, and SSA countries like Kenya, Lesotho, and Swaziland, have been quite passive in preparing for the MFA phaseout and initiating upgrading. These limited responses can be at least partly explained by ownership structures: the apparel industries in these countries are largely foreign owned, depending on offshore owners with headquarters in China; Hong Kong SAR, China; Korea; Taiwan, China; and so forth.

Overview of Case Study Countries

The following chapters and the background country papers in part 2 discuss in detail the nine country case studies. They give an overview of the structure, development, and upgrading experiences of their apparel industries post-MFA and particularly assess the impact of the MFA phaseout on employment and wages. This section starts with a short overview of the nine case studies based on the discussion of global developments in the apparel industry above. The case study countries include Bangladesh, Cambodia, Honduras, India, Mexico, Morocco, Pakistan, Sri Lanka, and Vietnam.

Development of the Apparel Industries

Different developments in the apparel industries in the country cases post-MFA can be shown by the percentage change between 2004 and 2008 of apparel export values to the world, share of world apparel exports, and employment in the apparel industry (figure 3.7). On the basis of this information, we can classify the countries into three groups:

- *Growing suppliers* have increased global market share since the early 1990s; post-MFA they increased export value, market share, and employment. Bangladesh, India, Vietnam, and, to a lesser extent, Cambodia are part of this group. Employment in the apparel industry between 2004 and 2008 grew in Bangladesh by 40 percent, in Cambodia by 20 percent, in India by 48 percent, and in Vietnam by

Figure 3.7   Country Cases: Change in Export Value, Market Share, and Employment, 2004–08

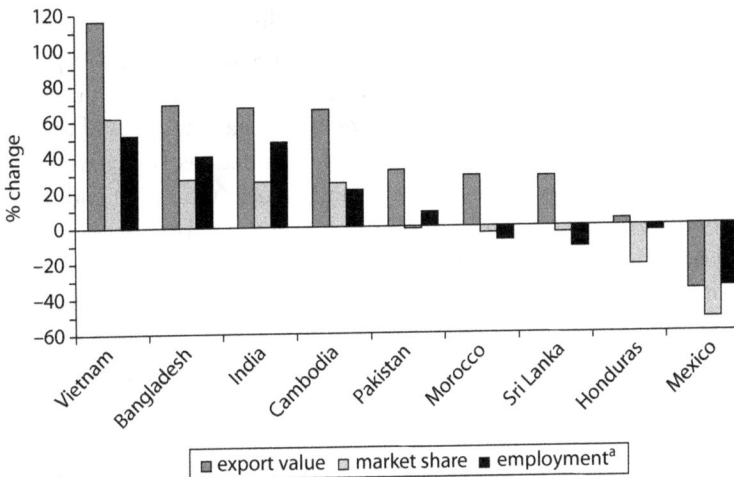

Source: For export data, United Nations Commodity Trade Statistics Database (UN Comtrade); for employment data, various sources; see background country papers (Staritz and Frederick 2011a, 2011b, 2011c, 2011d, 2011e, 2011f, 2011g, 2011h, 2011i).
a. An average of 2003–05 employment is used for 2004 for Sri Lanka.

52 percent. During the same period, Bangladesh's apparel exports and market share increased by 69 percent and 27 percent, respectively; Cambodia's by 66 percent and 24 percent; India's by 67 percent and 25 percent; and Vietnam's by 116 percent and 62 percent.

• *Stagnating suppliers* have increased export value and maintained market share post-MFA. Morocco, Pakistan, and Sri Lanka are part of this group, increasing their export values by 28 percent, 32 percent, and 28 percent, respectively, over 2004–08; their market shares remained relatively stable; employment in Pakistan went up by 8 percent, and in Morocco and Sri Lanka, it decreased by 8 percent and 12 percent, respectively.

• *Declining suppliers* lost significant market share and experienced stable or declining export value and employment post-MFA. Honduras and Mexico are part of this group. Honduras increased exports by 4 percent but experienced a decline in market share of 22 percent and in employment of 3 percent between 2004 and 2008. In Mexico, exports decreased by 36 percent, market share by 52 percent, and employment by 40 percent between 2004 and 2008.

Structure of Apparel Industries and Upgrading Experiences

The case study countries differ with regard to the structure of their apparel industries and upgrading experiences, including functional, channel (end market), product, and supply chain (backward linkages) upgrading. The following paragraphs discuss, first, the importance of the industry in each country (table 3.8) and, second, the main characteristics of the industry in the country cases, including labor costs, functions, backward linkages, ownership, export diversification, and unit values (tables 3.9 and 3.10).

Importance of apparel industry: Apparel exports in Bangladesh, Cambodia, Honduras, and Sri Lanka account for a large share of total merchandise exports—71.1 percent, 84.8 percent, 48.6 percent, and 40.9 percent, respectively, in 2008 (table 3.8). Other countries have more diversified export structures, in particular India and Mexico, where apparel exports account for 6.1 percent and 1.7 percent, respectively, of total merchandise exports in 2008. Apparel employment is large in all country cases, and it is even much more significant when informal employment is included. For instance, in India, total formal and informal employment in the apparel and textile industries was around 35 million, while formal employment was only 2 million (and of that, 700,000 in apparel) in 2008. Apparel employment accounted for 40 percent of total

Table 3.8   Significance of Apparel Industry and Employment

Country	Share of total exports (%)			Apparel employment	Textile+Apparel employment	Apparel's share of manufacturing employment (%)	
	2000	2004	2008	2008	2008	ILO	Current
Bangladesh	79.3	54.5	71.1	3,100,000	4,200,000	—	40
Cambodia[a]	69.8	70.8	84.8	281,855	281,855	38.2 (2005)	30
Honduras	68.0	35.8	48.6	83,712	83,712	—	79
India	14.1	10.5	6.1	675,000	2,037,143	6.2 (2001)	—
Mexico	5.2	3.8	1.7	289,351	750,000	12.3 (2000)	8
Morocco	32.3	30.9	16.6	149,477	200,000	17.8 (2002)	31
Pakistan	23.8	22.6	19.2	2,000,000	2,500,000	42.9 (2001)	38
Sri Lanka	51.8	48.0	40.9	280,000	301,000	34.2 (2000)	21
Vietnam	12.6	15.5	14.3	758,274	937,350	—	—

Sources: Data reflect the apparel industry only unless otherwise noted. Apparel's share of total exports: World Trade Organization (WTO) International Trade Statistics. Apparel and textile+apparel employment: various sources; see background country papers. Apparel's share of manufacturing employment: Ernst, Hernández Ferrer and Zult (2005); Pakistan's share represents textiles and apparel.
Note: ILO = International Labour Organization, — = not available.
a. Employment for Cambodia only represents apparel, and share of employment in the report represents industrial rather than manufacturing employment.

manufacturing employment in Bangladesh in 2008, 30 percent in Cambodia, 79 percent in Honduras, 31 percent in Morocco, 38 percent in Pakistan (including textile employment), and 21 percent in Sri Lanka. In India and Pakistan, the textile industry is similar to or more important than the apparel industry in terms of exports and employment generation; in Pakistan, this situation is largely based on the production of made-up textiles, including towels and bed linen.

Labor costs: Labor costs per hour differ between the country cases, ranging from $0.22 in Bangladesh to $2.54 in Mexico in 2008 (table 3.9). Lower labor costs locations include (besides Bangladesh) Cambodia ($0.33), Pakistan ($0.37), and Vietnam ($0.38). India and Sri Lanka range in the middle, with $0.51 and $0.43, respectively. Higher labor cost locations are Honduras ($1.77), Mexico, and Morocco ($2.24).

Functions performed: As discussed above, apparel-producing countries can be categorized by the functional capabilities of the majority of apparel manufacturing firms within the country. In the country cases, Cambodia is largely limited to CMT activities. Bangladesh, Honduras, Morocco, Pakistan, and Vietnam are also concentrated in CMT production, but there have been important upgrading processes to OEM. A third group of countries is concentrated in OEM production, such as Mexico; India and Sri Lanka are also focused on OEM, with some upgrading into ODM.

Table 3.9 Industry Characteristics and Upgrading (Functional and Supply Chain)

Country	Labor cost ($/hour) 2002	2008	Functions performed	Backward linkages	Ownership structure (%)	Firms Number (2008)	Size
Bangladesh	0.39	0.22	CMT (ca. 70%)/OEM	Cotton knitted fabric and yarn, limited cotton woven fabric	Domestic (98)	4,743	Varies
Cambodia	—	0.33	CMT (75–90%)	No	Foreign (93)	284	Varies
Honduras	1.48	1.77	CMT/OEM	Limited cotton knitted fabric	Foreign (85)	133	Varies
India	0.38	0.51	OEM/ODM	Cotton fiber through fabric and man-made fibers	Domestic (majority)	77,000	Small
Mexico	2.45	2.54	CMT/OEM	Limited cotton fiber through woven fabric	Domestic and foreign	10,159	Varies
Morocco	—	2.24	CMT (50–70%)/OEM	Limited knitted fabric and woven (denim) fabric	Domestic (majority)	880	SME (75%)
Pakistan	0.41	0.37	CMT/OEM	Cotton fiber through fabric	Domestic (98)	—	Small
Sri Lanka	0.48	0.43	OEM/ODM	Limited knitted fabric	Domestic (80)	350	Varies
Vietnam	—	0.38	CMT (ca. 70%)/OEM	Limited knitted fabric	Private/SOE partnership (76); foreign (18)	3,174	Varies

Sources: Various sources; see country background papers (Staritz and Frederick 2011a, 2011b, 2011c, 2011d, 2011e, 2011f, 2011g, 2011h, 2011i). Hourly labor rate: Jassin-O'Rourke Group 2008.

Note: For comparison of hourly labor rates: China 2002: $0.78 (coastal average). China 2008: $0.88 (inland average). — = not available. CMT = cut-make-trim; OEM = original equipment manufacturing; ODM = original design manufacturing; SME = small and medium enterprises; SOE = state-owned enterprise.

Table 3.10   Export Diversification and Unit Values

Country	Export share to countries other than EU-15 and United States (%)			Unit values average, 2000–08		Unit values change, 2004–08 (%)	
	2000	2005	2008	EU-15 (€/kg)	United States ($/doz)	EU-15	United States
Bangladesh	6.0	10.0	15.4	7.9	36.3	0.0	−1.7
Cambodia	7.2	8.5	13.7	14.1	49.8	−6.7	−25.4
Honduras	1.6	4.3	7.8	—	20.8	—	−6.2
India	21.7	17.5	19.7	14.9	56.3	12.1	−19.9
Mexico	2.3	5.1	8.0	—	46.0	—	10.4
Morocco	1.8	5.5	9.3	19.0	—	22.2	—
Pakistan	7.4	7.8	12.3	7.9	36.1	−5.1	−9.4
Sri Lanka	5.2	5.6	10.0	16.4	60.4	15.2	−21.7
Vietnam	49.7	20.2	20.3	15.1	47.3	−12.0	−10.5

Sources: United Nations Commodity Trade Statistics Database (UN Comtrade), U.S. International Trade Commission (USITC), Eurostat.

Note: — = not available. EU-15 = the 15 member states of the European Union (EU) as of December 31, 2003, before the new member states joined the EU: Austria, Belgium, Denmark, Finland, France, Germany, Greece, Ireland, Italy, Luxembourg, the Netherlands, Portugal, Spain, Sweden, and the United Kingdom.

Backward linkages: The country cases can be differentiated into fiber-producing countries, including India and Pakistan, and nonfiber-producing countries. In India and Pakistan, the textile industry is as important as the apparel industry or even more important, accounting for 46 percent and 66 percent, respectively, of total textile and apparel exports in 2008. Some nonfiber-producing countries have invested strongly into backward linkages into textiles to improve delivery time and competitiveness—for example, Bangladesh and Vietnam. Generally, backward linkages are more developed in the knit segment than in the woven segment due to the higher capital intensity of woven fabric production.

Ownership structures: In countries such as Cambodia and Honduras, the apparel industry is dominated by foreign-owned firms—93 percent of Cambodian factories and 85 percent of Honduran factories. Ownership structures are important because they determine how supplier firms are linked to global production and distribution networks (Staritz 2011). Factories in Cambodia and Honduras are integrated into production networks through their foreign parent companies. This organization secures access to global buyers and input sourcing networks but also limits the decision power and the functions performed locally. The parent companies are generally in charge of input sourcing, product development and design, logistics, merchandising, and marketing and have direct relationships with buyers. In the other country cases, the majority or at least an important part of firms are locally owned. In India and Pakistan, an important part of the apparel and textile industries consists of small-scale, informal firms—in India, informal employment is estimated at 90 percent of total textile and apparel employment.

Export market diversification: All country cases are concentrated on the EU-15 and U.S. markets, with generally more than 80 percent of total exports going to these two markets (table 3.10). However, apparel industries in all countries have diversified export markets post-MFA. Bangladesh, India, and Vietnam have the most diversified end markets. Regional suppliers are concentrated in only one of the two largest markets—Honduras and Mexico on the U.S. market, Morocco on the EU-15 market.

Product diversification and unit values: Cambodia, India, Mexico, Sri Lanka, and Vietnam are above the world average unit value of $45 per dozen to the U.S. market for the period 2000–08; Bangladesh, Honduras, and Pakistan are below the world average (table 3.10). Between 2004 and 2008, U.S. unit values declined for all countries except Mexico, where they increased by 10.4 percent. This different position with regard to unit values shows on the one hand product upgrading and specialization in products with different unit values, but on the other hand it can also show declining cost competitiveness. In the EU-15 market, Morocco is above the world average unit value of €17.5 per kilogram for the period 2000–08; all other countries are below the world average (which is relatively high due to the importance of intra–EU-15 trade). Most countries increased their EU-15 unit values between 2004 and 2008; only Cambodia, Pakistan, and Vietnam experienced a decline, by 6.7 percent, 5.1 percent, and 12.0 percent, respectively. Supplier countries such as Bangladesh and Pakistan are in the low unit value segment, and supplier countries such as India and Sri Lanka are in the higher unit value segment. In contrast to Honduras, which has relatively low unit values in the U.S. market, Morocco has relatively high unit values in the EU-15 market that can be related to its role as a "fast fashion" supplier.

Trade Regulations and Proactive Policies

Trade preferences have an important role in the apparel industry, as discussed above. The case study countries enjoy varying market access preferences to the main export markets of the EU-15 and the United States and are part of different regional groups and agreements (table 3.11).

Table 3.11 Market Access Preferences

Country	Regional group	Regional agreements	Bilateral FTAs	GSP	WTO member
Bangladesh	SAARC	SAFTA	—	Australia, Canada, New Zealand, Norway, Switzerland, Japan, EU (EBA); LDCs	Yes
Cambodia	ASEAN	ASEAN: Japan, Australia-New Zealand, and China	—	Australia, Canada, New Zealand, Norway, Switzerland, Japan, EU (EBA); LDCs	Yes (2004)
Honduras	DR-CAFTA	Mexico-CA3: Guatemala, El Salvador, Honduras	—	EU, Canada	Yes
India	SAARC	SAFTA	Sri Lanka	EU (GSP for apparel only; textiles omitted)	Yes
Mexico	NAFTA	Mexico-CA3	EU	Japan, Turkey, Belarus, New Zealand, Russian Federation	Yes
Morocco	OPT, Euro-Mediterranean Partnership	EU: Euro-Mediterranean Partnership and EFTA, Algadir	U.S., Turkey, UAE		Yes
Pakistan	SAARC	SAFTA	China, Sri Lanka, Malaysia	EU (GSP); U.S. Reconstruction Opportunity Zone (ROZ)	Yes
Sri Lanka	SAARC	SAFTA	India, Pakistan	EU (GSP+: mid-2005–10; GSP 2010–present)	Yes
Vietnam	ASEAN	ASEAN: Japan, Australia-New Zealand, and China	Vietnam-Japan Economic Partnership Agreement	EU (GSP)	Yes (2007)

Source: Authors.

Note: — = not available. FTA = free trade agreement; GSP = Generalized System of Preferences; WTO = World Trade Organization; SAARC = South Asian Association for Regional Cooperation; SAFTA = South Asian Free Trade Agreement; EBA = Everything but Arms; LDCs = least developed countries; ASEAN = Association of South East Asian Nations; DR-CAFTA = Dominican Republic–Central America Free Trade Agreement; CA3 = Guatemala, Honduras, and El Salvador; NAFTA = North American Free Trade Agreement; OPT = Outward Processing Trade; EFTA = European Free Trade Association; UAE = United Arab Emirates; EU = European Union; GSP+ = GSP that offers preferential market access to vulnerable developing countries.

The countries also differ with regard to upgrading efforts and proactive policies to support upgrading by the private and the public sector (table 3.12). Bangladesh, India, Sri Lanka, and Vietnam have been very active in developing industry strategies and enhancing upgrading along several dimensions. Other countries, such as Cambodia (with the exception

Table 3.12   Policies in the Context of the MFA Phaseout

Country	Initiator	Program
Bangladesh	National government and industry associations (BGMEA/BKMEA)	National Coordination Council (NCC), Post-MFA Action Program (PMAP); EPZ Program
Cambodia	Industry association (GMAC); ILO	Government/Private Sector Forum, Garment Sector Strategy but not implemented; Better Factories Cambodia
Honduras	National and U.S. government	DR-CAFTA; CBI preferences; FTZ policy
India	National government and industry associations	National Textile Policy 2000 (Technology Upgradation Fund Scheme [TUFS], Integrated Textile Parks, Technology Mission on Cotton and Non-Cotton Fibers and Yarns, Product Development and Design Capabilities, Integrated Skill Development Scheme)
Mexico	National and U.S. government	NAFTA; Maquiladora and PITEX Policy
Morocco	National government and EU; industry association (AMITH)	Euromed; Framework Agreement, Plan Emergence, Fibre Citoyenne Code
Pakistan	National government and industry associations	Textile Vision 2005; Technology Upgradation Fund; Textile Policy 2009–14
Sri Lanka	National government and industry association (JAAF)	Five-Year Strategy; Garments without Guilt
Vietnam	National government and industry association (VITAS); ILO/IFC	Ten-Year Strategy; Better Work Vietnam

Source: Authors, based on Staritz and Frederick 2011a, 2011b, 2011c, 2011d, 2011e, 2011f, 2011g, 2011h, 2011i.
Note: BGMEA = Bangladesh Garment Manufacturers and Exporters Association; BKMEA = Bangladesh Knitwear Manufacturers and Exporters Association; MFA = Multi-fibre Arrangement; EPZ = export processing zone; GMAC = Garment Manufacturers' Association in Cambodia; ILO = International Labour Organization; DR-CAFTA = Dominican Republic–Central America Free Trade Agreement; CBI = Caribbean Basin Initiative; FTZ = free trade zone; NAFTA = North American Free Trade Agreement; PITEX = Temporary Importation Program to Produce Articles for Exportation; AMITH = The Moroccan Association of Textile and Apparel Industries; JAAF = Joint Apparel Association Forum; VITAS = Vietnam Textile and Apparel Association; IFC = International Finance Corporation.

of the Better Factories Cambodia program supported by the International Labour Organization [ILO] and the International Finance Corporation [IFC]), Honduras, Mexico, and Morocco, have been less active in preparing for the MFA phaseout and initiating upgrading.

Figure 3.8 provides a rough overview of the discussion above on the nine case study countries. It highlights differences in the structure of the apparel industry and in particular different upgrading experiences and proactive policies. The figure is based on a mix of empirical evidence and judgment from the authors. It shows, based on the experiences of the case study countries, that cost competitiveness and preferential market access have remained major competitiveness factors but that the

Figure 3.8   Factors Affecting Post-MFA Competitiveness: Country Comparison

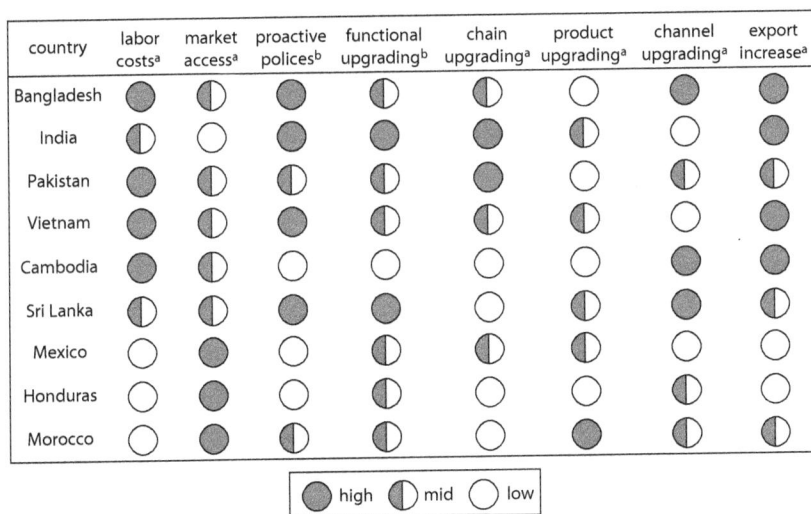

country	labor costs[a]	market access[a]	proactive polices[b]	functional upgrading[b]	chain upgrading[a]	product upgrading[a]	channel upgrading[a]	export increase[a]
Bangladesh	high	mid	high	mid	mid	low	high	high
India	mid	low	high	high	high	mid	low	high
Pakistan	high	mid	mid	mid	high	low	mid	mid
Vietnam	high	mid	high	mid	mid	mid	low	high
Cambodia	high	mid	low	low	low	low	high	high
Sri Lanka	mid	mid	high	high	mid	mid	high	mid
Mexico	low	high	low	mid	mid	mid	low	low
Honduras	low	high	low	mid	low	low	mid	low
Morocco	low	high	mid	mid	low	high	mid	mid

● high   ◑ mid   ○ low

Source: Authors. For labor costs: hourly labor rate (including social charges) (2008) by Jassin-O'Rourke Group (2008); for market access: various sources on market access agreements specific to the United States and the EU-15 (see country background papers—Staritz and Frederick 2011a, 2011b, 2011c, 2011d, 2011e, 2011f, 2011g, 2011h, 2011i); for chain upgrading: various sources on textile production and other input industries (see country background papers); for product upgrading: average unit values to the United States and the EU-15 (2000–08) from United Nations Commodity Trade Statistics Database (UN Comtrade), U.S. International Trade Commission (USITC), and Eurostat; for channel upgrading: change in export share to countries other than the United States and the EU-15 (2000–08) from UN Comtrade, USITC, and Eurostat; for export increase: total exports from UN Comtrade (2004–08).

Note: For each category a "high" ranking indicates the country is competitive in this area compared to other country cases. EU-15 = the 15 member states of the European Union (EU) as of December 31, 2003, before the new member states joined the EU: Austria, Belgium, Denmark, Finland, France, Germany, Greece, Ireland, Italy, Luxembourg, the Netherlands, Portugal, Spain, Sweden, and the United Kingdom.
a. Based on empirical evidence.
b. Based on the judgment of the authors on the basis of industry data and documents (see discussion in country background papers—Staritz and Frederick 2011a, 2011b, 2011c, 2011d, 2011e, 2011f, 2011g, 2011h, 2011i).

different dimensions of upgrading and proactive policies have also played a crucial role in how the countries have fared post-MFA. With regard to proactive policies, the public and private sectors in Bangladesh, India, Sri Lanka, and Vietnam have been active in preparing for heightened competition and developing upgrading strategies. Functional upgrading has played a particularly important role in helping countries' apparel industries remain competitive post-MFA, specifically for the higher-cost countries of India and Sri Lanka. However, countries such as Cambodia still have been able to increase exports and market share post-MFA without important upgrading experiences and proactive policies. This short overview of the case study countries underscores three points in particular: (i) that the "success" or "failure" story of countries is not exactly the same because several dimensions are involved in increasing exports and competitiveness; (ii) that public and private proactive policies supporting the apparel industry play a crucial role in apparel export growth; and (iii) that upgrading strategies (at the firm, industry, and policy level) are necessary to increase apparel exports and ensure sustainable competitiveness. However, besides these general conclusions, appropriate policies and upgrading strategies will depend on the specific country context.

Conclusions

The global apparel industry has expanded rapidly since the early 1970s, and many developing countries have been integrated into the apparel GVC. With the MFA phaseout at the end of 2004, the most significant change in the recent history of global apparel trade took place, reshaping the environment for global apparel trade. Competitive dynamics and buyers' sourcing policies have changed, with crucial implications for the structure of the global apparel industry and for reallocations of production and employment between countries and within countries. Competition and price pressures have intensified, and global buyers have increased their demands for high levels of manufacturing and nonmanufacturing capabilities, short lead times, production flexibility, and labor and environmental compliance.

In this context, cost competitiveness (particularly labor costs) and preferential market access have remained major competitiveness factors, but they are not the whole story. Upgrading—particularly to increase functional capabilities, establish backward linkages to important input sectors such as textiles, produce more sophisticated products, and diversify end markets—is crucial in understanding how different suppliers have fared post-MFA. Most countries' apparel sectors that increased market shares post-MFA have upgraded their industries to meet buyers' increasing requirements. Firms play a key role in upgrading efforts. However, proactive government policies have been critical to support firm and industry upgrading.

The MFA phaseout has led to global consolidation whereby leading apparel supplier countries and firms have strengthened their position in the apparel GVC. Low-cost Asian apparel exporter countries such as Bangladesh, China, India, and Vietnam and to a lesser extent Cambodia and Indonesia have increased their market share in the EU-15 and the United States. This increase has been primarily at the expense of regional suppliers, such as Caribbean, Central American, and Mexican suppliers to the United States and North African and CEE suppliers to the EU-15. Higher-cost Asian apparel exporter economies (such as Hong Kong SAR, China; Korea; Malaysia; the Philippines; Taiwan, China; and Thailand), as well as SSA apparel suppliers and several LICs in different regions, have also lost market share after the MFA phaseout. At the firm level, larger and more capable suppliers that provide broader functions have benefited at the expense of smaller firms focusing on dependent assembly activities, leading to a consolidation of supplier firms in many countries. In particular, CMT suppliers have faced challenges in the global apparel industry post-MFA.

Notes

1. The EU-15 is the 15 member states of the European Union (EU) as of December 31, 2003, before the new member states joined the EU: Austria, Belgium, Denmark, Finland, France, Germany, Greece, Ireland, Italy, Luxembourg, the Netherlands, Portugal, Spain, Sweden, and the United Kingdom.

2. In producer-driven chains (which are common in capital- and technology-intensive products such as automobiles, electronics, and machinery), large, integrated, and often multinational firms coordinate production networks. Control is generally embedded in lead firms' control over production technology.

3. FOB is technically an international trade term meaning that, for the quoted price, goods are delivered on board a ship or to another carrier at no cost to the buyer.

4. For example, the North American Free Trade Agreement (NAFTA), the Caribbean Basin Initiative (CBI), and the Dominican Republic–Central America Free Trade Agreement (DR-CAFTA) in the case of the United States;

the EU itself, the Euro-Mediterranean Partnership, and the EU Customs Union in the case of the EU.

5. For example, the Association of South East Asian Nations (ASEAN), the South Asian Association for Regional Cooperation (SAARC), Mercosur, the Andean Community, and several agreements in SSA, including the Southern African Development Community (SADC), the East African Community (EAC), and the Economic Community of West African States (ECOWAS).

6. The **EBA amendment** became effective in March 2001 and extended duty- and quota-free access to all products originating in LDCs, except arms and ammunition. In general, ROOs under the EU GSP require double transformation, that is, two significant processes to be performed within the beneficiary country. However, in January 2011, EU ROOs changed to single transformation for LDCs. **GSP+** offers preferential market access to vulnerable developing countries. To benefit from this scheme, countries need to demonstrate that their economies are "poorly diversified and therefore vulnerable and dependent." In addition, the beneficiary nation needs to have ratified and implemented the 16 core conventions of human and labor rights and at least 7 of the 11 conventions on good governance and protection of the environment or undertake actions to combat drug trafficking and production. The GSP+ came into operation in December 2005 and provides duty-free access to over 7,200 products to the EU market. The group of **African, Caribbean, and Pacific (ACP)** countries has traditionally received more generous tariff preferences in the EU market. The Lomé Convention (signed in 1975 and renewed three times) was replaced by the Cotonou Agreement in 2000, which eliminates import duties on apparel meeting its ROO. A central part of the Cotonou Agreement was the negotiation of economic partnership agreements (EPAs), and several countries signed interim EPAs in 2008 and 2009. For countries that signed an interim EPA, ROO changed to single transformation.

7. **AGOA** includes SSA countries and was signed in May 2000 and subsequently extended and modified three times, currently running until 2015. In terms of improved market access, the impact differs between lesser developed countries (defined as countries that had a gross national product (GNP) per capita of less than $1,500 in 1998) and others. For lesser developed countries, it matters whether they are able to access the preferences on apparel products, since most other products liberalized under AGOA had already been liberalized under the GSP. AGOA ROO requires triple transformation. A special rule applies to lesser developed countries, allowing them duty-free access for apparel made from fabrics originating anywhere in the world—the third country fabric (TCF) provision—initially granted until September 2004 but extended to September 2007 and again to September 2012.

8. The global economic crisis started in 2008 but evolved particularly in 2009, and is thus only partly captured in the data shown. The phaseout of the China safeguards took place at the end of 2008 and is thus not captured in the data shown.

9. The HHI can range between $1/n2*10,000$ (all countries have the same share) and 10,000 (one country exports all), where n designates the total number of countries exporting this product (Milberg and Winkler 2010).

References

Background Papers

Staritz, Cornelia, and Stacey Frederick. 2011a. "Background Global Value Chain Country Papers: Bangladesh." Background paper to *Sewing Success? Employment, Wages, and Poverty following the End of the Multi-fibre Arrangement*, World Bank, Washington, DC.

———. 2011b. "Background Global Value Chain Country Papers: India." Background paper to *Sewing Success? Employment, Wages, and Poverty following the End of the Multi-fibre Arrangement*, World Bank, Washington, DC.

———. 2011c. "Background Global Value Chain Country Papers: Vietnam." Background paper to *Sewing Success? Employment, Wages, and Poverty following the End of the Multi-fibre Arrangement*, World Bank, Washington, DC.

———. 2011d. "Background Global Value Chain Country Papers: Pakistan." Background paper to *Sewing Success? Employment, Wages, and Poverty following the End of the Multi-fibre Arrangement*, World Bank, Washington, DC.

———. 2011e. "Background Global Value Chain Country Papers: Cambodia." Background paper to the book *Sewing Success? Employment, Wages, and Poverty following the End of the Multi-fibre Arrangement*, World Bank, Washington, DC.

———. 2011f. "Background Global Value Chain Country Papers: Sri Lanka." Background paper to the book *Sewing Success? Employment, Wages, and Poverty following the End of the Multi-fibre Arrangement*, World Bank, Washington, DC.

———. 2011g. "Background Global Value Chain Country Papers: Honduras." Background paper to the book *Sewing Success? Employment, Wages, and Poverty following the End of the Multi-fibre Arrangement*, World Bank, Washington, DC.

———. 2011h. "Background Global Value Chain Country Papers: Mexico." Background paper to the book *Sewing Success? Employment, Wages, and Poverty following the End of the Multi-fibre Arrangement*, World Bank, Washington, DC.

———. 2011i. "Background Global Value Chain Country Papers: Morocco." Background paper to the book *Sewing Success? Employment, Wages, and Poverty following the End of the Multi-fibre Arrangement*, World Bank, Washington, DC.

Sources

Abernathy, Frederick H., Anthony Volpe, and David Weil. 2006. "The Future of the Apparel and Textile Industries: Prospects and Choices for Public and Private Actors." *Environment and Planning A* 38 (12): 2207–32.

Bair, Jennifer, and Gary Gereffi. 2003. "Upgrading, Uneven Development, and Jobs in the North American Apparel Industry." *Global Networks* 3 (2): 143–69.

Barrientos, Stephanie, Gary Gereffi, and Arianna Rossi. 2008. "What Are the Challenges and Opportunities for Economic and Social Upgrading?" Concept note for research workshop, "Capturing the Gains," University of Manchester, U.K.

Cattaneo, Olivier, Gary Gereffi, and Cornelia Staritz. 2010. *Global Value Chains in a Post-Crisis World: A Development Perspective.* Washington, DC: World Bank.

Dickerson, Kitty G. 1999. *Textiles and Apparel in the Global Economy.* Upper Saddle River, NJ: Merrill.

Ernst, Christoph, Alfons Hernández Ferrer, and Daan Zult. 2005. "The End of the Multi-fibre Arrangement and its Implication for Trade and Employment." International Labour Organization, Geneva.

Frederick, Stacey. 2010. "Development and Application of a Value Chain Research Approach to Understand and Evaluate Internal and External Factors and Relationships Affecting Economic Competitiveness in the Textile Value Chain." Doctoral dissertation, North Carolina State University, Raleigh, NC.

Frederick, Stacey, and Gary Gereffi. 2011. "Upgrading and Restructuring in the Global Apparel Value Chain: Why China and Asia Are Outperforming Mexico and Central America." *International Journal of Technological Learning, Innovation, and Development* 4 (1–2): 67–95.

Gereffi, Gary. 1994. "The Organization of Buyer Driven Global Commodity Chains: How U.S. Retailers Shape Overseas Production Networks." In *Commodity Chains and Global Capitalism,* ed. Gary Gereffi and Miguel Korzeniewicz, 95–122. Westport, CT: Praeger.

———. 1999. "International Trade and Industrial Upgrading in the Apparel Commodity Chain." *Journal of International Economics* 48 (1): 37–70.

Gereffi, Gary, and Stacey Frederick. 2010. "The Global Apparel Value Chain, Trade and the Crisis—Challenges and Opportunities for Developing Countries." In *Global Value Chains in a Postcrisis World: A Development Perspective,* ed. Olivier Cattaneo, Gary Gereffi, and Cornelia Staritz, 157–208. Washington, DC: World Bank.

Gereffi, Gary, John Humphrey, Raphael Kaplinsky, and Timothy J. Sturgeon. 2001. "Introduction: Globalisation, Value Chains and Development." *IDS Bulletin* 32 (3): 1–8.

Gereffi, Gary, John Humphrey, and Timothy J. Sturgeon. 2005. "The Governance of Global Value Chains." *Review of International Political Economy* 12 (1): 78–104.

Gereffi, Gary, and Olga Memedovic. 2003. "The Global Apparel Value Chain: What Prospects for Upgrading by Developing Countries?" United Nations Industrial Development Organization, Sectoral Studies Series, Vienna.

Humphrey, John, and Hubert Schmitz. 2002. "How Does Insertion in Global Value Chains Affect Upgrading in Industrial Clusters?" *Regional Studies* 36 (9): 1017–27.

Jassin-O'Rourke Group, L. 2008. "Global Apparel Manufacturing Labor Cost Analysis 2008, Textile and Apparel Manufacturers & Merchants." http://www.tammonline.com/researchpapers.htm.

Kaplinsky, Raphael, and Mike Morris. 2006. "Dangling by a Thread: How Sharp Are the Chinese Scissors?" Report prepared for the Department for International Development Trade Division, Institute of Development Studies, Brighton, U.K.

Milberg, William, and Deborah Winkler. 2010. "Trade, Crisis, and Recovery: Restructuring Global Value Chains." In *Global Value Chains in a Postcrisis World: A Development Perspective*, ed. Olivier Cattaneo, Gary Gereffi, and Cornelia Staritz, 23–72. Washington, DC: World Bank.

Morris, Mike. 2006. "Globalisation, China, and Clothing Industrialisation Strategies in Sub-Saharan Africa." In *The Future of the Textile and Clothing Industry in Sub-Saharan Africa*, ed. Herbert Jauch and Rudolf Traub-Merz, 36–53. Bonn: Friedrich-Ebert-Stiftung.

Staritz, Cornelia. 2011. "Making the Cut? Low-Income Countries and the Global Clothing Value Chain in a Post-Quota and Post-Crisis World." Study, World Bank, Washington, DC.

Staritz, Cornelia, Gary Gereffi, and Olivier Cattaneo. 2011. *Shifting End Markets and Upgrading Prospects in Global Value Chains.* Special Issue, *International Journal of Technological Learning, Innovation and Development* 4(1–3).

Textiles Intelligence. 2009. "World Trade in Textiles and Clothing." Presentation by Sam Anson at the World Free Zones Conference, Hyderabad, India, December.

CHAPTER 4

Success and Upgrading after the End of the MFA

Ana Luisa Gouvea Abras

Introduction

This chapter analyzes the evolution of employment, wages, and working conditions in the textile and garment (T&G) sector in four developing economies that faced the end of the Multi-fibre Arrangement (MFA) quotas: Bangladesh, India, Pakistan, and Vietnam. In these four countries, T&G remains an important sector in terms of export value and employment (mostly female) and as a channel for social and economic upgrading for unskilled workers. Employment in T&G in the late 2000s ranged from approximately 937,350 workers in Vietnam to 2.5 million in Pakistan, 3.1 million in Bangladesh, and 35.0 million in India. The large T&G Asian countries analyzed in this chapter share several characteristics. The first is the substantial and increasing relevance of T&G in providing jobs and

The author of this chapter is grateful for comments provided by Gladys Lopez-Acevedo, Raymond Robertson, and Yevgeniya Savchenko. Regressions with Bangladeshi and Indian firm-level data were performed by Hong Tan and Yevgeniya Savchenko. Kalpana Mehra prepared the household data set working files. The background information for the industry evolution section draws extensively from the country background papers of Cornelia Staritz and Stacey Frederick (Staritz and Frederick 2011a, 2011b, 2011c, 2011d).

export revenues. The second is success in expanding exports in a more competitive market. The third is the active role of the government in promoting the sector.

In the following sections, we discuss trends in T&G employment for male and female workers, industry structure, wages, and working conditions. Results from the qualitative research are difficult to generalize, but we are able to identify a *positive relationship between industry successes and proactive state policies*. The government played a crucial role in developing the sector since its inception. The state also helped in preparing T&G firms for the more competitive market after 2004. In the aftermath of the phaseout, the countries studied modernized their industries, increased capabilities, and moved up in the global value chain (GVC). In all the large Asian T&G industries analyzed, sector employment and export revenues increased after the MFA phaseout. These outcomes are surprising given the decline in average unit value of apparel exports and heightened international competition, and they should be interpreted in light of country internal factors. Quantitative results indicate that the phaseout favored T&G workers. The average wage in T&G is found to be similar or higher than wages in other labor-intensive sectors. Moreover, the industry wage premium increased for T&G workers in all countries. Wages and working conditions do not always move in the same direction, and we find a negative change in T&G working conditions in comparison to other sectors in the period post-MFA in three out of the four countries.

Every successful upgrading T&G export country is successful in its own way. In the case of the Indian T&G sector, for instance, employment growth was concentrated among female workers in informal apparel jobs. The expansion of informal apparel production was concomitant with a statistically significant negative change in firm productivity indicators. The number of apparel firms also increased in Bangladesh. Nevertheless, we find in Bangladesh a negative change in employment in apparel and a positive change in value added and employment in textile firms in comparison to firms in other sectors of the economy.

Interestingly, the female share of employment in T&G tends to either follow the expansion of the industry or not be affected. Regression results suggest a statistically significant positive change post-MFA in comparison to other sectors in the economy in the female share of workers in Indian apparel and Bangladeshi textile industries, a negative change in Bangladeshi apparel and Vietnamese textiles, and no change in the T&G female share of industry employment in Pakistan. The empirical exercises clearly indicate that modernization of the industry can go either way in terms of impact on employment. Nevertheless, the employment adjustment is likely to happen through the less costly margin: the female intensity in industry employment.

We focus the analysis on wages and employment, since labor earnings are often the main source of income and determinant of economic well-being for unskilled workers in developing countries. Previous research has documented the relationship between poverty reduction and employment in the T&G sector (see, for example, Kabeer and Mahmud 2004 and Kabeer and Van Ahn 2006). The end of the MFA raised concern about the consequences of job turnover in T&G on poverty. According to model simulations for Bangladesh, a 25.0 percent decline in ready-made garment export volume would lead to a 6.0 percent decrease in wage payments to unskilled female labor in nonagricultural sectors and a 0.5 to 1.0 percent decline in the real incomes of urban poor households (Arndt et al. 2002). This chapter considers the link between MFA phaseout and poverty via wages and employment changes.

The chapter is organized as follows. The following section provides information on industry evolution, focusing on the relevance of the T&G sector and its development, export and end market dynamics, and sector policy orientation after 2004. The third section discusses empirical analysis of changes in employment, within-industry structure, wages, and working conditions. The fourth section concludes.

Industry Evolution, Policies, and Post-MFA Development

Industry Evolution
The large Asian T&G exporters share several features. The first is the strong relevance of the sector for employment and export revenue. The Bangladeshi apparel sector has been the country's main source of growth of exports and formal employment for the past three decades. The industry directly employs 3.1 million people, constituting 40 percent of manufacturing employment; indirectly more than 10.0 million people are dependent on the apparel sector. Apparel exports were Vietnam's largest exports in the period 2005 to 2009 and accounted for 17 percent of Vietnam's total exports in 2009. The sector is the largest formal employer in the country, providing jobs for 937,350 people. In 2009, T&G in India accounted for roughly 4 percent of the gross domestic product (GDP), 14 percent of industrial production, and 14 percent of total exports, and it was the largest net foreign

exchange earner. Only agriculture has a greater significance in terms of employment, and an estimated 35 million workers are (formally and informally) employed in the textile and apparel sectors (Ministry of Textiles 2010). T&G is also the backbone of Pakistan's economy. The sectors accounted for around 54 percent of total exports and provided direct employment to around 2.5 million people (with 2.0 million in the apparel sector) in 2009–10, representing 38 percent of total manufacturing employment (PRGMEA 2010).

The second common aspect is that T&G played an important role in the initial phase of manufacturing development in these economies and generally involved active government participation. For instance, the Vietnamese government was responsible for the creation of state-owned apparel firms. The Indian state directed T&G production through a series of restrictions on exports and firm licensing. In Bangladesh and Pakistan, the state promoted credit subsidies and increased capacities. Despite the similarities, however, internal factors help explain the development and expansion of the T&G sector, as is discussed below for each of the four countries in turn.

Bangladesh has a long history of textile and made-to-order apparel production, mostly for the domestic market. The Bangladeshi apparel export sector started on a large scale in the late 1970s and early 1980s when manufacturers in the Republic of Korea; Taiwan, China; and elsewhere in East Asia started to invest in and source from Bangladesh, motivated by MFA quota hopping and by access to Bangladesh's abundant supply of low-cost labor. A ready-made apparel industry for the domestic market only developed more recently in Bangladesh. Two of the first exporters—Read Garments and Jewel Garments—developed from this domestic-oriented ready-made apparel industry.

The MFA, preferential market access to the European Union (EU), and specific government support policies were crucial in starting the export-oriented apparel sector in Bangladesh. Two government policies put in place in 1980 were particularly important. First, the government introduced the system of bonded warehouse facilities through which firms can delay the payment of tariffs until they are ready to consume inputs imported earlier, and if the inputs are used for producing exports, they are not required to pay the tariff (Ahmed 2009a). Second, back-to-back letters of credit (L/C) were introduced through which exporters are able to open L/C in a local bank for the import of inputs against the export orders placed in their favor by the final apparel importers (master L/C).

Until the 1980s, India's textile and apparel sectors were also initially geared toward the domestic market, as with Bangladesh. In contrast to many Asian low-cost exporters that are concentrated in apparel, Indian firms have significant textile production and a raw material base that partly feeds into apparel exports. Among the industries studied in this chapter, only firms in Pakistan also have major textile production and extensive cotton agriculture.

The Indian state played an important role in shaping the textile and apparel sectors. Policies included a strict licensing regime (firms were required to obtain permission before establishing or expanding operations), reservation policies (apparel production was reserved for the small-scale industry), and control of exports and imports. In the mid-1980s the textile and apparel industries began to be liberalized and subsequently integrated into world markets (Tewari 2005). In contrast to other apparel-exporting countries such as Bangladesh, this integration was not based on (quota-hopping) foreign investment and preferential market access, but was driven by local firms that—induced by changing government policies—restructured themselves and extended their reach from the domestic to export markets.

The domestic market is still important for T&G firms in India and increasingly so in the context of rising incomes. Local as well as foreign retail chains cater to the emerging middle class. The focus on the domestic market furthered the development of broader functions, including product development, design, and even branding. The development of the industry was also driven by specific domestic policies, in particular the National Textile Policy 2000, which includes measures such as the creation of a Technology Upgrading Fund and Integrated Textile Parks.

Apparel production and export in Pakistan started relatively late compared to other large South Asian exporters. Until the 1980s, cotton-based textiles dominated Pakistan's exports. Pakistan is the fourth largest of the world's 70 cotton-growing countries (behind China, India, and the United States). The dominance of textiles was driven by expanding cotton production in light of the agrarian "green revolution" in the 1960s as well as by various government efforts to promote textile manufacturing during the 1970s and 1980s. The growth of textile capacities influenced the growth of the apparel sector, as apparel exports were largely dependent on locally available cotton yarns and fabrics.

Pakistan's T&G development comes from a mix of strong global industry dynamics and internal industry-specific factors. The country historically focused on cotton-based textile and apparel products and only recently developed noncotton apparel production. Apparel exporters are heavily dependent on the EU and U.S. markets, and export concentration has increased. The sector's trajectory also has to be assessed in the broader context of Pakistan's recent history, including its geopolitical position as a front state in the "war on terror" and natural disasters (such as the earthquake in 2005 and flooding in 2010). These events led to temporary preferential market access and aid inflows to Pakistan.

The development of Vietnam's apparel sector differs from that of other large Asian exporters because of its recent socialist history. The French laid the foundations for the textile and apparel industries in Vietnam in the late nineteenth century. The sector only started to develop on a larger scale after the end of the First and Second Indochina Wars (1946–75) and in the context of the Council for Mutual Economic Assistance (CMEA). During the 1980s, the sector evolved on the basis of the cooperation program between Vietnam, the Soviet Union, and Eastern European countries. Vietnam's role was to assemble apparel products and some textiles such as embroidered products for export to the Soviet Union and Eastern Europe. This cooperation program did not last long because of the collapse of CMEA in the late 1980s, which had negative repercussions on Vietnam's apparel sector (Huy et al. 2001). A series of reforms were adopted starting in 1986, which gained momentum after the collapse of the Soviet bloc in 1989. The "doi-moi" (renovation) reforms were intended to transform Vietnam into a "socialist market economy under state guidance" (Staritz and Frederick 2011d) and included the gradual liberalization of the domestic economy and the development of a private sector as well as the shift toward a more market-based system of foreign trade.

In Vietnam, the adoption of the "doi-moi" reforms marked the beginning of the export-led growth trajectory, in which the apparel sector has occupied a key role. A new era of export-led growth began alongside the attraction of foreign investment. However, state-owned enterprises (SOEs) still played a crucial role in the economy and the industrial development strategy. This reform process continued throughout the 1990s as Vietnam increasingly integrated into the global economy and exports grew as a result of the gradual normalization of trade relations with the rest of the world.

Export Dynamics

Except for the case of India, expectations were gloomy for apparel export post-MFA in large T&G Asian countries. Nevertheless, those countries were able to increase export value and expand or maintain market share after 2004 (table 4.1). From 2004 to 2008, export value grew 69 percent in Bangladesh, 67 percent in India, 32 percent in Pakistan, and 116 percent in Vietnam. Over the same period, firms in Pakistan kept their global apparel market share approximately constant, while firms in India, Bangladesh, and Vietnam increased their share by 19 percent, 20 percent, and 35 percent, respectively. From the late 1980s until 2004, Bangladesh's apparel exports increased significantly. While apparel export earnings accounted for around $1.0 million in 1978, exports increased to $7.9 billion in 2004. Between 2004 and 2005, export values increased and market share remained stable and increased afterward. Total apparel exports increased to $8.0 billion in 2005, a 1 percent increase from 2004, and rose again to $10.4 billion in 2006. The share of Bangladesh in global apparel exports decreased from 3.2 percent to 3.0 percent between 2004 and 2005 but then increased again to 3.6 percent in 2006.

Dynamics similar to Bangladesh can be seen in Vietnamese apparel exports since the early 1990s. Import data from Vietnam's trading partners

Table 4.1   Export Dynamics

	1995	2004	2006	2008
Bangladesh's apparel exports to the world				
Total value ($, million)	2,544	7,945	10,415	13,464
Share of world exports (%)	1.7	3.2	3.6	4.0
India's apparel exports to the world				
Total value ($, million)	4,233	7,298	10,705	12,210
Share of world exports (%)	2.8	2.9	3.7	3.6
India's textile exports to the world				
Total value ($, million)	4,031	7,690	8,614	10,430
Share of world exports (%)	2.9	4.2	4.3	4.7
Pakistan's apparel exports to the world				
Total value ($, million)	1,279	2,665	3,081	3,504
Share of world exports (%)	0.8	1.1	1.1	1.0
Pakistan's textile exports to the world				
Total value ($, million)	3,848	5,679	6,699	6,825
Share of world exports (%)	2.8	3.1	3.4	3.1
Vietnam's apparel exports to the world				
Total value ($, million)	831	4,408	5,931	9,541
Share of world exports (%)	0.5	1.8	2.1	2.8

Source: United Nations Commodity Trade Statistics Database (UN Comtrade).

show an increase from $831.0 million in 1995 to $4.4 billion in 2004. Against the background of extended quotas in the U.S. market, Vietnam's performance post-MFA is particularly astonishing. Total apparel exports increased to $4.7 billion in 2005, a 7.5 percent increase from 2004, and rose further to $5.9 billion in 2006. The share of Vietnam in global apparel exports increased from 0.5 percent in 1995 to 1.8 percent in 2004. Vietnam's share of global apparel exports remained stable at 1.8 percent between 2004 and 2005 and increased to 2.1 percent in 2006.

Unlike other large Asian exporters that concentrated in apparel products, Pakistani and Indian firms enjoy strong textile production. The period from the 1990s leading to the MFA phaseout was characterized by an overall increase of Pakistani textile and apparel exports. However, the performance was uneven for the two sectors, and textile exports dominated, accounting for 70 percent of overall textile and apparel exports in 2004. Pakistani textile exports grew rapidly during the first half of the 1990s but stagnated in the second half of the 1990s and in the early 2000s, before surging in 2003 and 2004 in light of increased exports to the EU and the United States (Nordås 2005). Textile exports increased from $3.9 billion in 1995 to $5.7 billion in 2004, while apparel exports grew more steadily, from $1.3 billion in 1995 to $2.7 billion in 2004. Over the same period, textile exports increased their share in the world market from 2.8 percent to 3.1 percent, while apparel exports slightly increased their share in the world market, from 0.8 percent to 1.1 percent. Between 2004 and 2006, Pakistan increased its apparel export value from $2.7 billion to $3.1 billion, while total textile export value rose from $5.7 billion to $6.7 billion over the same period. Since the phaseout, Pakistan has kept a fairly constant participation in the world's apparel and textile market.

Indian textile and apparel exports have grown strongly from 1985 onward. Apparel exports rose from $914.0 million in 1985 to $2.5 billion in 1990 at an annual compound growth rate of 19.3 percent (Tewari 2005). Textile exports followed a similar path, increasing from around $1.0 billion in 1985 to $2.2 billion in 1990. Indian firms benefited from the MFA phaseout. The value of apparel exports went from $7.3 billion in 2004 to $10.7 billion in 2006, while textile export values rose from $7.7 billion to $8.6 billion over the same period. The increase in apparel exports was particularly strong during the first two years, with annual growth rates of 29.7 percent (2005) and 13.1 percent (2006). As a result, Indian apparel increased its global market share from 2.9 percent in 2004 to 3.7 percent in 2006. But growth slowed in 2007 and 2008, partly due to the appreciation of the Indian rupee and rising manufacturing costs

(Textiles Intelligence 2008). Textile export growth was strongest in 2006 and 2007, with annual growth rates of 10.1 percent and 14.9 percent, respectively. From 2004 to 2006, India's global share of textile exports increased from 4.2 percent to 4.3 percent.

End Markets and Export Products

The overall export figures mask a significant change in the composition of apparel and textile exports from large Asian countries over the past few decades. Bangladeshi and Vietnamese exports initially concentrated on woven products and more recently moved into knitted apparel items. Generally, firms in Pakistan and India moved away from the export of unprocessed cotton and increased the local value added of their largely cotton-based textile and apparel production. The growth of textile capacities influenced the growth of the apparel capacities. In terms of end markets, Bangladeshi producers historically focused on the U.S. market while Vietnamese producers started exporting to Japan and then expanded to the EU. The importance of the United States as an end market has decreased for Bangladeshi and increased for Vietnamese firms. In India and Pakistan, concentration toward EU-15 and U.S. markets is still high but has decreased since 2000.[1]

In the 1980s, the Bangladeshi industry only produced woven apparel products, but from the early 1990s on, exports of knit apparel products, principally sweaters and T-shirts, experienced rapid growth. In 1991, knitted apparel was 15 percent of total apparel exports and increased in 2004 to nearly 50 percent. The growth of knit products was particularly spurred by preferential market access to the EU.

Until the early, 1990s the United States was the main export destination for Bangladesh's apparel products, but in the 1990s, the EU-15 surpassed the United States as the top export market. Bangladesh's apparel exports, both woven and knit, are highly concentrated in a few products (for example, trousers, sweaters, T-shirts, and shirts), and product concentration levels have increased since 2000. The product concentration of Bangladesh's apparel exports is much higher than in competitor countries such as China and India. In the EU-15 and the U.S. market, cotton products dominate. From 2004 to 2006, the EU-15 share of Bangladesh's total apparel exports decreased from 64 percent to 60 percent, while the U.S. export share increased from 25 percent to 29 percent.

Vietnam's apparel exports are almost equally divided between woven and knit apparel items, with 53.8 percent and 46.2 percent shares, respectively, in 2009. Until 2000, woven items dominated, accounting for around 75–80 percent of total exports. Vietnam's woven and knit apparel exports are concentrated in a few products (for example, trousers, sweaters, T-shirts, and shirts); however, the concentration is lower than in competitor countries such as Bangladesh and Cambodia.

In the 1990s, Japan and the EU-15 were Vietnam's only important end markets; up to 2002, exports did not go to the United States. In the early 2000s, Japan's share decreased and the United States emerged as an important export market, accounting for 60.7 percent of total exports in 2004. Export growth to the United States was moderated by quotas until the end of 2006. Nevertheless, Vietnam extended its share in the U.S. market from 3.7 percent in 2004 to 4.3 percent in 2006. In 2009, the U.S. market absorbed 55.6 percent of Vietnamese apparel exports, compared to only a 3.3 percent share in 2000. In contrast, the shares of the EU-15 and Japan fell from 47.0 percent and 36.4 percent in 2000 to 21.2 percent and 10.7 percent in 2009, respectively.

Until the 1980s, Pakistani exports were dominated by cotton-based textiles, in particular raw cotton as well as cotton yarn and fabrics. Pakistan is concentrated in the production of made-up textiles (for example, bed, bath, and kitchen linens), ranking second behind China in terms of export value. As a result, apparel exports only account for around 30 percent of total textile and apparel exports, but they have increased since the late 1990s.

Pakistan's apparel exports are highly concentrated with regard to end markets. In 2009, 87.0 percent of apparel exports went to the United States and the EU-15, with 43.6 percent of exports going to the United States and 43.4 percent to the EU-15. The concentration toward the United States and the EU-15, however, has decreased; those two markets accounted for 92.6 percent in 2000.

Notwithstanding its late integration into the global economy, India has developed into the second-largest global exporter of textiles and apparel. Historically, textile exports dominated, based on India's large raw material base, in particular cotton. But during the past three decades, apparel exports have increased in importance and now account for more than half of total textile and apparel exports. India's woven and knit apparel exports are concentrated in a few products (for example, T-shirts, shirts, dresses, and sweatshirts). Export concentration levels to the United States and EU-15 have generally increased since 2000; however, they are still lower than in most competitor countries.

The EU has been the major export market for Indian producers, accounting for 54.2 percent of apparel and 29.5 percent of textile exports in 2009. The second most important export market is still the United

States, with 25.7 percent of apparel and 24.6 percent of textile exports. The role of the EU-15 as the key apparel export market increased from 39.3 percent in 2000, while the share of the U.S. market decreased from 38.9 percent over the same period.

Trade Agreements

The T&G sectors in Bangladesh, India, and Pakistan enjoyed preferential market access to the EU through the Generalized System of Preferences (GSP). This agreement contributed to the growth of exports from large Asian apparel and textile producers to the EU. Nevertheless, the importance of the European GSP system has decreased over time.

In Bangladesh, the EU GSP system has provided quota-free and tariff-free access to the EU market since the early 1980s, and since 2001 through the Everything but Arms (EBA) initiative.[2] This access helped to make the EU the largest export destination of Bangladeshi apparel products. More recently, in January 2011, Bangladeshi firms qualified for GSP+ status in the EU market (GSP+ offers preferential market access to vulnerable developing countries). With this, the rules of origin (ROO) changed to single transformation. Currently only around half of apparel exports to the EU use preferential market access facilities. Bangladeshi products also have duty-free market access to Australia, Canada, Japan, New Zealand, and Norway. In the United States, Bangladeshi producers face most favored nation (MFN) tariffs. Indian exporting firms enjoyed preferential market access to the EU for textile and apparel exports via the EU's GSP scheme until 2006. While textile products lost their preferential status from January 2006 and onward, apparel exports continued to enjoy preferential rates 20 percent lower than MFN rates. Indian producers do not enjoy any special preferences to the U.S. market, as almost their entire textile and apparel items are excluded from the GSP scheme in the United States.

Pakistani firms also have preferential market access to the EU market via the EU's GSP scheme. In addition to normal GSP status, Pakistani products were granted special preferences under the "special arrangement to combat drug production and trafficking" against the background of 9/11 (EC's Delegation to Pakistan 2004). Hence, between 2002 and 2005, Pakistani products were granted duty-free access to the EU for 95 percent of the tariff lines under the scheme (Siegmann 2006). Pakistani producers lost their preferential status in 2005 in light of pressures at the World Trade Organization (WTO), where India successfully challenged part of the EU's GSP system. Since then, Pakistani firms have received special preferences under the normal GSP, granting duty-free access in 60 percent of tariff lines (CARIS 2008). Pakistan is also included in the U.S. GSP system. However, most key Pakistani export products from the textile and apparel sectors are excluded, so the effects are limited (Fakhar 2005).

A multitude of regional cooperation and trade agreements are under various stages of implementation in South Asia, the most important being the South Asian Association for Regional Cooperation (SAARC).[3] Despite these regional integration efforts, the potential for regional trade and investment in the apparel and textile sectors still remains largely untapped. The ROO stipulations that the EU offered in the context of SAARC in 1995 and 2001 were largely rejected. At the regional level, the South Asian Free Trade Agreement (SAFTA) is the key agreement to further integration between South Asian countries. It was signed in 2004 by the then-members of the SAARC, including Bangladesh, Bhutan, India, the Maldives, Nepal, Pakistan, and Sri Lanka. The signatories agreed to phase out tariffs on practically all trade in goods (but not services) by the end of 2016 (CARIS 2008). However, so far there has been little tangible progress in implementing SAFTA. In particular, long-standing political issues between India and Pakistan impede the potential gains derived from regional integration. Instead, a number of bilateral agreements have been signed between SAFTA members. Most of them involve India, and trade flows within SAARC are focused toward India (Weerakoon 2010).

Because of its position as a socialist economy, Vietnam had a different trajectory in terms of trade agreements compared to other large Asian T&G exporters. Vietnam's accession to the WTO occurred only in 2007. Nevertheless, preferential market access for Vietnamese products was granted by Japan, the EU since 1992, and the United States since 2001, all of which have played a key role in promoting the T&G sector. In the United States (Vietnam's most important export market), Vietnam's apparel exports still face MFN tariffs. Vietnam's export development has also been influenced by the growth of regional trade arrangements, most importantly the Association of South East Asian Nations (ASEAN), which it joined in 1995 (the same year that WTO accession talks formally began). Exports to ASEAN have been duty free since 2009. As a member of ASEAN, Vietnam is part of the ASEAN-China Free Trade Agreement (ACFTA). ACFTA was signed in 2002 and is being implemented in stages. ASEAN also has a trade agreement with the Republic of Korea.

Proactive Policies

A strong feature of the large Asian T&G exporters is the active role of the government in promoting the sector since its inception. More recently, these countries invested in preparing industries for the increase in competition after 2004. In the context of the MFA phaseout, credit subsidies (Pakistan), creation of textile parks and upgrading funds (India), L/Cs and training programs (Bangladesh), and investment in modernization by SOEs (Vietnam) were implemented. Though not all initiatives achieved their end goal, the large Asian T&G producers were able to increase T&G export value and expand or maintain market share after 2004.

The Bangladesh government has provided support to the apparel and textile sectors on different levels after 2004. The government allotted $3 million for training programs for productivity improvement of workers in the apparel sector. During the second half of 2007, the apparel sector opened L/Cs for the purchase of machinery valued at $200 million and the textile sector for $236 million (Saheed 2008). Since 2006, the government has invested in the provision of bonded warehouse facilities, concessionary duty rates, and tax exemptions for the import of capital machinery.

In anticipation of the MFA phaseout, the Pakistani state launched a comprehensive policy framework—Textile Vision 2005—in 1999–2000. To meet the challenges of the MFA phaseout and to boost competitiveness, a number of measures, including technology and skill upgrading, were proposed to shift toward higher-value textile and apparel products. However, implementation was slow and selective, with an emphasis on textile investments in equipment and technology. The Pakistani government also deployed several measures to stabilize the industry (IFPRI 2008). The government provided preferential short- and long-term financing, which became increasingly important when interest rates and inflation started to increase significantly in 2006–07. A 6 percent research and development cash subsidy was introduced in 2005 for apparel exporters, which was in the following years extended to the textile industry. Roughly $500 million was spent under this scheme until 2008; however, it failed to "induce technological upgrading" (GoP 2008b). This failure can be related to a dramatic change in the domestic environment in 2007–08, when the cost of financing increased significantly, with interest rates going up to 35 percent, cotton prices surging, and inflation rising. According to industry representatives, the government's support was vital to help the industry fulfill its export commitments against rising financing, utility, and raw material costs (*Just-style* 2008).

Vietnamese firms' positive development after MFA can be explained by its accession to the WTO in 2007, which improved market access and cost competitiveness. But Vietnam's apparel sector has also restructured and upgraded production processes, capabilities, and backward linkages. The government initiated a comprehensive development strategy for the sector to cope with the post-MFA context. At an aggregate level, investments during the 1990s and 2000s promoted significant productivity increases in Vietnam's apparel and textile sector (AFTEX 2010). Some SOEs, in particular Vinatex, have invested heavily to modernize equipment and production processes. Since 2005, Vinatex has invested $800–900 million in modernization.

The development of the Indian T&G industry after 2000 was also driven by specific domestic policies, in particular the National Textile Policy 2000, which promoted the industry's development. The most important measures of this policy are the Technology Upgrading Fund established in 1999 to promote technical modernization of the sector; the Technology Mission on Cotton launched in 2000 to improve quality and raise productivity in the cotton sector; the Integrated Textile Parks launched in 2005 to provide state-of-the-art infrastructure to local and international manufacturers; the gradual reduction of import tariffs and support of man-made fibers (MMF) and yarns production; and the support of product development, design, and branding capabilities (Singh 2008).

Empirical Results

This section discusses the changes in employment, within-industry structure, wages, and working conditions after the phaseout. We use household and firm-level data to test for statistical differences in employment, industry wage premiums, female and male wage differential, and average working conditions in T&G jobs before and after the MFA phaseout. We also present the qualitative evidence on industry upgrading and firm dynamics.

Employment and Firm Outcomes

Several empirical patterns worthy of attention are common across the countries studied. First, employment in T&G increased after the phaseout. In Pakistan, jobs in T&G grew from 1.3 million in 2000 to 2.5 million in 2009, while in Vietnam, they rose from 354,707 in 2000 to 937,350 in 2008, according to official statistics.[4] In Bangladesh, apparel employment increased from 1.6 million in 2000 to 3.1 million in 2009, and in India, T&G jobs increased from 34 million in 2001 to 35 million in 2009.

Second, the female share of workers in the T&G industry is substantial (annex table 4A.1). Female employment has a lower bound of at least one-fourth of the T&G sector. That is the case even in countries with low female labor force participation, such as Bangladesh and Pakistan. Moreover, most countries kept a fairly constant share of female employment in the industry after the MFA phaseout.

Although employment increased, the quantitative analysis of employment composition and firm performance shows mixed results (see annex for full results). Employment and number of firms in apparel increased in Bangladesh and India. In the regression exercises, we focus the analysis on the changes in the T&G variables of interest—employment, female share of employment, wages per worker, and so forth—in the period post-MFA in comparison to the other sectors in the economy. Bearing this comparison in mind, the results indicate that the female share of employment in apparel fell in the period post-MFA in Bangladesh but rose in India. In Vietnam, we find a statistically significant negative change in textile employment and in the textile share of female employment. Finally, in Pakistan, sales per worker and employment fell post-MFA in comparison to other sectors.

The basic statistics from Bangladeshi firm data (annex table 4A.3) indicate a growing importance of the T&G industry over time. The number of T&G firms grew from 1995 to 2005, especially garments firms, which doubled in 10 years. The share of T&G employment in total industry employment increased 8 percent over the same period, reaching almost 75 percent. Regression results also indicate a positive change in wage per worker in T&G after 2005 when compared to the other sectors in the economy (annex table 4A.10). Analogously, the female share in the industry increased in textile firms and fell in garment firms (table 4.2).

The regression results for Pakistan suggest that overall and male employment, as well as T&G sales, and the female share of workers among textile workers fell in the post-MFA period (table 4.2, table 4.3 and annex table 4A.7) when compared to other sectors of the economy. Results using the Enterprise Survey indicate substantial churning of T&G jobs, with a tendency to larger reallocation of female employees. In results not reported for other countries and sectors with Enterprise Surveys, we see large female reallocation in the economy and higher T&G churning compared to other industries (annex tables 4A.7 and 4A.8).

Regression exercises with industry data from Vietnam show in comparison with other sectors a statistically significant negative change in the T&G employment in the period post-MFA (annex table 4A.9). The female

Table 4.2   Female Share in Textile and Apparel Industry Employment

	Bangladesh	India		Pakistan	Vietnam
	All	All	Informal	All	All
Time	0.0506***	0.0163	0.016	0.018**	0.042**
	(0.009)	(0.017)	(0.017)	(0.009)	(0.017)
Time*apparel	−0.246***	0.086**	0.087**	−0.004	n.a.
	(0.020)	(0.034)	(0.035)	(0.009)	
Time*textiles	0.0817***	0.007	0.007	−0.028***	n.a.
	(0.011)	(0.040)	(0.040)	(0.008)	
Time*T&G	n.a.	n.a.	n.a.	n.a.	0.020
					(0.036)
Constant	0.408***	0.358***	0.357***	0.387***	0.276***
	(0.083)	(0.079)	(0.080)	(0.002)	(0.020)
R-squared	0.403	0.69	0.693	0.043	0.839

Source: Authors' calculations.
Note: Disaggregated cell data by industry, size, age categories, state, year. State absorbed, size, and industry dummies included. Pakistan—household weights by industry and WDR (World Development Report) labor force numbers. Vietnam—industry-level data, Vietnam Statistical Office, several years. India—firm-level data. Industry dummies included. Time dummy equal to 1 from 2005 on; n.a. = not applicable. T&G = textiles and garments.
*** $p < 0.01$, ** $p < 0.05$.

share of employment also changed over the same period, but the change was positive in the apparel and negative in the textile sector (tables 4.2 and 4A.9). The phaseout did not appear to affect the number of T&G firms in comparison to the size of other sectors in the economy (table 4.3).

Firm-level data for India show an increase in the number of plants and employment in T&G, and in apparel firms in particular (figures 4.1 and 4.2). The female share in informal apparel employment increased over time and converged to the same level as in textiles (around 30 percent in 2005; see figure 4.3). The empirical analysis indicates that apparel firms—especially informal ones—carried the changes in employment after 2005. When compared to other sectors in the economy, the share of females in apparel overall and the female share in informal apparel firms increased in the period post-MFA.[5] The increase in the female share of employment in India is concomitant with a statistically significant negative change in apparel firm performance relative to other sectors, using measures such as output per worker, average wage per worker, and value added or capital per worker. These results are consistent with an increase in competition post-MFA, because competition may reduce average firm performance and a firm's ability to discriminate (Becker 1971).

Within-industry dynamics: Unit value change. As expected with the intensification of competition in T&G export, unit values of apparel

Table 4.3 Firm Outcomes

	India				Bangladesh	Vietnam	Pakistan
	Output per worker		Average wage per worker		log (wage/ worker)	number of firms	log (sales)
	All	Informal	All	Informal			
Time	0.167**	0.168**	0.284***	0.284**	0.0543**	0.829***	0.518***
	0.000	0.000	0.000	(0.140)	(0.022)	(0.079)	(0.173)
Time*textiles	−0.049	−0.0490207	0.384	0.385	0.321***	−0.129	n.a.
	0.000	0.000	0.000	(0.252)	(0.028)	(0.080)	
Time*apparel	−0.354***	−0.353***	−0.369*	−0.370*	0.109**	−0.1	n.a.
	0.000	0.000	0.000	0.211	(0.055)	(0.079)	
Time*T&G	n.a.	n.a.	n.a.	n.a.	n.a.	n.a.	−0.456*
							(0.235)
Constant	8.153***	8.151***	4.349***	4.346***	9.484***	5.469***	15.316***
	0.000	0.000	0.000	(0.092)	(0.060)	(0.053)	(0.793)
R-squared	0.634	0.6117	0.623	0.616	0.159	0.46	0.175
Number of observations	27,160	8,582	26,543	7,973	14,410	442	755

Source: Authors' calculations.

Note: Disaggregated cell data by industry, size, age categories, state, year. State absorbed, size, and industry dummies included. India—firm-level data. Pakistan—household weights by industry and WDR (World Development Report) labor force numbers. Vietnam—industry-level data, Vietnam Statistical Office, several years. Industry dummies included. Time is a dummy equal to 1 from 2005 on; n.a. = not applicable. T&G = textiles and garments.

*** $p < 0.01$, ** $p < 0.05$, * $p < 0.1$.

Figure 4.1   Number of Plants in Formal and Informal Textile and Apparel Sectors in India

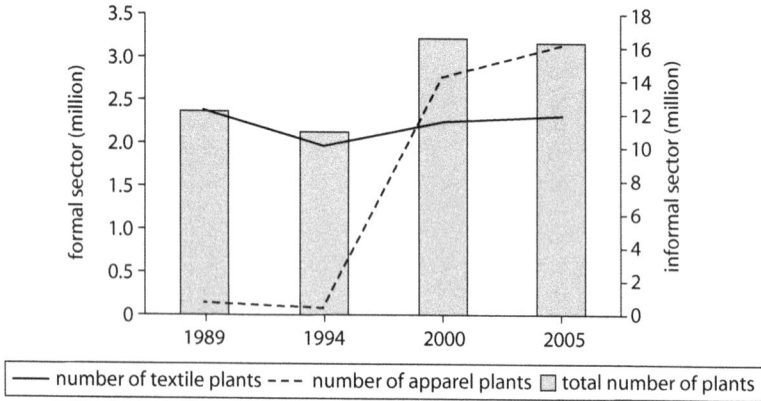

number of textile plants --- number of apparel plants ☐ total number of plants

Source: Authors' calculations.
Note: Firm-level data in two-digit NIC National Industry Classification and year cells.

Figure 4.2   Total Employment in Formal and Informal Textile and Apparel Sectors in India

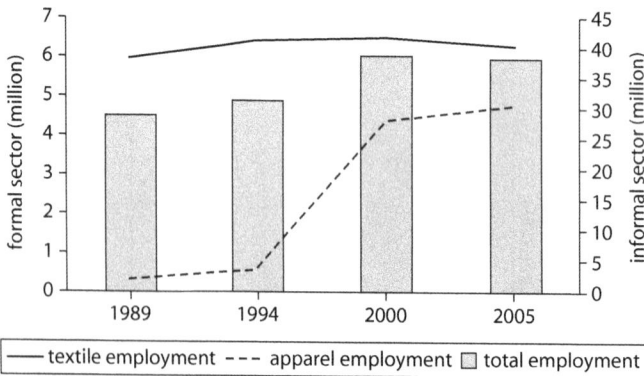

textile employment --- apparel employment ☐ total employment

Source: Authors' calculations.
Note: Firm level data in two-digit NIC National Industry Classification and year cells.

exports have declined since 2000 (annex table 4A.6). This decline occurred in large Asian countries regardless of whether the country produced apparel export products of lower value compared to the world average, as in the case of Bangladesh, or produced more sophisticated and higher-value export products, as in the case of India. In the aftermath of the MFA phaseout from 2004 to 2007, the average price of export

Figure 4.3   Female Share in Industry Employment in Formal and Informal Textile and Apparel Sectors in India

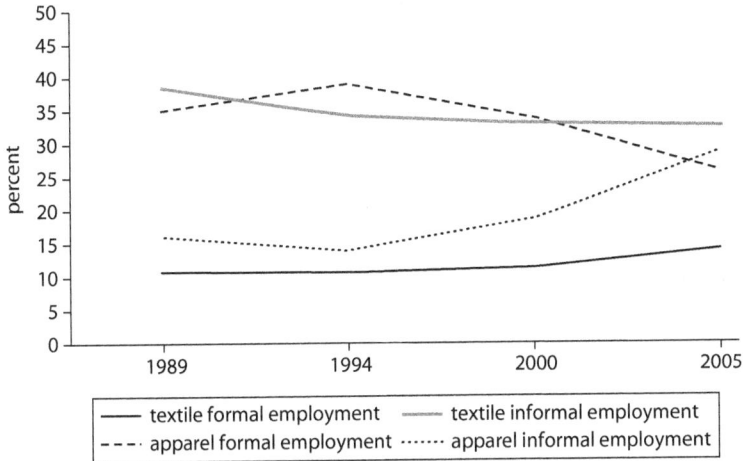

Source: Authors' calculations.
Note: Firm-level data in two-digit NIC National Industry Classification and year cells.

apparel to U.S. markets fell 11 percent in Bangladesh, 13 percent in India, and 6 percent in Pakistan and Vietnam.

The unit prices of Bangladesh's main export products are comparatively low—in general lower than the world average, including unit values of apparel exports from China and also India and Sri Lanka. In the case of EU-15 exports, only Pakistan had lower unit values in 2005; Cambodia, China, India, Sri Lanka, and Vietnam had higher unit values (Tewari 2008). This pattern is related to Bangladesh being cost competitive but also concentrating in basic products, while these other countries export higher-value products. Average unit prices decreased significantly in 2001–02 because of China's entry into the WTO, and they continued to decline post-MFA. Between 2004 and 2007, the average price of export apparel fell from $2.60 to $2.31 per unit, a decline of 11 percent. Average unit prices for woven fell from $3.26 to $2.92 and for knit from $1.95 to $1.90 for the same time period, declines of 10 percent and 3 percent, respectively.

Average unit values of Pakistani apparel exports in the U.S. market decreased considerably post-MFA. The drop was particularly pronounced in the more important knitwear segment, while woven apparel registered an increase in average unit values after the quota. Unit prices in the EU-15 remained relatively stable. According to the government's own assess-ment, the Pakistani apparel industry was not able to take advantage of the quota-free environment, in which other factors (for example, quality and fast turnaround) became more important in global sourcing. Instead, the industry remained entrapped in a low-value, low-productivity vicious cycle in which low labor costs remained the focus of doing business (GoP 2008a). Between 2004 and 2007, the average price of export apparel to the United States fell from $36.30 to $34.00 per dozen, a decline of 6 percent. Unit values to the EU-15 stayed approximately con-stant at €7.90 per kilogram.

The unit values of Vietnam's apparel exports to the United States and the EU-15 generally declined or stagnated post-MFA. The average unit values to the United States decreased from $56.90 per dozen in 2004 to $53.70 in 2007, a 6 percent decline. In the case of the EU-15, unit values dropped 18 percent between 2004 and 2007 (and even more in woven exports), but by 2009, prices recovered to slightly above 2004 values.

India's apparel export unit values are high compared to main com-petitor countries in the EU-15 and the U.S. market. This difference is related to India's more sophisticated and higher-value export basket, in particular compared to countries such as Bangladesh and Pakistan. But the high unit prices can also be explained by relatively high costs for power, transportation, and logistics; taxes (value added tax [VAT], excise, and so forth); and labor. In terms of the development of average apparel unit prices, patterns differ in the two main export markets. Unit values of Indian woven and knit apparel exports to the EU-15 generally increased between 2004 and 2009, particularly until 2006, with a slight decline afterward. As in the case of Bangladesh, unit values of Indian apparel exports to the United States have fallen since 2000, with a par-ticularly large decline in 2002 related to China's WTO accession. The continued decline is largely due to the rising importance of knitted apparel exports, which experienced slumping unit values. Between 2004 and 2007, the average price of export apparel to the United States fell from $56.20 to $49.00 per dozen, a decline of 13 percent. Over the same period, unit values to the EU-15 increased from €14.1 per kilo-gram to €16.1 per kilogram, a 14 percent increase.

Upgrading and firm dynamics. The large Asian T&G exporters are dif-ferent in terms of position in the GVC. Bangladesh and Vietnam are concentrated in the lower end of the chain, performing cut-make-trim

(CMT) activities. India and Pakistan are higher up in the GVC with a set of vertically integrated operations. The T&G sector in all four countries has received attention via various policy initiatives since the early 2000s because of its key role in the economy. Many of these policies were geared toward technologically upgrading the sector. In the aftermath of the phaseout, India, Pakistan, and Vietnam modernized their T&G industry and increased capabilities, while the Bangladeshi T&G industry successfully moved up in the value chain. The large Asian exporters are different in terms of firm dynamics. We discuss each country's firm ownership structure and the role of foreign direct investment (FDI) in turn.

FDI played a central role in establishing the Bangladeshi apparel industry; nevertheless, the industry is now dominated by locally owned firms. FDI in the T&G sector still accounts for the lion's share of total aggregated investment (around 75 percent), mostly directly toward firms in export processing zones (EPZs). Despite the dominance of FDI in EPZs, the vast majority of apparel firms is located outside of EPZs and is locally owned. In 2005, only 1 percent of apparel firms operated in EPZs, and around 65 percent of those had foreign ownership (World Bank 2005a).

Bangladeshi apparel firms' decision to upgrade differs somewhat from that of firms in other large Asian countries, since firms invested not only in technology modernization but also in moving up the value chain. Ten years ago, the majority of firms were CMT firms. A World Bank study (World Bank 2005b) states that in 2005, two-thirds of apparel firms in Bangladesh were involved in CMT production. Today, an important share of apparel firms can be classified as free on board (FOB) firms. In contrast to CMT, FOB firms are capable of sourcing and financing inputs and providing all production services, finishing, and packaging for delivery to the retail outlet. Apart from important progress in upgrading from CMT to FOB production, progress in developing more advanced capabilities in design and branding has been limited in the Bangladeshi apparel sector. Some firms, particularly large and foreign-owned firms in EPZs, offer product development and design as well as merchandising and marketing services and work closely with buyers to design and develop products. Some of these firms also achieved product upgrading and produce more complex and higher-value apparel product.

According to the General Statistics Office of Vietnam, the number of apparel firms increased from 579 in 2000 to 3,174 in 2008, while the number of textile firms rose from 408 to 1,577 over the same period.

Better Work Vietnam (2011) states that there were 3,719 textile and apparel firms in 2009, of which 2,424 were apparel firms. In terms of ownership, there are three types of firms in Vietnam—SOEs, locally owned private firms, and foreign-owned firms. The relevance of SOEs has dropped over time, although they still have a central role, and the largest SOE—Vinatex—accounted for more than 20 percent of total exports in 2009. SOEs tend to be large, often employing several thousands of workers. SOEs have had several advantages over private firms because of their direct access to the state system. Locally owned private firms are usually medium-size owner-managed firms. Firms with foreign participation have increased since the late 1990s.

Using evidence from 23 interviews, Goto (2007) concludes that an average apparel supplier in Vietnam produced 67 percent CMT and 33 percent FOB, based on total sales amount. However, the importance of CMT is understated because it accounted in volume terms for 95 percent of production compared to 5 percent from FOB. The three types of apparel firms discussed above fulfill generally different functions in the GVC. Domestic private firms tend to be locked into CMT positions, while the larger SOEs have more functional responsibility in the chain as mostly FOB producers. Foreign-owned subsidiaries tend to cater to the needs of their headquarters. There is limited room for functional upgrading of these plants because higher-value functions remain with the overseas headquarters.

At an aggregate level, investments during the 1990s and 2000s promoted significant productivity increases in Vietnam's apparel and textile sector (AFTEX 2010), but these productivity gains were unevenly distributed across the different types of firms. Foreign-owned firms generally use more modern production processes and machinery. Some SOEs, in particular Vinatex, have invested heavily to modernize equipment and production processes. Since 2005, Vinatex has invested $800 million–$900 million in modernization, including renovating and improving obsolete facilities, resulting in higher productivity and product quality.

India and Pakistan are two of the few countries (besides China and Turkey) that have a significant raw material base and vertically integrated manufacturing capacities, which explains their higher position in the GVC. A set of globally competitive apparel exporters has emerged that manage vertically integrated operations, including product developing, design, and branding, and produce for domestic as well as international markets.

In terms of manufacturing capabilities, India's apparel sector offers a wide range of activities and high flexibility. Smaller to medium-size firms can provide small batches with high-fashion content and customized, design-intensive orders. Larger firms can provide high-volume and mass-produced series. Smaller and larger firms now offer product development, design, and even branding capabilities that are increasingly demanded by global buyers.

However, the industry is divided. On the one hand, there is a relatively small formal segment characterized by more developed, often larger firms with higher capital intensity and often better working conditions. On the other hand, there is a large informal segment where firms employ fewer than 10 workers. The informal sector accounts for the vast majority of employment but only 31 percent of total production. Domestic deregulation, liberalization, and increasing international competition in the context of the MFA phaseout, as well as increasing demands from global buyers, have, however, furthered the consolidation of the industry (Singh 2008; Tewari 2008).

The involvement of foreign investors in India's textile and apparel industries remains marginal. Initially, this lack of involvement was related to the government's inward-looking policy, which oriented the sector toward the domestic market and restricted FDI. India's textile and apparel exports continue to be largely driven by domestic firms. As part of the trend toward modernization in the textile sector through the adoption of new technology and the installation of advanced production facilities, India is now one of the world's top importers of T&G machinery.

The Pakistani textile and apparel complex remains strongly centered on textiles, although the apparel industry has increased in importance over the past decade. The textile and apparel industry has been modernized with the help of the government; hence, it uses modern spinning, weaving, and, lately, finishing technologies. Pakistan's apparel sector retains a significant cottage industry. Industry estimates state that around 70 to 80 percent of production units consist of small enterprises in workers' homes. The rest of the sector is mainly composed of large, integrated firms that are generally involved in the knit segment (SMEDA 2002, cited in USITC 2004).

As in the case of India, FDI has not played an important role in Pakistan's textile and apparel industries. In recent years, the government has adopted several measures to attract FDI to help modernize the economy. However, despite having an overall liberal and friendly FDI regime, the political insecurities inhibit foreign investment. Given the sector's important role, several policies were implemented in light of the quota phaseout to promote technology upgrading. According to the Textile Commission's Office, the cumulative investment over the 10-year period

1999–2009 amounted to roughly $7.5 billion, and Pakistan is now a strong importer of T&G machinery.

Inter-industry Wage Differential and Female Wages

The T&G sector is often perceived as exploiting its workers through low wages and subjecting them to coercive or unhealthy treatment, commonly known as "sweatshop" working conditions (see discussion in Carr 2001 and Brown, Deardorff, and Stern 2004). Previous work has analyzed apparel wage and working conditions in several countries (Robertson et al. 2009). Interestingly, Robertson et al. find that apparel wage premiums are higher than the average premiums in all countries studied. Moreover, the data suggest that higher wages in apparel do not seem to be offered to workers as a substitute for poor working conditions.

An inspection of the data from household surveys in large Asian exporters shows that the wages in T&G usually are above wages for agricultural jobs and close to values for other labor-intensive sectors such as sales. Also, average years of education and average wage in T&G are comparable to economywide numbers for education and wages. However, this homogeneity hides between-group differences. Female educational attainment and wages tend to be lower than for male workers in T&G (annex table 4A.1).

Groups of workers in different labor-intensive sectors do not necessarily share the same characteristics, but even after considering the effect of

Figure 4.4   Inter-industry Wage Differential (IIWD) in Labor-Intensive Sectors

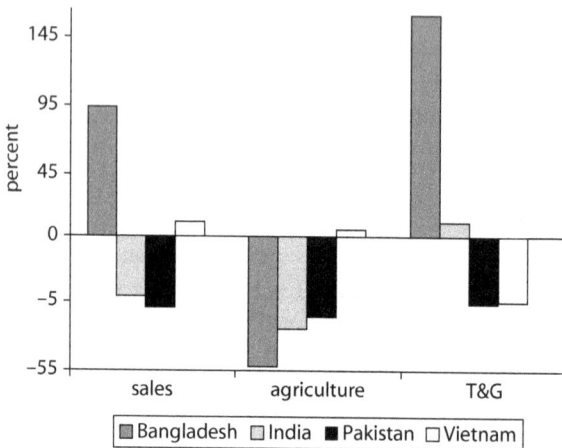

Sources: Authors' calculations. Industry dummy coefficients from wage regressions. Household data, late 2000s.
Note: Percent difference from the average wage in the economy.

experience, gender, and education, the data show that workers in agriculture tend to receive on average a lower wage, while workers in T&G receive a premium (figure 4.4). This difference suggests that moving from agriculture into T&G jobs is a channel for social and economic upgrading. The T&G wage premium is substantial in cases of a growing sector, such as T&G in Bangladesh. Regressions indicate that the inter-industry wage differential (IIWD) in T&G jobs increased after the phaseout in the countries studied in this chapter. The rising premium is consistent with an increase in demand for T&G workers (see the annex for labor force statistics and results).

The Bangladeshi T&G industry premium increased substantially over time.[6] At the end point of the data analyzed, T&G workers made 150 percent more than the average Bangladeshi worker (table 4.4), after controlling for demographic characteristics that affect wage levels. Also, returns to education did not increase (see annex table 4A.2), but the female-male wage gap narrowed (table 4.5). Bangladesh is an interesting case in the sense that the unit apparel price fell, but that fall was not followed by a decrease in industry wage premium. We interpret this result as a mix of different effects. First, it is partially an effect of proactive government policies used to counteract the end of the MFA, which kept the garment firms competitive when compared to other industries in Bangladesh and T&G producers in other countries. Those policies involved preferential agreements with the United States and Europe as well as government investment in programs to bolster apparel exports. Second, the Bangladeshi government pushed T&G wages up by announcing an increase in the minimum wage in T&G from Tk930 ($16) in 1994 to Tk1,662 ($24) in 2006. Despite the change in the minimum wage, the increased wage is still among the lowest in the world for garment workers. Average apparel labor costs per hour in 2008 in India were more than twice as high and four times higher in China when compared to Bangladeshi wages (Jassin-O'Rourke Group 2008). Backward links also help explain success in face of the MFA phaseout: T&G relies on local producers, who could not easily shift investments to other countries after the phaseout.

In Pakistan, the empirical results show a spike in the textile and clothing wage premium in 2005 followed by a decline at the end of the period. Overall, the IIWD for T&G improved from 2003 to 2008. There was no improvement in the economywide returns to female workers, and returns to education showed no major improvement (see annex table 4A.2). The lack of effect of the MFA on the gender gap is to be expected, since Pakistan's T&G industry has a low share of female workers. Over the sample period, the female workers comprised over 75 percent of the

Table 4.4 Textile and Apparel Industry Premiums

	1999	2000	2001	2002	2003	2004	2005	2006	2007	2008	2008 (LFS)	2009	Change
Textile and apparel industry premium dummy coefficient													
Bangladesh	—	0.134**	—	**0.387**	—	—	0.343**	—	—	—	—	**1.545**	+
		(0.034)		**(0.023)**			(0.058)					**(0.034)**	
India	0.015	—	—	—	—	-0.046*	-0.124**	—	0.084**	—	—	—	+
	(0.015)					(0.019)	(0.016)		(0.012)				
Pakistan	—	—	0.001	—	-0.046*	—	0.076**	—	—	-0.085**	0.019	—	+
			(0.017)		(0.019)		(0.025)			(0.013)	(0.022)		
Vietnam	—	—	—	0.097*	—	-0.340**	—	-0.092	—	-0.076**	—	—	+
				(0.039)		(0.061)		(0.061)		(0.030)			

Source: Authors' calculations based on household surveys, several years.

Note: Sample of workers with positive wages, ages 10–69. Standard errors in parentheses. Comparison points highlighted in bold. The pre-MFA (Multi-fibre Arrangement) comparison point is chosen as close to 2005 as data allow to better identify the immediate post-MFA change. Last column indicates direction of change over time. Pakistan results separated in 2008 into LSMS (Living Standard Measurement Survey) and LFS (Labor Force Survey),

— = not available.

** *p* < 0.01, * *p* < 0.05.

Table 4.5 Male–Female Wage Gap

	1999	2000	2001	2002	2003	2004	2005	2006	2007	2008	2008 (LFS)	2009	Change
Female dummy coefficient													
Bangladesh	—	-0.586* (0.080)	—	**-0.429*** **(0.023)**	—	—	-0.373* (0.067)	—	—	—	—	**0.158** **(0.100)**	+
India	-0.478* (0.024)	—	—	—	—	**-0.489*** **(0.039)**	-0.400* (0.023)	—	**-0.403*** **(0.019)**	—	—	—	+
Pakistan	—	—	-0.493* (0.122)	—	**-0.563*** **(0.103)**	—	-0.721* (0.094)	—	—	-0.473* (0.058)	**-0.630*** **(0.082)**	—	–
Vietnam	—	—	—	-0.127* (0.021)	—	**-0.138*** **(0.025)**	—	-0.135* (0.021)	—	-0.215* (0.031)	—	—	–

Source: Authors' calculations based on household surveys, several years.

Note: Sample of workers with positive wages, ages 10–69. Standard errors in parentheses. Comparison points highlighted in bold. The pre-MFA (Multi-fibre Arrangement) comparison point is chosen as close to 2005 as data allow to better identify the immediate post-MFA change. Last column indicates direction of change over time. Pakistan results separated in 2008 into LSMS (Living Standard Measurement Survey) and LFS (Labor Force Survey).

— = not available.

* $p < 0.01$,

workforce in Vietnamese T&G, and the industry is considered a gateway for women to acquire savings and increase their economic independence. The T&G industry premium dropped in 2004 and did not recover to the early 2000s level. The modest recovery in the industry premium in 2008 is consistent with the observed decline in unit values of Vietnamese apparel exports to the United States and stagnant unit prices of exports to the EU-15. Returns to females in the economy did not increase. It is interesting to note that the drop in the textile premium in 2004 was followed four years later by an increase in the female-male wage gap.

Since India relied on quota-restricted EU and U.S. markets, the MFA phaseout was expected to favor India's apparel and textile exports. India can be considered a case of relative success, with an industry premium that flipped from negative to positive after 2004 and a decrease in the female-male wage gap in the period right before and after the phaseout. This improvement occurred despite the steady decline since the early 2000s in apparel unit prices exported to the United States.

We also consider two other aspects of male and female wages in the T&G sector: the ratio of female and male raw earnings and the difference between male and female residual wage at the industry level (annex tables 4A.4 and 4A.5). We use a measure of residual wages to control for the characteristics of female workers, such as education and experience, which might influence female wages. If the MFA phaseout raised female labor demand compared to men, we should expect a decrease in the earning gaps for similar workers. A decrease in the gap is also a potential consequence of more competition in the sector, leading to less ability of employers to discriminate against female employees. We find that in T&G the ratio of female and male raw earnings either stayed constant or increased post-MFA. However, the difference in male-female residual earnings only decreased post-MFA in comparison to other sectors in India.

Working Conditions

It is interesting to ask whether the post-MFA success of T&G in large Asian exporters translated into better working conditions. In this section, we construct measures of working conditions using household and labor force surveys to identify possible changes after the quota phaseout. We try to maximize the use of the data, constructing country-specific measures of working conditions. We identify several variables that are potentially related to conditions: employment status, injury at work, child labor, overtime, ratio of in-kind over cash pay, and ratio of benefits over cash pay. Conditions are considered favorable to the worker if he or she (i) is paid

Table 4.6   Textile and Apparel Working Conditions

		Working conditions (2)	Working conditions (female workers) (3)
		(1)	
Bangladesh	Time*T&G	0.078*	0.063*
		(0.010)	(0.016)
	Time*T&G*Female	n.a.	−0.088*
			(0.022)
India	Time*T&G	−0.034*	−0.031*
		(0.004)	(0.005)
	Time*T&G*Female	n.a.	0.000
			(0.012)
Pakistan	Time*T&G	−0.001	0.003
		(0.003)	(0.004)
	Time*T&G*Female	n.a.	−0.025*
			(0.005)
Vietnam	Time*T&G	0.007	−0.007
		(0.009)	(0.019)
	Time*T&G*Female	n.a.	0.025
			(0.022)

Source: Authors' calculations.
Note: Workers 10–69 years old. Standard errors in parentheses. Time is a dummy equal to 1 from 2005 on. T&G is a dummy for textile and garment industries. Bangladesh data from 2002 and 2005–06. India data from 1999–2000, 2004, and 2007–08. Vietnam data from 2002, 2004, 2006, and 2008. Pakistan data from 2003–04 and 2008; n.a. = not applicable.
* $p < 0.01$.

as a regular employee with fixed wages, (ii) is not under the age of 14, (iii) reports no work-related injuries, (iv) works no more than 40 hours a week (or less than six days a week), (v) has a low ratio of in-kind over cash work, and (vi) has a high ratio of benefits over cash pay. To measure average working conditions in a job, we assign a dummy variable equal to 1 for each good condition and average the respective dummies for each worker (table 4.6).

The reader should take cross-country and time comparisons with a grain of salt. It is not always possible to construct the same variable definition with different surveys. For instance, overtime for Indian workers has to be defined with the available information on days worked during the week, instead of the usual hours worked used in other countries. Information on less standard benefits for workers such as holiday or bonus pay is also less frequent in household surveys. Since the definitions of the dependent variable are not homogeneous across countries, the analysis also includes as a robustness check one working condition at a time in a probit regression instead of the average for each worker. The reader can then assess whether average results should come from a potentially more relevant condition (such as child labor) or a less relevant condition (such as bonus pay). We focus on the data immediately before and after the phaseout in early 2005. Though more recent information is available, we avoid using recent data years to not mix the impact of the financial crisis with the changes in working conditions in T&G after the end of quotas.

Defining the threshold for good working conditions is not easy. The International Labour Organization (ILO) provides guidelines, but countries are free to ratify their own rules. For example, the appropriate age or the maximum bearable hours of work will vary by country or even industry and gender. We use strict rules where overtime starts to count at more than 40 hours per week, and child labor is defined as age 14 and below. We err on the side of including more workers in the pool of bad working conditions by abiding to stringent definitions. We assume that this "measurement error" is unlikely to change over time and across groups.

We measure working conditions in Bangladesh as the average of a dummy for holding a regular paid job and a dummy for 40 or less workweek hours. The two surveys used are from 2002 and 2005–06. The regression exercises assess the changes in average working conditions for T&G workers in the period post-MFA in comparison to the other sectors in the economy (column 2 in table 4.6). The results are narrowed to consider the relative change in working conditions for female to male in T&G post-MFA compared to other sectors (column 3 in table 4.6). Overall, Bangladeshi working conditions improved when we consider the pool of all workers in T&G who report positive hours. The improvement did not reach women in T&G (column 3 in table 4.6). When we restrict the sample to wage earners, results not reported here show a statistically significant negative effect of the MFA, with no difference between genders. The difference between wage earners and all employees is to be expected if there is a pool of women on nonregular pay in the sector.

Curiously, the economywide returns to being female and the T&G industry premium all move in the same positive direction, while working conditions for women and the share of female employment show a statistically significant negative change over time in comparison to other sectors. We speculate from further inspection of the data that female workers increasingly face a tradeoff in which they obtain jobs and higher wages at the expense of a nonregular paid (hence less stable) position in T&G.

As we have seen previously, India also expanded production by relying on informality and female employment.

To analyze working conditions in Pakistan's apparel sector, we identify four potentially related variables: employment status, injury at work, child labor, and overtime. When compared to the other sectors, working conditions for the pool of T&G workers did not improve while the women in T&G were affected by a decline in working conditions post-MFA. The result is consistent with the observation that the gender gap did not improve in Pakistan's apparel sector, and in the case of the residual wage gap at the industry level, the difference between male and female workers in T&G increased. With regard to policy, as in several other countries, the Pakistani government tried to anticipate the MFA phaseout with a comprehensive policy framework—Textile Vision 2005—which started in 1999–2000. However, another channel seems to have counteracted the phaseout, which is more consistent with the lack of large improvement in IIWD: the government relaxed labor restrictions, and the sector increasingly relied on long daily work hours and temporary contracts.

We measure working conditions in Vietnam in three ways. The first two are standard—no overtime or child labor—and the other one refers to the share of extra pay such as New Year, holidays, and social benefits over the wage earnings. A higher-than-economywide average share of benefits suggests a job with more social protection, which should be valued by workers. Using all available surveys, we find no statistically significant change in T&G working conditions in the period post-MFA in comparison to other sectors. Results hold also with a probit specification on the dummies for benefit pay ratio and overtime.

The benefits brought by internal policies and the end of quota restrictions did not seem to translate into better working conditions in India. We measure working conditions with dummies for the relative position of in-kind over cash pay, no child labor, and no overtime as measured by a workweek of less than six days. Results indicate that average T&G working conditions have declined in the period post-MFA in comparison to other sectors, with no statistically significant difference between genders (table 4.6). This outcome should not be surprising given the high share of informal labor, amounting to 90 percent of total employment in T&G. In fact, as discussed before, informal garment firms carry the weight of the sectoral changes in employment after the phaseout. The results for in-kind over cash pay and no overtime dummies hold in a probit specification for robustness check.

Final Remarks

This chapter discussed the trends in T&G employment for male and female workers, industry structure, wages, and working conditions in Bangladesh, India, Pakistan, and Vietnam after the MFA quota phaseout. In these countries, the government had an active role in developing the sector and preparing T&G firms for the more competitive market after 2004. A mix of state policies in the form of subsidies and upgrading funds and internal country factors are related to the modernization of the T&G sector.

Modernization meant different things for the countries studied. Overall, the quantitative analysis indicates that the phaseout favored T&G firms and workers. In all the large Asian industries analyzed, we find that T&G employment, export revenues, and the industry wage premium improved after the MFA phaseout. However, we find that changes in working conditions vary across countries.

The analysis of employment data indicates that firms had different strategies facing the increase in competition. The regression exercises assess the changes in the firm performance and employment in T&G in the period post-MFA in comparison to the other sectors in the economy. Results indicate a positive change in informal apparel and female share of employment in the industry in India. The expansion of informal apparel is consistent with the negative change after the phase-out in firm-level outcomes and working conditions found in the data, since the sector is usually associated with lower labor productivity and compliance with labor laws. In Bangladesh, we also observe an expansion in the number of firms and employment in T&G. Nevertheless, the regression analysis indicates a negative change post-MFA in employment and the female share of workers in the case of garment firms, and a positive change in textile firms compared to other sectors. The results for Bangladesh are surprising since textile products tend to have higher value-added and more skilled workers. Nevertheless, the industry was capable of absorbing an increasing share of female workers and offering higher wages. In the case of Vietnam and Pakistan, the results show a negative change in T&G employment and textile female share in employment in the period post-MFA in comparison to other sectors.

Annex

Table 4A.1 Basic Education and Employment Statistics

	Bangladesh			India				Pakistan				Vietnam			
	2000	2005	2009	1999	2002	2005	2009	2001	2003	2005	2008	2002	2004	2006	2008
Employment and education															
Females in labor force, share	0.10	0.24	0.25	0.29	0.27	0.28	0.26	0.15	0.17	0.23	0.21	0.50	0.49	0.49	0.49
Years of formal education	3.86	4.95	4.36	4.25	4.86	4.73	5.88	4.05	4.21	4.54	4.97	6.32	8.38	8.50	8.69
Female years of education in T&G	2.35	4.61	5.35	3.60	5.19	4.77	5.80	2.74	2.88	2.93	3.58	7.78	8.50	8.64	8.74
Male years of education in T&G	4.95	7.98	6.45	5.70	5.90	5.90	6.20	4.94	5.50	5.74	6.451	8.63	9.99	10.24	9.45
Average years of education in T&G	4.08	6.71	6.03	5.06	5.69	5.53	6.04	4.39	4.77	4.74	5.62	8.00	8.88	9.21	8.89
Employment share of the industry															
Agriculture	0.41	0.42	0.35	0.51	0.48	0.45	0.49	0.14	0.14	0.15	0.18	0.61	0.58	0.55	0.54
T&G	0.06	0.02	0.05	0.03	0.04	0.04	0.04	0.03	0.02	0.02	0.02	0.01	0.01	0.00	0.03
Female share of employment in T&G	0.38	0.33	0.35	0.32	0.34	0.36	0.33	0.27	0.29	0.29	0.25	0.75	0.80	0.75	0.81
Mean log wage in T&G	7.39	7.85	9.26	5.96	6.07	7.10	6.41	10.25	10.32	10.10	10.63	6.06	5.93	6.62	6.96
Mean log wage in agriculture	7.07	7.60	6.54	5.20	5.30	6.70	5.70	9.90	10.00	10.10	10.50	5.37	6.11	6.35	6.77
Mean log wage	7.41	7.66	7.92	5.96	6.11	7.26	6.38	10.44	10.54	10.48	10.83	5.95	6.52	6.79	7.14

Source: Authors' calculations. Household surveys.

Note: Workers 10–69 years old. Education refers only to workers in the labor force for whom we have information on industry of main occupation. Weighted results. T&G = textiles and garments.

Table 4A.2 Wage Regression Results, Returns to Education

	1999	2000	2001	2002	2003	2004	2005	2006	2007	2008	2008 (LFS)	2009	Change
Bangladesh	—	0.050*	—	**0.031***	—	—	0.013*	—	—	—	—	**0.045***	+
		(0.003)		**(0.001)**			(0.005)					**(0.003)**	
India	0.047*	—	—	—	—	**0.051***	0.030*	—	**0.043***	—	—	—	—
	(0.001)					**(0.001)**	(0.001)		**(0.001)**				
Pakistan	—	—	0.032*	—	**0.039***	—	0.044*	—	—	0.018*	**0.040***	—	+
			(0.002)		**(0.002)**		(0.001)			(0.001)	**(0.001)**		
Vietnam	—	—	—	0.012*	—	**0.038***	—	0.028*	—	0.052*	—	—	+
				(0.001)		**(0.007)**		(0.006)		(0.008)			

Source: Authors' calculations. Household surveys, several years.

Note: Sample of workers with positive wages, ages 10–69. Standard errors in parentheses. Comparison points highlighted in bold. The pre-MFA (Multi-fibre Arrangement) comparison point is chosen as close to 2005 as data allow to better identify the immediate post-MFA change. Last column indicates direction of change over time. Pakistan results separated in 2008 into LSMS (Living Standards Measurement Survey) and LFS (labor force survey); — = not available.

* $p < 0.01$.

Table 4A.3 Bangladeshi Firm-Level Statistics

Industry	Firm distribution weighted			Industry share by number of firms			Industry share by employment		
	1995	2001	2005	1995	2001	2005	1995	2001	2005
Beverages and food	5,662	5,681	6,790	23.67	24.52	19.56	12.54	9.70	7.57
Chemicals and pharmaceuticals	307	578	800	1.28	2.50	2.30	1.87	5.01	2.58
Garments	2,372	3,550	5,002	9.91	15.32	14.41			
Leather	198	268	283	0.83	1.16	0.82	0.59	0.64	0.57
Metals and machinery	1,532	1,221	2,023	6.40	5.27	5.83	5.99	2.35	2.65
Other manufacturing	3,588	5,081	7,033	15.00	21.93	20.26	11.58	14.15	12.39
Other services	197		2	0.83	0	0.01	0.31	0	0
Textiles	10,067	6,790	12,777	42.08	29.31	36.81	67.12	68.15	74.23
Total	23,923	23,169	34,710	100	100	100	100	100	100

Source: Authors' calculations. Firm-level data.

Table 4A.4   Residual Wage Differentials in Textile and Apparel

	Bangladesh	India	Pakistan	Vietnam
Time*T&G	0.375*	−0.078*	0.338*	0.189**
	(0.141)	(0.035)	(0.136)	(0.061)
Constant	−0.705**	0.319**	0.864**	0.180**
	(0.191)	(0.025)	(0.125)	(0.038)
R-squared	0.58	0.097	0.465	0.064
Number of observations	57	60	55	45

Source: Authors' calculations. Household surveys, several years.
Note: Includes year and industry dummies. Standard errors in parentheses. Time is a dummy equal to 1 from 2005 on. T&G = textiles and garments.
**$p < 0.01$, *$p < 0.05$.

Table 4A.5   Raw Earnings Gaps in Textile and Apparel, Female-Male Ratio

percent

	Bangladesh	India	Pakistan	Vietnam
Before 2005	60	55	48	89
After 2005	76	63	44	87

Source: Authors' calculations. Household surveys, several years.
Note: Individuals age 10–69. Bangladesh had no weights for 2002 data, and the year was dropped. Individuals who did not work in the week before interview were dropped in the data from India. No weights for India 2007. Individuals who reported not working in the year before interview in the Vietnam data were dropped from the sample.

Table 4A.6   Unit Values of Apparel Imports to the European Union and the United States

	1999	2000	2001	2002	2003	2004	2005	2006	2007	2008	2009
India											
EU: euro/kg	14.1	16.1	12.5	14.3	13.2	14.1	15.4	17.0	16.1	15.8	16.2
U.S.: $/dozen	63.3	71.0	67.5	56.5	57.5	56.2	52.6	51.1	49.0	45.0	41.2
Pakistan											
EU: euro/kg	7.8	8.7	8.6	8.2	7.8	7.9	7.5	7.6	7.7	7.5	7.7
U.S.: $/dozen	43.0	40.0	39.6	37.3	36.6	36.3	34.9	33.0	34.0	32.9	31.6
Vietnam											
EU: euro/kg	18.7	20.8	18.6	17.3	13.3	14.2	13.4	13.9	11.7	12.5	14.7
U.S.: $/dozen	32.0	26.9	26.8	47.6	48.6	56.9	58.1	56.4	53.7	50.9	45.0

Source: Several sources; metadata from country background papers; Staritz and Frederick 2011a, 2011b, 2011c, 2011d.
Note: Kg = kilogram

Table 4A.7   Pakistani Employment Results

	Female share in total employment	Log (employment)	Log (male employment)	Log (female employment)
Time*T&G	−0.042	−0.293*	−0.340**	−0.375
	(0.033)	(0.174)	(0.100)	(0.593)
Time	−0.024	−0.037	0.196**	(0.296)
	(0.019)	(0.101)	(0.068)	(0.265)
Constant	0.524**	16.644**	16.270**	15.204**
	(0.115)	(0.116)	(0.075)	(0.271)
R-squared	0.837	0.964	0.983	1
Number of observations	59	60	60	59

Source: Authors' calculations. Household data, several years.
Note: Employment levels are constructed using household weights by industry and WDR World Development Report labor force numbers. Data cells at the industry, gender, year levels. Industry dummies included. Standard errors in parentheses. Sample with workers 15–64 years old. Time is a dummy equal to 1 from 2005 on; T&G = textiles and garments.
**$p < 0.01$, *$p < 0.1$.

Table 4A.8   Pakistani Enterprise Survey Results

	Log (sales)		Job creation	Job destruction
Time*T&G	−0.456*			
	(0.235)	All	32%	11%
Time	0.518**			
	(0.173)	Female	48%	10%
Constant	15.316**			
	(0.793)	Male	31%	11%
R-squared	0.175			
Number of observations	755	Number of T&G firms	222	222

Source: Authors' calculations. Enterprise survey. Panel 2002 and 2007.
Note: All job creation and job destruction numbers for T&G (textiles and garments). Time is a dummy equal to 1 from 2005 on.
**$p < 0.01$, *$p < 0.1$.

Table 4A.9   Vietnamese Employment Results

	Female share in total employment	Log (employment)	Log (male employment)	Log (female employment)
Time*textiles	−0.007*	−0.264*	−0.190*	−0.317*
	(0.001)	(0.061)	(0.057)	(0.072)
Time*apparel	0.024*	0.022	−0.015	0
	(0.001)	(0.061)	(0.056)	(0.072)
Assets per worker	0	0.041	0.072	0.006
	(0.000)	(0.103)	(0.103)	(0.107)
Time	0	0.538*	0.494*	0.578*
	(0.001)	(0.061)	(0.056)	(0.072)
Constant	0.018*	10.183*	9.646*	9.124*
	(0.000)	(0.044)	(0.043)	(0.045)
R-squared	0.043	0.398	0.384	0.371
Number of observations	442	442	442	442

Source: Authors' calculations. Industry level data, several years.
Note: Industry dummies. Standard errors in parentheses. Time is a dummy equal to 1 from 2005 on.
* $p < 0.01$.

Table 4A.10   Bangladeshi Firm-Level Results

	Log (value added)	Log (labor)	Log (wage per worker)	Female share in the industry
Time	0.294***	−0.0142	0.0543**	0.0506***
	(0.040)	(0.010)	(0.022)	(0.009)
Time*apparel	−0.122	−0.0463*	0.109**	−0.246***
	(0.077)	(0.025)	(0.055)	(0.020)
Time*textiles	0.121**	0.0482***	0.321***	0.0817***
	(0.057)	(0.014)	(0.028)	(0.011)
Constant	12.65***	2.577***	9.484***	0.408***
	(0.095)	(0.037)	(0.060)	(0.083)
R-squared	0.669	0.943	0.159	0.403
Number of observations	13959	14439	14410	13959

Source: Authors' calculations. Firm-level data.
Note: Industry, size, and location dummies. Standard errors in parentheses. Time is a dummy equal to 1 from 2005 on.
***$p < 0.01$, **$p < 0.05$, *$p < 0.1$.

Notes

1. The EU-15 are the 15 member states of the European Union (EU) as of December 31, 2003, before the new member states joined the EU: Austria, Belgium, Denmark, Finland, France, Germany, Greece, Ireland, Italy, Luxembourg, the Netherlands, Portugal, Spain, Sweden, and the United Kingdom.

2. Everything but Arms (EBA) is an initiative of the EU under which all imports to the EU from least developed countries are duty and quota free, with the exception of armaments. The EBA is part of the EU Generalized System of Preferences (GSP).

3. Other agreements include the South Asian Preferential Trading Agreement (SAPTA) and the Bay of Bengal Initiative for Multi-Sectoral Economic Cooperation (BIMSTEC) involving Bangladesh, Bhutan, India, Myanmar, Nepal, Sri Lanka, and Thailand.

4. Numbers from Better Work Vietnam (2011) state that 2 million people are employed in textiles and garments and that the sector was the largest provider of formal employment in Vietnam in 2009.

5. Results using the subset of firms in the formal sector are not statistically significant.

6. Bangladeshi data cover the 2000–09 period. BHIES (Bangladesh Household Income and Expenditure Survey) 2010 was not used in the analysis because the world apparel industry was affected by the global financial crisis and the China safeguard removal in 2008–09; thus, we would not be able to single out the MFA affect. Moreover, the response of the apparel sector to those shocks may be a topic for a separate study.

References and Other Sources

Bangladesh

Adhikari, Ratnakar, and Chatrini Weeratunge. 2006. "Textiles and Clothing Sector in South Asia: Coping with Post-Quota Challenges." In *South Asian Yearbook of Trade and Development*. B. L. Das, B. S. Chimni, Saman Kelegama, and Mustafizur Rahman, 109–47. New Delhi: Centre for Trade and Development (CENTAD).

———. 2007. "Textiles and Clothing in South Asia: Current Status and Future Potential." *South Asia Economic Journal* 8 (2): 171–203.

Ahmed, Nazneen. 2005. "Impact of the MFA Expiry on Bangladesh." In *South Asia after the Quota System: Impact of the MFA Phase-out*, ed. Saman Kelegama. Colombo: Institute of Policy Studies of Sri Lanka.

———. 2009a. "Sustaining Ready-made Garment Exports from Bangladesh." *Journal of Contemporary Asia* 39 (4): 597–618.

———. 2009b. "The Role of Economic Zones in Tackling Labor Compliance." *The Daily Star*, November 10.

———. 2009c. "Elected Workers' Association in EPZs." *The Daily Star*, December 11.

Ahmed, Nazneen, and Jack H. M. Peerlings. 2009. "Addressing Workers' Rights in the Textile and Apparel Industries: Consequences for the Bangladesh Economy." *World Development* 37 (3): 661–75.

Anson, Robin, and Guillame Brocklehurst. 2008. Part 1 of "World Markets for Textile Machinery: Fabric Manufacture." *Textile Outlook International* 137: 98–138.

———. 2010a. Part 2 of "World Markets for Textile Machinery: Woven Fabric Manufacture." *Textile Outlook International* 146: 89–106.

———. 2010b. Part 3 of "World Markets for Textile Machinery: Knitted Fabric Manufacture." *Textile Outlook International* 147: 120–54.

Arnold, John. 2010. "Effects of Trade Logistics on the Strategy of the Garments Industry for Product and Market Diversification." Background paper prepared for the Bangladesh Trade Note, Dhaka, World Bank.

Bair, Jennifer, and Gary Gereffi. 2003. "Upgrading, Uneven Development, and Jobs in the North American Apparel Industry." *Global Networks* 3 (2): 143–69.

Bakht, Zaid, Mohammad Yunus, and Md. Salimullah. 2002. "Machinery Industry in Bangladesh." IDEAS Machinery Industry Study Report 4, Tokyo Institute of Development Economies Advanced School, Tokyo.

Bangladesh (Department of Textiles). 2009. *Survey of the Bangladesh Textile Industry to Assess the Requirement of Textile Technologists.* Dhaka, Bangladesh: Bangladesh DOT.

BEPZA (Bangladesh Export Processing Zone Authority). 2010. *Annual Report: 2008–09.* Dhaka: BEPZA.

BIDS (Bangladesh Institute of Development Studies). 2011. "Trade Liberalization, Changes in Industrial Structure, and Job Creation in Bangladesh." Background paper for the "South Asia Regional Flagship on More and Better Job," BIDS, April, Dhaka.

Brocklehurst, Guillame, and Robin Anson. 2010. Part 1 of "World Markets for Textile Machinery: Yarn Manufacture." *Textile Outlook International* 145: 80–117.

Elmer, Diepak. 2010. "The RMG Skills Formation Regime in Bangladesh: A Background Paper." Background paper prepared for the Bangladesh Trade Note, Dhaka, World Bank.

Gereffi, Gary. 1994. "The Organization of Buyer Driven Global Commodity Chains: How U.S. Retailers Shape Overseas Production Networks." In *Commodity Chains and Global Capitalism*, ed. Gary Gereffi and Miguel Korzeniewicz, 95–122. Westport, CT: Praeger.

———. 1999. "International Trade and Industrial Upgrading in the Apparel Commodity Chain." *Journal of International Economics* 48 (1): 37–70.

———. 2005. "The Global Economy: Organization, Governance, and Development." In *The Handbook of Economic Sociology*, ed. Neil J. Smelser and Richard Swedberg, 160–82. Princeton, NJ: Princeton University Press.

Gereffi, Gary, John Humphrey, Raphael Kaplinsky, and Timothy J. Sturgeon. 2001. "Introduction: Globalisation, Value Chains and Development." *IDS Bulletin* 32 (3): 1–8.

Gereffi, Gary, John Humphrey, and Timothy J. Sturgeon. 2005. "The Governance of Global Value Chains." *Review of International Political Economy* 12 (1): 78–104.

Gereffi, Gary, and Olga Memodovic. 2003. "The Global Apparel Value Chain: What Prospects for Upgrading by Developing Countries?" United Nations Industrial Development Organization (UNIDO), Sectoral Studies Series, Vienna.

Gereffi, Gary, and Frederick Stacey. 2010. "The Global Apparel Value Chain, Trade and the Crisis—Challenges and Opportunities for Developing Countries." In *Global Value Chains in a Postcrisis World: A Development Perspective*, ed. Olivier Cattaneo, Gary Gereffi, and Cornelia Staritz, 157–208. Washington, DC: World Bank.

GTZ (German Technical Corporation). 2009. "Skill Development Overview: Productivity and Income Gains through Skill Development." PROGRESS fact sheet, GTZ, Dhaka, Bangladesh.

Haider, Mohammed Ziaul. 2007. "Competitiveness of the Bangladesh Ready-Made Garment Industry in Major International Markets." *Asia Pacific Trade and Investment Review* 3 (1): 3–27.

IMF (International Monetary Fund). 2008. *The Ready-Made Garment Industry in Bangladesh: An Update*, by Jonathan Dunn. IMF Report, Washington, DC.

Just-style. 2010a. "Asian Woven Fabric Industry Moves Upmarket—Research." *Just-style.com*, September 20.

———. 2010b. "Bangladesh: Garment Factories Resume Operations." *Just-style.com*, August 3.

———. 2010c. "Bangladesh in Brief: Apparel Industry Snapshot." *Just-style.com*, August 2.

———. 2010d. "Continuing Protests Blight Bangladesh Pay Deal." *Just-style.com*, August 2.

———. 2010e. "Update: Bangladesh Garment Wages to Rise 80%." *Just-style.com*, July 29.

Kabeer, Naila, and Simeen Mahmud. 2004. "Globalization, Gender and Poverty: Bangladeshi Women Workers in Export and Local Markets." *Journal of International Development* 16: 93–109.

Knowles, A., C. Reyes, and K. Jackson. 2008. "Gender, Migration and Remittances: A Bangladeshi Experience." In *Southern Perspectives on Development: Dialogue or Division?* ed. Alec Thorton and Andrew McGregor, 229–46. Auckland: Centre for Development Studies, University of Auckland.

Quddus, Munir, and Salim Rashid. 2000. *Entrepreneurs and Economic Development: The Remarkable Story of Garment Exports from Bangladesh.* Dhaka: The University Press Limited.

Rahman, Mustafizur, Debapriya Bhattacharya, and Khondakar Golam Moazzem. 2008. "Dynamics of Ongoing Changes in Bangladesh's Export Oriented RGM Enterprises: Findings from an Enterprise Level Survey." Unpublished manuscript, Dhaka: Centre for Policy Dialogue (CPD).

World Bank. 2010. *Export Bulletin.* Dhaka: World Bank, Bangladesh country office.

India

AEPC (Apparel Export Promotion Council). 2009. Presentation to Apparel Export Promotion Council, Apparel House, Institutional Area Sector-44, Gurgaon-122003 Haryana.

CARIS (Centre for the Analysis of Regional Integration at Sussex). 2008. "The Impact of Trade Policies on Pakistan's Preferential Access to the European Union." Report for the European Commission, Department of Economics, University of Sussex.

Euromonitor. 2009. "Clothing-India: Country Sector Briefing." London: Euromonitor International.

Hirway, Indira. 2008. "Trade and Gender Inequalities in Labour Market: Case of Textile and Garment Industry in India." Paper prepared for the International Seminar on Moving towards Gender Sensitization of Trade Policy, organized by United Nations Conference on Trade and Development, New Delhi, February 25–27.

IFPRI (International Food Policy Research Institute). 2008. "Cotton-Textile-Apparel Sectors of India: Situations and Challenges Faced." IFPRI Discussion Paper 00801, IFPRI, Washington, DC.

Italia (Italian Trade Commission). 2009. "The Textile Industry and Related Sector Report 2009." Italian Trade Commission, www.ice.gov.it.

Ministry of Textiles. 2006a. "Report of the Working Group on the Textiles and Jute Industry for the Eleventh Five-Year-Plan." December, www.planningcommission.gov.in.

———. 2006b. Study for the Ministry of Textiles. Indian Council for Research on International Economic Relations (ICRIER), New Delhi, India.

———. 2008. "Varieties of Global Integration: Navigating Institutional Legacies and Global Networks in India's Garment Industry." *Competition & Change* 12 (1): 49–67.

———. 2009a. "Assessing the Prospects for India's Textile and Clothing Sector." July, www.texmin.nic.in.

————. 2009b. "The Textiles and Clothing Industry." In *Study on Intraregional Trade and Investment in South Asia*. Manila: Development Partnership Program for South Asia, Asian Development Bank.

Tewari, Meenu, and Manjeeta Singh. Forthcoming. Textile Ministry Study. Indian Council for Research on International Economic Relations (ICRIER), New Delhi, India.

Thoburn, John. 2009. "The Impact of World Recession on the Textile and Garment Industries of Asia." Working Paper 17/2009, United Nations Industrial Development Organization, Research and Statistics Branch, Vienna, Austria.

Verma, Samar. 2005. "Impact of the MFA Expiry on India." In *South Asia after the Quota-System: Impact of the MFA Phase-out*, ed. Saman Kelegama. Colombo: Institute of Policy Studies.

Pakistan

Abdullah, Ahmed. 2009. "Pakistan: South Korea Invests in Garment Technology Centre." *Just-style*, October 15.

ADB (Asian Development Bank). 2004. "Industrial Competitiveness. The Challenge for Pakistan." ADB Institute–Pakistan Resident Mission Seminar Paper, Tokyo, Japan.

Amjad, Rashid. 2005. "Skills and Competitiveness: Can Pakistan Break Out of the Low-Level Skills Trap?" *Pakistan Development Review* 44 (4): 387–409.

CFR (Council on Foreign Relations). 2010. "China-Pakistan Relations, Backgrounder." Council on Foreign Relations. http://www.cfr.org/china/china -pakistan-relations/p10070.

Elliott, Kimberly Ann. 2010. "Stimulating Pakistani Exports and Job Creation. Special Zones Won't Help Nearly as Much as Cutting Tariffs across the Board." Center for Global Development, Washington, DC.

FBS (Federal Bureau of Statistics). 2009. "Compendium on Gender Statistics in Pakistan 2009." FBS, Islamabad.

Ghayur, Sabur. 2009. "Evolution of the Industrial Relations System in Pakistan." International Labour Organization (ILO) Working Paper, New Delhi, India.

GoP (Government of Pakistan). 2000. Textile Vision 2005. Government of Pakistan.

————. 2010. "Chapter 3: Manufacturing." In *Economic Survey*. Ministry of Textiles, Government of Pakistan, Islamabad.

Hamdani, Khalil. 2009. "Foreign Direct Investment Prospects for Pakistan." PowerPoint presentation, Pakistan Institute of Development Economics, Islamabad.

Hisam, Zeenat. 2010. "Organising for Labour Rights. Women Workers in Textile/ Readymade Garments Sector in Pakistan and Bangladesh." Report published by Pakistan Institute of Labour Education & Research and South Asia Alliance for Poverty Eradication (SAAPE), Karachi.

Hufbauer, Gary Clyde, and Shahid Javed Burki. 2006. "Sustaining Reform with a US-Pakistan Free Trade Agreement." Peterson Institute for International Economics, Washington, DC.

ILO (International Labour Organization). 2005. "Promoting Fair Globalization in Textiles and Clothing in a post-MFA Environment." Report for discussion at the Tripartite Meeting on Promoting Fair Globalization in Textiles and Clothing in a Post-MFA Environment, ILO, Geneva.

———. 2010. "Women Continue to Face Discrimination in the World of Work." ILO, Islamabad Office, Press Release, December 6. http://www.ilo.org /islamabad/info/public/pr/lang--en/WCMS_150228/index.htm. Accessed February 21, 2011.

Khan, Zubair. 2003. "Impact of post-ATC Environment on Pakistan's Textile Trade." New York: United Nations Development Programme (UNDP), Asia Pacific Regional Initiative on Trade, Economic Governance and Human Development (Asia Trade Initiative).

PTJ (Pakistan Textile Journal). 2010a. "Pak-China Economic and Trade Relations." Pakistan Textile Journal, September.

———. 2010b. "Pakistan: The Third Largest Spinner Country in Asia." Pakistan Textile Journal, February.

Saheed, Hassen. 2009. "Prospects for the Textile and Garment Industry in Pakistan." Textile Outlook International 142: 55–102.

Sekhar, Uday. 2010. "Denim Fabric: Global Trade and Leading Players." Textile Outlook International 146: 32–55.

———. 2009. "The Trade and Gender Interface: A Perspective from Pakistan." Sustainable Development Policy Institute, Islamabad, Pakistan.

SMEDA (Small and Medium Development Authority). 2002. "Apparel Sector Brief." Lahore: Small and Medium Development Authority, Government of Pakistan.

UNDP (United Nations Development Programme). 2008. "Current Status and Prospects of Female Employment in the Apparel Industry Pakistan." Baseline study submitted to the Gen Prom Pakistan, New York.

USA-ITA (U.S. Association of Importers of Textiles and Apparel). 2010. "White Paper of the U.S. Association of Importers of Textiles and Apparel (USA-ITA) on the Need for Meaningful Pakistan-Afghan ROZs." http://www.usaita.com /pdf/82_20100113120548.pdf.

USITC (United States International Trade Commission). 2004. "Textiles and Apparel: Assessment of the Competitiveness of Certain Foreign Supplier to the U.S. Market." Publication 3671, USITC, Washington, DC.

Weerakoon, Dushni. 2010. "SAFTA—Current Status and Prospects." In *Promoting Economic Cooperation in South Asia: Beyond SAFTA*, ed. Sadiq Ahmed, Saman Kelegama, and Ejaz Ghani. Washington, DC: World Bank.

Vietnam

Adams, Wilson. 2010. "Textiles and Clothing in Vietnam: Riding the Crest of a Wave." *Textile Outlook International* 146 (August).

BMI (Business Monitor International). 2009. "Vietnam Textile & Clothing Report Q4 2009." Part of BMI's industry Report & Forecast Series, August, London.

CIEM (Central Institute for Economic Management). 2010. *Vietnam Competitiveness Report*, by Christian Ketels, Nguyen Dinh Cung, Nguyen Thi Tue Anh, and Do Hong Hanh. Report, CIEM, Hanoi, Vietnam.

GTAI (Germany Trade and Investment Agency). 2010. *Vietnam's Textil und Bekleidungsbranche wächst weiter zweistellig*, by Stefanie Schmitt. Report, GTAI, Berlin.

ILO (International Labour Organization). 2009. "Sectoral Coverage of the Global Economic Crisis—Implications of the Global Financial and Economic Crisis on the Textile and Clothing Sector." ILO, Geneva.

———. 2010. "Labor and Social Trends in Viet Nam 2009/10." ILO, Hanoi.

Martin, Michael F. 2010. "U.S.-Vietnam Economic and Trade Relations: Issues for the 112th Congress." Congressional Research Service, Washington, DC.

Nadvi, Khalid, John Thoburn, Tat T. Bui, Thi T. H. Nguyen, Thi H. Nguyen, Hong L. Dao, and Enrique B. Armas. 2004a. "Vietnam in the Global Garment and Textile Value Chain: Impacts on Firms and Workers." *Journal of International Development* 16 (1): 111–23.

———. 2004b. "Challenges to Vietnamese Firms in the World Garment and Textile Value Chain, and the Implications for Alleviating Poverty." *Journal of the Asia Pacific Economy* 9 (2): 249–67.

Saheed, Hassen. 2007. "Prospects for the Textile and Garment Industry in Vietnam." *Textile Outlook International* 129: 12–50.

Schaumburg-Mueller, Henrik. 2009. "Garment Exports from Vietnam: Changes in Supplier Strategies." *Journal of the Asia Pacific Economy* 14 (2): 162–71.

Statistical Yearbook of Vietnam. 2010, 2008. http://www.gso.gov.vn/default_en .aspx?tabid= 515&idmid=5&ItemID=11974.

Thoburn, John. 2009. "The Impact of World Recession on the Textile and Garment Industries of Asia." Working Paper 17/2009, United Nations

Industrial Development Organization (UNIDO) Research and Statistics Branch, Vienna.

———. 2010. "Vietnam as a Role Model for Development." Research Paper 2009/300, World Institute for Development Economics Research of the United Nations University (UNU-WIDER), Helsinki.

Thomson, Lotte. 2007. "Accessing Global Value Chains? The Role of Business–State Relations in the Private Clothing Industry in Vietnam." *Journal of Economic Geography* 7: 753–76.

Vietnam Business News. 2010. "FDI Rushes into Vietnam." http://vietnambusiness .asia/ fdi-rushes-into-vietnam%E2%80%99s-textile-and-garment-sector/.

Additional Readings

AFTEX (ASEAN Federation of Textile Industries). 2010. "Vietnam's Garment and Textile Industry." AFTEX, Kuala Lumpur, Malaysia.

Arndt, Channing, Paul Dorosh, Marzia Fontana, and Sajjad Zohir. 2002. "Opportunities and Challenges in Agriculture and Garments: A General Equilibrium Analysis of the Bangladesh Economy." TMD Discussion Paper 07. Paper from the "Bangladesh and the WTO" project implemented by researchers from the International Food Policy Research Institute (IFPRI) and the Bangladesh Institute of Development Studies (BIDS), Washington, DC.

Becker, Gary S. 1971. *The Economics of Discrimination*. 2nd ed. Chicago: University of Chicago Press.

Better Work Vietnam. 2011. http://www.betterwork.org/sites/VietNam/English/ Pages/index.aspx.

Brown, Drusilla, Alan Deardorff, and Robert Stern. 2004. "The Effects of Multinational Production on Wages and Working Conditions in Developing Countries." In *Challenges to Globalization: Analyzing the Economics*, ed. Robert E. Baldwin and L. Alan Winters, 279–330. Chicago: University of Chicago Press.

Carr, Marilyn. 2001. "Globalization and the Informal Economy: How Global Trade and Investment Impact on the Working Poor." Background paper commissioned by the ILO Task Force on the Informal Economy, International Labour Office, Geneva, Switzerland.

CARIS (Centre for the Analysis of Regional Integration). 2008. "The Impact of Trade Policies on Pakistan's Preferential Access to the European Union." Report for the EC, Centre for the Analysis of Regional Integration at Sussex, Department of Economics, University of Sussex, U.K.

Goto, Kenta. 2007. "Industrial Upgrading of the Vietnamese Garment Industry: An Analysis from the Global Value Chains Perspective." Working Paper. 07-1,

Ritsumeikan Center for Asia Pacific Studies (RCAPS). http://www.apu.ac.jp/rcaps/.

EC's Delegation to Pakistan. 2004. "European Union-Pakistan Trade Relations." http://www.delpak.cec.eu.int/eupaktrade/New-EU-Pak-Trade-May-04.htm.

Fakhar, Huma. 2005. "The Political Economy of the EU GSP Scheme: Implications for Pakistan." In *South Asian Yearbook of Trade and Development 2005.* New Delhi, India: Centre for Trade and Development (Centad).

GoP (Government of Pakistan). 2008a. "Textiles and Clothing Trade 2002–07." Research, Development and Advisory Cell, Ministry of Textiles, Government of Pakistan, Islamabad.

———. 2008b. "Investment in Imported Textile Machinery." Research, Development and Advisory Cell, Ministry of Textiles, Government of Pakistan, Islamabad.

IFPRI (International Food Policy Research Institute). 2008. "Cotton-Textile-Apparel Sectors of Pakistan, Situations and Challenges Faced." Discussion Paper 00800, IFPRI, Washington, DC.

Jassin-O'Rourke Group, L. 2008. "Global Apparel Manufacturing Labor Cost Analysis 2008, Textile and Apparel Manufacturers & Merchants." http://www.tammonline.com/researchpapers.htm.

Just-style. 2008. "Pakistan: Extends R&D Subsidy for Apparel Exports." August 8.

Kabeer, Naila, and Simeen Mahmud. 2004. "Globalization, Gender, and Poverty: Bangladeshi Women Workers in Export and Local Markets." *Journal of International Development* 16: 93–109

Kabeer, Naila, and Tran Thi Van Anh. 2006. "Global Production, Local Markets: Gender, Poverty and Export Manufacturing in Vietnam." GEM-IWG Working Paper 06-3, International Working Group on Gender, Macroeconomics, and International Economics. Salt Lake City, Utah.

Ministry of Textiles. 2010. *Annual Report* 2009/10. New Delhi, www.texmin.nic.in.

Nordås, Hildegunn Kyvik. 2005. "Labour Implications of the Textiles and Clothing Quota Phase-Out." ILO Working Paper 224, International Labour Organization, Geneva, January.

PRGMEA (Pakistan Readymade Garments Manufacturers and Exporters Association). 2010. "Pakistan's Garment Sector. An Overview." PowerPoint presentation. http://www.prgmea.org.

Robertson, Raymond, Drusilla Brown, Pierre Gaelle, and Maria Laura Sanchez-Puerta. 2009. "Globalization, Wages and the Quality of Jobs: Five Country Studies." World Bank, Washington, DC.

Saheed, Hassen. 2008. "Prospects for the Textile and Garment Industry in Bangladesh." *Textile Outlook International* 135: 12–48.

Siegmann, Karin Astrid. 2006. "Pakistan's Textile Sector and the EU." *South Asian Journal* 13 (September).

Singh, J. N. 2008. "Indian Textile and Clothing Sector Poised for a Leap." In *Unveiling Protectionism: Regional Responses to Remaining Barriers in the Textiles and Clothing Trade*, ed. ESCAP. Studies in Trade and Investment, United Nations Economic and Social Commission for Asia and the Pacific (ESCAP), Bangkok.

Staritz, Cornelia, and Stacey Frederick. 2011a. "Background Global Value Chain Country Papers: Bangladesh." Background paper to the book *Sewing Success? Employment, Wages, and Poverty following the End of the Multi-fibre Arrangement*, World Bank, Washington, DC.

———. 2011b. "Background Global Value Chain Country Papers: India." Background paper to the book *Sewing Success? Employment, Wages, and Poverty following the End of the Multi-fibre Arrangement*, World Bank, Washington, DC.

———. 2011c. "Background Global Value Chain Country Papers: Vietnam." Background paper to the book *Sewing Success? Employment, Wages, and Poverty following the End of the Multi-fibre Arrangement*, World Bank, Washington, DC.

———. 2011d. "Background Global Value Chain Country Papers: Pakistan." Background paper to the book *Sewing Success? Employment, Wages, and Poverty following the End of the Multi-fibre Arrangement*, World Bank, Washington, DC.

Tewari, Meenu. 2005. "Post-MFA Adjustments in India's Textile and Apparel Industry: Emerging Issues and Trends." Working paper, Indian Council for Research on International Economic Relations (ICRIER), New Delhi, India, July.

———. 2008. "Deepening Intraregional Trade and Investment in South Asia—The Case of the Textile and Clothing Industry." Working Paper 213, India Council for Research on International Economic Relations, New Delhi.

Textiles Intelligence. 2008. *Textile Outlook International*, May–June 2008, No. 135. www.textilesintelligence.com.

USITC (United States International Trade Commission). 2004. "Textiles and Apparel: Assessment of the Competitiveness of Certain Foreign Supplier to the U.S. Market." Publication 3671, USITC, Washington, DC.

Vu Quoc Huy, Vi Tri Thanh, Nguyen Thang, Cu Chi Loi, Nguyen Thi Thanh Ha, and Nguyen Van Tien. 2001. "Trade Liberalisation and Competitiveness of Selected Industries in Vietnam Project: Textile and Garment Industry in Vietnam." Institute of Economics, Hanoi/International Development Research Center, Canada.

Weerakoon, Dushni. 2010. "SAFTA—Current Status and Prospects." In *Promoting Economic Cooperation in South Asia: Beyond SAFTA*, ed. Sadiq Ahmed, Saman Kelegama, and Ejaz Ghani, 71–88. Washington, DC: World Bank.

World Bank. 2005a. "Bangladesh Growth and Export Competiveness." Report 31394-BD, Poverty Reduction and Economic Management Sector Unit, South Asia Region, World Bank, Washington, DC.

———. 2005b. "End of MFA Quotas—Key Issues and Strategic Options for Bangladesh Readymade Garment Industry." Bangladesh Development Series Paper 2, Poverty Reduction and Economic Management Unit, World Bank Office, Dhaka.

Empirical Results
Black, Sandra, and Elizabeth Brainerd. 2002. "Importing Equality? The Impact of Globalization on Gender Discrimination." IZA Discussion Paper 556, Institute for the Study of Labor, Bonn.

Robertson, Raymond. 2010. "Apparel Wages before and after the Better Factories Cambodia Program." Working Paper, World Bank, Washington, DC.

CHAPTER 5

The Challenge to Major Exporters after the MFA Phaseout

Elisa Gamberoni

Introduction

The end of the Multi-fibre Arrangement (MFA) regime induced a reshuffling of resources toward more competitive producers. As a result, some of the previous major exporters who were heavily tied to one import market thanks to preferential access were challenged by the increased competition, particularly from Asian economies. This chapter focuses on three of them: Honduras, Mexico, and Morocco.

The apparel and textile sector represents an important source of export earnings and is a major source of employment in the three countries. In 2003, Mexican textile and clothing exports accounted for 6 percent of total Mexican exports and about 10 percent of overall employment. Similarly, in Honduras, textile and clothing exports in 2003 accounted for 5.0 percent of total exports and 6.0 percent of employment, while in

The author is grateful for comments provided by Gladys Lopez-Acevedo, Raymond Robertson, and Yevgeniya Savchenko. The chapter was based on contributions by Ana Luisa Gouvea (figures and regressions on wage and working conditions for Honduras); country background papers (Staritz and Frederick 2011a, 2011b, 2011c); Monica Tinajero (figures and regressions on employment for Mexico); and Jimerson Asencio (figures and regressions on wage and working conditions for Mexico).

Morocco, textile and clothing exports constituted about 32.0 percent of total exports and 31.2 percent of manufacturing employment on average for the period 2003–07 (Rossi 2010). The sector is also a key source for female employment. The clothing industry employed about 14 percent of total Honduran female workers and about 18 percent of Mexican female workers in 2003. The sector is highly female intensive: in 2003, female workers made up 44.0 percent of all textile and clothing workers in Mexico and 60.0 percent in Honduras, and in Morocco, the women accounted for 83.6 percent of total apparel workers in 2007 (Rossi 2010).

Available studies point to the importance of the apparel sector for poverty reduction through the effects on wages, particularly for female workers, and job creation. De Hoyos, Bussolo, and Núñez (2008) show that during 2002–06, workers in the *maquila*[1] sector in Honduras earned wages about 30 percent higher than those of workers outside the sector. The authors, using a simulation exercise, show that poverty in Honduras would have been 1.5 percentage points higher had the *maquila* sector not existed. This beneficial effect of the *maquila* sector is due to the wage premium paid to all apparel workers, to the premium paid to women in particular, and to job creation.

This chapter starts by investigating the evolution of the apparel sector in Honduras, Mexico, and Morocco. It then looks at the trend of both the wage premium and employment in the apparel sector compared to the rest of the economy following the MFA phaseout for Honduras and Mexico. Data limitation prevents us from providing an accurate picture for Morocco, but we provide some relevant statistics when feasible.

Results from the qualitative analysis suggest that these countries experienced a drop in apparel exports following the MFA phaseout, but this drop was reversed in the case of Morocco. While it is difficult to establish causality, Morocco's apparel export performance seems to have benefited from proactive policy in terms of preferential market access to other big markets, less restrictive rules of cumulation to qualify for preferential access, and ability to attract foreign direct investment (FDI). These in turn have helped Morocco to diversify its export portfolio in terms of both products and markets.

The quantitative analysis shows that in Honduras and Mexico the wage premium and the share of workers employed in textile and clothing sectors decreased compared to other sectors in the period post-MFA. The analysis also reveals gender-differentiated effects. Compared to other sectors, the share of female workers and the intensity in the use of female workers in the textile and garment production process decreased in the period post-MFA. Preliminary evidence for Mexico also suggests a negative relation between female intensity and value-added per worker. In the case of Honduras, we also find large job destruction rates for unskilled workers in the period post-MFA, particularly for the clothing sector. This result, together with the results on female workers, suggests that there might be a negative relation between skilled activities and the female intensity of production. However, we do not see substantial differences in the education levels between men and women employed in the industry in the years under analysis.

Finally, we present results for working conditions in the apparel industry. Working conditions appear to have deteriorated in the Mexican and Honduran apparel industries compared to other sectors in the period post-MFA.

The chapter is structured as follows. Section one discusses the industry evolution in the period before and after the MFA and the type of proactive policies implemented to sustain export competitiveness in the apparel sector following the end of the MFA. Section two discusses trends in employment and intersectoral reallocation, section three focuses on the intraindustry reallocation, section four focuses on the wage premium, and section five considers working conditions. Given the importance of the sector for female workers, we also document gender-specific trends. Section six concludes.

Industry Evolution and Export Performance following the MFA Phaseout

This section documents the evolution of the apparel sector in all three countries.[2] We first analyze the factors that led to the establishment of the industry and the markets and products in which the countries specialized. We then discuss the impact of the end of the MFA and the type of policies adopted by the countries to help firms counteract increased competition.

In all three countries, the industry flourished thanks to the presence of preferential market access to key markets (the United States in the case of Honduras and Mexico and the European Union [EU] in the case of Morocco) and a mix of industrial policies. In Mexico, the initial development of the export-oriented apparel sector began in the mid-1960s, driven by preferential access to the U.S. market through the "807" production-sharing agreement and the establishment of the *maquiladora* program along the U.S. border. With the entry into force of the North American Free Trade Agreement (NAFTA) in 1994, access was significantly expanded, permitting Mexico to export apparel quota free and duty free to both the United States and Canada. In Honduras, initial development of the export-oriented apparel sector began in the mid-1980s with the U.S.-Caribbean preferential trade agreements known as the Caribbean Basin Initiative (CBI). During this time, apparel assembly plants emerged thanks to reduced duty rates and quota-free access to the United States. In Morocco, initial development of the export-oriented apparel sector began with a broad set of domestic policy changes, which led to a more export-oriented development model in the first half of the 1980s, and preferential access to the EU-15 through the so-called Outward Processing Trade (OPT).[3] The instrument, launched in the mid-1970s, allowed for reduced duties and higher quotas of assembled apparel items to the EU market. In 2000, OPT preferential market access switched to duty-free access and double transformation rules of origin (ROO) under the Euromed Association Agreement.

Apparel exports' destination were concentrated geographically: Honduras, Mexico, and Morocco focused mainly on the markets that offered preferential access. Mexico's exports of apparel have been almost entirely destined for the U.S. end market, although the concentration has been slowly decreasing over the past decade. The United States accounted for 97.7 percent of exports in 1995, decreasing to 94.0 percent in 2005. Canada and the EU-15 are the only other two markets representing more than 1 percent of exports. The United States has also been the key market for Honduras, receiving 98.4 percent of exports in 1995. This concentration has dropped in recent years, and 87.8 percent of exports went to the United States in 2009. Other export markets include Canada, El Salvador, Mexico, and in recent years, the EU.

Morocco's apparel exports have been traditionally for the EU-15 market, although this dependency has decreased over the past 15 years. In 1995, 97.0 percent of total apparel exports went to the EU-15, dropping to 86.9 percent by 2009. Exports to the U.S. market were highest in 2000, accounting for 4.1 percent of total apparel exports, but they decreased by the mid-2000s, a trend in part reversed thanks to the entry into force of the U.S.-Morocco free trade agreement (FTA) in 2006.

Similarly, product concentration has characterized the clothing exports of these countries. Honduras mainly exports knitwear products (predominantly cotton-based apparel, including sweatshirts, T-shirts, socks, and underwear). Mexican apparel exports for the United States are also highly concentrated, with the top 10 export products accounting for 73.3 percent of total apparel exports in 2009. For Morocco, apparel exports are concentrated in woven products, which have accounted for roughly three-quarters of Morocco's overall apparel exports since the mid-1990s. Key export products are cotton-based denim trousers (jeans) and shirts and T-shirts, which accounted together for more than 30 percent of total exports in 2009. Although Morocco's exports are still predominantly cotton based, its share of noncotton exports has increased, and Morocco is becoming an important EU supplier of man-made fiber (MMF) apparel (Textiles Intelligence 2009a). All top 10 products accounted for 49.8 percent of total exports in 2009, which is low compared to competitor countries.

Backward linkages (probably encouraged by the rules of origins associated with the market access advantage) played a role in fostering the concentration of exports in products and markets. For example, in Honduras, U.S. preferential access for assembled apparel was granted to cut apparel, provided it was sewn with U.S. thread and the fabric was formed in the United States from U.S. yarn. This development encouraged firms to move cutting operations to Honduras in addition to sewing. Investment in the apparel sector began in the early 2000s, coinciding with increased U.S. preferential access for a limited quantity of apparel produced from knitted fabrics in a CBI country. Mexico's export industry seems to be the result of a regional production-sharing model based on the tariff preference schemes. The production networks were created and held together by large U.S. brand manufacturers and textile firms, which moved the most labor-intensive parts of the apparel supply chain to nearby, low-wage countries. Because of the 807/9802 legislation, firms in Mexico initially only engaged in the sewing process of the supply chain. NAFTA, which allowed export apparel quota free and duty free provided that the yarn, fabric, and apparel assembly stages occurred in one of the NAFTA countries, led to initial investments in the apparel sector, mostly by U.S. firms. In Morocco, the persistence of sourcing relations with EU textile suppliers established under OPT, which provided for preferential access as long as inputs (such as yarn and fabrics) were sourced from the EU, did not encourage significant backward linkages but rather a deep-seated division of labor whereby Moroccan suppliers were largely limited to the assembly and cut-make-trim (CMT) role.

The MFA phaseout eroded the preference and the market positions of the three countries. For Mexico, the end of the MFA exacerbated a negative trend in apparel exports that had started in 2001 due to competition from China following its accession to the World Trade Organization

(WTO) and from other low-cost Asian countries (including Bangladesh and Vietnam) in the U.S. market. The MFA phaseout at the end of 2004 had additional negative effects on Honduras and Mexico. The majority of their exports to the United States were integrated in the final phaseout of the MFA system, thus insulating them from competing countries subject to quotas until the end of 2004. Morocco was generally anticipated as a regional supplier country to be among the losers post-MFA (Nordås 2004), and indeed Morocco's apparel exports declined strongly during the first months of 2005.

The end of the MFA is associated with a drop in the number of exporting apparel firms, either due to foreign subsidiary reallocation (in Honduras and Mexico) or to reconsolidation of locally owned firms (in Morocco). In Mexico, the decline in the number of firms is partially tied to the type of apparel firm that originally invested. Mexico's trouser industry was built on national brands owned by U.S. brand manufacturers such as VF (Wrangler and Lee) and Levi's (Levi's and Dockers) that opened foreign assembly plants in Mexico. However, the size of the U.S. consumer market for national brands has decreased significantly in the past decade due to consumer preferences. Men's trousers are one of the few categories in which brand manufacturers still exist, and national brands maintain a sizable consumer base, partially explaining Mexico's ability to maintain its leading export position in this category despite declines in nearly every other category (Frederick and Gereffi 2011). Also, over the past decade, Levi's has closed all of its own manufacturing plants and has shifted to a brand marketer model, and VF is slowly shifting production to Asian countries such as Bangladesh that can produce comparable products at lower prices. In Honduras, as quotas have phased out, many of the U.S.-branded manufacturers and other lead firms have moved to an outsourcing model of production, in which Asia has been a desirable location, or they have purchased and built factories in Asia. In Morocco, the number of apparel firms in 2002 was estimated at 1,200 (USITC 2004; World Bank 2006), but according to official data, there were 880 registered apparel firms operating in Morocco in 2008 (Rossi 2010).

Although the three countries lost competitiveness following the end of the MFA, the Morocco apparel industry managed to recover by 2006 (figure 5.1). While it is difficult to attribute causality, a mix of industrial policy implemented during the MFA phaseout period and immediately after the end of the MFA has clearly played a role for Morocco. The critical situation of the industry in the first months of 2005 prompted the

Figure 5.1   Export Evolution in Honduras, Mexico, and Morocco, 2002–07

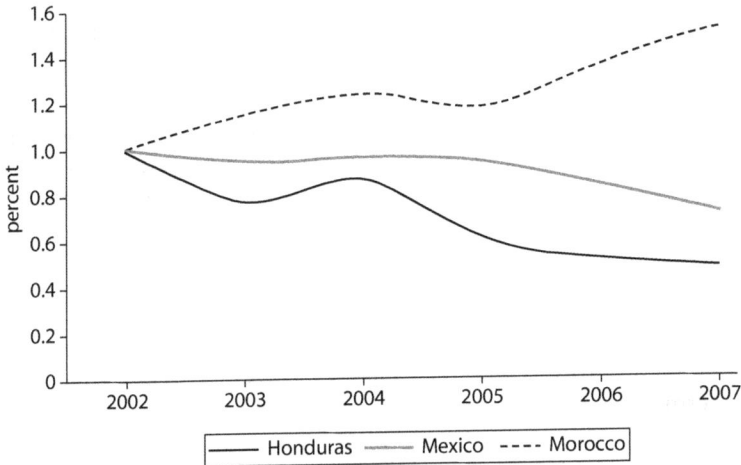

Source: United Nations Commodity Trade Statistics Database (Comtrade), chapters 50–63.
Note: 2002 is used as the base year.

Moroccan government to devise the Plan Emergence to boost strategic industrial sectors, in particular apparel, and foster Morocco's position in world markets. The plan provided for improving the educational system, the transportation infrastructure, and the bureaucratic environment for the private sector (World Bank 2006). The plan, together with previous efforts such as the creation of a Financial Restructuring Fund (Fonds de Soutien aux Entreprises du Secteur du Textile-Habillement, FORTEX) and a Business Upgrading Fund (Fonds National de la Mise à Niveau, FOMAN), aimed at supporting firm restructuring and upgrading (technical, equipment, and human resources upgrading) and at moving away from the dependent status as a CMT supplier and becoming a full-package supplier. These aims are reflected in the call for strengthening different skill sets, including design, sales, and input sourcing skills (World Bank 2006).

The apparel industry also lobbied for more liberal ROO, which was successful in mid-2005 when the country obtained a short-term permission to use Turkish fabrics for duty-free exports to the EU. This was made permanent with the adoption of the simplified Pan-Euro-Mediterranean ROO later that year.[4] Enhanced trade liberalization via bilateral FTAs with the United States and Turkey also improved market access and input sourcing possibilities. Moreover, while most apparel firms are Moroccan owned, foreign investment in the sector has increased since the government encouraged FDI via a set of incentive policies, particularly since the early 2000s (USAID 2008). New large (foreign and domestic) investment projects that benefited from state incentives have increased in terms of employment generation—19 projects created on average 182 jobs in 2006, while 17 projects created on average 469 jobs in 2007 (GoM 2008). The increased sourcing to Morocco post-MFA by fast-fashion retailers, particularly from Spain (for example, Inditex/Zara and Mango), was also important. Their increasing role has not only increased export levels but also promoted changes in the types of products exported. Unit values of apparel exports from Morocco increased, related to the higher-quality and fashion products of these buyers (see below). Hence, exports to the principal market—the EU-15—decreased in volume terms post-MFA, whereas values increased.

By contrast, the Mexican government has generally provided limited support to the apparel sector since the MFA phaseout (USITC 2004). In 2001, the Mexican government issued the National Development Plan (NDP), effective through 2006. It identified 12 priority sectors vital to the competitiveness of the country, and fiber, textile, and apparel were included because they are major generators of employment and attract manufacturing investment (USITC 2004). In November 2006, the Mexican government issued a new decree to regulate the operation of the *maquiladora* industry aimed at streamlining the sector. The Temporary Importation Program to Produce Articles for Exportation (Programa de Importación Temporal para Producir Artículos de Exportación, PITEX) and the *maquiladora* program were combined to form the Maquiladora Manufacturing and Export Services (Industria Manufacturera, Maquiladora y de Servicios de Exportación, IMMEX), which consolidates program benefits and facilitates interaction with government authorities (Textiles Intelligence 2009b). The government also acknowledged the need to reduce the flow of contraband and other counterfeit and illegally imported textile and apparel shipments into Mexico, primarily from China (Textiles Intelligence 2009b).[5]

During the MFA phaseout period, Honduras mainly focused on improving preferential market access to the United States. The end of the MFA coincided with the implementation of the Dominican Republic–Central America Free Trade Agreement (DR-CAFTA), which went into effect in 2006 for Honduras. Based on NAFTA, the agreement grants duty-free access to textiles and apparel into a U.S.-DR-CAFTA country, provided that the yarn production and all operations forward (that is, fabric production through apparel assembly) occur in the United States and/or the DR-CAFTA region. Another policy implemented at the end of the MFA includes the 2007 private-public partnership between the Instituto Politécnico Centroamericano (IPC), the chemical firm Clariant, and the Germany-based banking group DEG to create the Clariant Textile Center. Other firms that have invested in the IPC are Lectra, which contributed to the school's pattern design and scanning laboratory, and Rimoldi, which helped to equip the sewing laboratory (*Apparel Magazine* 2007). Other incentives for foreign investors were already present for several years: Honduras offers foreign investors exemption from all export taxes, local sales and excise taxes, and taxes on profits and profit repatriation, and it permits unrestricted capital repatriation and currency conversion. Moreover, since 1984, firms are allowed to import inputs free of duty for exporting firms. Additional incentives were provided in 1997–98, when the government granted firms a 10-year income tax holiday and expanded the Free Trade Zone area and its benefits to the entire country (USITC 2004).

Employment and Intersector Reallocation

Trade theory predicts that liberalization will shift resources across and within industries. In this section, we focus on resources shifting across industries and analyze changes in the share of labor employed in the apparel sector compared to other sectors in the period post-MFA. We also analyze these changes in the share of male and female workers and in the share of female workers engaged in the production process (female intensity of production). The apparel sector has generally been considered beneficial for female employment. For example, using household and firm-level data for 1990–2000 in Mexico, Aguayo-Tellez, Airola, and Juhn (2010) show that while women's wages remained stable, female employment increased, and this increase appears related to the liberalization efforts of Mexico, particularly for NAFTA, in female-intensive sectors such as clothing.

Employment in the apparel sector has generally dropped in Honduras and Mexico during the MFA phaseout period. In Honduras, employment in the apparel sector has been very erratic: it increased between 1994 and 2000, declined between 2000 and 2003, picked back up until 2007, and dropped again in 2008–09. In Mexico, sectoral employment has steadily declined since 1999, with the most significant drops occurring between 2000 and 2003. Between 2005 and 2008, employment growth fell on average 8 percent a year.

Morocco employment dropped in the textile sector but increased in the clothing sector. Formal employment in Morocco's apparel sector grew throughout the 1990s until the mid-2000s, with strong increases in the second half of the 1990s. Apparel employment peaked in 2003 with a registered workforce of 168,480, and it then declined to 153,010 in 2007. In the textile sector, employment declined strongly in the 1990s, particularly in the late 1990s, and remained at a substantially lower level of around 40,000 workers throughout the 2000s, accounting for one-quarter of total textile and apparel employment (Staritz and Frederick 2011c).

Compared to the rest of the economy, the apparel sector represents a smaller source of employment in the post-MFA period for Honduras and Mexico,[6] as shown by a fixed effect regression (table 5.1). Compared with other sectors, the share of Honduran workers employed in the textile and clothing sector decreased by about 0.4 percent in the post-MFA period, but the result is significant only at 12.0 percent. In Mexico, the same share decreased by 0.7 percent compared to the rest of the economy.

While the changes do not appear large, the above analysis masks gender differences. Compared to other sectors, the share of female workers in the textile and clothing sectors has decreased in the period post-MFA, particularly in Honduras (table 5.2).

We also find a decrease in the share of female workers engaged in the textile and garment production process compared to the other sectors in the period post-MFA (table 5.3). This phenomenon has been observed in other studies, particularly for high-income Asian countries and as the

Table 5.1   Share of Workers at the Sector Level, Honduras and Mexico
percent

	Honduras	Mexico
Time*T&G	−0.426	−0.70**
	(0.031)	(0.17)
Time	0.028	0.13*
	(0.252)	(0.07)
Constant	0.047**	9.09**
	(0.003)	(0.05)
Number of observations	57	66

Source: Authors' calculations. Estimation based on the National Statistical Office (Instituto Nacional de Estadística y Geografía—INEGI) Annual Industry Survey for 2003–08 (Mexico) and the Multipurpose Continuous Household Survey (Encuesta Permanente de Hogares de Propósitos Múltiples—EPHPM) for 2001, 2003, 2005, 2007 (Honduras).
Note: Regression controlling for sector fixed effects. Time is a dummy equal to 1 from 2005 onward. T&G is a dummy equal to 1 for the textile and the garment sector. Robust standard errors. Standard errors in parentheses. T&G = textile and garments.
** $p < 0.01$, * $p < 0.05$.

Table 5.2   Share of Workers at the Sector Level, by Gender, Honduras and Mexico

percent

| | Honduras | | Mexico | |
	Share of female workers in overall female workers	Share of male workers in overall male workers	Share of female workers in overall female workers	Share of male workers in overall male workers
Time*T&G	−2.950**	0.389	−1.381**	−0.493*
	(1.012)	(0.391)	(0.27)	(0.19)
Time	0.21	−0.026	0.25*	0.09
	(0.150)	(0.305)	(0.12)	(0.08)
Constant	5.710**	44.912**	9.091**	9.091**
	(0.085)	(1.854)	(0.085)	(0.059)
Number of observations	57	60	66	66

Source: Authors' calculations. Estimation based on the National Statistical Office (Instituto Nacional de Estadística y Geografía—INEGI) Annual Industry Survey for 2003-08 (Mexico) and the Multipurpose Continuous Household Survey (Encuesta Permanente de Hogares de Propósitos Múltiples—EPHPM) for 2001, 2003, 2005, 2007 (Honduras).
Note: Regression controlling for sector fixed effects. Time is a dummy equal to 1 from 2005 onward. Textiles and garments (T&G) is a dummy equal to 1 for the textile and garment sector. Robust standard errors. Standard errors in parentheses.
** $p < 0.01$, * $p < 0.05$.

Table 5.3   Female Intensity at the Sector Level, Honduras and Mexico

percent

	Honduras	Mexico
Time*T&G	−6.386*	−0.94*
	(0.003)	(0.49)
Time	0.865	0.89**
	(0.621)	(0.21)
Constant	4.772**	29.5**
	(0.015)	(0.15)
Number of observations	60	66

Source: Authors' calculations. Estimation based on the National Statistical Office (Instituto Nacional de Estadística y Geografía—INEGI) Annual Industry Survey for 2003–08 (Mexico) and the Multipurpose Continuous Household Survey (Encuesta Permanente de Hogares de Propósitos Múltiples—EPHPM) for 2001, 2003, 2005, 2007 (Honduras).
Note: Regression controlling for sector fixed effects. Time is a dummy equal to 1 from 2005 onward. T&G (textiles and garments) is a dummy equal to 1 for the textile and garment sector. Robust standard errors. Standard errors in parentheses.
** $p < 0.01$, * $p < 0.05$.

industry upgrades. Tejani and Milberg (2010) show that the female intensity of manufacturing is lower when the level of manufacturing value-added or capital intensity in production is higher. The authors suggest that this fact is not completely due to difference in skills between men and women, since education gaps have narrowed in these economies. Rather, these differences seem to be based on discrimination and vertical segregation of women (Tejani and Milberg 2010), the different content of education (Berik 2011), and the fact that firms prefer to invest in training for male workers, "consistent with the view that men deserve the more secure employment and are less likely to leave paid work to fulfill domestic responsibilities" (Seguino and Growth 2006).

Intrasector Reallocation

Analysis based at the sector level might understate the magnitude of the reallocation process. Indeed, trade theory suggests that employers reallocate not only across sectors but also within a sector. Accordingly, in this section, we analyze the evolution in job creation and destruction among firms in the industries.

Evidence on job churning suggests that women are subject to more volatile employment status following liberalization and are more vulnerable to external demand shocks. Levinsohn (1999), for example, analyzes the impact of trade liberalization in Chile and finds that gross job reallocation rates are often over twice as high for women than for men. We thus analyze whether this is the case also for the end of the MFA. Additionally, based on the previous evidence at the sector level, we also analyze whether female intensity correlates negatively with the skill intensity of the production.

The analysis of job creation and destruction rates at the firm level reveals a lot of churning within the apparel sector, which is, however, in line with the average of all other sectors (table 5.4). Job creation and destruction rates between 2004 and 2007 suggest that the clothing and textile sector did not experience overall net job destruction in Honduras, although net job creation was lower than in other sectors. Churning rates within the sector were also lower than the average for other sectors. Additional information for Honduras reveals that for the apparel sector, skilled workers faced a large net job creation while unskilled workers faced large losses. These results appear to mimic the rest of the economy: on average, skilled workers face net job creation while unskilled workers face net job destruction.

In Honduras, the churning rate for skilled and unskilled workers, together with the previous evidence on the female intensity of the sector, suggests a negative relationship between women and skill levels. In contrast, information from household data does not detect major differences

Table 5.4   Honduran Job Creation and Destruction Rates

Workers	Sector	Job creation	Job destruction	Total	Net
All workers	Clothing	9.7	4.7	14.5	4.9
	Textile	5.7	3.9	9.6	1.7
	Average other sectors	14.4	8.3	22.8	6.1
Skilled workers	Clothing	74.6	1.1	75.7	73.6
	Textile	12.9	17.3	30.2	−4.3
	Average other sectors	42.3	13.3	55.7	29.0
Unskilled workers	Clothing	8.7	36.2	45.1	−27.5
	Textile	22.1	27.7	49.9	−5.6
	Average other sectors	10.9	42.8	53.8	−31.9

Source: Authors' calculations based on World Bank Enterprise Survey data for 2003 and 2007.

in the education levels of male and female workers. In 2003, for example, the average education level of female workers employed in the sector was about 7.0 years, compared to 7.6 years for male workers. As stated above, however, authors have argued that while the gap in education levels is narrowing, the content of education may differ (Berik 2011), meaning that female workers' characteristics do not match the skill demand.

In Mexico, the textile and clothing sectors both faced net job destruction, but churning rates were in line with the rest of the economy (table 5.5).

The limited evidence on aggregate employment figures for Mexico seems again to mask gender-differentiated effects. Between 1998 and 2008, women's share of total workers in the apparel sector decreased from 64.2 percent to 59.0 percent. Similar trends exist for the textile manufacturing industries (yarn, fabric, finishing), in which the female share dropped from 32.1 percent to 27.0 percent. However, in textile product manufacturing (carpets, rugs, linens), the share of female employment increased from 46.7 percent to 60.4 percent in the same time period. Firm-level analysis on churning rates also suggests that women faced net job destruction within the clothing sector and net job creation within the textile sector. By contrast, men experienced job destruction in both sectors, particularly in the textile sector. Importantly, women experienced higher net job creation in other sectors compared to men (table 5.6), but in the textile sector they also faced a churning rate double that of male workers.

Regression analysis at the firm level also confirms a lower female intensity in the textile and garment production process compared to other sectors in the period post-MFA (table 5.7, column 1). In particular,

Table 5.5   Mexican Job Creation and Destruction Rates, All Workers

Sector	Job creation	Job destruction	Total	Net
Textile	7.6	13.2	20.7	−5.6
Clothing	9.8	16.1	25.9	−6.3
Average other sectors	12.8	9.8	22.6	2.9

Source: Authors' calculations based on the National Statistical Office (Instituto Nacional de Estadística y Geografía—INEGI) Annual Industry Survey, 2003–08.

Table 5.6   Mexican Intra-industry Job Creation and Job Destruction Rates

Gender	Sector	Job creation	Job destruction	Total	Net
Female	Textile	26.0	25.0	51.0	1.0
	Clothing	11.6	19.6	31.3	−8.0
	Average other sectors	23.3	15.7	39.1	7.5
Male	Textile	8.5	16.2	24.7	−7.6
	Clothing	16.2	19.5	35.7	−3.4
	Average other sectors	12.9	11.3	24.3	1.6

Source: Authors' calculations based on the National Statistical Office (Instituto Nacional de Estadística y Geografía—INEGI) Annual Industry Survey, 2003–08

Table 5.7   Share of Female Workers in Total Workers at the Firm Level

percent

	Share of female workers in total workers	
Time*T&G	−0.52*	1.92*
	(0.24)	(1.05)
Time	0.54**	0.58**
	(0.09)	(0.09)
Log value added per worker	n.a.	−0.17*
		(0.09)
Time*T&G log value added per worker	n.a.	−0.51*
		(0.21)
Constant	15.28**	16.25
	(5.24)	(5.19)
Number of observations	41,080	40,474

Source: Authors' calculations. Estimation based on the National Statistical Office (Instituto Nacional de Estadística y Geografía—INEGI) Annual Industry Survey, 2003–08.
Note: Regressions controlling for firm fixed effects, region dummies, size of the firm dummies, sector fixed effects. Time is a dummy equal to 1 from 2005 onward. T&G is a dummy equal to 1 for the textiles and garment sector. Robust standard errors. Standard errors in parentheses, n.a. = not applicable.
** $p < 0.01$, * $p < 0.05$.

this seems to be the case for more productive firms, proxied by value added per worker (table 5.7, column 2). The results of the regression in column 2 additionally suggests that higher value-added firms are generally associated with a lower female-intensity production in the whole economy, in line with the findings of Aguayo-Tellez, Airola, and Juhn (2010), who show a negative relation of women's wage bill share to capital intensity and value added in the period 1990–2000, and the findings of Tejani and Milberg (2010), who show a negative correlation between female intensity of production and value added per worker at the sector level.

While data limitations prevent us from conducting a similar analysis on Morocco, studies reveal gender discrimination in the textile and clothing sector. This discrimination includes, in particular, reduced access to on-the-job training, which is generally scheduled at times that are difficult for women with families, and the fact that female workers are more likely to be hired by the informal sector, representing 90 percent of home workers (ILO 2006a). Similarly, women are often employed in lower-skill tasks (ILO 2006a), reflecting vertical segregation.

Unit Values and Wages

Studies for Honduras suggest that wages in the apparel industry are better than several alternative employment options in the economy. For example, Marcouiller and Robertson (2009) find that workers in the apparel sector earn 10–20 percent more than the average Honduran wage gained by workers with similar characteristics. The authors find that young women with little schooling do better in the apparel industry than similar workers on average in the economy for the same type of occupation.

Analysis of the data indeed reveals a wage premium in the case of textiles and apparel in Honduras, but this advantage has decreased during the MFA phaseout. Honduran workers in the textile and clothing industries enjoy higher wages compared to the economywide average, but between 2001 and 2003, the wage premium dropped by 2.8 percent (figure 5.2, panel a). After a slight increase between 2003 and 2005 (0.1 percent), the wage premium for the textile and clothing sector dropped by 13.5 percent between 2005 and 2007.

In Mexico, by contrast, workers in the apparel sector received lower wages than the rest of the economy, and the decline in the wage premium started before the end of the MFA phaseout. Between 1999 and 2003, the sector wage dropped by 5.5 percent and between 2003 and 2006 by an additional 2.0 percent (figure 5.2, panel b).

Controlling for occupation, education, age, and sector of employment, female workers in the economy generally have a lower wage than their male counterparts. Coefficients from the female dummy on a regression

Figure 5.2   Textile and Clothing Wage Premium, Honduras and Mexico, Various Years

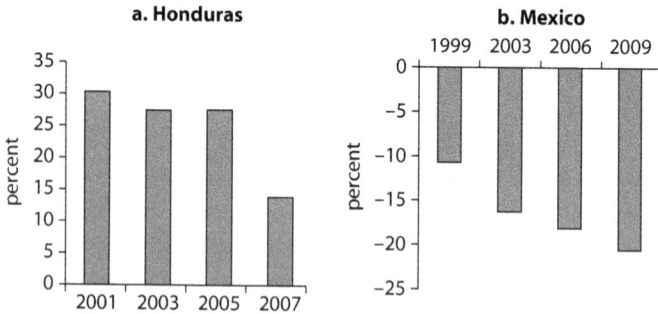

Source: Authors' calculations. Estimation based on the Multipurpose Continuous Household Survey (Encuesta Permanente de Hogares de Propósitos Múltiples—EPHPM), 2001, 2003, 2005, 2007 (Honduras) and the National Urban Labor Survey (Encuesta Nacional de Empleo Urbano—ENEU), 2003, 2006 (Mexico).
Note: Coefficients of the textile and clothing sector dummy. See annex tables 5A.1 and 5A.2 for more details.

of wages suggest that on average female workers earn 33 percent less than their male counterparts in Honduras (annex table 5A.1). Similarly, in Mexico, the female workers earn 27 percent less than the male workers (annex table 5A.2).

Again, the absence of data for Morocco prevents us from conducting a similar analysis. However, the International Labour Organization (ILO) (2006a) reports that women working in textiles are generally paid 25 percent less than their male counterparts and that 22.6 percent of women interviewed said they earned below the minimum wage, compared with 5.3 percent of men (ILO 2006a).

Working Conditions

There is limited analysis in the literature of the working conditions of the apparel industry, but results in the case of Honduras suggest that industry working conditions are similar to the rest of the economy. Marcouiller and Robertson (2009) do not find any systematic differences in Honduras between apparel and textile firms and others with respect to social benefits (13-month salary, vacation, social security, and other benefits) as a percent of total labor costs, either for skilled or unskilled production workers. Similarly, VerBeek (2001), comparing existing employees in the Honduras *maquiladora* industry with first-time applicant workers, does not find any difference between the two groups in terms of overtime, stress of work, and other related working conditions. In Mexico, Gereffi (2005), looking at the Torreón industrial cluster, suggests that large retailers and marketers do not want their brands associated with the exploitation of workers or with unsafe working conditions, and several companies had imposed very detailed codes of conduct, including compliance with local labor laws, with the threat to lose contracts in case of breach of these rules.

This section looks at working conditions defined as no overtime work, absence of child labor, and in-kind pay over cash pay or regular cash payment. We focus the quantitative analysis on Honduras and Mexico given the absence of data for Morocco, for which we provide evidence obtained from other studies. Institutions and laws governing these three dimensions in the three countries generally prohibit child labor and impose restrictions on the number of working hours. On child labor, all three countries have ratified ILO Convention 182 concerning the prohibition of child labor and immediate action for the elimination of the worst forms of child labor. In Honduras, the minimum legal work age is 16 (14 if in school), and minors may not work more than 30 hours per week (Marcouiller and Robertson 2009). In Mexico, the minimum legal age is 14, and special provisions apply for workers 14–16 years old, including the limitation of work to 6 hours per day and never later than 10 p.m.[7] Moreover, under the NAFTA, Mexico agreed to trade sanctions if it fails to enforce its own laws regulating child labor practices (Brown 2001). In Morocco, the minimum legal age is 15 with special provisions for minors age 15–16, who cannot work at night or more than 10 hours per day.[8]

Hours of work and overtime are also generally subject to law. According to the ILO working time database, in Honduras, the limit is 44 hours per week and a maximum of 12 hours per day. In Mexico, the legal limit is 48 hours per week with overtime set at a maximum of 3 hours per day, while in Morocco, the limit is 44 hours or 2,288 hours per year with overtime established at 10 hours per day. All countries limit the use of overtime and establish percentages for the increase in salary (ILO Working Time database).

There is very limited information on child labor in the textile and clothing industry, but it remains a pressing issue. In summarizing available studies, the U.S. Department of Labor reports that approximately 3.4 percent of children in Morocco under the age of 15 were engaged in child labor. While the majority work in rural areas, several children 12 years or younger are known to work as carpet weavers (U.S. Department of Labor 2004). The ILO (2006a) reports that child labor is virtually nonexistent in the formal sector, but it is a problem in informal units. In Honduras, the ILO survey on child labor indicates that in 2002, about 356,241 children between 5 and 17 years old worked in an economic activity, and about 123,195 are minors aged 14 years or less. While the principal economic activities are agriculture, forestry, hunting, and fishing, the manufacturing industry employs 8.2 percent of all minor workers. In Mexico, there is a very limited number of studies on the subject, and the U.S. Bureau of International Labor Affairs reports that "there is only limited evidence of the existence of child labor in *maquilas* currently producing goods for export although there have been past reports of child labor," and it suggests the need for more documentation because the majority of investigation took place at the beginning of the 1990s.[9]

Overall working conditions in the textile and clothing sector have deteriorated in Honduras and Mexico, compared to other sectors in the period post-MFA. We proxy the dependent variable with an indicator that represents the average value of three dummies: a dummy equal to 1 for no overtime work (40 hours), a dummy equal to 1 for a large ratio of cash versus in-kind payments, and a value greater than 1 if the individual is at least 14 years old. In both Honduras and Mexico, working conditions (proxied by the indicator) in the textile and clothing sector have worsened following the end of the MFA compared to other sectors (table 5.8).

Table 5.8   Working Conditions in Honduras and Mexico

	Honduras		Mexico	
Female	−0.001	0.009**	0.042**	0.097**
	(0.003)	(0.003)	(0.000)	(0.001)
Female*T&G		−0.005		−0.072**
		(0.009)		(0.003)
Female*time		−0.026**		−0.123**
		(0.004)		(0.001)
Time*T&G	−0.055**	−0.057**	−0.019**	−0.052**
	(0.007)	(0.010)	(0.002)	(0.003)
Time*T&G*female		0.029*		0.100**
		(0.014)		(0.004)
Time	0.017**	0.013**	−0.276**	−0.230**
	(0.003)	(0.003)	(0.000)	(0.000)
R-squared	0.17	0.171	0.441	0.456
Number of observations	41,246	41,246	811,714	811,714

Source: Authors' calculations. Estimations based on the Multipurpose Continuous Household Survey (Encuesta Permanente de Hogares de Propósitos Múltiples—EPHPM), 2001, 2003, 2005, 2007 (Honduras) and the National Urban Labor Survey (Encuesta Nacional de Empleo Urbano—ENEU), 2003, 2006 (Mexico).
Note: Regressions controlling for occupation, age, age square, education, marital status, and sector dummies (not reported). The dependent variable represents the average value of three dummies: a dummy equal to 1 for no overtime work (40 hours), a dummy equal to 1 for a large ratio of cash versus in-kind payments, and a value greater than 1 if the individual is at least 14 years old. Time is a dummy equal to 1 from 2005 onward. T&G is a dummy equal to 1 for the textile and the garment sector. Standard errors in parentheses.
** $p < 0.01$, * $p < 0.05$.

Compared to other sectors, female workers in the textile and clothing sectors relative to male workers have instead a higher probability of receiving cash rather than in-kind payments in Honduras and a higher probability of receiving regular payments in Mexico. However, compared to other sectors, female apparel workers relative to men are more likely to be engaged before the age of 14 in Mexico in the period post-MFA (table 5.9).

Conclusion

This chapter analyzes the evolution of the textile and clothing sector, trends in intersector and intrasector reallocation, and the wage premium for Honduras, Mexico, and Morocco following the end of the MFA. Analysis for Morocco was limited due to the lack of data.

The qualitative analysis suggests that only Morocco managed to implement policies that expanded products and markets for textile and clothing exports and upgraded the industry. In Honduras and Mexico, by contrast, the end of the MFA coincided with the loss of the textile and clothing exports, particularly for Mexico.

The quantitative analysis for Honduras and Mexico reveals that, in line with loss of exports, labor—particularly female labor—reallocated across and within the apparel sector following the end of the MFA. Data available for Mexico also reveal a negative relation between the female intensity of production and value added per worker. In Honduras, we observe lower female intensity in the textile and clothing sectors compared to other sectors and large job destruction for unskilled workers in the period post-MFA. Taken together, these results also suggest a negative relation between skill demand and the intensity in the use of female workers in the production process as documented by other authors. Moreover, the data do not reveal significant differences in education levels between male and female workers in the sector. The analysis for Honduras and Mexico also reveals a declining trend in the wage premium and worse working conditions in the textile and clothing sectors compared to other sectors in the period post-MFA.

The results thus validate the expectations in terms of labor reallocation and wage trends. However, the analysis also indicates gender difference in the adjustment process. Further analysis might shed light on this issue.

Table 5.9 Female and Male Workers' Conditions in Honduras and Mexico

	Honduras			Mexico		
	Individuals over 14 years old	High ratio of cash/in-kind payment	No overtime	Individuals over 14 years old	Regular payment	No overtime
Female	−0.0000002	−0.025**	0.165**	0.428**	0.173**	0.616**
	(0.000)	(0.006)	(0.005)	(0.019)	(0.005)	(0.005)
Time	0.0000013**	−0.004	0.061**	−0.069**	−1.465**	−1.701**
	(0.000)	(0.005)	(0.005)	(0.016)	(0.005)	(0.009)
Female*T&G	0.0000014	0.022**	−0.036*	−0.137	−0.556**	−0.035
	(0.000)	(0.013)	(0.020)	(0.118)	(0.026)	(0.027)
Female*time	0.0000012**	−0.090	0.004	0.050*	−0.324**	−0.571**
	(0.000)	(0.008)	(0.007)	(0.027)	(0.007)	(0.012)
Time*T&G	−0.0000068	−0.171**	0.034	0.556**	−0.494**	0.183**
	(0.000)	(0.025)	(0.023)	(0.177)	(0.036)	(0.066)
Time*T&G*female	0.0000023	0.048**	0.004	−0.396*	0.614**	0.125
	(0.000)	(0.015)	(0.031)	(0.221)	(0.046)	(0.081)
Number of observations	77,588	41,749	83,327	726,500	811,714	764,287

Source: Authors' calculations. Estimations based on the Multipurpose Continuous Household Survey (Encuesta Permanente de Hogares de Propósitos Múltiples, EPHPM), 2001, 2003, 2005, 2007 (Honduras) and the National Urban Labor Survey (Encuesta Nacional de Empleo Urbano, ENEU), 2003, 2006 (Mexico).

Note: Probit regressions controlling for occupation, age and age square (except for the child labor regressions), education, marital status, and sector dummies (not reported). Time equals 1 for the years from 2005 onward, and apparel equals 1 for the textile and clothing sector. T&G is a dummy equal to 1 for the textile and the garment sector. Standard errors in parentheses.

** $p < 0.01$, * $p < 0.1$.

156

Annex

Table 5A.1   Wage Premium Regressions, Honduras

	Log (wage)			
	2001	2003	2005	2007
Hours	0.008*	0.012*	0.013*	0.011*
	(0.000)	(0.001)	(0.001)	(0.000)
Female	−0.413*	−0.349*	−0.367*	−0.391*
	(0.026)	(0.036)	(0.042)	(0.023)
Age	0.093*	0.114*	0.131*	0.118*
	(0.005)	(0.009)	(0.011)	(0.005)
Age-squared	−0.001*	−0.001*	−0.002*	−0.001*
	(0.000)	(0.000)	(0.000)	(0.000)
Education	0.093*	0.100*	0.081*	0.103*
	(0.003)	(0.004)	(0.003)	(0.003)
T&G	0.264*	0.242*	0.243*	0.131
	(0.022)	(0.034)	(0.031)	(0.019)
Mills	0.340*	0.489*	0.509*	0.453*
	(0.050)	(0.078)	(0.091)	(0.046)
Constant	4.976*	4.358*	4.115*	4.511*
	(0.144)	(0.255)	(0.288)	(0.141)
Number of observations	13,847	5,597	5,254	16,543

Source: Authors' calculations. Estimations based on the Multipurpose Continuous Household Survey (Encuesta Permanente de Hogares de Propósitos Múltiples—EPHPM).
Note: Occupation and industry dummies (except for textiles and garments [T&G]) not reported. Standard errors in parentheses.
* $p < 0.01$.

Table 5A.2   Wage Premium Regressions, Mexico
log wage

	1999	2003	2006	2009
Female dummy	−0.348*	−0.350*	−0.301*	−0.263*
	(0.005)	(0.006)	(0.006)	(0.007)
Hours	0.013*	0.013*	0.013*	0.014*
	(0.000)	(0.000)	(0.000)	(0.000)
Age	0.086*	0.083*	0.067*	0.059*
	(0.001)	(0.001)	(0.001)	(0.002)
Age–squared	−0.001*	−0.001*	−0.001*	−0.001*
	(0.000)	(0.000)	(0.000)	(0.000)
Education	0.049*	0.045*	0.042*	0.040*
	(0.000)	(0.000)	(0.000)	(0.000)
T&G	−0.113*	−0.177*	−0.200*	−0.230*
	(0.005)	(0.006)	(0.007)	(0.008)

(continued next page)

Table 5A.2   *(continued)*

	1999	2003	2006	2009
Mills	0.281*	0.276*	0.139*	0.088*
	(0.009)	(0.011)	(0.011)	(0.014)
Constant	5.380*	5.851*	6.404*	6.638*
	(0.024)	(0.031)	(0.033)	(0.042)
Number of observations	449,924	415,680	348,607	305,660

Source: Authors' calculations. Estimations based on the National Urban Labor Survey (Encuesta Nacional de Empleo Urbano—ENEU), 1999, 2003, 2006, 2009.
Note: Occupation and industry dummies (except for textiles and garments [T&G]) not reported. Standard errors in parentheses.
* $p < 0.01$.

Notes

1. The *maquiladora* sector is composed of plants that assemble imported duty-free inputs for exports. In Honduras, the textile industry was the most important industry in terms of activity of the *maquiladora* sector, accounting for 61.2 percent of all the firms in 2002 (Banco Central de Honduras 2002).

2. The description of the evolution of the industry is taken from Staritz and Frederick (2011a, 2011b, 2011c).

3. The EU-15 includes the 15 member states of the European Union (EU) as of December 31, 2003, before the new member states joined the EU: Austria, Belgium, Denmark, Finland, France, Germany, Greece, Ireland, Italy, Luxembourg, the Netherlands, Portugal, Spain, Sweden, and the United Kingdom.

4. CEDITH (Cercle Euro-Méditerranéen des Dirigeants du Textile et de l'Habillement), News Archive, http://www.cedith.com/spip.php?page=archives.

5. Estimates suggest that 6 out of 10 apparel products sold in Mexico are illegally obtained (stolen, smuggled, or pirated), costing the sector around $13 billion. Much of the illegal apparel in Mexico is sold at street markets and is estimated to account for 26.9 percent of total sales (Chamber of the Garment Industry 2009).

6. Unfortunately, we were not able to include the information on Morocco in this and some of the following tables due to lack of data. We decided not to omit Morocco from the analysis since it represents an important case in the global apparel situation.

7. U.S. Bureau of International Labor Affairs, http://www.dol.gov.

8. U.S. Bureau of International Labor Affairs, http://www.dol.gov.

9. U.S. Bureau of International Labor Affairs, http://www.dol.gov.

References

Background Papers

Staritz, C., and S. Frederick. 2011a. "Background Global Value Chain Country Papers: Honduras." Background paper to the book *Sewing Success? Employment, Wages, and Poverty following the End of the Multi-fibre Arrangement*. Washington, DC: World Bank.

———. 2011b. "Background Global Value Chain Country Papers: Mexico." Background paper to the book *Sewing Success? Employment, Wages, and Poverty following the End of the Multi-fibre Arrangement*, World Bank, Washington, DC.

———. 2011c. "Background Global Value Chain Country Papers: Morocco." Background paper to the book *Sewing Success? Employment, Wages, and Poverty following the End of the Multi-fibre Arrangement*. Washington, DC: World Bank.

Sources

Aguayo-Tellez, Ernesto, Jim Airola, and Chinhui Juhn. 2010. "Did Trade Liberalization Help Women? The Case of Mexico in the 1990s." Working Paper 16195, National Bureau of Economic Research, Cambridge, MA.

Apparel Magazine. 2007. "IPC Training Center Expands in Honduras." *Apparel Magazine* 48 (11): 34.

Banco Central de Honduras. 2002. "Actividad Maquiladora en Honduras 2002." Tegucigalpa, Honduras.

Berik, Gunseli. 2011. "Gender Aspects of Trade." In *Trade and Employment: From Myths to Facts*, ed. M. Jansen, R. Peters, and J. M. Salazar-Xirinachs. Geneva: International Labour Organization–European Commission.

Brown, Drusilla. 2001. "Child Labor in Latin America: Policy and Evidence." *World Economy* 24 (6), 761–68.

Chamber of the Garment Industry (Cámara Nacional de la Industria del Vestido, CNIV). 2009. Presentation, Mexico City, Mexico.

de Hoyos, Rafael, Marizio Bussolo, and Oscar Núñez. 2008. "Can Maquila Booms Reduce Poverty? Evidence from Honduras." Policy Research Working Paper 4789, World Bank, Washington, DC.

Frederick, Stacey, and Gary Gereffi. 2011. "Upgrading and Restructuring in the Global Apparel Value Chain: Why China and Asia Are Outperforming Mexico and Central America." *International Journal of Technological Learning, Innovation, and Development* 4 (1–2): 67–95.

Gereffi, Gary 2005. "Export-Oriented Growth and Industrial Upgrading—Lessons from the Mexican Apparel Case: A Case Study of Global Value Chain Analysis." http://www.soc.duke.edu/~ggere/web/torreon_report_worldbank.pdf.

GoM (Government of Morocco). 2008. "Bilan de la Commission des Investissements 2007." Ministère des Affaires Économique et Générales, April.

ILO (International Labour Organization). 2006a. "Country Brief Morocco.
Decent Work Pilot Programme." http://www.ilo.org/public/english/bureau/
dwpp/countries/morocco/index.htm.

———. 2006b. "Final DWPP Country Brief." http://www.ilo.org/public/english
/bureau/dwpp/countries/morocco/index.htm.+ILO Working Time Database.
International Labour Organization, Geneva. http://www.ilo.org/travaildata-
base/servlet/ workingtime.

Levinsohn, J. 1999. "Employment Responses to International Liberalization in
Chile." *Journal of International Economics* 47: 321–44.

Marcouiller, Douglas, and Raymond Robertson. 2009. "Globalization and Working
Conditions: Evidence from Honduras." In *Globalization, Wages, and the
Quality of Jobs: Five Country Studies*, ed. Raymond Robertson, Drusilla Brown,
Pierre LeBorgne, and Maria L. Sanchez-Puerta, 175–202. Washington, DC:
World Bank.

Nordås, Hildegunn Kyvik. 2004. "The Global Textile and Clothing Industry post
the Agreement on Textiles and Clothing." Discussion Paper 5, World Trade
Organization, Geneva.

Rossi, Arianna. 2010. "Economic and Social Upgrading in Global Production
Networks: The Case of the Garment Industry in Morocco." Unpublished dissertation, University of Sussex, U.K.

Seguino, Stephanie, and Caren Growth. 2006. "Gender Equity and Globalization:
Macroeconomic Policy for Developing Countries." *Journal of International
Development* 18: 1–24.

Tejani, Sheba, and William Milberg. 2010. "Global Defeminization? Industrial
Upgrading, Occupational Segmentation and Manufacturing Employment in
Middle-Income Countries." Schwartz Center for Economic Policy Analysis
(SCEPA) Working Paper 2010-1, The New School, New York.

Textiles Intelligence. 2009a. *Textile Outlook International*, May–June 2008, No.
135. www.textilesintelligence.com.

———. 2009b. "Trade and Trade Policy: The World's Leading Clothing Exporters."
Global Apparel Markets 5: 39–69.

U.S. Department of Labor. 2004. "Morocco Labor Rights Report." http://white
.oit.org.pe/ipec/documentos/hon___sintesis.pdf.

USAID (United States Agency for International Development). 2008. "Apparel
Exports to the United States: A Comparison of Morocco, Jordan, and Egypt."
USAID, Washington, DC.

USITC (United States International Trade Commission). 2004. "Textiles and
Apparel: Assessment of the Competitiveness of Certain Foreign Suppliers to
the U.S. Market." Publication 3671, USITC, Washington, DC.

VerBeek, Kurt A. 2001. "Maquiladoras: Exploitation or Emancipation? An Overview of the Situation of Maquiladora Workers in Honduras." *World Development* 29 (9): 1553–67.

World Bank. 2006. "Morocco, Tunisia, Egypt and Jordan after the End of the Multi-Fiber Arrangement: Impact, Challenges and Prospects." Report 35376 MNA, World Bank, Washington, DC.

CHAPTER 6

The Rise of Small Asian Economies in the Apparel Industry

Yevgeniya Savchenko

Introduction

This chapter analyzes two Asian countries, Cambodia and Sri Lanka. The export-oriented apparel sector is the key manufacturing industry in both countries. In Cambodia, apparel exports accounted for 70 percent of total manufacturing exports, and the sector employed around 325,000 workers in 2008, which represented almost 30 percent of total industrial employment. In Sri Lanka, the apparel sector contributed 40 percent of total exports and employed 270,000 workers, or 13 percent of industrial employment in 2008.[1] Female workers dominate apparel sector employment in both countries—83 percent of apparel employment in Cambodia and 73 percent in Sri Lanka.[2] The MFA (Multi-fibre Arrangement) phaseout was a major concern for both countries because of the expected competition from cheaper Chinese products.[3] However, despite an initial slowdown in apparel export growth in 2005, Cambodian apparel exports

The author of this chapter is grateful for comments provided by Gladys Lopez-Acevedo, Raymond Robertson, Ana Luisa Gouvea Abras, and Cornelia Staritz. The empirical analysis was conducted by Elisa Gamberoni, Ana Luisa Gouvea Abras, Hong Tan, and Yevgeniya Savchenko. The first section on apparel sector structure is based on country background papers of Cornelia Staritz and Stacey Frederick (2011a, 2011b).

grew on average at almost 14 percent annually between 2005 and 2008, and Sri Lanka experienced more moderate but still healthy 6 percent annual growth.

One key difference between these countries is that Cambodian and Sri Lankan apparel industries had different strategies to facilitate the MFA phaseout and achieved different outcomes. The Sri Lankan apparel sector upgraded to full-service provider, moved to higher-value products, and consolidated the industry at the expense of small firms. The Cambodian apparel industry increased employment and expanded the number of firms after the MFA phaseout by remaining a supplier of less sophisticated cheap products and by being attractive to buyers through a good labor compliance record due to the Better Factories Cambodia program.

Poverty has considerably declined in Cambodia and Sri Lanka over the past 15 years (World Bank 2006, 2007), which some studies have linked to the development of the garment sector. Yamagata (2006), using a 2003 survey of export-oriented manufacturing firms in Cambodia, shows that employment in the apparel industry had a substantial impact on poverty reduction in Cambodia. The wage of an entry garment worker in Cambodia was higher than the amount of income needed for two people to live above the overall poverty line in Phnom Penh. Education entry barriers are not high for the garment sector, making it possible for people with little education to work in the industry. The proportion of apparel workers living on less than 1 dollar (purchasing power parity, PPP) a day in Cambodia and Sri Lanka is lower than in other low-skilled sectors.[4] One-quarter of Cambodian apparel workers were living on less than 1 PPP dollar a day in 2007, compared to 55 percent of agricultural and 48 percent of service workers. In Sri Lanka, only 11 percent of apparel workers lived on less than 1 PPP dollar a day in 2008, compared to 21 percent of agricultural and 17 percent of service workers.

The empirical analysis shows that the apparel wage premium dropped immediately following the MFA phaseout in both countries. However, in the following years, the industry wage premium improved, although it never regained pre-MFA phaseout levels. The male-female wage gap was declining before the MFA phaseout, but it widened after the phaseout in both countries. The share of females in apparel industries of both countries was not affected by the MFA phaseout, suggesting that labor shedding in Sri Lanka and employment increases in Cambodia were proportional for men and women. Apparel sector working conditions deteriorated in Cambodia following the MFA phaseout. In Sri Lanka, the results were mixed, depending on the measurement.

The rest of the chapter is structured as follows. Section one describes the apparel industry structure in Cambodia and Sri Lanka, section two presents findings on employment changes in apparel, section three describes the within-industry changes, section four analyzes the apparel sector wages, section five describes changes in working conditions, and section six concludes.[5]

Apparel Sector Structure in Cambodia and Sri Lanka

This section presents the apparel sector structure in Cambodia and Sri Lanka.[6] First, it describes the historical development of the sector and the factors that determined the sector characteristics, such as foreign direct investment (FDI) and the preferential market access. Then, we document the apparel export dynamics in both countries before and after the MFA, describe end market and export product orientation, and describe backward linkages (input sources). The section concludes with a description of the domestic policies that were designed to prepare the apparel sectors of both countries for the MFA phaseout.

Development of the Sector

Cambodian and Sri Lankan apparel industries thrived under the MFA, driven by both foreign investments and government efforts to develop the sector. Due to decades of political and civil unrest, Cambodia was a latecomer to the apparel industry. Although Cambodia was manufacturing apparel during the French colonial era, the modern industry was established only in the mid-1990s by investors from Hong Kong SAR, China; Malaysia; Singapore; and Taiwan, China. Foreign investors were attracted by unused quota under the MFA and preferential market access, as well as by the relatively low labor costs stemming from Cambodia's large labor surplus. Sri Lanka, on the other hand, has a longer tradition in the apparel sector. Before 1977, the Sri Lankan apparel sector was very small, with a few locally owned firms producing low-end apparel for the domestic market using inputs from the local state-controlled textile industry (Kelegama and Wijayasiri 2004; Kelegama 2009; Staritz and Frederick 2011b). In 1977, Sri Lanka was the first South Asian country to liberalize its economy. Moreover, the government was very supportive of the apparel sector, in particular through the Board of Investors (BOI),[7] and created a favorable investment environment for not only foreign but also domestic investors. Trade liberalization, together with unused MFA quotas, immediately attracted foreign investors from East Asia—Hong Kong SAR, China, in particular—who relocated their production to Sri Lanka. Also, European manufacturers saw a window of opportunity to reduce labor costs by moving to Sri Lanka. Government support programs also encouraged the development of local apparel firms.

FDI played a major role in establishing and developing the apparel industry in both countries, but subsequently the patterns diverged. In Sri Lanka, FDI in apparel came either through foreign ownership or joint ventures, which have been common among the largest local apparel manufacturers. According to BOI data, FDI accounted for about 50 percent of total investment (cumulative) in the apparel sector—either wholly owned or jointly owned in the early 2000s (USITC 2004). Joint ventures brought crucial technology, know-how, and skills to Sri Lanka. However, the industry soon became dominated by local firms. In 1999, around 80–85 percent of factories were locally owned (Kelegama and Wijayasiri 2004). Today, FDI plays a more limited role in the apparel sector, but it has recently increased in the textile sector.

By contrast, the apparel sector in Cambodia is dominated by FDI. About 93 percent of factories are foreign owned, led by Taiwan, China (25 percent); Hong Kong SAR, China (19 percent); China (18 percent); and other Asian economies (Natsuda, Goto, and Thoburn 2009). Cambodians own only 7 percent of apparel firms, and these are mostly smaller firms (accounting for around 3 percent of sectoral employment) that generally work on a subcontracting basis for larger foreign-owned firms. The vast majority of owners as well as managers are foreigners, and locals are predominant only at low-skilled jobs. According to a survey of 164 apparel factories in 2005,[8] 30 percent of top managers were from mainland China; 21 percent from Taiwan, China; 15 percent from Hong Kong SAR, China; and only 8 percent from Cambodia (Yamagata 2006). The Garment Manufacturers' Association in Cambodia (GMAC) estimates that 80 percent of middle managers are also foreigners.

Preferential market access to the United States and the European Union (EU) was central to the development of the apparel sector in both countries. When the sector started in Cambodia, it faced no quota restrictions to the United States and the EU because it was not part of the MFA system. In 1996, Cambodia, as a nonmember of the World Trade Organization (WTO), was granted most favored nation (MFN) status for the U.S. and the EU market. The major industry takeoff was spurred by the U.S.-Cambodian Bilateral Trade Agreement of 1999, under which favorable quota execution was linked to compliance with labor regulations. The two governments agreed that if the Cambodian government was able to secure compliance by apparel factories with the country's labor laws and internationally agreed-upon labor standards, quotas would be increased on an annual basis. Decisions for quota increases were based on a monitoring program—the Garment Sector Working Conditions Improvement Project—conducted by the International Labour Organization (ILO). In 2000 and 2001, a 9 percent increase of all quota categories was established. In 2001, the trade agreement was extended for three additional years, from 2002 to 2004. Across-the-board quota increases of 9 percent, 12 percent, and 14 percent were awarded for those years (Polaski 2009). Although Cambodia has preferential access to the EU market, it is not as well utilized as access to the U.S. market because the double transformation rules of origin (ROO)[9] cannot be fulfilled by all apparel exports. Thus, the utilization rate is very low, at around 10 percent (UNCTAD 2003). Cambodia also enjoys duty-free market access to Australia, Canada, Japan, New Zealand, and Norway. At the regional level, Cambodia is a member of the Association of South East Asian Nations (ASEAN).

Preferential access to the EU market under Generalized System of Preferences (GSP) schemes contributed to steady growth of Sri Lanka's apparel industry and its increased presence in the European market. In March 2001, the EU granted Sri Lanka quota-free market access, but it still faced duties. In February 2004, the EU granted Sri Lanka a 20 percent duty concession for its compliance with international labor standards, in addition to an earlier 20 percent duty concession granted under the GSP General Agreement.[10] In July 2005, Sri Lanka qualified as the first South Asian country for the GSP+ scheme for vulnerable countries, permitting duty-free entry to the EU market. This development contributed to the strong growth of exports to the EU and made the EU the largest export destination of Sri Lankan apparel products. Despite participation in multiple regional agreements, such as the South Asian Association for Regional Cooperation (SAARC) and the Indo–Sri Lanka Bilateral Free Trade Agreement (ILBFTA),[11] the potential for regional apparel trade and investment in Sri Lanka is still not fully realized.

Export Dynamics

Apparel exports grew remarkably in Cambodia and Sri Lanka during the MFA era. After the Cambodian apparel industry took off in the mid-1990s, exports quadrupled within a decade, growing from $578.0 million in 1998 to $2.4 billion in 2004 (figure 6.1). According to GMAC, apparel accounted for only 3 percent of total exports in the early 1990s,

Figure 6.1   Apparel Exports to the World, Volume and Annual Growth

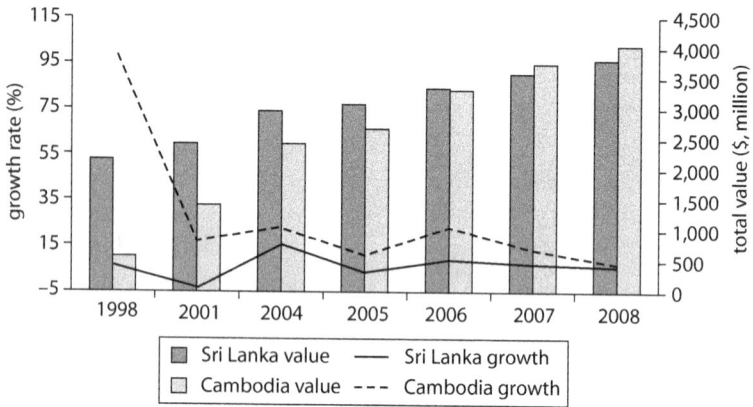

Source: United Nations Commodity Trade Statistics Database (UN Comtrade).
Note: Growth rate reflects change from previous year.

but by 2003, it constituted 76.4 percent. Between 2000 and 2004, apparel exports grew at an annual average rate of 20.5 percent. The share of Cambodia in global apparel exports increased from 0.3 percent in 1998 to 1.0 percent in 2004. Sri Lanka, already a seasoned apparel exporter in the mid-1990s, experienced healthy but more moderate growth than Cambodia, with exports rising from $1.7 billion in 1995 to $3.0 billion in 2004 (figure 6.1). However, in the late 1990s, export growth decelerated, and exports even declined in 2001 and 2002.[12] The share of Sri Lanka in global apparel exports increased from 1.1 percent in 1995 to 1.3 percent in 2001, but then decreased to 1.2 percent in 2004.

Despite pessimistic expectations for apparel sectors post-MFA, both countries continued increasing apparel exports, though growth slowed somewhat. Sri Lankan exports were expected to decrease by half and that 40 percent of firms would close in 2005 (Kelegama and Epaarachchi 2002). However, although exports were weak in the first half of 2005, apparel exports grew by 3.7 percent over the entire year. From 2004 to 2008, apparel exports as a share of total exports remained above 40 percent, and the share of Sri Lanka in global apparel exports remained quite stable at around 1.1–1.2 percent. Apparel exports grew 6 percent annually on average, and value increased by almost $1 billion over 2005–08. In Cambodia immediately after the MFA removal, total apparel exports increased to $2.7 billion in 2005 and to $4.0 billion in 2008, a rise of almost 14 percent annually. Cambodia's share of global apparel exports remained stable at 1.0 percent between 2004 and 2005, and it increased to 1.1 percent in 2006 and 1.2 percent in 2007. One of the contributors to continued growth post-MFA was the reimposition of quotas[13] on certain categories of apparel imports from China to the United States and the EU between 2005 and 2008, which limited the impact of the MFA phaseout.

End Markets

End markets of both countries are highly concentrated in the United States and the EU, with 87–90 percent of total Cambodian and Sri Lankan apparel exports going to those two destinations. The type of preferential agreements that Cambodia and Sri Lanka signed with the United States and the EU can explain the pattern of export concentration. The United States used to be the largest market for Sri Lankan apparel exports, but the composition has changed considerably since the MFA phaseout. The current largest export market—the EU-15—increased its share from 33.5 percent in 2004 to 48.8 percent in 2008, while the United States decreased its share from 55.3 percent to 41.2 percent.[14] The rest of the world increased its share from 5.2 percent in 2000 to 10.0 percent in 2008. The importance of the EU market increased because the EU granted Sri Lanka GSP+ status in 2005. Additional reasons for the shift to EU markets was that EU buyers generally demand more services and involvement in the sourcing and design process, are more prepared to pay higher prices for good quality, and are generally more relationship driven in their sourcing policies (Gibbon 2003, 2008).

The high concentration of Cambodian apparel exports in the U.S. end market is due to the preferential quotas that Cambodia had with the United States as a result of the U.S.-Cambodian Bilateral Trade Agreement. In 2008, 86.3 percent of apparel exports went to the United States and the EU-15, with 61.9 percent of all exports going to the United States and 24.4 percent to the EU-15. The only other important end market is Canada, which had a 6.1 percent share in 2008. Although the United States still dominates Cambodia's apparel exports, its share decreased from 70.4 percent in 2000 to 62.0 percent in 2008, while the EU-15 share increased from 22.4 percent to 24.4 percent in the same time period. Canada's share also increased, from 0.9 percent in 2000 to 6.1 percent in 2008. The increase in apparel exports to Canada since 2003 is related to the extension of Canada's GSP scheme to cover textiles and apparel in January 2003. In addition to preferential quotas, the interests of the parent foreign companies that control the Cambodian apparel sector explain the high concentration of Cambodian apparel exports in the U.S. market. Those parent companies, typically based in Hong Kong SAR, China; the Republic of Korea; and Taiwan, China, are largely concentrated in the U.S. market and have well-established relationships with U.S. buyers. Moreover, in contrast to Sri Lanka, the Cambodian apparel sector is tailored to a different demand sector. Orders from U.S. mass market retailers are large, and price is the most important criteria; quality and lead time are also central but not as important. In general, EU orders are smaller, demand more variation, and have different standards with regard to quality, fashion content, and lead times.

Export Products

Export products in both Cambodia and Sri Lanka are characterized by high concentration in a few items, though of different value-added products: the Sri Lankan apparel industry focuses on higher value-added products, whereas the Cambodian industry focuses on lower value-added items. After the MFA phaseout, the Sri Lankan apparel industry took over a lingerie products niche and gradually shifted away from woven to knit apparel production. Exports of lingerie products, including underwear, bras, and swimwear, have almost doubled since the end of the MFA, accounting for nearly a quarter of total EU-15 and U.S. exports in 2008. Sri Lanka's apparel exports are concentrated in relatively few products, namely underwear, trousers, and sweaters. The top five product categories accounted for 40 percent of total EU-15 apparel exports and for 47 percent in the U.S. market in 2008. Product concentration has increased since 2000. However, Sri Lanka's product concentration is lower than in most Asian competitor countries. Moreover, knit products grew in importance compared with woven products as a share of Sri Lankan apparel exports. In 1995, woven exports accounted for 72 percent of total apparel exports, but the share declined to 61 percent in 2004. By 2008, knit and woven accounted for an equal share of total apparel exports. Cambodia, on the other hand, concentrates on exporting lower value-added products, both woven and knit. The top five product categories accounted for 52.5 percent of the U.S. and 66.3 percent of the EU-15 apparel exports in 2008. The most important products in both markets are trousers, sweatshirts, and T-shirts. In the EU market, sweaters are particularly important, accounting for 53.3 percent of total exports in 2003, and different types of sweaters represent the top two apparel export products. This fact is related to the double transformation ROO required for preferential market access to the EU, which can be fulfilled for sweaters. From 1995 to 2004, knit and woven exports accounted for similar values. Woven exports, however, have stagnated since 2004, whereas knit exports have continued to increase. Nearly three-quarters of Cambodia's apparel exports were knit products in 2008.

Backward Linkages

Both Cambodian and Sri Lankan apparel industries have very weak domestic backward linkages and import most of the inputs for the apparel production. Despite government efforts to support a local textile sector, the Sri Lankan apparel sector still relies heavily on textile input imports. On average, over 65 percent of material input (excluding labor) used in the industry is imported (Kelegama 2009). In the early 2000s, an estimated 80–90 percent of fabric and 70–90 percent of accessories were imported (Kelegama and Wijayasiri 2004). In 2005, the ratio of imported yarn and fabric to apparel exports was 60 percent, and yarn and fabric imports accounted for a fourth of overall imports to Sri Lanka (Tewari 2008). There have been major changes in expanding the local supply base. Local accessory sourcing has increased importantly—40–50 percent of knit fabric is produced locally—but all woven fabric is still imported. The top textile importers to Sri Lanka are China (30.6 percent); the EU-15 (11.7 percent); Hong Kong SAR, China (14.2 percent); India (17.4 percent); and Pakistan (7.6 percent).

In Cambodia, over 90 percent of textile inputs are imported. Moreover, most of the accessory, packaging, and presentation materials are imported. Cambodia's fabric imports in 2008 accounted for an estimated 25 percent of the country's total merchandise imports (Natsuda, Goto, and Thoburn 2009). The major textile import sources in 2008 were China (41.5 percent); Hong Kong SAR, China (29.4 percent); Korea (8.6 percent); Malaysia (5.7 percent); and Thailand (5.5 percent). The high dependency of Cambodian backward linkages on imports can be explained by foreign ownership and concentration of the industry in cut-make-trim (CMT) production, which gives apparel firms located in Cambodia limited decision power with regard to input sourcing, as these decisions are made at the headquarters.

Proactive Policies

The Sri Lankan apparel sector actively prepared for the MFA phaseout by restructuring and functionally upgrading the industry, and the government played an important role in this process. The Cambodian government was less proactive than the Sri Lankan government, with most of the policies oriented toward attracting FDI rather than upgrading the apparel industry. Moreover, Sri Lankan government was very efficient in implementing policies, whereas in Cambodia, the implementation is still lagging.[15]

Sri Lankan post-MFA policies. In 2002, Sri Lanka's main apparel industry players and the government developed the Five-Year Strategy to face the MFA phaseout and the associated heightened competition in the global apparel sector. An important aspect of this strategy was the Joint Apparel Association Forum (JAAF) established by the government and the five industry associations,[16] which consolidated different associations under one roof and enabled an industrywide response to challenges posed by the MFA phaseout (Wijayasiri and Dissanayake 2008).

The key focus areas of the Five-Year Strategy included backward integration, human resource and technology advancement, trade, small and medium enterprises (SMEs), finance, logistics and infrastructure, and marketing and image building (JAAF 2002; Kelegama 2005b, 2009). The strategy had five main objectives:

- Increase the industry turnover from its 2001 level of $2.3 billion to $4.5 billion by 2007, which required a growth rate of 12.0 percent between 2003 and 2007 (lower than the growth rate of 18.5 percent between 1989 and 2000).
- Transform the industry from a contract manufacturer to a provider of fully integrated services, including input sourcing, product development, and design, as buyers demand more functions from suppliers.
- Focus on high value-added apparel instead of low-cost apparel and penetrate premium market segments.
- Establish an international reputation as a superior manufacturer in four product areas: sportswear, casual wear, children's wear, and intimate apparel.
- Consolidate and strengthen the industry.

The strategy proposed initiatives at three levels to reach these objectives (Fonseka 2004). At the macro level, initiatives included reducing the costs of utilities, instituting labor reforms, developing Electronic Data Interchange (EDI) facilities at the port and at customs, developing infrastructure, and building strong lobbies in Sri Lanka's main markets, such as Belgium, India, the United Kingdom, and the United States. At the industry level, the government encouraged branding and promotion, research and development, market intelligence, greater market diversification, backward linkages technological upgrading, building design, and product development skills, as well as enhanced productivity and reduced lead times. Finally, at the firm level, efforts were directed at reducing manufacturing costs, upgrading technology and human resources, and forming strong strategic alliances.

To shift the industry from a contract manufacturer to a fully integrated services supplier,[17] the Five-Year Strategy identified the following key steps: encourage backward integration, improve human resource capital and technology, change labor laws and regulation, promote Sri Lanka's image as a supplier with high labor standards, cater to the needs of SMEs, strengthen bilateral and multilateral links with key countries, lobby the government for improved infrastructure, and mobilize funds to implement change.

Human resource development was seen as particularly important in the post-MFA environment (Kelegama 2009). The government wanted to increase worker productivity in the apparel sector through strengthening marketing capabilities, creating design capabilities, improving productivity within firms, developing technical competence, enhancing skills, and encouraging a cohesive focus for apparel and textile education. As a result, multiple initiatives in the area of skill training have been implemented, which built on existing training facilities (Kelegama 2009).[18] See box 6.1.

As part of the Five-Year Strategy, two initiatives have been undertaken to improve working conditions and the international and local image of the apparel industry—an international image-building campaign "Garments without Guilt" in 2006 and a local image-building campaign *Abhimani* ("pride") in 2008.

Cambodian post-MFA policies. The government of Cambodia supported the development of the apparel sector, but proactive policies were mainly oriented only at attracting FDI. The government approved the establishment of 100 percent foreign-owned firms in Cambodia in 1994, improved the business environment, and provided favorable policies for foreign investors, including duty-free imports for export sectors, the provision of tax holidays and financial incentives, the introduction of laws to establish export processing zones (EPZs), and one-stop services to simplify investment procedures (Natsuda, Goto, and Thoburn 2009). Besides FDI-oriented policies, state capacity for proactive policies to

Box 6.1

Initiatives to Improve Human Capital in the Sri Lankan Apparel Industry

- **To strengthen the marketing competencies,** the JAAF, in collaboration with the Chartered Institute of Marketing, initiated an industry-specific professional marketing qualification (Wijayasiri and Dissanayake 2008).
- **To strengthen design capabilities,** the JAAF (with the support of the Sri Lankan government) initiated a Fashion Design and Development program, a four-year degree course conducted at the Department of Textile & Clothing Technology at the University of Moratuwa in collaboration with the London College of Fashion.
- **To increase firm productivity,** the JAAF (with the support of the Sri Lankan government) initiated the Productivity Improvement Program in 2004.[a] The objective is to promote "leaner" and more effective organizations, which would result in higher productivity, lower costs, better quality, and on-time delivery (Wijayasiri and Dissanayake 2008).
- **To strengthen technical capacity,** the JAAF entered into an agreement with the North Carolina State University (NCSU) College of Textiles in 2004 to deliver an NCSU-affiliated diploma in collaboration with the Clothing Industry Training Institute and the Textile Training & Service Centre. The Sri Lanka Institute of Textile and Apparel also organizes the following:
  - The Apparel Industry Suppliers Exhibition, a biannual exhibition for machinery suppliers to show new technology to support technology transfer in Sri Lanka
  - The Fabric and Accessory Sourcing Exhibition, a fabric and accessories supplier exhibition showcasing new technology developments in fabric and textiles around the world and improving the awareness of the local textiles manufacturers about global trends
  - A magazine (*Apparel Update*)
  - A conference (Apparel South Asia)
- Several programs have been established in the context of the MFA phaseout, supported by donors. For instance, USAID created four model training centers within the 31 vocational training centers, which provide training for the textile and apparel sectors (out of a total of 189 vocational training centers).

Source: Staritz and Frederick 2011b.
Note: JAAF = Joint Apparel Association Forum; MFA = Multi-fibre Arrangement; USAID = United States Agency for International Development.
a. Prior to this program, the International Labour Organization (ILO) launched the Factory Improvement Program (FIP) in 2002 with funding from the U.S. Department of Labor and the Swiss Secretariat for Economic Affairs. FIP is a training program that aims to help factories increase competitiveness, improve working conditions, and strengthen communication and collaboration between managers and workers. The Employers' Federation of Ceylon, together with the ILO, has implemented the program with JAAF as a collaborating partner (Wijayasiri and Dissanayake 2008).

support local involvement and links in the apparel sector and upgrading of the apparel sector has been rather weak, in particular compared to competitor countries such as Bangladesh, China, Sri Lanka, and Vietnam.

The major achievement in proactive policies was Better Factories Cambodia, which grew out of a trade agreement between Cambodia and the United States. Under the agreement, the United States allowed Cambodia better access to the U.S. markets in exchange for improved working conditions in the garment sector. This project has put in place institutional structures that facilitate collaboration between the government, industry associations, firms, and trade unions. Better Factories Cambodia is managed by the ILO and supported by the government, the GMAC, and unions. The project works closely with other stakeholders, including international buyers. It monitors and reports on working conditions in Cambodian garment factories according to national and international standards and helps factories to improve working conditions and productivity.

To facilitate the post-MFA transition, the government prepared the Cambodian Garment Industry Development Strategy in 2005; however, implementation is lagging. The main goal of the strategy is "to create an environment in which the Cambodian garment industry can develop and sustain export competitiveness and diversify its offer in niche markets, to retain greater value within the country, and to empower employees by fairly distributing the benefits" (Staritz and Frederick 2011a). The objectives of the strategy include the following:

- Strengthening the institutional and information base of the apparel sector by bringing together key stakeholders
- Improving access to major markets and forming close public-private partnerships
- Reducing transaction costs
- Shortening lead times and increasing value added by building links to a domestic textile industry and encouraging local investment throughout the supply chain
- Improving and expanding marketing efforts to a larger number of countries and buyers
- Improving productivity by establishing a skills development program
- Addressing general infrastructure issues within the country that add to product costs, such as the high cost of electricity and port charges

The strategy was accompanied by a work plan and management framework involving various stakeholders, including the National Export

Council of Cambodia, the GMAC, labor unions, and the ILO. Despite its ambitious goals, this strategy has not been implemented so far.

Although the apparel industry is the engine of growth in Cambodia, investments in systematic skill training have been limited. Existing training centers are largely focused on teaching women to sew and reducing injury and downtime rather than driving productivity improvements and upgrading to broader functions and higher value-adding activities (Rasiah 2009). The only two broader formal training institutes are the Cambodia Garment Training Center (CGTC) and the Cambodia Skills Development Center (CASDEC).[19]

Employment

This section presents the employment characteristics in the apparel industry in Cambodia and Sri Lanka and contrasts the trends in employment in both countries before and after the MFA. Labor populations employed in the apparel sectors of Cambodia and Sri Lanka share a number of characteristics. First, the share of population employed in the textiles and apparel industry was relatively small and remained stable after the end of the MFA: 5 percent in Cambodia and 6 percent in Sri Lanka (table 6.1). Second, the apparel sector is female dominated. The share of employment in apparel is 83 and 73 percent of women in Cambodia

Table 6.1   Labor Force Characteristics, Cambodia and Sri Lanka

	Cambodia				Sri Lanka		
	2004	2007	2008	2009	2002	2006	2008
Employment and education							
Females in labor force (%)	50	49	48	50	32	31	34
Years of education	5.51	6.07	6.05	5.98	8.44	8.56	8.81
Female years of education in T&G	6.12	6.26	5.80	6.39	10.03	10.01	10.18
Male years of education in T&G	7.55	8.62	7.22	7.28	10.20	10.33	10.46
Average years of education in T&G	6.39	6.67	6.10	6.55	10.08	10.11	10.26
Employment share of the industry							
Agriculture (%)	58	49	43	53	20	12	18
T&G (%)	4	5	6	5	6	6	6

Source: Authors' calculations.
Note: T&G = textiles and garments.

(2009) and Sri Lanka (2008), respectively. In both countries, this share was much higher than the proportion of females in the total labor force: 50 percent in Cambodia and 34 percent in Sri Lanka. Moreover, the share of females in apparel remained relatively stable in both countries after MFA removal. Third, the labor force working in apparel was more educated than the country average. In Cambodia, an average person had 6.0 years of education, while an apparel sector employee had 6.5 years of education. Although this sector has slightly more education than the country average, the skill of the workforce in the apparel sector is of major concern at both the worker and managerial levels (box 6.2).

In Sri Lanka, where the population is more educated on average than in Cambodia, an average person had 8.8 years of education compared to 10.3 years for an apparel sector worker. Education of the apparel workforce increased after the end of the MFA in both countries. But this change most likely reflected an overall increase in education rather than one specific to the apparel industry, since the national education levels went up as well. Within the apparel sector there was a gender gap in

Box 6.2

Shortage of Skill in the Cambodian Apparel Sector

A critical reason for the relatively low labor productivity in Cambodia's apparel sector is the lack of skills of workers and managers. Skilled sewing operators are in high demand, but the lack is more severe at the supervisory, management and technical, and design and fashion skill levels. The vast majority of top and middle managers as well as technically skilled workers and supervisors are foreigners. Around 5,000 Chinese apparel technicians and supervisors are dispatched to apparel factories in Cambodia through Chinese human resource agencies (Natsuda, Goto, and Thoburn 2009). These foreign workers have brought experience, which was critical for the rapid establishment of the apparel sector in Cambodia; however, they may now pose a challenge to upgrading and productivity improvements because of their limited training and skills in production processes or industrial engineering, outdated and unsuitable management practices, and communication barriers with regard to language and culture (Nathan Associates 2007). Another problem is that the transmission of knowledge to local workers is slowed by language difficulties; little learning probably takes place.

Source: Staritz and Frederick 2011a.

education. In Cambodia in 2009, women had on average 6.4 years of education, while men had 7.3 years. This gap was smaller for Sri Lanka, with 10.2 and 10.5 years of schooling of female and male workers in 2008, respectively.

In both countries, employment in the apparel sector grew under the MFA. The post-MFA dynamics were quite different: while in Cambodia the number of workers in the industry continued to grow because of industry expansion, in the Sri Lanka sector, employment declined because of industry consolidation. Employment in Cambodia's apparel sector mushroomed from under 19,000 workers in 1995 to almost 270,000 in 2004 (Staritz and Frederick 2011a). Growth continued after the MFA phaseout, with operating employment reaching 353,017 workers in 2007 (figure 6.2). After 2007, however, employment declined to 324,871 in 2008. It is estimated that besides these direct jobs, 242,000 indirect jobs have been created through the apparel sector: 113,000 in the services sector, including transportation and trade; 37,000 in nonapparel manufacturing, particularly in construction; and 92,000 in the agriculture sector (EIC 2007, cited in Natsuda, Goto, and Thoburn 2009). Unfortunately, we were not able to conduct a regression analysis to study the changes in employment at the industrial level for Cambodia because we lacked the time series or panel industrial or enterprise data.

Figure 6.2   Total Employment in the Apparel Sector

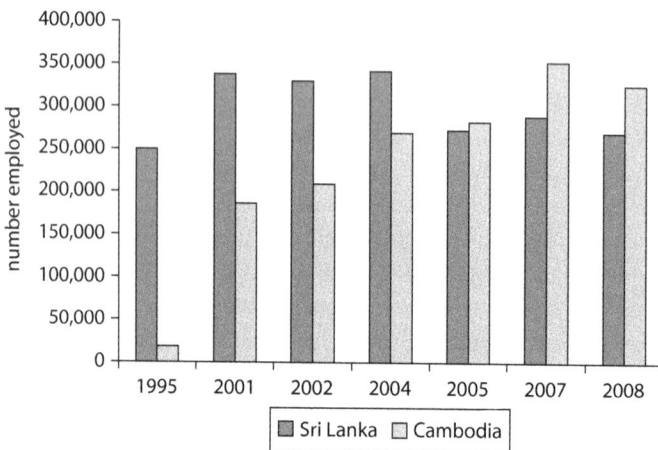

Source: Kelegama 2005a, 2005b, 2006, 2009; Tait 2008; *Just-style* 2009; Saheed 2010; Garment Manufacturers' Association in Cambodia (GMAC).
Note: For Cambodia, we present operating employment numbers.

Employment levels in Sri Lanka's apparel sector increased from 102,000 in 1990 to 340,367 in 2004, accounting for more than a third of manufacturing employment in 2004 (Staritz and Frederick 2011b). As the industry started consolidating[20] in terms of firms after the end of the MFA, employment declined by nearly 20 percent to 270,000 in 2008 (figure 6.2). The regression analysis of Sri Lanka industrial data supports these numbers and shows the 28 percent drop of employment in the textile and apparel industry post-MFA; however, this result is not significant (see the annex). The insignificance of the result may be due to the fact that the apparel industry was preparing for the consolidation even before the official MFA termination.

Industry employment in Sri Lanka is still female dominated, even though the share of females has declined. More than 90 percent of apparel workers in Sri Lanka were women in the 1980s and 1990s,[21] although that figure declined to below 80 percent in the second half of the 2000s. Nonetheless, the industry regression analysis for Sri Lanka shows that the post-MFA drop in the share of female production workers in textiles and garments was not significant (see the annex). Somewhat paradoxically, despite the consolidation of the industry, the Sri Lankan apparel industry experiences labor shortages that are related to the poor domestic image of the apparel industry, including perceived low wages and poor working conditions. The estimates show around 150,000 vacancies in the industry across all skill groups (Wijayasiri and Dissanayake 2008). Around 150,000 apparel workers, mostly skilled workers, have sought employment in foreign countries, including Bangladesh, Kenya, the Maldives, Mauritius, and the Middle East, as they find higher wages and better economic and social opportunities abroad (Kelegama and Wijayasiri 2004).

Within-Industry Changes

This section presents changes within the apparel sector following the end of the MFA in Cambodia and Sri Lanka. First, we show that the unit values in both countries declined post-MFA. Then we consider changes in the global value chain position and show that the Sri Lankan apparel industry moved up the value chain, while the Cambodian industry remained at the same position. Finally, in terms of firm dynamics, the number of Cambodian firms continued to grow after the MFA, whereas in Sri Lanka it declined mostly at the expense of the SMEs.

Unit Value Dynamics

In both Cambodia and Sri Lanka, unit values show declining trends post-MFA. Sri Lankan apparel export unit prices to the United States declined sharply post-MFA, from $59 to $42 per dozen over the 2004–08 period (figure 6.3). A slight rise in EU unit values over 2004–05 was followed by a moderate decrease (Staritz and Frederick 2011b). In spite of this decline, Sri Lanka's apparel exports have generally higher unit values than those of other Asian apparel exporter countries, reflecting the higher value-added production that Sri Lanka specializes in. Unit values of apparel exports from India and Sri Lanka to the EU are higher than those of Asian competitor countries, including Bangladesh, Cambodia, China, Pakistan, and Vietnam (Tewari 2008).

On the other hand, the unit prices of Cambodia's main export products are lower than the world average. For EU-15 exports, unit prices in 2005 were lower than in India, Sri Lanka, and Vietnam, but higher than in Bangladesh, China, and Pakistan (Tewari 2008). One of the reasons for the low prices of Cambodian apparel exports is the concentration in basic products, while other countries export higher-value products. Unit prices went down after the end of the MFA, with the U.S. import prices experiencing sharper declines than those of the EU. Between 2004 and 2008,

Figure 6.3   Unit Values of Sri Lanka's Apparel Exports to the EU-15 and the United States

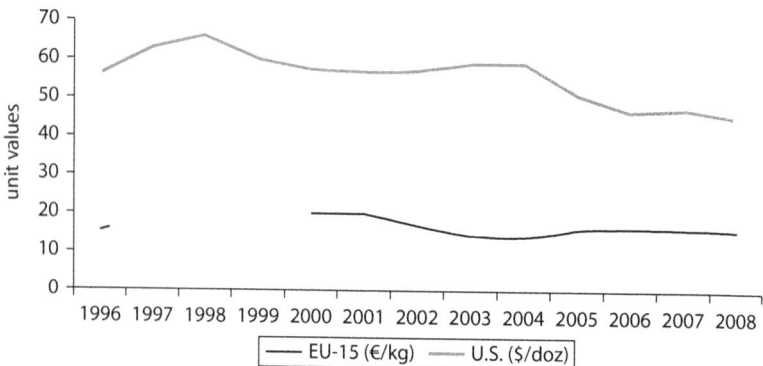

Source: EU-15: Eurostat; United States: U.S. International Trade Commission (USITC).
Note: For products exported to the United States, volume data were "not available" for four products, and for five products, volumes were reported in "numbers." Both are measured in numbers that were converted into dozens. EU-15 = the 15 member states of the European Union (EU) as of December 31, 2003, before the new member states joined the EU: Austria, Belgium, Denmark, Finland, France, Germany, Greece, Ireland, Italy, Luxembourg, the Netherlands, Portugal, Spain, Sweden, and the United Kingdom; kg = kilogram; doz = dozen.

the average price of apparel exports to the United States fell by 25 percent, from \$52 to \$39 per dozen, while the average price of apparel exports to the EU-15 declined 7 percent, from €13.4 to €12.5 per kilogram, according to U.S. International Trade Commission (USITC) and Eurostat data (Staritz and Frederick 2011a) (figure 6.4).

Global Value Chain Position and Industry Upgrading

Cambodian and Sri Lankan apparel industries are located on the opposite ends of the global apparel value chain. The Sri Lankan apparel sector made significant upgrading efforts, including process, product, functional, social, and to a lesser extent supply chain upgrading.[22] In contrast, Cambodia's apparel sector is concentrated in the lowest stage of the apparel-making value chain—CMT production. To some extent, the differences can be explained by the industry ownership. Sri Lankan firms are mostly locally owned and thus have a lot of decision-making power in terms of sector strategies. By contrast, most of the factories in Cambodia are foreign owned and consequently have limited leverage and autonomy in terms of strategic decision making or in attracting orders, since most of the decisions are made at the headquarters of the

Figure 6.4   Unit Values of Cambodia's Apparel Exports to the EU-15 and the United States

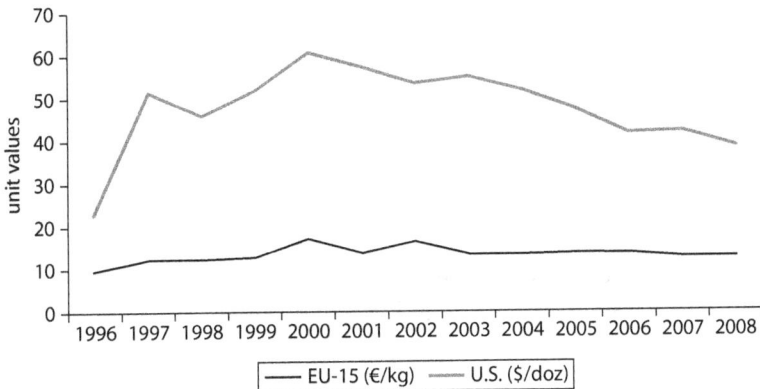

Source: EU-15: Eurostat; United States: U.S. International Trade Commission (USITC).
Note: For U.S. values, only products measured in dozens included. EU-15 = the 15 member states of the European Union (EU) as of December 31, 2003, before the new member states joined the EU: Austria, Belgium, Denmark, Finland, France, Germany, Greece, Ireland, Italy, Luxembourg, the Netherlands, Portugal, Spain, Sweden, and the United Kingdom; kg = kilogram; doz = dozen.

parent companies. In addition, Sri Lankan large manufacturers invested in new technology while Cambodian firms use the primitive equipment supplied by parent companies, a factor that also contributes to the difference in functional position in the global value chain of the two countries.

Functional upgrading of the Sri Lankan apparel sector was a central part of the post-MFA Five-Year Strategy to transform the industry from a contract manufacturer to a provider of fully integrated services. The initial steps in this direction were taken by large manufacturers such as Brandix and MAS, which, in the early 1990s, started to increase their capabilities and develop broader services, and today they offer design and marketing.[23] An important part of the apparel sector in Sri Lanka now provides full manufacturing services, including input sourcing, and has at least an understanding of product development and design. In addition, the apparel sector in Sri Lanka upgraded to higher-value products. Large manufacturers made a conscious effort to upgrade to middle and high value-added or niche products, in particular lingerie and to a lesser extent active wear.

On the other hand, Cambodia's apparel sector remained concentrated on CMT production, in which apparel firms receive all inputs (mostly fabrics and accessories) from buyers or parent companies and just perform the sewing and then export the final products. However, an important share of CMT firms is also in charge of cutting the fabric and performing some finishing activities, including washing and packing. GMAC reports that 60 percent of the factories (typically subsidiaries of companies overseas) are only involved in CMT production, 25 percent in free on board (FOB), and 15 percent in subcontracting arrangements. Very few apparel firms are involved in the design or product development process in Cambodia.

Locally owned Sri Lankan large manufacturers have a lot of leverage in defining the development strategies of the industry. After the MFA phaseout, they established their own brands and opened plants abroad. The establishment of own brands was a significant innovation because, until then, Sri Lanka's apparel industry did not possess any brands. For instance, MAS developed a range of intimate wear under the brand Amante in 2007. The brand caters to middle-income and upper-income consumers and competes with international brands such as Triumph, Etam, and La Senza (Wijayasiri and Dissanayake 2008). Investments in overseas plants further upgraded companies to an intermediary role, whereby firms in Sri Lanka manage and organize regional and international production and sourcing networks. Sri Lankan apparel manufacturers have opened factories in Jordan, Kenya, Madagascar, the Maldives, Mauritius, and more recently in Bangladesh, India, and elsewhere in South Asia.[24]

In contrast, Cambodian factories are largely integrated into triangular manufacturing networks where global buyers source from transnational producers with headquarters located in China; Hong Kong SAR, China; Korea; Malaysia; Singapore; or Taiwan, China that organize manufacturing networks on a global scale. Thus, factories in Cambodia are integrated into apparel global value chains through their foreign parent companies, where the production orders are received together with the fabric and accessories inputs and delivery instructions. This type of integration has secured access to the supply chains of global buyers and input sourcing networks, but it has also limited decision power and the functions performed in Cambodia. Production, sales, and management decisions are largely made at the headquarters of the parent companies. The parent companies are generally in charge of input sourcing, product development and design, logistics, merchandising, and marketing, and they have the direct relationships with buyers.

The technology levels of Sri Lanka's apparel sector vary, with the large manufacturers using the latest technology as they have invested in new technology and workforce development, while SMEs possess lower technology (JAAF 2002). As a part of JAAF's Productivity Improvement Plan, the large manufacturers in Sri Lanka have been implementing lean manufacturing methods in their production processes to reduce waste and lead times and to lower production costs, and they have also invested in supply chain enabling (Wijayasiri and Dissanayake 2008).

The Cambodian apparel industry uses very old technology—most machinery is secondhand from parent companies. An Asian Development Bank (ADB) study in 2004 concluded that the technology employed in Cambodia's apparel firms is at the lowest level in sewing and inspection, and few attachments are applied to machines that could aid workers to operate more effectively, in both volume and quality terms (ADB 2004). Interview evidence from Cambodia shows that equipment and machinery are mostly relocated to Cambodia after use in plants in China; Hong Kong SAR, China; Malaysia; Taiwan, China; and Thailand within triangular manufacturing networks, or imported secondhand by the few local producers. Only knitting machinery and equipment (weft and warp knitting) were imported by some firms firsthand from Germany and Taiwan, China (Rasiah 2009).

Firm Dynamics

Because of their different industry strategies, Cambodian and Sri Lankan firms experienced different post-MFA firm dynamics. A number of Cambodian firms continued to grow after the MFA phaseout, whereas in Sri Lanka, pre-MFA firms' growth was followed by post-MFA consolidation of the industry, mostly at the expense of SMEs. Cambodian apparel sector firms mushroomed over 1994–2004, with the number of operating firms increasing from 20 to 219. The growth of firms continued after the MFA phaseout as well, reaching 284 firms in 2008. The number of factories in Cambodia employing more than 5,000 workers more than doubled between 2004 and 2005. Just over one-quarter of factories employ less than 500 workers, while most employ between 500 and 2,000 workers (Natsuda et al. 2009).

In Sri Lanka, on the other hand, the number of apparel firms increased from around 142 in 1990 to their highest level of above 1,061 in 2001. From then on, the number of firms has declined, reaching around 830 in 2004 and 350 in 2008. This decline was due to the structural change in the industry, with the number of small firms shrinking and the industry consolidating within larger firms. The industrial data regression analysis for Sri Lanka confirms the negative change post-MFA on the number of plants (see the annex table 6A.1). The coefficient, however, was not significant, corroborating the fact that Sri Lanka prepared for the MFA phaseout ahead of time and that industry consolidation was part of the strategy.

Wages

In this section, we investigate the changes in wage levels as well as the male-female wage differential and apparel sector premiums before and after the MFA phaseout. The analysis shows that on average wages were higher in textiles and garments than in agriculture in both countries (table 6.2). In Cambodia, wages paid in apparel were higher than average wages in the economy. However, in Sri Lanka, apparel wages were slightly lower than the economywide average.

The average labor cost is relatively high in Sri Lanka—$0.43 per hour (including social charges) in 2008 (Staritz and Frederick 2011b). This figure is twice as high as in Bangladesh and also higher than in Cambodia, Pakistan, and Vietnam, but lower than in China and India. Average labor costs are comparatively low in Cambodia: the base minimum wage of a production worker is $0.33 per hour, including benefits and overtime

Table 6.2   Wage Levels in Local Currency, Cambodia and Sri Lanka

	Cambodia				Sri Lanka		
	2004	2007	2008	2009	2002	2006	2008
Mean log wage in T&G	12.24	12.45	12.53	12.45	8.35	8.75	8.86
Mean log wage in agriculture	11.05	11.6	11.72	11.61	7.82	8.31	8.68
Mean log wage	11.74	12.31	12.47	12.22	8.34	8.83	8.94

Source: Authors' calculations.
Note: T&G = textiles and garments.

(Nathan Associates 2007).[25] Cambodia ranked second after Bangladesh among regional competitor countries in 2008. These low wage levels are, however, accompanied by relatively low labor productivity. A World Bank study in 2004 concluded that firms and workers in Cambodia are generally less productive than in Bangladesh, China, India, and Pakistan and that Cambodia's low labor costs do not wholly compensate for the low productivity of its workers (World Bank 2004).

Tables 6.3 and 6.4 present results of wage regressions for Cambodia and Sri Lanka, respectively. The regression analysis was carried out using the methodology described in chapter 2. For our analysis, we used six rounds of Cambodian Socio-Economic Household Surveys that cover the 1996–2009 period, Sri Lankan 2002 and 2006 Household Income and Expenditure Surveys, and 2002 and 2008 Sri Lankan Labor Force Surveys.

In Cambodia, the female wage gap decreased over time: in 1996, female wages were 26.6 percent lower than those of males, but in 2009, women were paid only 11.5 percent less than men (table 6.3). The wage gap went up after the MFA phaseout from 12.0 to 13.3 percent over 2004–08; however, it decreased in 2009 to 11.5 percent. The gender wage differential in Sri Lanka also increased after the end of the MFA. In 2002, women earned 40 percent less than men (table 6.4). The difference went up to 55 percent in 2006, and even though it decreased in 2008 to 44 percent, it was still higher than the pre-MFA phaseout level.

In both countries, working in apparel pays a positive premium compared to the economy average; however, the premium dipped immediately after the MFA phaseout. In Cambodia, the wage premium for working in apparel was negative in 1996, most likely because the industry was just established and had operated for only three years. In 1999, the apparel wage premium increased significantly, coinciding with Cambodia signing trade agreements with the United States and the EU

Table 6.3   Wage Premium Regressions, Cambodia

	Log(wage)					
	1996	*1999*	*2004*	*2007*	*2008*	*2009*
Female dummy	−0.266**	−0.141**	−0.120**	−0.128**	−0.133**	−0.115**
Hours	0.010**	0.011**	0.016**	0.014**	0.017**	0.017**
Age	0.059**	0.044**	0.038**	0.052**	0.066**	0.056**
Education	0.053**	0.042**	0.009**	0.079**	0.066**	0.050**
Textiles and apparel	−0.301**	0.781**	0.287**	0.354**	0.374**	0.130*
Hazard	−0.000	0.094	−0.085	0.362*	0.132	0.040
Constant	10.640**	9.973**	10.747**	9.942**	9.930**	10.394**
Number of observations	4,706	3,000	7,068	2,294	1,287	3,800

Source: Authors' calculations based on Cambodian Socio-Economic Household Surveys.
Note: The grand mean effects of the industries are calculated; additional controls include age squared, hours of work, industry, and occupation dummies.
** $p < 0.01$, * $p < 0.05$.

Table 6.4   Wage Premium Regressions, Sri Lanka

	Log(wage)		
	2002	*2006*	*2008*
Female dummy	−0.401**	−0.553**	−0.443**
Age	0.111**	0.154**	0.118**
Education	0.040**	0.039**	0.041**
Textiles and apparel	0.196**	0.050**	0.082**
Hazard	0.525**	0.790**	0.528**
Constant	6.070**	5.742**	6.181**
Number of observations	12,213	17,828	14,998

Source: Authors' calculations based on Sri Lankan 2002 and 2006 Household Income and Expenditure Surveys and 2008 Labor Force Survey.
Note: The grand mean effects of the industries are calculated; additional controls include age squared, industry, and occupation dummies. Hours worked were not available in Sri Lankan surveys.
** $p < 0.01$.

and significantly increasing its exports. The apparel wage premium declined considerably in 2004[26] compared to 1999. However, it went up over 2007–08. The textile and apparel industry premium in Sri Lanka in 2002 was positive as compared to the economy average and equal to 0.196 (see table 6.4). The premium went down in 2006 to 0.05, but it increased to 0.08 in 2008. The increase in the apparel wage premium in 2008 might be associated with the industry switch to higher-value goods (lingerie).

Working Conditions

In this section, we investigate whether the MFA phaseout had any implications for employee working conditions. Working conditions directly impact worker's well-being through the number of hours worked overtime, a hazardous work environment, social benefits, or workplace discrimination. But they also have an indirect impact on employment and wage opportunities through the demand side: buyers might pay lower prices or refuse to buy at all if they know that producers exploit child labor or mistreat employees.

Cambodian and Sri Lankan governments had different strategies to improve working conditions in the apparel sector. Sri Lanka, as a part of the Five-Year Strategy, designed an international image-building campaign, Garments without Guilt, in 2006 and a local image-building campaign *Abhimani* ("pride") in 2008 to improve the image of the apparel sector and working conditions. Despite these efforts, working conditions are still far from ideal. As mentioned earlier, labor costs in Sri Lanka are lower than in China and India. Besides low wages, issues such as the lack of appointment letters, long working hours, high work intensity, and in particular the right of association and collective bargaining (as many firms are reluctant to recognize trade unions) have been problematic in parts of the apparel sector, particularly in smaller firms (Staritz and Frederick 2011b). Kelegama and Wijayasiri (2004) find that unfilled vacancies in the apparel industry can to some extent be explained by poor working conditions, as workers migrate to foreign countries in search of higher wages and better working conditions.

Cambodia has a good record of labor compliance because of the Better Factories Cambodia program begun in 1999. Through this program, compliance with international labor standards was directly linked to apparel export quotas that Cambodia received from the United States. In a 2004 Foreign Investment Advisory Service survey of the 15 largest U.S. and EU buyers of Cambodian apparel, Cambodia was rated the highest on "level of labor standards" and "protecting the rights of workers to organize unions" among Asian apparel-exporting countries, including Bangladesh, China, Thailand, and Vietnam (Staritz and Frederick 2011a). Better Factories Cambodia is the most comprehensive and systematic monitoring effort governing any country's apparel sector. All factories in the sector are registered with the program, and a team of local Khmer-speaking inspectors is engaged in a constant 10-month cycle of monitoring visits that culminate in factory reports and a publicly available synthesis report.

The process is streamlined via a computerized information management system that buyers and suppliers can access. The monitoring checklist (based on Cambodian labor law and the ILO core labor standards) covers over 480 items. The MFA phaseout coincided with the expiration of the U.S. quotas in 2004, which eliminated the incentive motive of Better Factories Cambodia (Staritz and Frederick 2011a). However, Cambodia continued with the program to keep up with the good labor standards compliance reputation. Despite a good record in labor compliance, there are still problems. As Miller et al. (2007) conclude, social audits positively impact child labor, forced labor, and health and safety, but they have a more limited impact on freedom of association and collective bargaining, discrimination, living wages, and working hours. Low wages and excessive working hours have prevailed in Cambodia, as well as problems establishing collective bargaining.

We measure working conditions as an average for a dummy for working above age of 14, and a dummy of less than or equal to a 40-hour workweek (table 6.5, columns 1–4). In both cases, regressions are pooled across different survey years. Time is a dummy for 2005 and later years. The results show that the working condition index in Cambodia has deteriorated in the textile and garment industry post-MFA by 5.2 percent compared to other industries (table 6.5, column 1). This figure might also reflect the fact that the end of the U.S. quotas removed the incentive motive to comply with labor standards operating through the Better Factories Cambodia program. On the other hand, working conditions in the textile and garment industry post-MFA in Sri Lanka improved by 2.3 percent compared to other industries, which might be a sign of the impact of the Garments without Guilt campaign. Even though the post-MFA changes in female working conditions relative to male working conditions and compared with other industries are positive in both countries, they are not significant, suggesting that women's working conditions in textiles and garments were not affected differently than those of men after the MFA phaseout. Using Sri Lanka's household survey, we can also use an alternative measure of working conditions (table 6.5, columns 5–6): the share of bonuses and allowances over cash earnings and the share of food stamps over cash pay. Good working conditions correspond to having a higher-than-average performance pay ratio and a lower-than-average food stamps ratio. Our dependent variable represents an average between those two variables. The analysis shows that this index of working conditions in the textile and garment industry compared to other industries worsened post-MFA by 3 percent in

Table 6.5 Working Conditions Regressions, Cambodia and Sri Lanka

| | Cambodia | | Sri Lanka | | | |
| | Household surveys | | Labor force surveys | | Household surveys | |
	(1)	(2)	(3)	(4)	(5)	(6)
Female	0.031**	0.032**	0.066**	0.059**	0.010**	0.038**
	(0.002)	(0.002)	(0.002)	(0.004)	(0.003)	(0.004)
Time	0.045**	0.046**	-0.009**	-0.014**	-0.451**	-0.435**
	(0.002)	(0.003)	(0.002)	(0.003)	(0.003)	(0.003)
Female*T&G	n.a.	-0.036**	n.a.	-0.029*	n.a.	-0.008
		(0.012)		(0.015)		(0.014)
Female*time	n.a.	-0.001	n.a.	0.015**	n.a.	-0.060**
		(0.004)		(0.005)		(0.005)
Time*T&G	-0.052**	-0.069**	0.023**	0.01	-0.030**	-0.062**
	(0.008)	(0.018)	(0.009)	(0.017)	(0.009)	(0.016)
Time*T&G*female	n.a.	0.022	n.a.	0.01	n.a.	0.085**
		(0.020)		(0.020)		(0.020)
Constant	0.779**	0.779**	0.737**	0.739**	0.630**	0.631**
	(0.016)	(0.016)	(0.015)	(0.015)	(0.029)	(0.029)
R-squared	0.09	0.091	0.122	0.123	0.559	0.561
Number of observations	84,724	84,724	49,348	49,348	34,585	34,585

Source: Authors' calculations.

Note: Standard errors in parentheses. Additional controls include age, age squared, marital status, education, industry, and occupation dummies. T&G is a dummy variable equal to 1 in the textiles and garments sector and 0 in other sectors. Time is a dummy equal to 1 from 2005 on. n.a. = not applicable.

** $p < 0.01$, * $p < 0.1$.

Sri Lanka. However, the working conditions improved for women post-MFA by 8.5 percent relative to men and compared to other industries (table 6.5, column 6).

Conclusions

Despite gloomy post-MFA expectations, the apparel industries of both Cambodia and Sri Lanka managed to increase export volumes, maintain world market shares, and grow at a healthy rate, outcomes that may have poverty-reducing implications. The resilience can be explained by several factors. The United States and the EU established safeguard quotas against imports from China from 2005 until the end of 2008, which mitigated the impact of the MFA phaseout. Other factors such as proactive policies, industry ownership, and background were important too.

Because of the different post-MFA development strategies and niches that Cambodia and Sri Lanka occupy in the global apparel market, the post-MFA implications for employment were different. As a part of the Five-Year Strategy, Sri Lanka consolidated the apparel industry, which resulted in a decline in employment even though the overall volume of production and exports grew. In Cambodia, employment in apparel continued to grow after the MFA phaseout; however, the labor force is low skilled and has low labor productivity compared to other countries in the region. We did not observe major changes in male-female apparel industry employment composition post-MFA—the sector remained a female-dominated industry in both countries.

The unit values of apparel exports have declined post-MFA as a result of increasing competition in the sector at the global level. Male-female wage differentials were declining under the MFA in both countries. The gap widened right after the MFA phaseout but later decreased. A similar trend can be observed in the garment industry premium in both countries. Workers in the apparel industry were receiving a premium comparable to that of an average worker. This premium decreased in both countries right after the MFA phaseout, but it slightly recovered in the following years. Finally, in terms of working conditions, we found mixed results. In Cambodia, working conditions worsened in the textile and garment industry compared to other industries after the MFA phaseout, while in Sri Lanka, results are mixed and depend on how working conditions are measured.

Given the transition patterns of the Cambodian and Sri Lankan apparel industries, more research is needed to learn if these countries were able to maintain the growth of the apparel sector that boomed under the MFA. Major concerns for industry development are the lifting of China safeguards and the consequences of the 2008 financial crisis, which might impact the apparel industry through the demand side.

Annex

Table 6A.1   Industry Data Regression Analysis, Sri Lanka

	Number of plants	Log labor	Female share
Time	−9.61	0.04	0.07***
	(10.376)	(0.127)	(0.019)
Time*T&G	−33.51	−0.28	−0.06
	(22.707)	(0.278)	(0.040)
Food, beverage, tobacco	144.46	1.35***	0.32***
	(17.485)	(0.208)	(0.034)
Textiles, garments, leather	113.15***	1.18***	0.62***
	(20.371)	(0.246)	(0.036)
Wood products, furniture	41.35**	0.43**	0.08**
	(18.138)	(0.219)	(0.032)
Paper, printing, publishing	−3.05	−0.12	0.11***
	(20.430)	(0.250)	(0.036)
Chemicals, petrol, rubber	44.01**	0.38*	0.23***
	(18.545)	(0.223)	(0.033)
Nonmetal products	91.30***	0.98***	0.23***
	(19.221)	(0.232)	(0.034)
Basic metals	−12.19	−0.45	−0.04
	(36.759)	(0.450)	(0.065)
Log output	n.a	n.a	−0.03***
			(0.006)
Constant	96.19***	4.90***	0.58***
	(19.199)	(0.188)	(0.094)
Number of observations	560	560	560
R-squared	0.3112	0.4199	0.5526

Source: Authors' calculations.
Note: Standard errors in parentheses. The Sri Lanka manufacturing sector data unit of observation is a summary (cell data) by industry, firm size, and provincial location due to confidentiality restrictions. The data are pooled across three years: 1993, 1998, and 2007. Time is a dummy equal to 1 for 2007 and zero for 1993 and 1998. T&G is a dummy variable equal to 1 in the textiles and garments sector and 0 in other sectors. Omitted group for industry is metal products and machinery. Additional controls include firm size and location for number of plants and female share regression, and firm size for log labor. n.a. = not applicable.
*** $p < 0.01$, ** $p < 0.05$, * $p < 0.1$.

Notes

1. Authors' calculations using data from World Development Indicators.

2. Data from household surveys.

3. Experts estimated that Sri Lankan apparel exports would decrease by half and that 40 percent of firms would close in 2005 (Kelegama and Epaarachchi 2002). For Cambodia, the problem was exacerbated by the fact that the industry was mostly foreign owned. The foreign investors could have reallocated the production to cheaper places, say China, after expiration of Cambodian preferential quotas.

4. Calculations by Ana Luisa Gouvea Abras.

5. The empirical analysis for the sections was conducted by Elisa Gamberoni, Ana Luisa Gouvea Abras, Hong Tan, and Yevgeniya Savchenko.

6. This section is heavily based on Staritz and Frederick (2011a, 2011b).

7. At the time of the takeoff of apparel exports, the BOI was named Greater Colombo Economic Commission (GCEC); in 1992, it was renamed BOI.

8. A total of 164 firms represented 84 percent of exporting firms in Cambodia.

9. Staritz (2011), p. 11: "ROO requirements under EU preferential trade agreements vary. In general, ROO under the EU GSP require two significant processes to be performed within the beneficiary country, which often requires a product to be reclassified from one four-digit tariff heading to another. For the clothing sector this means that production, including cutting and sewing, must be combined with another process such as manufacture of fabrics or yarns. Thus, ROO require that clothing items undergo a double transformation in the beneficiary country, that is, assembly plus at least one preassembly operation."

10. Moldova is the only other country that has succeeded in achieving GSP concessions for labor standards.

11. Other agreements include the South Asian Preferential Trading Agreement (SAPTA); the Bay of Bengal Initiative for Multi-Sectoral Economic Cooperation (BIMSTEC) involving Bangladesh, Bhutan, India, Myanmar, Nepal, Sri Lanka, and Thailand; and since 2004, the South Asian Free Trade Agreement (SAFTA).

12. This decline was related to lower demand in developed countries but more importantly to bomb attacks at the Colombo International Airport in July 2001 that triggered the imposition of war-risk insurance charges (Kelegama and Wijayasiri 2004). The reduction in orders and escalating insurance costs hit the industry severely, and as a result, several small and medium enterprises closed in the early 2000s.

13. The implication of China safeguards removal is not part of our focus. However, it is an interesting question in itself. Contrary to the pessimistic

implications of the China safeguards removal for the apparel sectors of smaller countries, recent studies show that the influence might not be that significant. "China still dominates the business. It supplies nearly half of the European Union's garment imports and 41 percent of America's. But more orders are shifting to lower-wage economies such as Cambodia and Vietnam, where garment factories are mushrooming. Vietnam is already the second-largest supplier of clothes to America" (*Economist* 2011).

14. The EU-15 includes the 15 member states of the European Union (EU) as of December 31, 2003, before the new member states joined the EU: Austria, Belgium, Denmark, Finland, France, Germany, Greece, Ireland, Italy, Luxembourg, the Netherlands, Portugal, Spain, Sweden, and the United Kingdom.

15. This section is based on Staritz and Frederick (2011a, 2011b).

16. Industry associations included the Sri Lanka Apparel Exporters Association (SLAEA), the National Apparel Exporters Association, the Sri Lanka Chamber of Garment Exporters, the Free Trade Zone Manufacturers Association, and the Sri Lanka Garment Buying Office Association.

17. The functions of a fully integrated services supplier include input sourcing and supply chain management, product development and design, and customer relationship management, as well as strong manufacturing skills.

18. In addition to these formal training programs, a variety of small-scale programs are run by nongovernmental organizations to train mostly women for employment in the industry, such as the American Center for International Labor Solidarity, the Indian organization Community and Police, and the Italian-run Don Bosco. Furthermore, the government-run vocational training authority offers three- to six-month courses. Large firms such as Brandix and MAS have their own training institutes: Brandix College of Clothing Technology (in collaboration with the Royal Melbourne Institute of Technology) and MAS Institute of Management and Technology.

19. CGTC was opened in April 2002 and is managed by GMAC and supported by eight organizations. The principal course is "Training of Garment Industry Supervisors"; more recently, a new course for "Skill Development at Entry" was established. CASDEC offers training in technical and industrial engineering, especially targeting middle management, and also works directly with firms offering assistance for production management, including workflow, planning, controls, and supervision. This center was funded by the United States Agency for International Development (USAID) but is now largely financially self-sufficient.

20. Consolidating of the apparel industry in the case of Sri Lanka means concentrating the apparel production in a fewer number of plants, mostly large. This phenomenon was accompanied by a decrease in the number of small firms and employment.

21. See Staritz and Frederick (2011b).

22. This section is heavily based on Staritz and Frederick (2011a, 2011b).

23. They established their own design centers with in-house designers who work closely with the design teams of brand owners, interpreting their designs, making suggestions, and sometimes even giving ideas. MAS has even established design studios in Hong Kong SAR, China; the United Kingdom; and the United States to offer design solutions to its main customers—Victoria Secret, Gap, and Speedo. Brandix has not opened design centers abroad but has opened marketing offices in New York and London to improve links with buyers (Wijayasiri and Dissanayake 2008).

24. For instance, Brandix and MAS set up textile and apparel industrial parks in India. Both manufacturers had already established plants in other countries, but their investments in India are on a much larger scale than previous initiatives, which were mainly driven by availability of quotas. The Brandix India Apparel City located in Andra Pradesh covers 1,000 acres and was set up in 2006 with the backing of the state government. It is expected to generate a turnover of $1.2 billion and employ over 60,000 people. It aims to become India's largest vertically integrated textile and apparel venture, housing the total supply chain from fiber through spinning, knitting and weaving, trimming and accessories, apparel making and embellishment, to logistics and store services. MAS signed a Memorandum of Understanding (MOU) in 2006 to invest $200 million to set up a 750-acre park in Andra Pradesh (Wijayasiri and Dissanayake 2008).

25. For labor cost comparisons with other countries, see chapter 3.

26. Robertson et al. (2009) also document a positive wage premium for Cambodian apparel sector in 2004.

References

Background Papers

Staritz, Cornelia, and Stacey Frederick. 2011a. "Background Global Value Chain Country Papers: Cambodia." Background paper to the book *Sewing Success? Employment, Wages, and Poverty following the End of the Multi-fibre Arrangement*, World Bank, Washington, DC.

———. 2011b. "Background Global Value Chain Country Papers: Sri Lanka." Background paper to the book *Sewing Success? Employment, Wages, and Poverty following the End of the Multi-fibre Arrangement*. Washington, DC: World Bank.

Sources

ADB (Asian Development Bank). 2004. "Cambodia's Garment Industry: Meeting the Challenges of the Post-Quota Environment." ADB, Manila.

The Economist. 2011. "Textiles in South-East Asia: Good Darning, Vietnam." June 4.

Fonseka, Tilak. 2004. "Forward Integration and Supply Capacity of the Garment Industry." In *Ready-Made Garment Industry in Sri Lanka: Facing the Global Challenge*, ed. Saman Kelegama. Colombo: Institute of Policy Studies.

Gibbon, Peter. 2003. "The African Growth and Opportunity Act and the Global Commodity Chain for Clothing." *World Development* 31 (11): 1809–27.

———. 2008. "Governance, Entry Barriers, Upgrading: A Re-interpretation of Some GVC Concepts from the Experience of African Clothing Exports." *Competition & Change* 12 (1): 29–48.

JAAF (Joint Apparel Association Forum). 2002. *5 Year Strategy for the Sri Lankan Apparel Industry*. Colombo: JAAF.

Just-style. 2009. "Sri Lanka: Apparel Firms in Bullish Mood over GSP+." *Just-style .com*, December 4.

Kelegama, Saman. 2005a. "Impact of the MFA Expiry on Sri Lanka." In *South Asia after the Quota System: Impact of the MFA Phase-out*, ed. Saman Kelegama. Colombo: Institute of Policy Studies.

———. 2005b. "Ready-Made Garment Industry in Sri Lanka: Preparing to Face the Global Challenges." *Asia-Pacific Trade and Investment Review* 1: 1, 51–68.

———. 2006. *Development under Stress: Sri Lankan Economy in Transition*. New Delhi: Sage Publications India.

———. 2009. "Ready-made Garment Exports from Sri Lanka." *Journal of Contemporary Asia* 39 (4): 579–96.

Kelegama, Saman, and Roshen Epaarachchi. 2002. "Garment Industry in Sri Lanka." In *Garment Industry in South Asia—Rags or Riches? Competitiveness, Productivity, and Job Quality in the Post-MFA Environment*, ed. Gopal Joshi. Delhi: International Labour Organization (ILO).

Kelegama, Saman, and Janaka Wijayasiri. 2004. "Overview of the Garment Industry in Sri Lanka." In *Ready-Made Garment Industry in Sri Lanka: Facing the Global Challenge*, ed. Saman Kelegama. Colombo: Institute of Policy Studies.

Miller, Doug, Veasna Nuon, Charlene Aprill, and Ramon Certeza. 2007. "'Business as Usual?': Governing the Supply Chain in Clothing post-MFA Phase-out. The Case of Cambodia." Discussion Paper 6, Global Union Research Network, Geneva.

Nathan Associates. 2007. "Factory-Level Value Chain Analysis of Cambodia's Apparel Industry." U.S. Agency for International Development (USAID), Washington, DC.

Natsuda, Kaoru, Kenta Goto, and John Thoburn. 2009. "Challenges to the Cambodian Garment Industry in the Global Garment Value Chain." Working Paper 09-3, Ritsumeikan Center for Asia Pacific Studies (RCAPS), Ritsumeikan Asia Pacific University, Beppu, Japan.

Polaski, Sandra. 2009. "Harnessing Global Forces to Create Decent Work in Cambodia." International Labour Organization and International Finance Corporation, Washington, DC.

Rasiah, Rajah. 2009. "Can Garment Exports from Cambodia, Laos and Burma Be Sustained?" *Journal of Contemporary Asia* 39 (4): 619–37.

Robertson, Raymond, Drusilla Brown, Gaëlle Pierre, and Laura Sanchez-Puerta, eds. 2009. *Globalization, Wages, and the Quality of Jobs: Five Country Studies.* Washington, DC: World Bank.

Saheed, Hassen. 2010. "Prospects for the Textile and Clothing Industry in Sri Lanka." *Textile Outlook International* 147: 79–119.

Staritz, Cornelia. 2011. *Making the Cut? Low-Income Countries and the Global Clothing Value Chain in a Post-Quota and Post-Crisis World.* World Bank, Washington, DC.

Tait, Niki. 2008. "Textiles and Clothing in Sri Lanka: Profiles of Five Companies." *Textile Outlook International* 133: 59–81.

Tewari, Meenu. 2008. "Deepening Intraregional Trade and Investment in South Asia—The Case of the Textile and Clothing Industry." Working Paper 213, India Council for Research on International Economic Relations, New Delhi.

UNCTAD (United Nations Conference on Trade and Development). 2003. "Trade Preferences for LDCs: An Early Assessment of Benefits and Possible Improvements." The United Nations, New York and Geneva.

USITC (United States International Trade Commission). 2004. *Textile and Apparel: Assessment of the Competitiveness of Certain Foreign Suppliers to the U.S. Market,* vol. 1. Washington, DC: USITC.

Wijayasiri, Janaka, and Jagath Dissanayake. 2008. "Trade, Innovation and Growth: The Case of the Sri Lankan Textile and Clothing Industry." Organisation for Economic Co-operation and Development (OECD), Institute of Policy Studies, Colombo.

World Bank. 2004. "Cambodia Seizing the Global Opportunity: Investment Climate Investment and Reform Strategy for Cambodia." Report 27925, World Bank, Washington, DC.

———. 2006. "Cambodia Poverty Assessment: Halving Poverty by 2015?" World Bank, Washington, DC.

———. 2007. "Sri Lanka Poverty Assessment: Engendering Growth with Equity: Opportunities and Challenges." World Bank, Washington, DC.

———. 2009. World Development Indicators, World Bank, Washington, DC.

Yamagata, Tatsufumi. 2006. "The Garment Industry in Cambodia: Its Role in Poverty Reduction through Export-Oriented Development." Institute of Developing Economies Discussion Paper 62, Institute of Developing Economies, Japan External Trade Organization (JETRO), Chiba.

CHAPTER 7

Conclusions

Gladys Lopez-Acevedo and Yevgeniya Savchenko

Apparel and Poverty

Understanding the effects of globalization and trade on job creation, job destruction, and changes in the quality of jobs is essential for the design of sustainable poverty reduction strategies. The apparel sector is particularly important for poverty reduction. Seventy percent of worldwide apparel exports in 2008 came from developing countries, making the sector a critical engine of growth. It often provides entry into formal employment for the unskilled, the poor, and women because of the relatively low technology and the labor-intensive nature of the work.

The phaseout of the Multi-fibre Arrangement (MFA) at the end of 2004 led to substantial reallocation of production and employment worldwide. However, few studies examine the development of the apparel value chain post-MFA (Gereffi and Frederick 2010; Frederick and Gereffi 2011; Staritz 2011), and most analyses do not focus on the implications of the MFA phaseout for employment and workers.

This book examines the changes in employment, wages, interindustry changes, working conditions, and government policies enacted after the

The authors of this chapter are grateful for comments provided by Raymond Robertson and Cornelia Staritz.

MFA phaseout. Case studies were conducted in nine countries: Bangladesh, Cambodia, Honduras, India, Mexico, Morocco, Pakistan, Sri Lanka, and Vietnam. The analysis used administrative data as well as the latest available industry, enterprise, labor, and household surveys.

Changes following the End of the MFA: Overview of Country-Level Results

The end of the MFA was associated with changes in apparel industries across the countries studied in this book, such as increased exports and decreased apparel prices, and led to a reallocation of production and employment between and within countries. Apparel exports in the nine countries studied increased by 41.8 percent in the four years following the MFA removal, from $41.4 billion in 2004 to $58.7 billion in 2008. There were winners and losers. From 2004 to 2008, some countries previously restricted by the quota system were able to expand their supply—for example, Bangladesh by 69 percent, India by 67 percent, and Pakistan by 32 percent (figure 7.1). Other countries contracted their exports over the same period—for example, Mexico by 36 percent.

Figure 7.1   Country Cases: Change in Export Value, Market Share, and Employment, 2004–08

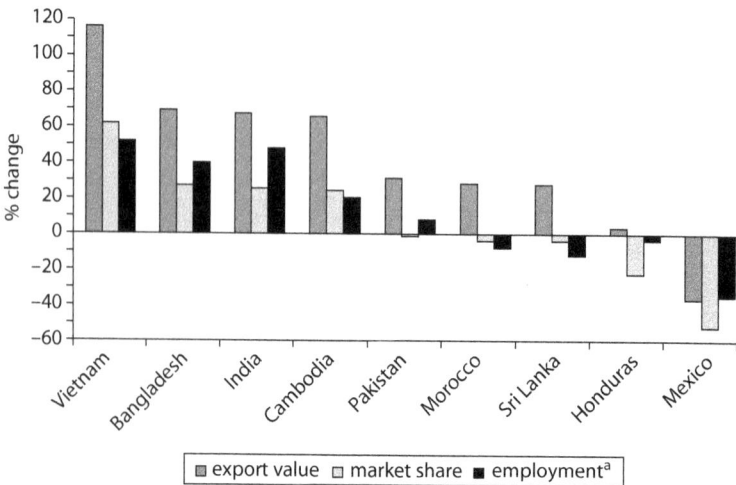

Source: For export data: United Nations Commodity Trade Statistics Database (UN Comtrade); for employment data: various sources; see background country papers (Staritz and Frederick 2011a, 2011b, 2011c, 2011d, 2011e, 2011f, 2011g, 2011h, 2011i).
a. An average of 2003–05 employment is used for 2004 for Sri Lanka.

Cost competitiveness increased after the MFA phaseout due to rising supply, and, as a result, world average apparel unit values declined. Under the MFA, many countries (such as Bangladesh and Cambodia) expanded apparel industries to take advantage of nonexistent or excess quotas, leading to oversupply after the MFA removal. This expansion, together with low-cost and highly competitive apparel supply from China, heightened global cost competition post-MFA and led to a decline in world apparel unit values.

The end of the MFA was followed by substantial reallocation of production among countries, with buyers changing their sourcing policies and moving sourcing to countries with more competitive apparel sectors. Some developing countries were able to significantly increase their global apparel market share (figure 7.1). For example, over the 2004–08 period, Bangladesh increased its world apparel share from 3.2 to 4.0 percent, Cambodia from 1.0 to 1.2 percent, India from 2.9 to 3.6 percent, and Vietnam from 1.8 to 2.8 percent. However, apparel export shares of other countries declined: over the same period, Honduras's share fell from 1.2 to 0.8 percent, Mexico's from 2.9 to 1.4 percent, and Morocco's from 2.8 to 2.3 percent. Apparel market shares of Pakistan and Sri Lanka remained stable at around 1.1 percent over the same time period.

There were also significant changes within countries in terms of employment, wage premiums, and position in the global value chain. Some countries were able to expand employment in apparel over 2004–08 (figure 7.1). For example, apparel employment in Bangladesh increased by 40.0 percent, in Cambodia by 20.4 percent, in India by 48.0 percent, in Pakistan by 8.0 percent, and in Vietnam by 52.0 percent. By contrast, apparel employment in other countries contracted over the same period: in Honduras by 3.2 percent, in Mexico by 34.8 percent, in Morocco by 7.7 percent, and in Sri Lanka by 12.0 percent.

Main Findings and Policy Implications

The empirical analysis suggests that changes in employment and wages generally coincided with the change in exports, but other factors, such as upgrading and domestic policy, also seem to vary with worker outcomes (table 7.1; detailed results are in annex table 7A.1). For example, Sri Lanka followed a deliberate policy to consolidate the industry and focus on higher-value production. These changes corresponded with an increase in total apparel exports but falling total employment. In Vietnam and Bangladesh, total employment increased, but women's

Table 7.1   Summary of Results

Country	Across-country changes	Within-country changes			
	Exports (value and market share, 2004–08)	Total employment	Wage premium	Upgrading	Working conditions
Bangladesh	Improved	Improved	Improved	Yes	Improved (declined for women)
India	Improved	Improved	Improved	Yes	Declined
Pakistan	Stagnant	Improved	Improved	Yes	Declined for women
Vietnam	Improved	Improved	Improved	Yes	No change
Cambodia	Improved	Improved	Declined	No change	Declined
Sri Lanka	Stagnant	Declined	Declined	Yes	Mixed
Honduras	Declined	Declined	Declined	No change	Declined
Mexico	Declined	Declined	Declined	No change	Declined
Morocco	Stagnant	Declined	—	Yes	—

Source: Authors' formulation.

Note: Wage premium is the interindustry wage differential in textiles and garments. Upgrading is broadly defined as moving to higher-value activities in global value chains. Countries that were less active in preparing for the MFA (Multi-fibre Arrangement) phaseout and initiating upgrading are classified as having "No change."
— = not available. Definitions of working conditions are detailed in the annex table 7A.1 of this chapter. The change in working conditions in the textile and garment industry is based on comparison with other industries post-MFA. The change in working conditions for women in the textile and garment industry is relative to men and compared with other industries post-MFA.

share of total employment declined, possibly as a result of a shift toward knit apparel and upgrading. These results show that shifts in the value chain that correspond to increasing employment and exports may actually result in fewer jobs for women or those workers most likely to be closest to poverty. On the other hand, shifting out of apparel is not necessarily negative. If the country is moving into more advanced manufacturing, moving out of apparel may be a sign of economic development. This may be the case for Mexico.

Table 7.1 also shows that labor demand clearly increased in Bangladesh, India, Pakistan, and Vietnam. Apparel firms in these countries increased exports, and in so doing increased employment and wages. In contrast, labor demand fell in Honduras, Mexico, and Sri Lanka, since apparel firms in these countries exported less and employment and the wage premium fell.

Chapter 4 found that Bangladesh, India, Pakistan, and Sri Lanka increased apparel exports after the end of the MFA/ATC (Multi-fibre Arrangement/Agreement on Textiles and Clothing). Interestingly, the apparel-specific wage premium increased in all four countries following the end of the MFA/ATC. The increase in the apparel-specific wage premium is followed by a closing of the male-female wage gap throughout the economy, not just in the apparel sector. This result is consistent with the idea that the increase in apparel exports coincides with an increase in the demand for the factor used intensively in apparel—women—which may then have significant long-run poverty-reducing effects.

The countries featured in chapter 5—Honduras, Mexico, and Morocco—tended to concentrate on single export markets (the United States in the case of Honduras and Mexico, and the European Union [EU] for Morocco). Honduras and Mexico both entered free trade agreements with the United States and seemed to have relied on these agreements instead of a more proactive policy that might have encouraged upgrading. In both countries, apparel exports and the estimated wage premium in the apparel sector fell after the end of the MFA/ATC. In Honduras, this premium has been identified as a critical factor in the success of the *maquila* sector in lifting people out of poverty, so the loss of apparel exports—and apparel jobs—has potentially significant adverse effects on poverty in Honduras.

Chapter 6 illustrated that while Cambodia's apparel sector remained focused on the lower end of the value chain, the Sri Lankan government worked with the private sector to encourage upgrading and focusing on higher value-added items. Interestingly, employment expanded in Cambodia and fell in Sri Lanka, although the total value of exports increased in both. This comparison highlights the importance of understanding industry structure and policies. Policies to move up the value chain may cause the industry to move away from precisely those entry-level positions that give opportunities for people to exit poverty, raising the question of what other policies might be needed to complement policies that facilitate moving up the value chain.

Finally, the case studies that follow the main findings provide a detailed description of the apparel sector in the nine countries under consideration.

Taken as a whole, we can summarize the book's results in four points. First, export gains in the apparel industry were not simply due to industry relocation from higher-wage countries to lower-wage countries. Global buyers seeking to maximize profits try to minimize costs by picking the "best" sources for their products. Since apparel is a very labor-intensive industry, shifts in apparel production might have been driven primarily by wage differences across countries. This book shows, however, that only about a third of the variation in cross-country changes in exports is explained by wage differences. Countries that gained the most, including Bangladesh, India, Pakistan, and Vietnam, implemented proactive policies specific to the apparel industry. While wage differences explain some of the production shifts, domestic policies targeting the apparel sector, ownership type, and functional upgrading of the industry also played an important role. These results highlight the importance of performing in-depth country studies to describe factors driving the changes in wages and employment that occurred after the end of the MFA.

Second, changes in exports usually, but not always, matched changes in wages and employment. This fact is especially important for policy because it shows that simply using exports as a metric of "success" in terms of helping the poor is not sufficient. While rising exports correlated with rising wages and employment in the large Asian countries, rising exports coincided with falling employment in Sri Lanka. Mexico had falling exports and employment in apparel but seems to have been able to absorb these workers into other industries. This does not seem to be the case in Honduras, where falling apparel exports correlated with falling wages and employment. The implication is that facilitating the movement into higher-value economic areas in the face of rising global competition is important.

Third, this book identifies the specific ways that changes in the global apparel market affected earnings. De Hoyos, Bussolo, and Núñez (2008) and Robertson et al. (2009) demonstrate that the apparel premium over other industries is the critical component of wages that helps lift workers from poverty. This book shows that these premiums change in predictable ways: rising (in most cases) in countries that "gain" and falling in countries that "lose." This fact means that not only are employment opportunities generally lost when exports contract and gained when exports expand, but one of the most important features that made these "good" jobs—the wage premiums—are also lost (or gained). This change represents a double impact for workers in developing countries.

Fourth, in terms of policies, the countries that had larger increases in apparel exports were those that promoted apparel sector upgrading; those that did not promote upgrading had smaller increases or even falling exports. Although this fact may imply that upgrading facilitates competitiveness, upgrading does not always correspond with increases in employment or wages. In some cases, the opposite might be true (as in Sri Lanka, where functional and product upgrading of the sector coincided with employment decline, particularly for women). Apparel industries in other countries (such as Bangladesh and Cambodia) were able to expand employment while staying at lower levels of the value chain. Since upgrading often requires workers with more advanced skills, the decline in labor demand affects mostly the low-skilled poor. In Honduras, where neither proactive upgrading nor workforce development programs were present, increased competition and subsequent production shifts represented real losses to workers. Having a vision for the evolution of the textile and apparel sector that incorporates developing worker skills is important. A further notable finding is that in an industry driven by reputation-sensitive buyers in importing countries, concern for labor conditions and worker treatment may be not only a labor rights issue but also a competitive advantage, as the case of Cambodia suggests.

One policy-related concern is that the opportunities for pro-poor apparel production may be short lived and are highly sensitive to changes in the global economic environment. It is important to identify how the change in policy is affecting workers and through which channels they are being affected so that the appropriate policy responses can be applied.[1] For economies that are gaining, it is important to know who is benefiting and what conditions are necessary for the poor to benefit from the change in policy. If the poor are not benefiting, policy makers need to ask why and to determine what, if anything, might be done to help the poor capture some of the gains.

Directions for Future Work

The present book aims to contribute to the body of analysis of the implications of the MFA phaseout. Future work can move in a number of directions.

First, a crucial extension of this report would be a study of post-MFA economic structure and welfare. The economy of any country has a complex structure consisting of three main sectors—agriculture, manufacturing, and services. Apparel is one of many industries in manufacturing. Changes in the apparel sector might lead to a reallocation of employment to other sectors, which in its turn can trigger changes in relative wages and have implications for total welfare in the economy. This book considers only changes in the apparel sector and does not analyze the multisectoral implications of the MFA removal. An important extension of this book would be a study of how post-MFA changes in the apparel labor and product markets affected the overall structure of and welfare in the economy and employment and wage opportunities in other sectors.

Second, further analysis of how the various shocks after 2008 affected the apparel sector would be useful. The objective of the current book was to understand the immediate post-MFA changes in the apparel sector of nine country case studies. However, the apparel sector was affected by a number of shocks that occurred after 2008—the last year covered in this book. At the end of 2008, the China safeguards for apparel were removed, allowing China, already the largest apparel exporter, to further increase export volumes and heighten competition in the global apparel market. Moreover, the world apparel sector experienced a major demand shock as the global financial crisis hit in 2008. The aftermath of the crisis resulted in decreased purchasing power and demand from industrial countries. Staritz (2011) and Gereffi and Frederick (2010) analyze first the general effects and implications of the China safeguard phaseout and the financial crisis implications for the global apparel sector at the macro level. Further analysis is needed to uncover how these shocks affected wages and employment for workers in apparel-exporting countries. Because of the lack of data, this book does not address these shocks.

Third, further work is needed on the efficacy of domestic policies in the short and long term. This book highlights different policies that governments of case study countries implemented to prepare for the MFA phaseout, which included workforce skill development programs among others. In general, it seems that in countries where those policies were successfully implemented, employment and wage premiums went up. However, this book does not directly evaluate the impact of the policies on employment and wages in the sector and does not provide a comparative analysis of which policies were more effective. Further work is needed to identify how changes in domestic policies affected workers and which policies were most efficient in improving workers' welfare in the short and long term. Opportunities for pro-poor apparel production may be short lived and are highly sensitive to changes in the global economic environment. It is important to identify how and through what channels policy changes are affecting workers so that the appropriate responses can be applied.

Moreover, there should be more analysis of the effects of specific policies and interventions in the apparel sector that aim to improve working conditions. One such effort at data collection and analysis is the Better Work program run by the International Finance Corporation (IFC) and the International Labour Organization (ILO), which operates in close collaboration with local and international stakeholders, including unions and buyers. The program is quickly expanding operations in several low-income developing countries with the aim of improving working conditions and access to international markets. Better Work is making a commendable effort in systematically gathering data that will improve our understanding of specific changes within the apparel industry in developing countries.

Annex

Table 7A.1 Detailed Summary of Results

| | Across-country changes | | | Within-country changes | | | | |
| | Exports (2004–08) | | | | | | Working conditions (post-MFA change) | |
Country	Improvement	% change	Total employment	Year	Wages (premium)	Upgrading	Improved	Premium
Bangladesh	Improved		Improved		Improved	Improved	Improved (declined for women)	
	Value	69	1.6 million in 2000 to	2005	0.343***		Average	0.078***
	Market share	27	3.1 million in 2009	2009	1.545***		Female	-0.088***
India	Improved		Improved		Improved	Improved	Declined	
	Value	67	34 million in 2001 to	2004	-0.046**		Average	-0.034***
	Market share	25	35 million in 2009	2007	0.084***		Female	-0.003
Pakistan	Stagnant		Improved		Improved	Improved	Declined for women	
	Value	32	1.3 million in 2000 to	2003	-0.046**		Average	-0.001
	Market share	-1	2.5 million in 2009	2008	0.019		Female	-0.025***
Vietnam	Improved		Improved		Improved	Improved	No change	
	Value	116	354,707 in 2000 to	2004	-0.340***		Average	0.007
	Market share	62	937,350 in 2008	2008	-0.076***		Female	0.025
Cambodia	Improved		Improved		Declined	No change	Declined	
	Value	66	187,103 in 2001 to	1999	0.781***		Average	-0.069***
	Market share	24	324,871 in 2008	2008	0.374***		Female	0.022

Country	Across-country changes			Within-country changes				
	Exports (2004–08)		Total employment	Year	Wages (premium)	Upgrading	Working conditions (post-MFA change)	
	Improvement	% change					Improved	Premium
Sri Lanka	Stagnant		Declined		Declined	Improved	Mixed	
Value		28	338,704 in 2001 to	2002	0.196***		Average	0.023***/0.030***
Market share		–4	270,000 in 2008	2008	0.082***		Female	0.010/0.085***
Honduras	Declined		Declined		Declined	No change	Declined	
Value		4	125,000 in 2000 to	2001	0.302***		Average	–0.055***
Market share		–22	103,377 in 2007	2007	0.140***		Female	0.029**
Mexico	Declined		Declined		Declined	No change	Declined	
Value		–36	821,846 in 2000 to	1999	–0.106		Average	–0.019***
Market share		–52	489,985 in 2007	2009	–0.181		Female	0.100***
Morocco	Stagnant		Declined		—	Improved	—	
Value		28	199,478 in 2000 to		—		—	
Market share		–4	191,809 in 2007		—		—	

Source: Authors' formulation.

Note: Wage premium is the interindustry wage differential in textiles and garments. Upgrading is broadly defined as moving to higher-value activities in global value chains. Countries that were less active in preparing for the Multi-fibre Arrangement (MFA) phaseout and initiating upgrading are classified as having "No change." — = not available. Definition of working conditions is as follows: Bangladesh: average of two dummies—holding a regular paid job and no overtime work (40 hours). Pakistan: average of four dummies—holding a regular paid job, no injury at work, no child labor (child labor is working at age 14 or younger) and no overtime work (40 hours). Vietnam: average of three dummies—no overtime work (40 hours), no child labor (child labor is working at age 14 or younger), and dummy equal to 1 if a job has higher than economywide average share of benefits over total wage payments. India: average of three dummies—no child labor (child labor is working at age 14 or younger), no overtime work (workweek of less than six days), and dummy equal to 1 if a job has higher than economywide average share of cash over in-kind wage payments. Honduras and Mexico: average value of three dummies—a dummy equal to 1 for no overtime work (40 hours), a dummy equal to 1 for larger-than-average ratio of cash versus in-kind payments, and a value greater than 1 if the individual is at least 14 years old. Cambodia: an average of two dummies—working above age of 14 and no overtime work (40 hours). Sri Lanka: two measures were used: measure 1—an average for a dummy for working above age of 14, and a dummy for no overtime work (40 hours) (working conditions using this variable improved); measure 2—an average of higher-than-average performance pay ratio and a lower-than-average food stamps ratio (working conditions using this variable declined). The change in average working conditions in the textile and garment industry is based on comparison with other industries post-MFA. The change in working conditions for women in the textile and garment industry is relative to men and compared with other industries post-MFA.

*** $p < 0.01$, ** $p < 0.05$, * $p < 0.01$.

Note

1. The recent World Bank (2011) report "More and Better Jobs in South Asia" suggests that "South Asian countries would benefit from reorienting their labor market policies from protecting jobs to protecting workers."

References

Background Papers

Staritz, Cornelia, and Stacey Frederick. 2011a. "Background Global Value Chain Country Papers: Bangladesh." Background paper to the book *Sewing Success? Employment, Wages, and Poverty following the End of the Multi-fibre Arrangement*, World Bank, Washington, DC.

———. 2011b. "Background Global Value Chain Country Papers: Cambodia." Background paper to the book *Sewing Success? Employment, Wages, and Poverty following the End of the Multi-fibre Arrangement*, World Bank, Washington, DC.

———. 2011c. "Background Global Value Chain Country Papers: Honduras." Background paper to the book *Sewing Success? Employment, Wages, and Poverty following the End of the Multi-fibre Arrangement*, World Bank, Washington, DC.

———. 2011d. "Background Global Value Chain Country Papers: India." Background paper to the book *Sewing Success? Employment, Wages, and Poverty following the End of the Multi-fibre Arrangement*, World Bank, Washington, DC.

———. 2011e. "Background Global Value Chain Country Papers: Mexico." Background paper to *Sewing Success? Employment, Wages, and Poverty following the End of the Multi-fibre Arrangement*, World Bank, Washington, DC.

———. 2011f. "Background Global Value Chain Country Papers: Morocco." Background paper to *Sewing Success? Employment, Wages, and Poverty following the End of the Multi-fibre Arrangement*, World Bank, Washington, DC.

———. 2011g. "Background Global Value Chain Country Papers: Pakistan." Background paper to *Sewing Success? Employment, Wages, and Poverty following the End of the Multi-fibre Arrangement*, World Bank, Washington, DC.

———. 2011h. "Background Global Value Chain Country Papers: Sri Lanka." Background paper to *Sewing Success? Employment, Wages, and Poverty following the End of the Multi-fibre Arrangement*, World Bank, Washington, DC.

———. 2011i. "Background Global Value Chain Country Papers: Vietnam." Background paper to *Sewing Success? Employment, Wages, and Poverty following the End of the Multi-fibre Arrangement*, World Bank, Washington, DC.

Sources

de Hoyos, Rafael, Marizio Bussolo, and Oscar Núñez. 2008. "Can Maquila Booms Reduce Poverty? Evidence from Honduras." World Bank Policy Research Working Paper 4789, World Bank, Washington, DC.

Frederick, Stacey, and Gary Gereffi. 2011. "Upgrading and Restructuring in the Global Apparel Value Chain: Why China and Asia Are Outperforming Mexico and Central America." *International Journal of Technological Learning, Innovation, and Development* 4 (1–2): 67–95.

Gereffi, Gary, and Stacey Frederick. 2010. "The Global Apparel Value Chain, Trade and the Crisis—Challenges and Opportunities for Developing Countries." In *Global Value Chains in a Postcrisis World: A Development Perspective*, 157–208, ed. Olivier Cattaneo, Gary Gereffi, and Cornelia Staritz. Washington, DC: World Bank.

Robertson, Raymond, Drusilla Brown, Gaëlle Pierre, and Laura Sanchez-Puerta, eds. 2009. *Globalization, Wages, and the Quality of Jobs: Five Country Studies.* Washington, DC: World Bank.

Staritz, Cornelia. 2011. "Making the Cut? Low-Income Countries and the Global Clothing Value Chain in a Post-Quota and Post-Crisis World." Working Paper, World Bank, Washington, DC.

World Bank. 2011. *More and Better Jobs in South Asia.* Washington, DC: World Bank.

Summaries of the Country Case Studies on Apparel Industry Development, Structure, and Policies

Cornelia Staritz and Stacey Frederick

The authors of the chapters in part 2 are grateful for comments provided by Gladys Lopez-Acevedo, Raymond Robertson, Elisa Gamberoni, Ana Luisa Gouvea Abras, and Yevgeniya Savchenko. The authors would like to thank Meenu Tewari for very useful comments on the Bangladesh and Sri Lanka chapters.

CHAPTER 8

Bangladesh

Overview

- The export-oriented apparel sector has been the main source of growth in exports and formal employment for the past three decades in Bangladesh. The industry directly employs 3.1 million people, comprising 40 percent of manufacturing employment; indirectly more than 10 million people are dependent on the apparel sector.

- The Multi-fibre Arrangement (MFA), preferential market access to the European Union (EU), and specific government support policies were crucial in starting the export-oriented apparel sector in Bangladesh. Bangladesh's apparel export sector started in the late 1970s and early 1980s when manufacturers in the Republic of Korea and other East Asian countries began to invest in and source from Bangladesh, motivated by MFA quota hopping and by access to Bangladesh's abundant supply of low-cost labor. Local entrepreneurs followed and established apparel firms, motivated by markets guaranteed by quotas, low investment requirements, and initial technology and know-how transfer from foreign investors, in particular, from the Republic of Korea.

- Although expectations for Bangladesh's apparel exports post-MFA were gloomy, the apparel sector increased its export value and market share after 2004. Also, during the global economic crisis, Bangladesh's apparel sector has been one of the few winners, increasing market shares in both the United States and the EU-15.[1]

- Bangladesh's main competitive advantage is low labor costs—the lowest among main apparel exporter countries in the world. But besides low costs, Bangladesh's apparel sector has other competitive strengths, including a comparatively long experience in the sector, local ownership and entrepreneurship, backward linkages to local textile suppliers (particularly in the knit segment), and capabilities in addition to cut-make-trim (CMT) production that have secured profitability relative to other sectors and countries even in the more competitive post-MFA period. There have been important upgrading processes in the context of the MFA phaseout, including process, functional, and supply chain upgrading. However, there remain important challenges related to the skills gap, particularly at the management, technological, and design and fashion skill levels, as well as challenges related to lead times, labor compliance, and concentration in basic products and in the end markets of the EU-15 and the United States.

Development of the Apparel Industry[2]

Bangladesh has a long experience in textile and made-to-order apparel production, mostly for the domestic market. However, a ready-made apparel industry for the domestic market only developed more recently. Two of the first exporters—Reaz Garments and Jewel Garments—developed from this domestic-oriented ready-made apparel industry. The apparel export sector started on a large scale in the late 1970s and early 1980s when Korean, Taiwanese, and other East Asian manufacturers started to invest in and source from Bangladesh, motivated by MFA quota hopping and by access to Bangladesh's abundant supply of low-cost labor. Quddus and Rashid (2000) see the breakthrough of the apparel export industry occurring in 1978, when the Bangladeshi entrepreneur Quader of the company Desh was invited by the chairman of Daewoo, a then-large apparel manufacturer from (quota-restricted) Korea, to collaborate in the production and export of apparel. As part of this collaboration, in 1979, Daewoo provided training to Desh supervisors and managers at its plants in Korea, thus creating an important initial transfer of technology and skills. In the mid-1980s, the sector developed into a sound industry, and a period of rapid export growth began, with apparel becoming the main export product of Bangladesh in the late 1980s.

Besides the abundant availability of low-cost labor, the MFA quota system, preferential market access to the EU, and specific government support policies have played central roles in the initial development of Bangladesh's apparel sector. Bangladesh faced no quota restrictions for apparel and textile exports to the EU (with the partial exception of the United Kingdom and France, which imposed quotas from 1985 to 2001) and Norway and none for textile exports to the United States and Canada. For apparel exports to the United States, quota restrictions for 30 product categories were imposed in 1985 after a triple-digit growth rate during the previous five years, with exports to the United States rising to $150 million. However, in export tax equivalents, the quotas amounted to 7.6 percent in 2003, which is low compared to India (20.0), China (36.0), and Pakistan (10.3) (Mlachila and Yang 2004). Another important factor in the growth of Bangladesh's apparel sector was duty-free market access to the EU under the Generalized System of Preferences (GSP) scheme since the early 1980s. Although exports to the EU were lower than those to the United States throughout the 1980s, the picture changed in the 1990s, and by the mid-1990s, exports to the EU accounted for over 50 percent of total apparel exports.

Two government policies, both put in place in 1980, were particularly important in the development of Bangladesh's apparel export sector. First, the government introduced the system of bonded warehouses, through which firms can delay the payment of tariffs until they are ready to consume inputs imported earlier; and if the inputs are used for producing exports, they are not required to pay the tariff (Ahmed 2009). Second, back-to-back letters of credit (L/C) were introduced through which exporters are able to open L/C in a local bank for the import of inputs against the export orders placed in their favor by the final apparel importers (master L/C). Thus, by showing the export order, firms can get credit to pay for imported inputs. At the time of payment for the final good, the cost of the imported items along with interest and other charges would be deducted by the local bank from the proceeds. Hence, manufacturers were spared the financial involvement in the purchase of imported inputs, and the financial outlay for apparel manufacturing was reduced to wages, energy, transport, and other overhead costs (Ahmed 2009; World Bank 2005b). These policies were particularly crucial for the establishment of local firms in the apparel sector in Bangladesh.

From the late 1980s until 2004, Bangladesh's apparel exports increased significantly. Whereas apparel exports accounted for around $1 million in 1978 (Ahmed 2009), import data from Bangladesh's trading partners show that exports increased to $2,544 million in 1995 and to $7,945 million in 2004 (table 8.1). The share of Bangladesh in global apparel exports increased from 1.7 percent in 1995 to above 3.2 percent in 2004. However, the overall export figures mask a significant change in the composition of Bangladesh's apparel exports with regard to export products and end markets. In the 1980s, Bangladesh produced only woven apparel products, but starting from the early 1990s there was rapid growth in exports of knit apparel products, principally sweaters and T-shirts. In 1991, the share of knitted apparel was 15 percent of total apparel exports (Ahmed 2009); in 1995, it was 31 percent; and in 2004, knit exports nearly reached 50 percent. The growth of knit products was particularly spurred by preferential market access to the EU. Until the early 1990s, the United States was the main export destination for Bangladesh's apparel products, but in the 1990s, the EU-15 surpassed the United States as the number one export market. The share of total apparel exports going to the EU-15 remained above 50 percent (or approximately $US1 billion) in the second part of the 1990s and reached 64 percent (or approximately $US4 billion) in 2004 (figure 8.1).

Apparel exports grew from less than 1 percent of total exports in the early 1980s to 75 percent of total exports in 2004 (table 8.2). Along with the increase in exports, the number of apparel firms increased from around 130 in 1984 to nearly 4,000 in 2004. Employment grew from 0.1 million in 1985 to 2.0 million in 2004 (table 8.2).

Expectations on the impact of the MFA phaseout on Bangladesh's apparel exports had been pessimistic. However, export values increased and market share remained stable between 2004 and 2005 and increased afterward. Looking at data for imports by Bangladesh's trading partners, total apparel exports increased to $8,026 million in 2005, which accounts for a 1 percent increase from 2004 (table 8.1). The share of Bangladesh in global apparel exports decreased from 3.2 to 3.0 percent between 2004 and 2005 but then increased again to 3.6 percent in 2006. However, although aggregate exports increased, different types of firms were affected differently. Mostly larger firms

Table 8.1 Bangladeshi Apparel Exports to the World

	1995	1998	2001	2004	2005	2006	2007	2008	2009
Total value ($, million)	2,544	3,704	5,032	7,945	8,026	10,415	11,181	13,464	14,189
Annual growth rate (%)	—	10.6	3.5	25.3	1.0	29.8	7.3	20.4	5.4
Share of world exports (%)	1.7	2.1	2.6	3.2	3.0	3.6	3.5	4.0	4.8
Woven and knit value ($, million)									
Woven	1,762	2,394	2,968	4,035	3,991	5,051	5,222	6,016	6,412
Knit	782	1,310	2,064	3,911	4,035	5,365	5,959	7,448	7,778
Woven and knit share of total import value (%)									
Woven	69.3	64.6	59.0	50.8	49.7	48.5	46.7	44.7	45.2
Knit	30.7	35.4	41.0	49.2	50.3	51.5	53.3	55.3	54.8

Source: United Nations Commodity Trade Statistics Database (UN Comtrade). Imports reported by partner countries.
Note: UN Comtrade classification, Harmonized Commodity Description and Coding System (HS 1992): Woven Apparel, HS62; Knitted Apparel, HS61. Growth rate reflects change from previous year. — = not available.

Figure 8.1   Bangladeshi Apparel Exports to the EU-15 and the United States

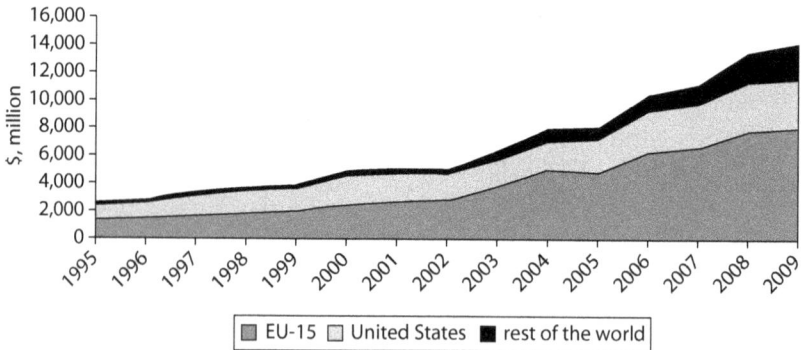

Source: United Nations Commodity Trade Statistics Database (UN Comtrade); imports reported by partner countries.
Note: EU-15 = the 15 member states of the European Union (EU) as of December 31, 2003, before the new member states joined the EU: Austria, Belgium, Denmark, Finland, France, Germany, Greece, Ireland, Italy, Luxembourg, the Netherlands, Portugal, Spain, Sweden, and the United Kingdom.

had prepared themselves for the MFA phaseout and had invested in new technology and machinery, developed broader capabilities, and established direct relationships with buyers. Smaller and subcontracting firms were not well prepared, and several closed in the context of the MFA phaseout. Thus, export growth post-MFA was higher for larger firms than for medium and smaller firms (Rahman, Bhattacharya, and Moazzem 2008).The industry is generally highly concentrated—in 2004, the top 500 firms exported nearly 75 percent of total apparel exports; the top 650, more than 80 percent (World Bank 2005b).

These aggregate numbers also mark important changes in the composition of Bangladesh's apparel exports. In relation to products, the post-MFA export increase was based on knit exports. While knit exports increased by 3 percent in 2005, woven exports declined by 1 percent. Regarding end markets, while exports to the United States, which were previously quota restricted, increased by 21 percent in 2005 (table 8.3), exports to the EU-15 fell by 5 percent from 2004 to 2005 (table 8.4). However, exports to the EU-15 increased again in 2006. Still, from 2004 to 2006, the EU-15 share of Bangladesh's total apparel exports decreased from 64 to 60 percent; the U.S. export share increased from 25 to 29 percent (figure 8.1). The increase in exports to the United States post-MFA can be explained by the lifting of U.S. quotas, because Bangladesh had reached quota limits in several product categories in the U.S. market before the MFA phaseout.

Table 8.2   Bangladeshi Apparel Industry: Factories, Employment, and Share of Total Exports

Year	Number of apparel factories	Employment (million workers)	Share of apparel exports in total exports (%)
1981	—	—	0.4
1982	—	—	1.1
1984	134	0.040	3.9
1985	384	0.115	12.4
1986	594	0.198	16.1
1987	629	0.283	27.7
1988	685	0.306	35.2
1989	725	0.317	36.5
1990	759	0.335	32.5
1991	834	0.402	50.5
1992	1,163	0.582	59.3
1993	1,537	0.804	60.6
1994	1,839	0.827	61.4
1995	2,182	1.200	64.2
1996	2,353	1.290	65.6
1997	2,503	1.300	67.9
1998	2,726	1.500	73.3
1999	2,963	1.500	75.7
2000	3,200	1.600	75.6
2001	3,480	1.800	75.1
2002	3,618	1.800	76.6
2003	3,760	2.000	75.0
2004	3,957	2.000	74.8
2005	4,107	2.000	74.2
2006	4,220	2.200	75.1
2007	4,490	2.400	75.6
2008	4,743	2.800	75.8
2009	4,825	3.100	79.3

Source: Ready-made garment (RMG) factories and employment data from Bangladesh Garment Manufacturers and Exporters Association (BGMEA); share of exports 1984–2009 from BGMEA; 1981 share of exports from Ahmed (2009) and 1982 share of exports from Yunus (2010).
Note: Years refer to fiscal years ending June 30. — = not available. Data for 1983 are unavailable.

The impact of the global economic crisis that started in 2008 but evolved particularly in 2009 has to be assessed together with the phase-out of the China safeguards at the end of 2008. Bangladesh was relatively resilient to the crisis and increased its share in global apparel exports. Looking at import data by Bangladesh's trading partners, total apparel exports increased by 20.4 percent in 2008 and by 5.4 percent in 2009. Bangladesh's share in global apparel trade increased from 3.5 to 4.8 percent between 2007 and 2009 (table 8.1). Apparel exports to the

Table 8.3   U.S. Apparel Imports from Bangladesh

	1996	1998	2001	2004	2005	2006	2007	2008	2009
Total value ($, million)	1,021	1,498	1,930	1,872	2,268	2,809	2,999	3,355	3,345
Annual growth rate (%)	—	13	−1	6	21	24	7	12	0
Share of total U.S. apparel imports (%)	2.7	3.0	3.3	2.8	3.2	3.8	4.0	4.6	5.2
Woven and knit value ($, million)									
Woven	797	1,167	1,450	1,373	1,681	2,075	2,180	2,413	2,497
Knit	224	331	481	499	587	734	819	942	849
Woven and knit share of total import value (%)									
Woven	78	78	75	73	74	74	73	72	75
Knit	22	22	25	27	26	26	27	28	25

Source: United States International Trade Commission (USITC).
Note: Apparel imports represented by Harmonized Commodity Description and Coding System (HS) Codes 61 and 62; General Customs Value; growth rate reflects change from previous year; — = not available.

Table 8.4   EU-15 Apparel Imports from Bangladesh

	1996	1998	2001	2004	2005	2006	2007	2008	2009
Total value (€, million)	1,132	1,635	2,794	3,689	3,509	4,556	4,344	4,667	5,036
Growth rate (%)	—	12	9	20	−5	30	−5	7	8
Share of total EU-15 imports (%)	2.0	2.5	3.4	4.3	3.9	4.6	4.3	4.5	5.1
Woven and knit value (€, million)									
Woven	625	868	1,325	1,522	1,328	1,678	1,499	1,513	1,669
Knit	506	767	1,469	2,167	2,181	2,878	2,845	3,154	3,366
Woven and knit share of total import value (%)									
Woven	55	53	47	41	38	37	35	32	33
Knit	45	47	53	59	62	63	65	68	67

Source: Eurostat.
Note: Apparel imports represented by Harmonized Commodity Description and Coding System (HS) Codes 61 and 62; growth rate reflects change from previous year. EU-15 = the 15 member states of the European Union (EU) as of December 31, 2003, before the new member states joined the EU: Austria, Belgium, Denmark, Finland, France, Germany, Greece, Ireland, Italy, Luxembourg, the Netherlands, Portugal, Spain, Sweden, and the United Kingdom. — = not available.

EU-15 increased by 7 percent in 2008 and 8 percent in 2009 (table 8.4). Apparel exports to the United States increased by 12 percent in 2008 and stagnated in 2009 (table 8.3). Imports to the United States from Bangladesh's competitor countries such as India, Sri Lanka, and Vietnam decreased by 7.4 percent, 17.5 percent, and 2.9 percent, respectively, in 2009. Imports from China, however, increased by 2.5 percent in 2009.

The positive development of Bangladesh's apparel exports post-MFA can be explained by several factors. Bangladeshi firms could better respond to falling prices post-MFA than firms in other countries by squeezing profits and wages and reinforcing relationships with buyers. Thus, Bangladesh remained cost competitive, particularly with its very low labor costs—the lowest of important apparel exporter countries. But Bangladesh's apparel sector has also experienced important restructuring and upgrading with regard to production processes, capabilities, and backward linkages, which reinforced Bangladesh's competitive position. Further, the large share of local ownership in Bangladesh played an important role because production is more locally embedded and local entrepreneurs could not easily shift production to other countries post-MFA. In the context of the global economic crisis, the "Wal-Mart effect" and the "China effect" were cited to explain Bangladesh's positive export development. The "Wal-Mart effect" describes how consumers during a recession substitute more expensive products with cheaper ones offered by discounters such as Wal-Mart. Wal-Mart is the largest buyer of apparel from Bangladesh. While the retail sector has suffered considerably during the crisis, sales by Wal-Mart increased in 2008 and 2009. The "China effect" describes how buyers have shifted orders from China to Bangladesh as Bangladesh has become the world's lowest-cost producer. China had lost some of its competitive edge in the basic apparel market due to the appreciation of its currency, rising labor costs, and labor shortages.

Structure of the Apparel Industry

Types of Firms
Although foreign direct investment (FDI) played a central role in establishing the apparel industry in Bangladesh and acted as a catalyst given its important role through technology and know-how transfer, the industry is now dominated by locally owned firms. Of the 4,220 firms in Bangladesh at the end of 2006, only 83 were wholly or partially foreign owned. Until 2005, FDI was restricted to export processing zones (EPZs), and within EPZs, it was conditional upon associated investment in backward linkage industries (spinning and/or weaving or knitting, dyeing, and finishing). The revised industrial policy in 2005 removed these restrictions, but there is no evidence of any significant FDI outside of the EPZs since the removal (IMF 2008). Aggregate FDI in the textile and apparel sector in EPZs from 1983 to 2006 is estimated at around $500 million, which accounts for around 75 percent of total aggregated investment in

textile and apparel factories in EPZs. Despite the dominance of FDI in EPZs, the vast majority of apparel firms are located outside of EPZs and are locally owned. In 2005, 1 percent of apparel firms operated in EPZs, and around 65 percent of those had foreign ownership (World Bank 2005b).

There have been important changes with regard to functions performed by Bangladesh apparel firms. Ten years ago, the majority of firms were CMT firms. A World Bank study (World Bank 2005b) states that in 2005, two-thirds of apparel firms in Bangladesh were involved in CMT production. Today, an important share of apparel firms can be classified as FOB (free on board) firms. In contrast to CMT, FOB firms are capable of sourcing and financing inputs and providing all production services, finishing, and packaging for delivery to the retail outlet. Being in charge of input sourcing and financing is an important step because input sourcing on suppliers' accounts has become the standard in global sourcing of most buyers. Besides important progress in upgrading from CMT to FOB production, Bangladeshi firms have only made limited progress in developing more advanced capabilities in design and branding. However, some firms, particularly large and foreign-owned firms in EPZs, offer product development and design as well as merchandising and marketing services and work closely with buyers to design and develop products. Some of these firms have also achieved product upgrading and produce more complex and higher-value apparel such as dresses, suits, jackets, and technical apparel. However, the majority of firms have very limited or nonexistent product development, design or marketing, and merchandising capabilities.

End Markets

Bangladesh's apparel exporters are highly concentrated with regard to export markets. The EU-15 and the United States comprise 82.6 percent of Bangladesh's total apparel exports, with the EU-15 accounting for 57.1 percent and the United States for 24.7 percent in 2009 (table 8.5). Woven products mainly go to the U.S. market and knit products mainly to the EU-15. The only other important end markets are Canada (4.4 percent) and Turkey (2.9 percent).

The largest export market—the EU-15—increased its share from 51.0 percent in 2000 to 57.1 percent in 2009. The United States, however, decreased its share from 42.9 percent to 24.7 percent between 2000 and 2009. Canada more than doubled its export share in the same time period, reaching 4.4 percent in 2009. Turkey also increased its

Table 8.5   Top Five Bangladeshi Apparel Export Markets, 1995, 2000, 2005, 2008, and 2009

Country/ region	Customs value ($, million)					Market share (%)				
	1995	2000	2005	2008	2009	1995	2000	2005	2008	2009
World	2,544	4,862	8,026	13,464	14,189					
EU-15	1,355	2,481	4,801	7,823	8,108	53.3	51.0	59.8	58.1	57.1
United States	1,064	2,088	2,422	3,562	3,510	41.8	42.9	30.2	26.5	24.7
Canada	65	101	360	530	619	2.6	2.1	4.5	3.9	4.4
Turkey	n.a.	n.a.	n.a.	339	415	n.a.	n.a.	n.a.	2.5	2.9
Poland	n.a.	n.a.	n.a.	220	278	n.a.	n.a.	n.a.	1.6	2.0
Switzerland	9	36	60	n.a.	n.a.	0.4	0.7	0.8	n.a.	n.a.
Norway	19	n.a.	53	n.a.	n.a.	0.8	n.a.	0.7	n.a.	n.a.
Singapore	n.a.	55	n.a.	n.a.	n.a.	n.a.	1.1	n.a.	n.a.	n.a.
Top five share	2,514	4,760	7,697	12,474	12,930	98.8	97.9	95.9	92.6	91.1

Source: United Nations Commodity Trade Statistics Database (UN Comtrade).
Note: Exports represented by countries' imports. n.a. = not applicable (indicates country not in top 5 in given year). EU-15 = the 15 member states of the European Union (EU) as of December 31, 2003, before the new member states joined the EU: Austria, Belgium, Denmark, Finland, France, Germany, Greece, Ireland, Italy, Luxembourg, the Netherlands, Portugal, Spain, Sweden, and the United Kingdom.

export share, and the rest of the world increased their share from 2.1 percent in 2000 to 8.9 percent in 2009 (figure 8.2).[3]

Export Products

In the 1980s, Bangladesh produced only woven apparel products. But since the early 1990s, Bangladesh has diversified its apparel exports to knit products. In 2004, knit exports accounted for nearly 50 percent; in 2009, for 55 percent. Bangladesh's apparel exports, woven and knit, are highly concentrated in a few products. The top five product categories accounted for 68 percent of total EU-15 apparel exports in 2009 and for 56 percent in the U.S. market; the top 10 product categories for 82 percent and 71 percent, respectively (table 8.6 and table 8.7). Product concentration levels have increased since 2000. The top export product categories to the EU-15 and the United States are overlapping—7 of the top 10 products appear in the EU-15 and the U.S. list. The product concentration of Bangladesh's apparel exports is much higher than of competitor countries such as China and India. In the EU-15 and the U.S. markets, cotton products dominate. Of the top 10 export products to the EU-15, 9 are cotton based, and only 1 is based on man-made fibers (MMF). In the U.S. market, the top 10 products include 8 cotton-based

Figure 8.2   Top Five Bangladeshi Apparel Export Markets, 2000 and 2009
% market share

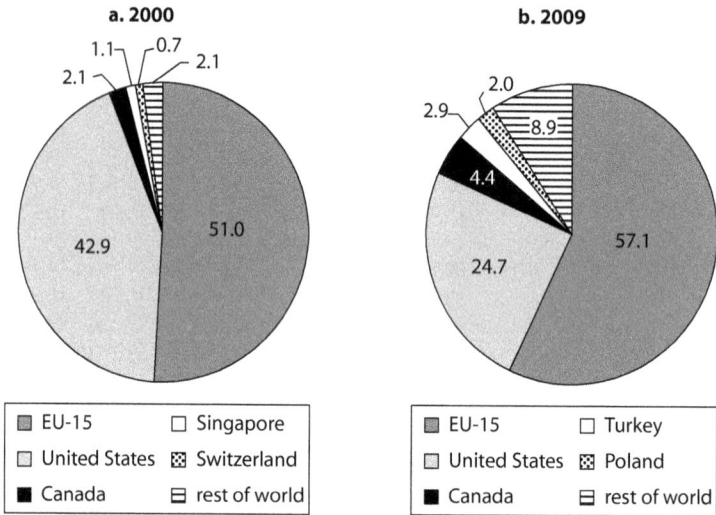

a. 2000

b. 2009

EU-15	Singapore
United States	Switzerland
Canada	rest of world

EU-15	Turkey
United States	Poland
Canada	rest of world

Source: United Nations Commodity Trade Statistics (UN Comtrade).
Note: Exports represented by countries' imports. EU-15 = the 15 member states of the European Union (EU) as of December 31, 2003, before the new member states joined the EU: Austria, Belgium, Denmark, Finland, France, Germany, Greece, Ireland, Italy, Luxembourg, the Netherlands, Portugal, Spain, Sweden, and the United Kingdom.

products and 1 product based on MMF and 1 on synthetics. In the EU-15 market, knit products dominate—7 out of the top 10 export products are knit apparel products, the most important ones being T-shirts and tank tops, sweaters and sweatshirts, and shirts. The most important woven export products are trousers and shorts. In contrast to the EU-15 market, woven products are more important in the U.S. market—6 out of the top 10 products are woven products, the most important ones being trousers and shorts, and shirts. The most important knit products are sweaters and sweatshirts, and T-shirts and tank tops. For both markets, cotton-based products and, for knitwear, T-shirts, sweaters, and shirts and, for woven, trousers are the leading export products.

The unit prices of Bangladesh's main export products are comparatively low, in general lower than the world average. Unit value analysis shows that unit values of apparel exports from China and also India and Sri Lanka are considerably higher for most products than from Bangladesh. In the case of EU-15 exports, a comparison with competitor countries shows that only Pakistan had lower unit values in 2005; Cambodia, China, India, Sri Lanka, and Vietnam account for higher unit values

Table 8.6 Top 10 U.S. Apparel Imports from Bangladesh, 1996, 2000, 2005, 2008, and 2009

HS code	HS description			Customs value ($, million)					Market share (%)				
	Gender	Fiber	Product	1996	2000	2005	2008	2009	1996	2000	2005	2008	2009
Total				**1,021**	**1,942**	**2,268**	**3,355**	**3,345**					
620342	M&B	COT	Trousers	104	184	307	817	890	10.2	9.5	13.6	24.4	26.6
620462	W&G	COT	Trousers	53	148	213	447	464	5.2	7.6	9.4	13.3	13.9
620520	M&B	COT	Shirts	162	236	330	336	320	15.9	12.2	14.6	10.0	9.6
611020	All	COT	Sweaters	n.a.	99	114	202	179	n.a.	5.1	5.0	6.0	5.4
610910	All	COT	T-Shirts	n.a.	n.a.	52	136	127	n.a.	n.a.	2.3	4.1	3.8
620920	Baby	COT	Garments	n.a.	n.a.	n.a.	76	100	n.a.	n.a.	n.a.	2.3	3.0
620343	M&B	SYN	Trousers	34	61	64	84	77	3.3	3.2	2.8	2.5	2.3
620630	W&G	COT	Shirts	57	141	112	68	76	5.6	7.3	4.9	2.0	2.3
620821	W&G	COT	Underwear	n.a.	51	n.a.	101	76	n.a.	2.7	n.a.	3.0	2.3
611030	All	MMF	Sweaters	35	123	84	88	61	3.4	6.3	3.7	2.6	1.8
620193	M&B	MMF	Jackets	51	82	65	n.a.	n.a.	5.0	4.2	2.9	n.a.	n.a.
620293	W&G	MMF	Jackets	32	49	n.a.	n.a.	n.a.	3.1	2.5	n.a.	n.a.	n.a.
620530	M&B	MMF	Shirts	n.a.	n.a.	50	n.a.	n.a.	n.a.	n.a.	2.2	n.a.	n.a.
621142	W&G	COT	Garments	36	n.a.	n.a.	n.a.	n.a.	3.5	n.a.	n.a.	n.a.	n.a.
610510	M&B	COT	Shirts	36	n.a.	n.a.	n.a.	n.a.	3.5	n.a.	n.a.	n.a.	n.a.
Top 10 share				**600**	**1,174**	**1,391**	**2,355**	**2,370**	**58.6**	**60.6**	**61.3**	**70.2**	**70.8**

Source: United States International Trade Commission (USITC).

Note: U.S. imports from Bangladesh by General Customs Value; top 10 determined by top 10 customs values in each year; n.a. = not applicable (indicates product not in the top 10 in given year); — = not available. Harmonized Commodity Description and Coding System (HS) numbers beginning with 61 indicate knitted garments and 62 indicate nonknitted (woven) garments. M&B = men and boys; W&G = women and girls; All = all genders; COT = cotton; SYN = synthetic; MMF = man-made fiber.

Table 8.7 Top 10 EU-15 Apparel Imports from Bangladesh, 1996, 2000, 2005, 2008, and 2009

HS Code	HS Description Gender	Fiber	Product	Customs value ($, million) 1996	2000	2005	2008	2009	Market share (%) 1996	2000	2005	2008	2009
Total				**1,474**	**2,567**	**3,509**	**4,667**	**5,036**					
610910	All	COT	T-Shirts	269	565	861	1,269	1,307	18.3	22.0	24.5	27.2	26.0
611020	All	COT	Sweaters	26	93	340	626	689	1.7	3.6	9.7	13.4	13.7
620342	M&B	COT	Trousers	48	258	438	571	648	3.3	10.1	12.5	12.2	12.9
611030	All	MMF	Sweaters	110	346	544	449	448	7.5	13.5	15.5	9.6	8.9
620462	W&G	COT	Trousers	24	115	273	295	301	1.6	4.5	7.8	6.3	6.0
610510	M&B	COT	Shirts	23	103	128	219	229	1.6	4.0	3.7	4.7	4.6
620520	M&B	COT	Shirts	197	228	180	198	227	13.4	8.9	5.1	4.2	4.5
610610	W&G	COT	Shirts	n.a.	n.a.	n.a.	89	94	n.a.	n.a.	n.a.	1.9	1.9
610462	W&G	COT	Trousers	n.a.	n.a.	n.a.	77	117	n.a.	n.a.	n.a.	1.7	2.3
611120	Babies	COT	Garments	n.a.	n.a.	n.a.	n.a.	79	n.a.	n.a.	n.a.	n.a.	1.6
620530	M&B	MMF	Shirts	145	185	104	78	n.a.	9.8	7.2	3.0	1.7	n.a.
620343	M&B	SYN	Trousers	n.a.	n.a.	52	n.a.	n.a.	n.a.	n.a.	1.5	n.a.	n.a.
620463	W&G	SYN	Trousers	n.a.	53	46	n.a.	n.a.	n.a.	2.1	1.3	n.a.	n.a.
620193	M&B	MMF	Jackets	50	65	n.a.	n.a.	n.a.	3.4	2.5	n.a.	n.a.	n.a.
620293	W&G	MMF	Jackets	40	n.a	n.a	n.a	n.a	2.7	n.a.	n.a.	n.a.	n.a.
Top 10 share				**932**	**2,011**	**2,966**	**3,871**	**4,139**	**63.2**	**78.3**	**84.5**	**83.0**	**82.2**

Source: Eurostat.

Note: Top 10 determined by top 10 values in each year; n.a. = not available (indicates product not in the top 10 in given year); — = not applicable. Harmonized Commodity Description and Coding System (HS) numbers beginning with 61 indicate knitted garments and 62 indicate nonknitted (woven) garments. M&B = men and boys; W&G = women and girls; All = all genders; COT = cotton; SYN = synthetic; MMF = man-made fiber. EU-15 = the 15 member states of the European Union (EU) as of December 31, 2003, before the new member states joined the EU: Austria, Belgium, Denmark, Finland, France, Germany, Greece, Ireland, Italy, Luxembourg, the Netherlands, Portugal, Spain, Sweden, and the United Kingdom.

(Tewari 2008). This fact is related to Bangladesh being cost competitive but also to being concentrated in basic products, while these other countries export higher-value products. Figure 8.3 shows the development of unit prices for knit and woven exports. Average unit prices decreased significantly in 2001–02, a development related to China's entry to the World Trade Organization (WTO). Also, post-MFA unit prices continued to decline. Between 2004 and 2007, the average price of exporter apparel fell from $2.60 to $2.31 per unit, representing a decline of 11 percent over three years. Average unit prices for woven fell from $3.26 to $2.92 and for knit from $1.95 to $1.90 for the same time period, accounting for declines of 10 percent and 3 percent, respectively. Between 2007 and 2009, the average price of apparel exports fell from $2.31 to $2.23 per unit, representing a decline of over 3 percent over two years. Average unit prices for woven fell from $2.92 to $2.91 and for knit from $1.90 to $1.84 for the same time period, accounting for declines of 0.3 percent and 3.0 percent, respectively. Thus, in contrast to the post-MFA period, the downward price pressure was more evident in the knitted apparel segment after the global financial crisis in 2008/09.

Backward Linkages

Bangladesh's apparel sector is almost self-sufficient in accessories and support services. Local sources are able to meet about 80 percent of the

Figure 8.3   Average Unit Values of Bangladeshi Woven and Knit Apparel Exports

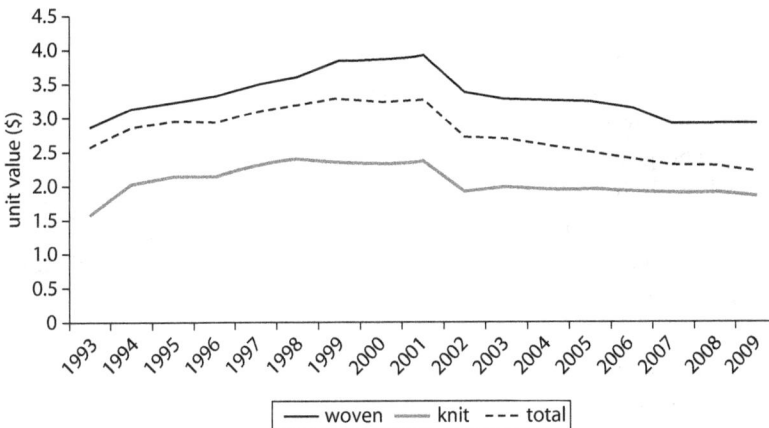

Sources: Until 2007 from Bangladesh Garment Manufacturers and Exporters Association (BGMEA); also included in DOT (2009) until 2008.
Note: Unit values calculated.

domestic apparel industry's demand for apparel accessories such as thread, buttons, labels, bags, tapes, shirt board, and cartons (Saheed 2008). But Bangladesh's apparel sector relies on imported fabric and yarn inputs because the local textile industry is unable to supply its requirement in terms of quality, quantity, and variety. Important developments have, however, taken place in the local textile sector, and there are differences between the woven and knit segments. Bangladesh has a well-established supply chain for knitted apparel. Domestic suppliers can fulfill 85–90 percent of the fabrics required and 75 percent of the yarn required for knit exports (Knowles, Reyes, and Jackson 2008; DOT 2009). A dyeing and finishing sector has also emerged to support the knit industry. However, despite the fact that the woven apparel industry emerged nearly a decade before the knit industry, the domestic woven fabric industry is not as developed as the knit fabric industry. Woven fabric manufacturers can only supply about 25 percent of the requirement needs for the woven apparel sector (DOT 2009); however, this percentage has increased since 2007, when the local industry could only supply 15 percent (Saheed 2008). Both knit and woven fabric mills are nearly exclusively involved in cotton-based fabrics; the production of man-made fabrics is very limited in Bangladesh. Cotton is almost completely imported because there is no local cotton industry. As a result of increasing backward linkages, particularly in knit, the value of cotton imports has increased more rapidly than the value of textile imports (Arnold 2010).

The different situation with regard to local linkages in the knit and woven fabric industries can be explained by different investment requirements. A knit fabric mill, including a dyeing and finishing unit of a viable minimum economic size, requires an investment of at least $3.5 million, while the investment required for a similar factory for woven fabric production amounts to at least $35.0 million (World Bank 2005b; Ahmed 2009). The government granted cash incentives in 1994 for exports of apparel made from locally produced yarn and fabric, which encouraged investments in composite knitting mills and spinning (World Bank 2005b). Other incentives that encouraged investment in the knit textile industry included low (subsidized) interest rates and government support in terms of investment in land development, power, and infrastructure. Because of the larger costs of investments in woven mills, a similar development did not happen in the woven segment. However, more recently, investment in the woven textile industry has also increased, in particular through FDI and in integrated spinning and weaving mills, but the remaining demand-and-supply gap is still large.

Table 8.8 compares domestic to total fabric consumption in the export-oriented apparel sector between 1998 and 2008. Domestic fabrics accounted for less than 20 percent of total fabric consumption in 1998; this share increased to over 50 percent in 2004 and to 71 percent in 2008. Table 8.9 shows the domestic production of yarn and fabric between 1973 and 2008. Although Bangladesh is not a cotton-growing country, it increased the production of yarn from 39 million kilograms in 1973 to 710 million kilograms in 2008 (18 times higher). Similarly, production of fabrics for domestic and export markets increased from 702 million meters in 1973 to 5,800 million meters in 2008 (12 times higher). However, an important part of this fabric is used for the domestic market (World Bank 2005b).

During the second half of 2007, the apparel sector opened L/C for the purchase of machinery valued at $200 million and the textile sector for $236 million, amounting to a total of $436 million (Saheed 2008). In the apparel sector, firms have invested in new computerized cutting and spreading machinery, high-quality sewing machines, and barcode-enabled inventory management systems to improve the production process, increase productivity, and keep prices low. In the textile sector, there has been a trend toward modernization through the adoption of new technology and the installation of advanced production facilities. In the woven fabric sector, deliveries of shuttleless looms to Asian mills increased by 47 percent in 2009. This surge was led by Bangladesh and China, which accounted for 19.4 percent and 59.0 percent, respectively, of total shipments in 2009 (*Just-style* 2010a). Bangladesh has also significantly increased purchases of machinery for knitted fabric production in recent years. In 2008 and 2009, Bangladesh ranked between second and fourth place in shipments of single and double jersey circular knitting machinery. It is the number one importer of hand knitting and semiautomatic flat knitting machinery, accounting for over half of global imports of such machinery. With regard to the spinning industry, Bangladesh was the third-largest purchaser of spindles in 2007 (behind China and India), and the third- and fourth-largest purchaser of short-staple spindles in 2008 and 2009, respectively (Saheed 2008).

With regard to imports in 2009, more than half of imported textile inputs came from China (59.5 percent). The next most important suppliers include India (11.6 percent); Hong Kong SAR, China (9.2 percent); Pakistan (8.4 percent); and Thailand (3.2 percent) (table 8.10).[4] Intraregional (South Asia) trade in textile inputs has increased in recent years. For Bangladesh, regional textile imports accounted for 20 percent

Table 8.8 Bangladeshi Domestic Production and Consumption of Fabrics, 1998–2008

	Availability of fabric in the domestic market (meters, million)			Fabric consumed by export-oriented RMG industry (meters, million)				Domestic consumption for local market (meters, million)[a]
Fiscal year	Domestic production	Imports (official and unofficial)	Total available	Woven	Knit	Total	Use of domestic production (%)[a]	
1998[b]	1,356	—	—	—	—	—	18	—
1999[b]	1,424	—	—	—	—	—	23	—
2000[b]	1,599	—	—	—	—	—	29	—
2001	1,800	—	—	—	—	—	33	—
2002	2,050	598	2,648	240	718	958	38	1,690
2003	2,200	686	2,966	301	833	1,134	40	1,832
2004	2,750	683	3,433	334	1,154	1,488	54	1,945
2005	3,400	725	4,057	375	1,621	1,996	64	2,061
2006	4,090	985	5,075	504	2,365	2,869	66	2,260
2007	4,910	1,130	6,040	631	2,945	3,576	68	2,464
2008	5,800	1,240	7,040	711	3,587	4,298	71	2,742

Source: DOT 2009.

Note: RMG = ready-made garment; — = not available.

a. Use of domestic textile production in the export-oriented industry is calculated as 1 − (textile imports/total textile use). We assume that the large majority of textile imports are used for export production.

b. Figures for 1998–2001 are from Gherzi et al. 2002 and Bangladesh Textile Mills Association (BTMA) Annual Report 2004, cited in World Bank 2005b.

Table 8.9   Bangladeshi Domestic Production of Yarn and Fabrics, 1973–2008

Fiscal year	Yarn production (kg, million)	Fabric production (meters, million)
1973	39	702
1984	67	983
1994	140	1048
1998[a]	213	1356
1999[a]	229	1424
2000[a]	251	1599
2001[a]	252	1800
2002	298	2,050
2003	340	2,200
2004	380	2,750
2005	450	3,400
2006	537	4,090
2007	594	4,910
2008	710	5,800

Source: DOT 2009.
Note: kg = kilogram.
a. Figures for 1998–2001 are from Gherzi et al. 2002 and Bangladesh Textile Mills Association (BTMA) Annual Report 2004, cited in World Bank 2005b.

Table 8.10   Top 10 Textile Suppliers to Bangladesh, 1995, 2000, 2005, 2008, and 2009

Country/ economy/ region	Customs value ($, million)					Market share (%)				
	1995	2000	2005	2008	2009	1995	2000	2005	2008	2009
World	**1,343**	**1,549**	**2,442**	**3,542**	**3,081**					
China	224	465	1,176	1,983	1,832	16.7	30.0	48.2	56.0	59.5
India	287	213	281	526	356	21.3	13.7	11.5	14.9	11.6
Hong Kong SAR, China	353	309	370	355	284	26.3	19.9	15.2	10.0	9.2
Pakistan	76	n.a.	172	282	260	5.7	n.a.	7.1	8.0	8.4
Thailand	n.a.	n.a.	n.a.	97	99	n.a.	n.a.	n.a.	2.7	3.2
Korea, Rep.	255	274	134	n.a.	n.a.	19.0	17.7	5.5	n.a.	n.a.
Indonesia	n.a.	76	n.a.	n.a.	n.a.	n.a.	4.9	n.a.	n.a.	n.a.
Top five share	**1,195**	**1,337**	**2,133**	**3,243**	**2,832**	**88.9**	**86.3**	**87.4**	**91.6**	**91.9**

Source: United Nations Commodity Trade Statistics Database (UN Comtrade).
Note: SITC Standard International Trade Classification 65 Rev3; n.a. = not applicable (indicates country not in top 5 in given year).

of total textile imports in 2009, which increased from 18 percent in 2000. India is the largest regional textile supplier, accounting for 11.6 percent of total textile imports, followed by Pakistan with 8.4 percent in 2009.

Employment

Employment levels in Bangladesh's apparel sector increased significantly, from a little more than 100,000 in 1985 to 3.1 million workers in 2009 (figure 8.4). There was no negative employment growth rate over the whole period, only years when employment levels stagnated, namely, 1999, 2002, 2004, and 2005. A recent study by the Bangladesh Department of Textiles (DOT) identified 4.2 million employees in the textile and apparel industry in 2009 (DOT 2009). Employees were split into three categories: textile technologists, nontechnical workers, and general workers. General workers constitute 93 percent of all workers, making this the largest category, with 3.9 million workers. The distribution of employment per subsector shows the importance of the apparel sector, which accounts for 3.1 million workers, including 2.5 million in the ready-made garment (RMG) segment and nearly 600,000 in the sweater segment, representing together 74 percent of total workers in textile- and apparel-related sectors. The knitting industry accounts for 12.0 percent of total employment, spinning for 5.8 percent, dyeing for 2.4 percent, weaving for 2.4 percent, and the power loom segment for 1.2 percent (table 8.11).

Figure 8.4   Employment in the Bangladeshi Apparel Sector

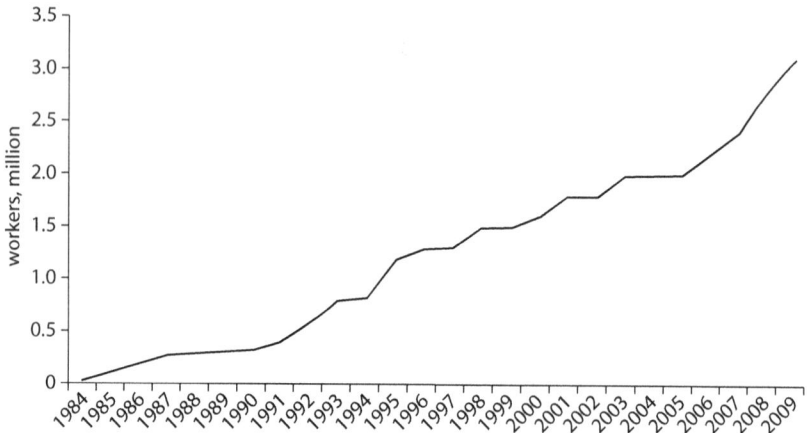

Source: Bangladesh Garment Manufacturers and Exporters Association (BGMEA).
Note: Years refer to fiscal years ending June 30.

Table 8.11 Bangladeshi Textile and Apparel Workers, by Subsector and Type

Subsectors	Textile technologists Employees (#)	Share (%)	Nontechnical persons Employees (#)	Share (%)	General workers Employees (#)	Share (%)	Total employees (#)
Spinning	1,595	0.6	17,678	7.2	226,536	92.2	245,809
Weaving	291	0.3	9,640	9.6	90,792	90.1	100,723
Composite	103	0.7	2,088	14.7	12,036	84.6	14,227
Power loom	6	0.0	17,048	34.4	32,482	65.6	49,536
Knitting industry	1,054	0.2	33,583	6.4	486,173	93.3	520,810
Terry towel	72	0.4	1,546	8.4	16,886	91.3	18,504
Dyeing (mechanized)	980	1.0	9,442	9.2	92,675	89.9	103,097
Dyeing (semimechanized)	326	0.9	1,868	4.9	35,943	94.2	38,137
Synthetic yarn	18	0.2	1,022	13.1	6,741	86.6	7,781
Sewing thread	2	0.1	475	15.0	2,689	84.9	3,166
Silk industry	12	0.3	549	14.6	3,201	85.1	3,762
Sweater industry	161	0.0	37,620	6.3	559,739	93.7	597,520
RMG industries	438	0.0	128,525	5.1	2,374,559	94.8	2,503,522
Textile education/training	390	37.5	650	62.5	0	0.0	1,040
Buying house	102	0.5	20,557	99.5	0	0.0	20,659
Other organization	94	100.0	0	0.0	0	0.0	94
Total	**5,644**	**0.1**	**282,291**	**6.7**	**3,940,452**	**93.2**	**4,228,387**

Source: DOT 2009.
Note: RMG = ready-made garment.

With regard to the gender distribution of employment, it is widely stated that more than 90 percent of apparel workers were women in the 1980s and 1990s. The female employment share has, however, decreased since the 1990s. According to the Census of Manufacturing Industries (CMI) 1999–2000, female employment accounted for 66.5 percent of total apparel industry employment in 1999. In the 2000s, the share of female employment further declined, reaching 62 percent for the RMG sector and 42 percent for the sweater subsector, and only slightly above 50 percent for all textile- and apparel-related sectors in 2009. Women accounted for 54 percent of the total general workforce in textile- and apparel-related sectors in 2009. The highest share of female workers is found in the RMG and the spinning segments, where women constitute 62 percent and 51 percent of workers, respectively. In all other subsectors, women constitute less than 50 percent of the workforce (table 8.12). However, this figure is still very high compared to the average female share in manufacturing of 35 percent. The changing female intensity of employment is related to changes in the composition of apparel exports from woven to knit. The woven segment employs mostly women workers, and the knit segment—and even more the sweater segment—mostly men.

With regard to average labor costs per hour, Bangladesh accounted for the lowest labor costs in a comparison with competitor countries in 2008.

Table 8.12   Bangladeshi Apparel General Workers: Male and Female Workers by Subsector, 2009

Subsector	General workers (#)		Share of workforce (%)		Total general workers (#)
	Male	Female	Male	Female	
Spinning	110,070	116,466	49	51	226,536
Weaving	70,395	20,397	78	22	90,792
Composite	6,816	5,220	57	43	12,036
Power loom	28,885	3,597	89	11	32,482
Knitting industry	261,849	224,324	54	46	486,173
Terry towel	9,936	6,950	59	41	16,886
Dyeing (mechanized)	64,582	28,093	70	30	92,675
Dyeing (semi-mechanized)	21,531	14,412	60	40	35,943
Synthetic yarn	4,109	2,632	61	39	6,741
Sewing thread	2,003	686	74	26	2,689
Silk industry	1,791	1,410	56	44	3,201
Sweater industry	324,017	235,722	58	42	559,739
RMG industries	894,299	1,480,260	38	62	2,374,559
Total	**1,800,283**	**2,140,169**	**46**	**54**	**3,940,452**

Source: DOT 2009.
Note: RMG = ready-made garment.

Average apparel labor costs per hour in 2008 were $0.22; in comparison, rates in India were more than twice as high and four times higher in China (Jassin-O'Rourke Group 2008). The minimum wage accounted for Tk 1,662 ($24) in 2008, which was increased to Tk 3,000 ($43) in November 2010 as a reaction to widespread labor unrest (*Just-style* 2010b). The increased wage is still among the lowest in the world. However, low wages are accompanied by relatively low levels of labor productivity. Average annual value addition per worker in Bangladesh was estimated at $2,500 compared to nearly $7,000 for a group of similar Chinese factories in 2005 (World Bank 2005a). But even after adjusting for productivity differences across countries, Bangladesh's apparel industry retains a significant per unit labor cost advantage (World Bank 2005b).

A critical reason for the relatively low productivity in Bangladesh's apparel sector is the lack of skills among workers, supervisors, and managers. With regard to production workers, the skill gap is estimated at 25 percent at the operator level, which translates into around 500,000 missing skilled operators (given that, of the 3.1 million workers in the apparel sector, there are around 2.0 million operators)(Bangladesh Garment Manufacturers and Exporters Association [BGMEA]). The skill gap is particularly high in the area of middle management and technical and design or fashion skills such as pattern masters, product developers, designers, textile engineers, production managers, or merchandising and marketing professionals. These skills are critical for diversification of production and upgrading to higher-value products and activities. No specific estimates are available for the skill gap in these professions. However, the Ministry of Labor estimates that around 17,000 foreigners work in the apparel industry in Bangladesh to cover part of that gap (Elmer 2010). These expatriates are mostly technically experienced workers from China; India; Korea; Pakistan; the Philippines; Sri Lanka; Taiwan, China; and Turkey (BGMEA). The skill gap in the apparel sector is related to the rapid expansion of apparel exports and to capacity and supply limitations in the skill development and training system in Bangladesh.

Bangladesh has had a bad record with regard to labor compliance in the apparel sector. Wages and working conditions have long been a source of concern, as can be seen in frequent strikes and labor unrest in Bangladesh's apparel sector. The labor protests in summer 2010 marked an escalation in apparel industry violence (*Just-style* 2010c). The most common labor issues in Bangladesh's apparel sector are low wages, lack of appointment letters, long working hours, lack of holidays, late payment, no maternity leave, and no dormitories for workers. Government investigations found that 30 percent of factories are noncompliant. Also, over

90 percent of the factories claiming to be compliant have one or more problematic conditions, including delays in promotion and pay raises after training entry-level workers, irregular or reduced pay, low overtime benefits, long working hours, poor working conditions, absence of paid leave and medical facilities, absence of maternity benefits, absence of occupational safety and protection, absence of conveyance and housing, and neglect of trade unionism and labor laws (*Just-style* 2010c).

A main issue with regard to labor compliance is low wages. Although Bangladesh has had a minimum wage since 1994, there is no mechanism that adjusts it to inflation and other macroeconomic changes, and there had been no adjustments until October 2006. Responding to labor unrest, the government announced a minimum wage increase from Tk 930 ($16) in 1994 to Tk 1,662 in 2006 ($24),[5] but this wage still falls short of living wage estimates, particularly in a context of persistently high inflation driven by food prices. Protestors in 2010 demanded minimum wages to be raised to Tk 5,000 ($72) a month, which was reduced from initial demands of Tk 6,200 ($89). Also, a group of global buyers, motivated by fears that sweatshop allegations could taint their reputations as socially responsible companies, sent a letter to the Bangladeshi prime minister in February 2010 stating that "swift action" was needed to tackle the problem. In July 2010, the Bangladesh Ministry of Labor and Employment agreed to increase the minimum wage to Tk 3,000 ($43) per month as of October 31, 2010, an increase of 80 percent (*Just-style* 2010b). This increase was based on recommendations of the Minimum Wage Board, which includes representatives from the government, industry, and workers.[6] It is estimated that this wage increase will add 7 percent to the production costs of apparel producers (*Just-style* 2010b). However, the new wage falls short of the $75 per month that workers are demanding, and it remains to be seen whether it will be enough to end labor unrest. Trade unions and campaigners expressed disappointment at the scale of the proposed increase.

Several other steps taken to address working conditions in Bangladesh have led to improvements in labor compliance since the 1990s. BGMEA and the Bangladesh Knitwear Manufacturers and Exporters Association (BKMEA) have taken initiatives to monitor workers' rights in factories, but on a very limited scale. Twenty counselors work for BGMEA, which is a very small number for an industry with nearly 5,000 firms. BGMEA has worked with the International Labour Organization (ILO), the United Nations Development Programme (UNDP), the German Technical Corporation (GTZ), and the EU toward meeting social compliance requirements in its member factories. The Ministry of Commerce has taken the initiative to form a National Forum on Social Compliance in the Textile and Garment Industry, along with issue-based Task Forces on Social Compliance and a Compliance Monitoring Cell (World Bank 2005b). These initiatives were later replaced by the Social Compliance Forum for RMG, instituted in the Ministry of Commerce; the Compliance Monitoring Cell, instituted in the Export Promotion Bureau, works under the Forum. The most comprehensive program has been implemented in EPZs since 2005, against international pressure, particularly aggressive lobbying by the American Federation of Labor and Congress of Industrial Organizations (AFL-CIO), and financed by the World Bank, and it has led to significant progress in monitoring and enforcing labor standards in EPZ firms. Around 60 counselors are appointed by the Bangladesh Export Processing Zone Authority (BEPZA) to work in the eight EPZs and prepare monthly reports on compliance for every factory. The counselors work in teams of two, and each team is responsible for around 10 factories, which they visit on a daily or weekly basis. They provide orientation to management with respect to compliance, raise awareness among workers, support the establishing of workers' associations,[7] monitor social compliance, and arbitrate between workers and management in cases of disputes. This program has worked effectively in the EPZ context, but it is questionable how this limited program can be extended to the whole sector in Bangladesh given the Department of Labor's limited resources for an adequate number of inspectors and enforcement options compared to EPZ authorities.

Trade Regulations and Proactive Policies

Preferential Market Access
Bangladesh enjoys preferential market access to the EU through the GSP, which has provided quota-free and tariff-free access to the EU market since the early 1980s and since 2001 through the EBA (Everything but Arms) initiative. This system contributed to the growth of exports to the EU and made the EU the largest export destination of Bangladeshi apparel products. Preferential market access to the EU, however, requires the fulfillment of double transformation rules of origin (ROO), which could not be fulfilled by all apparel exports, in particular woven products. Currently only around half of the apparel exports to the EU use preferential market access facilities. The utilization rate varies between knit and woven apparel, accounting for around 90 percent for knit exports and only for 16 percent for woven exports. However, Bangladesh

qualified for GSP+ status in the EU market in January 2011. With this development, the ROO changed from double to single transformation for least developed countries (LDCs), including Bangladesh, in January 2011. Bangladesh also enjoys duty-free market access to Australia, Canada, Japan, New Zealand, and Norway. In Japan, the ROO concerning its GSP changed in April 2011 from triple to double transformation for knit products (Harmonized Commodity Description and Coding System [HS] Code 61) from Bangladesh. In the U.S. market, however, Bangladesh faces most favored nation (MFN) tariffs.

At the regional level, there exists a multitude of regional cooperation and trade agreements under various stages of implementation in South Asia, the most important one being the South Asian Association for Regional Cooperation (SAARC).[8] However, despite these regional integration efforts, the potential for regional trade and investment in the apparel and textile sectors still remains largely unused. The limited efforts in regional integration can be seen in the rejection of the regional cumulation in ROO stipulations that the EU offered in the context of SAARC in 1995 and 2001. In India, Bangladesh benefits from a duty-free export quota of 8 million pieces. However, Bangladesh has not used the whole quota. In 2009, only half of the quota was used because of the existence of nontariff barriers, including high specific duties.

Proactive Policies

Institutions and policies at various national levels have been crucial in the development of Bangladesh's apparel sector. Generally, the government and the industry associations have been very active in supporting the apparel and textile sectors. International institutions have had an important role in funding and implementing policies related to infrastructure but most important, skill development, often in cooperation with the government or industry associations.

In the context of the MFA phaseout, projects to support the apparel and textile sectors increased on different levels. In 2003, the Ministry of Commerce commissioned a report (from the industry consultant firm Gherzi) to identify the strengths and weaknesses of the apparel sector and to identify areas of improvement for increasing productivity. The report made 14 strategic recommendations relating to human resource development, infrastructure development, and governance (BIDS 2011). To design a policy strategy, the government formed a National Coordination Council (NCC) in 2004. The NCC produced a report in 2005 with recommendations for implementation (table 8.13). These recommendations were approved

Table 8.13   Apparel- and Textile-Specific Projects in Post-MFA Bangladesh

National Coordination Council (NCC)

Sponsor: Government;
timeline: 2005–15

Recommendations for implementation:

- Enterprise debt-to-equity ratios should be fixed at 70/30 or any rate considered favorable.
- Weaving, dyeing, and finishing sector investments should be given priority to bank loans.
- Textile investment interest rates should be fixed at 9% by state-owned and private banks.
- Currency conversion rates (U.S. dollar and taka) for exported products should be restricted within a maximum range of 50 paisa.
- Imported spare parts/machinery, dyes, chemicals, and sizing materials used in the textile sector should be available duty and tax free.
   ◦ Customs duties on imported textile fibers, yarns, and fabrics have been reduced from five levels (0%, 5%, 15%, 25%, and 37.5%) to four levels (0%, 5%, 12%, and 25%). Import duties on textile machinery, the majority of spares and accessories, dyes, chemicals, and raw cotton have been reduced to zero.
- In lieu of duty drawback and bond facilities, cash assistance rates should increase to 10%.
- Technical skill shortages in the textile sector should be addressed by (i) setting up more technical and vocational institutes; (ii) upgrading the Bangladesh College of Textile Engineering and Technology (CTET) to a textile university; (iii) opening textile facilities in all technical universities; and (iv) including textiles as a subject in the curriculum of all technical schools, colleges, and technical institutes.
- Textiles and apparel should be the priority sector for establishing high-tech industrial parks, apparel villages, and export processing zones (EPZs), all with the necessary infrastructural facilities.
- The scheme for tax holidays should be continued.
- Environmental protection should be encouraged and achieved by setting up effluent treatment plants (ETPs) facilitated by duty-free provision of equipment/parts, low-interest bank loans, formation of a committee from government departments and associations to encourage clustering of industrial regions, and value added tax (VAT) exemptions for electricity and gas charges, together with carriage, freight, and insurance.

(continued next page)

Table 8.13 *(continued)*

Government Post-MFA Action Program (PMAP)

Sponsor: Government, Ministry of Commerce (MOC); timeline: 2005–10

Program components:

- Skill and Quality Development Program (SQDP): Training is given in several areas, such as compliance, quality management, and marketing, in order to improve the performance of the sector; to target about 22,000 workers.
- Displaced Workers Rehabilitation Program (DWRP): to assist and retrain those who might lose their jobs ($15 million).
- Small Enterprise Capacity Enhancement Program (SECEP): This has two subcomponents—(i) to assist capacity enhancement of smaller producers by helping them form strategic partnerships, mergers, and productivity improvement programs; and (ii) a Technological Capacity Development Program to help small and medium enterprizes (SMEs) in the apparel and textile sector to access improved technology to enhance their competitiveness ($3 million).
- Support and capacity building in the primary textile sector (PTS) to improve quality and reduce costs ($4 million).
- Support to the handloom sector to make it more competitive by setting up separate design and development centers for both handloom and PTS ($4 million).
- Support to Forward Linkage Industries (SFLI) to enable them to provide better service to the apparel sector, including trade facilitation as well as marketing tools.
- Support to New Market Opportunity (SNMO).

Bangladeshi Government Support Measures

Sponsor: Government; start: 2006

Support measures:

- Provision of bonded warehouse facilities.
- Technological upgrading (concessional duty rates and tax exemptions for the import of capital machinery).
- Cash subsidies for the use of local fabrics as inputs for exporting apparel firms.
- Export Credit Guarantee Scheme covering risk on export credits at home and commercial and political risks occurring abroad.

- Support of market promotion efforts of apparel exporters.
- Subsidies for utility charges.
- Market Diversification: Bangladesh and India MOU (Memorandum of Understanding) allows Bangladesh to export 8 million pieces of Bangladesh-produced garments to India duty free per year. This is a small amount in the total exports, but it is viewed as a means to begin to reduce dependence on the traditional U.S. and EU markets.
- Apparel exporters receive small cash incentives for exports to new destinations (outside of the EU, the United States, and Canada) in the period 2009 to 2012.

BGMEA Strategy to Increase Apparel Exports

Sponsor: BGMEA;
timeline: 2008–13

BGMEA persuades domestic manufacturers to do the following:

- Increase labor productivity
- Diversify product lines and export markets
- Invest in research and development and human resources
- Place renewed emphasis on product quality
- Strengthen CSR (Corporate Social Responsibility) policies

The strategy also involves lobbying the government to improve domestic infrastructure—including gas, electricity, and roads—and implement policies to encourage domestic and foreign investment in the textile and apparel industries. BGMEA also supports efforts to enter new markets by sending missions to South Africa and Brazil and inviting missions from Japan.

Sources: Saheed 2008, Adhikari and Weeratunge 2007, World Bank 2005b, BIDS 2011.
Note: BGMEA = Bangladesh Garment Manufacturers and Exporters Association.

by the government and have been the core policy guidelines for the over-all development of the sectors in the post-MFA era (from 2005 to 2015).

The Ministry of Commerce prepared a five-year Post-MFA Action Program (PMAP) of $40 million to support the apparel sector in the context of the quota phaseout in early 2004. The objective of this strategic program was to help the industry retain its existing market shares as well as to expand markets in the post-MFA period through implementation of several activities under six different components (table 8.13). However, not all initiatives materialized, largely because of lack of support from donors (BIDS 2011).

Beginning in 2006, the Bangladeshi government took additional support measures to bolster the apparel sector. For instance, the government allotted Tk 200 million ($2.89 million) to fund training programs for productivity improvement of workers The BGMEA has also provided support to apparel firms in the context of its strategy to increase apparel exports. Table 8.13 gives an overview of these post-MFA recommendations and measures.

Notes

1. The EU-15 is the 15 member states of the European Union (EU) as of December 31, 2003, before the new member states joined the EU: Austria, Belgium, Denmark, Finland, France, Germany, Greece, Ireland, Italy, Luxembourg, the Netherlands, Portugal, Spain, Sweden, and the United Kingdom.

2. This section is partly based on Staritz (2011).

3. The Bangladesh Garment Manufacturers and Exporters Association (BGMEA) reports that, in 2009, Bangladesh exported apparel products worth $240 million to Turkey, $82 million to Mexico, $49 million to Australia, $43 million to South Africa, and $40 million to Brazil. Exports to Japan more than doubled, to $74 million (World Bank 2010). But despite these promising developments, exports to these markets remain marginal.

4. Taiwan, China, is also an important textile supplier, but data on Taiwanese imports are not reported in the United Nations Commodity Trade Statistics Database (UN Comtrade).

5. Since 1982, EPZs have been under different labor laws that are known as Instructions 1 and 2. In the EPZ, the minimum wage for workers in the apparel sector is $30, but the average wage paid is generally higher.

6. Factory owners, represented by the BGMEA, only agreed to the minimum wage raise if it was underpinned by a series of benefits to support their businesses, including 120 days' delayed implementation of the new wages,

the withdrawal of their advance income tax and value added tax (VAT), reduced charges for utility and port services, lower bank interest rates, and the creation of a $70 million fund to build dormitories for workers (*Just-style* 2010d).

7. A problem, however, is that these workers' associations lack some trade union rights and are not connected to outside unions. Thus, they do not fulfill the core labor standards of the ILO.

8. These agreements include the South Asian Association for Regional Cooperation (SAARC); the South Asian Preferential Trading Agreement (SAPTA); the Bay of Bengal Initiative for Multi-Sectoral Economic Cooperation (BIMSTEC), involving Bangladesh, Bhutan, India, Myanmar, Nepal, Sri Lanka, and Thailand; and, since 2004, the South Asian Free Trade Agreement (SAFTA).

References

Adhikari, R., and C. Weeratunge. 2007. "Textiles and Clothing Sector in South Asia: Coping with Post-quota Challenges." In *South Asian Yearbook of Trade and Development 2006—Multilateralism at Cross-roads: Reaffirming Development Priorities*, ed. B. S. Chimni, B. L. Das, Saman Kelegama, and M. Rahman, 109–47. New Delhi: Centre for Trade and Development and Wiley India.

Ahmed, Nazneen. 2009. "Sustaining Ready-made Garment Exports from Bangladesh." *Journal of Contemporary Asia* 39 (4): 597–618.

Arnold, John. 2010. "Effects of Trade Logistics on the Strategy of the Garments Industry for Product and Market Diversification." Background paper prepared for the Bangladesh Trade Note, World Bank, Dhaka.

Bakht, Z., M. Yunus, and M. Salimullah. 2002. "Machinery Industry in Bangladesh." Machinery Industry Study Report 4, Tokyo Institute of Development Economies Advanced School, Tokyo.

BEPZA (Bangladesh Export Processing Zone Authority). 2010. *Annual Report: 2008–09.* Bangladesh Export Processing Zone Authority, Dhaka.

BIDS (Bangladesh Institute of Development Studies). 2011. "Trade Liberalization, Changes in Industrial Structure, and Job Creation in Bangladesh." Background paper by Bangladesh Institute of Development Studies, Dhaka, for the book *More and Better Jobs in South Asia*, Washington, DC: World Bank.

DOT (Department of Textiles). 2009. *Survey of the Bangladesh Textile Industry to Assess the Requirement of Textile Technologists.* Dhaka, Bangladesh: Bangladesh Department of Textiles.

Elmer, Diepak. 2010. "The RMG Skills Formation Regime in Bangladesh: A Background Paper." Background paper, Bangladesh Trade Note, World Bank, Dhaka.

IMF (International Monetary Fund). 2008. *The Ready-made Garment Industry in Bangladesh: An Update*, by Jonathan Dunn. Report for International Monetary Fund, Washington, DC.

Jassin-O'Rourke Group, L. 2008. "Global Apparel Manufacturing Labor Cost Analysis 2008, Textile and Apparel Manufacturers & Merchants." http://tammonline.com/files/GlobalApparelLaborCostSummary2008.pdf.

Just-style. 2010a. "Asian Woven Fabric Industry Moves Upmarket—Research." September 20.

———. 2010b. "Update: Bangladesh Garment Wages to Rise 80%." July 29.

———. 2010c. "Bangladesh in Brief: Apparel Industry Snapshot." August 2.

———. 2010d. "Continuing Protests Blight Bangladesh Pay Deal." August 2.

Knowles, A., C. Reyes, and K. Jackson. 2008. "Gender, Migration and Remittances: A Bangladeshi Experience." In *Southern Perspectives on Development: Dialogue or Division?* ed. A. Thorton and A. McGregor, 229–46. Auckland: Centre for Development Studies, University of Auckland.

Mlachila, Montfort, and Yongzheng Yang. 2004. "The End of Textiles Quotas: A Case Study on the Impact on Bangladesh." Working Paper WP/04/108, International Monetary Fund, Washington, DC.

Quddus, Munir, and Salim Rashid. 2000. *Entrepreneurs and Economic Development: The Remarkable Story of Garment Exports from Bangladesh.* Dhaka: The University Press Limited.

Rahman, Mustafizur, Debapriya Bhattacharya, and Khondaker Golam Moazzem. 2008. "Dynamics of Ongoing Changes in Bangladesh's Export-Oriented RGM Enterprises: Findings from an Enterprise-Level Survey." Unpublished manuscript, Centre for Policy Dialogue, Dhaka.

Saheed, Hassen. 2008. "Prospects for the Textile and Garment Industry in Bangladesh." *Textile Outlook International* 135: 12–48.

Staritz, Cornelia. 2011. "Making the Cut? Low-Income Countries and the Global Clothing Value Chain in a Post-Quota and Post-Crisis World." Study, World Bank, Washington, DC.

Tewari, Meenu. 2008. "Deepening Intraregional Trade and Investment in South Asia—The Case of the Textile and Clothing Industry." Working Paper 213, India Council for Research on International Economic Relations, New Delhi.

World Bank. 2005a. "Bangladesh Growth and Export Competiveness." Report 31394-BD, Poverty Reduction and Economic Management Sector Unit, South Asia Region, World Bank, Washington, DC.

———. 2005b. "End of MFA Quotas—Key Issues and Strategic Options for Bangladesh Readymade Garment Industry." Bangladesh Development Series

Paper 2, Poverty Reduction and Economic Management Unit, World Bank, Dhaka.

———. 2010. "Export Bulletin," Bangladesh country office, World Bank, Dhaka.

Yunus, Mohammad. 2010. "Knitwear Industry in Bangladesh: A Case Study of Firms in Narayanganu." Report prepared for the Institute of Human Development, Delhi, Bangladesh Institute of Development Studies, Dhaka.

CHAPTER 9

Cambodia

Overview

- Cambodia is a latecomer to apparel exporting as it only became an apparel exporter in the mid-1990s following almost three decades of political and social unrest. However, by the late 1990s, apparel was playing a leading role in Cambodia's development process. Apparel rapidly developed into the largest export sector, accounting for almost 70 percent of Cambodia's total merchandise exports. It has been the main source of growth of formal employment since the late 1990s, with a workforce of around 300,000 and a nearly 30 percent share of industrial employment.

- The Multi-fibre Arrangement (MFA), preferential market access, and a large supply of low-cost labor were crucial in the development of Cambodia's apparel sector. The growth of the sector was driven by foreign direct investment (FDI), as foreign investors were attracted by MFA quota hopping and preferential market access, in particular through the U.S.-Cambodia Bilateral Textile Agreement, in which quota increases were linked to improvements in working conditions, as well as by Cambodia's low labor costs.

- Although expectations were gloomy for Cambodia's apparel exports post-MFA, Cambodia increased export value and market share after 2004. However, in the context of the global economic crisis and the phaseout of the China safeguards at the end of 2008, Cambodia's apparel exports declined in 2009. Besides these "external" reasons, "internal" factors are also important in explaining the decline, in particular the specific integration of Cambodia into apparel global value chains (GVCs) dominated by foreign investments and expatriates with management decisions largely taken in head offices in East Asia, cut-make-trim (CMT) production, and a disintegrated apparel industry with limited local or regional linkages.

- Cambodia's main competitive advantages are low labor costs, preferential market access (today particularly to the European Union [EU]), and a reputation for good labor compliance due to the Better Factories Cambodia program of the International Labour Organization (ILO) and the International Finance Corporation (IFC). Main challenges are the relatively low productivity level compared to its main competitors such as Bangladesh and Vietnam; the skill gap, in particular with regard to technological, design and fashion, and management skills; long lead times and limited backward integration; concentration with regard to the end market of the United States and to a lesser extent the EU-15[1] and in relatively simple low-value products.

- Proactive government policies are—with the exception of the ILO/IFC collaboration in Better Factories Cambodia—limited compared to other main Asian apparel exporter countries.

Development of the Apparel Industry[2]

Cambodia only became an apparel exporter in the mid-1990s. Although the origins of the Cambodian apparel industry go back to the French colonial area (1863–1953), the current foundation of the apparel industry was established by foreign investors from Hong Kong SAR, China; Malaysia; Singapore; and Taiwan, China. They were attracted by unused quota under the MFA and preferential market access as well as by the relatively low labor costs stemming from Cambodia's large labor surplus. When the sector started in Cambodia, it faced no quota restrictions to the United States and the EU as it was not part of the MFA system. In 1996, Cambodia, as a nonmember of the World Trade Organization (WTO), was granted most favored nation (MFN) status for the U.S. and the EU markets.

In 1999, Cambodia received quota- and duty-free access for apparel exports to the EU market under the three-and-a-half-year EU-Cambodian Textile Agreement and from 2001 onward under the Everything but Arms (EBA) initiative for least developed countries (LDCs). However, the major takeoff of the industry resulted from the U.S.-Cambodia Bilateral Textile Agreement, which was concluded in 1999.

As exports from Cambodia to the United States increased rapidly, negotiations were started between the United States and the Cambodian government in 1998 to bring Cambodia under the MFA quota system. The U.S. and Cambodian negotiators agreed on the U.S.-Cambodian Bilateral Trade Agreement on Textile and Apparel for the three-year period from 1999 to 2001 that established fixed quotas for the 12 largest categories of apparel exports from Cambodia to the United States. These quotas were, however, the most generous on a per capita basis among all countries given Cambodia's commitment to improve core labor standards. The two governments agreed that if the Cambodian government was able to secure compliance by apparel factories with the country's labor laws and internationally agreed labor standards, quotas would be increased on an annual basis. The decisions for quota increases were based on a monitoring program—the Garment Sector Working Conditions Improvement Project—conducted by the ILO. In 2000 and 2001, a 9 percent increase of all quota categories was decided. In 2001, the trade agreement was extended for three additional years, from 2002 to 2004. Across-the-board quota increases of 9 percent, 12 percent, and 14 percent were awarded for those years (Polaski 2009). The U.S.-Cambodia Textile Agreement and the ILO monitoring program were central for the initial growth of the apparel sector in Cambodia thanks to the generous and increased quotas that secured exports to the U.S. market, as well as the exposure the agreement provided to consumers, buyers, and manufacturers on Cambodia's capabilities as an apparel-exporting country.

Apparel exports have increased significantly since the mid-1990s. Import data from Cambodia's trading partners show an increase from $63 million in 1995 to $2,434 million in 2004 (table 9.1). Between 2000 and 2004, apparel exports grew at an annual average growth rate of 20.5 percent. The share of Cambodia in global apparel exports increased from 0.3 percent in 1998 to 1.0 percent in 2004. Since 1998, the United States has been Cambodia's most important end market, accounting for 62 percent of total exports (or around $1,400 million) in 2004; the EU-15 was the second-biggest end market, with 30 percent (or around $700 million) (figure 9.1).

Table 9.1 Cambodian Apparel Exports to the World

	1995	1998	2001	2004	2005	2006	2007	2008	2009
Total value ($, million)	63	578	1,430	2,434	2,696	3,324	3,765	4,043	3,473
Annual growth rate (%)	—	101.4	17.8	23.7	10.8	23.3	13.3	7.4	−14.1
Share of world exports (%)	0.0	0.3	0.7	1.0	1.0	1.1	1.2	1.2	1.2
Woven and knit value ($, million)									
Woven	30	240	689	1,108	1,106	1,128	1,156	1,130	905
Knit	33	338	741	1,326	1,590	2,196	2,609	2,913	2,568
Woven and knit share of total import value (%)									
Woven	47.6	41.5	48.2	45.5	41.0	33.9	30.7	27.9	26.1
Knit	52.4	58.5	51.8	54.5	59.0	66.1	69.3	72.1	73.9

Source: United Nations Commodity Trade Statistic Database (UN Comtrade).

Note: Exports represented by imports reported by partner countries. Apparel classification: Harmonized Commodity Description and Coding System (HS) 1992: Woven: HS62; Knit: HS61; growth rate reflects change from previous year; — = not available.

Figure 9.1   Cambodian Apparel Exports to the EU-15 and the United States

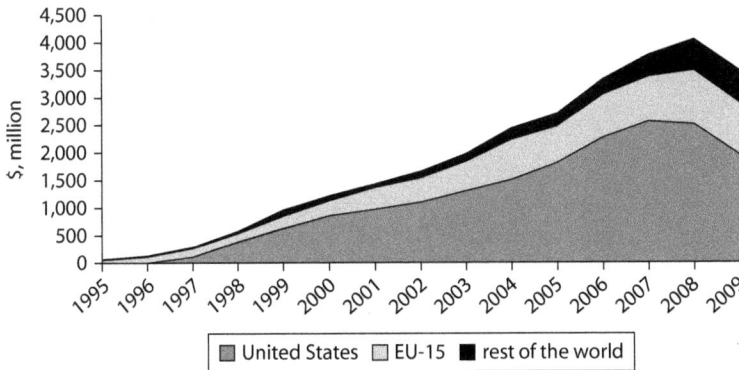

Source: United Nations Commodity Trade Statistic Database (UN Comtrade).
Note: Exports represented by imports reported by partner countries. Apparel classification: Harmonized Commodity Description and Coding System (HS) 1992: Woven: HS62; Knit: HS61. EU-15 = the 15 member states of the European Union (EU) as of December 31, 2003, before the new member states joined the EU: Austria, Belgium, Denmark, Finland, France, Germany, Greece, Ireland, Italy, Luxembourg, the Netherlands, Portugal, Spain, Sweden, and the United Kingdom.

Apparel exports grew from less than 3.0 percent of total exports in the early 1990s to 76.4 percent in 2003. The number of apparel firms increased from around 20 in 1995 to 219 in 2004.[3] Employment grew from 18,703 workers in 1995 to 269,846 in 2004 (table 9.2).

Expectations regarding the impact of the MFA phaseout on Cambodia's apparel exports were pessimistic, yet Cambodia managed to increase its export value and market share after 2004. Looking at import data by Cambodia's trading partners, total apparel exports increased to $2,696 million in 2005, which accounted for a 10.8 percent increase from 2004 (table 9.1). Cambodia's share of global apparel exports remained stable at 1.0 percent between 2004 and 2005 and increased to 1.1 percent in 2006 and 1.2 percent in 2007. This increase was based on knit exports, as woven exports stagnated in 2005. Exports to the United States increased by 20.1 percent in 2005, while exports to the EU-15 declined by 8.2 percent. In 2006, exports to the United States and the EU-15 increased by 25.2 percent and 16.3 percent, respectively (tables 9.2 and 9.3). Along with total exports, the number of operating firms increased from 219 in 2004 to 247 in 2005, and total employment increased from around 270,000 to 283,906 in 2005 (table 9.2). However, while total net employment increased, there was considerable employment adjustment within the industry. As buyers consolidated their suppliers between and

Table 9.2   Cambodian Apparel Industry: Factories, Employment, and Share of Total Exports

Year	Number of firms		Employment		Apparel share of total exports (%)
	Registered	Operating	Registered	Operating	
1995	—	20	—	18,703	3.0
1997	—	67	—	51,578	23.9
2001	233	185	200,861	187,103	71.2
2002	248	188	226,484	210,440	—
2003	266	197	254,355	233,969	76.5
2004	300	219	300,043	269,846	—
2005	351	247	328,466	283,906	74.5
2006	398	290	379,293	334,063	70.9
2007	432	292	414,789	353,017	69.4
2008	455	284	407,927	324,871	—
2009	487	243	405,249	281,855	—
2010	515	262	451,900	319,383	—

Source: Garment Manufacturers' Association in Cambodia (GMAC). Garment exports' share of total exports and 1995–97 firm and employment data from Arnold and Shih 2010.
Note: Figures represent numbers in December of given year; — = not available.

Table 9.3   U.S. Apparel Imports from Cambodia

	1996	1998	2001	2004	2005	2006	2007	2008	2009
Total value ($, million)	2	359	920	1,418	1,702	2,131	2,421	2,371	1,869
Growth rate (%)	—	265.0	14.7	15.4	20.1	25.2	13.6	−2.0	−21.2
Share of all U.S. apparel imports (%)	0.0	0.7	1.6	2.1	2.4	2.9	3.2	3.2	2.9
Woven and knit value ($, million)									
Woven	2	170	516	776	828	834	836	786	586
Knit	1	188	404	642	875	1,297	1,584	1,585	1,283
Woven and knit share of total import value (%)									
Woven	75.0	47.5	56.1	54.7	48.6	39.1	34.5	33.1	31.3
Knit	25.0	52.5	43.9	45.3	51.4	60.9	65.5	66.9	68.7

Source: United States International Trade Commission (USITC).
Note: Apparel imports represented by Harmonized Commodity Description and Coding System (HS) Codes 61 and 62; General Customs Value; growth rate reflects change from previous year; — = not available.

within countries and sourced from fewer but larger factories, smaller factories closed in Cambodia and the remaining factories increased in size post-MFA. The number of factories in Cambodia employing more than 5,000 workers more than doubled between 2004 and 2005. Just over one-quarter of factories employ less than 500 workers, and most factories employ between 500 and 2,000 workers (Natsuda, Goto, and Thoburn 2009).

When the MFA was phased out at the end of 2004, so was the U.S.-Cambodia Bilateral Textile Agreement that was based on the quota system. But the Cambodian government and apparel firms decided to continue the ILO monitoring program. The focus shifted from the U.S. Department of Labor to the Cambodian government, manufacturers, and buyers, and the project expanded to include capacity-building and training programs for government officials, managers, and workers (Polaski 2009). However, one of the main incentives of the program was lost at the end of 2004 when the MFA phased out—access to higher quotas for improvements in working conditions. Since then, the primary incentive for buyers has been labor compliance and the associated "reputation risk insurance" as the ILO monitoring program has higher credibility than buyers' own codes of conducts.

The impact of the global economic crisis that started in 2008 but evolved particularly in 2009 has to be assessed together with the phase-out of the China safeguards at the end of 2008. Cambodia's apparel sector was hit hard by these two developments. Looking at import data by Cambodia's trading partners, total apparel exports increased by 7.4 percent in 2008 but declined by 14.1 percent in 2009 (table 9.1). Apparel exports to the United States fell by 2.0 percent in 2008 and 21.2 percent in 2009, and apparel exports to the EU-15 increased by 5.7 percent in 2008 and declined by 2.4 percent in 2009 (tables 9.3 and 9.4). The reduction in exports is mirrored by factory closures. While 292 factories were operating in 2007, in 2008, the number decreased to 284 and in 2009, to 243 (table 9.2). Beginning in November 2008, a wave of factory closures ended a trend of relatively steady growth, and within a year's time, the number of operating factories dropped from a peak of 313 in October 2008 to a low of 241 in November 2009, with most of the remaining factories running at only 60–70 percent of their capacity (Better Factories Cambodia 2010). Altogether around 70 factories have closed since the start of the global economic crisis in 2008, and around 75,500 workers have lost their jobs, which represents 20 percent of the total workforce in the sector. Employment declined from 353,017 in 2007 to 324,871 in 2008 and to 281,855 by the end of 2009 (table 9.2).

The developments in 2008–09 draw a rather gloomy picture of the apparel sector in Cambodia. However, data from the Ministry of Commerce for 2010 suggest that the industry has hit the bottom. In January 2010, for the first time since December 2008, apparel exports

Table 9.4   EU-15 Apparel Imports from Cambodia

	1995	1998	2001	2004	2005	2006	2007	2008	2009
Total value									
(€, million)	43	151	395	517	475	552	524	554	541
Growth rate (%)	—	6.8	39.9	23.3	−8.2	16.3	−5.0	5.7	−2.4
Share of all									
EU-15 apparel									
imports (%)	0.1	0.2	0.5	0.6	0.5	0.6	0.5	0.5	0.6
Woven and knit value (€, million)									
Woven	19	44	114	134	99	99	83	83	70
Knit	24	107	281	383	376	453	442	471	470
Woven and knit share of total import value (%)									
Woven	44.5	28.9	28.8	26.0	20.8	17.9	15.8	15.0	13.0
Knit	55.5	71.1	71.2	74.0	79.2	82.1	84.2	85.0	87.0

Source: Eurostat.
Note: Apparel imports represented by Harmonized Commodity Description and Coding System (HS) Codes 61 and 62; growth rate reflects change from previous year; — = not available. EU-15 = the 15 member states of the European Union (EU) as of December 31, 2003, before the new member states joined the EU: Austria, Belgium, Denmark, Finland, France, Germany, Greece, Ireland, Italy, Luxembourg, the Netherlands, Portugal, Spain, Sweden, and the United Kingdom.

increased (by 7.3 percent) compared to the same month of the previous year. For the whole year 2010, exports increased by 22.7 percent compared to the previous year. Throughout 2010, the number of operating apparel firms started to increase again, reaching 262 by December (Better Factories Cambodia 2010). Also, apparel sector employment increased again in 2010, accounting for 319,383 workers in December 2010.

The export growth post-MFA phaseout and the end of the U.S.-Cambodia Bilateral Textile Agreement has to be viewed in the context of the reimposition of quotas on certain categories of apparel imports from China to the United States and the EU between 2005 and 2008, which cushioned the impact of the MFA phaseout. For the United States, over 40 percent of Cambodia's exports occurred in categories in which the United States imposed safeguards on apparel exports from China. Furthermore, Vietnam, a main competitor of Cambodia, continued to be subject to quotas in the U.S. market after 2004 because it was not a member of the WTO. However, in January 2007, Vietnam became a WTO member, and at end of 2008, the China safeguards were phased out, which together with the decline in demand due to the global economic crisis affected Cambodia's apparel exports negatively. Cambodia has remained an important apparel exporter post-MFA, with its competitive advantages largely based on low labor costs and preferential market access, particularly to the EU. Productivity and overall competitiveness levels have, however, increased at a lower rate than in its main competitors Bangladesh and Vietnam.

Structure of the Apparel Industry

Types of Firms

The apparel sector in Cambodia is dominated by FDI; almost 95 percent of the factories are foreign owned. In 2008, the main nationalities were Taiwan, China (25 percent, 86 factories); Hong Kong SAR, China (19 percent, 68 factories); and China (18 percent, 65 factories), followed by the Republic of Korea (10 percent); Malaysia (5 percent); and Singapore (4 percent) (figure 9.2). Firms from "greater China," including China; Hong Kong SAR, China; and Taiwan, China, accounted for over 60 percent of all apparel factories in Cambodia. Overall Chinese investment, including Hong Kong SAR, China, accounted for 59 percent of approved

Figure 9.2   Ownership Nationality of Cambodian Apparel Factories, 2008
% market share

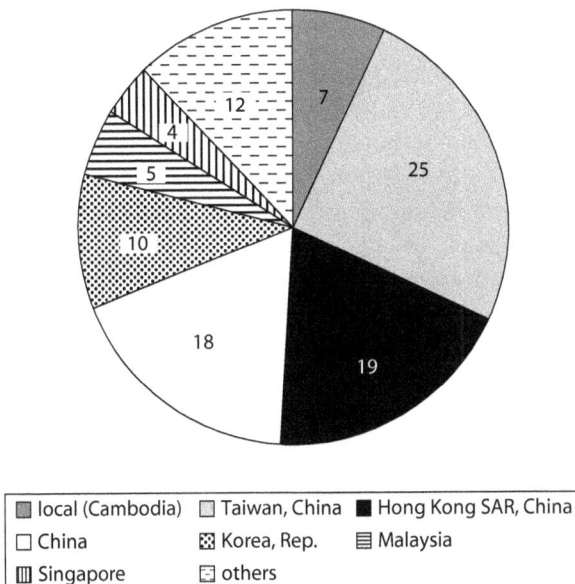

local (Cambodia)   Taiwan, China   Hong Kong SAR, China
China   Korea, Rep.   Malaysia
Singapore   others

Source: Garment Manufacturers' Association in Cambodia (GMAC).

investment in the apparel sector in the period 2000 to 2005; Taiwanese investment accounted for 23 percent (Natsuda, Goto, and Thoburn 2009). Only 7 percent of apparel firms are owned by Cambodians, and these are mostly smaller firms (around 3 percent of employment is accounted for by Cambodian-owned firms) and generally work on a sub-contracting basis for larger foreign-owned firms. The vast majority of owners as well as managers are foreigners. According to a survey of 164 apparel factories in 2005, 30 percent of top managers were from mainland China; 21 percent from Taiwan, China; 15 percent from Hong Kong SAR, China; and only 8 percent from Cambodia (Yamagata 2006). The Garment Manufacturers' Association in Cambodia (GMAC) esti-mates that 80 percent of middle managers are also foreigners.

Ownership structure is important because it determines how supplier firms are linked to international production and distribution networks (Natsuda, Goto, and Thoburn 2009). Factories in Cambodia are largely integrated into triangular manufacturing networks where global buyers source from transnational producers with headquarters located in China; Hong Kong SAR, China; the Republic of Korea; Malaysia; Singapore; or Taiwan, China. These producers organize manufacturing networks on a global scale. Thus, factories in Cambodia are integrated into apparel GVCs through their foreign parent companies, where the production orders are received together with the fabric and accessories inputs and delivery instructions. This type of integration has secured access to the supply chains of global buyers and input sourcing networks, but it has also limited the decision-making power and functions performed in Cambodia. Production, sales, and management decisions are largely made at the headquarters of the parent companies. Unlike locally owned facto-ries, foreign-owned factories in Cambodia have limited leverage and autonomy in terms of strategic decision making or in attracting orders; these negotiations are generally conducted with the buyers at the head-quarters of the parent companies (Natsuda, Goto, and Thoburn 2009). The parent companies are generally in charge of input sourcing, product development and design, logistics, merchandising, and marketing, and they have the direct relationships with buyers. Transnational producers are able to leverage the skills and expertise of their home offices and other production locations for value-adding activities, which reduces the need for capacity building, investment, and upgrading in Cambodia (Nathan Associates 2007).

Hence, Cambodia's apparel sector is concentrated in CMT produc-tion. Under CMT, apparel firms receive all inputs (mostly fabrics and accessories) from buyers or parent companies, just perform the sewing, and then export the final products. However, a significant number of CMT firms are also in charge of cutting the fabric and of some finishing activities, including washing and packing. According to a survey in 2006, 139 out of 164 apparel firms (87 percent) were engaged in CMT production (Yamagata 2006). The Asian Development Bank (ADB) estimates that over 70 percent of apparel exports were based on CMT in 2004 (ADB 2004). GMAC supports these figures, stating that 60 percent of the factories are only involved in CMT production, which are typically subsidiaries of companies overseas, 25 percent in free on board (FOB) and 15 percent in subcontracting arrangements. In contrast to CMT, FOB firms are capable of sourcing and financing inputs and provide all production services, as well as finishing and packaging for delivery to the retail outlet. This is an important step because input sourcing on suppliers' accounts has become the standard in global sourcing post-MFA. Firms without broader capabilities and in particular without sourcing capabilities face challenges in the global apparel sector post-MFA. Original design manufacturing (ODM) firms carry out all steps involved in the production of a product, including design and product development. Very few apparel firms are involved in the design or the product development process in Cambodia.

An ADB study in 2004 concludes that the level of technology employed in Cambodia's apparel firms is at the lowest level in sewing and inspection, and few attachments are applied to machines that could aid workers to operate more effectively, both in volume and quality terms (ADB 2004). Interview evidence from Cambodia shows that equipment and machinery are mostly relocated to Cambodia after use in plants in China; Hong Kong SAR, China; Malaysia; Taiwan, China; and Thailand within triangular manufacturing networks, or imported secondhand by the few local producers. Only knitting machinery and equipment (weft and warp knitting) were imported by some firms firsthand from Germany and Taiwan, China (Rasiah 2009). This fact is supported by the increase in shipments of knit machinery to Cambodia over the 2000–09 time frame. In 2009, Cambodia ranked sixth globally for shipments of hand-knitting and semiautomatic flat knitting machinery and fifth for shipments of electronic flatbed knitting machines. Flat knitting machines are purchased by apparel firms and used for the production of knitwear, largely sweaters, which do not require a separate fabric step. However, for both product categories, imports peaked in the early to mid-2000s and have decreased since to around 2005 levels (Brocklehurst and Anson 2010).

End Markets

Cambodia's apparel exports are highly concentrated in a few end markets. In 2009, 83.2 percent of apparel exports went to the United States and the EU-15, with 56.0 percent of exports going to the United States and 27.2 percent to the EU-15 (table 9.5). The only other important end market is Canada, which had a share of 7.2 percent in 2009. Although the United States still strongly dominates Cambodia's apparel exports, its share decreased from 70.4 percent in 2000 to 56.0 percent in 2009. The share of the EU-15 increased from 22.4 percent to 27.2 percent in the same time period. Canada's share significantly increased, from 0.9 percent in 2000 to 7.2 percent in 2009. Also, the rest of the world increased its share from 6.4 percent to 9.6 percent of total apparel exports (figure 9.3).

The high export concentration to the United States—and to a lesser extent to the EU-15—can be explained by several factors. First, due to the U.S.-Cambodia Bilateral Textile Agreement, Cambodia had a favorable quota access to the U.S. market. Access to the EU market has also been on a preferential basis since 1999—even more as it has been quota and duty free—but it is subject to double transformation rules of origin (ROO), which has been difficult to fulfill for Cambodia's apparel exporters. The exception in this regard is sweaters, which can fulfill the EU's ROO and account for an important share of EU exports. The increase in apparel exports to Canada since 2003 has been related to the extension of Canada's Generalized System of Preferences (GSP) scheme to cover textiles and apparel in January 2003. Second, transnational producers based in Hong Kong SAR, China; Korea; and Taiwan, China, which are the main investors in Cambodia's apparel sector, are largely concentrated on the U.S. market and have well-established relationships with the U.S. buyers. Third, the end markets are different and demand different capabilities. Orders from the U.S. mass market retailers are large and price is the most important criterion; quality and lead time are also central but not as important. In general, the EU orders are smaller and demand more variation and different standards with regard to quality, fashion content, and lead times.

Export Products

Nearly three-quarters of Cambodia's apparel exports are knit products. From 1995 to 2004, knit and woven exports accounted for similar values. Woven exports, however, have stagnated since 2004, whereas knit exports have continued to increase. Cambodia's apparel exports, both woven and

Table 9.5 Top Five Cambodian Apparel Export Markets, 1995, 2000, 2005, 2008, and 2009

Country/region	Customs value ($, million)					Market share (%)				
	1995	2000	2005	2008	2009	1995	2000	2005	2008	2009
World	63	1,214	2,696	4,043	3,473					
United States	1	854	1,807	2,503	1,946	0.8	70.4	67.0	61.9	56.0
EU-15	53	272	660	986	945	83.8	22.4	24.5	24.4	27.2
Canada	0	11	106	246	249	0.7	0.9	3.9	6.1	7.2
Poland	n.a.	n.a.	n.a.	47	56	n.a.	n.a.	n.a.	1.2	1.6
Japan	n.a.	n.a.	n.a.	n.a.	45	n.a.	n.a.	n.a.	n.a.	1.3
Mexico	n.a.	n.a.	n.a.	32	n.a.	n.a.	n.a.	n.a.	0.8	n.a.
Singapore	7	61	45	n.a.	n.a.	11.3	5.0	1.7	n.a.	n.a.
Switzerland	n.a.	n.a.	16	n.a.	n.a.	n.a.	n.a.	0.6	n.a.	n.a.
Norway	2	4	n.a.	n.a.	n.a.	2.6	0.3	n.a.	n.a.	n.a.
Top five share	**63**	**1,202**	**2,634**	**3,813**	**3,241**	**99.3**	**99.0**	**97.7**	**94.3**	**93.3**

Source: United Nations Commodity Trade Statistics Database (UN Comtrade).

Note: Harmonized Commodity Description and Coding System (HS) 1992: Codes 61 and 62; exports represented by country imports from Cambodia. n.a. = not applicable (indicates country not in top five for given year). EU-15 = the 15 member states of the European Union (EU) as of December 31, 2003, before the new member states joined the EU: Austria, Belgium, Denmark, Finland, France, Germany, Greece, Ireland, Italy, Luxembourg, the Netherlands, Portugal, Spain, Sweden, and the United Kingdom.

Figure 9.3   Top Three Cambodian Apparel Export Markets, 2000 and 2009
% market share

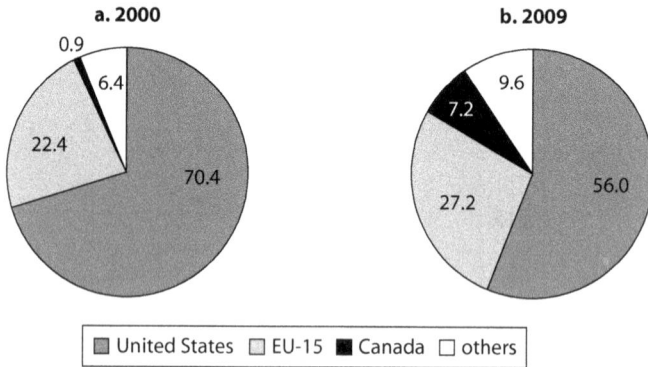

a. 2000

b. 2009

United States   EU-15   Canada   others

Source: United Nations Commodity Trade Statistics Database (UN Comtrade).
Note: Harmonized Commodity Description and Coding System (HS) 1992: Codes 61 and 62; exports represent
partner imports from Cambodia. EU-15 = the 15 member states of the European Union (EU) as of December 31,
2003, before the new member states joined the EU: Austria, Belgium, Denmark, Finland, France, Germany,
Greece, Ireland, Italy, Luxembourg, the Netherlands, Portugal, Spain, Sweden, and the United Kingdom.

knit, are highly concentrated in a few products. The top 5 product categories accounted for 48.2 percent of total Cambodian apparel exports to the
U.S. market and for 64.8 percent to the EU-15 market in 2009; the top 10
product categories, for 64.2 percent and 75.5 percent, respectively (tables
9.6 and 9.7). However, the product concentration levels have declined in
both markets since 2000. The top export product categories to the United
States and the EU-15 are overlapping—6 of the top 10 products appear in
the U.S. and the EU-15 lists. In the U.S. and the EU-15 markets, knit products dominate, accounting for 8 of the top 10 products. The most important products in both markets are trousers, sweatshirts, and T-shirts. In the
EU market, sweaters are particularly important, accounting for 51.8 percent of total exports in 2009 and representing the top two apparel export
products. This is related to the double transformation ROO required for
preferential market access to the EU that can be fulfilled for sweaters. Of
the top 10 export products to the United States, 9 are cotton based and
only 1 based on man-made fiber (MMF). In the EU-15 market, the situation is more diversified—the top 10 products include 5 cotton, 2 synthetic,
1 MMF, and 1 wool-based product (as well as 1 product based on textile
materials not elsewhere specified or indicated [NESOI]).

The unit prices of Cambodia's main export products are comparatively low, in general lower than the world average. In the case of EU-15
exports, a comparison with competitor countries shows that Bangladesh,

Table 9.6 Top 10 U.S. Apparel Imports from Cambodia, 1998, 2000, 2005, 2008, and 2009

HS code	Product	Customs value ($, million)					Market share (%)				
		1998	2000	2005	2008	2009	1998	2000	2005	2008	2009
Total		**359**	**802**	**1,702**	**2,371**	**1,869**					
611020	Sweatshirts	79	120	222	462	323	22.0	15.0	13.0	19.5	17.3
620462	Trousers	36	123	315	310	204	9.9	15.3	18.5	13.1	10.9
620342	Trousers	84	147	125	203	156	23.5	18.3	7.4	8.6	8.3
610462	Trousers	12	n.a.	n.a.	155	125	3.2	n.a.	n.a.	6.5	6.7
610910	T-Shirts	11	n.a.	n.a.	114	93	3.1	n.a.	n.a.	4.8	5.0
611030	Sweatshirts	24	59	60	97	71	6.6	7.3	3.5	4.1	3.8
610510	Shirts	11	15	n.a.	78	68	3.1	1.8	n.a.	3.3	3.6
610610	Shirts	16	n.a.	66	78	59	4.5	n.a.	3.9	3.3	3.2
611420	Garments	n.a.	n.a.	n.a.	60	53	n.a.	n.a.	n.a.	2.5	2.9
610220	Jackets	n.a.	n.a.	n.a.	n.a.	46	n.a.	n.a.	n.a.	n.a.	2.5
610832	Pajamas	n.a.	n.a.	60	52	n.a.	n.a.	n.a.	3.5	2.2	n.a.
610831	Pajamas	n.a.	20	82	n.a.	n.a.	n.a.	2.4	4.8	n.a.	n.a.
620452	Skirts	n.a.	18	55	n.a.	n.a.	n.a.	2.2	3.2	n.a.	n.a.
620520	Shirts	n.a.	44	44	n.a.	n.a.	n.a.	5.5	2.6	n.a.	n.a.
620630	Shirts	n.a.	17	42	n.a.	n.a.	n.a.	2.1	2.5	n.a.	n.a.
611120	Garments	n.a.	13	n.a.	n.a.	n.a.	n.a.	1.6	n.a.	n.a.	n.a.
620193	Jackets	11	n.a.	n.a.	n.a.	n.a.	3.1	n.a.	n.a.	n.a.	n.a.
611010	Sweatshirts	10	n.a.	n.a.	n.a.	n.a.	2.7	n.a.	n.a.	n.a.	n.a.
Top 10 share		**293**	**574**	**1,071**	**1,609**	**1,199**	**81.7**	**71.6**	**62.9**	**67.9**	**64.2**

Source: United States International Trade Commission (USITC).

Note: n.a. = not applicable (indicates product not in top 10 in given year). Product descriptions shortened to fit table. Sweatshirts also represent sweaters, pullovers, vests, and similar articles. Harmonized Commodity Description and Coding System (HS) numbers beginning with 61 indicate knitted garments and 62 indicate nonknitted (woven) garments.

Table 9.7 Top 10 EU-15 Apparel Imports from Cambodia, 1998, 2000, 2005, 2008, and 2009

HS code	Product	Customs value (€, million)					Market share (%)				
		1998	2000	2005	2008	2009	1998	2000	2005	2008	2009
Total		**151**	**282**	**475**	**554**	**541**					
611020	Sweatshirts	13	42	73	173	144	8.5	15.0	15.5	31.2	26.7
611030	Sweatshirts	49	104	187	123	136	32.1	36.7	39.3	22.1	25.1
610910	T-Shirts	13	17	36	40	40	8.3	6.1	7.6	7.2	7.4
620342	Trousers	8	26	25	20	16	5.2	9.1	5.4	3.5	2.9
610990	T-Shirts	6	11	11	13	14	3.7	3.9	2.3	2.3	2.7
610462	Trousers	n.a.	n.a.	n.a.	11	14	n.a.	n.a.	n.a.	2.0	2.6
611011[a]	Sweatshirts	n.a.	7	10	16	13	n.a.	2.3	2.1	2.8	2.4
620463	Trousers	3	11	25	12	11	2.2	4.0	5.3	2.2	2.1
610220	Jackets	n.a.	n.a.	n.a.	10	11	n.a.	n.a.	n.a.	1.8	2.0
610463	Trousers	n.a.	n.a.	n.a.	n.a.	9	n.a.	n.a.	n.a.	n.a.	1.7
620462	Trousers	n.a.	8	10	10	n.a.	n.a.	2.8	2.1	1.8	n.a.
610520	Shirts	3	n.a.	13	n.a.	n.a.	2.2	n.a.	2.6	n.a.	n.a.
620343	Trousers	n.a.	7	7	n.a.	n.a.	n.a.	2.5	1.6	n.a.	n.a.
610230	Jackets	n.a.	6	n.a.	n.a.	n.a.	n.a.	2.0	n.a.	n.a.	n.a.
611212	Track suits	6	n.a.	n.a.	n.a.	n.a.	3.8	n.a.	n.a.	n.a.	n.a.
620193	Jackets	5	n.a.	n.a.	n.a.	n.a.	3.2	n.a.	n.a.	n.a.	n.a.
620293	Jackets	4	n.a.	n.a.	n.a.	n.a.	2.9	n.a.	n.a.	n.a.	n.a.
Top 10 share		**109**	**238**	**398**	**427**	**408**	**72.4**	**84.3**	**83.8**	**77.0**	**75.5**

Source: Eurostat.

Note: n.a. = not applicable (indicates product not in top 10 in given year). EU-15 = the 15 member states of the European Union (EU) as of December 31, 2003, before the new member states joined the EU: Austria, Belgium, Denmark, Finland, France, Germany, Greece, Ireland, Italy, Luxembourg, the Netherlands, Portugal, Spain, Sweden, and the United Kingdom. Harmonized Commodity Description and Coding System (HS) numbers beginning with 61 indicate knitted garments and 62 indicate nonknitted (woven) garments. Sweatshirts also represent sweaters, pullovers, vests, and similar articles.

a. Code represents HS611010: 1995–2001.

China, and Pakistan had lower unit values in 2005; India, Sri Lanka, and Vietnam had higher unit values (Tewari 2008). This fact is related to Cambodia being relatively cost competitive but also being concentrated in basic products, while other countries export higher-value products. Figure 9.4 shows the development of unit prices based on data from Cambodia's Ministry of Economy and Finance. Average unit prices of Cambodia's total apparel exports have declined since 2004. According to United States International Trade Commission (USITC) data, between 2004 and 2007, the average price of apparel exports to the United States fell from $52.00 to $42.10 per dozen, representing a decline of 19 percent over three years. Between 2007 and 2009, the average price of apparel exports to the United States fell again to $37.10 per dozen, representing a decline of over 12 percent over two years. According to Eurostat data, the average price of apparel exports to the EU-15 declined from €13.40 to €12.80 per kilogram between 2004 and 2007, representing a decline of 4 percent. Between 2007 and 2009, the average price of apparel exports to the EU-15 fell only slightly to $12.60 per kilogram, accounting for a decline of 2 percent. Thus, in contrast to the United States, in the EU-15, average price declines were less severe for Cambodia's apparel exports post-MFA.

Backward Linkages
Backward linkages from the apparel to the textile sector, including yarn and fabric production, are very limited in Cambodia. Over 90 percent of

Figure 9.4   Average Unit Values of Cambodian Apparel Exports, 2001–10

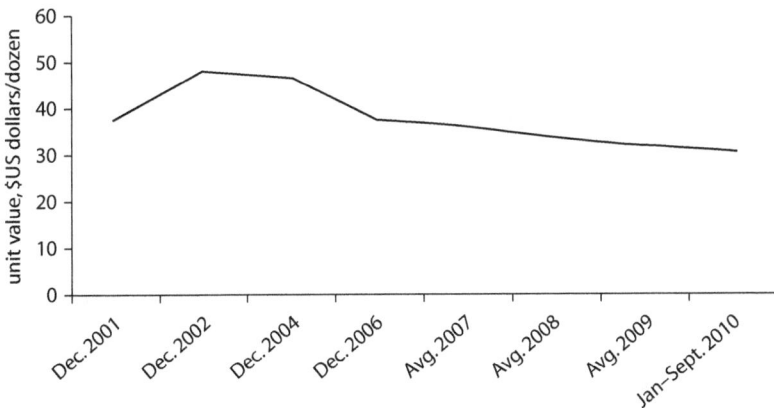

Source: Cambodia's Ministry of Economy and Finance (MEF); Monthly Bulletin of Statistics.
Note: Apparel represented by "Clothing (all kinds)."

fabric and yarn inputs are imported, and there is very minimal mill capacity. Also, the large majority of accessories, packaging, and presentation materials are imported. The domestic material content is largely limited to cardboard cartons, hangers, and poly bags. Cambodia's fabric imports in 2008 accounted for 25 percent of the country's total merchandise imports (Natsuda, Goto, and Thoburn 2009). Cambodia's apparel industry imported textiles were worth $1.3 billion in 2008 and $1.08 billion in 2009. In 2009, 46.1 percent of textile imports came from China; 25.1 percent from Hong Kong SAR, China; 11 percent from Korea; 7.1 percent from Thailand; and 5.6 percent from Malaysia (table 9.8).[4] Regional sourcing has remained quite stable, accounting for 17.5 percent of total textile imports in 2000 and 16.6 percent in 2008. Most regional textile imports come from Malaysia, Thailand, and Vietnam. Increased regional sourcing faces challenges because Cambodia's apparel sector has strong relations with East Asian textile producers due to foreign ownership, triangular manufacturing networks, and concentration in CMT. This situation gives apparel firms located in Cambodia limited decision-making power with regard to input sourcing, as these decisions are made at the headquarters.

Employment

Employment levels in Cambodia's apparel sector have increased significantly, from under 19,000 workers in 1995 to 353,017 workers in

Table 9.8   Top Five Textile Suppliers to Cambodia, 1995, 2000, 2005, 2008, and 2009

Country/ economy/ region	Customs value ($, million)					Market share (%)				
	1995	2000	2005	2008	2009	1995	2000	2005	2008	2009
World	67	401	930	1,325	1,080					
China	4	76	344	550	498	6.2	19.0	37.0	41.5	46.1
Hong Kong SAR, China	4	204	330	390	271	5.8	51.0	35.4	29.4	25.1
Korea, Rep.	n.a.	38	69	114	119	n.a.	9.4	7.4	8.6	11.0
Thailand	16	n.a.	56	73	76	23.6	n.a.	6.0	5.5	7.1
Malaysia	11	24	48	75	60	16.5	6.1	5.1	5.7	5.6
Singapore	30	21	n.a.	n.a.	n.a.	44.9	5.2	n.a.	n.a.	n.a.
Top five share	**64**	**363**	**846**	**1,202**	**1,024**	**97.0**	**90.6**	**91.0**	**90.7**	**94.8**

Source: United Nations Commodity Trade Statistics Database (UN Comtrade)
Note: Standard International Trade Classification (SITC) 65 Rev. 3. Imports represented by partner country export values. n.a. = not applicable (indicates country not in the top 5 in given year).

2007. After 2007, however, employment declined, reaching 281,855 in 2009. However, in 2010 employment increased again, reaching 319,383 in December 2010 (figure 9.5). With regard to the gender distribution of employment, it is widely stated that between 80 and 85 percent of apparel workers are women, which contrasts significantly from other manufacturing sectors, where men account for the large majority of workers. Female employment in the apparel sector has had crucial impacts on the economic and social roles of women in Cambodia. The export-oriented apparel sector has been one of the few avenues to paid and formal employment for women (in addition to the tourism sector), in particular for women from poor households in rural areas. The sector is mostly drawing on young, unmarried, and largely uneducated women. It is estimated that, besides these direct jobs, 242,000 indirect jobs have been created through the apparel sector: 113,000 in the services sector, including transportation and trade; 37,000 in nonapparel manufacturing, in particular in construction; and 92,000 jobs in the agriculture sector (EIC 2007, cited in Natsuda, Goto, and Thoburn 2009).

Absolute labor costs are comparatively low in Cambodia, and there is a large supply of workers. The base minimum wage of a production worker in Cambodia was $50.00 per month, which is $1.92 per day if 26 days are worked each month (8 hours of work per day, 6 days per week), leading to an average hourly wage of $0.24. Including benefits and average overtime, the average wage accounts for $77.00 per month, $2.67 per day, or $0.33 per hour (Nathan Associates 2007;

Figure 9.5   Employment in Cambodian Apparel Operating Factories

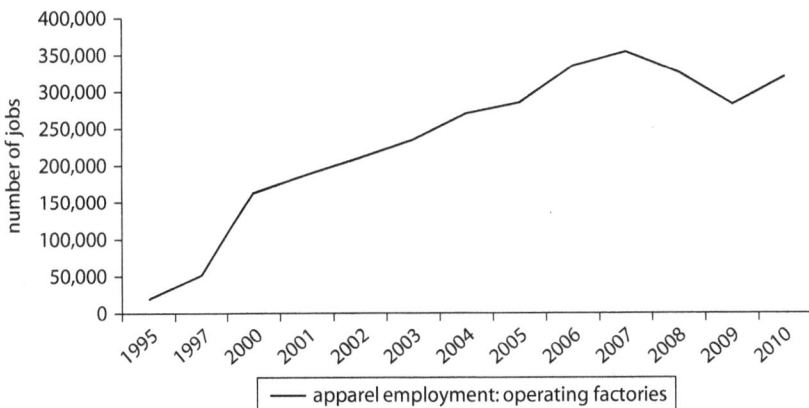

Sources: Garment Manufacturers' Association in Cambodia (GMAC); 1995–97 data from Arnold and Shih 2010.

Jassin-O'Rourke Group 2008). With regard to the average labor costs per hour, Cambodia ranked second after Bangladesh in a comparison with regional competitor countries in 2008. In October 2010, the minimum wage was increased from $50 to $61 per month due to protests and a planned nationwide strike in July 2010. These low wage levels are, however, accompanied by relatively low labor productivity. Cambodia's labor productivity is estimated to be 65 percent of China's, while Bangladesh's and Vietnam's were at 75 percent and 95 percent, respectively (Natsuda, Goto, and Thoburn 2009). A World Bank study in 2004 concluded that firms and workers in Cambodia are generally less productive than in Bangladesh, China, India, and Pakistan and that Cambodia's low labor costs do not wholly compensate for the low productivity of its workers (World Bank 2004).

A critical reason for the relatively low labor productivity in Cambodia's apparel sector is lack of skills of workers and managers. There is a high demand for skilled sewing operators, but the lack is more severe at the supervisory, management, technical, and design and fashion skill level. Managers and supervisors have a crucial role in defining factory productivity levels, labor relations, and the potential for upgrading. The vast majority of (top and middle) managers as well as technically skilled workers and supervisors are foreigners in Cambodia's apparel sector. Around 5,000 Chinese apparel technicians and supervisors are dispatched to apparel factories in Cambodia through Chinese human resource agencies (Natsuda, Goto, and Thoburn 2009). These foreign workers have brought experience, which was critical for the rapid establishment of the apparel sector in Cambodia; however, they may now pose a challenge to upgrading and productivity improvements because of their limited training and skills in production processes or industrial engineering, outdated and unsuitable management practices, and communication barriers with regard to language and culture (Nathan Associates 2007). Another problem is that the transmission of knowledge to local workers is slowed by language difficulties; the little learning possible probably does not take place.

Given the U.S.-Cambodia Bilateral Textile Agreement and the related ILO monitoring program, which changed to Better Factories Cambodia after the phaseout of the MFA, Cambodia's apparel sector has a reputation for good labor compliance. The Foreign Investment Advisory Services (FIAS) conducted a survey on sourcing criteria with the 15 largest U.S. and EU buyers that account for 45 percent of Cambodia's apparel exports in 2004 (FIAS 2004). The survey showed that Cambodia was rated the highest on "level of labor standards" and "protecting the rights of workers to organize unions" among Asian apparel-exporting countries, including Bangladesh, China, Thailand, and Vietnam. The ILO monitoring program in Cambodia is the most comprehensive and systematic monitoring effort governing any country's apparel sector. All factories in the sector are registered with the program, and a team of local Khmer-speaking inspectors is engaged in a constant 10-month cycle of monitoring visits, which culminate in factory reports and a publicly available synthesis report. The process is streamlined via a computerized information management system that buyers and suppliers can access. The monitors checklist (based on Cambodian labor law and the ILO core labor standards) covers over 480 items.

Despite a good record in labor compliance, there are still problems. As Miller et al. (2008) conclude, social audits have some impacts on child labor, forced labor, and health and safety but tend to have a more limited impact on freedom of association and collective bargaining, discrimination, living wages, and working hours. Low wages and excessive working hours have prevailed in Cambodia, as well as problems to establish collective bargaining. In the context of the global economic crisis, orders have decreased, and several firms had to close and reduce their workforce. In addition to job losses, wages declined due to cuts in regular working hours (including work suspensions and mandatory leave) and reduced overtime. Furthermore, duration of contracts was shortened and payments were delayed (Better Factories Cambodia 2010). Job losses, decreasing job security, and reduced wages have contributed to an increase in the number of strikes. In 2008, there were 30 percent more strikes reported than in 2007 (from 80 in 2007 to 105 in 2008).[5] Most strikes involved claims for higher wages, layoff compensation, payments for entitlements, nondiscrimination against union members, and rehiring of retrenched workers. There have been protests demanding higher minimum wages and a planned nationwide strike organized by the local Free Trade Union (FTU), which led to an agreement between the government, employers, and five large progovernment unions in July 2010 to increase the minimum wage.

Trade Regulations and Proactive Policies

Preferential Market Access
Cambodia has enjoyed quota- and duty-free market access to the EU—from 1999 to 2001 under the three-and-a-half-year EU-Cambodian

Textile Agreement and from 2001 onward under the EBA initiative. Preferential market access to the EU, however, requires the fulfillment of double transformation ROO, which cannot be fulfilled by all apparel exports. Thus, the utilization rate is very low, at around 10 percent (UNCTAD 2003). The use of duty concessions could be maximized by increasing regional input sourcing based on the EU GSP's regional cumulation, as the EU allows for regional cumulation in the context of the Association of South East Asian Nations (ASEAN). Cambodia faces duties in the U.S. market (averaging 11.4 percent) but enjoyed preferential quotas between 1999 and 2004 through the U.S.-Cambodia Bilateral Textile Agreement. Cambodia also enjoys duty-free market access to Australia, Canada, Japan, New Zealand, and Norway. At the regional level, Cambodia is a member of ASEAN.

Proactive Policies

The most important national institutional actors in Cambodia's apparel sector include the government, the industry association GMAC, and trade unions—most important, the five national labor federations, including the Cambodian Federation of Independent Trade Unions, the Cambodian Union's Federation, the Free Trade Union of Workers of the Kingdom of Cambodia, the Cambodian Labor Union Federation, and the National Independent Federation of Textile Unions in Cambodia.[6] Important international institutional actors acting in Cambodia include the ILO, the IFC, the World Bank, and the ADB, as well as some donors, in particular the United States Agency for International Development (USAID) and the ADF. In particular, Better Factories Cambodia has had an important role in the development of the sector in Cambodia and has put in place institutional structures that facilitate collaboration between the government, industry associations, firms, and trade unions. The Government-Private Sector Forum (sponsored by the IFC), which is a platform that enables local firms to identify problems and propose solutions, also has had an important role in the development of the apparel sector.

The government has generally supported the development of the apparel sector. It approved the establishment of 100 percent foreign-owned firms in Cambodia in 1994, improved the business environment, and provided favorable policies for foreign investors. Policies to spur investment include duty-free imports for export sectors, the provision of tax holidays and financial incentives, the introduction of laws to establish export processing zones (EPZs), and one-stop services to simplify investment procedures (Natsuda, Goto, and Thoburn 2009). Besides FDI-attraction policies, proactive state policies to support local involvement and linkages in and upgrading of the apparel sector have been rather weak, in particular compared to competitor countries such as Bangladesh, China, Sri Lanka, and Vietnam.

The government prepared a sector strategy—the Cambodian Garment Industry Development Strategy—in 2005 to cope with the post-MFA context. The vision statement for the strategy was "to create an environment in which the Cambodian garment industry can develop and sustain export competitiveness and diversify its offer in niche markets, to retain greater value within the country, and to empower employees by fairly distributing the benefits." The objectives of the strategy included (i) strengthening the institutional and information base of the apparel sector by bringing together key stakeholders, (ii) improving access to major markets and forming close public-private partnerships, (iii) reducing transaction costs, (iv) shortening lead times and increasing value added by building linkages to a domestic textile industry and encouraging local investment throughout the supply chain, (v) improving and expanding marketing efforts of the Cambodian sector to a larger number of countries and buyers, (vi) improving productivity by establishing a skills development program, and (vii) addressing general infrastructural issues within the country that add to product costs, such as the high cost of electricity and port charges. The strategy was accompanied by a work plan and management framework involving various stakeholders, including the NECC (National Export Council of Cambodia), the GMAC, labor unions, and the ILO (Cambodia MIC 2006). This far-reaching strategy has, however, not been implemented so far.

Although the apparel industry is the engine of growth in Cambodia, investments in systematic skill training have been limited. The existing training centers are largely focused on teaching women to sew and reducing injury and downtime rather than on driving productivity improvements and upgrading to broader functions and higher value-adding activities (Rasiah 2009). The only two broader formal training institutes are the Cambodia Garment Training Center (CGTC) and the Cambodia Skills Development Center (CASDEC, previously Garment Industry Productivity Center [GIPC]). CGTC was opened in April 2002 and is managed by GMAC and supported by eight organizations.[7] The principal course provided is Training of Garment Industry Supervisors; more recently a new course for Skill Development at Entry was established. CASDEC offers training in technical and industrial engineering that especially targets middle management, and it also works directly with firms by offering assistance for production management, including workflow, planning, controls, and supervision. This center was funded by USAID but is now largely financially self-sufficient.

In response to the crisis, the Cambodian government initiated a few programs in an effort to maintain apparel exports and keep jobs. In November 2008, the government announced cuts to export fees on apparel and other related bureaucratic costs by 10 percent, following a request by GMAC. To mitigate the fall in demand in Western markets, especially in the United States and the EU, as well as to sustain employment levels, the government has also supported diversification to new markets. The Ministry of Commerce and representatives of Cambodia's apparel industry went on an expo trip to Japan in late November 2008. In 2009, the government suspended a 1 percent tax on factory expenditures (advanced profit tax), effective January 1, 2009, for two years until 2011 (Chandararot, Sina, and Dannet 2009).

Notes

1. The EU-15 is the 15 member states of the European Union (EU) as of December 31, 2003, before the new member states joined the EU: Austria, Belgium, Denmark, Finland, France, Germany, Greece, Ireland, Italy, Luxembourg, the Netherlands, Portugal, Spain, Sweden, and the United Kingdom.

2. This section is partly based on Staritz (2011).

3. The Garment Manufacturers' Association in Cambodia (GMAC) reports the number of officially registered firms and effectively operating firms, the difference being temporarily closed firms and firms in closure. Numbers reported in this paper refer to effectively operating firms.

4. Textile imports from Taiwan, China, are also high, but the United Nations Commodity Trade Statistics Database (UN Comtrade) does not report data on Taiwan, China.

5. This number, however, decreased to 58 in 2009, which can be largely explained by factory closures.

6. Many trade unions are associated with the apparel industry in Cambodia. One or more independent unions usually work in each firm. The independent unions are members of federations of unions. All apparel industry unions are affiliated with one of the five federations named.

7. Including the Cambodian Ministry of Commerce, the Cambodian Chamber of Commerce, GMAC, and five Japanese organizations (Japan External Trade Organization [JETRO], Marubeni, JUKI Corporation, Japan Overseas Development Corporation [JODC], and The Association for Overseas Technical Scholarship [AOTS]).

References

ADB (Asian Development Bank). 2004. "Cambodia's Garment Industry: Meeting the Challenges of the Post-Quota Environment, October 2004." Report, Asian Development Bank, Manila.

Arnold, Dennis, and Toh Shih. 2010. "A Fair Model of Globalization? Labor and Global Production in Cambodia." *Journal of Contemporary Asia* 40 (3): 401–24.

Better Factories Cambodia. 2010. "Cambodia's Garment Industry Struggles in the Face of the Global Economic Downturn." Report, Phnom Penh.

Brocklehurst, G., and R. Anson. 2010. "World Markets for Textile Machinery: Yarn Manufacture, Part 1." *Textile Outlook International* (145): 80–117.

Cambodia MIC (Ministry of Commerce). 2006. "Cambodia National Export Strategy: 2007–2010." Report, Cambodia's Ministry of Commerce and the International Trade Center, Phnom Penh.

Chandararot, Kang, Sok Sina, and Liv Dannet. 2009. "Rapid Assessment of the Impact of the Financial Crisis in Cambodia." International Labour Organization (ILO) Asia-Pacific Working Paper Series, Bangkok.

EIC (Economic Institute of Cambodia). 2007. *Export Diversification and Value Addition*. Phnom Penh: Economic Institute of Cambodia.

FIAS (Foreign Investor Advisory Service). 2004. "Cambodia—Corporate Social Responsibility and the Apparel Sector Buyer Survey Results." Foreign Investor Advisory Service, International Finance Corporation, and World Bank, Washington, DC.

Jassin-O'Rourke Group, L. 2008. "Global Apparel Manufacturing Labor Cost Analysis 2008, Textile and Apparel Manufacturers & Merchants," Available at http://www.tammonline. com/researchpapers.htm.

Miller, Doug, Veasna Nuon, Charlene Aprill, and Ramon Certeza. 2008. "Governing the Supply Chain in Clothing Post MFA Phase Out. The Case of Cambodia." Global Union Research Network Discussion Paper 6, Revised Version (February), International Labour Organization, Geneva.

Nathan Associates. 2007. "Factory-Level Value Chain Analysis of Cambodia's Apparel Industry." Report, United States Agency for International Development, Washington, DC.

Natsuda, Kaoru, Kenta Goto, and John Thoburn. 2009. "Challenges to the Cambodian Garment Industry in the Global Garment Value Chain." Working Paper 09–3, Ritsumeikan Center for Asia Pacific Studies (RCAPS), Beppu-City.

Polaski, Sandra. 2009. "Harnessing Global Forces to Create Decent Work in Cambodia." Report, International Labour Organization and International Finance Corporation, Washington, DC.

Rasiah, Rajah. 2009. "Can Garment Exports from Cambodia, Laos, and Burma Be Sustained?" *Journal of Contemporary Asia* 39 (4): 619–37.

Staritz, Cornelia. 2011. "Making the Cut? Low-Income Countries and the Global Clothing Value Chain in a Post-quota and Post-crisis World." Study, World Bank, Washington, DC.

Tewari, Meenu. 2008. "Deepening Intraregional Trade and Investment in South Asia—The Case of the Textile and Clothing Industry." Working Paper 213, India Council for Research on International Economic Relations, New Delhi.

UNCTAD (United Nations Conference on Trade and Development). 2003. "Trade Preferences for LDCs: An Early Assessment of Benefits and Possible Improvements." United Nations, New York and Geneva.

World Bank. 2004. "Cambodia Seizing the Global Opportunity: Investment Climate Investment and Reform Strategy for Cambodia." Report 27925, World Bank, Washington, DC.

Yamagata, Tatsufumi. 2006. "The Garment Industry in Cambodia: Its Role in Poverty Reduction through Export-Oriented Development." Institute of Developing Economies Discussion Paper 62, Institute of Developing Economies, Japan External Trade Organization, Chiba.

CHAPTER 10

Honduras

Overview

- The apparel industry in Honduras relies almost entirely on exports to the United States, making it a typical regional supplier that exports to one major market in geographical proximity based on short lead times and regional trade agreements. Honduras has developed to be the largest apparel supplier to the United States within the Dominican Republic–Central America Free Trade Agreement (DR-CAFTA) region, displacing the Dominican Republic over the past 15 years.

- Initial development of the export-oriented apparel sector in Honduras began in the mid-1980s with the onset of the first of a series of U.S. preferential trade agreements with Caribbean Basin countries known as the Caribbean Basin Initiative (CBI). During this time, apparel assembly plants emerged due to reduced duty rates and quota-free access to the U.S. market beginning in 1986. In 2000, U.S. preferential access for apparel assembled in CBI countries switched to duty-free access, and duty-free access was extended to apparel cut in a CBI country provided it was sewn with U.S. thread and the fabric was formed in the United States from U.S. yarn. This development encouraged firms to move cutting operations to Honduras in addition to sewing.

- Investment in the textile sector began in the early 2000s, coinciding with increased U.S. preferential access for a limited quantity of apparel produced from knitted fabrics in a CBI country. During this time, five textile mills for knitted fabrics were established; three were owned by the Republic of Korean, one was Canadian, and the largest firm was a joint venture between a Honduran and U.S. firm (Fruit of the Loom). The first and still the only yarn plant was also set up by a Taiwanese firm in 1999. Investment in the textile industry increased with the passing of DR-CAFTA in 2005, which permitted duty-free access for apparel imported from Honduras that used fabric or yarn from the United States or a DR-CAFTA country. Since 2005, seven new knit textile fabric plants, all from large North American brand manufacturers, have opened in Honduras. DR-CAFTA was the first legislation that encouraged firms to acquire textile sourcing and production skills, allowing firms to move into original equipment manufacturing (OEM) and full-package production models.

- U.S. trade legislation helped Honduras to create an export-oriented apparel industry; however, it has not helped the country to upgrade into higher value-adding activities. Many firms are owned by U.S. brand manufacturers, and they have transferred limited functional capabilities to their Central American operations. Exports are concentrated in basic knitwear products such as T-shirts, socks, and underwear, with a focus on the men's market.

- The Multi-fibre Arrangement (MFA), regional trade agreements with the United States, the government's attractive foreign direct investment (FDI) and export processing zone (EPZ) policies, and relatively low labor costs were crucial in the development of the export-oriented apparel sector in Honduras. Since the MFA phaseout, the DR-CAFTA region, including Honduras, has lost competitiveness compared to Asian countries and has experienced declining exports.

Development of the Apparel Industry

Honduras's export-oriented apparel sector began in the mid-1980s following the first of a series of U.S. trade preferences for Caribbean and Central American countries known collectively as the Caribbean Basin Initiative (CBI). The first of these programs was the U.S.-Caribbean Basin Economic Recovery Act (CBERA). CBERA came into effect on January 1, 1984, and granted benefits to 20 countries and territories in the Caribbean Basin, including Honduras. This was a production-sharing arrangement (commonly referred to as 807) that permitted U.S. firms to export cut textile fabrics to Honduras and reimport sewn products, only paying duty on the minimal value added (that is, labor) in Honduras.

Known as 807A, U.S. preferential treatment was expanded two years later in 1986 to provide essentially quota-free access as well as reduced-duty rates for apparel assembled in CBI countries from U.S. fabrics. This expansion remained in effect from 1986 through 2000. During this time, *maquila*-style firms emerged in Honduras that only performed the sewing activity in the apparel supply chain. Growth of this type of firm was also spurred by Honduran incentives to attract FDI to the country. In 1987, Honduras established an EPZ program, and in 1998, it expanded this concept to make the entire country a free trade zone (USITC 2004).

The addition of quota-free access to the U.S. market under the 807A legislation provided Honduras and the other CBI countries with an advantage over competing Asian suppliers still subject to MFA quotas. It also made Honduras an attractive location for U.S. brand manufacturers. During this time, many U.S. brand manufacturers began moving their apparel assembly plants to nearby low-wage countries in the CBI region. The first foreign apparel companies started coming to Honduras in the San Pedro Sula area in the late 1980s. Van Heusen has been cited as the first company to open in a free zone, followed by other names such as OskKosh and Springtown Apparel (from Georgia, United States), which manufactured knit T-shirts and underwear for Jockey and J.C. Penney (Cedrone 1994). These firms were mostly from the United States, and relocations were motivated by the low labor costs in Honduras (compared to the United States), FDI incentives, and the regional trade agreements in the context of the CBI.

Sixteen years after the 807A provision, CBI was substantially expanded through the U.S.-Caribbean Basin Trade Partnership Act (CBTPA). CBTPA entered into force in October 2000 and remained the main trade agreement with the Central American countries until the passage of DR-CAFTA in 2005–06.[1] CBTPA allowed for duty- and quota-free access to the U.S. market for apparel assembled in a CBI country from U.S.-formed and -cut fabric (807A+) or for apparel cut and assembled in a CBI country using U.S. thread provided the fabric was formed in the United States using U.S. yarn. CBTPA permitted duty-free access to CBI apparel, and unlike the previous agreement, it permitted the cutting operation to be performed in a CBI country.

CBTPA also included a new provision that granted duty-free access to a *limited* quantity of apparel assembled in CBI countries from knitted fabrics formed within the region from yarns produced in the United States. With the exception of a few local firms producing for the local market, this provision sparked the first developments in the textile sector. Five textile mills for knitted fabrics were established between 1997 and 2004, and the first and still the only yarn plant was set up in 1999.

The years of the CBTPA legislation (2000–05) coincided with the second half of the MFA quota phaseout. During this time, Honduran shipments to the United States were concentrated in basic apparel, particularly knit tops (for example, T-shirts) and underwear, which together accounted for 72 percent of the total quantity of U.S. sector imports from Honduras in 2002. In terms of value, 85 percent of the U.S. apparel imports from Honduras entered under preferential duty provisions in 2002 (USITC 2004). Preferential access to the U.S. market was an advantage for Honduran exporters, as the majority of U.S. exports were in categories that were not phased out until the last rounds, giving Honduras an edge over Asian competitors (USITC 2004).

Apparel exports have increased significantly since the mid-1990s. Import data from Honduras's trading partners show an increase from $970 million in 1995 to $2,926 million in 2004 (table 10.1). The share of Honduras in global apparel exports increased from 0.6 percent in 1995 to 1.2 percent in 2004. Woven exports were higher than knit exports in 1995, but from then onward, knit exports increased and accounted for nearly three-quarters by 2004. With regard to end markets, Honduras's apparel exports that are strongly concentrated toward the U.S. market accounted for nearly 96 percent of total apparel exports in 2004. Table 10.2 shows the development of apparel exports to the United States. Honduras's apparel exports to the United States hit their peak in 2004, accounting for $2,743 million and representing 4.1 percent of total U.S. apparel imports. Table 10.3 shows the share of different DR-CAFTA countries in imports to the United States. Honduras's share increased from 19 percent in 1995 to 28 percent in 2004, making Honduras the largest apparel exporter from the region.

Along with the development of exports, the number of firms and employment in the apparel sector increased in the 1990s and early 2000s. In 1994, Honduran firms employed 50,000 workers (USITC 2004) and there were 130 members of the Honduran Apparel Manufacturers Association (Cedrone 1994). In 2003, members of the Honduran Apparel Manufacturers Association included 157 apparel producers, 9 textile

Table 10.1 Honduran Apparel Exports to the World

	1995	1998	2001	2004	2005	2006	2007	2008	2009
Total value ($, million)	970	1,984	2,558	2,926	2,897	2,777	2,891	3,035	2,457
Annual growth rate (%)	—	13.2	1.4	7.8	–1.0	–4.2	4.1	5.0	–19.1
Share of world exports (%)	0.6	1.1	1.3	1.2	1.1	1.0	0.9	0.9	0.8
Woven and knit value ($, million)									
Woven	503	699	743	769	732	645	648	620	505
Knit	467	1,286	1,815	2,157	2,165	2,132	2,243	2,416	1,952
Woven and knit share of total import value (%)									
Woven	51.8	35.2	29.0	26.3	25.3	23.2	22.4	20.4	20.6
Knit	48.2	64.8	71.0	73.7	74.7	76.8	77.6	79.6	79.4

Source: United Nations Commodity Trade Statistics Database (UN Comtrade).
Note: Exports represented by imports reported by partner countries. Apparel classification: Harmonized Commodity Description and Coding System (HS) 1992: Woven: HS62; Knit: HS61. Growth rate reflects change from previous year. — = not available.

Table 10.2 U.S. Apparel Imports from Honduras

	1996	1998	2001	2004	2005	2006	2007	2008	2009
Total value ($, million)	1,240	1,903	2,438	2,743	2,685	2,518	2,587	2,675	2,107
Annual growth rate (%)	—	12.8	0.9	6.8	−2.1	−6.2	2.8	3.4	−21.2
Share of all U.S. apparel imports (%)	3.3	3.8	4.2	4.1	3.8	3.4	3.4	3.7	3.3
Woven and knit value ($, million)									
Woven	508	668	714	729	669	599	602	535	420
Knit	732	1,234	1,724	2,013	2,016	1,919	1,985	2,140	1,687
Woven and knit share of total import value (%)									
Woven	41.0	35.1	29.3	26.6	24.9	23.8	23.3	20.0	19.9
Knit	59.0	64.9	70.7	73.4	75.1	76.2	76.7	80.0	80.1

Source: United States International Trade Commission (USITC).

Note: Apparel imports represented by Harmonized Commodity Description and Coding System (HS) Codes 61 and 62; General Customs Value. Growth rate reflects change from previous year. — = not available.

Table 10.3 U.S. Apparel Imports from DR-CAFTA by Country

Country/region	Customs value ($, million)					Share of DR-CAFTA total (%)				
	1995	2000	2004	2005	2009	1995	2000	2004	2005	2009
DR-CAFTA	4,745	8,973	9,509	9,104	6,145					
Honduras	918	2,323	2,673	2,622	2,032	19.4	25.9	28.1	28.8	33.1
El Salvador	582	1,583	1,720	1,619	1,298	12.3	17.6	18.1	17.8	21.1
Guatemala	682	1,487	1,947	1,816	1,103	14.4	16.6	20.5	19.9	17.9
Nicaragua	74	336	595	716	892	1.6	3.7	6.3	7.9	14.5
Dominican Republic	1,731	2,425	2,059	1,849	613	36.5	27.0	21.7	20.3	10.0
Costa Rica	757	819	516	482	206	16.0	9.1	5.4	5.3	3.4

Source: Office of Textiles and Apparel (OTEXA): Multi-fibre Arrangement (MFA) Category 1: All Apparel Imports.

Note: DR-CAFTA = Dominican Republic–Central America Free Trade Agreement.

mills, and numerous suppliers of equipment, components, and services to the industry (table 10.4). Apparel producers employed 90,000 workers and textile mills an estimated 4,500 (USITC 2004). In 2000, apparel exports represented 68 percent of total exports, but this figure declined to around 46 percent in 2009 (WTO 2010). According to the Asociación Hondureña de Maquiladores (AHM) in 2003, 90 percent of Honduras's 215 export-processing plants were dedicated to apparel production (Bair and Peters 2006).

The Multi-fibre Arrangement/Agreement on Textiles and Clothing (MFA/ATC) transition period was unique for Honduras and the CAFTA countries because it occurred at the same time as the implementation of DR-CAFTA, which went into effect on April 1, 2006, for Honduras. The DR-CAFTA agreement was based on the North American Free Trade Agreement (NAFTA) and initiated free trade between the United States and six countries of the Caribbean Basin region—Costa Rica, the Dominican Republic, El Salvador, Guatemala, Honduras, and Nicaragua. For textiles and apparel to receive duty-free entry into a U.S.–DR-CAFTA country, products must meet the rules of origin (ROO) of the agreement. The textile and apparel ROO is known as yarn-forward, which requires that the yarn production and all operations

Table 10.4   Honduran Apparel Industry: Factories and Employment

Year	Number of firms	Employment	Female employment (% share and number employed)
1997	—	87,000	—
1998	—	110,000	—
1999	—	120,000	—
2000	145	125,000	—
2001	154	110,000	—
2002	155	107,000	
2003	162	90,618[a]	57.9 (52,437)
2004	168	95,319	53.9 (51,392)
2005	153	100,311	56.7 (56,886)
2006	160	100,537	56.8 (57,095)
2007	169	103,377	56.4 (58,355)
2008	133	92,276	56.9 (55,370)
2009	132	83,712	54.4 (45,564)

Sources: Central Bank of Honduras (number of firms 2000–2009 and employment 2003–09); employment 1994–2002 from USITC 2004.
Note: — = not available.
a. The decline between 2002 and 2003 may be explained by the switch in data sources.

forward (that is, fabric production through apparel assembly) occur in either the United States or the DR-CAFTA region.[2] There are some exceptions that generally allow fibers, yarns, or fabrics to be sourced from outside the region. For example, CAFTA includes a cumulation provision, which allows fabric manufactured in Mexico or Canada to be used in woven apparel products (Office of Textiles and Apparel, OTEXA). Since DR-CAFTA was implemented in the same year as the MFA phaseout (2005), it is difficult to separate the effects of the two. However, despite the increase in preferential access to the United States, exports still declined post-MFA.

During the MFA phaseout transition years, Honduras's apparel exports decreased by 1.0 percent in 2005 and by 4.2 percent in 2006, and Honduras's share of global apparel exports declined from 1.2 percent in 2004 to 1.0 percent in 2006 (table 10.1). In the United States, exports decreased by 2.1 percent in 2005 and by 6.2 percent in 2006, reducing Honduras's apparel market share in the U.S. market from 4.1 percent in 2004 to 3.4 percent in 2006 (table 10.2). As quotas have phased out, many of the U.S. branded manufacturers and other lead firms that originally moved into Honduras have moved into an outsourcing model of production, in which Asia has been a desirable location, or they have purchased and built factories in Asia. Hanesbrands, a U.S.-based manufacturer and marketer, stated when it went public in 2006 that it planned on closing U.S. facilities, consolidating Central American plants, and increasing investment and sourcing relationships in Asia. Hanesbrands (from the United States) has mills in Thailand and Vietnam and a fabric mill in China. Gildan (from Canada) purchased its first mill in Bangladesh in 2010.

In 2007 and 2008, exports increased back to values similar to those in 2004–05, but the global economic crisis together with the phaseout of the China safeguards impacted exports again negatively. Honduras's global apparel exports and U.S. exports declined by 19.1 percent and by 21.2 percent, respectively, between 2008 and 2009. Honduras's *maquila* sector as a whole lost 30,000 jobs during the global economic crisis, but in 2010, leading industry executives anticipated growth in Honduras's textile and apparel *maquila* industry due to recent investments in the northern industrial area and recovering U.S. exports (Freeman 2010).

Honduras's recent political unrest has raised concerns for textile and apparel producers in the region. In June 2009, Honduras president Manuel Zelaya was removed from office by the Honduran military and replaced by a de facto president, Roberto Micheletti. In July 2009,

Nike Inc., Adidas Group, Gap Inc., and Knights Apparel sent letters to the U.S. government outlining their concerns over the political instability in a country where U.S. companies produce millions of dollars in apparel annually (Ellis 2009). The apparel and footwear companies called on the U.S. secretary of state and other stakeholders to put pressure on the new government to "fully respect" freedom of the press, freedom of speech, freedom of movement, freedom of assembly, and freedom of association. In October 2009, a coalition of trade associations[3] called on the U.S. secretary of state to increase pressure on the Honduran government to resolve the coup before the textile and apparel industries deteriorated further. The groups warned that if the current standoff continued, the textile and apparel sectors in Honduras could be permanently damaged. The associations' members reported that their financing costs increased as uncertainty in Honduras fueled a loss of confidence in the region. The letter stated that textile and apparel imports from Honduras and textile exports to Honduras had both fallen more than 30 percent (Casabona 2009).

Overview of DR-CAFTA Countries

The following provides a brief description of each of the countries in the DR-CAFTA region, and the preceding table 10.3 presents U.S. imports from each country and their share of regional totals.

Honduras was the leading apparel exporter to the U.S. market, representing 33 percent of the total apparel import value from DR-CAFTA countries in 2009. Honduras is primarily a supplier of basic knit apparel, predominantly for men, including T-shirts and underwear. Investment in the country is largely from U.S. brand apparel manufacturers that set up operations to take advantage of low labor costs, which, along with preferential tariff and quota access, have allowed products to be produced and exported to the United States for less than the cost of manufacturing them entirely in the United States.

El Salvador has followed a very similar path to that of Honduras. It was the second-largest apparel exporter from the region to the United States in 2009, representing 21 percent of total exports. The majority of U.S. exports are knit shirts and underwear (mostly cotton). El Salvador is the second most significant exporter of women's woven trousers and has the third-largest number of textile firms in the region.

The Dominican Republic held a similar position to Honduras in the U.S. market in 1995, with a 36.5 percent share of the DR-CAFTA region with a similar product offering. However, over the past 15 years, the Dominican Republic's exports have steadily declined, and Honduras and the Dominican Republic have essentially switched places. Today, Dominican Republic exports represent only 10 percent of total regional exports to the United States. The Dominican Republic, El Salvador, and Honduras all have similar labor rates.

Guatemala plays a very different role than any of the other exporters in the region. Guatemala is primarily a supplier of women's apparel for U.S. retailers and brand marketers. Firm ownership is dominated by Korean (130 of a total of 244 firms are Korean owned) or Guatemalan apparel manufacturers that put together full-package products for U.S. brands. Many independent sourcing agents and the sourcing arm of the U.S. retailers have locations in Guatemala. Guatemala is also the major source of woven fabric manufacturing in the region. It has a very strong industry organization—VESTEX—that has been critical in marketing the country as a full-package supplier and in promoting local firms through an annual sourcing trade event and with ads in apparel publications. Guatemala was one of the top three apparel exporters from the region, accounting for 18 percent of total U.S. apparel exports.

Nicaragua is also unique in that growth in the apparel export sector really only began with the passage of DR-CAFTA. In the DR-CAFTA legislations, Nicaragua was granted a tariff preference level (TPL) for certain woven products. This legislation permits local apparel manufacturers to use fabric from anywhere in the world and not just from the United States. The majority of U.S. exports are men's and women's cotton knit shirts, followed by men's and women's cotton trousers. Nicaragua is now the leading DR-CAFTA exporter of men's blue denim trousers.

Costa Rica's role in the export industry was more prominent in 1995 and years prior, but it plays a very limited, niche role in the U.S. market today. Exports are dominated by hosiery, underwear, and swimwear, with a majority of products made from man-made fiber (MMF). Costa Rica has a TPL for swimwear, and it is the only DR-CAFTA country with a textile product in its top 10 exports to the U.S. market (specialty yarn). Prior to 2008, the largest import category from Costa Rica was men's blue denim cotton woven trousers, but this export fell off completely in 2008. Costa Rica has the highest labor rates in the region and was the last to implement the DR-CAFTA legislation. The country is moving on to focus on other industries such as electronics and tourism.

Structure of the Apparel Industry

Types of Firms

The majority of the apparel firms in Honduras are North American brand manufacturers that started setting up sewing facilities in the late 1980s to take advantage of preferential access to the United States. Based on employment figures provided in the AHM directory, five North American–based brand manufacturers (for details see following text) employ approximately 38,000 workers. Given the overall employment figure of 83,712 workers in the Honduran apparel industry in 2009, these firms represent roughly 45 percent of all employment. Honduras also has several large, Honduran-owned apparel firms, including the Kattan Group, Lovable Group, and GrupoKarim's (for details see following text). These three locally owned firms employ roughly 17 percent of the total. Further, there are also firms owned by Asian investors, mostly from the Republic of Korea and Taiwan, China. Korean firms were early investors in the textile industry and represent three of the fabric plants in Honduras today. These companies include Shin Sung, established in 1997, and Woong Chun and Cottonwise, both set up around 2002 (AHM 2010; Bair and Peters 2006). This breakdown by country investment is similar to AHM figures from 2002–03 in which U.S.-owned companies accounted for 54 percent of the apparel industry workforce; Korea 17 percent; Honduras 15 percent; Canada 5 percent; and other Asian sources 10 percent (USITC 2004). In 2001, cumulative investment in the apparel sector totaled $1.4 billion, of which $751 million was FDI and $670 million was local investment. The United States was the major foreign investor, accounting for 26 percent ($370 million) of the FDI total, followed by Korea with 10 percent ($146 million).

The Honduran apparel industry primarily consists of locally owned firms capable of producing under a cut-make-trim (CMT) or OEM production model and U.S.-owned firms that own both apparel assembly plants and textile facilities in Honduras and other Central American countries. These locations produce solely for their parent companies, so the skills generally associated with OEM are limited to the sourcing or producing practices of the lead firm that owns the factory.

The development of assembly subcontracting networks within North America has been promoted by several policies that actually impede opportunities for Honduran firms to upgrade. In the 1980s, Honduras began with just the assembly portion of the CMT model. With the passage of CBTPA in 2000, firms moved into cutting and sewing in Honduras due to the extension of preferential access that permitted cutting to occur within CBI countries. Under CBTPA, specified quantities of knitted garments could also enter the United States duty and quota free from regionally knitted fabrics in the CBI region, leading to a few investments in the knitted fabric industry from Honduran, Korean, Taiwanese, and U.S. investors. With the passing of the DR-CAFTA trade legislation in 2005, four of the five major brand manufacturers opened local factories to produce knitted fabrics. Fruit of the Loom/Russell, Gildan, Anvil, and Delta Apparel have all set up textile manufacturing facilities in Honduras to supply cut-and-sew plants. Hanesbrands has facilities in neighboring El Salvador, which likely accounts for a significant share of the increase in fabric exports from El Salvador to Honduras after 2005.

The other category of firms is primarily made of locally owned firms that are export oriented and produce for the regional market. These companies are capable of OEM production and have limited fabric manufacturing, but they also produce goods based on the CMT model. This group of companies, though limited in number, has been the most dynamic in recent years, witnessing expansion in both production capacity and employment for most of the post-2000 period (Bair and Peters 2006). The trade agreement in 2000 also permitted local firms to produce and export apparel to the United States without having a strong tie to a U.S. apparel manufacturer. This development led a few investors to begin establishing or expanding knitting operations in Honduras to make T-shirts, underwear, and other knitwear for U.S. exports under the full-package production model.

Beyond backward linkages into the textile industry, there has been limited movement into original design manufacturing (ODM) or original brand manufacturing (OBM) activities. Since the majority of the firms in Honduras are owned by brand manufacturers, it is highly unlikely that locations in Honduras will acquire design or branding capabilities unless the lead firm moves these operations from North America to Central America. A few local firms produce original brands for the Central American market. The Lovable Group produces domestic brands for the regional market, and the Kattan Group has a licensing agreement with Phillips-Van Heusen (PVH) to produce and sell apparel in the Central American region.

North American Brand Manufacturers in Honduras

Hanesbrands is a U.S.-based manufacturer and marketer of innerwear and outwear for men, women, and children. Hanesbrands produces a variety of products, including sweatshirts, underwear, bras, hosiery, and T-shirts (table 10.5). It is the owner of many well-known apparel brands, including Hanes, Playtex, Bali, barely there, Just My Size, Wonderbra, Duofold, Champion, C9 by Champion, and Hanes Beefy-T. In 2008, 27 percent of Hanesbrands sales were from T-shirts (Textiles Intelligence 2008). Hanesbrands has a significant presence in Central America, primarily in the Dominican Republic, El Salvador, and Honduras. Since Hanesbrands became an independent, public company in 2006, it has focused on closing North American facilities, consolidating Central American facilities, and expanding capacity in Asia. Hanesbrands has 10 apparel assembly plants in Honduras. Other Central American facilities include 6 apparel plants and 1 textile plant each in the Dominican Republic and El Salvador. Hanesbrands has around 12,000 workers in Honduras (Hanesbrands 2011). In February 2009, Hanes started a continuing education program, and more than 1,000 Honduran employees participate at no cost. The employees attend classes on Saturdays in the towns of Villanueva and Choloma near San Pedro Sula in schools close to the plants where they work. The program is available to associates at Hanesbrands apparel manufacturing and sewing facilities (Hanesbrands 2011).

Fruit of the Loom, Russell, and **VF Intimates** are all part of the "Fruit of the Loom" division owned by Berkshire Hathaway. Fruit of the Loom

Table 10.5   Hanesbrands Factories in Honduras

Local name	Activity	Products	Employees	Location
Jasper de Honduras	Sewing	T-shirts, fleece and jersey outerwear, sports shirts	2,175	ZIP Honduras
Confecciones del Valle	Sewing	Bras, underwear	2,100	ZIP Buena Vista
Hanes Choloma	Sewing	Sportswear	1,850	ZIP Choloma
Manufacturera San Pedro Sula	Sewing	T-shirts	1,350	ZIP Buena Vista
Jogbra Honduras	Sewing	Women's sportswear and bras	1,300	ZIP Buena Vista
Confecciones Atlántida	Sewing	Men's boxers and T-shirts	898	ZOLI ManufactureraCeibeña
Industrial Embroidery	Accessories	Embroidery, screen printing, labels	668	ZOLI Inhdelva
HBI Socks de Honduras	Service	Socks	4	ZIP Búfalo

Sources: AHM 2010, BCH 2010, and Hanesbrands 2011.

manufactures and sells T-shirts, underwear, and activewear primarily for men, but for women and children as well (table 10.6). Fruit of the Loom/ Russell owns all eight of its factories in Honduras rather than subcontracting to outside manufacturers (Fibre2Fashion 2009). Fruit of the Loom employs 10,875 workers in its Honduran factories (AHM 2010).

Gildan, a Canadian company, is a vertically integrated manufacturer of T-shirts, sweatshirts, underwear, and socks. In 2008, 77 percent of sales were from T-shirts (Textiles Intelligence 2008). Gildan currently has seven locations in Honduras: two apparel sewing facilities, two textile plants, two sock manufacturing plants, and one distribution center (table 10.7). Gildan employs a little over 10,000 workers in Honduras. It opened its first factory in Honduras for sewing in 1998. Around 2003, this number had increased to three, and Gildan had added the first fabric plant. In 2007, Honduras added the first sock mill, and the number of factories in Honduras hit its peak of eight. Since 2007, Gildan has been consolidating and upgrading its Honduran operations. Its other investments in Central America include two sewing plants in Nicaragua and one textile and one sewing facility in the Dominican Republic. Gildan also has cut-and-sew outsourcing relationships with apparel contractors in Haiti that work closely with their owned facilities in the Dominican Republic.

Table 10.6   Fruit of the Loom and Russell Corporation Factories in Honduras

Local name	Activity	Products	Employees	Location
Confecciones Dos Caminos	Sewing	Day wear	2,173	ZIP Búfalo
Caracol Knits	Textile mill	Knit fabric	1,900	ZOLI Caracol Knits
El Porvenir Manufacturing	Sewing	Underwear	1,627	ZIP El Porvenir
Desoto Knits	Sewing	Socks, packaging	1,241	ZOLI R.L.A. Manufacturing
RLA Russell Manufacturing	Textile mill	Fabric	1,069	ZOLI R.L.A. Manufacturing
Jerzees Buena Vista	Sewing	Fleece	927	ZIP Buena Vista
Manufacturas Villanueva	Service	Packaging	868	ZIP Villanueva
VFI de Honduras	Sewing	Underwear, lingerie, sleepwear	670	ZIP Choloma
Coral Knits	Textile mill	Fabric	400	ZOLI Caracol Knits
Total			**10,875**	

Sources: AHM 2010, BCH 2010.

Table 10.7   Gildan Factories in Honduras

Local name	Activity	Products	Employees	Location
Gildan Activewear San Miguel	Sewing	Sportswear	4,000	ZOLI América
Gildan Activewear Villanueva	Sewing	Fleece and pants	2,381	ZIP Villanueva
Gildan Hosiery	Hosiery, knit	Socks	1,400	ZOLI San Miguel VI
Gildan Choloma Textile	Textile mill	Fabric producer	1,000	ZOLI San Miguel VI
Gildan Honduras Textile Company	Textile mill	Fabric	869	ZOLI San Miguel VI
Prewett Mills Honduras	Hosiery, knit	Socks	581	Villanueva
Gildan Distribution Center	Distribution center		—	Choloma
Total			**10,231**	

Sources: AHM 2010, BCH 2010.
Note: — = not available.

Anvil Knitwear is a U.S.-based company that designs, manufactures, markets, and distributes T-shirts, polo shirts, fleece tops, and athletic shorts for men, women, and children (table 10.8). Anvil has three manufacturing facilities: two in Honduras and one cut-and-sew facility in Nicaragua (Textiles Intelligence 2009). Anvil has had a presence in Honduras since 1996, when it opened the Star, S.A. facility. For the first five years, this plant only performed sewing, but with the new trade legislation, cutting was added to the local production process. In 2005, the AKH, S.A. plant was built to knit and finish fabrics to support the Star, S.A. plant. Anvil employs nearly 2,500 workers in Honduras. Both of Anvil's factories are certified by the Worldwide Responsible Accredited Production (WRAP). Anvil Knitwear was also the first company worldwide to receive the organization's new WRAP certificate for its textile mill, located in Honduras (Fibre2Fashion 2010).

Delta Apparel produces T-shirts and other basic activewear. Delta Apparel owns two apparel assembly plants and one textile plant operational in 2007 in Honduras (table 10.9). Other regional manufacturing occurs at plants in El Salvador and Mexico. Delta employs around 2,300 employees at its factories in Honduras.

Several other large apparel manufacturers with at least one operation in Honduras include VF Corporation (Red Kap; Workwear Division), Jockey, NH Apparel, Garan (also owned by Berkshire Hathaway), Dickies, and Bay Island Sportswear.

Table 10.8   Anvil Knitwear Factories in Honduras

Local name	Activity	Products	Employees	Location
AKH, S.A.	Textile mill	Knit fabric: produce, dye, finish	546	ZOLI Green Valley: Est. 2005
Star, S.A.	Sewing	T-shirts (knit fabric: cut, sew)	1,930	ZIP El Porvenir: Est. 1996
Total			**2,476**	

Source: AHM 2010.

Table 10.9   Delta Apparel Factories in Honduras

Local name	Activity	Products	Employees	Location
Ceiba Textiles	Textile mill	Knit, dye, finish, cut, sew	441	ZOLI Green Valley: Est. 2007
Delta Apparel Honduras	Sewing	Blank T-shirts	986	ZIP Buena Vista
Delta Cortés	Sewing	Blank T-shirts	902	ZIP Buena Vista
Total			**2,329**	

Source: AHM 2010; BCH 2010.

Honduran Manufacturing Firm Groups in Honduras

The Kattan Family has been credited with establishing the local apparel industry (see table 10.10) in the 1920s by starting the first small sewing shop in downtown San Pedro Sula to service the Central American market. The company expanded in the local market over the next 40 years until a six-day war with El Salvador in the late 1960s resulted in the removal of Honduras from the region's common market. This event spurred the Kattans to begin seeking opportunities to export to the United States. The Kattans' first relationship with a U.S. firm was with Phillips-Van Heusen in 1965, when the company acquired a licensing agreement to produce and sell PVH products in Central America. In 1985, the Kattans started their first U.S. joint venture with Cluett Peabody (The Arrow Co.) (Cedrone 1994). In 1994, the Kattan family owned seven plants, five of which were joint ventures with companies including Warnaco Inc. (Menswear Division), PVH, and Corporation Textile of Foshan. Today, major customers include Hanesbrands and Gildan (knit shirts) and PVH, Oxford Industry brands, and Carhartt, among others (woven shirts).

GrupoKarim's owns the only yarn facility in Honduras, previously owned by a Taiwanese firm. GrupoKarim's is headquartered in Honduras

Table 10.10   Major Local Firms in Honduras

Parent company	Number of local firms	Category	Products	Employees
Kattan Group	4–6	Assembly (3) Finishing (1)	Woven and knit dress shirts, bottoms; laundry finishing services; Phillips-Van Heusen (PVH) license	~4,000
GrupoKarim's	4	Assembly (1) Yarn (1) Chemicals (1) Recycling (1)	Acquired Formosa Spinning 9/2010; only yarn mfg. in Honduras. Apparel: uniforms, polo shirts	2,000
Lovable Group	9	Sewing (6) Textiles (2) Service (1)	Lingerie, underwear, T-shirts, knit fabric, elastic, embroidery, screenprinting	~8,000
Total				**~14,000**

Source: AHM 2010; company websites.

and has facilities for assembly, textile chemical production, yarn spinning and fabric production, and recycling within the country. The group also has operations in other Central American countries.

The Lovable Group is an exporter and a brand designer and product developer for intimate apparel in Honduras and the Central American region. The company was established in 1964, and today it has nine facilities in Honduras, ranging from assembly to fabric and elastic. The company owns two textile mills, Elcatex and Elca.

End Markets

Honduras's apparel exports are predominantly destined for the United States, although this volume has decreased over the past 15 years. In 1995, 98.4 percent of exports went to the United States, but this figure dropped to 87.8 percent by 2009 (table 10.11). Since 2005, exports to El Salvador and Mexico have increased with the implementation of DR-CAFTA in 2005. Canada is the other main export destination, largely driven by Gildan, a Canadian-owned knitwear manufacturer with significant manufacturing facilities in Honduras. The EU-15[4] accounted for 2.1 percent of total apparel exports, a share that has increased from 0.8 percent in 2000 (figure 10.1).

Export Products

Knitwear products dominate Honduras's export portfolio, with a concentration in cotton-based apparel including sweatshirts (fleece products), T-shirts, socks, and underwear. In 1995, knit exports accounted for

Table 10.11 Top Five Honduran Apparel Export Markets, 1995, 2000, 2005, 2008, and 2009

Country/region	Customs value ($, million)					Market share (%)				
	1995	2000	2005	2008	2009	1995	2000	2005	2008	2009
World	970	2,524	2,897	3,035	2,457					
United States	954	2,462	2,744	2,741	2,156	98.4	97.6	94.7	90.3	87.8
Mexico	n.a.	3	18	46	65	n.a.	0.1	0.6	1.5	2.6
El Salvador	n.a.	n.a.	n.a.	38	65	n.a.	n.a.	n.a.	1.2	2.6
Canada	7	24	52	63	62	0.7	0.9	1.8	2.1	2.5
EU-15	4	21	30	57	52	0.4	0.8	1.0	1.9	2.1
Morocco	n.a.	n.a.	n.a.	n.a.	n.a.	n.a.	n.a.	n.a.	n.a.	n.a.
Costa Rica	n.a.	n.a.	23	n.a.	n.a.	n.a.	n.a.	0.8	n.a.	n.a.
Japan	1	7	n.a.	n.a.	n.a.	0.1	0.3	n.a.	n.a.	n.a.
Guatemala	1	n.a.	n.a.	n.a.	n.a.	0.1	n.a.	n.a.	n.a.	n.a.
Top five share	968	2,517	2,867	2,944	2,400	99.8	99.7	99.0	97.0	97.7

Source: United Nations Commodity Trade Statistics Database (UN Comtrade).

Note: Harmonized Commodity Description and Coding System (HS) 1992: Codes 61 and 62); exports represented by country imports from Honduras. n.a. = not applicable (indicates country not in top five for given year); EU-15 = the 15 member states of the European Union (EU) as of December 31, 2003, before the new member states joined the EU: Austria, Belgium, Denmark, Finland, France, Germany, Greece, Ireland, Italy, Luxembourg, the Netherlands, Portugal, Spain, Sweden, and the United Kingdom.

Figure 10.1   Top Four Honduran Apparel Export Markets, 2000 and 2009
% market share

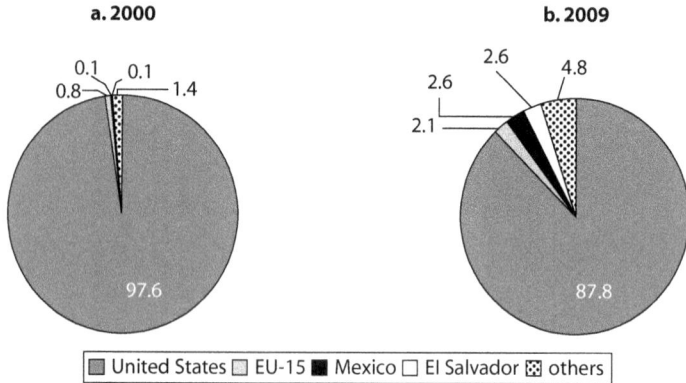

a. 2000

0.1 0.1
0.8   1.4
97.6

b. 2009

2.6   4.8
2.6
2.1
87.8

■ United States □ EU-15 ■ Mexico □ El Salvador ▨ others

Source: United Nations Commodity Trade Statistics Database (UN Comtrade).
Note: Harmonized Commodity Description and Coding System (HS) 1992: Codes 61 and 62; exports represented by country imports. EU-15 = the 15 member states of the European Union (EU) as of December 31, 2003, before the new member states joined the EU: Austria, Belgium, Denmark, Finland, France, Germany, Greece, Ireland, Italy, Luxembourg, the Netherlands, Portugal, Spain, Sweden, and the United Kingdom.

48.2 percent of total apparel exports, in 2004 for 73.7 percent, and in 2009 for 79.4 percent. In 2008, Honduras was a top 10 country source for 2 of the top 10 U.S. apparel import categories (Brocklehurst 2009). The largest U.S. import category in 2008, cotton sweaters, constituted 19.3 percent of the total apparel import value (table 10.12). Honduras was the eighth-largest supplier by value for 2008 in this category. Of the top 10 countries, Honduras was the lowest-cost supplier, at $1.69 per piece (Brocklehurst 2009). Honduras was also the leading U.S. supplier of the third-largest U.S. import category by volume, men and boys cotton knitted shirts. However, Honduras performed the worst of the top 10 suppliers in 2008 compared to 2007, experiencing a 5.3 percent decline in value and a 6.4 percent decline in volume. Similar to the women and girls (W&G) category, Honduras is also the lowest-cost supplier of this product, at an average of $1.52 per piece (Brocklehurst 2009). The development of unit prices for Honduras's top 10 apparel export products to the United States are depicted in table 10.13.

For the DR-CAFTA region as a whole in 2009, the leading export to the U.S. market was knitted cotton shirts, representing 38 percent of all U.S. textile and apparel imports from the region (OTEXA 2011). This product provides an interesting case study into the competitive dynamics for similar products within the region. In general, U.S. T-shirt imports are

Table 10.12 Top 10 U.S. Imports from Honduras, 1996, 2000, 2005, 2008, and 2009

HS Code	Product	Customs value ($, million)					Market share (%)				
		1996	2000	2005	2008	2009	1996	2000	2005	2008	2009
Total		**1,240**	**2,416**	**2,685**	**2,675**	**2,107**					
611020	Sweatshirts	144	459	606	517	415	11.6	19.0	22.6	19.3	19.7
610910	T-Shirts	183	499	644	625	400	14.7	20.7	24.0	23.4	19.0
611030	Sweatshirts	n.a.	n.a.	108	240	197	n.a.	n.a.	4.0	9.0	9.4
611595	Socks NESOI[a]	n.a.	n.a.	n.a.	143	169	n.a.	n.a.	n.a.	5.4	8.0
610821	Underwear	39	n.a.	75	96	102	3.1	n.a.	2.8	3.6	4.8
621210	Bras	66	128	146	110	86	5.3	5.3	5.5	4.1	4.1
621010	Garments	n.a.	55	n.a.	n.a.	76	n.a.	2.3	n.a.	n.a.	3.6
620343	Trousers	n.a.	n.a.	83	86	69	n.a.	n.a.	3.1	3.2	3.3
610711	Underwear	71	133	114	99	66	5.7	5.5	4.3	3.7	3.1
620530	Shirts	n.a.	n.a.	67	n.a.	59	n.a.	n.a.	2.5	n.a.	2.8
620342	Trousers	120	143	129	89	n.a.	9.7	5.9	4.8	3.3	n.a.
610990	T-Shirts	n.a.	123	101	80	n.a.	n.a.	5.1	3.8	3.0	n.a.
610510	Shirts	80	121	n.a.	n.a.	n.a.	6.4	5.0	n.a.	n.a.	n.a.
620520	Shirts	96	112	n.a.	n.a.	n.a.	7.7	4.6	n.a.	n.a.	n.a.
620462	Trousers	54	75	n.a.	n.a.	n.a.	4.3	3.1	n.a.	n.a.	n.a.
610462	Trousers	43	n.a.	n.a.	n.a.	n.a.	3.5	n.a.	n.a.	n.a.	n.a.
Top 10 share		**896**	**1,847**	**2,074**	**2,084**	**1,639**	**72.2**	**76.4**	**77.2**	**77.9**	**77.8**

Source: United States International Trade Commission (USITC).
Note: General Customs Value; n.a. = not applicable (indicates product not in the top 10 in given year). Harmonized Commodity Description and Coding System (HS) numbers beginning with 61 indicate knitted garments and 62 indicate nonknitted (woven) garments.
a. Socks NESOI (not elsewhere specified or indicated): HS code changed from 611592 to 611595 in 2007.

Table 10.13   Unit Values of Honduran Apparel Exports to the EU-15 and the United States

Year	EU-15 unit values (€/kg)			U.S. unit values ($/dozen)		
	Knit	Woven	Total	Knit	Woven	Total
1995	17.8	24.7	20.1			
1996	23.9	23.5	23.6	17.8	44.0	23.5
1997	29.7	33.3	32.9	18.0	44.6	23.3
1998	29.1	33.3	32.2	18.2	42.9	22.9
1999	24.4	35.0	29.2	17.9	41.6	22.0
2000	6.8	33.5	7.6	18.3	48.4	22.5
2001	6.9	53.8	7.9	18.6	48.1	22.7
2002	6.8	32.3	7.8	17.8	45.2	21.5
2003	5.3	38.4	6.1	17.0	45.0	20.4
2004	5.1	31.8	5.6	17.3	47.3	20.9
2005	5.7	26.3	6.3	16.5	48.1	19.8
2006	5.3	18.9	6.2	16.8	48.3	19.9
2007	5.6	30.8	6.0	16.6	50.6	19.9
2008	4.2	26.1	4.6	17.0	48.3	19.6
2009	4.0	31.7	4.2	18.5	45.9	21.2

Sources: Eurostat, volumes reported in kilograms; United States International Trade Commission (USITC), only includes products in which the first unit of quantity is reported in dozens.
Note: EU-15 = the 15 member states of the European Union (EU) as of December 31, 2003, before the new member states joined the EU: Austria, Belgium, Denmark, Finland, France, Germany, Greece, Ireland, Italy, Luxembourg, the Netherlands, Portugal, Spain, Sweden, and the United Kingdom.

increasing from Guatemala, Haiti, and Nicaragua. Imports are decreasing from the Dominican Republic, El Salvador, Honduras, and Mexico (Textiles Intelligence 2008). Mexico declined first because lead firms moved to nearby Central American countries. Next, firms moved out of the Dominican Republic and Costa Rica, then El Salvador. Now lead firms are moving to lower-cost Latin American countries or contracting with manufacturers in Asia.

Backward Linkages

The United States supplies most of the cotton fabrics and almost all of the cotton yarn used by the Honduran textile and apparel sector, while China; Korea; and Taiwan, China, primarily provide MMF woven fabrics (USITC 2004). Fabric imports increased from El Salvador, Guatemala, and Mexico with the passage of DR-CAFTA. In 2004, these countries represented 0.9 percent, 1.0 percent, and 0.2 percent, respectively, of textile exports to Honduras. By 2009, El Salvador increased to 5.5 percent, Guatemala to 4.5 percent, and Mexico to 1.5 percent. On the other hand, China's share dropped from 2.1 percent to 1.6 percent; Hong Kong SAR, China, dropped from 5.1 percent to 0.9 percent; and Korea went from 6.7 percent to 0.9 percent between 2004 and 2009 (table 10.14).

The Caribbean countries do not produce woven fabrics (except for some limited amounts believed to be for local consumption). The region does have a small knit fabric industry whose development was facilitated by the regional fabric provision implemented in 2000 under the CBTPA. Honduras has several integrated knit apparel facilities that produce fabric as well as finished apparel, and in 2002, it was the largest supplier of regional knit fabric for U.S. apparel imports from the region, thus qualifying for CBTPA benefits under the regional fabric provision. In 2003, there were nine textile manufacturers in Honduras. Six of these manufacturers also produced apparel, and one produced yarn (Bair and Peters 2006). Based on available information, there is only one yarn-producing facility in Honduras; it is now owned by GrupoKarim's but was originally established by Formosa, a Taiwanese firm, in 1999. Honduras also has a handful of sundries (zippers, buttons, labels, and so on) providers, and two major global thread manufacturers are also present in the country (A&E and Coats). Table 10.15 gives an overview of textile mills in Honduras.

Employment

Employment in the apparel sector has been very erratic in Honduras. Employment increased between 1994 and 2000, declined between 2000 and 2003, picked back up until 2007, and dropped again in 2008–09. The female employment share accounted for around 56 percent throughout

Table 10.14   Top Five Textile Suppliers to Honduras, 1995, 2000, 2005, 2008, and 2009

Country/ economy/ region	Customs value ($, million)					Market share (%)				
	1995	2000	2005	2008	2009	1995	2000	2005	2008	2009
World	208	497	1,235	1,634	1,112					
United States	87	263	1,013	1,368	888	41.8	53.0	82.0	83.7	79.9
El Salvador	7	18	n.a.	52	61	3.4	3.6	n.a.	3.2	5.5
Guatemala	n.a.	n.a.	26	52	50	n.a.	n.a.	2.1	3.2	4.5
China	19	42	36	41	32	9.0	8.5	2.9	2.5	2.9
Mexico	n.a.	n.a.	n.a.	n.a.	16	n.a.	n.a.	n.a.	n.a.	1.5
Korea, Rep.	66	111	53	25	n.a.	31.7	22.4	4.3	1.5	n.a.
Hong Kong SAR, China	11	24	39	n.a.	n.a.	5.2	4.8	3.2	n.a.	n.a.
Top five	189	458	1,167	1,539	1,048	91.1	92.2	94.5	94.2	94.2

Source: United Nations Commodity Trade Statistics Database (UN Comtrade).
Note: Standard International Trade Classification SITC Rev. 3; imports represented by countries exports to Honduras; n.a. = not applicable (indicates country not in top 5 in given year).

Table 10.15 Evolution of Textile Mills in Honduras

Parent name	Local name	Products	Employment	Ownership	Location	Established	Source
—	Textiles Rio Lindo	Fabric	—	China	—	1951	Bair and Peters (2006)
Lovable Group	ELCATEX	Cotton and polyester circular knit fabric	2,500	Honduras	ZOLI Elcatex	1964	AHM (2010)
Shin Sung	Shin Sung Honduras	Fabric	238	Korea, Rep.	ZOLI San Miguel VI	1997	AHM (2010)
Diban Group	Industrias Continental	Knit fabric and apparel	110	Honduras	ZOLI Industrias Continental	2000	AHM (2010)
Fruit of the Loom	Caracol Knits	Knit fabric	1,900	United States and Honduras	ZOLI Caracol Knits	2001	AHM (2010)
Woong Chun	Woong Chun Honduras	Cotton and polyester circular and warp knit fabric	504	Korea, Rep.	ZOLI Woong Chun Honduras	2002	AHM (2010)
Cottonwise	Cottonwise Textiles	Fabric	135	Korea, Rep.	ZIP San José	~2002	AHM (2010)
Gildan	Gildan Honduras Textiles	Fabric for activewear and underwear	869	Canada	ZOLI San Miguel VI	2003	AHM (2010)
Anvil Knitwear	AKH	Knit fabric and dye, finish	546	United States	ZOLI Green Valley	2005	AHM(2010); BCH (2010)
Fruit of the Loom/Caracol Knits	Coral Knits	Fabric	400	Honduras	ZOLI Caracol Knits	~2005	AHM (2010)

		Product	Employees	Country	ZOLI location	Year	Source
Fruit of the Loom/Russell	RLA Russell Manufacturing	Fabric	1,069	United States	ZOLI RLAManufacturing	~2005	AHM (2010)
Gildan	Gildan Choloma Textile	Fabric for activewear and underwear	1,000	Canada	ZOLI San Miguel VI	2006	AHM (2010)
Delta Apparel	Ceiba Textiles	Knit, dye, finish, cut, and sew	441	United States	ZOLI Green Valley	2007	AHM(2010); BCH (2010)
Bay Island Sportswear	Simtex International	Circular knit fabric (finished)	340	United States	ZOLI Green Valley	2008	AHM (2010)
Roman Knit	RKH	Knit fabric	198	United States and Costa Rica	ZOLI Green Valley	2009	AHM(2010); BCH (2010)
Yarn, Thread, and Elastic Manufacturers							
Grupo Karim's	Former Yangtex: Formosa	Yarn: Ring spun combed cotton; cotton/poly blend	1,417	Honduras (Taiwan, China)	ZIP Formosa	1999	Bair and Peters (2006); AAPN
American & Efird	Hilos A&E de Honduras	MMF sewing thread distributor	14	United States	ZOLI Elcatex	<2001	AHM (2010)
Coats NA	Coats Honduras	Cotton & MMF sewing thread	300	England	ZOLI Inhdelva	<2001	AHM (2010)
Lovable Group	ELCA	Yarn dyeing; narrow knit fabric; elastics	299	Honduras	ZOLI Elcatex	~2005	AHM (2010)
	TelasElasticas	Knitted and woven elastic		Honduras	ZOLI Green Valley Industrial	2009	BCH (2010)

Source: Authors.

Note: AHM (2011) lists 14 textile mills (March 10).

— = not available; AAPN: American Apparel Producers' Network.

the 2000s. The number of firms has also fluctuated, but in a narrow band between about 130 and 165 firms over the 2000 to 2009 time frame (figure 10.2). Labor costs in Honduras averaged around $1.77 per hour in 2008. Compared to other regional suppliers, Honduras's hourly rates are less than those of Costa Rica ($3.35) and Mexico ($2.54), more than Nicaragua ($1.00) and Haiti ($0.52), and essentially on a par with El Salvador ($1.79), the Dominican Republic ($1.75), and Guatemala ($1.65) (Jassin-O'Rourke Group 2008).

Honduras was in the news a few times over the past decade for lead firms denying workers the right to unionize. In 2005, Gildan was accused of closing its El Porvenir factory to resist unionizing workers. In 2009, Fruit of the Loom's Russell Athletic was in the forefront of a student protest for similar actions. A sustained national student campaign was led by United Students against Sweatshops (USAS) that enlisted university pressure on apparel supplier Russell Athletic to reopen a plant it owned in Honduras that it had closed to avoid recognizing a union of its employees; the campaign ended in a victory for labor rights. The students and their universities based their stance on the conclusion of an in-depth, on-site investigation of the plant closing by the Worker Rights Consortium (WRC), the investigative labor rights watchdog with which 175 American universities and colleges are affiliated and which USAS helped found earlier this decade. The WRC concluded that Russell's decision to close the plant was clearly intended as a measure to avoid allowing its workers to organize a union, a clear violation of the WRC's and the universities' codes of conduct for suppliers (Fibre2Fashion 2009).The event marked

Figure 10.2   Employment and Firms in the Honduran Apparel Sector

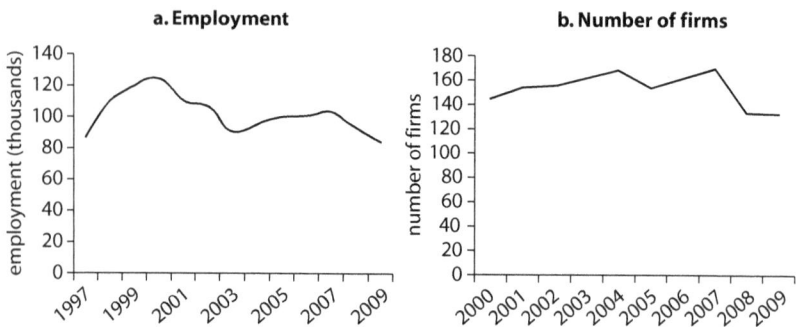

Sources: Central Bank of Honduras (various years) and United States International Trade Commission (USITC 2004).

the first time a factory that was shut down to eliminate a union was later reopened after a worker-activist campaign and the first companywide neutrality agreement in the history of the Central America apparel export industry (Fibre2Fashion 2009).

Honduras has been in the news several times in the past three years regarding workers' discontent with international buyers in the region scaling back purchases, which has led to local factory closures or closing operations. In January 2009, two of Nike's subcontractors, Hugger and Vision Tex, closed operations. After a student protest against Nike, Nike created a $1.5 million fund for workers previously employed by those factories in Honduras, who lost their jobs when the firms closed. National Mills, a U.S.-owned firm and supplier to PVH, closed its Honduras operation, leaving many workers unpaid with owed severance and other payments. PVH agreed to withhold payment of outstanding invoices to National Mills until it met its obligations to the workers. A representative committee was established, including the trade union and its lawyers, as well as the former factory manager and another representative of management staff. National Mills passed ownership of the plant and equipment to this committee for sale to interested buyers and, after constant pressure from PVH, agreed to use the outstanding payment to meet its commitments to the workforce (Forstater 2010).

Trade Regulations and Proactive Policies

Preferential Market Access

Beginning in 1984, the United States initiated the first of a series of trade programs known collectively as the CBI (table 10.16). The CBI is a vital element in U.S. economic relations with Central American and the Caribbean countries. CBERA permitted production sharing whereby U.S. firms shipped cut textile pieces ready to be sewn to the CBI region for assembly and the same firm reimported the assembled apparel under heading 9802.00.80 of the Harmonized Tariff Schedule of the United States (HTS) and, prior to 1989, item 807.00 of the former Tariff Schedules of the United States (TSUS). Often referred to as 807 or 9802 production sharing, the scheme provided preferential access to U.S. firms as duty was only applied to the value added abroad. In the case of apparel sewing, this is mainly the value of labor (Bair and Peters 2006). The tariff heading provides a duty exemption for U.S. components incorporated in imports of assembled goods. The fabric for making the apparel parts

Table 10.16   CBI Trade Preference Programs, Past to Present

Provision	Thread	Yarn	Fabric	Cut	Sew	HTS code	Program	In effect
TSUS 807.00: tariff only applied to value added in assembly if fabric cut in the United States	—	—	—	United States	CBI	—	807	1984–88
TSUS replaced by HTS; former 807 now 9802; tariff only applied to value added in assembly if fabrics cut in the United States; HS codes before 2002	—	—	—	United States	CBI	9802.00.8065 9802.00.8066	807	1988–2001
Articles assembled from fabric cut in the United States; HS codes after 2002	—	—	—	United States	CBI	9802.00.8068	807	2002–present
CBERA and Special Access Programs (807 and 807A)								
Articles assembled from fabric cut in the United States	—	—	—	United States	CBI	9802.00.8068	807	1984–present
Guaranteed access level (essentially quota free); tariff on value added only	—	—	United States	United States	CBI	9802.00.8015	807A	1986
Guaranteed access level (essentially quota free); tariff on value added only	—	—	United States	United States	MEX	9802.00.9000	807A	1988
Trade and Development Act of 2000: U.S.-Caribbean Basin Trade Partnership Act (CBTPA)								
Apparel assembled from U.S.-formed and -cut fabric from U.S. yarn	—	United States[a]	United States	United States	CBI	9802.00.8044	807A+	2000
Apparel assembled and further processed from U.S.-formed and -cut fabric from U.S. yarn	—	United States[a]	United States	United States	CBI	9820.11.03	807A+	2000

300

Apparel cut and assembled from U.S. fabric, yarn, and thread	United States	United States[a]	United States	CBI	CBI	9820.11.06	809	2000
Apparel knit-to-shape from U.S. yarn and knit apparel cut and assembled from regional or U.S. fabric from U.S. yarn		United States	CBI	CBI	CBI	9820.11.09	TRQ	2000
Knitted or crocheted apparel cut and assembled from U.S. fabric, yarn, and thread	United States	United States	United States	CBI	CBI	9820.11.18	809	2000
Nonunderwear T-shirts made of regional fabric from U.S. yarn	—	United States	CBI	CBI	CBI	9820.11.12	TRQ	2000
Bras cut and assembled in the United States and/or CBI	—	—	75% United States	United States/CBI	States/CBI	9820.11.15		2000
Apparel cut (or knit-to-shape) and assembled from fabric or yarn not formed in the United States as identified in NAFTA	—	—	—	CBI	CBI	9820.11.24	Short supply	2000
Apparel cut (or knit-to-shape) and assembled from fabric or yarn not available in the United States in commercial quantities	—	—	—	CBI	CBI	9820.11.27	Short supply	2000
Handloom, handmade, or folklore articles	—	—	—	CBI	—	9820.11.30		2000
Special Rules: Interlining, de minimis	—	—	—	—	—	19 CFR 10.223(b)		2000

Source: Office for Textiles and Apparel (OTEXA 2011).

Note: CBI = Caribbean Basin Initiative; HTS = Harmonized Tariff Schedule of the United States; TSUS = Tariff Schedules of the United States; HS = Harmonized Commodity Description and Coding System; CBERA = Caribbean Basin Economic Recovery Act; NAFTA = North American Free Trade Agreement; Special Rules: Interlining de minimis; 19 CFR 10.223(b) is a code TRQ = Tariff Rate Quota; — = not available.

a. Nylon filament yarn (other than elastomeric yarn) from Canada, Israel, and Mexico may qualify.

could be of either U.S. or foreign origin as long as it was cut in the United States, exported ready for assembly, and not advanced in value abroad except by assembly and incidental operations (USITC 2004).

In 1986, the United States created a "special access program" within the framework of the former TSUS item 807.00 (known as 807A), providing virtually unlimited market access for apparel assembled in the CBI region from "fabric wholly formed and cut in the United States." Rather than being charged against regular quotas, 807A imports entered under preferential quotas known as "guaranteed access levels" (GALs) (USITC 2004).

In 2000, Honduras received additional preferential access to the U.S. market with the advent of the U.S. Trade and Development Act of 2000. Title II of the U.S.-CBTPA extended preferential treatment, initially granted under CBERA, to certain apparel made in the CBI countries and exported to the United States. Effective October 1, 2000, CBTPA granted unlimited duty- and quota-free treatment to apparel assembled in CBI countries that met one of the following criteria: (i) the fabric was both cut and formed in the United States;[5] or (ii) the fabric was formed in the United States from U.S. yarn, cut in an eligible CBI country, and assembled using U.S. thread. CBTPA was intended to provide the Caribbean Basin countries with trade preferences that were more on par with the NAFTA legislation passed in 1994 (Bair and Peters 2006). CBTPA also included a new provision that granted duty-free access to a *limited* quantity of apparel assembled in Caribbean countries from knitted fabrics formed within the region from yarns produced in the United States. On August 6, 2002, the United States initiated a new agreement, the Trade Act of 2002, which in section 3107(a) amended the CBTPA apparel provisions by greatly expanding the quantity caps on apparel made from regionally knitted fabrics. Nevertheless, in 2002, U.S. imports of apparel using regional fabrics accounted for less than 5 percent of total apparel imports from the region. In 2002, the tariff preference level (TPL) for goods using regional fabrics was fully utilized for T-shirts, but the TPL for other knit apparel, which accounted for most of the regional fabric provision, only had a utilization rate of 51 percent (USITC 2004).

DR-CAFTA went into effect on April 1, 2006, for Honduras. For textiles and apparel to receive duty-free entry into a U.S.–DR-CAFTA country, products must qualify as originating under the terms of the agreement. Originating goods are goods that meet the ROO of the agreement. The ROO is known as the yarn-forward standard, which requires that the yarn production and all operations forward (that is, fabric production through apparel assembly) occur in either the United States or the DR-CAFTA region. There are some exceptions that generally allow fibers, yarns, or fabrics to be sourced from outside the region (OTEXA 2011).

All of the Central American countries currently benefit from the EU's GSP+ scheme; however, the EU and Central America concluded negotiations for an Association Agreement in May 2010 that includes a comprehensive trade pillar. The text of the agreement is currently undergoing legal review. Textiles and apparel are, however, currently not significant items traded between the EU and Central American countries.

Proactive Policies

Honduras offers foreign investors exemption from all export taxes, local sales and excise taxes, and taxes on profits and profit repatriation, and it permits unrestricted capital repatriation and currency conversion. Other incentives include the 1984 Temporary Import Regime (RIT), which permitted firms to import inputs free of duty, provided the final products were exported out of Central America. In 1997, the government amended the RIT to allow firms to export to other Central American countries and also granted firms a 10-year income tax holiday. In 1998, the government expanded the free-trade zone (FTZ) area and its benefits to include the entire country. As a result, virtually all firms in the apparel sector are registered as an EPZ, and many are located near the deepwater port of Puerto Cortes, the closest major port to Miami in Central America (USITC 2004).

Instituto Politécnico Centroamericano (IPC) is a Honduras-based educational institution with programs geared to developing workers for the textile and apparel manufacturing industries. In May 2007, IPC announced a new private-public partnership with chemical firm Clariant and the Germany-based banking group DEG to create the Clariant Textile Center. Other firms that have invested in the IPC are Lectra, which contributed to the school's pattern design and scanning laboratory, and Rimoldi, which helped to equip the sewing laboratory (*Apparel Magazine* 2007).

Notes

1. CBTPA is effective until September 2020 and remains the preferential trade agreement for Caribbean countries not included in DR-CAFTA.
2. The ROO of the U.S.–DR-CAFTA Agreement are found on pages 44–66 of Annex 4.1—Specific Rules of Origin (OTEXA 2011).

3. Including American Apparel & Footwear Association, the American Manufacturing Trade Action Coalition, the Hosiery Association, the National Cotton Council, the National Council of Textile Organizations, the National Textile Association, the National Retail Federation, and the U.S. Association of Importers of Textiles and Apparel.

4. The EU-15 is the 15 member states of the European Union (EU) as of December 31, 2003, before the new member states joined the EU: Austria, Belgium, Denmark, Finland, France, Germany, Greece, Ireland, Italy, Luxembourg, the Netherlands, the Portugal, Spain, Sweden, and the United Kingdom.

5. Essentially this amounts to an extension of the 807 special access program, giving 807A exports duty-free as well as quota-free status.

References

AHM (Asociación Hondureña de Maquiladores). 2010. "AHM Online Directory." http://www.ahm-honduras.com/directorio/Directory.aspx.

Apparel Magazine. 2007. "IPC Training Center Expands in Honduras."Apparel Magazine 48 (11): 34.

Bair, Jennifer, and Enrique Peters. 2006. "Global Commodity Chains and Endogenous Growth: Export Dynamism and Development in Mexico and Honduras." World Development 34 (2): 203–21.

BCH (Banco Central de Honduras). 2001–2010. "Actividad Económica de la Industria de BienesparaTransformación (Maquila) y Actividades Conexas en Honduras." Annual publication. http://www.bch.hn/actividad_maquiladora .php.

Brocklehurst, G. 2009. "Trends in U.S. Textile and Clothing Imports." Textile Outlook International 144: 122–97.

Casabona, Lisa. 2009. "Trade Groups Lobby Clinton on Honduras." Women's Wear Daily 198 (90): 13.

Cedrone, Lisa. 1994. "Honduras on the Move." (Honduran apparel industry, special report: Sourcing the Caribbean & Latin America.) Bobbin (November): 33–37.

DeCoster, Jozef. 2003. "Profile of the Maquila Apparel Industry in Honduras." Textile Outlook International 108: 11–45.

Ellis, Kristi. 2009. "Companies Urge Obama Administration to Help Settle Upheaval in Honduras." Women's Wear Daily 198 (20): 13.

Fibre2Fashion. 2009. "Honduras: WE WON! USA Signs Historic Agreement with Russell Athletic." November 24. http://www.fibre2fashion.com.

———. 2010. "Honduras: Anvil's Textile Mill Passes WRAPe Audit." April 23. http://www.fibre2fashion.com.

Forstater, Maya. 2010. "Implications of the Global Financial and Economic Crisis on the Textile and Clothing Sector." International Labor Organization Sectoral Activities Programme Report, Geneva.

Freeman, Ivan. 2010. "Central America: Nicaragua, Honduras See Maquila Expansions." *Just-style.com*, June 18, 2010.

Hanesbrands. 2011. "Hanesbrands Celebrates First Graduating Class of Honduras Employees in Company's Continuing Education Program." Press Release, January 11, Winston-Salem, N.C. http://www.hanesbrands.com/hbi/docs /newsreleases/HBI%20Honduras%20Employee%20Graduation%20 Program%20Press%20Release%2001-11-11%20FINAL.htm.

Jassin-O'Rourke Group, L. 2008. "Global Apparel Manufacturing Labor Cost Analysis 2008, Textile and Apparel Manufacturers & Merchants." http://www .tammonline.com/researchpapers.htm.

Just-style.com. 2008. "U.S. to Impose Safeguard on Socks from Honduras." April 30.

OTEXA (Office of Textiles and Apparel). 2011. Office of Textiles and Apparel, U.S. International Trade Administration. http://otexa.ita.doc.gov.

Textiles Intelligence. 2008. "World Trade in T-shirts." *Global Apparel Markets* 1: 9–30.

———. 2009. "Profile of Anvil Knitwear: An Environmentally Responsible Apparel Producer." *Performance Apparel Markets*, 4th Quarter: 64–74.

USITC (United States International Trade Commission). 2004. *Assessment of the Competitiveness of Certain Foreign Suppliers to the U.S. Market* (Publication 3671). Washington, DC: Office of Industries and Office of Economics. http:// www.usitc.gov/publications/332/pub3671.pdf.

WTO (World Trade Organization). 2010. International Trade Statistics 2010. Geneva, Switzerland. Available from www.wto.org/english/res_e/statis_e /its2010_e/its10_toc_e.htm.

CHAPTER 11

India

Overview

- The textile and apparel industries have been of great importance for decades in India's economy. In 2009, the industries accounted for roughly 4 percent of gross domestic product (GDP), 14 percent of industrial production, and 14 percent of total exports, and they were the largest net foreign exchange earners. Only agriculture has a greater significance in terms of employment, and an estimated 35 million workers are formally and informally employed in the textile and apparel industries (Ministry of Textiles 2010).

- In line with the general policy direction that had prevailed until the early 1990s, the textile and apparel industries had been largely oriented toward the domestic market. But in the mid-1980s, reforms in the textile and apparel industries marked the beginning of a deregulation and liberalization period and subsequent integration into world markets (Tewari 2005). In contrast to other apparel-exporting countries, this integration was not based on (quota-hopping) foreign investment and preferential market access but was driven by local firms that—induced by changing government policies—restructured themselves and extended their reach from the domestic to export markets.

- Notwithstanding its late integration, India developed into the second-largest global exporter of textile and apparel. In 2009, exports of textiles and apparel amounted to $8,392 million and $11,881 million, respectively. Historically, textile exports dominated because of India's large raw material base, particularly in cotton. But during the past three decades, apparel exports have increased in importance and now account for more than half of total textile and apparel exports. The European Union (EU) has been the major export market, accounting for 54.2 percent of apparel and 29.5 percent of textile exports in 2009. The second most important export market is the United States, with 25.7 percent of apparel and 24.6 percent of textile exports.

- Since India faced quota restrictions in its main export markets of the EU and the United States, it was thought that the Multi-fibre Arrangement (MFA) phaseout would boost India's apparel and textile exports (Nordås 2004; USITC 2004). As predicted, India's apparel and textile exports grew strongly post-MFA. But despite absolute growth in value terms, India was outperformed by other low-cost Asian competitors, including Bangladesh, Cambodia, China, and Vietnam, that have expanded more significantly since 2005. In the context of the global economic crisis, apparel and textile exports declined but not as strongly as in other apparel-exporting countries, and, hence, India's global market share rose by 0.4 percent between 2008 and 2009 to 4.0 percent in apparel and by 0.2 percent to 4.9 percent in textiles.

- In addition to these global industry dynamics, "internal" industry-specific factors are important in understanding the industries' development. The inward-oriented policies that prevailed until the mid-1980s shaped the sector in important ways. The domestic market is still important and increasingly so in the context of rising incomes and local as well as foreign retail chains aiming to cater to the emerging Indian middle class. The focus on the domestic market also furthered the development of broader functions, including product development, design, and even branding. The development of the industries was also driven by specific domestic policies, in particular the National Textile Policy 2000, which includes measures such as the Technology Upgradation Fund and Integrated Textile Parks.

- The main competitive advantages of India's textile and apparel industries include a large raw material base, in particular cotton, and related to this a vertically integrated fiber-textile-apparel supply chain, broader functions with regard to manufacturing as well as design and even branding, a large pool of unskilled and also skilled workers, local entrepreneurship, and relatively supportive government policies. The main challenges to India's textile and apparel industries are export concentration to the EU-15[1] and the U.S. markets; concentration in cotton-based production; the inability to take advantage of scale economies due to the small size of firms and the large informal sector; relatively low productivity and skill levels; absence of technological upgrading in the small-scale and informal sector; and cumbersome bureaucratic and regulatory procedures with regard to exporting.

Development of the Apparel Industry

India is a latecomer to textile and apparel export production. Until the 1980s, India's textile and apparel sectors were geared toward the domestic market. In this regard, the Indian state played a key role in shaping the textile and apparel sectors via a set of policies that included a strict licensing regime (firms were required to obtain permission before establishing or expanding operations), reservation policies (in particular, apparel production was reserved to the small-scale industry), and control of exports and imports. In this way, the government heavily influenced the size, location, and scale of the textile and apparel industries from the late 1960s to the mid-1980s (Tewari 2005; Singh 2008). In particular, it effectively limited the scale of apparel operations, and hence, almost the entire industry was classified as small scale, catering to the needs of the domestic market and providing jobs in rural areas. The strong domestic orientation during this period is underlined by the export trajectory of textiles and apparel. Until the mid-1980s, exports remained limited, accounting for a small share of total production.

Textile and apparel exports grew strongly from 1985 onward. Apparel exports rose from $914.0 million in 1985 to $2.5 billion in 1990 at an annual compound growth rate of 19.3 percent (Tewari 2005). Textile exports grew at a similar path, from around $1.0 billion in 1985 to $2.2 billion in 1990. This export surge was induced by a major shift in India's industrial policy, which started to deregulate the textile and apparel industries to boost competitiveness. This policy change preceded the overall turn of India's development strategies in the early 1990s and helped to reshape firms' capabilities before the external sector reforms took off. Policies included an increase in the limits of allowed investments and the provision of special funds and preferential credit lines to facilitate imports of modern equipment and machinery with a view to support technological modernization. Licensing requirements were gradually removed, the reservation policies (particularly for apparel) were discontinued, and exporters could increasingly draw on imported inputs and machinery due to tariffs reductions. As a result, the consolidation, modernization, and capital intensity of the sectors were furthered (Tewari 2005).

Against this background, the period from the 1990s leading to the MFA phaseout was characterized by an overall increase of textile and apparel exports. India's apparel sector grew throughout the 1990s and early 2000s, although not as strongly as during the second half of the 1980s. Apparel exports almost doubled, from $4,233 million in 1995 to $7,298 million in 2004, but India's share in world markets remained relatively stable at around 2.9 percent (table 11.1). With regard to the composition of apparel exports, woven apparel dominated, but knitted apparel exports increased in importance and accounted for roughly 40 percent in 2004—up from 26 percent in 1995. Textile exports increased from $4,031 million in 1995 to $7,690 million in 2004. With regard to the main textile subcategories, made-up textiles in particular increased their share in total textile exports from 18.1 percent in 1995 to 27.5 percent in 2004 (table 11.2). The largest export category in 2004 was yarn, accounting for 29.5 percent, followed by made-up textiles (27.5 percent), woven fabrics (22.6 percent), and floor coverings (15.5 percent). Besides showing continued export growth, India's textile and apparel exports were highly constrained by quotas in their main export markets, with India being one of the top constrained countries along with China and Pakistan.

Figure 11.1 shows the importance of different segments in India's total textile and apparel exports. From 1995 onward, woven apparel has been the largest export segment, followed by knitted apparel and made-up textiles. In the second half of the 1990s, cotton yarn exports were the number two export segment, particularly in 1997. However, in the 2000s, cotton yarn exports stagnated. Cotton fabric and man-made fiber (MMF) yarn and fabric were also important export segments in the period 1995–2004, but apparel and made-up textiles clearly dominated (table 11.3 and figure 11.1).

As expected, India benefited from the MFA phaseout, as indicated by the constant growth of apparel and textile exports since 2005. The increase in apparel exports was particularly strong during the first two years, with annual growth rates of 29.7 percent (2005) and 13.1 percent (2006) (table 11.1). As a result, India increased its global markets share

Table 11.1 Indian Apparel Exports to the World

	1995	1998	2001	2004	2005	2006	2007	2008	2009
Total value ($, million)	4,233	4,321	5,094	7,298	9,468	10,705	11,428	12,210	11,883
Annual growth rate (%)	—	5.0	-0.7	13.0	29.7	13.1	6.8	6.8	-2.7
Share of world exports (%)	2.8	2.4	2.6	2.9	3.5	3.7	3.6	3.6	4.0
Woven and knit value ($, million)									
Woven	3,133	2,817	3,171	4,329	5,768	6,283	6,324	6,702	6,621
Knit	1,100	1,503	1,924	2,969	3,701	4,421	5,105	5,508	5,262
Woven and knit share of total import value (%)									
Woven	74.0	65.2	62.2	59.3	60.9	58.7	55.3	54.9	55.7
Knit	26.0	34.8	37.8	40.7	39.1	41.3	44.7	45.1	44.3

Source: United Nations Commodity Trade Statistics Database (UN Comtrade).
Note: Exports represent imports reported by partner countries. Apparel classifications: Harmonized Commodity Description and Coding System (HS) 1992: Woven: HS62; Knit: HS61. Growth rate reflects change from previous year. — = not available.

Table 11.2   Indian Textile Exports to the World

	1995	1998	2001	2004	2005	2006	2007	2008	2009
Total value ($, million)	4,031	5,323	5,588	7,690	7,822	8,614	9,897	10,430	8,392
Annual growth rate (%)	—	−6.7	−2.5	18.0	1.7	10.1	14.9	5.4	−19.5
Share of world exports (%)	2.9	3.7	3.8	4.2	4.1	4.3	4.6	4.7	4.9
Specific Textile Subgroup Value ($, million)									
Yarn	1,240	1,975	1,859	2,271	2,085	2,382	2,949	3,216	2,245
Woven fabric	1,202	1,352	1,354	1,739	1,629	1,704	1,834	1,897	1,535
Knit fabric	59	62	54	70	63	94	111	116	108
Made-up textiles	729	1,033	1,330	2,113	2,408	2,597	2,934	3,108	2,820
Floor coverings	714	783	812	1,190	1,275	1,453	1,665	1,632	1,298
Specific Textile Subgroup Market Share (%)									
Yarn	30.8	37.1	33.3	29.5	26.7	27.7	29.8	30.8	26.8
Woven fabric	29.8	25.4	24.2	22.6	20.8	19.8	18.5	18.2	18.3
Knit fabric	1.5	1.2	1.0	0.9	0.8	1.1	1.1	1.1	1.3
Made-up textiles	18.1	19.4	23.8	27.5	30.8	30.1	29.6	29.8	33.6
Floor coverings	17.7	14.7	14.5	15.5	16.3	16.9	16.8	15.6	15.5

Source: United Nations Commodity Trade Statistics Database (UN Comtrade).
Note: Textiles represented by Standard International Trade Classification Rev. 3 code 65 and 65 subgroups. Exports represent world imports from India. Shares do not sum to 100 percent because four-digit SITC subgroups not significant for India are omitted. — = not available.

Figure 11.1   Indian Textile and Apparel Exports by HS Categories, 1995–2009

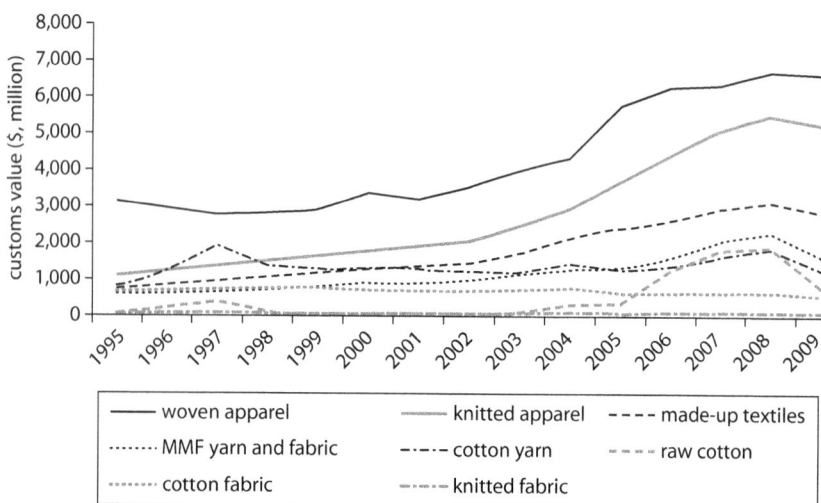

Source: United Nations Commodity Trade Statistics Database (UN Comtrade).
Note: Harmonized Commodity Description and Coding System (HS) 1992: Codes 50–63; exports represented by partner country imports. MMF = man-made fiber.

Table 11.3 Indian Textile and Apparel Exports by HS Categories, 1995, 2000, 2005, 2008, and 2009

HS code	Description	Customs value ($, million)					Market share (%)				
		1995	2000	2005	2008	2009	1995	2000	2005	2008	2009
50–63	Total	8,301	10,977	17,794	24,951	21,420					
62	Woven apparel	3,133	3,350	5,768	6,702	6,619	37.7	30.5	32.4	26.9	30.9
61	Knitted apparel	1,100	1,780	3,701	5,508	5,262	13.3	16.2	20.8	22.1	24.6
63	Made-up textiles	724	1,281	2,418	3,134	2,842	8.7	11.7	13.6	12.6	13.3
54–55	MMF yarn and fabric	591	927	1,310	2,256	1,641	7.1	8.4	7.4	9.0	7.7
5204–07	Cotton yarn	806	1,317	1,235	1,822	1,296	9.7	12.0	6.9	7.3	6.1
5201–03	Raw cotton	51	69	334	1,880	797	0.6	0.6	1.9	7.5	3.7
5208–12	Cotton fabric	658	666	632	663	560	7.9	6.1	3.6	2.7	2.6
60	Knitted fabric	59	53	64	116	108	0.7	0.5	0.4	0.5	0.5
Total		**7,123**	**9,444**	**15,462**	**22,081**	**19,124**	**85.8**	**86.0**	**86.9**	**88.5**	**89.3**

Source: United Nations Commodity Trade Statistics Database (UN Comtrade).

Note: Harmonized Commodity Description and Coding System (HS) 1992: Codes 50–63; exports represented by partner country imports. MMF = man-made fiber.

from 2.9 percent in 2004 to 3.7 percent in 2006. But growth slowed down in 2007 and 2008, partly due to the appreciation of the Indian rupee and rising manufacturing costs (Textiles Intelligence 2008). Textile export growth was the strongest in 2006 and 2007, with annual growth rates of 10.1 percent and 14.9 percent, respectively (table 11.2). From 2004 to 2008, India's global share of textile exports increased from 4.2 percent to 4.7 percent. Notwithstanding India's apparel and textiles export growth post-MFA, the general assessment is that India could have done better—in particular if one considers the scenarios and predictions preceding the MFA phaseout that saw India as the major winner besides China (Thoburn 2009).

The general picture of strong growth during the first two years after quotas were lifted is mirrored in India's two key apparel export markets, namely, the EU-15 and the United States. Total apparel exports to the EU-15 increased from $1,588 million in 1995 to $2,434 million in 2004 and continued to expand post-MFA phaseout (table 11.4). The strong

Table 11.4   EU-15 Apparel Imports from India

	1995	1998	2001	2004	2005	2006	2007	2008	2009
Total value (€, million)	1,588	1,575	2,162	2,434	3,201	3,755	3,774	3,826	4,027
Total quantity (kg, million)	108	110	173	173	208	221	234	242	249
Share of all EU-15 apparel imports (%)	3.2	2.4	2.7	2.9	3.5	3.8	3.7	3.7	4.1
Annual Growth Rate (%)									
Value	—	2.1	7.8	5.1	31.5	17.3	0.5	1.4	5.2
Quantity	—	1.9	38.8	−1.6	20.4	6.1	5.9	3.2	2.9
Woven and knit value (€, million)									
Woven	1,135	940	1,170	1,225	1,710	1,990	1,906	1,964	2,153
Knit	453	634	992	1,209	1,491	1,765	1,868	1,862	1,873
Woven and knit share (%)									
Woven	71.5	59.7	54.1	50.3	53.4	53.0	50.5	51.3	53.5
Knit	28.5	40.3	45.9	49.7	46.6	47.0	49.5	48.7	46.5
Woven and knit quantity (kg, million)									
Woven	65	54	73	67	82	89	93	96	104
Knit	43	56	100	107	127	132	141	145	145

Source: Eurostat.
Note: Apparel represented by Harmonized Commodity Description and Coding System (HS) Codes 61 and 62; growth rate reflects change from previous year. kg = kilogram. EU-15 = the 15 member states of the European Union (EU) as of December 31, 2003, before the new member states joined the EU: Austria, Belgium, Denmark, Finland, France, Germany, Greece, Ireland, Italy, Luxembourg, the Netherlands, Portugal, Spain, Sweden, and the United Kingdom. — = not available.

growth rates in 2005 (31.5 percent) and 2006 (17.3 percent) translated into a market share of 3.8 percent in 2006. The MFA phaseout also gave a boost to apparel exports to the U.S. market, where India increased its market share from 3.4 percent in 2004 to 4.4 percent in 2006 (table 11.5). But since 2007, exports have declined in value terms in the U.S. market. In 2007, this decline was in particular driven by an appreciation of the Indian rupee against the U.S. dollar. Between December 2006 and December 2007, the Indian rupee rose by 13 percent against the dollar, while, for instance, the Bangladeshi taka depreciated by 1.3 percent (Textiles Intelligence 2008). While knitted apparel has continued to grow, the export value of woven apparel has declined after an initial surge in 2005.

As in most apparel-exporting countries, India's apparel and textile exports were negatively affected by the slump in global demand in the context of the global economic crisis. Total apparel exports from India dropped by 2.7 percent in 2009 (table 11.1). Despite this absolute loss in value terms, India extended its share in world markets from 3.6 percent in 2008 to 4.0 percent in 2009. Notwithstanding the difficult economic environment, exports to the EU-15 market increased in value terms from €3,826 million in 2008 to €4,027 million in 2009, while exports declined by 7.6 percent in the U.S. market. Textile exports decreased from $10,430 million in 2008 to $8,392 million in 2009, which amounts

Table 11.5   U.S. Apparel Imports from India

	1996	1998	2001	2004	2005	2006	2007	2008	2009
Total value ($, million)	1,250	1,560	1,781	2,277	3,058	3,242	3,223	3,122	2,886
Annual growth rate (%)	—	11.4	–3.8	10.7	34.3	6.0	–0.6	–3.1	–7.6
Share of all U.S. apparel imports (%)	3.3	3.1	3.0	3.4	4.3	4.4	4.3	4.3	4.5
Woven and knit value ($, million)									
Woven	938	1,111	1,276	1,598	2,121	2,080	1,904	1,791	1,649
Knit	312	449	506	680	937	1,163	1,319	1,331	1,237
Woven and knit share of total import value (%)									
Woven	75.1	71.2	71.6	70.2	69.4	64.1	59.1	57.4	57.1
Knit	24.9	28.8	28.4	29.8	30.6	35.9	40.9	42.6	42.9

Source: United States International Trade Commission (USITC).
Note: Apparel imports represented by Harmonized Commodity Description and Coding System (HS) Codes 61 and 62; General Customs Value; growth rate reflects change from previous year. — = not available.

to a decline of 19.5 percent. This decline can be attributed to shrinking global demand but also to the significant decline in exports of raw cotton, which was related to government policies that sought to ensure availability of affordable cotton inputs for textile and apparel production (see following text). However, as with apparel, India actually increased its global share in the textile market, from 4.7 percent in 2008 to 4.9 percent in 2009.

Exports were hampered not only by deteriorating opportunities on traditional export markets related to the global economic crisis but also by rising input costs. In particular, raw cotton prices have surged since mid-2007 (*Just-style* 2008). Given the dependence on cotton as a major input into textile and apparel production, this surge has negatively affected Indian textile and apparel firms. To ensure the availability of adequate inputs for textile and apparel exporters, the government introduced several measures. A 14.5 percent import duty on raw cotton was dropped to facilitate imports. Duty drawbacks for exporters of raw cotton were dropped, and additional administrative measures to control export of raw cotton were introduced (*Just-style* 2008). In 2010, India's government even introduced an export ban on raw cotton that was later extended to cotton yarn, which provided Indian apparel exporters with a relative price advantage over major competitors (*Just-style* 2010a).

The development of the industry in the 2000s and post-MFA was also driven by specific domestic policies, in particular the National Textile Policy 2000, which promoted the industry's development. The most important measures of this policy are the Technology Upgradation Fund established in 1999 to promote technical modernization of the sector, the Technology Mission on Cotton launched in 2000 to improve quality and raise productivity in the cotton segment, the Integrated Textile Parks announced in 2005 to provide state-of-the-art infrastructure to local and international manufacturers, the gradual reduction of import tariffs and support of man-made fiber (MMF) and yarn production, and the support of product development, design, and branding capabilities (see following text, Singh 2008).

Prospects for India's textile and apparel exports look positive, despite the export declines in 2009. In particular, government and industry efforts in nurturing product development, design, and branding capabilities have started to pay off. The domestic market is still important, and increasingly so in the context of rising incomes and the emergence of an Indian middle class. Between 2003 and 2007, consumer expenditure on apparel rose by approximately 7 percent per year in India, and domestic apparel expenditures accounted for about two and a half times the value of apparel exports in 2007 (Textiles Intelligence 2008). In 2008, the value of the domestic market was estimated at Rs 306.7 billion, up from Rs 79.8 billion in 2003 (Euromonitor 2009).[2] Against this background, the most capable firms have developed brands for the domestic market and are also entering their traditional export markets by buying up brands in the United States and the EU (Singh 2008). The domestic market is supplied by not only local but also foreign retailers and brand marketers, including DKNY, Gant, Arrow, and Marks & Spencer. Given the prospects of the Indian market, retailers are increasingly looking to gain presence, which up to now is only possible via joint ventures and other arrangements (for example, licensing or franchising) as the domestic retail sector is not yet fully liberalized (Italia 2009). These foreign retailers have largely switched from importing to sourcing from local suppliers to supply the domestic markets. More generally, the boundaries between the domestic and export markets are becoming porous, as domestic demand is getting increasingly quality conscious (Tewari 2008).

Structure of the Apparel Industry

Types of Firms

India is one of the few countries (besides China, Pakistan, and Turkey) that have a significant raw material base and vertically integrated manufacturing capacities. A set of globally competitive apparel exporters has emerged that manages vertically integrated operations, including product developing, design and branding, and production, both for the domestic market and for international markets (Singh 2008). In terms of manufacturing capabilities, India's apparel sector offers a wide range of capabilities and high flexibility. Smaller to medium-size firms can provide small batches with high-fashion content and customized, design-intensive orders. Larger firms can provide high-volume and mass-produced series. Smaller and larger firms have developed product development, design, and even branding capabilities that are increasingly demanded by global buyers (Tewari 2009).

However, the industry is divided into two segments: (i) a relatively small formal segment characterized by more developed, often larger firms with higher capital intensity and often better working conditions; and (ii) a large informal segment where firms employ fewer than 10 workers. The importance of the informal segment and the different productivity levels of the two segments are reflected in the high share of the informal sector in total employment (90 percent) and the high share of the formal sector in total production (69 percent) (Hirway 2008). This highly fragmented structure can be related to government policies until the mid-1980s that favored small-scale operations and partly to cumbersome regulations in the formal sector. According to a United Nations Development Programme (UNDP) report, by the mid-2000s, about 80 percent of units in the apparel sector were small (employing fewer than 11 workers), 14 percent were medium (10–49 workers), and 6 percent were large (employing more than 49 workers) (UNDP 2006, cited in Hirway 2008). However, domestic deregulation, liberalization, and increasing international competition in the context of the MFA phaseout, as well as increasing demands from global buyers, have furthered the consolidation of the industry (Tewari 2005; Singh 2008).

Despite its fragmented structure, the apparel industry shows some degree of geographical concentration, in particular around Tirupur, Ludhiana, Bangalore, Delhi/Noida/Gurgaon, Mumbai, Kolkata, Jaipur, and Indore. Tirupur, Ludhiana, and Kolkata are major centers for knitted apparel, while Bangalore, Delhi/Noida/Gurgaon, Mumbai, Jaipur, and Indore are major centers for woven apparel (Ministry of Textiles 2006). Table 11.6 highlights the product specialization of some of these regions.

With regard to the different production segments, in 2006, India had 6,500 ginning units that were almost all small scale, 1,161 small-scale spinning and 1,566 large-scale spinning units, 3.6 million handloom and 400,000 power loom units, 2,300 largely decentralized processing units, and 77,000 apparel units that were largely small scale (table 11.7). The yarn manufacturing sector is almost wholly in the formal sector,[3] the fabric manufacturing sector is almost wholly in the informal sector with the share of composite mills in total fabric manufacturing being below

Table 11.6   Major Hubs in Indian Textile and Apparel Sectors

Location	Profile
Tirupur and surrounding cities	Cotton knitwear export
Mumbai and Sholapur	Power loom weaving export
Ludhiana and Kanpur	Woolen knitwear export
Kolkata	Apparel and hosiery cotton
Bangalore	Leading manufacturers turning out varieties of products

Source: Italia 2009.

Table 11.7 Number of Firms and Capacities in Indian Textile and Apparel Sectors, 2006

Sector	Number of units	Size
Ginning	6,500 (2001)	Almost all are in the small-scale industry
Spinning	1,161, small scale	39 million spindles
	1,566, large scale	621,000 rotors
Weaving	3.5 million in handloom segment	3.9 million handlooms
	400,000 in power loom segment	2.1 million power looms
		0.1 million looms in the formal sector
Processing	2,300	Majority are operating decentralized; only around 200 are vertically integrated units
Apparel	77,000	Largely small-scale units

Sources: IFPRI 2008.

5 percent, and the share of informal power looms is above 50 percent.[4] Over 60 percent of all apparel units are only engaged in sewing operations. In the mid-2000s, apparel units employing over 50 machines accounted for only 6 percent of all apparel manufacturing firms; 80 percent used fewer than 20 machines (Verma 2005).

Despite this high level of fragmentation, there are important large players in India's textile and apparel sectors. Table 11.8 gives an overview of the top 15 textile and apparel firms in India in 2010.

The involvement of foreign investors in India's textile and apparel industries remains marginal. Initially, this situation was related to the government's inward-looking policy, which oriented the sector toward the domestic market and restricted foreign direct investment (FDI). With the overall policy change in the early 1990s, the orientation toward FDI changed as well. With regard to the textile and apparel industries, one of the last major restrictions on foreign participation was lifted in 2001 when 100 percent foreign ownership was allowed and additional licensing requirements were abolished (USITC 2004). However, FDI has not really picked up, despite government efforts to attract FDI in the context of the National Textile Policy 2000. According to information from the Ministry of Commerce and Industry, over the period 1991–2009, cumulative FDI in textiles and apparel accounted for $1.11 billion, which equals roughly 0.77 percent of total FDI inflows (table 11.9). While FDI inflows into textile and apparel have increased in value terms since 2001—with slight dips in 2003 and 2007—they never amounted to more than 2 percent of total annual FDI inflows. FDI contributed only a bit more than 2 percent of total investment in the sectors between 2001 and 2006

Table 11.8   Top 15 Indian Textile and Apparel Firms

Rank	Company	Turnover 2010 (in Rs 10 mil = crores)
1	Aditya Birla Nuvo Ltd., Mumbai[a]	15,769
2	JBF Industries Ltd., Mumbai[a]	4,965
3	Century Textiles & Industries Ltd., Mumbai	4,545
4	Alok Industries Ltd., Mumbai	4,319
5	S Kumars Nationwide Ltd., Mumbai	3,861
6	Vardhman Textiles Ltd., Ludhiana	3,399
7	Arvind Ltd., Ahmedabad	3,300
8	Raymond Ltd., Mumbai	2,585
9	SRF Ltd., Delhi/ National Capital Region (NCR)	2,579
10	Indo Rama Synthetics (India) Ltd., Delhi/National Capital Region (NCR)	2,558
11	Garden Silk Mills Ltd., Surat	2,521
12	Welspun India Ltd., Vapi	2,064
13	House of Pearl Fashions Ltd., Delhi/ National Capital Region (NCR)	1,878
14	Abhishek Industries Ltd., Ludhiana	1,835
15	Bombay Rayon Fashions Ltd., Mumbai	1,821

Source: The Economic Times, Top 500 List for 2010, data from http://economictimes.indiatimes.com/et500list.cms.
Note: Ranked by turnover in 2010. Crore = 10 million.
a. Diversified activities.

Table 11.9   Foreign Direct Investment (FDI) in Indian Textile and Apparel Sectors

Year	Total FDI ($, billion)	T&A FDI ($, billion)	FDI share of T&A (%)
1991–2000	18.89	0.244	1.29
2001	3.73	0.004	0.11
2002	3.79	0.046	1.21
2003	2.53	0.018	0.71
2004	3.75	0.039	1.04
2005	4.36	0.079	1.81
2006	11.12	0.118	1.06
2007	19.16	0.100	0.52
2008	33.03	0.200	0.61
2009	27.10	0.200	0.74
Total 1991–2009	**144.83**	**1.110**	**0.77**

Source: Department of Industrial Policy and Promotion, Ministry of Commerce and Industry, Government of India cf. Ministry of Textiles, available at http://texmin.nic.in/fdi/fdi_home.htm.
Note: T&A = textiles and apparel.

(Ministry of Textiles 2009). In short, India's textile and apparel exports continue to be largely driven by domestic firms.

The Indian textile and apparel industries have received considerable support given their important role in the domestic economy. In particular, the Technology Upgradation Fund Scheme (TUFS) set up in 1999 has been an important source of investment for technological modernization. According to the Ministry of Textiles, cumulative investment under the TUFS over the period 1999–2008 amounted to roughly Rs 698,280 (US$15.29 million based on an average foreign exchange rate of 0.022 for the concerned period), with the spinning and composite mill sector receiving more than 54 percent of the total while apparel received a relatively small share of 7.7 percent (table 11.10). The trend toward modernization in the textile sector through the adoption of new technology and the installation of advanced production facilities can also be seen by looking at global shipment data (see following text).

End Markets

The largest market for India's textile and apparel products is the domestic market. In 2007, two-thirds of textiles and apparel output in India were for domestic sales, with one-third destined for exports (Tewari 2008). With regard to India's apparel exports, end markets are concentrated. In 2009, 79.9 percent of apparel exports went to the EU-15 and the United States, with 54.2 percent of exports going to the EU-15 and 25.7 percent to the United States (table 11.11). Canada, Japan, and the United Arab Emirates were other important end markets, accounting for 3.0 percent, 2.5 percent, and 1.6 percent, respectively. The role of the EU-15 as the key export market increased from 39.3 percent in 2000 to 54.2 percent in 2009. At the same time, the share of the U.S. market decreased from 38.9 percent to 25.7 percent. The shares of Canada, Japan, and the United Arab Emirates also decreased; exports to the rest of the world increased from 10.3 percent to 12.9 percent of total apparel exports (figure 11.2). India's textile exports

Table 11.10   Cumulative Investments under TUFS, 1999–2008

Sector	Share of total investment (%)
Spinning mills	33.9
Composite mills	20.6
Weaving	7.8
Processing of fibers, yarn, fabrics, garments, and made-ups	8.9
Made-ups	1.0
Technical textiles	1.5
Apparel	7.7
Others	18.6

Source: Ministry of Textiles 2009.
Note: TUFS = Technology Upgradation Fund Scheme.

Table 11.11 Top Five Indian Apparel Export Markets, 1995, 2000, 2005, 2008, and 2009

Country/region	Customs value ($, million)					Market share (%)				
	1995	2000	2005	2008	2009	1995	2000	2005	2008	2009
World	4,233	5,131	9,468	12,210	11,883					
EU-15	2,185	2,019	4,531	6,483	6,443	51.6	39.3	47.9	53.1	54.2
United States	1,274	1,998	3,284	3,316	3,054	30.1	38.9	34.7	27.2	25.7
United Arab Emirates	n.a.	180	229	361	358	n.a.	3.5	2.4	3.0	3.0
Canada	140	238	326	311	300	3.3	4.6	3.4	2.6	2.5
Japan	152	136	n.a.	182	193	3.6	2.6	n.a.	1.5	1.6
Saudi Arabia	n.a.	n.a.	156	n.a.	n.a.	n.a.	n.a.	1.7	n.a.	n.a.
Switzerland	104	n.a.	n.a.	n.a.	n.a.	2.5	n.a.	n.a.	n.a.	n.a.
Top five share	**3,855**	**4,570**	**8,526**	**10,655**	**10,348**	**91.1**	**89.1**	**90.1**	**87.3**	**87.1**
SAARC	1	5	19	11	28	0.0	0.1	0.2	0.1	0.2

Source: United Nations Commodity Statistics Database (UN Comtrade).

Note: Apparel represented by Harmonized Commodity Description and Coding System (HS) 1992: Codes 61 and 62; exports represented by partner country imports; n.a. = not applicable (indicates country not in top five in given year). For South Asian Association for Regional Cooperation (SAARC) region, several countries' data are not available in all years. EU-15 = the 15 member states of the European Union (EU) as of December 31, 2003, before the new member states joined the EU: Austria, Belgium, Denmark, Finland, France, Germany, Greece, Ireland, Italy, Luxembourg, the Netherlands, Portugal, Spain, Sweden, and the United Kingdom.

are more diversified with regard to end markets. In 2009, India's main textile export markets were also the EU-15 (29.5 percent) and the United States (24.6 percent), which together accounted for 54.4 percent of total textile exports (table 11.12). Brazil, China, Sri Lanka, Turkey, and the United Arab Emirates are also important export markets. While the market shares of traditional Asian export destinations, in particular Hong Kong SAR, China and the Republic of Korea, have gone down, demand from the countries previously named has increased since 2005 (figure 11.3).

Tables 11.11 and 11.12 show that although intraregional trade in apparel has remained marginal, intraregional trade in textiles has increased in importance. In 2005, less than 0.5 percent of total apparel exports in South Asia were exported to other South Asian countries. In contrast, around 6.3 percent of the region's textile exports were geared toward other South Asian countries (Tewari 2009). For India, only 0.2 percent of total apparel exports went to the South Asian Association for Regional Cooperation (SAARC) region in 2009, compared to 0.1 percent in 2000. Nepal is the leading apparel export destination, followed by Bangladesh and Sri Lanka. With regard to textiles, 3.9 percent of India's total textile

Figure 11.2   Top Five Indian Apparel Export Markets, 2000 and 2009
% market share

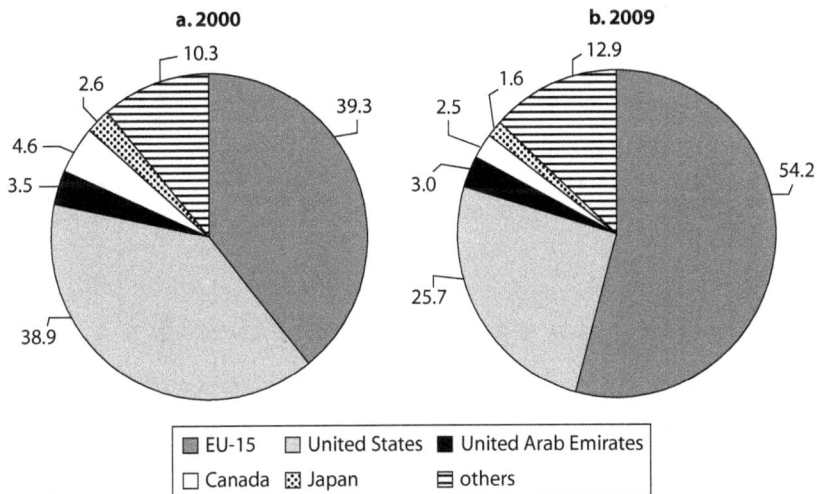

Source: United Nations Commodity Statistics Database (UN Comtrade).
Note: Apparel represented by Harmonized Commodity Description and Coding System (HS) 1992: Codes 61 and 62; exports represented by partners' imports. EU-15 = the 15 member states of the European Union (EU) as of December 31, 2003, before the new member states joined the EU: Austria, Belgium, Denmark, Finland, France, Germany, Greece, Ireland, Italy, Luxembourg, the Netherlands, Portugal, Spain, Sweden, and the United Kingdom.

Table 11.12 Top 10 Indian Textile Export Markets, 1995, 2000, 2005, 2008, and 2009

Country/economy/region	Customs value ($, million)					Market share (%)				
	1995	2000	2005	2008	2009	1995	2000	2005	2008	2009
World	4,031	5,732	7,822	10,430	8,392					
EU-15	1,813	1,865	2,468	3,120	2,476	45.0	32.5	31.6	29.9	29.5
United States	655	1,210	2,036	2,408	2,065	16.3	21.1	26.0	23.1	24.6
Turkey	103	136	292	546	383	2.6	2.4	3.7	5.2	4.6
United Arab Emirates	n.a.	216	277	366	292	n.a.	3.8	3.5	3.5	3.5
China	n.a.	195	142	221	275	n.a.	3.4	1.8	2.1	3.3
Brazil	n.a.	n.a.	n.a.	399	272	n.a.	n.a.	n.a.	3.8	3.2
Sri Lanka	n.a.	n.a.	134	240	256	n.a.	n.a.	1.7	2.3	3.1
Korea, Rep.	126	268	245	235	220	3.1	4.7	3.1	2.3	2.6
Canada	n.a.	116	169	179	151	n.a.	2.0	2.2	1.7	1.8
Hong Kong SAR, China	115	229	127	n.a.	150	2.9	4.0	1.6	n.a.	1.8
Egypt	n.a.	n.a.	n.a.	266	n.a.	n.a.	n.a.	n.a.	2.6	n.a.
Japan	185	174	157	n.a.	n.a.	4.6	3.0	2.0	n.a.	n.a.
Mauritius	101	114	n.a.	n.a.	n.a.	2.5	2.0	n.a.	n.a.	n.a.
Bangladesh	145	n.a.	n.a.	n.a.	n.a.	3.6	n.a.	n.a.	n.a.	n.a.
Australia	83	n.a.	n.a.	n.a.	n.a.	2.0	n.a.	n.a.	n.a.	n.a.
Singapore	80	n.a.	n.a.	n.a.	n.a.	2.0	n.a.	n.a.	n.a.	n.a.
Top 10 share	**3,406**	**4,524**	**6,048**	**7,980**	**6,541**	**84.5**	**78.9**	**77.3**	**76.5**	**77.9**
SAARC	149	150	271	267	327	3.7	2.6	3.5	2.6	3.9

Source: United Nations Commodity Statistics Database (UN Comtrade).

Note: SITC Standard International Trade Classification Rev. 3; exports represented by countries' imports from India; n.a. = not applicable (indicates country not in top 10 in given year). EU-15 = the 15 member states of the European Union (EU) as of December 31, 2003, before the new member states joined the EU: Austria, Belgium, Denmark, Finland, France, Germany, Greece, Ireland, Italy, Luxembourg, the Netherlands, Portugal, Spain, Sweden, and the United Kingdom; SAARC = South Asian Association for Regional Cooperation.

Figure 11.3   Top 10 Indian Textile Export Markets, 2000 and 2009
% market share

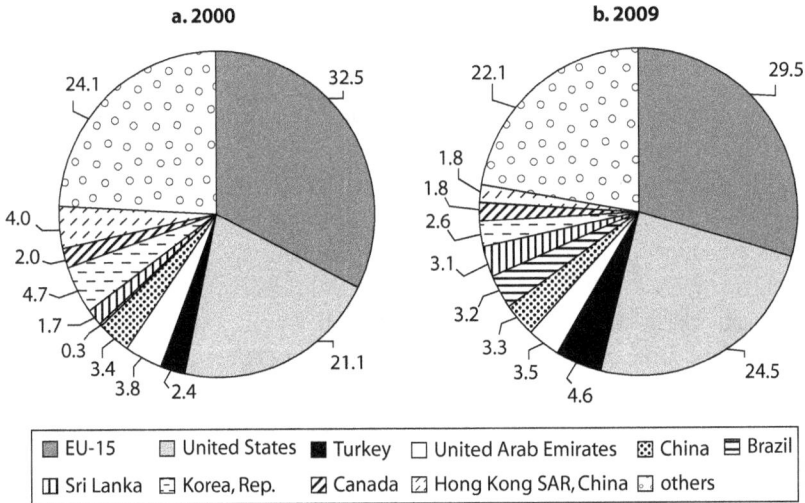

a. 2000

24.1
32.5
4.0
2.0
4.7
1.7
0.3
3.4
3.8   2.4
21.1

b. 2009

22.1
29.5
1.8
1.8
2.6
3.1
3.2
3.3
3.5
4.6
24.5

| ⊞ EU-15 | ▢ United States | ■ Turkey | ☐ United Arab Emirates | ⊠ China | ⊟ Brazil |
| ⊞ Sri Lanka | ⊟ Korea, Rep. | ▨ Canada | ▨ Hong Kong SAR, China | ▢ others |

Source: United Nations Commodity Statistics Database (UN Comtrade).
Note: SITC Standard International Trade Classification 65, Rev. 3; exports represented by partner country imports from India. EU-15 = the 15 member states of the European Union (EU) as of December 31, 2003, before the new member states joined the EU: Austria, Belgium, Denmark, Finland, France, Germany, Greece, Ireland, Italy, Luxembourg, the Netherlands, Portugal, Spain, Sweden, and the United Kingdom.

exports went to the SAARC region in 2009, compared to 2.6 percent in 2000, with the main market being Sri Lanka.

Export Products

Historically, India had been known as an exporter of textiles, but apparel exports have increased in importance since the mid-1980s. Since then, apparel exports have roughly equaled textile exports in value terms. In 2009, woven and knitted apparel constituted the majority of textile and apparel exports, accounting together for 55.5 percent, followed by made-up textiles (13.3 percent), man-made (MM) yarn and fabric (7.7 percent), and cotton yarn (6.1 percent) (table 11.3). With regard to apparel exports, woven apparel accounted for 55.7 percent and knitted apparel for 44.3 percent of total apparel exports. Traditionally, woven apparel had been of greater significance in India's apparel export basket, with a share of 74 percent in 1995. While both apparel categories grew in absolute value terms in the 2000s, knitted exports increased in relative importance (table 11.1). India's apparel exports, woven and knit, are concentrated in a few products. The top 5 product categories accounted for 41.2 percent of total U.S. apparel exports in 2009 and for 44.4 percent in the EU-15 market; the top 10 product categories, for 64.0 percent and 60.2 percent, respectively (tables 11.11 and 11.12). Product concentration levels to the United States and EU-15 have generally increased since 2000; however, they are still lower than in most competitor countries.

The top apparel export product categories to the United States and the EU-15 are overlapping—8 of the top 10 products appeared in the U.S. and the EU-15 lists in 2009. The most important products in both markets are shirts and T-shirts, sweatshirts, dresses, and trousers. In the U.S. market, knit items account for 4 out of the top 10, and in the EU-15 for 5 out of the top 10 (tables 11.13 and 11.14). In the EU-15 market, shirts and T-shirts are particularly important, accounting for 36.7 percent of total exports in 2009 and representing the top two apparel export products. In both the EU-15 and the U.S. markets, cotton products dominate, reflecting India's strong domestic cotton-based textile industry. Although local capacities for noncotton fabrics have increased and the tariffs on imports of noncotton inputs were reduced, cotton-based products still accounted for an estimated 78 percent of total apparel exports in 2009 (AEPC 2009).

With regard to unit values of apparel exports, India's unit values are high compared to main competitor countries in the EU-15 and the U.S. markets. This fact is related to India's more sophisticated and higher-value export basket, in particular compared to countries such as Bangladesh and Pakistan. But the high unit prices can be also explained by higher landed costs, which are particularly related to relatively high power and energy costs, transportation and logistics costs, taxes (for example, value added tax [VAT] and excise), and labor costs. In terms of the development of average apparel unit prices, patterns differ in the two main export markets (table 11.15). Unit values of woven and knit apparel exports to the EU-15 generally increased between 2004 and 2009, particularly until 2006, with a slight decline afterward. In contrast, unit values of apparel exports to the United States have fallen since 2000, with a particularly large decline in 2002 related to China's World Trade Organization (WTO) accession. The continued decline is largely due to the rising importance of knitted apparel exports, which experienced strongly declining unit values. In contrast, woven exports decreased in absolute value terms but their average unit values increased from 2005 to 2008 before dropping to the 2004 level in 2009.

Table 11.16 shows India's top textile export categories.

The top three textile export product groups are made-up textiles, yarn, and floor coverings, which together accounted for 75.8 percent of

Table 11.13 Top 10 EU-15 Apparel Imports from India, 1996, 2000, 2005, 2008, and 2009

HS code	Product	Customs value (€, million)					Market share (%)				
		1996	2000	2005	2008	2009	1996	2000	2005	2008	2009
Total		1,540	2,005	3,201	3,826	4,027					
610910	T-Shirts	146	186	526	652	616	9.5	9.3	16.4	17.0	15.3
620630	Shirts	116	88	255	400	473	7.5	4.4	8.0	10.5	11.7
620442	Dresses	46	n.a.	n.a.	219	273	3.0	n.a.	n.a.	5.7	6.8
620520	Shirts	255	166	211	259	259	16.5	8.3	6.6	6.8	6.4
611020	Sweatshirts	65	108	163	176	170	4.2	5.4	5.1	4.6	4.2
620342	Trousers	n.a.	n.a.	83	158	148	n.a.	n.a.	2.6	4.1	3.7
611120	Garments	n.a.	52	91	127	132	n.a.	2.6	2.8	3.3	3.3
610510	Shirts	41	n.a.	n.a.	134	131	2.6	n.a.	n.a.	3.5	3.3
610831	Pajamas	67	124	110	124	130	4.4	6.2	3.5	3.2	3.2
620462	Trousers	n.a.	63	94	n.a.	94	n.a.	3.1	2.9	n.a.	2.3
620452	Skirts	n.a.	n.a.	246	103	n.a.	n.a.	n.a.	7.7	2.7	n.a.
620640	Shirts	78	63	92	n.a.	n.a.	5.1	3.1	2.9	n.a.	n.a.
620444	Dresses	111	50	n.a.	n.a.	n.a.	7.2	2.5	n.a.	n.a.	n.a.
621420	Scarves	n.a.	49	n.a.	n.a.	n.a.	n.a.	2.4	n.a.	n.a.	n.a.
620459	Skirts	35	n.a.	n.a.	n.a.	n.a.	2.3	n.a.	n.a.	n.a.	n.a.
Top 10 share		960	950	1,870	2,352	2,424	62.4	47.4	58.4	61.5	60.2

Source: Eurostat.

Note: n.a. = not applicable (indicates product not in the top 10 in given year). Harmonized Commodity Description and Coding System (HS) numbers beginning with 61 indicate knitted garments and 62 indicate nonknitted (woven) garments. EU-15 = the 15 member states of the European Union (EU) as of December 31, 2003, before the new member states joined the EU: Austria, Belgium, Denmark, Finland, France, Germany, Greece, Ireland, Italy, Luxembourg, the Netherlands, Portugal, Spain, Sweden, and the United Kingdom.

Table 11.14　Top 10 U.S. Apparel Imports from India, 1996, 2000, 2005, 2008, and 2009

HS code	Product	Customs value ($, million)					Market share (%)				
		1996	2000	2005	2008	2009	1996	2000	2005	2008	2009
Total		**1,250**	**1,852**	**3,058**	**3,122**	**2,886**					
611020	Sweatshirts	94	171	271	345	332	7.5	9.2	8.9	11.0	11.5
620630	Shirts	215	286	336	261	261	17.2	15.5	11.0	8.4	9.1
620462	Trousers	n.a.	43	133	252	219	n.a.	2.3	4.3	8.1	7.6
610510	Shirts	122	143	215	245	200	9.8	7.7	7.0	7.9	6.9
620520	Shirts	164	188	288	213	175	13.1	10.2	9.4	6.8	6.1
610910	T-Shirts	31	n.a.	99	198	164	2.5	n.a.	3.2	6.3	5.7
620442	Dresses	31	n.a.	n.a.	131	153	2.4	n.a.	n.a.	4.2	5.3
620342	Trousers	n.a.	n.a.	132	217	149	n.a.	n.a.	4.3	7.0	5.2
620452	Skirts	n.a.	44	281	78	97	n.a.	2.4	9.2	2.5	3.4
610711	Underwear	n.a.	n.a.	70	124	96	n.a.	n.a.	2.3	4.0	3.3
620640	Shirts	45	67	78	n.a.	n.a.	3.6	3.6	2.5	n.a.	n.a.
621142	Garments	52	71	n.a.	n.a.	n.a.	4.2	3.9	n.a.	n.a.	n.a.
620459	Skirts	43	48	n.a.	n.a.	n.a.	3.5	2.6	n.a.	n.a.	n.a.
620444	Dresses	68	65	n.a.	n.a.	n.a.	5.4	3.5	n.a.	n.a.	n.a.
Top 10 share		**865**	**1,127**	**1,902**	**2,065**	**1,847**	**69.2**	**60.9**	**62.2**	**66.1**	**64.0**

Source: United States International Trade Commission (USITC).

Note: U.S. General Customs Value; Harmonized Commodity Description and Coding System (HS) numbers beginning with 61 indicate knitted garments and 62 indicate nonknitted (woven) garments; n.a. = not applicable (indicates product not in the top 10 in given year).

Table 11.15   Unit Values of Indian Apparel Exports to the EU-15 and the United States

Year	EU-15 unit values (€/kg)			U.S. unit values ($/dozen)		
	Knit	Woven	Total	Knit	Woven	Total
1995	10.6	17.3	14.7	—	—	—
1996	10.5	16.1	13.6	52.9	67.4	63.1
1997	11.2	17.2	14.3	63.8	68.7	67.3
1998	11.4	17.4	14.3	64.9	66.9	66.3
1999	11.5	17.2	14.1	57.0	66.2	63.3
2000	12.8	19.9	16.1	65.9	72.9	71.0
2001	9.9	16.0	12.5	62.8	69.4	67.5
2002	11.4	17.7	14.3	48.8	60.2	56.5
2003	10.5	16.6	13.2	43.7	65.3	57.5
2004	11.3	18.4	14.1	40.1	67.4	56.2
2005	11.8	20.9	15.4	34.4	68.0	52.6
2006	13.4	22.2	17.0	33.3	72.2	51.1
2007	13.2	20.5	16.1	33.1	72.7	49.0
2008	12.8	20.4	15.8	29.5	72.7	45.0
2009	12.9	20.8	16.2	26.8	67.1	41.2

Sources: Eurostat and United States International Trade Commission (USITC).
Note: kg = kilogram; — = not available. EU-15 = the 15 member states of the European Union (EU) as of December 31, 2003, before the new member states joined the EU: Austria, Belgium, Denmark, Finland, France, Germany, Greece, Ireland, Italy, Luxembourg, the Netherlands, Portugal, Spain, Sweden, and the United Kingdom.

India's total textile exports in 2009. In 2009, the made-up textiles group held the largest market share. Within this group, the largest subgroup was household linens (also called bed, bath, and kitchen linens). This subcategory has increased significantly over the past 15 years. In 1995, this subcategory only represented 11.1 percent of all textile exports, but the share increased to 21.0 percent in 2009. Figure 11.4 shows the top four items within this subcategory. The most significant shift has been the increase in market share of cotton bath and kitchen linens and the decrease in woven cotton table linens.

Backward Linkages

India has a significant raw material base and is one of the few countries worldwide that has a vertically integrated sector across all stages of fiber-textile-apparel production, which sets it apart from most other apparel-exporting countries. In the National Textile Policy 2000, it is stated that the sector has a "unique position as a self-reliant industry, from the production of raw materials to the delivery of finished products,

Table 11.16　Top Three Indian Textile Export Categories, 1995, 2000, 2005, 2008, and 2009

Categories	Customs value ($, million)					Market share (%)				
	1995	2000	2005	2008	2009	1995	2000	2005	2008	2009
Total textiles: 65	4,031	5,732	7,822	10,430	8,392					
Yarn: 651	1,240	1,994	2,085	3,216	2,245	30.8	34.8	26.7	30.8	26.8
Floor coverings: 659	714	801	1,275	1,632	1,298	17.7	14.0	16.3	15.6	15.5
Household linens: 658.4	446	639	1,374	1,868	1,759	11.1	11.2	17.6	17.9	21.0
Top three share	**2,399**	**3,435**	**4,734**	**6,716**	**5,303**	**59.5**	**59.9**	**60.5**	**64.4**	**63.2**

Source: United Nations Commodity Trade Statistics Database (UN Comtrade).
Note: SITC Standard International Trade Classification Rev. 3, codes 65, 651, 659, and 658.4; exports represented by partner country imports.

Figure 11.4   Top Four Indian Linen Export Products, 1995, 2000, 2005, and 2009
% market share

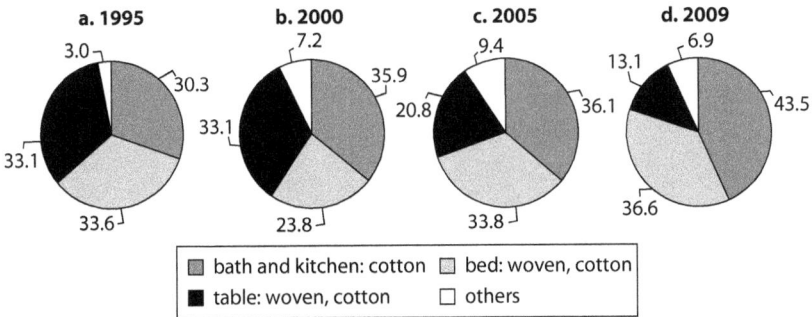

a. 1995
3.0
30.3
33.1
33.1
33.6

b. 2000
7.2
35.9
33.1
23.8

c. 2005
9.4
20.8
33.8

d. 2009
6.9
13.1
36.1
43.5
36.6

■ bath and kitchen: cotton   ▨ bed: woven, cotton
■ table: woven, cotton   □ others

Source: United Nations Commodity Trade Statistics Database (UN Comtrade).
Note: SITC Standard International Trade Classification Rev. 3, codes 65842, 65845, and 65847; exports represented by world imports from India.

with substantial value-addition at each stage of processing with a major contribution to the country's economy" (Government of India 2000). Thus, backward linkages from the apparel sector to the textile and even fiber sectors are well developed. India's domestic raw material and textile base is significant and only topped by China. India is the second-largest producer of cotton (23 percent of world market), the largest producers of jute (63 percent), the fifth-largest producer of synthetic fiber and yarn (6.5 percent), and number nine in wool production (2 percent) (IFPRI 2008). Backward linkages are reflected in the low import intensity of India's apparel exports, which accounted for barely 2 percent in the early 2000s (Tewari 2005). At present, 90 percent of apparel made in India (including domestic and export sales) employs local fabric (Tewari 2008). However, in recent years the share of imported inputs has increased, largely due to increased imports of accessories and fabrics, in particular MMF-based fabrics. As depicted in table 11.17, the rise in textile imports has been largely based on rising imports from China, which accounted for almost two-thirds of total textile imports in 2009 (up from 15 percent in 2000). In contrast, traditional sources of textile imports, including the EU-15; Hong Kong SAR, China; Indonesia; and Korea, have declined in importance.

In the formal textile sector, there has been a trend toward modernization through the adoption of new technology and the installation of advanced production facilities. This trend can be seen in increased imports and world share of machinery for woven fabric, knit fabric, and

Table 11.17 Top Five Textile Suppliers to India, 1995, 2000, 2005, 2008, and 2009

Country/economy/region	Customs value ($, million)					Market share (%)				
	1995	2000	2005	2008	2009	1995	2000	2005	2008	2009
World	359	786	2,287	2,873	2,906					
China	26	118	1,210	1,807	1,848	7.3	15.0	52.9	62.9	63.6
EU-15	69	109	204	238	188	19.1	13.9	8.9	8.3	6.5
Nepal	n.a.	n.a.	n.a.	n.a.	157	n.a.	n.a.	n.a.	n.a.	5.4
Korea, Rep.	75	139	123	117	117	21.0	17.7	5.4	4.1	4.0
Thailand	n.a.	n.a.	n.a.	105	92	n.a.	n.a.	n.a.	3.6	3.2
Hong Kong SAR, China	49	84	141	103	n.a.	13.7	10.7	6.2	3.6	n.a.
Indonesia	28	78	112	n.a.	n.a.	7.7	9.9	4.9	n.a.	n.a.
Top five share	**247**	**529**	**1,790**	**2,370**	**2,401**	**68.7**	**67.2**	**78.3**	**82.5**	**82.6**

Source: United Nations Commodity Trade Statistics Database (UN Comtrade).

Note: SITC Standard International Trade Classification Rev. 3; imports represented by countries' exports to India; n.a. = not applicable (indicates country not in top five in given year). EU-15 = the 15 member states of the European Union (EU) as of December 31, 2003, before the new member states joined the EU: Austria, Belgium, Denmark, Finland, France, Germany, Greece, Ireland, Italy, Luxembourg, the Netherlands, Portugal, Spain, Sweden, and the United Kingdom.

yarn production (Brocklehurst 2009). India ranked third in shipments of single and double jersey circular knitting machinery (after China and Mauritius, tables 11.18 and 11.19) and in shipments of shuttleless looms (after China and Bangladesh, table 11.20) in 2009. With regard to the spinning industry, India was the second-largest purchaser of short-staple spindles in 2009 (behind China; table 11.21). India increased its capacity of short-staple spindles to 36,943 and ranked second only after China in global capacity of short-staple spindles in 2009, accounting for 16.8 percent of the world capacity (table 11.22). The government has also tried to address quality concerns related to the cotton sector. In particular, a Technology Mission was established to improve the quality of Indian cotton, which was perceived as low due to inadequate storage, outdated equipment, and production methods (USITC 2004). The government also tried to further domestic capacities to meet the growing demand in MMF fibers and textiles. In this regard, the Technology Mission was extended to encompass in particular the growing markets of technical textiles. However, fiber and textile production is still dominated by cotton-based products.

Employment

With an estimated 35 million employees, the textile and apparel industries are the second most important source of employment in India (after agriculture). Their significance is even higher if one considers the estimated 55 million jobs in upstream cotton and jute agriculture (Ministry of Textiles 2006). In the National Textile Policy 2000, it is stated that the sector has a "vast potential for creation of employment opportunities in the agricultural, industrial, organized and decentralized sectors, and rural and urban areas, particularly for women and the disadvantaged" (Government of India 2000).

Figure 11.5 shows the development of formal employment in the textile and apparel sectors of establishments with 10 or more workers from 1974 to 2008. It shows a steady increase in apparel employment since the mid-1980s and a decline in textile employment until the early 2000s. From the mid-2000s onward, employment in apparel and textiles has strongly increased, reaching a total employment level of above 2 million in 2008. In 2008, the textile sector accounted for two-thirds of total textile and apparel employment. These data are not comparable with data reported by the Ministry of Textiles for the years 2001 and 2006, which also include establishments with fewer than 10 workers as well as informal employment and show a much larger employment level. As indicated

Table 11.18 **Indian Knit Textile Industry: Shipments of Single Jersey Circular Knitting Machinery**

Country/region	Shipments (# machines)			Share of world (%)			Global rank		
	2000–2009	2008	2009	2000–2009	2008	2009	2000–2009	2008	2009
World	113,251	12,705	13,144	100.0	100.0	100.0	n.a.	n.a.	n.a.
China	62,274	8,031	8,437	55.0	63.2	64.2	1	1	1
Mauritius	1,346	21	1,042	1.2	0.2	7.9	12	34	2
India	5,601	519	587	4.9	4.1	4.5	3	3	3
Bangladesh	5,094	802	580	4.5	6.3	4.4	4	2	4
Indonesia	2,990	408	420	2.6	3.2	3.2	6	6	5
Vietnam	1,427	52	207	1.3	0.4	1.6	11	20	8
Mexico	800	52	37	0.7	0.4	0.3	18	20	19
Pakistan	1,044	4	15	0.9	0.0	0.1	15	46	28
Morocco	—	44	12	—	0.3	0.1	—	24	32
Honduras	863	—	—	0.8	—	—	17	—	—

Source: Brocklehurst and Anson 2010c.
Note: Cambodia and Sri Lanka data not available; n.a. = not applicable; — = not available.

Table 11.19 Indian Knit Textile Industry: Shipments of Double Jersey Circular Knitting Machinery

Country/region	Shipments (# machines)			Share of world (%)			Global rank		
	2000–09	2008	2009	2000–09	2008	2009	2000–09	2008	2009
World	85,706	8,447	12,292	100.0	100.0	100.0	n.a.	n.a.	n.a.
China	58,342	6,373	9,149	68.1	75.4	74.4	1	1	1
Mauritius	1,457	13	1,271	1.7	0.2	10.3	5	29	2
India	3,241	333	454	3.8	3.9	3.7	2	2	3
Bangladesh	2,287	264	264	2.7	3.1	2.1	4	3	4
Indonesia	1,030	124	148	1.2	1.5	1.2	10	5	5
Vietnam	496	65	60	0.6	0.8	0.5	15	10	11
Mexico	422	19	18	0.5	0.2	0.1	19	24	22
Morocco	—	32	11	—	0.4	0.1	—	20	26
Pakistan	384	—	—	0.4	—	—	20	—	—
Honduras	234	n.a.	n.a.	0.3	n.a.	n.a.	28	n.a.	n.a.

Source: Brocklehurst and Anson 2010c.
Note: Cambodia and Sri Lanka data not available; n.a. = not applicable; — = not available.

Table 11.20   Indian Woven Textile Industry: Shipments of Shuttleless Looms

Country/region	Shipments (# machines)					Share of world (%)			Global rank				
	2000–09	2006	2007	2008	2009	2000–09	2006	2009	2000–09	2006	2007	2008	2009
World	579,176	66,633	68,213	44,754	43,417	100.0	100.0	100.0	n.a.	n.a.	n.a.	n.a.	n.a.
China	377,728	42,152	46,236	28,597	25,600	65.2	63.3	59.0	1	1	1	1	1
Bangladesh	26,871	3,854	4,219	3,068	8,411	4.6	5.8	19.4	2	3	2	3	2
India	26,091	5,662	3,994	3,302	3,464	4.5	8.5	8.0	3	2	3	2	3
Vietnam	6,717	1,357	826	508	748	1.2	2.0	1.7	10	6	9	10	5
Pakistan	11,956	2,424	1,100	767	383	2.1	3.6	0.9	6	5	7	6	6
Morocco	1,018	173	154	33	28	0.2	0.3	0.1	26	20	20	40	27
Mexico	1,871	228	95	29	19	0.3	0.3	<0.1	22	17	31	43	31

Sources: Anson and Brocklehurst 2008, Brocklehurst and Anson 2010b.

Note: Cambodia, Honduras, and Sri Lanka data not included; n.a. = not applicable.

Table 11.21 Indian Shipments of Short-Staple Spindles

Country/region	Shipments (# machines)			Share of world (%)			Global rank		
	2000–09	2008	2009	2000–09	2008	2009	2000–09	2008	2009
World	80,210	8,640.3	7,204.4	100.0	100.0	100.0	n.a.	n.a.	n.a.
China	41,585	3,687.3	5,036.6	51.8	42.7	69.9	1	1	1
India	16,085	2,527.7	1,372.2	20.1	29.3	19.0	2	2	2
Vietnam	1,993	579.3	111.1	2.5	6.7	1.5	6	4	3
Bangladesh	3,613	642.1	107.5	4.5	7.4	1.5	4	3	4
Myanmar	199	19.3	88.6	0.2	0.2	1.2	17	17	5
Mexico	415	26.9	27.6	0.5	0.3	0.4	12	15	13
Pakistan	5,549	238.0	16.5	6.9	2.8	0.2	3	6	16
Cambodia	79	—	—	0.1	—	—	27	—	—
Morocco	67	—	—	0.1	—	—	32	—	—

Source: Brocklehurst and Anson 2010a.

Note: Honduras and Sri Lanka data are not available; n.a. = not applicable; — = not available.

Table 11.22   Installed Capacity of Indian Short-Staple Spindles, 2009

Country/region	Installed machines (#)	Share of world (%)	Global rank
World	219,529	100.0	n.a.
China	104,228	47.5	1
India	36,943	16.8	2
Pakistan	11,366	5.2	3
Indonesia	7,950	3.6	4
Bangladesh	7,276	3.3	5
Turkey	6,550	3.0	6
Mexico	3,540	1.6	9
Vietnam	1,940	0.9	11
Morocco	450	0.2	32

Source: Brocklehurst and Anson 2010a.
Note: Cambodia, Honduras, and Sri Lanka data are not available; n.a. = not applicable.

Figure 11.5   Employment in Indian Textile and Apparel Sectors, 1974–2008

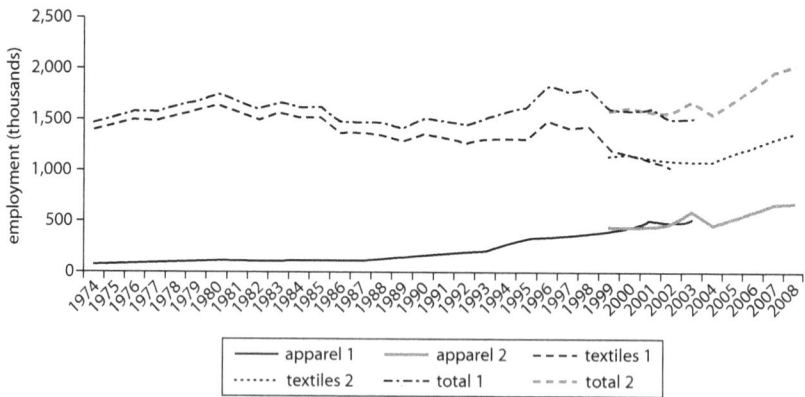

Sources: Data from 1974–2003: ASI Employment Data from ASI CD-ROM cited in Tewari (2006); data from 1999–2008: ASI Publication 2009/10. Note: ASI data only includes establishments with 10 or more workers and does not include informal employment.
Note: ASI data include only establishments with 10 or more workers and do not include informal employment.

in table 11.23, textile employment decreased in absolute numbers between 2001 and 2006, a decrease that can be largely attributed to the reduction of employment in the handloom segment of the industry. At the same time, apparel employment increased from approximately 3.5 million in 2001 to 5.6 million in 2006, accounting for 16.8 percent (see figure 11.6) of total textile and apparel employment.

As previously discussed, the textile and apparel industries are divided into a relatively small formal segment characterized by more developed,

Table 11.23   Employment in Indian Textile and Apparel Sectors, 2001 and 2006

	2001		2006	
Segment	Number of jobs (million)	Share (%)	Number of jobs (million)	Share (%)
Cotton, man-made fiber, and yarn textile and mill sector (including small-scale spinning and exclusively weaving units)	1.07	3.1	0.94	2.8
Man-made fiber and filament yarn industry (including texturizing industry)	0.11	0.3	0.16	0.5
Decentralized power loom sector	4.15	12.1	4.86	14.7
Handloom sector	12.00	34.9	6.50	19.6
Knitting sector	0.30	0.9	0.43	1.3
Processing sector	0.24	0.7	0.29	0.9
Woolen sector	1.20	3.5	1.50	4.5
Apparel sector (including woven and knitted)	3.54	10.3	5.57	16.8
Sericulture	5.57	16.2	5.95	17.9
Handicraft sector	5.84	17.0	6.57	19.8
Jute industry	0.40	1.2	0.40	1.2
Total	**34.42**	**100.0**	**33.17**	**100.0**

Sources: Hirway 2008; Ministry of Textiles 2006.

Figure 11.6   Employment in Indian Textile and Apparel Sectors, 2001 and 2006

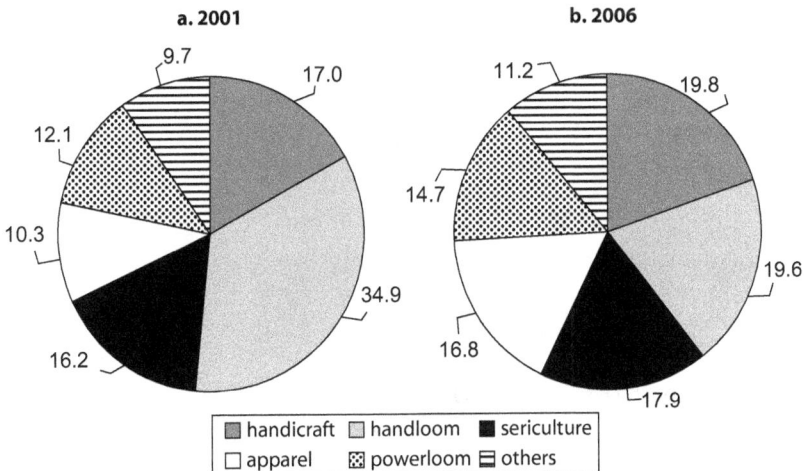

Sources: Hirway 2008; Ministry of Textiles 2006.

often larger firms with higher capital intensity and often better working conditions and a large informal segment, together accounting for about 90 percent of employment (Hirway 2008). The textile and apparel industries have traditionally been one of the major means of employment for women. The participation of women is particularly high in the hand-loom weaving, sericulture, handicraft, and more recently the power loom and apparel segments (Ministry of Textiles 2006). However, the large majority of female employment participation has taken place in the informal sector. As indicated in table 11.24, the female share in the informal segment, in both textiles and apparel, is higher than the male share (Hirway 2008). According to official data, the employment share of women in the whole apparel industry (formal and informal segments) accounted for 38 percent but was substantially higher than the average share of female employment in total manufacturing, which ranged between 15 and 17 percent between 1999 and 2005 (ILO LaborStat 2010).

With regard to wages and working conditions, there appears to be a bifurcation between the formal and the informal sector. Workers in the formal industry generally enjoy relatively good working conditions, including decent wages and social security payments, and are generally represented by trade unions. In contrast, the majority of workers in the informal sector receive lower wages and are largely deprived of additional social protection measures (Hirway 2008). As the majority of women are employed in the informal sector, the gender wage gap is evident across all segments of the industry (table 11.25). Child labor has also

Table 11.24   Employment in Indian Formal and Informal Textile and Apparel Segments, 2000

	Formal	Informal
Textiles Employment (%)		
Male	15.98	84.02
Female	2.60	97.40
Total	11.29	88.71
Apparel Employment (%)		
Male	7.26	92.74
Female	6.64	93.36
Total	7.09	92.91
Textiles and Apparel Employment (%)		
Male	13.61	86.39
Female	3.43	96.57
Total	**10.24**	**89.76**

Sources: National Sample Survey Organization (NSSO) Round 1999–2000, cf. Hirway 2008.

Table 11.25   Average Daily Earnings in Indian Textile and Apparel Industries

Industry	1974–79			1985–92			2002–05		
	Male earnings (Rs)	Female earnings (Rs)	M/F ratio	Male earnings (Rs)	Female earnings (Rs)	M/F ratio	Male earnings (Rs)	Female earnings (Rs)	M/F ratio
Cotton textiles	14.58	11.63	1.25	42.78	29.74	1.44	78.12	73.24	1.07
Woolen textiles	13.76	8.22	1.67	35.83	35.96	1.00	69.31	59.24	1.17
Silk textiles	10.42	7.10	1.47	30.63	25.15	1.22	63.98	39.56	1.62
Synthetic textiles	—	—	—	44.63	42.28	1.06	62.38	40.86	1.53
Jute textiles	14.66	15.59	0.94	42.44	42.00	1.01	89.73	85.99	1.04
Garments	11.27	7.12	1.58	34.01	18.61	1.83	60.60	37.83	1.60
Coefficient of variation	*0.17*	*0.37*	*0.46*	*0.16*	*0.25*	*0.64*	*0.17*	*0.37*	*0.46*

Sources: Occupational Wage Survey, Labor Bureau, Government of India; cf. Hirway 2008.

Note: — = not available; Rs = rupees.

been a recurring issue in the Indian textile and apparel industries, as highlighted by several nongovernmental organizations (NGOs) and most recently by the U.S. Department of Labor (*Just-style* 2010c). Average labor costs in India were around $0.51 per hour in 2008 (Jassin-O'Rourke Group 2008).

Trade Regulations and Proactive Policies

Preferential Market Access

India enjoyed preferential market access to the EU for textile and apparel exports via the EU's Generalized System of Preferences (GSP) scheme until 2006. While textile products lost their preferential status from January 2006 onward, apparel exports continue to enjoy preferential rates 20 percent lower than most favored nation (MFN) rates. India successfully challenged the EU's old GSP system in a WTO court case in the first half of the 2000s, claiming that Pakistan was granted special preferences under the scheme. Along the same line, India together with other countries put pressure on the EU to abandon plans that would grant Pakistan special preferences in light of the floods that hit Pakistan in summer 2010 (*Just-style* 2010d). Currently, India is negotiating a free trade agreement (FTA) with the EU that would promote trade liberalization in goods and services, including elimination of tariffs on textile and apparel exports. According to the Indian Apparel Export Promotion Council (AEPC), such an agreement would boost apparel exports to the EU by $3 billion and create up to 2.5 million new jobs (*Just-style* 2010e). With regard to the U.S. market, India does not dispose of any special preferences, as almost all textile and apparel items are excluded from the United States' GSP scheme. The Japanese market has not been of great importance for textile and apparel exports. However, this situation is likely to change because India and Japan signed an FTA in February 2011 after more than six years of negotiation. Under the Comprehensive Economic Partnership Agreement (CEPA), 94 percent of tariffs between the two countries will be eliminated over the next 10 years. Tariffs of around 11 percent for apparel will be eliminated immediately (*Just-style* 2011a).

Besides India's efforts to improve its market access to key Northern markets, it has increasingly looked to enter new Southern markets via a set of bilateral and regional agreements, in particular in the Asian region. Table 11.26 gives an overview of India's bilateral and regional trade agreements.

Table 11.26   Indian Bilateral and Regional Trade Agreements

Country (group)	Type of agreement	Status
East and Southeast Asia		
China	JSG	Completed in 2005
	JTF to develop Trade Agreement	Ongoing
Indonesia	JSG	Completed in 2009
	Aim for a CECA	Ongoing
Japan	CEPA	Signed in 2011
Malaysia	CECA	Signed in 2011
Singapore	CECA	Signed in 2005
Korea, Rep.	CEPA	Signed in 2009
Thailand	Framework Agreement	Signed in 2003
	Aim for a CECA	Ongoing
South Asia		
Afghanistan	PTA	Signed in 2003
Bangladesh	Trade Agreement	Signed in 2006
Bhutan	FTA (replaced former agreement from 1995)	Signed in 2006
Maldives	Trade Agreement	Signed in 1981
Nepal	FTA (replaced former agreement from 1991)	Signed in 2009
Sri Lanka	FTA	Signed in 1998
	CEPA	Ongoing
Others		
Australia	JSG	Completed in 2008
	Aim for an FTA	Ongoing
Chile	PTA	Signed in 2006
Finland	Agreement on Economic Cooperation (replaced agreement from 1974)	Signed in 2010
Mauritius	JSG	Completed in 2004
	CEPA	Ongoing
Mongolia	Trade Agreement	Signed in 1996
New Zealand	JSG for CECA/FTA	Ongoing
Regional Agreements		
APTA	PTA	Signed in 1975 (amended in 2005)
ASEAN	FTA	Signed in 2009
GCC	Framework Agreement	Signed in 2004
	Aim for an FTA	
MERCOSUR	PTA	Signed in 2004
SACU	PTA	Ongoing
SAFTA	FTA	Signed in 2004

Sources: Authors; Ministry of Commerce and Industries website http://india.gov.in/sectors/commerce/ministry_commerce.php; Weerakoon 2010.
Note: APTA = Asia-Pacific Trade Agreement; ASEAN = Association of South East Asian Nations; GCC = Gulf Cooperation Council; MERCOSUR = Common Southern Market (Mercado Común del Sur); SACU = Southern Africa Customs Union; SAFTA = South Asian Free Trade Agreement; CECA = Comprehensive Economic Cooperation Agreement; CEPA = Comprehensive Economic Partnership Agreement; FTA = Free Trade Agreement; PTA = Preferential Trade Agreement; JSG = Joint Study Group; JTF = Joint Task Force.

At the regional level, the South Asian Free Trade Agreement (SAFTA) is the key agreement to further regional integration between South Asian countries. It was signed in 2004 by the then members of SAARC, including Bangladesh, Bhutan, India, Maldives, Nepal, Pakistan, and Sri Lanka. The signatories agreed to phase out tariffs on practically all trade in goods (with services excluded) by the end of 2016 (CARIS 2008). However, so far there has been little sign of tangible progress in implementing SAFTA. In particular, long-standing political issues between India and Pakistan impede the potential gains derived from regional integration. Instead, a number of bilateral agreements have been signed between SAFTA members, and most of them involve India, which is less surprising given the fact that trade flows within SAARC are focused toward India (Weerakoon 2010).

As part of India's Look East policy, which aims to foster ties with the wider Asian region, India started negotiations on trade liberalizations with the Association for South East Asian Nations (ASEAN). In August 2009, India signed an FTA with the 10 ASEAN member countries, including Brunei, Burma, Cambodia, Indonesia, the Lao People's Democratic Republic, Malaysia, the Philippines, Singapore, Thailand, and Vietnam, which entered into force in January 2010. In the context of the agreement, tariffs will be phased out for a range of products, including textiles and apparel items, over a six-year period. The FTA is expected to promote export diversification by opening new markets for exporters in the Asian region and to increase the availability of inputs for local apparel manufacturers (*Just-style* 2009).

Proactive Policies

At the national level, institutions and policies at several levels have been crucial in the development of India's textile and apparel sectors. The most important national actors include the government and its ministries and agencies responsible for the textile and apparel sectors (in particular the Ministry of Textiles) and industry associations. Industry associations include the Apparel and Handloom Exporters Association, the Apparel Export Promotion Council (AEPC) established in 1978, the Apparel Exporters and Manufacturers Association, the Clothing Manufacturers Association of India (CMAI), the Confederation of Indian Apparel Exporters (CIAE), the Confederation of Indian Textile Industry (CITI), the Cotton Textiles Export Promotion Council (Texprocil), the International Garment Fair Association, the Knitwear Technology Mission (KTM), the

Synthetic and Rayon Textiles Promotion Council (SRTEPC), and the Textile Association. Regionally, India is one of seven founding members of the Asian Apparel Federation (AAF), established in 2007 to promote the development of Asia's apparel industry.

The policy change in the mid-1980s marked the beginning of the restructuring and modernization of India's textile and apparel sectors, which was deepened in the context of broader deregulation and liberalization policies since the early 1990s (Tewari 2005). This policy change started with the textile and apparel sectors and was formulated in the National Textile Policy 1985, which had large implications for the growth of the sectors. Since then, the Indian government has deployed several measures to promote the industries' development. The National Textile Policy 2000 is a key policy initiative in this regard. It was established in the context of "the new challenges and opportunities presented by the changing global environment, particularly the initiation of the process of gradual phasing out of quantitative restrictions on imports and the lowering of tariff levels for an integration of the world textile and clothing markets by end of 2004, and the need for a focused approach to maximizing opportunities and strengths inherent in the situation" (Government of India 2000). The objective of the National Textile Policy 2000 was to facilitate the textile and apparel industries to attain and sustain a global standing in the manufacture and export of textiles and apparel. To achieve these objectives, the following thrust areas were identified (Government of India 2000):

- Technological upgradation
- Enhancement of productivity
- Quality consciousness
- Strengthening of the raw material base
- Product diversification
- Increase in exports and innovative marketing strategies
- Financing arrangements
- Maximizing employment opportunities
- Integrated human resource development.

Some of the most important measures include the following (Singh 2008; Tewari and Singh forthcoming):

- *Technology Upgradation Fund Scheme:* In 1999, the government established a Technology Upgradation Fund Scheme (TUFS) to promote technical modernization and upgradation of the textile and apparel sectors. The scheme provides credit at reduced rates, that is, reimbursement of 5 percent interest paid on loans for technological upgrading of textile machinery. In this way, the government has assisted textile firms by ensuring that they are not overburdened by the high interest rates prevailing in India. The TUFS was initially planned for five years but was subsequently extended up to March 2007 and to March 2012. The modified structure of TUFS provides for a higher level of assistance to segments that have a larger potential for growth, such as apparel, technical textiles, and processing.

- *Integrated Textile Parks:* In 2005, the government announced the Scheme for Integrated Textile Parks (SITP), which has the objective to consolidate individual units in a cluster and to provide state-of-the-art infrastructure to local and international manufacturers. SITP was launched by merging two early schemes, the Apparel Parks for Exports Scheme (APES) and the Textile Center Infrastructure Development Scheme (TCIDS), that were initiated in 2002. Although 19 TCIDS and 12 APES projects were taken up, the progress was slow (Tewari and Singh forthcoming). Under SITP, initially 40 textile parks all over the country were announced, but their implementation has been lagging behind official schedules (*Just-style* 2010b). In late 2010, the Indian government claimed that some production had started in 25 of the 40 approved parks. Three projects have been completed, including Brandix & Pochampally Handloom Park Ltd. at Andhra Pradesh, Gujarat Eco Textile Park in Gujarat, and Palladam Hi-Tech Weaving Park in Tamil Nadu (Tewari and Singh forthcoming). However, up to now these 25 parks have together generated only 15,000 jobs. The country's textile minister, Dayanidhi Maran, claimed in 2009 that the program would create 800,000 new jobs (*Just-style* 2010b).

- *Technology Mission on Cotton:* In February 2000, the Technology Mission on Cotton was launched by the government to address the issues of raising productivity, improving quality, and reducing contamination in cotton. The Mission, consisting of four Mini Missions, was intended to run for five years. It was then extended up to March 2007 for Mini Mission I and II and to March 2009 for Mini Mission III and IV. Mini Mission I consists of research and development on cotton, Mini Mission II of dissemination of technology to farmers, Mini Mission III of the development of market yards, and Mini Mission IV of the modernization of ginning and pressing units (Tewari and Singh forth-coming). The efforts have provided positive results, as cotton produc-tion has increased substantially since mid-2005 and contamination has been reduced.

- *Technology mission on noncotton fibers and yarns:* Given the rising global and local demand for noncotton fibers and yarns, the government furthered the domestic production of noncotton fibers and yarns and pursued a policy of gradual reduction of import tariffs on man-made fibers and yarns. In this way, Indian apparel and fabric manufacturers should get access to noncotton inputs at more competitive prices. More recently, the government announced that it would invest Rs 2 billion (US$43.8 million) in a five-year project to boost the country's technical textiles industry, including four new centers of excellence for specialty materials (*Just-style* 2011b).

- *Product development and design capabilities:* India's textile and apparel industries have been supported by a variety of public-private institutions, in particular research and training institutes that were cre-ated during the inward-looking period. They supported the promotion of standards, including environmental and social standards, via their vast, decentralized networks and contributed to skill formation at the worker and management levels. The current training infrastructure consists of engineering colleges, Indian Institutes of Technology (IITs) and polytechnics, and agencies like apparel training and development centers (ATDCs), powerloom service centers (PSCs), weaving service centers (WSCs), industrial training institutes (ITIs), and textile research associations (TRAs) (Tewari and Singh forthcoming). Joint government and industry efforts also targeted the creation of design capabilities. As early as 1984, the National Institute of Fashion Technology (NIFT) was launched in partnership with the Fashion Institute of Technology in New York. The NIFT, together with the National Institute of Design (NID), has produced a rising number of fashion designers and manag-ers who have played an increasing role in the Indian and larger South Asian apparel industry (Tewari 2008).

- *Integrated Skill Development Scheme:* The Integrated Skill Devel-opment Scheme was launched in September 2010 and covers all segments, including textiles and apparel, handicrafts, handlooms, jute, sericulture, and technical textiles. The scheme covers basic training, skill upgradation, advanced training in emerging technologies, training of trainers, orientation toward modern technology, retraining, managerial skill, entrepreneurship development, and so forth. A total of 58 ATDCs across the country that provide trained manpower in the fields of pattern making and cutting techniques, production supervision, and quality control techniques to the apparel industry have been identified as implements for this scheme (Tewari and Singh forthcoming).

- *Mega clusters:* In 2008–09, the government decided to scale up infrastructure and production by taking up six centers for development as mega clusters in Varanasi and Sibsagar for handlooms; Bhiwandi and Erode for power looms; and Narsapur and Moradabad for handicrafts. Five more mega clusters—two for handicrafts at Srinagar (J&K) and Mirzapur-Badohi (UP), two for handlooms at Virudhnagar (TN) and Murshidabad (WB), and one for power looms at Bhilwara (Raj)—were announced for 2009–10. The scheme for mega clusters aims to give support to weavers and artisans by providing raw material support, design inputs, upgradation of technology, infrastructure development, marketing support, welfare support, and so forth. The scheme will be implemented over a five-year period (Tewari and Singh forthcoming).

Notes

1. The EU-15 is the 15 member states of the European Union (EU) as of December 31, 2003, before the new member states joined the EU: Austria, Belgium, Denmark, Finland, France, Germany, Greece, Ireland, Italy, Luxembourg, the Netherlands, Portugal, Spain, Sweden, and the United Kingdom.

2. Men's outerwear constitutes the majority of the domestic apparel market, accounting for a value share of 45 percent of total retail sales. One reason for this large share is the fact that branded apparel coverage is limited for women in India. Women's apparel in India is still dominated by traditional attire, such as the saree, which has yet to have an impact in the branded segment (Euromonitor 2009).

3. "Despite the thrust given by the Textile Policy of 1985 to the spinning sector, resulting in considerable modernization, 80 percent capacity utilization, and a 20 percent share of global cotton yarn exports, cotton spinning still suffers the problems of over-capacity and of obsolete spindleage. This Textile Policy 2000 will continue the effort to modernize and upgrade technology to international levels" (Government of India 2000).

4. "Despite a 58 percent global share of looms, consisting of 3.5 million hand-looms and 1.8 million powerlooms, technology still remains backward. The Textile Policy 2000 will support the modernization of this sector, critical to the survival of the Indian textile industry and its export thrust. Clustering of production facilities in the decentralized sector will be encouraged to achieve optimum size and adopt appropriate technology. Efforts will be made to restore the organized mill industry to its position of pre-eminence to meet international demand for high value, large volume products" (Government of India 2000).

References

AEPC (Apparel Export Promotion Council). 2009. Presentation on Export Trends, Haryana, India. http://www.aepcindia.com.

Anson, Robin, and Guillaume Brocklehurst. 2008. Part 2 of "World Markets for Textile Machinery: Fabric Manufacture." *Textile Outlook International* 137: 98–138.

Brocklehurst, Guillaume. 2009. "Trends in U.S. Textile and Clothing Imports." *Textile Outlook International* 144: 122–97.

Brocklehurst, Guillaume and Robin Anson. 2010a. Part 1 of "World Markets for Textile Machinery: Yarn Manufacture." *Textile Outlook International* 145: 80–117.

———. 2010b. Part 2 of "World Markets for Textile Machinery: Woven Fabric Manufacture." *Textile Outlook International* 146: 89–106.

———. 2010c. Part 3 of "World Markets for Textile Machinery: Knitted Fabric Manufacture." *Textile Outlook International* 147: 120–54.

CARIS (Centre for the Analysis of Regional Integration at Sussex). 2008. "The Impact of Trade Policies on Pakistan's Preferential Access to the European Union." Report for the European Council Centre for the Analysis of Regional Integration at Sussex, Department of Economics, University of Sussex.

Euromonitor. 2009. "Clothing—India: Country Sector Briefing." Report, London Euromonitor International, London.

Government of India. 2000. "National Textile Policy." New Delhi.

Hirway, Indira. 2008. "Trade and Gender Inequalities in Labour Market: Case of Textile and Garment Industry in India." Paper prepared for the International Seminar on Moving towards Gender Sensitization of Trade Policy, organized by the United Nations Conference on Trade and Development (UNCTAD), New Delhi, February 25–27.

IFPRI (International Food Policy Research Institute). 2008. "Cotton-Textile-Apparel Sectors of India: Situations and Challenges Faced." Discussion Paper 00801, IFPRI, Washington, DC.

ILO (International Labour Organization). 2010. ILO LaborStat: http://laborsta .ilo.org.

Italia. 2009. "The Textile Industry and Related Sector Report 2009." Italian Trade Commission. http://www.ice.gov.it.

Jassin-O'Rourke Group, L. 2008. "Global Apparel Manufacturing Labor Cost Analysis 2008, Textile and Apparel Manufacturers & Merchants." http://www .tammonline.com/researchpapers.htm.

Just-style. 2008. "Government Ends Raw Cotton Import Duty." July 11.

———. 2009. "Textiles to Benefit from ASEAN Trade Deal." August 19.

———. 2010a. "Indian Cotton Controls Mask Higher Input Costs." May 4.

———. 2010b. "Indian Cotton Curb Sparks New Wave of Protectionism." December 9.

———. 2010c. "US Labour "Blacklisting" a Wake-up Call to India?" July 22.

———. 2010d. "Pakistan Tariff Waiver Gains Initial Support." December 15.

———. 2010e. "Apparel Exporters Renew Calls for EU Trade Pact." July 13.

———. 2011a. "Apparel Exporters to Benefit from Japan Trade Pact." February 21.

———. 2011b. "Launches Five-Year Technical Textiles Plan." January 21.

Ministry of Textiles. 2006. "Report of the Working Group on the Textiles and Jute Industry for the Eleventh Five-Year-Plan." December. http://planningcommis-sion.gov.in.

———. 2009. "Assessing the Prospects for India's Textile and Clothing Sector." July. http://www.texmin.nic.in.

———. 2010. *Annual Report* 2009/10. New Delhi. http://www.texmin.nic.in.

Nordås, H. K. 2004. "The Global Textile and Clothing Industry post the Agreement on Textiles and Clothing." Discussion Paper 5, World Trade Organization, Geneva.

Singh, J. N. 2008. "Indian Textile and Clothing Sector Poised for a Leap." In *Unveiling Protectionism: Regional Responses to Remaining Barriers in the Textiles and Clothing Trade*, 157–70. Bangkok: United Nations Economic and Social Commission for Asia and the Pacific.

Tewari, Menu. 2005. "Post-MFA Adjustments in India's Textile and Apparel Industry: Emerging Issues and Trends." Working Paper, Indian Council for Research on International Economic Relations, New Delhi.

———. 2006. Study for the Ministry of Textiles, Indian Council for Research on International Economic Relations, New Delhi.

———. 2008. "Varieties of Global Integration: Navigating Institutional Legacies and Global Networks in India's Garment Industry." *Competition & Change* 12 (1): 49–67.

———. 2009. "The Textiles and Clothing Industry." In *Study on Intraregional Trade and Investment in South Asia*, ed. African Development Bank, 40–69. Tunis-Belvedère, Tunisia: African Development Bank.

Tewari, Menu, and Manjeeta Singh. Forthcoming. Textile Ministry Study, Indian Council for Research on International Economic Relations, New Delhi.

Textiles Intelligence. 2008. *Textile Outlook International*, No. 135.

Thoburn, John. 2009. "The Impact of World Recession on the Textile and Garment Industries of Asia." Working Paper 17/2009, Research and Statistics Branch, United Nations Industrial Development Organization, Vienna.

USITC (United States International Trade Commission). 2004. "Textiles and Apparel: Assessment of the Competitiveness of Certain Foreign Suppliers to the U.S. Market." U.S. International Trade Commission Publication 3671, Washington, DC.

Verma, Samar. 2005. "Impact of the MFA Expiry on India." In *South Asia after the Quota System: Impact of the MFA Phase-out*, ed. Saman Kelegama. Colombo: Institute of Policy Studies.

Weerakoon, Dushni. 2010. "SAFTA: Current Status and Prospects." In *Promoting Economic Cooperation in South Asia: Beyond SAFTA*, ed. Sadiq Ahmed, Saman Kelegama, and Ejaz Ghani, 71–88. Washington, DC: World Bank.

CHAPTER 12

Mexico

Overview

- Initial development of the export-oriented apparel sector in Mexico began in the mid-1960s, driven by preferential access to the U.S. market through the "807" production-sharing agreement and the establishment of the *maquiladora* program along the U.S. border. In 1994, access was significantly expanded with the passage of the North American Free Trade Agreement (NAFTA), permitting Mexico to export apparel quota and duty free to both Canada and the United States provided that the yarn, fabric, and apparel assembly stages occurred in one of the three countries. This expansion also led to initial investments in the textile sector, mostly from U.S. firms.

- NAFTA occurred at the beginning of the Multi-fibre Arrangement (MFA) phaseout and provided Mexican exporters with a timely advantage over quota-constrained countries. As a result of NAFTA, apparel exports experienced rapid growth from 1994 to 2000. However, exports have steadily declined since 2001. This decline can be attributed to several factors, including China's accession to the World Trade Organization (WTO), the temporary recession in the United States, and the beginning of expanded market access for the Caribbean Basin countries in 2000 under the U.S.-Caribbean Basin Trade Partnership Act (CBTPA).

- Post-MFA, the trend of declining export value, employment, and factories continued. Export values declined at an increasing rate in the 2005–09 time frame, with the largest contraction occurring in 2009 (–15.3 percent). Post-MFA declines can be attributed to the end of the quota system in 2005 and partially to the implementation of the Dominican Republic–Central America Free Trade Agreement (DR-CAFTA). More recent declines in the 2008–09 period have been caused primarily by the end of Chinese safeguards at the end of 2008, the economic recession, and also the H1N1 virus outbreak in Mexico.

- Mexico has relied almost entirely on the United States for exports because of its two main competitive advantages in the apparel industry— proximity and preferential access to the U.S. market. However, exporters have not been able to turn their geographic proximity to the U.S. market into a lasting source of competitive advantage. This failure can be attributed to a lack of broad supplier upgrading because of being locked into assembly versus more advanced full-package capabilities, as well as a lack of diversification beyond the U.S. market. Despite declines in exports and market share, Mexico has some advantages in terms of products (men's blue denim jeans) and close connections with lead firms in the U.S. market that have sustained Mexico's position among the leading U.S. exporters.

Development of the Apparel Industry

Export-oriented apparel production originally started in Mexico in 1965 under the Border Industrialization Program as a means of attracting foreign investment, increasing exports, and alleviating the high unemployment along the U.S.-Mexico border that resulted from the termination of the U.S. Bracero program in 1964 (Rice 1998). This program permitted Mexican factories to temporarily import raw materials and machinery duty free provided the resulting products were to be exported. During this time, Mexican exports also benefited from the U.S. special tariff scheme known as the "807 program," which permitted U.S. firms to import apparel and only pay duty on the value added in the exporting country provided the fabric used was cut in the United States. These programs led to growth in apparel employment, factories, and exports destined for the United

States. The program also encouraged some U.S. apparel manufacturers to set up foreign assembly operations in Mexico.

The export industry began in the 1960s, but it accelerated during the 1980s due to several factors: the so-called *maquiladora* policy was expanded to include factories outside the border region; the Mexican peso depreciated significantly against the U.S. dollar; and in 1988, Mexican exports were essentially granted quota-free access to the U.S. market provided the apparel products were made using U.S.-manufactured and -cut fabric. Shortly thereafter (1990), the Mexican government enacted a new policy known as the Temporary Importation Program to Produce Articles for Exportation (Programa de Importación Temporal para Producir Artículos de Exportación—PITEX) that provided similar import privileges as the *maquiladora* program to factories more oriented toward domestic apparel sales. Whereas both programs allow firms to engage in domestic sales, the share allowed under the PITEX program is higher. PITEX holders still had to maintain a certain percentage or value of export sales; however, they were not required to adhere to the employment requirements of the *maquila* program (Rice 1998).

Mexico's most significant apparel export growth occurred during the 1990s, specifically in 1994 with the passage of NAFTA, which permitted quota- and duty-free access to the U.S. market provided the textile components from yarn-forward were made in Canada, Mexico, or the United States. NAFTA led to upstream investments in the apparel value chain, primarily in the cotton fabric and yarn sectors. Given the benefit of quota-free access to the U.S. market, Mexican exporters were not directly impacted by the MFA phaseout. As the most sensitive U.S. imports were only phased in at the end of the phaseout in 2005, NAFTA provided participants in the apparel value chain in Mexico with a 10-year advantage over other U.S. apparel exporters.

Apparel exports from Mexico experienced significant growth in the 1990s, reaching a peak value in 2000 of $8,924 million (table 12.1). Import data from Mexico's trading partners show an increase from $2,871 million in 1995 to $8,372 million in 2001, although this increase marked the first year of the trend in the 2000s of declining export values. Mexico's share of global apparel exports increased from 1.9 percent in 1995 to 4.3 percent in 2001. Woven apparel exports have remained consistently ahead of knitted apparel exports throughout the 1990s and 2000s. Ratios have varied marginally over the 1995–2009 time span, with woven and knit export shares fluctuating between ranges of 58–64 percent and 42–36 percent, respectively.

Table 12.1 Mexican Apparel Exports to the World

	1995	1998	2001	2004	2005	2006	2007	2008	2009
Total value ($, million)	2,871	6,928	8,372	7,285	6,683	5,952	5,129	4,634	3,923
Annual growth rate (%)	55.3	27.0	−6.2	−2.6	−8.3	−10.9	−13.8	−9.6	−15.3
Share of world exports (%)	1.9	3.9	4.3	2.9	2.5	2.1	1.6	1.4	1.3
Woven and knit value ($, million)									
Woven	1,857	4,008	4,871	4,382	4,112	3,542	3,117	2,834	2,476
Knit	1,014	2,920	3,500	2,903	2,570	2,410	2,012	1,799	1,448
Woven and knit share of total import value (%)									
Woven	64.7	57.9	58.2	60.1	61.5	59.5	60.8	61.2	63.1
Knit	35.3	42.1	41.8	39.9	38.5	40.5	39.2	38.8	36.9

Source: United Nations Commodity Trade Statistics Database (UN Comtrade).

Note: Exports represented by imports reported by partner countries. Apparel classifications: Harmonized Commodity Description and Coding System (HS) 1992: Woven: HS62; Knit: HS61; growth rate reflects change from previous year.

Mexico's exports have been almost entirely destined for the U.S. end market, although the concentration has been slowly decreasing over the past decade. The United States accounted for 97.7 percent of exports in 1995, decreasing to 94.0 percent in 2005. Canada and the EU-15 are the only other two markets representing more than 1 percent of exports.[1] In the U.S. market, Mexico's exports increased from US$3,743 million in 1996 to a peak of US$8,618 in 2000 (figure 12.1). From 1998 to 2002, Mexico was the largest source of apparel imports into the U.S. market, reaching a market share of 14.8 percent in 1999 (table 12.2).

The fall in Mexican apparel exports since 2001 can largely be attributed to fierce competition from China and other low-cost Asian countries (including Bangladesh and Vietnam) in its main export market, the United States. When China joined the WTO in 2001, a number of quotas were removed in accordance with the Agreement on Textiles and Clothing (ATC), allowing China more open access to the U.S. market ("Trade and Trade Policy" 2009). Additional factors explaining the export decline in the early 2000s were the temporary recession in the United States and the beginning of expanded market access for the Caribbean Basin countries in 2000 under the U.S.-Caribbean Basin Trade Partnership Act.

Figure 12.1   Mexican Apparel Exports to Canada, the EU-15, and the United States

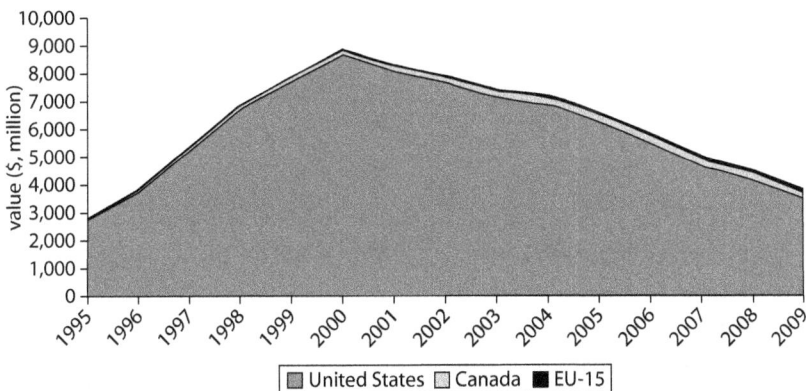

Source: United Nations Commodity Trade Statistics Database (UN Comtrade).
Note: Exports represented by imports reported by partner countries. Apparel classifications: Harmonized Commodity Description and Coding System (HS) 1992: Woven: HS62; Knit: HS61. EU-15 = the 15 member states of the European Union (EU) as of December 31, 2003, before the new member states joined the EU: Austria, Belgium, Denmark, Finland, France, Germany, Greece, Ireland, Italy, Luxembourg, the Netherlands, Portugal, Spain, Sweden, and the United Kingdom.

Table 12.2 U.S. Apparel Imports from Mexico

	1996	1998	2001	2004	2005	2006	2007	2008	2009
Total value ($, million)	3,743	6,702	8,028	6,845	6,230	5,448	4,630	4,129	3,482
Annual growth rate (%)	—	27.8	–6.9	–3.6	–9.0	–12.6	–15.0	–10.8	–15.7
Share of all U.S. apparel imports (%)	9.9	13.5	13.7	10.2	8.8	7.4	6.1	5.6	5.4
Woven and knit value ($, million)									
Woven	2,281	3,884	4,672	4,137	3,842	3,237	2,814	2,533	2,208
Knit	1,462	2,819	3,356	2,708	2,389	2,211	1,816	1,596	1,274
Woven and knit share of total import value (%)									
Woven	60.9	57.9	58.2	60.4	61.7	59.4	60.8	61.4	63.4
Knit	39.1	42.1	41.8	39.6	38.3	40.6	39.2	38.6	36.6

Source: U.S. International Trade Commission (USITC).

Note: Apparel represented by Harmonized Commodity Description and Coding System (HS) Codes 61 and 62: customs value; growth rate reflects change from previous year. — = not available.

The end of the MFA phaseout had additional negative effects on Mexico. The majority of Mexico's exports to the United States were integrated into the MFA system in Phase IV, thus insulating Mexico from competing countries subject to quotas until the end of 2004. Furthermore, most of Mexico's exports were also protected from Chinese exports in the U.S. market throughout the safeguard period 2005–08. Thus, the phaseout of the MFA and the end of China safeguards in 2004 and 2008, respectively, had large impacts on Mexico's apparel exports.

Trends since the MFA phaseout in 2005 should be assessed in light of both the Chinese safeguards and the global economic crisis. In addition, the H1N1 outbreak had an effect on exports. Trends occurring during the MFA phaseout had continued to 2009. Global exports since 2005 have continued to decline, shrinking from $7,285 million in 2004 to $3,923 million in 2009. Exports have slightly increased to Australia, the EU-15, and Japan since 2005, but these countries are still marginal markets for Mexico, accounting for less than 5 percent of total apparel exports. In the U.S. market, Mexico experienced the most dramatic decrease in market share during the 2000–09 period, falling from 14.6 percent in 2000 to just 5.4 percent in 2009. Estimates suggest that Mexico reported between 36,000 and 80,000 job losses in 2008–09 alone, largely because of the global economic crises (MSN 2009; Forstater 2010).

The combination of preferential market access to the United States and Mexico's export-oriented industrial and investment policies led to significant export growth that placed Mexico among the top sources of U.S. apparel imports for nearly two decades, but it subsequently also limited Mexico's ability to move up the value chain. While preferential market access was important in giving regional suppliers such as Mexico an entry point to the U.S. market, the assembly subcontracting model based on these agreements has also been criticized. Its detractors claim that while these activities generate badly needed employment opportunities and access to foreign currency, they trap developing countries in low value-added activities that provide minimal opportunities for upgrading, few linkages to domestic manufacturers or suppliers, and strong incentives to keep labor costs low (Bair and Peters 2006). The Mexican apparel industry did not fully capitalize on the 10-year advantage it had over nearly every other apparel-exporting country in the U.S. market during the MFA phaseout period. The free trade agreement protected Mexico's industry and allowed it to grow for the first six years, but the agreement did not provide long-term benefits to remain competitive when other countries were no longer constrained by quotas.

Post-MFA, apparel buyers have desired to work with fewer, larger, and more capable suppliers that have the network to coordinate supply chains in strategic locations around the world. Mexico is not part of a global network and is not tied into a strategic regional network. Many of the production operations in Central America and the Caribbean were set up by U.S. firms as a way of preserving U.S. textile factories and maintaining a foothold in apparel manufacturing, but low-cost competition has made these networks increasingly uncompetitive (Anson 2010). Many of the U.S. brand manufacturers that set up the apparel assembly base in Mexico have shifted to a sourcing rather than manufacturing business model and have looked to more capable suppliers in Asia (Frederick and Gereffi 2011).

Structure of the Apparel Industry

Types of Firms

In 2009, there were 11,500 textile- and apparel-related firms in Mexico, with 9,380 in apparel and 2,120 in textiles (figure 12.2). Together the textile and apparel sectors represent 9.5 percent of all manufacturing firms in Mexico. In the apparel sector, 73.5 percent of firms are considered "micro" and employ between 1 and 10 workers. Only 2.3 percent

Figure 12.2   Number of Firms in the Mexican Textile Apparel Sector

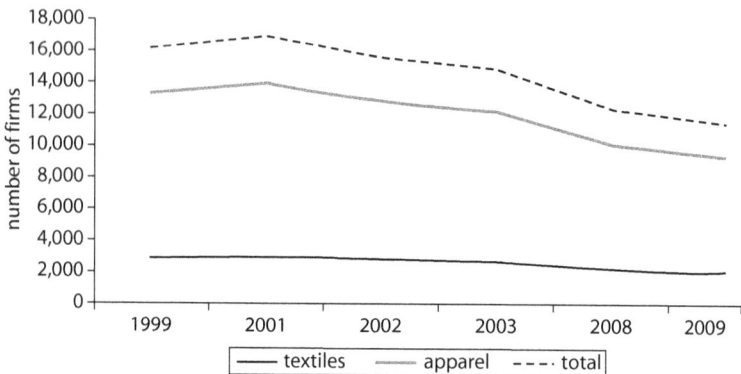

Sources: National Statistical Office (Instituto Nacional de Estadística y Geografía, INEGI), 1999–2007; Banco Nacional de Comercio Exterior (BANCOMEXT); and Cámara Nacional de la Industriadel Vestido (CNIV), 2008–09.

are considered large (over 250 employees). In 1999, the ratios were quite similar; 80 percent were micro and 1.9 percent were considered large (CNIV 2009). The number of firms has declined since 2001—from 17,002 textile and apparel firms in 2001 to 11,500 in 2009. The large majority of these firms are apparel firms, accounting for 82.2 percent in 2001 and 81.6 percent in 2009 (INEGI 2001; CNIV 2009).

Mexico's export industry emerged as part of a regional production-sharing model based on tariff preference schemes, including the 807/9802 scheme and later NAFTA. The production networks based on these schemes were created and held together by large U.S. brand manufacturers and textile firms with a desire to keep domestic textile manufacturing in business by moving the most labor-intensive parts of the apparel supply chain to nearby, low-wage countries. Because of the 807/9802 legislation, firms in Mexico initially engaged only in the sewing process in the supply chain. These firms, which perform labor-intensive assembly of foreign components, are often referred to as *maquilas*.

Most apparel manufacturers in Mexico operate under the traditional *maquiladora* model, performing only the cut-make-trim (CMT) tasks; only a small share operates as part of original equipment manufacturing (OEM) full-package networks.[2] Studies of the Mexican apparel industry discovered some evidence of full-package networks between manufacturers in Mexico and U.S. buyers, including retailers such as J.C. Penney and the Gap (Bair and Gereffi 2003). The development of full-package capabilities and the competitiveness of the Mexican industry more generally are highly uneven across the industrial landscape of Mexico's textile and apparel sector. The full-package capabilities that do exist are primarily limited to specific geographic clusters in a limited range of products, mostly men's blue denim jeans. The primary example is the Torreon region, which emerged as a relatively integrated apparel manufacturing network linking local apparel firms, textile mills, and U.S. buyers (Bair and Gereffi 2001). The Torreon region developed full-package capabilities for jeans, but there is little evidence that full-package production has evolved anywhere else in the country.

An important share of apparel and textile firms is locally owned. With regard to foreign ownership, the United States is the largest foreign investor in the textile and apparel sectors in Mexico, holding between 51 percent and 87 percent of all inward foreign investment in the sectors over the 2001–09 time period (table 12.3). In 2009, Luxembourg, Japan, and Spain were the next largest investors, with values of $18 million, $9 million, and $3 million, respectively, or 22 percent, 12 percent, and

Table 12.3 Mexican Textile and Apparel Foreign Investment Value by Country of Origin, 2001–09

Country/economy of origin	Investment value ($, million)								Share of new investment only (%)							
	'01	'03	'04	'05	'06	'07	'08	'09	'01	'03	'04	'05	'06	'07	'08	'09
Total	222	225	226	252	327	45	122	76	n.a.	n.a.	n.a.	n.a.	n.a.	n.a.	n.a.	n.a.
Divestment	-3	-3	-48	0	-1	-93	-74	-2	n.a.	n.a.	n.a.	n.a.	n.a.	n.a.	n.a.	n.a.
New investment	225	228	274	253	327	138	197	78	n.a.	n.a.	n.a.	n.a.	n.a.	n.a.	n.a.	n.a.
United States	134	183	229	144	168	120	151	43	59	80	84	57	51	87	77	55
Luxembourg	0	0	0	0	0	0	0	18	0	0	0	0	0	0	0	22
Japan	0	0	0	1	1	0	6	9	0	0	0	0	0	0	3	12
Spain	23	-1	1	9	3	8	18	3	10	-1	0	3	1	6	9	4
Germany	1	0	1	1	114	-57	3	3	0	0	0	0	35	-41	1	3
Taiwan, China	9	9	6	6	5	6	-8	2	4	4	2	2	1	5	-4	3
Korea, Rep.	12	0	1	1	0	0	0	0	5	0	0	0	0	0	0	0
United Kingdom	8	1	8	3	31	-22	12	0	3	0	3	1	9	-16	6	0
Netherlands Antilles	12	31	-41	86	0	0	-63	0	5	13	-15	34	0	0	-32	0

Source: National Statistical Office (Instituto Nacional de Estadística y Geografía, INEGI), 2001–03, 2007, 2004–09, 2010.

Note: n.a. = not applicable.

4 percent of all new investment for the year. Large investments have also come from other EU-15 countries, including Germany, the Netherlands, and the United Kingdom, but divestments occurred in recent years. The Republic of Korea and Taiwan, China, have also made smaller investments representing $12 million or less, predominantly in the years leading up to the MFA phaseout in 2005.

This decline in apparel exports and number of firms is partially tied to the type of apparel firm that originally invested in Mexico. Apparel products can be divided into two main categories, national brands available at a variety of different department store retail outlets and private labels sold exclusively through one specialty or mass merchant retailer. Mexico's trouser industry was built on national brands owned by U.S. brand manufacturers such as VF (Wrangler & Lee) and Levi's (Levi's and Dockers), which opened foreign assembly plants in Mexico. The size of the U.S. consumer market for national brands has decreased significantly in the last decade due to consumer preferences and a shift in retailing to specialty stores catered to specific demographic segments. Men's trousers are one of the few categories in which brand manufacturers still exist, and national brands maintain a sizable consumer base, partially explaining Mexico's ability to maintain its leading export position in this category despite declines in nearly every other category (Frederick and Gereffi 2011). Further working against Mexico, over the past decade, is the fact that Levi's has closed all of its owned manufacturing plants and has shifted to a brand marketer model, and VF is slowly shifting production to Asian countries such as Bangladesh that can produce comparable products at lower prices. Most private label brands that have emerged established sourcing networks in Asia rather than with regional suppliers because they did not have preexisting relationships with U.S. textile or apparel manufacturers (Frederick and Gereffi 2011).

End Markets

Mexico's exports are predominantly destined for the United States, although the concentration has been slowly decreasing over the past decade. The United States accounted for 97.7 percent of exports in 1995, decreasing to 94 percent in 2005 and 89.4 percent in 2009 (table 12.4 and figure 12.3). Canada and the EU-15 are the only other two markets, representing more than 1 percent of exports. With the signing of the NAFTA agreement, exports to Canada increased from 1.5 percent in 2000 to 4.2 percent by 2005 and to 6.1 percent by 2009. In 2000, Mexico and the EU signed a free trade agreement, which

Table 12.4 Top Five Mexican Apparel Export Markets, 1992, 1995, 2000, 2005, 2008, and 2009

Country/region	Customs value ($, million)						Market share (%)					
	1992	1995	2000	2005	2008	2009	1992	1995	2000	2005	2008	2009
World	1,138	2,871	8,924	6,683	4,634	3,923						
United States	1,107	2,805	8,695	6,282	4,164	3,508	97.3	97.7	97.4	94.0	89.9	89.4
Canada	11	25	135	280	282	238	1.0	0.9	1.5	4.2	6.1	6.1
EU-15	16	19	27	57	99	92	1.4	0.7	0.3	0.9	2.1	2.3
Japan	2	7	27	20	16	15	0.2	0.2	0.3	0.3	0.3	0.4
Australia	1	n.a.	n.a.	n.a.	n.a.	9	0.0	n.a.	n.a.	n.a.	n.a.	0.2
Korea, Rep.	n.a.	n.a.	n.a.	6	15	n.a.	n.a.	n.a.	n.a.	0.1	0.3	n.a.
Costa Rica	n.a.	4	6	n.a.	n.a.	n.a.	n.a.	0.2	0.1	n.a.	n.a.	n.a.
Top five share	**1,13**	**2,860**	**8,890**	**6,646**	**4,576**	**3,862**	**100.0**	**99.6**	**99.6**	**99.4**	**98.7**	**98.4**

Source: United Nations Commodity Trade Statistics Database (UN Comtrade).

Note: Apparel represented by Harmonized Commodity Description and Coding System (HS) 1992: Codes 61 and 62; exports represented by partner country imports; EU-15 = the 15 member states of the European Union (EU) as of December 31, 2003, before the new member states joined the EU: Austria, Belgium, Denmark, Finland, France, Germany, Greece, Ireland, Italy, Luxembourg, the Netherlands, Portugal, Spain, Sweden, and the United Kingdom; n.a. = not applicable (indicates country not in top five in given year).

Figure 12.3   Top Four Mexican Apparel Export Markets, 2000 and 2009
% market share

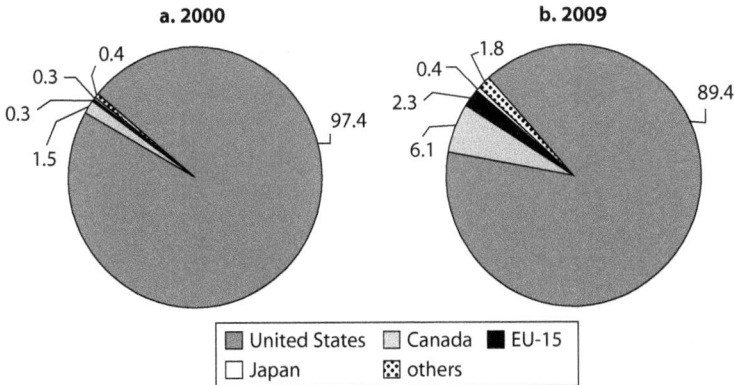

a. 2000

0.4
0.3
0.3
1.5
97.4

b. 2009

1.8
0.4
2.3
6.1
89.4

United States   Canada   EU-15
Japan   others

Source: United Nations Commodity Trade Statistics Database (UN Comtrade).
Note: Apparel represented by Harmonized Commodity Description and Coding System (HS) 1992: Codes 61 and 62; exports represented by partner country imports. EU-15 = the 15 member states of the European Union (EU) as of December 31, 2003, before the new member states joined the EU: Austria, Belgium, Denmark, Finland, France, Germany, Greece, Ireland, Italy, Luxembourg, the Netherlands, Portugal, Spain, Sweden, and the United Kingdom.

facilitated the boost in exports from Mexico to the EU after 2000 (Frederick and Gereffi 2011). However, although the EU-15 has been Mexico's third-largest export market since the late 1990s, Mexico represents less than 1 percent of the EU-15 apparel imports. Mexico's top five export markets represented 99.6 percent of all exports in 1995, and this number has only decreased to 98.4 percent in 2009. Mexico has a domestic apparel market but has yet to develop a strong local market for domestic brands. One of the major weaknesses in the domestic market is a very high level of contraband and counterfeit apparel. A 2005 study suggested that 58 percent of all apparel sold in Mexico entered the country as contraband, largely originating in China (BMI 2009).

Export Products

Mexico's main export items to the United States are highlighted in table 12.5. Exports are highly concentrated, with the top 10 export products accounting for 73.3 percent of total apparel exports in 2009. Exports are predominantly concentrated in the top 3 categories, which accounted for over 50 percent of all U.S. apparel imports from Mexico in 2009. These products include woven cotton trousers for men and women and cotton knit T-shirts. All but 2 of the top 10 U.S. export categories in 2009 declined in value between 2005 and 2009. The two

Table 12.5 Top 10 U.S. Apparel Imports from Mexico, 1996, 2000, 2005, 2008, and 2009

HS code	Product	Customs value ($, million)					Market share (%)				
		1996	2000	2005	2008	2009	1996	2000	2005	2008	2009
Total		**3,743**	**8,618**	**6,230**	**4,129**	**3,482**	**19.9**	**19.2**	**23.0**	**28.5**	**30.6**
620342	Trousers	745	1,657	1,431	1,177	1,067	9.9	11.2	9.2	11.9	11.6
610910	T-Shirts	371	963	570	491	403	12.1	17.0	16.3	10.5	10.4
620462	Trousers	451	1,462	1,013	435	361	5.8	4.9	4.5	5.4	4.0
611030	Sweatshirts	216	419	281	225	139	2.1	3.0	3.7	3.7	3.6
620343	Trousers	79	256	231	151	124	3.3	1.8	2.1	1.7	3.0
610990	T-Shirts	124	156	130	69	104	3.0	4.6	5.3	4.1	2.8
611020	Sweatshirts	112	394	332	170	98	3.0	4.6	5.3	2.3	2.7
611592[a]	Socks NESOI	n.a.	n.a.	n.a.	93	93	n.a.	n.a.	n.a.	2.3	2.7
621010	Garments	188	233	150	109	90	5.0	2.7	2.4	2.6	2.6
620311	Suits	n.a.	n.a.	n.a.	n.a.	73	n.a.	n.a.	n.a.	n.a.	2.1
611241	Swimwear	n.a.	n.a.	142	86	n.a.	n.a.	n.a.	2.3	2.1	n.a.
621143	Garments NESOI	n.a.	n.a.	114	n.a.	n.a.	n.a.	n.a.	1.8	n.a.	n.a.
621210	Bras	176	262	n.a.	n.a.	n.a.	4.7	3.0	n.a.	n.a.	n.a.
620463	Trousers	n.a.	140	n.a.	n.a.	n.a.	n.a.	1.6	n.a.	n.a.	n.a.
610463	Trousers	96	n.a.	n.a.	n.a.	n.a.	2.6	n.a.	n.a.	n.a.	n.a.
Top 10 share		**2,557**	**5,942**	**4,395**	**3,006**	**2,552**	**68.3**	**68.9**	**70.5**	**72.8**	**73.3**

Source: U.S. International Trade Commission (USITC).

Note: U.S. General Customs Value; Harmonized Commodity Description and Coding System (HS): Woven Apparel, HS62; Knitted Apparel, HS61. NESOI = not elsewhere specified or indicated; n.a. = not applicable (indicates product not in the top 10 in given year).

a. HS code changed from 611592 to 611595 in 2007.

products that increased were T-shirts made from textile materials elsewhere classified and men and boys (M&B) wool suits. Eight of the top 10 products were the same in both 1996 and 2009, indicating that Mexico has had little variation in its exports to the United States. Most of Mexico's main product exports primarily compete with China and other low-cost Asian countries, including Bangladesh and Vietnam, for U.S. market share.

Trousers. Collectively, cotton woven trousers are Mexico's main exports, representing 41 percent of U.S. apparel imports from Mexico in 2009. This category can be further broken into trousers for M&B and women and girls (W&G). M&B cotton woven trousers are one of the few product categories in which Mexico has been able to remain ahead of China through the end of 2009 in terms of U.S. market share, although Mexico's share has been steadily falling. In 2006, China took over the leading position from Mexico in the W&G trouser market. Other significant competitors in this market include Bangladesh, Vietnam, and to a lesser extent the Arab Republic of Egypt, which are all increasing their share in the U.S. market (USITC 2010).

Regarding the trouser market, Mexico's relationship with U.S. brand manufacturers has been both a curse and a blessing. On one hand, it permitted Mexico to establish long-term relationships with prominent U.S. brands in one of the leading U.S. apparel import categories. On the other hand, it has locked Mexico into the production of basic, mid-to low-price jeans, predominantly for the men's market rather than the larger women's market, whose products often sell at higher price points. In 2008, 50 percent of the U.S. jeanswear market was for women, 27 percent for men, and 23 percent for children (Newberry 2009). Furthermore, most jeans brands carry products for men, women, and children, so buyers prefer to purchase jeans from a country capable of supplying all three.

The market for trousers that are parts of uniforms (workwear or imagewear[3]) has performed better in Mexico because of the turnaround time and the small orders desired by the buyers. Manufacturers in Mexico and the CAFTA region are in a good position to produce school uniforms, public safety uniforms, and military apparel because of the proximity to the United States, allowing manufacturers to turn and replenish goods quickly (USITC 2004; BMI 2009). Similar to men's jeans, this product category is relatively standardized with a focus on functionality, thus limiting the need for firms to expand capabilities in design, style, or branding.

T-shirts. Mexico's second-largest export category to the United States, cotton knit T-shirts, provides an example of how U.S. trade preferences have led to competition among regional suppliers rather than collaboration. Mexico's main competitors in this category were primarily other Caribbean countries from 1995 to 2005. During this time, leading export positions shifted among the Dominican Republic, El Salvador, Guatemala, Haiti, and Honduras, and most recently Nicaragua and Peru. However, after the quota phaseout in 2005, China and Vietnam both emerged as rapidly growing competitors. While regional suppliers were busy taking market share from each other, Asian competitors moved into the picture and are slowly pushing out all of the regional suppliers. Regional suppliers have mostly taken market share from each other rather than focusing on growing one country's capabilities (Frederick and Gereffi 2011).

Sweaters and sweatshirts. Mexico's third-largest group of U.S. exports, representing 6.8 percent of total export value, includes knitted sweaters and sweatshirts made from cotton and man-made fiber (MMF). For both cotton and MMF, Mexico led China in U.S. market share until 2005. Other major country competitors include Indonesia and Vietnam, two countries that have decisively shifted focus to the U.S. market over the 2000–09 time frame.

Exports to the EU-15 are also dominated by cotton woven trousers, T-shirts, and woven wool suits and jackets (table 12.6). Although the overall value and volume of wool suit and jacket exports to the EU-15 are small, these products warrant high unit values, which have increased by around 50 euros per kilogram in each category over the 2000–09 time frame (table 12.7). In Canada, Mexico's third-largest export destination, exports reached an all-time high in 2006 but have declined since then. Productwise, knitted apparel and nonwoven fabrics and felts, classified under Harmonized Commodity Description and Coding System (HS) chapter 56, are Mexico's strongest export categories to Canada ("World Textile and Apparel Trade" 2009).

The unit values of knitted and woven apparel imports from Mexico into the United States generally increased from 1995 to 2004 and from 2005 to 2009 (table 12.7). This increase indicates that whereas Mexico's overall export value and volume may be decreasing to the United States, the products it is exporting are warranting higher returns. This fact does not bode well for increasing employment opportunities for the industry as a whole, but it may indicate that existing firms are improving their operations.

Table 12.6   Top 10 EU-15 Apparel Imports from Mexico, 2000, 2005, 2008, and 2009

		Customs value ($, million)				Market share (%)			
HS code	Product	2000	2005	2008	2009	2000	2005	2008	2009
Total		**30**	**38**	**59**	**59**				
610910	T-Shirts	4	7	8	9	14.6	18.9	13.5	14.7
620311	Suits	3	n.a.	6	8	10.4	n.a.	9.9	14.3
620462	Trousers	1	3	4	7	4.4	8.9	6.7	11.2
620342	Trousers	4	3	6	7	14.3	7.0	9.9	11.1
610990	T-Shirts	n.a.	1	2	4	n.a.	3.4	3.9	6.7
620331	Suit jackets	n.a.	n.a.	n.a.	2	n.a.	n.a.	n.a.	3.9
611030	Sweatshirts	n.a.	4	3	2	n.a.	10.5	4.4	3.8
611610	Gloves	n.a.	2	4	2	n.a.	5.6	7.1	3.4
620329	Ensembles	n.a.	n.a.	n.a.	2	n.a.	n.a.	n.a.	3.3
611241	Swimwear	2	2	n.a.	2	7.1	6.3	n.a.	2.7
620441	Dresses	n.a.	n.a.	5	n.a.	n.a.	n.a.	8.1	n.a.
611693	Gloves	n.a.	2	2	n.a.	n.a.	6.1	3.6	n.a.
620431	Suit jackets	n.a.	n.a.	1	n.a.	n.a.	n.a.	2.1	n.a.
610463	Trousers	n.a.	1	n.a.	n.a.	n.a.	3.0	n.a.	n.a.
611020	Sweatshirts	n.a.	1	n.a.	n.a.	n.a.	3.0	n.a.	n.a.
621210	Bras	1	n.a.	n.a.	n.a.	5.0	n.a.	n.a.	n.a.
610822	Underwear	1	n.a.	n.a.	n.a.	4.4	n.a.	n.a.	n.a.
620463	Trousers	1	n.a.	n.a.	n.a.	3.6	n.a.	n.a.	n.a.
620349	Trousers	1	n.a.	n.a.	n.a.	2.2	n.a.	n.a.	n.a.
620193	Jackets	1	n.a.	n.a.	n.a.	2.1	n.a.	n.a.	n.a.
Top 10 share		**20**	**27**	**41**	**44**	**68.0**	**72.8**	**69.1**	**75.0**

Source: Eurostat.
Note: Harmonized Commodity Description and Coding System (HS): Woven Apparel, HS62; Knitted Apparel, HS61. EU-15 = the 15 member states of the European Union (EU) as of December 31, 2003, before the new member states joined the EU: Austria, Belgium, Denmark, Finland, France, Germany, Greece, Ireland, Italy, Luxembourg, the Netherlands, Portugal, Spain, Sweden, and the United Kingdom. n.a. = not applicable (indicates product not in the top 10 in given year).

Backward Linkages

Mexico's imports of textile have increased from $1,204 million in 1995 to $4,060 million in 2009. The United States is by far the largest source of textile imports, although its share has declined. In 1995, the United States represented 79 percent of Mexico's textile imports, but this figure declined to 63 percent in 2009. China has primarily been responsible for taking over the U.S. share. In 1995, China was not even a top 5 supplier, but by 2009, China represented 18.3 percent of Mexico's textile imports (table 12.8). Mexico's textile imports have remained highly concentrated in the top 5 markets throughout the 1995–2009 period, only slightly decreasing from 95.4 percent in 1995 to 91.7 percent in 2009.

Under the production-sharing scheme,[4] textile inputs had to come from the United States. Mexican operations only performed the assembly

Table 12.7   Mexican Apparel Exports to the EU-15 and the United States

	EU-15 unit values ($/kg)			U.S. unit values ($/dozen)		
Year	Knit	Woven	Total	Knit	Woven	Total
1995	17.1	9.5	11.9	—	—	—
1996	18.6	16.5	17.4	29.0	50.0	39.2
1997	19.3	23.6	21.6	30.2	56.0	41.8
1998	18.8	24.1	21.8	30.5	60.4	43.1
1999	26.3	31.0	28.7	29.0	60.7	41.8
2000	24.2	32.5	28.5	29.5	62.9	43.6
2001	20.7	36.3	27.2	31.1	63.9	44.8
2002	17.8	23.3	20.4	30.7	64.1	44.8
2003	15.8	17.2	16.4	29.9	65.7	44.3
2004	16.8	15.5	16.3	29.2	68.5	45.2
2005	17.4	20.8	18.4	28.9	71.1	46.2
2006	17.5	46.4	25.1	29.8	73.5	46.6
2007	19.0	45.2	27.1	31.2	75.2	49.0
2008	24.4	45.5	33.0	30.7	78.8	49.9
2009	25.3	42.0	33.2	30.4	78.2	50.4

Sources: Eurostat, volumes reported in kilograms; U.S. International Trade Commission (USITC), volumes reported in dozens (only products for which the first unit of quantity is "volumes reported in dozens" are included in the table).
Note: — = not available. EU-15 = the 15 member states of the European Union (EU) as of December 31, 2003, before the new member states joined the EU: Austria, Belgium, Denmark, Finland, France, Germany, Greece, Ireland, Italy, Luxembourg, the Netherlands, Portugal, Spain, Sweden, and the United Kingdom.

(sewing) stage using precut fabric pieces from U.S. firms. Under this scheme, the U.S. firm reimports the final apparel product composed of its precut fabric pieces from Mexico, only paying a tariff on the minimal value added in Mexico (that is, labor). In 1988, benefits were also extended to include guaranteed access levels, which more or less equated to quota-free access to the U.S. market. Even though this was an advantage, this regulation discouraged the development of local input industries and linkages. This situation changed, however, with NAFTA. NAFTA rules of origin (ROO) made the incorporation of local inputs possible in apparel produced for the U.S. market. As a result, after NAFTA went into effect in 1994, foreign investors, including a number of U.S. textile companies, expressed an interest in developing Mexico's raw materials base, thereby increasing the quality and quantity of locally produced fabrics to fuel the country's apparel exports. U.S. firms started investing in yarn spinning (Parkdale Mills), while others were building new textile plants (Guilford Mills) or acquiring existing production capacity through joint ventures (Cone Mills and Galey & Lord) (Bair and Peters 2006). Denim is, however, one of the few export-quality fabrics manufactured in large quantities in Mexico, partly because of investments from foreign

Table 12.8 Top Five Textile Suppliers to Mexico, 1995, 2000, 2005, 2008, and 2009

Country/economy/region	Customs value ($, million)					Market share (%)				
	1995	2000	2005	2008	2009	1995	2000	2005	2008	2009
World	1,204	4,605	4,849	4,921	4,060					
United States	951	3,807	3,688	3,076	2,558	79.0	82.7	76.1	62.5	63.0
China	n.a.	112	353	835	744	n.a.	2.4	7.3	17.0	18.3
EU-15	63	181	311	388	275	5.2	3.9	6.4	7.9	6.8
Korea, Rep.	102	275	102	115	87	8.5	6.0	2.1	2.3	2.1
Brazil	n.a.	n.a.	45	86	58	n.a.	n.a.	0.9	1.7	1.4
Hong Kong SAR, China	n.a.	28	n.a.	n.a.	n.a.	n.a.	0.6	n.a.	n.a.	n.a.
Japan	17	n.a.	n.a.	n.a.	n.a.	1.4	n.a.	n.a.	n.a.	n.a.
Canada	17	n.a.	n.a.	n.a.	n.a.	1.4	n.a.	n.a.	n.a.	n.a.
Top five share	**1,149**	**4,404**	**4,499**	**4,499**	**3,723**	**95.4**	**95.6**	**92.8**	**91.4**	**91.7**

Source: United Nations Commodity Trade Statistics Database (UN Comtrade).

Note: Standard International Trade Classification Rev. 3 Code 65; imports represent world exports to Mexico; EU-15 = the 15 member states of the European Union (EU) as of December 31, 2003, before the new member states joined the EU: Austria, Belgium, Denmark, Finland, France, Germany, Greece, Ireland, Italy, Luxembourg, the Netherlands, Portugal, Spain, Sweden, and the United Kingdom. n.a. = not applicable (indicates not in the top five in given year).

companies such as Cone Mills, which is part owner of the denim mill located in the Laguna town of Parras.

As a regional supplier, Mexico suffers from the decline in competitiveness across the U.S. cotton-textile-apparel value chain. Because a majority of Mexico's top 10 U.S. apparel products are made from cotton (58 percent by value in 2009), producers have benefited from low raw material cotton costs due to extensive subsidies provided to U.S. cotton farmers. However, the United States is also suffering from an institutional strategy focused on insulating producers from competition in the short term rather than investing in long-term competitive capabilities, and as a result, U.S. cotton exports are losing their competitive edge (Frederick and Gereffi 2011). Furthermore, in recent years, several of the textile giants that invested in Mexico in the post-NAFTA period, including Burlington Industries, Guilford Mills, Galey & Lord, Cone Mills Corporation, and Dan River, have filed for Chapter 11 protection (Bair and Peters 2006).

Hence, more than 15 years after NAFTA, Mexico lacks the kind of developed fabric base required for world-class, full-package production, leaving the country's apparel exporters increasingly hard pressed to compete with their Asian, and especially Chinese, counterparts (Bair and Peters 2006). Mexico's lack of quality textile products is also reflected in its relatively stagnant investments in textile machinery. Mexico ranked 18th and 19th for single and double jersey knitting machine shipments, 32nd for electronic flatbed knitting shipments, 22nd for shuttleless loom shipments, and 12th for short-staple spinning machine shipments (Anson and Brocklehurst 2010a, 2010b; Brocklehurst and Anson 2010). However, it should be noted that among the regional U.S. suppliers composed of Mexico, Central America, and the Caribbean Basin countries, Mexico is the most significant producer of fabric and the only significant source of yarn.

Employment

Employment in the textile and apparel sectors has steadily declined since 1999, with the most significant drops occurring between 2000 and 2003. In 1999, there were 829,390 total employees, with around 78 percent in apparel and 22 percent in textiles. In 2009, total employment had dropped to 396,534, with 74 percent working in the apparel industry and 26 percent in textiles (figure 12.4 and table 12.9). Mexico is faced with higher labor costs ($2.54 per hour) and lower productivity than Asian competitors. Mexican apparel firms also lack strong management capabilities (USITC 2004; Jassin-O'Rourke Group 2008).

Figure 12.4   Employment in Mexican Textile and Apparel Industries

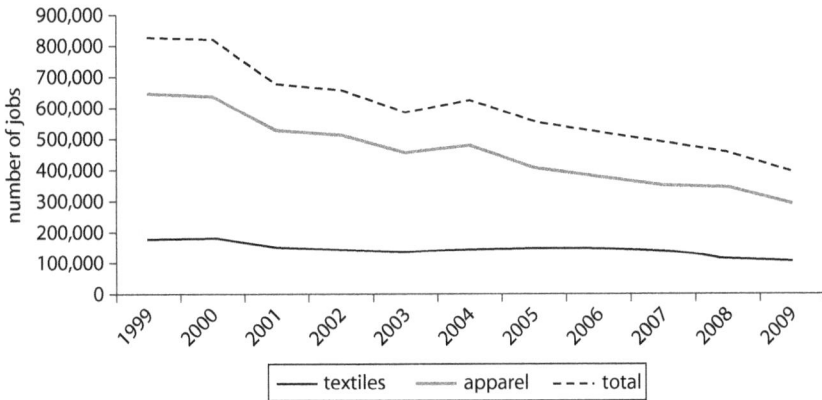

Sources: National Statistical Office (Instituto Nacional de Estadística y Geografía, INEGI), 1999–2007; Cámara Nacional de la Industriadel Vestido (CNIV), 2008–09.

Table 12.9   Employment in Mexican Textile and Apparel Industries

Year	Textiles	Apparel	Total
		Number of jobs	
1999	179,858	649,532	829,390
2000	181,846	640,000	821,846
2001	150,001	529,000	679,001
2002	146,000	514,000	660,000
2003	132,457	454,663	587,120
2004	144,262	482,396	626,658
2005	149,821	409,910	559,731
2006	147,471	378,682	526,153
2007	138,506	351,479	489,985
2008	113,748	343,533	457,281
2009	104,618	291,916	396,534

Sources: National Statistical Office (Instituto Nacional de Estadística y Geografía, INEGI), 1999–2007; Cámara Nacional de la Industriadel Vestido (CNIV), 2008–09.

Data from the Maquila Solidarity Network (MSN) state that the textile, apparel, and leather sector generated approximately 300,000 direct jobs in Mexico in 2009. This figure accounts for approximately 2 percent of national employment and 8 percent of total manufacturing jobs. Out of all manufacturing jobs, this sector is the largest employer of women, accounting for about 70 percent of jobs for women in manufacturing (MSN 2009). However, over the 10-year span ranging from 1998 to 2008, women's share of total workers in the apparel sector decreased

Table 12.10   Male and Female Share of Mexican Employment by Sector

Sector and year	Share of total employment (%)	
	Men	Women
Manufacture of textile inputs		
1998	67.9	32.1
2003	71.2	28.8
2008	73.0	27.0
Textile product manufacturing (nonapparel)		
1998	53.3	46.7
2003	45.4	54.6
2008	39.6	60.4
Apparel manufacturing		
1998	35.8	64.2
2003	39.8	60.2
2008	41.0	59.0

Source: National Statistical Office (Instituto Nacional de Estadística y Geografía, INGEI) 2009, 2010.

from 64.2 percent to 59.0 percent. Similar trends exist for the textile manufacturing industries (yarn, fabric, finishing), in which the female share dropped from 32.1 percent to 27.0 percent (table 12.10). However, in textile product manufacturing (carpets, rugs, linens), the share of female employment increased from 46.7 percent to 60.4 percent in the same time period. Textile product manufacturing is the smallest sector, employing just below 17 percent of total employment in 2008 (INEGI 2009, 2010).

Trade Regulations and Proactive Policies

Preferential Market Access

The start of Mexico's apparel export industry was facilitated by U.S. trade legislation promoting assembly subcontracting networks within North America based on preferential market access. This form of production is often referred to as 807/9802 production for the tariff classification this form of import falls under. U.S. firms are allowed to export cut parts of apparel to lower-wage countries for assembly (sewing) and reimport the final apparel under a regime known as production sharing. U.S. firms were permitted to export fabric pieces cut in the United States to another country and reimport the product with duty only assessed on the value added abroad (Bair and Peters 2006).

In 1986, the United States expanded the production-sharing clause and created a "special access program" within the framework of the former Tariff Schedules of the United States (TSUS) item 807 (known as 807A), providing virtually unlimited market access for apparel assembled in the Caribbean Basin Initiative (CBI) region from "fabric wholly formed and cut in the United States." Rather than being charged against regular quotas, 807A imports entered under preferential quotas known as "guaranteed access levels" (GALs) (USITC 2004). In 1988, these benefits were extended to Mexico in what is known as the special regime.

In 1994, NAFTA initiated free trade among three signatory countries, Canada, Mexico, and the United States, that met designated ROO requirements. NAFTA established new ROO specifying that an apparel product sewn in North America is eligible for quota- and duty-free treatment under NAFTA as long as it contains yarn and fabrics produced in any of the signatory countries (often referred to as yarn-forward ROO). Thus, Mexican apparel exports were not only granted duty-free access, but they could also contain fabrics and yarns produced in Mexico. The 807/9802 program still exists, but NAFTA provides better benefits and has all but replaced 807/9802 exports.

Besides the United States, Mexico also enjoys preferential access to a number of other countries. In 2000, Mexico signed a bilateral free trade agreement with the EU, the EU-Mexico Free Trade Agreement. As a result, Mexico's exports can enter the EU tariff free as long as they comply with ROO. Prior to this trade agreement, Mexico qualified for tariff preferences in the EU under the general Generalized System of Preferences (GSP) scheme. Mexico is also currently eligible for GSP preferences from Belarus, Bulgaria, Japan, New Zealand, the Russian Federation, and Turkey.

Proactive Policies

The Mexican government enacted two key programs to spur export-oriented production and attract foreign investment that had profound effects on the development and current structure of Mexico's apparel industry. The first program, the Border Industrialization Program, was enacted in 1965 to attract foreign investment, increase exports, and alleviate the high unemployment along the U.S.-Mexico border that resulted from the termination of the U.S. Bracero program in 1964 (Rice 1998). The Border Industrialization Program was modeled on an export processing zone (EPZ) already in existence in many Asian economies.[5] The goal of the Mexican government was to reduce unemployment by turning the isolated northern border of Mexico into a dynamic growth area by attracting foreign companies. The principal activity of these companies was assembly production, and the factories built under this program are referred to as *maquiladoras* or *maquilas*. Originally, *maquilas* were only allowed along the border region, but this limitation was gradually reduced over the next decade, and in 1983, the *maquiladora* industry was officially separated from the Border Industrialization Program and a Maquiladora Program was created to govern *maquilas* operating throughout Mexico. Under this program, firms (foreign or local) can "temporarily import" raw materials and auxiliaries (packaging, labels), tools and equipment, machinery, replacement parts, and lab equipment, and containers provided if the resulting products are exported (Rice 1998). The program was established to promote exports, but *maquilas* could also conduct limited domestic sales.[6] *Maquilas* also had informal requirements to employ and train certain levels of workers and stay current in their fiscal and labor obligations (Rice 1998). This program, combined with the 807/9802 U.S. tariff benefits, made Mexico a major trading partner for both exports of U.S. fabric and imports of apparel.

The second policy, the Temporary Importation Program to Produce Articles for Exportation, or the PITEX program, was enacted in 1990. PITEX was largely created to extend the import advantages provided under the *maquiladora* program to domestic producers, primarily in the interior of the country. PITEX is largely oriented toward national producers wishing to expand their domestic operations to include export manufacturing, while the Maquiladora Program is primarily intended for purely export companies.

Both programs are administered by and require authorization from the Secretary of Commerce and Industrial Development (SECOFI), with the Secretary of Finance and Public Credit (SHCP) playing a supporting role by monitoring compliance with the programs. Both programs permit local or foreign firms that directly or indirectly export products to import various items used in the production process of the exported products duty free because these items are considered "temporarily imported." The import benefits in the two programs are similar, but the export requirements differ. Under the PITEX program, to import raw materials, components, packaging, containers, and other items consumed during the production process, PITEX required the company to have foreign sales exceeding the equivalent of $500,000 or exports accounting for at least 10 percent of total sales. To import machinery, equipment, and instruments, the company must have foreign sales accounting for at least 30 percent of the value of its total sales. Additionally, domestic sales of goods utilizing items imported under the PITEX program are limited to 30 percent of the value of total export sales (Rice 1998).

Since the beginning of the MFA phaseout in 1995, the Mexican government has generally provided limited support, with few major programs to assist the textile and apparel sectors (USITC 2004). In 2001, the Mexican government issued the National Plan for Development (NDP), effective for the five-year period through 2006. It identified 12 strategic, priority sectors vital to the competitiveness of the country, of which fiber, textile, and apparel were included because they are major generators of employment and they attract manufacturing investment (USITC 2004). In November 2006, the Mexican government issued a new decree to regulate the operation of the *maquiladora* industry that was aimed at streamlining the sector. The PITEX program and the *maquiladora* program were combined to form the Industria Manufacturera, Maquiladora y de Servicios de Exportación (IMMEX) program, which consolidates the benefits of these programs and facilitates interaction with government authorities ("Trade and Trade Policy" 2009). The government also acknowledged the need to reduce the flow of contraband and other counterfeit and illegally imported textile and apparel shipments into Mexico, primarily from China ("Trade and Trade Policy" 2009).[7]

As part of China's accession to the WTO, importing countries were allowed to apply antidumping tariffs on imports. To protect the domestic industry, Mexico applied strict antidumping tariffs on a broad range of textile and apparel imports from China. The tariffs did not comply with WTO standards and varied from 533 percent for apparel and 501 percent for MMF yarns and fabrics to 379 percent for made-up textiles classified under HS63 and 331 percent for cotton and other vegetable fiber yarns and fabrics. Mexico eliminated these on October 15, 2008, after reaching a bilateral agreement with China. It replaced them with "transition tariffs" on a range of textiles, apparel, and other Chinese imports. The initial rates were lower but still high, at 110 percent for certain yarns and fabrics and 140 percent for certain apparel and made-up textiles. The tariffs were further reduced by 10 percent on an annual basis until they were eliminated on December 12, 2011 ("Trade and Trade Policy" 2009; "World Textile and Apparel Trade" 2009). Outside of China, Mexico has also had historically high most favored nation (MFN) tariff rates. In December 2008, Mexico lowered its MFN tariff rate on most textile and apparel imports. Tariffs on apparel and certain made-up textiles were lowered from 35 percent to 30 percent, with plans to further reduce these tariffs during 2010–13 ("Trade and Trade Policy" 2009).

Notes

1. The EU-15 is the 15 member states of the European Union (EU) as of December 31, 2003, before the new member states joined the EU: Austria, Belgium, Denmark, Finland, France, Germany, Greece, Ireland, Italy, Luxembourg, the Netherlands, Portugal, Spain, Sweden, and the United Kingdom.

2. Many cite lack of access to affordable credit as a reason for limited functional upgrading to OEM/full package, noting that without adequate financing it is not possible to purchase the raw materials.

3. Examples of imagewear buyers include the government, airlines, and major league sports teams.

4. This is the same production-sharing scheme that applied to Honduras.

5. For example, Hong Kong SAR, China; Malaysia; Singapore; the Philippines; Taiwan, China.

6. In 1997, *maquilas* were allowed to have domestic sales up to 70 percent of the value of their annual export sales from the preceding year, increasing 5 percent per year until 2001, when limits were removed.

7. Estimates suggest that 6 out of 10 apparel products sold in Mexico are illegally obtained (stolen, smuggled, or pirated), for which the allocation to the sector amounts to around $13 billion. Much of the illegal apparel sold in Mexico takes place in street markets and is estimated to account for 26.9 percent of total sales (CNIV 2009).

References

Anson, Robin. 2010. "Li & Fung Will Source Less Apparel from China and More from Bangladesh and Other Asian Countries." *Textile Outlook International* 144: 4–8.

Anson, Robin, and Guillaume Brocklehurst. 2010a. Part 2 of "World Markets for Textile Machinery: Woven Fabric Manufacture." *Textile Outlook International* 146: 89–106.

———. 2010b. Part 3 of "World Markets for Textile Machinery: Knitted Fabric Manufacture." *Textile Outlook International* 147: 120–54.

Bair, Jennifer, and Gary Gereffi. 2001. "Local Clusters in Global Chains: The Causes and Consequences of Export Dynamism in Torreon's Blue Jeans Industry." *World Development* 29 (11): 1885–1903.

————. 2003. "Upgrading, Uneven Development and Jobs in the North American Apparel Industry." *Global Networks* 3 (2): 143–70.

Bair, Jennifer, and Enrique Peters. 2006. "Global Commodity Chains and Endogenous Growth: Export Dynamism and Development in Mexico and Honduras." *World Development* 34 (2): 203–21.

Brocklehurst, Guillaume, and Robin Anson. 2010. Part 1 of "World Markets for Textile Machinery: Yarn Manufacture." *Textile Outlook International* 145: 80–117.

BMI (Business Monitor International). 2009. "Mexico Textiles and Clothing Report: Q4 2009." BMI, London.

CNIV (Cámara Nacional de la Industriadel Vestido). 2008–10. "Información Estadística." CNIV, Cuauhtemoc. http://www.cniv.org.mx/estadistica.php.

Forstater, Maya. 2010. "Sectoral Coverage of the Global Economic Crisis: Implications of the Global Financial and Economic Crisis on the Textile and Clothing Sector." Report, International Labour Organization, Geneva.

Frederick, Stacey, and Gary Gereffi. 2011. "Upgrading and Restructuring in the Global Apparel Value Chain: Why China and Asia Are Outperforming Mexico and Central America." *International Journal of Technological Learning, Innovation and Development 2011* 4 (/2/3): 67–95.

INEGI (Instituto Nacional de Estadística y Geografía). 1984–2010. "La Industria Textil y del Vestido en México." Instituto Nacional de Estadística y Geografía. http://www.inegi.org.mx.

Jassin-O'Rourke Group, L. 2008. "Global Apparel Manufacturing Labor Cost Analysis 2008." Textile and Apparel Manufacturers and Merchants. http://tammonline.com/files/GlobalApparelLaborCostSummary2008.pdf.

MSN (Maquila Solidarity Network). 2009. "How Will the Global Financial Crisis Affect the Garment Industry and Garment Workers?" Maquila Solidarity Network. Toronto, Ontario. http://en.maquilasolidarity.org/sites/maquilasolidarity.org/files/2009-02-25%20MSN-FinancialCrisis-Feb09-ENG.pdf.

Newberry, M. 2009. "Global Market Review of the Denim and Jeanswear Industries—Forecasts to 2016." *Just-style* Management Briefing, Aroq Limited, Bromsgove, U.K.

Rice, Justin. 1998. "PITEX and Maquiladora Import Programs: A Working Guide and Comparative Evaluation." Texas *International Law Journal* 33 (2): 365–80.

"Trade and Trade Policy: The World's Leading Clothing Exporters." 2009. *Global Apparel Markets* 5: 39–69.

USITC (U.S. International Trade Commission). 2004. *Assessment of the Competitiveness of Certain Foreign Suppliers to the U.S. Market* (Publication

3671). Washington, DC: Office of Industries and Office of Economics. www
.usitc.gov/publications/332/pub3671.pdf.

———. 2010. "USITC Interactive Trade and Tariff Database" (Dataweb). USITC.
http://dataweb.ustic.gov.

World Textile and Apparel Trade and Production: USA, Argentina, Brazil,
Colombia and Mexico." 2009. *Textile Outlook International* 142: 12–43.

CHAPTER 13

Morocco

Overview

- Morocco's apparel sector is heavily dependent on the EU-15[1] market, and thus is a typical regional supplier that exports to one major market in geographical proximity based on short lead times and regional trade agreements. Among the MENA-4 (Middle East and North Africa) countries, it ranks number two behind Tunisia and before the Arab Republic of Egypt and Jordan in terms of global as well regional exports to the EU-15.

- Initial development of the export-oriented apparel sector in Morocco began with a broad domestic policy change to a more export-oriented development model in the first half of the 1980s. Against this background, the so-called Outward Processing Trade (OPT) agreements became the key driver behind the rising apparel exports to the EU-15 market. Formally launched in the second half of the 1970s, this instrument of European Union (EU) trade policy allowed for preferential market access (via reduced duties and higher quotas) of assembled apparel items—as long as the inputs (such as yarns and fabrics) were sourced from the EU. In 2000, OPT preferential market access switched to duty-free access and double transformation rules of origin (ROO) under the Euromed Association Agreement. Given the persistence of sourcing relations with EU textile suppliers established under OPT, this change did not encourage the establishment of significant backward linkages in Morocco. However, investments in the textile sector have increased after the Multi-fibre Arrangement (MFA phaseout), in particular foreign direct investment (FDI) in the denim segment, which was supported by special government incentives.

- The EU's trade policies were a double-edged sword for Morocco's apparel sector. On the one hand, they secured a steady flow of orders under the production-sharing agreements (OPT), largely originating earlier with European branded manufacturers and later with retailers. On the other hand, they circumscribed the potential for functional upgrading and backward linkages of apparel exporters because they promoted a deep-seated division of labor whereby Moroccan suppliers were largely limited to the assembly and cut-make-trim (CMT) role.

- Expectations were pessimistic for Morocco's apparel exports MFA phaseout. However, although exports declined in 2005, they increased in the following three years. Compared to its regional competitor Tunisia, Morocco was slow to develop proactive policies in the context of the MFA phaseout. Key efforts in this regard were the Framework Agreement in 2002, which supported restructuring and upgrading, and the Plan Emergence in late 2005. The most important explanation for Morocco's sustained and increasing apparel exports post-MFA is the increasing role of fast-fashion retailers, particularly from Spain (for example, Inditex/Zara and Mango), which significantly increased sourcing from Morocco post-MFA. However, the global economic crisis hit Morocco's apparel exports severely, leading to an export decline of 19.4 percent in 2009.

Development of the Apparel Industry

Initial development of the export-oriented apparel sector in Morocco began with a broader domestic policy change to a more export-oriented development model in the first half of the 1980s. Since then, the apparel sector has been at the forefront of export-led industrial growth in Morocco. Apparel exports increased significantly from the early 1980s to the early 1990s. During the 1990s, growth continued, albeit at a slower pace. The slowdown is related to the increasing incorporation of former state-socialist countries in the Central and Eastern European (CEE) region that threatened market shares of Moroccan and other MENA apparel suppliers in the EU market. Nonetheless, the sector continued to expand in terms of exports and employment during the 1990s. Besides Morocco's geographical location, its comparatively low labor costs, and export-oriented policies, preferential trade agreements with the EU promoted its increasing integration into supply chains of EU-based apparel branded manufacturers and retailers (Stengg 2001).

The initial push came via the EU's OPT agreements, which were introduced in the late 1970s (Pellegrin 2001). This regulation allowed for cross-border production-sharing arrangements that permitted EU-based firms to temporarily export inputs for processing to an OPT-partner country and reimport products under preferential conditions. In the case of apparel, these preferential conditions were either reduced tariff rates (tariff OPT) or expanded quota access (economic OPT) for imports under the OPT regime. Tariff OPT suspended tariffs on the reimport of goods from the OPT-partner country into the EU when raw materials (such as yarns and fabrics) are temporarily exported from the EU country for processing undertaken in the OPT country and reimported into the same EU country as partially or fully finished goods. Economic OPT granted additional quotas for the import into the EU of specific products produced from EU-originating materials. Thus, in the context of OPT, EU-based firms could send inputs (textile) to one of the countries in question (for example, Morocco) for processing and could reimport the finished apparel without facing restrictions that pertain to "direct" imports from third countries into the EU. Under the OPT regime, MFA quotas were expanded, and tariffs on the reimports only needed to be paid on the value added abroad—provided that the textile inputs came from Western European countries. As a consequence, European buyers, in particular branded manufacturers, transferred labor-intensive operations like cutting, sewing, and packing to an "OPT country," whereas design, input purchasing, and marketing, as well as the production of textile inputs, remained in the EU.

The OPT regime was superseded and replaced when Morocco signed an Association Agreement with the EU in 1996, which entered into force in 2000. Under this Association Agreement, Moroccan apparel exports enjoyed duty-free access if they met the agreement's ROO. The EU's ROO demand "double transformation"; that is, in addition to apparel production (such as cutting and sewing), fabric production or yarn production also has to take place in the beneficiary country or in the EU to qualify for preferential market access. Given the limited textile capacities in Morocco, it was difficult to fulfill double transformation requirements in the local economy, and thus the majority of textile inputs continued to be sourced from the EU after 2000. The sourcing relationships established under OPT therefore did not significantly change with the new agreement, and Moroccan apparel exports continued to expand, largely based on inputs sourced from the EU (USAID 2004; World Bank 2006).

Notwithstanding slower growth—as compared to the first phase of export orientation in the 1980s—Morocco's apparel exports continued to rise throughout the 1990s and early 2000s. In 1995, apparel exports stood at $2,250 million and rose to $3,476 million by 2004 (table 13.1). While exports grew in value terms, Morocco's global market share decreased slightly, from 1.5 percent to 1.4 percent, during the same period. Woven apparel exports dominated Morocco's apparel exports, despite a small relative decline from 75.3 percent in 1995 to 71.0 percent in 2004. With regard to end markets, Morocco's apparel exports are strongly concentrated toward the EU-15 market, which accounted for nearly 93 percent of total apparel exports in 2004. Morocco's apparel exports to the EU-15 hit their peak in the first half of the 2000s, representing around 3.2 percent of total EU-15 apparel imports in 2001. This share declined to 2.8 percent by 2004 (table 13.2). Table 13.3 shows the share of the four main apparel-producing countries in MENA in the EU-15's total apparel imports. Tunisia is the number one MENA exporter to the EU-15, accounting for a share of 3.7 percent in 2000, which decreased, however,

Table 13.1   Moroccan Apparel Exports to the World

	1995	1998	2001	2004	2005	2006	2007	2008	2009
Total value ($, million)	2,250	2,563	2,654	3,476	3,326	3,588	4,232	4,463	3,599
Annual growth rate (%)	22.6	9.4	8.6	8.1	−4.3	7.9	17.9	5.4	−19.4
Share of world exports (%)	1.5	1.4	1.4	1.4	1.2	1.2	1.3	1.3	1.2
Woven and knit value ($, million)									
Woven	1,695	1,861	1,871	2,467	2,404	2,565	2,984	3,212	2,586
Knit	555	702	783	1,009	922	1,024	1,249	1,251	1,012
Woven and knit share of total import value (%)									
Woven	75.3	72.6	70.5	71.0	72.3	71.5	70.5	72.0	71.9
Knit	24.7	27.4	29.5	29.0	27.7	28.5	29.5	28.0	28.1

Source: United Nations Commodity Trade Statistics Database (UN Comtrade).
Note: Exports represented by imports reported by partner countries. Apparel classifications: Harmonized Commodity Description and Coding System (HS) 1992: Woven: HS62; Knitted: HS61; growth rate reflects change from previous year.

to 2.9 percent in 2005. Morocco is the number two exporter, with a share
of 3.3 percent in 2000 and 2.8 percent in 2005. The Arab Republic of
Egypt and, to a lesser extent, Jordan are important apparel exporter countries, but they largely export to the U.S. market (see following text).

Table 13.2   EU-15 Apparel Imports from Morocco

	1995	1998	2001	2004	2005	2006	2007	2008	2009
Total value (€, million)	1,631	2,038	2,624	2,417	2,262	2,370	2,544	2,386	1,991
Total quantity (kg, million)	95	118	145	134	124	122	122	108	91
Share of all EU-15 apparel imports (%)	3.2	3.1	3.2	2.8	2.5	2.4	2.5	2.3	2.0
Annual growth rate (%) of									
Value		8.4	11.4	−2.0	−6.4	4.8	7.3	−6.2	−16.6
Quantity		10.7	6.2	−3.2	−8.0	−1.1	0.1	−11.4	−15.7
Woven and knit value (€, million)									
Woven	1,232	1,486	1,856	1,742	1,647	1,723	1,811	1,722	1,444
Knit	400	552	768	675	615	647	733	664	547
Woven and knit share (%)									
Woven	75.5	72.9	70.7	72.1	72.8	72.7	71.2	72.2	72.5
Knit	24.5	27.1	29.3	27.9	27.2	27.3	28.8	27.8	27.5
Woven and knit quantity (kg, million)									
Woven	68	80	93	85	77	77	77	68	56
Knit	27	39	51	49	46	46	45	40	35

Source: Eurostat.
Note: Apparel represented by Harmonized Commodity Description and Coding System (HS) Codes 61 and 62; growth rate reflects change from previous year. kg = kilogram; EU-15 = the 15 member states of the European Union (EU) as of December 31, 2003, before the new member states joined the EU: Austria, Belgium, Denmark, Finland, France, Germany, Greece, Ireland, Italy, Luxembourg, the Netherlands, Portugal, Spain, Sweden, and the United Kingdom.

Table 13.3   EU-15 Apparel Imports from MENA Region

Country/ region	Customs value ($, million)					Market share (%)				
	1995	2000	2005	2008	2009	1995	2000	2005	2008	2009
World	65,239	69,556	110,711	148,487	133,215					
Tunisia	2,373	2,573	3,264	4,135	3,428	3.6	3.7	2.9	2.8	2.6
Morocco	2,183	2,300	3,085	3,952	3,127	3.3	3.3	2.8	2.7	2.3
Egypt, Arab Rep.	185	269	438	769	647	0.3	0.4	0.4	0.5	0.5
Jordan	14	17	10	15	11	0.0	0.0	0.0	0.0	0.0

Source: United Nations Commodity Trade Statistics Database (UN Comtrade).
Note: Apparel represented by Harmonized Commodity Description and Coding System (HS) 1992: Codes 61 and 62. MENA = Middle East and North Africa; EU-15 = the 15 member states of the European Union (EU) as of December 31, 2003, before the new member states joined the EU: Austria, Belgium, Denmark, Finland, France, Germany, Greece, Ireland, Italy, Luxembourg, the Netherlands, Portugal, Spain, Sweden, and the United Kingdom.

It was generally anticipated that Morocco as a regional supplier country would be among the losers post-MFA (Nordås 2004). Indeed, Morocco's apparel exports declined strongly during the first months of 2005, and declines would have probably continued for the whole year if the China safeguards had not reduced China's imports to the EU (ILO 2005). Overall, exports declined in 2005 by 4.3 percent but increased again in the following three years, accounting for growth rates of 7.9 percent, 17.9 percent, and 5.4 percent. The end of the phaseout of the China safeguards in 2008, but more important the global economic crisis, hit Morocco's apparel exports severely, leading to an export decline of 19.4 percent in 2009 (Textiles Intelligence 2009). In terms of global market share, Morocco regained some of the losses experienced immediately post-MFA phaseout, but the strong decline in export orders in 2009 meant a setback to the 2005 level of 1.2 percent. In terms of employment, it was estimated that more than 10,000 workers lost their job in the first quarter of 2009 (Business Monitor 2009).

Compared to its regional competitor Tunisia, Morocco started late in developing proactive policies in the context of the MFA phaseout, and these policies were initially triggered by industry groups, in particular the Moroccan Textile & Clothing Industries Association (AMITH) (Cammett 2007). Key efforts in this regard were the Framework Agreement concluded between the government and AMITH in 2002, which created a Financial Restructuring Fund and a Business Upgrading Fund to support firm restructuring and upgrading, and state subsidies with regard to social security and electricity costs (Cammett 2007; WTO 2009). The critical situation of the industry in the first months of 2005 promoted government action, and the "Plan Emergence" was devised to boost strategic industrial sectors, in particular apparel, and foster Morocco's position in world markets. The apparel industry also lobbied for more liberal ROO and was successful in mid-2005, when it obtained a short-term derogation to use Turkish fabrics for duty-free exports to the EU. This short-term derogation was made permanent with the adoption of the simplified Pan-Euro-Mediterranean ROO later that year.[2] Along the same lines, enhanced trade liberalization via bilateral free trade agreements (FTAs) with Turkey and the United States improved market access and input sourcing possibilities.

The most important explanation for Morocco's sustained apparel exports post-MFA is, however, the increasing role of fast-fashion retailers, particularly from Spain (for example, Inditex/Zara and Mango), which significantly increased sourcing from Morocco post-MFA. Their increasing role has not only maintained and increased export levels but also promoted changes in the types of products exported. Unit values of apparel exports from Morocco increased because of the higher quality and fashion products of these buyers (see following text). Hence, exports to the principal market—the EU-15—decreased in volume terms post-MFA, whereas values increased (table 13.2).

Overview of MENA-4 Countries

The MENA-4 countries (Egypt, Jordan, Morocco, and Tunisia) show different profiles in terms of their apparel end markets and the way they are integrated into apparel global value chains (GVCs). While Morocco and Tunisia are concentrated in apparel production and strongly integrated into EU-based production networks, exporting more than 90 percent of their apparel exports to the EU-15, the U.S. market is crucial for Jordan, with 93 percent of its exports shipped there. The Arab Republic of Egypt is serving both main markets, with 40 percent of its apparel exports going to the United States and 30 percent to the EU-15, and it has a more vertically integrated apparel sector related to its raw material base in cotton (World Bank 2006; USAID 2008). The following provides a brief description of each of the countries in the MENA-4 region.

Morocco's apparel sector is primarily Moroccan owned, though foreign investment increased in the mid-2000s, in particular from EU-15 countries. Morocco's apparel industry consists predominantly of small and medium enterprises (SMEs) and a small number of larger firms. In 2008, there were around 880 firms registered, which employed almost 150,000 workers. Firms are clustered around three regions (Casablanca, Rabat, and Tangiers) and besides some upgrading largely continue to operate as CMT suppliers for the EU-15 market. Post-MFA, Morocco's export dependence on the EU market has slightly declined.

Tunisia's apparel industry is also heavily dependent on the EU-15 market, with roughly 86 percent of exports going to France, Germany, Italy, and the United Kingdom in 2009. Around 2,100 firms are active in the textile and apparel industries, which employed more than 200,000 workers in 2008. In March 2009, around 1,300 export-oriented apparel firms were operational (Textiles Intelligence 2009). The share of foreign involvement has been on the rise. In particular, firms from Belgium, France, Germany, and Italy have some ownership ties with

Tunisian firms. The largest investor is Italian Benetton, which has been present in Tunisia since the early 1990s and accounted for around 10,000 jobs directly and indirectly in 2007. Tunisia fared slightly better than Morocco post-MFA in terms of export performance (*Think*Tunisia 2009). Almost 47 percent of Tunisia's apparel exports to the EU were woven suits in 2008 and 2009. Several Tunisian manufacturers offer integrated weaving facilities for fabrics made from high-quality Italian yarns. Buyers include Adidas, Calvin Klein, Lacoste, La Redoute, Etam, Kookai, Laura Ashley, Next, Prada, Puma, and Quicksilver (Textiles Intelligence 2009).

Jordan's apparel export industry emerged largely as a result of preferential market access to the United States and was driven by quota-hopping investors. In particular, duty-free access granted under the Qualifying Industrial Zone (QIZ) program (starting in 1998) and an FTA with the United States (implemented in 2000) provided the key incentive to develop Jordan into an export platform for the U.S. market. As a result, apparel exports to the United States surged until 2005, when they started to decline. Jordan's apparel sector is dominated by foreign investment, and migrant workers play an important role. In 2004, Asian investors (besides India) accounted for 40 percent, Indian for 22 percent, and U.S. investors for 3 percent of total investment in the sector. A total of 776 apparel firms were officially registered in the sector in the same year. According to industry estimates, roughly 70 percent of the firms operate as full-package suppliers; the remainder largely consists of CMT suppliers (USAID 2008).

Egypt has vertically integrated textile and apparel sectors ranging from cotton harvesting, spinning, and weaving to manufacturing of apparel and made-up textiles. The industry is predominantly Egyptian owned, but foreign involvement has been on the rise; in particular, Turkish and Indian textile firms have reportedly been established in Egypt. The rising foreign interest was promoted by the QIZ program, which allowed for preferential market access to the United States. Although the QIZ has not led to a similar export boom as in Jordan, Egypt's market share in the U.S. market has increased importantly related to QIZ. Most of the textile and apparel firms in Egypt are clustered around the Greater Cairo area and Alexandria and operate in export-processing and industrial zones. Large vertically integrated state enterprises play an important role, accounting for 100 percent of the spinning, 70 percent of the weaving, and 30 percent of the apparel industry (USAID 2008).

Structure of the Apparel Industry

Types of Firms

Historically, the center of Morocco's textile and apparel industry was the ancient capital city Fez, where *fassi* families controlled the sector (Rossi 2010). However, with the change to export orientation during the 1980s, they lost importance (Cammett 2007). Today, firms operating in and around Fez are largely oriented toward the domestic market and focus on traditional apparel items. In contrast, the export-oriented firms are clustered around Casablanca, Tangier, and Rabat and have modern facilities and better infrastructure, including ports (USAID 2008). Tangier is rapidly rising as an outsourcing location given its Free Trade Zone (FTZ) status, its new port infrastructure, and its attractive geographical location, in particular for Spanish firms.

According to official data, there were 880 registered apparel firms operating in Morocco, with a registered workforce of 149,477 workers in 2008 (Rossi 2010). In 2002, the number of apparel firms was estimated at 1,200, pointing to a consolidation process in the apparel sector (USITC 2004; World Bank 2006). Overall, the sector remains characterized by a majority share of SOEs (WTO 2009). The latest available survey-based data (from around 2000) indicate that roughly 43 percent of apparel firms employed less than 50 employees, 31 percent employed between 50 and 199 employees, and the remaining 26 percent employed more than 200 (Benabderrazik 2009). Most apparel firms are Moroccan owned, but foreign investment in the sector has increased since the government encouraged FDI via a set of incentive policies, particularly since the early 2000s (USAID 2008). New large (foreign and domestic) investment projects that benefited from state incentives have increased in terms of employment generation—in 2006, 19 projects created on average 182 jobs, while in 2007, 469 jobs were on average created by 17 projects (GoM 2008).

The majority of Moroccan apparel exporters are operating as CMT suppliers (Rossi 2010). According to industry information, most firms operate a production model named "co-traitance," which is an intermediate form between CMT and full package. Under this arrangement, the supplier can be responsible for fabric suggestion or some design additions, but the buyer is still responsible for inputs sourcing and the associated financial risks. The share of traditional CMT was estimated at 27 percent, while cotraitance accounted for 54 percent in 2007 (USAID 2008). In 2010, the share of CMT-like contractual arrangements was estimated to range between 50 and 70 percent of total turnover (GoM 2011). Hence, while the share of mere CMT assembly has declined in the last years, CMT-like production arrangements still account for the majority of the sector. In response to the FTA between Morocco and Turkey (which came into force in January 2006), Turkish firms have relocated production from Turkey to Morocco. The common model is to remain full-package manufacturing capacities in Turkey and relocate CMT production to Morocco to access the EU market duty free (Tokatli and Kizilgün 2009). Moroccan suppliers are generally quite dependent in terms of their client base. Some apparel suppliers make more than 80 percent of their export turnover with a single buyer (GoM 2011). Important buyers for Moroccan suppliers are Inditex/Zara, Mango, Marks & Spencer, Decathlon, Fruit of the Loom, Gap, and VF Corporation (Tokatli and Kizilgün 2009; Rossi 2010).

Investment in the apparel and textile sectors has generally declined from 2000 onward (figure 13.1). Total investment in the sector peaked in the late 1990s and, after a drop in 2000, has fluctuated around the same value. Its relative importance compared to other industrial sectors has decreased, however. Its share declined from roughly 25 percent of total industrial investment in 1998 to 9 percent in 2007.

End Markets

Morocco's apparel exports are traditionally geared toward the EU-15 market, although the dependency has decreased over the past 15 years. In 1995, 97 percent of total apparel exports went to the EU-15, but this share dropped to 86.9 percent by 2009 (table 13.4). Exports to the U.S.

Figure 13.1   Moroccan Total Investment by Major Industrial Sector

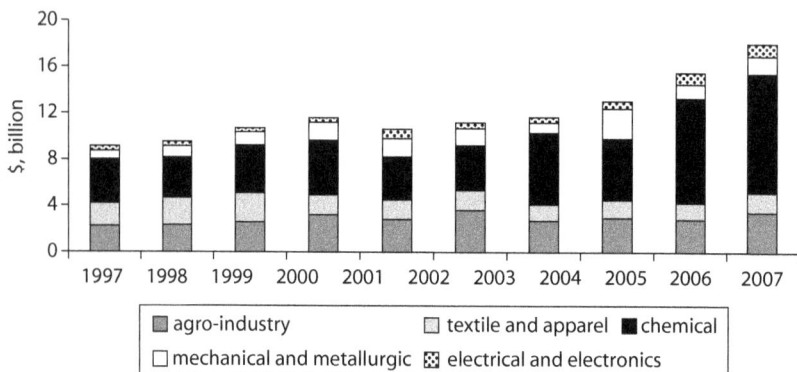

Source: Maroc en Chiffres, various years; Haut-Commissariat au Plan.

Table 13.4 Top Five Moroccan Apparel Export Markets, 1995, 2000, 2005, 2008, and 2009

Country/region	Customs value ($, million)					Market share (%)				
	1995	2000	2005	2008	2009	1995	2000	2005	2008	2009
World	**2,250**	**2,444**	**3,326**	**4,463**	**3,599**					
EU-15	2,183	2,300	3,085	3,952	3,127	97.0	94.1	92.8	88.6	86.9
United States	44	100	59	96	61	2.0	4.1	1.8	2.2	1.7
Mexico	n.a.	n.a.	24	61	53	n.a.	n.a.	0.7	1.4	1.5
Russian Federation	n.a.	n.a.	n.a.	50	48	n.a.	n.a.	n.a.	1.1	1.3
Poland	n.a.	n.a.	17	n.a.	42	n.a.	n.a.	0.5	n.a.	1.2
Turkey	n.a.	n.a.	26	43	n.a.	n.a.	n.a.	0.8	1.0	n.a.
United Arab Emirates	n.a.	n.a.	n.a.	n.a.	n.a.	n.a.	n.a.	n.a.	n.a.	n.a.
Norway	n.a.	4	n.a.	n.a.	n.a.	n.a.	0.2	n.a.	n.a.	n.a.
Czech Republic	3	4	n.a.	n.a.	n.a.	0.1	0.2	n.a.	n.a.	n.a.
Japan	n.a.	3	n.a.	n.a.	n.a.	n.a.	0.1	n.a.	n.a.	n.a.
Saudi Arabia	4	n.a.	n.a.	n.a.	n.a.	0.2	n.a.	n.a.	n.a.	n.a.
Canada	3	n.a.	n.a.	n.a.	n.a.	0.1	n.a.	n.a.	n.a.	n.a.
Top five share	**2,238**	**2,411**	**3,210**	**4,202**	**3,329**	**99.5**	**98.7**	**96.5**	**94.2**	**92.5**

Source: United Nations Commodity Trade Statistics Database (UN Comtrade).

Note: Harmonized Commodity Description and Coding System (HS) 1992: Codes 61 and 62; exports represented by partner country imports; n.a. = not applicable (indicates country not in top five for given year). EU-15 = the 15 member states of the European Union (EU) as of December 31, 2003, before the new member states joined the EU: Austria, Belgium, Denmark, Finland, France, Germany, Greece, Ireland, Italy, Luxembourg, the Netherlands, Portugal, Spain, Sweden, and the United Kingdom.

market were highest in 2000, accounting for 4.1 percent of total apparel exports, but decreased until the mid-2000s. With the entering into force of the U.S.-Morocco FTA in 2006, exports started to rise again but are still very modest, accounting for 1.7 percent in 2009. Besides Mexico, the significant markets of larger European economies, including Poland and the Russian Federation, are rising in importance (figure 13.2).

A more disaggregate view on the main export destinations within the EU-15 reveals a high concentration on a few EU-15 countries (figures 13.3 and 13.4). France, Spain, and to a lesser extent the United Kingdom have absorbed the large majority of apparel exports since 2000. France has been the traditional export market, accounting for roughly 40 percent of total apparel exports in 2000, but its share declined to roughly 30 percent in 2009. In contrast, Spain's role is increasing as an export market, as underlined by its constant increase in value terms, which became particularly pronounced post-MFA. In 2000, Spain accounted for only 10 percent of Morocco's total apparel exports, but its share reached more than 30 percent in 2009. Exports to the United Kingdom grew during the first half of the 2000s but

Figure 13.2   Moroccan Top Apparel Export Markets, 2000 and 2009

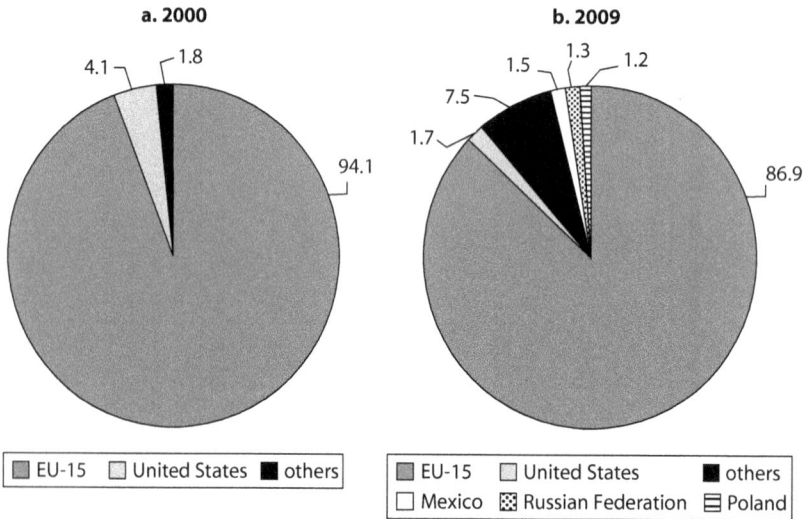

a. 2000

4.1   1.8

94.1

b. 2009

1.3
1.5   1.2
7.5
1.7
86.9

EU-15   United States   others

EU-15   United States   others
Mexico   Russian Federation   Poland

Source: United Nations Commodity Trade Statistics Database (UN Comtrade).
Note: Apparel represented by Harmonized Commodity Description and Coding System (HS) 1992: Codes 61 and 62.
EU-15 = the 15 member states of the European Union (EU) as of December 31, 2003, before the new member states joined the EU: Austria, Belgium, Denmark, Finland, France, Germany, Greece, Ireland, Italy, Luxembourg, the Netherlands, Portugal, Spain, Sweden, and the United Kingdom.

Figure 13.3   Top Five Export Destinations for Moroccan Apparel

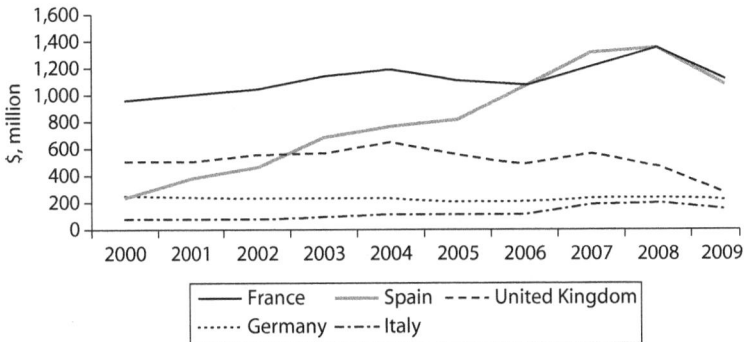

Source: United Nations Commodity Trade Statistics Database (UN Comtrade).
Note: Apparel represented by Harmonized Commodity Description and Coding System (HS) 1992: Codes 61 and 62.

Figure 13.4   Shares of Top Five Export Destinations for Moroccan Apparel

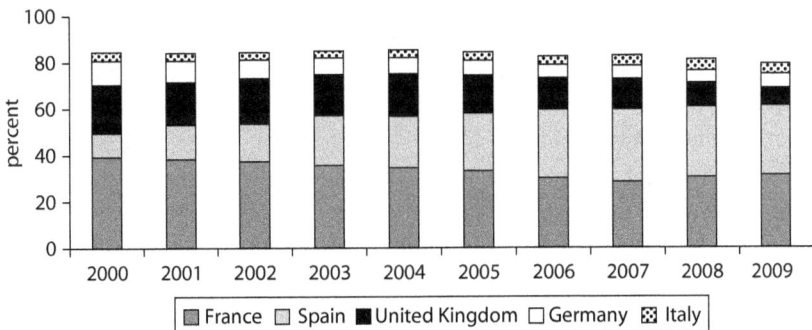

Source: United Nations Commodity Trade Statistics Database (UN Comtrade).
Note: Apparel represented by Harmonized Commodity Description and Coding System (HS) 1992: Codes 61 and 62.

declined post-MFA. Exports to Germany experienced a slight decrease until 2005 but have remained stable since then at a relatively low level. Italy has gradually increased in importance as an export destination since 2000, however also at a low level.

A key driver behind these developments is the increasing importance of fast-fashion buyers, in particular Inditex/Zara and Mango from Spain (Rossi 2010). Other important buyers include large French retailers such as Decathlon or the British Marks & Spencer.

Export Products

Apparel exports are concentrated in woven products, which have accounted for roughly three-quarters of Morocco's overall apparel exports since the mid-1990s (table 13.5). Key export products are cotton-based denim trousers (jeans) and shirts and T-shirts, which together accounted for more than 30 percent of total exports in 2009. Although Morocco exports are still predominantly cotton based, its share of noncotton-based exports has increased, and Morocco is becoming an important EU supplier of man-made fiber (MMF) apparel (Textiles Intelligence 2009). All top 10 products accounted for 49.8 percent of total exports in 2009, which is low compared to competitor countries. Product concentration has decreased since 2000, when the top 10 apparel products accounted for 56 percent of total apparel exports (table 13.5).

Average unit values of EU-15 exports increased post-MFA for woven and knitted apparel (table 13.6). This increase can be explained by the increasing importance of fast-fashion buyers, which generally source higher-quality and fashion products, but also by increasing costs. An early assessment of volume and unit price developments in 2006 suggests that Morocco could partially compensate its fall in export volumes with increasing unit prices, in particular in the fast-fashion segment (World Bank 2006). More generally, regional supplier countries such as Morocco, Tunisia, and Turkey are concentrated in higher-value apparel exports in the EU-15 market. Out of the top 10 EU supplier countries, Morocco had the second-highest average unit values, right behind Tunisia and before Turkey, in 2009. However, those three countries lost some of the EU demand for higher-end apparel items to Chinese suppliers in 2009, as the latter were actively looking to win such orders from European retailers, such as for men's woven suits (Textiles Intelligence 2009).

Backward Linkages

In the context of OPT, the EU-15 had developed into the key source for textile inputs. However, the EU-15's share of total textile imports declined from 93.0 percent in 1995 to 71.4 percent in 2009. During the same period, China's share rose from barely 1 percent in 1995 to 16 percent in 2009 (table 13.7). Post-MFA, India and Turkey emerged as additional new sources of textile inputs, with a share of 2.8 percent and 5.9 percent in 2009, respectively. Turkey's increasing role is related to the FTA concluded in 2004 between Morocco and Turkey and the adoption of the Pan-Euro-Mediterranean system of cumulation of ROO, which facilitates regional integration in the Mediterranean Basin. Traditional, albeit small, textile

Table 13.5 Top 10 EU-15 Apparel Imports from Morocco, 1996, 2000, 2005, 2006, and 2009

HS code	Product	Customs value (€, million)					Market share (%)				
		1996	2000	2005	2008	2009	1996	2000	2005	2008	2009
Total		**1,672**	**2,356**	**2,262**	**2,386**	**1,991**					
620462	Trousers	67	142	261	235	216	4.0	6.0	11.6	9.8	10.8
620342	Trousers	257	320	262	243	190	15.4	13.6	11.6	10.2	9.5
610910	T-Shirts	59	168	162	131	105	3.5	7.1	7.2	5.5	5.3
620630	Shirts	n.a.	n.a.	n.a.	109	101	n.a.	n.a.	n.a.	4.6	5.1
611030	Sweatshirts	99	141	102	94	91	5.9	6.0	4.5	3.9	4.6
620442	Dresses	n.a.	n.a.	n.a.	66	67	n.a.	n.a.	n.a.	2.8	3.4
621210	Bras	34	59	71	82	63	2.0	2.5	3.2	3.4	3.2
610990	T-Shirts	n.a.	n.a.	54	75	55	n.a.	0.0	2.4	3.1	2.8
620463	Trousers	59	163	104	72	53	3.5	6.9	4.6	3.0	2.6
620443	Dresses	n.a.	n.a.	n.a.	n.a.	52	n.a.	n.a.	n.a.	n.a.	2.6
620520	Shirts	88	80	67	69	n.a.	5.3	3.4	3.0	2.9	n.a.
620452	Skirts	n.a.	n.a.	77	n.a.	n.a.	n.a.	n.a.	3.4	n.a.	n.a.
620343	Trousers	51	76	58	n.a.	n.a.	3.0	3.2	2.6	n.a.	n.a.
620640	Shirts	79	111	n.a.	n.a.	n.a.	4.7	4.7	n.a.	n.a.	n.a.
620469	Trousers	n.a.	60	n.a.	n.a.	n.a.	n.a.	2.6	n.a.	n.a.	n.a.
611120	Garments	33	n.a.	n.a.	n.a.	n.a.	2.0	n.a.	n.a.	n.a.	n.a.
Top 10 share		**826**	**1,320**	**1,219**	**1,175**	**992**	**49.4**	**56.0**	**53.9**	**49.3**	**49.8**

Source: Eurostat.

Note: Apparel classification: Harmonized Commodity Description and Coding System (HS) 1992: Woven: HS62; Knit HS61; n.a. = not applicable (indicates product not in the top 10 in given year); EU-15 = the 15 member states of the European Union (EU) as of December 31, 2003, before the new member states joined the EU: Austria, Belgium, Denmark, Finland, France, Germany, Greece, Ireland, Italy, Luxembourg, the Netherlands, Portugal, Spain, Sweden, and the United Kingdom.

Table 13.6   Unit Values of EU-15 Apparel Imports from Morocco

Year	EU-15 unit values (€/kg)		
	Knit	Woven	Total
1995	14.70	18.20	17.20
1996	15.20	18.70	17.60
1997	15.00	18.70	17.60
1998	14.30	18.60	17.20
1999	13.70	12.60	12.90
2000	13.70	19.30	17.30
2001	14.90	19.90	18.10
2002	18.00	20.50	19.70
2003	14.30	19.70	17.80
2004	13.70	20.50	18.00
2005	13.20	21.30	18.30
2006	14.20	22.50	19.40
2007	16.20	23.50	20.80
2008	16.50	25.30	22.00
2009	15.40	25.90	21.80

Source: Eurostat.

Note: kg = kilogram; EU-15 = the 15 member states of the European Union (EU) as of December 31, 2003, before the new member states joined the EU: Austria, Belgium, Denmark, Finland, France, Germany, Greece, Ireland, Italy, Luxembourg, the Netherlands, Portugal, Spain, Sweden, and the United Kingdom.

Table 13.7   Top Five Textile Suppliers to Morocco, 1995, 2000, 2005, 2008, and 2009

Country/ economy/ region	Customs value ($, million)					Market share (%)				
	1995	2000	2005	2008	2009	1995	2000	2005	2008	2009
World	1,196	1,293	1,811	2,428	2,006					
EU-15	1,117	1,177	1,478	1,828	1,432	93.3	91.0	81.6	75.3	71.4
China	13	41	165	291	321	1.1	3.2	9.1	12.0	16.0
Turkey	n.a.	10	60	127	119	n.a.	0.8	3.3	n.a.	5.9
India	n.a.	n.a.	40	67	56	n.a.	n.a.	2.2	2.8	2.8
Korea, Rep.	13	14	11	n.a.	11	1.1	1.1	0.6	n.a.	0.5
Syrian Arab Repulic	n.a.	n.a.	n.a.	17	n.a.	n.a.	n.a.	n.a.	0.7	n.a.
Hong Kong SAR, China	11	12	n.a.	n.a.	n.a.	0.9	0.9	n.a.	n.a.	n.a.
United States	15	n.a.	n.a.	n.a.	n.a.	1.2	n.a.	n.a.	n.a.	n.a.
Top five share	**1,168**	**1,254**	**1,754**	**2,330**	**1,939**	**97.6**	**97.0**	**96.8**	**90.7**	**96.7**

Source: United Nations Commodity Trade Statistics Database (UN Comtrade).

Note: Standard International Trade Classification Rev. 3 Code 65; imports represent world exports to Morocco; n.a. = not applicable (indicates not in the top 5 in given year); EU-15 = the 15 member states of the European Union (EU) as of December 31, 2003, before the new member states joined the EU: Austria, Belgium, Denmark, Finland, France, Germany, Greece, Ireland, Italy, Luxembourg, the Netherlands, Portugal, Spain, Sweden, and the United Kingdom.

suppliers, including Hong Kong SAR, China; the Republic of Korea; and the United States, have dropped in significance since the mid-1990s.

Given the important role of production-sharing agreements with the EU in the development of Morocco's export apparel sector, the EU-15's dominant role as a source of textile inputs is not surprising. However, the picture is more differentiated when looking within the EU-15 (figure 13.5). Spain and Italy increased their textile exports to Morocco in the 2000s, while France and the United Kingdom both decreased in importance as textile input sources. Spain and Italy increased their shares from 15.2 percent and 6.4 percent, respectively, in 2000 to 20.7 percent and 14.8 percent, respectively, in 2009. In contrast, France and the United Kingdom decreased their shares from 33.8 percent and 20.1 percent, respectively, in 2000 to 14.9 percent and 1.9 percent, respectively, in 2009. Other EU-15 import sources, including Belgium, Germany, Portugal, have remained relatively stable in value terms.

With regard to backward linkages, investment in the textile sector has remained limited in Morocco. Before Morocco's turn to export orientation, there existed some capacities in textiles, including spinning, weaving, and dyeing capacities. These were, however, not relevant to EU-based buyers operating under OPT, which were primarily looking for proximate, lower-cost assembly (CMT) suppliers. Thus, given the prevalence of OPT contracts that relied on imported inputs from EU buyers, the existing textile capacities prior to the 1980s were not further developed.

Figure 13.5   Top 10 Textile Suppliers to Morocco

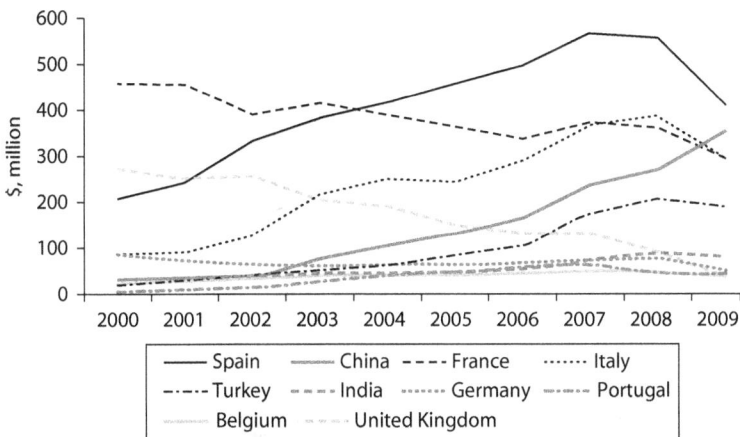

Source: United Nations Commodity Trade Statistics Database (UN Comtrade).
Note: Standard International Trade Classification Rev. 3 Code 65; gross textile imports as reported by Morocco, ranked by 2009 position.

The constant decline in terms of employment in the textile sector under-lines this stagnation (figure 13.6). However, there has been an increase in investments in the textile sector since the MFA, particularly through foreign investment from Italian and Spanish firms and in yarn spinning and fabric weaving, particularly in the denim segment (World Bank 2006). These investments were supported by special facilities for upgrading established by the government and the industry association in the early 2000s. Thus, some vertically integrated foreign projects have added new capacities that are explicitly targeted at export production (table 13.8). In contrast, the majority of the still existing old textile mills are state owned and are geared to the domestic market.

In particular, several large-scale textile projects by major international operators were implemented in Morocco. The first involves the Italian group Legler, which together with its Moroccan partner Atlantic Confec-tion invested in a denim spinning and weaving unit with a capacity of 24 million meters and 9,000 tons per annum, respectively. This $85.29 million project, which began operations in September 2006, is the largest integrated textile unit in the MENA region (USAID 2007). The Spanish Tavex, another top player in the global denim market and an early investor in Morocco, expanded its investments in Morocco (Tokatli and Kizilgün 2009). The $73 million investment increased the capacity of its Settat-based subsidiary Settavex by 47 million meters. A new dyeing facil-ity and warehouse for the storage of 3 million meters of fabric were also announced (*MEED* 2005). Besides these two denim-related investments, the U.S. firm Fruit of the Loom invested in a spinning, weaving, and

Figure 13.6   Employment in Moroccan Textile and Apparel Sector

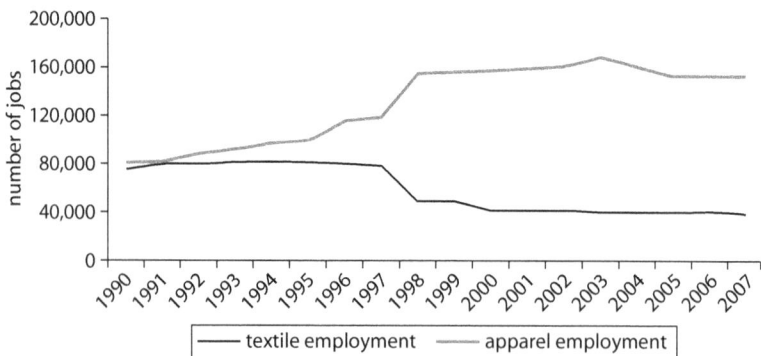

Source: Adapted from Bensaid and Ibourk (2009), cf. Rossi 2010.

Table 13.8   Major FDI Projects in Moroccan Textile and Apparel Industries, 2005–07

Company	Amount (DH, million)	Employment (expected)	Date signed
Legler (ITA)	782.6	800	May 2005
Settavex (ESP)	634	70	August 2005
Fruit of the Loom (U.S.)	1,477	1,150	February 2006
Polyfil	93.1	100	February 2007
Martelli (ITA)	257.4	250	August 2007
Martelli (ITA)	78.5	250	August 2007

Source: GoM 2007.
Note: FDI = foreign direct investment; DH = dirhams; ITA = Italy; ESP= Spain; U.S. = the United States.

dyeing unit at Skhirat (near Rabat) for T-shirts, sweatshirts, and tracksuits, which was expected to have an export turnover of $170 million per year starting with 2008–09. Fruit of the Loom was also planning to expand its assembly unit at Bouknadel at a cost of $159.2 million. These investment projects have benefited from government incentives, including the use of state land and financial support from the Hassan II Fund, and were partly motivated by the prospects of the U.S.-Morocco FTA.

Employment

The textile and apparel sectors are the largest employers in Morocco, accounting for about 200,000 jobs in the formal economy and at least as many in the informal sector (ILO 2006; Rossi 2010). Formal employment in Morocco's apparel sector grew throughout the 1990s until the mid-2000s, with strong increases in the second half of the 1990s. Apparel employment peaked in 2003 with a registered workforce of 168,480 and has since then declined, reaching 153,010 in 2007 (figure 13.6). The sector is a key job provider, accounting for 44.0 percent of total industrial employment on average for the period 2000–08 (GoM 2011) and for 31.2 percent of manufacturing employment on average for the period 2003–07 (Rossi 2010). The workforce is characterized by a high share of female workers, with women accounting for 83.6 percent of total apparel workers in 2007 (Rossi 2010). In terms of regional importance, Casablanca and Tangier account for the majority of workers, with the latter increasing in importance given its rise as an export hub (Rossi 2010). In the textile sector, employment declined importantly in the 1990s, particularly in the late 1990s, and remained at a substantially lower level of around 40,000 workers throughout the 2000s, accounting for one-quarter of total textile and apparel employment.

Average labor costs in Morocco were around $2.24 per hour in 2008. Compared to its main regional competitors, Morocco's hourly rates are lower than in Turkey ($2.44) but above those of Tunisia ($1.68), Jordan ($1.01), and Egypt ($0.83) (Jassin-O'Rourke Group 2008). Qualitative studies have highlighted reoccurring issues regarding the low level of wages—occasionally below the minimum wage—and various precarious types of employment. Particularly in smaller firms, which account for an estimated 70 percent of employment, working conditions seem to be problematic (ILO 2006). In terms of gender discrimination, women seem to face additional obstacles, including wage discrimination, reduced access to on-the-job training, long working hours, and poorer working conditions. Along the same line, female workers are more likely to be working in the informal sector (for example, they represent 90 percent of home workers) (ILO 2006). While child labor is virtually nonexistent in the formal segment of the industry, it is a problem in firms operating in the informal sector (ILO 2006). Morocco is criticized for violations of key trade union rights, including freedom of association and collective bargaining. In the legal area, Morocco has not ratified the International Labour Organization (ILO) Convention 87 on freedom of association and protection of the right to organize (ITUC 2009). Unionization is estimated at around 3 percent, and the few existing unions are male dominated and, hence, do not represent the prevalence of women workers in the industry (Rossi 2010).

Trade Regulations and Proactive Policies

Preferential Market Access

Morocco has benefited from preferential market access to the EU for more than three decades. Initially, the OPT agreements provided the background for increasing CMT exports to European countries. During the 1990s, these agreements were superseded and replaced by a broad regional strategy—the Euro-Mediterranean Partnership— which led to the conclusion of several bilateral and regional preferential trade agreements.

The origins of the OPT regime date back to the 1970s, when its initial objective was to help EU-based manufacturers adjust to increasing international competition (Pellegrin 2001). The OPT system promoted a production system that allowed producers in EU member states to outsource labor-intensive production steps to nearby countries with lower labor costs but to secure the survival of the more capital-intensive parts of the production process within the EU. This goal was typically achieved by applying complex tariff schedules and ROO to protect the more capital-intensive parts of the sectors (such as textiles) and reduce tariffs on labor-intensive stages (such as apparel) (Begg, Pickles, and Smith 2003). As a result of these OPT agreements, a specific division of labor emerged whereby low-cost regional countries such as Morocco were responsible for labor-intensive production steps whereas more capital-intensive and higher-value production was confined to the core countries of the EU. In the case of Morocco's apparel sector, predominantly firms from France supplied intermediate inputs (such as yarns and fabrics) to be assembled by Moroccan suppliers and subsequently reimported as semifinal or final products under preferential conditions (such as reduced tariff rates or expanded import quotas). This reflected in the parallel rise of textile imports from EU-15 countries, in particular France, Italy, Spain, and the United Kingdom, and apparel exports to the same group of countries.

Since the launch of the "Barcelona Declaration" in 1995, trade relations between the EU and the Mediterranean countries have been governed by the Euro-Mediterranean Partnership, including the EU member states and the Mediterranean countries Algeria, Egypt, Israel, Jordan, Lebanon, Morocco, the Palestinian Authority, Syrian Arab Republic, Tunisia, and Turkey. The partnership aims at fostering the political, economic, and social ties between EU member states and Southern Mediterranean countries. Its stated economic objective is to create a deep Euro-Mediterranean Free Trade Area that aims at substantially liberalizing trade between both the EU and Southern Mediterranean countries (North-South), and between Southern Mediterranean countries themselves (South-South). In this context, Morocco signed an Association Agreement with the EU in 1996 that entered into force in 2000 and aims primarily at liberalizing trade in goods.[3] To boost regional integration and cooperation, Egypt, Jordan, Morocco, and Tunisia concluded a regional FTA—the Agadir or Arab Mediterranean FTA—in 2004. Implementation started in 2007, but progress has been slow so far. Morocco is also a member of the Greater Arab Free Trade Area (GAFTA), which formally entered into force in 1998 but which still needs to be filled with content (Martín 2010). A bilateral FTA with Turkey was concluded in 2004 and entered into force in January 2006, which provided the background for rising textile imports from Turkey in recent years. See figure 13.7 for an overview of Morocco's trade agreements.

Figure 13.7   Preferential Trade Agreements in the Euro-Mediterranean Region

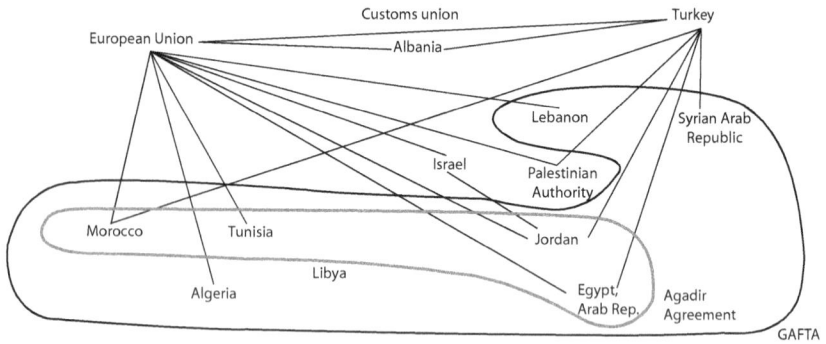

Source: World Trade Organization (WTO), cf. Martín 2010.
Note: GAFTA = Greater Arab Free Trade Area.

In 2004, Morocco signed an FTA with the United States that entered into force in 2006. The FTA foresees the elimination of U.S. duties for most textile and apparel products from Morocco. The provisions of the FTA are, however, less liberal than comparable agreements with other countries in the region (for example, Egypt and Jordan), which partly explains why Morocco is not performing as well as Egypt and Jordan on the U.S. market (USAID 2008).

First, the benefit of duty-free treatment is withheld from most textile and apparel products until 2011, except for some products eligible for duty-free entry under tariff rate quotas. Second, the ROO for duty-free access require that apparel items be assembled from inputs made either in the United States or Morocco, generally from the yarn stage forward ("yarn-forward rule," or triple transformation) (USITC 2004). However, the agreement contains limited allowances for the use of yarns and fabrics from a nonparty under a tariff preference level (TPL), but this TPL is only temporary. It is set at an initial level of 30 million square meters equivalent for the first four years of the FTA and is reduced gradually over the next six years. Hence, by 2016, all trade under the Morocco FTA must adhere to the "yarn-forward rule." There is also a special derogation for the use of cotton from Sub-Saharan African (SSA) countries to promote SSA cotton production and exports. But given the lack of sourcing relations to SSA and of textile capacities to process cotton, this provision has not prompted any tangible results so far (Benabderrazik 2009). In addition, Moroccan suppliers highlight the diverging requirements of U.S. and EU buyers, in particular with regard to order size, and language issues, which are obstacles in increasing orders from the United States (Benabderrazik 2009).

Proactive Policies

Compared to its regional competitor Tunisia, proactive policies emerged relatively late in Morocco and were initially triggered by industry groups, in particular the Moroccan Textile & Clothing Industries Association (AMITH) (Cammett 2007). Key efforts in this regard were the Framework Agreement concluded between the government and AMITH in 2002, as well as the industrial development strategy "Plan Emergence" introduced in 2005 and updated in 2008. The Framework Agreement created a Financial Restructuring Fund (Fonds de Soutien aux Entreprises du Secteur du Textile-Habillement, FORTEX) and a Business Upgrading Fund (Fonds National de la Mise à Niveau, FOMAN) to support firm restructuring and upgrading (technical, equipment, and human resources upgrading); called for a reform of the tax system; and required the state to cover 50 percent of employers' social security costs and a share of the electricity costs (Cammett 2007; WTO 2009). Prior to the Framework Agreement, the Hassan II fund was launched to encourage investment in a number of sectors, including textile and apparel, via a set of measures, in particular by subsidizing up to 50 percent of the land costs and up to 30 percent of the construction costs (AMITH 2006).

An industrial development strategy called "Plan Emergence" was introduced in late 2005 that sought to foster Morocco's position in world markets. The plan outlined a more active role for the government in horizontal issues such as improving the educational system, the transportation infrastructure, and the bureaucratic environment for the private sector (World Bank 2006). At the same time, the plan highlights priority sectors, including textiles and apparel, and calls for the creation of clusters and "picking winners" based on performance criteria and integration in global production networks (Cammett 2007). A key objective of these policies in the apparel sector was to move away from the dependent status as a CMT supplier and to become a full-package supplier, which is reflected in the call for strengthening different skill sets, including design, sales, and input sourcing skills (World Bank 2006). In 2008, the "Pacte nationale pour l'emergence industrielle 2009–2015" was announced, which restates many aims and issues from its predecessor (GoM 2009). With regard to textiles and apparel, the domestic market is additionally highlighted as a potential source of growth alongside export sales. The latter should increasingly focus on fast-fashion products and further develop jeans and sportswear exports to the EU-15, in particular to Italy and Northern Europe, as well as address EU-15 niche markets for lingerie and household textiles (GoM 2009). In the context of the global economic crisis, the government granted tax breaks and state aid to stabilize the sector (ILO 2009; *Just-style* 2011).

With regard to social upgrading, AMITH issued an industrywide code of conduct (CoC) and a related label called "Fibre Citoyenne" (FC) in 2003 as a reaction to increasing demand for labor compliance from global buyers. The label should be awarded to supplier firms that pass a social audit. Contentwise, the CoC/FC covers key labor rights such as the ban on child labor, forced labor, and discrimination, as well as the right to freedom of association. However, it fails to explicitly mention the right to collective bargaining. Global buyers have been interested in the CoC because it could become a substitute for their own social audits if adopted at the industry level. In 2007, the Spanish firm Inditex/Zara signed an International Framework Agreement with the International Textile, Garment & Leather Worker's Federation (ITGLWF), and in this context it committed to source only from FC-certified suppliers in Morocco. This step has promoted the label among Moroccan export firms and global buyers alike (Rossi 2010).

Notes

1. The EU-15 is the 15 member states of the European Union (EU) as of December 31, 2003, before the new member states joined the EU: Austria, Belgium, Denmark, Finland, France, Germany, Greece, Ireland, Italy, Luxembourg, the Netherlands, Portugal, Spain, Sweden, and the United Kingdom.
2. CEDITH (Cercle Euro-Méditerranéen des Dirigeants du Textile et de l'Habillement), News Archive. http://www.cedith.com/spip.php?page=archives.
3. EC (European Commission), DG Trade, Bilateral Relations with Morocco. http://ec.europa.eu/trade/creating-opportunities/bilateral-relations/countries/morocco/.

References

AMITH (Association Marocaine des Industries du Textile et de l'Habillement). 2006. "Guide de l'Investissment." http://www.textile.ma.

Begg, Robert, John Pickles, and Adrian Smith. 2003. "Cutting It: European Integration, Trade Regimes, and the Reconfiguration of Eastern and Central European Apparel Production." *Environment and Planning A* 35 (12): 2191–207.

Benabderrazik, Hassan. 2009. "Moroccan Textile and Apparel Exports: An Evaluation." In *Capitalizing on the Morocco-U.S. Free Trade Agreement: A Road*

Map to Success, ed. Gary Hufbauer and Claire Brunel, 79–112. Washington, DC: Peterson Institute for International Economics.

Business Monitor International. 2009. "Morocco Textile & Clothing Report Q4 2009." Business Monitor International, London.

Cammett, Melanie. 2007. "Business-Government Relations and Industrial Change: The Politics of Upgrading in Morocco and Tunisia." *World Development* 35 (11): 1889–903.

CCC. 2002. "Working Conditions in Morocco." English Summary. http://www.cleanclothes.org/component/content/article/7-resources/1101-working-conditions-in-morocco.

GoM (Government of Morocco). 2007. "Investissements directs étrangers dans le Monde et au Maroc." Ministère des Affaires Économiques et Générales, Rabat. http://www.ccsm.ma/photos/IDE%20dans%20le%20Monde%20et%20au%20Maroc%2016%20oct%2007%5B1%5D.pdf.

———. 2008. "Bilan de la Commission des Investissements 2007." Ministère des Affaires Économiques et Générales, Rabat.

———. 2009. "Revue Interface No. 14." Edition Special, Ministère de l'Industrie, du Commerce et des Nouvelles Technologies. http://www.mcinet.gov.ma/mciweb/BiblioGle/interface/interface14.pdf.

———. 2010. "Revue Interface No. 17." Edition Special, Ministère de l'Industrie, du Commerce et des Nouvelles Technologies. http://www.mcinet.gov.ma/mciweb/BiblioGle/interface/interface17.pdf.

———. 2011. "Rapport Economique et Financier." Ministère de l'Economie et des Finances. http://www.finances.gov.ma/.

ILO (International Labour Organization). 2005. "Promoting Fair Globalization in Textiles and Clothing in a Post-MFA Environment." Report for discussion at the Tripartite Meeting on Promoting Fair Globalization in Textiles and Clothing in a Post-MFA Environment, Geneva.

———. 2006. "Country Brief Morocco." Decent Work Pilot Programme, ILO, Geneva. http://www.ilo.org/public/english/bureau/dwpp/countries/morocco/index.htm.

———. 2009. "Implications of the Global Financial and Economic Crisis on the Textile and Clothing Sector." ILO, Geneva.

ITUC (International Trade Union Confederation). 2009. "Report for the WTO General Council Review of the Trade Policies of Morocco." ITUC, Brussels. http://www.ituc-csi.org/IMG/pdf/WTO_report_Morocco_Final_EN.pdf.

Jassin-O'Rourke Group, L. 2008. "Global Apparel Manufacturing Labor Cost Analysis 2008." Textile and Apparel Manufacturers and Merchants. http://tammonline.com/files/GlobalApparelLaborCostSummary2008.pdf.

Just-style. 2011. "Moroccan Industry Boosts Skills Amid Returning Demand." March 30.

Martín, Iván. 2010. "Economic Integration in the Mediterranean: Beyond the 2010 Free Trade Area." In *Med.2010, Mediterranean Yearbook*, 73–78. Barcelona: Fundación CIDOB/Institut Europeu de la Mediterrània (IEMed).

MEED (Middle East Economic Digest). 2005. "New Investments Offer Hope for Textiles." *MEED*, May 27.

Nordås, Hildegunn K. 2004. "The Global Textile and Clothing Industry post the Agreement on Textiles and Clothing." Discussion Paper 5, World Trade Organization, Geneva.

Pellegrin, Julie. 2001. *The Political Economy of Competitiveness in an Enlarged Europe*. Basingstoke/New York: Palgrave.

Rossi, Arianna. 2010. "Economic and Social Upgrading in Global Production Networks: The Case of the Garment Industry in Morocco." Unpublished dissertation, University of Sussex, U.K.

Stengg, Werner. 2001. "The Textile and Clothing Industry in the EU: A Survey." Enterprise Papers 2-2001, European Commission, the Enterprise Directorate General, Brussels.

Textiles Intelligence. 2009. "Trade and Trade Policy: The EU Clothing Import Markets and Its Ten Largest Suppliers." *Global Apparel Markets*, 3rd quarter.

*Think*Tunisia. 2009. "Textile and Clothing Industries." *Think*Tunisia. http://www .tunisianindustry.nat.tn/thinktunisia/html/en/industrietextile.html.

Tokatli, Nebahat, and Ömür Kizilgün. 2009. "Coping with the Changing Rules of the Game in the Global Textiles and Apparel Industries: Evidence from Turkey and Morocco." *Journal of Economic Geography* 10: 209–29.

USAID (United States Agency for International Development). 2004. "Changing International Trade Rules for Textiles and Apparel." Egyptian Market Access, USAID, Washington, DC.

———. 2007. "Morocco Is in the Race: Investment Trends 2003–2007." USAID, Washington, DC.

———. 2008. "Apparel Exports to the United States: A Comparison of Morocco, Jordan, and Egypt." USAID, Washington, DC.

USITC (United States International Trade Commission). 2004. "U.S.-Moroccan Free Trade Agreement: Potential Economywide and Selected Sectoral Effects." USITC, Washington, DC.

World Bank. 2006. "Morocco, Tunisia, Egypt and Jordan after the End of the Multi-Fiber Agreement: Impact, Challenges and Prospects." Report 35376 MNA, World Bank, Washington, DC.

WTO (World Trade Organization). 2009. "Trade Policy Review—Kingdom of Morocco." Report by the Secretariat, WTO, Geneva.

CHAPTER 14

Pakistan

Overview

- The textile and apparel industries have been the backbone of Pakistan's economy over the last decades. They accounted for around 54 percent of total exports and provided direct employment to around 2.5 million people (with 2 million in the apparel sector) accounting for 38 percent of total manufacturing employment in the 2009/10 fiscal year (PRGMEA 2010). The Textile Policy 2009–14 states that the textile and apparel sector "is the most important manufacturing sector of Pakistan and has the longest production chain—one-fourth of industrial value-added, employment to about 40 percent of industrial labor force, consumes more than 40 percent of banking credit, accounts for 8 percent of the GDP, an average share of about 60 percent in national export, and 12th rank in world textile exports."

- In contrast to many Asian low-cost apparel exporters that are concentrated in apparel production, Pakistan also has significant textile production and a raw material base that partly feeds into apparel exports. Pakistan is the fourth largest of the world's 70 cotton growing countries (behind China, India, and the United States), but given the rising demand of its local textile industry, it has become a net importer of cotton. Pakistan is concentrated in the production of made-up textiles (for example, bed, bath, and kitchen linens), ranking second behind China in terms of export value. As a result, apparel exports only account for around 30 percent of total textile and apparel exports, but they have increased since the late 1990s. In contrast to the textile sector, where male employment dominates, the apparel sector and the upstream cotton sector employ a higher share of women—in the cotton sector predominantly as cotton pickers and in the apparel sector as sewers.

- As in several other low-cost apparel-exporting countries, the Multi-fibre Arrangement (MFA) provided incentives to further the development of existing textile and apparel capacities. However, unlike with most other apparel exporters, the growth of the sector was not driven by quota-hopping foreign investors. Foreign direct investment (FDI) did not have an important role in the sector and was not actively promoted. Moreover, Pakistan generally did not have preferential access to the key end markets of the United States and the European Union (EU).

- The phaseout of the MFA was expected to benefit the textile sector, while the apparel industry was predicted to lose in light of the increased competition. But Pakistani textile and apparel exporters were able to capture larger market shares and increase export values in the first three years post-MFA phaseout. However, in the context of the global economic crisis and the phaseout of the China safeguards at the end of 2008, Pakistan's textile and apparel exports declined.

- Besides these global industry dynamics, "internal" industry-specific factors are important in understanding the sector's development. In particular, until recently Pakistan's historical focus on cotton-based textile and apparel products led production, neglecting the potential of noncotton-based apparel production. Also, apparel exporters are heavily dependent on the U.S. and the EU markets, and export concentration has increased productwise. In addition to these industry dynamics, the sector's trajectory has to be assessed in the broader context of Pakistan's recent history, including its geopolitical position as a front state in the "war on terror" and natural disasters (the earthquake in 2005, flooding in 2010). These events impacted the sector's performance and led to temporary preferential market access and aid inflows.

- The main competitive advantages of Pakistan's apparel and textile sectors are low labor costs, vertically integrated capabilities including raw cotton production, and supportive government policies through upgradation funds. The main challenges are relatively low productivity and product quality; the skill gap with regard to design, fashion, and technological and management skills; the inability to take advantage of scale economies due to the small size of firms and reliance on the cottage industry; export concentration to the United States and to a lesser extent the EU-15;[1] and relatively simple, low-value products. Political instability is also a detriment to the development of the sector, in particular with regard to FDI.

Development of the Apparel Industry

Apparel production and export in Pakistan started relatively late compared to that of other large South Asian apparel exporters. Until the 1980s, Pakistan's exports were dominated by cotton-based textiles, in particular raw cotton, as well as cotton yarn and fabrics. In 1979, textile exports accounted for $991 million and included predominantly raw cotton, yarn, and fabrics, while apparel exports amounted to $79 million. The dominance of textiles was driven by expanding cotton production in light of the agrarian "green revolution" in the 1960s as well as by various government efforts to promote textile capacities during the 1970s and 1980s. The growth of textile capacities influenced the growth of the apparel sector, as apparel exports were largely dependent on locally available cotton yarns and fabrics. This fact is reflected in Pakistan's relatively strong position in knitted apparel based on short cotton and low-count yarn. In contrast, apparel products based on manmade fiber (MMF) accounted for only a small share of production and export (Khan 2003).

The period from the 1990s leading to the MFA phaseout was characterized by an overall increase of textile and apparel exports. However, the performance was uneven for the two sectors, and textile exports dominated, accounting for 70 percent of overall textile and apparel exports in 2004. Textile exports grew rapidly during the first half of the 1990s but stagnated in the second half and in the early 2000s before surging in 2003 and 2004 in light of increased exports to the EU and the United States (Nordås 2005). Pakistani textile exports increased their share in the world market from 2.8 percent in 1995 to 3.1 percent in 2004 (table 14.1). Apparel exports grew more steadily, from $530 million in 1991 to $2,665 million in 2004. Pakistani apparel exports slightly increased their share in the world market, from 0.8 percent in 1995 to 1.1 percent in 2004 (table 14.2). The importance of knitted apparel

Table 14.1 Pakistani Textile Exports to the World

	1995	1998	2001	2004	2005	2006	2007	2008	2009
Total value ($, million)	3,848	3,801	4,267	5,679	5,976	6,699	7,127	6,825	6,252
Annual growth rate (%)	21.6	-3.1	4.0	17.4	5.2	12.1	6.4	-4.2	-8.4
Share of world exports (%)	2.8	2.6	2.9	3.1	3.1	3.4	3.3	3.1	3.6
Specific textile products: Value ($, million)									
Yarn	1,527	1,149	1,302	1,313	1,448	1,702	1,762	1,339	1,401
Woven fabric	1,434	1,496	1,383	1,960	1,917	1,986	2,081	2,082	1,758
Knit fabric	42	26	42	28	34	40	48	57	49
Made-up textiles	657	916	1,281	2,056	2,239	2,630	2,898	3,023	2,811
Floor coverings	171	193	230	280	296	303	304	284	190
Specific textile products: Market share (%)									
Yarn	39.7	30.2	30.5	23.1	24.2	25.4	24.7	19.6	22.4
Woven fabric	37.3	39.4	32.4	34.5	32.1	29.7	29.2	30.5	28.1
Knit fabric	1.1	0.7	1.0	0.5	0.6	0.6	0.7	0.8	0.8
Made-up textiles	17.1	24.1	30.0	36.2	37.5	39.3	40.7	44.3	45.0
Floor coverings	4.4	5.1	5.4	4.9	5.0	4.5	4.3	4.2	3.0

Source: United Nations Commodity Trade Statistics Database (UN Comtrade).
Note: Textiles represented by Standard International Trade Classification Rev. 3 code 65 and 65 subgroups. Exports represented by world imports from Pakistan. Shares do not sum to 100 percent because four-digit SITC subgroups not significant for Pakistan are omitted.

Table 14.2 Pakistani Apparel Exports to the World

	1995	1998	2001	2004	2005	2006	2007	2008	2009
Total value ($, million)	1,279	1,446	1,803	2,665	2,673	3,081	3,352	3,504	3,212
Annual growth rate (%)	15.8	7.6	4.1	16.9	0.3	15.3	8.8	4.5	−8.3
Share of world exports (%)	0.8	0.8	0.9	1.1	1.0	1.1	1.1	1.0	1.1
Woven and knit value ($, million)									
Woven	529	634	790	1,050	1,118	1,274	1,444	1,574	1,482
Knit	749	812	1,013	1,614	1,555	1,806	1,908	1,930	1,730
Woven and knit share of total import value (%)									
Woven	41.4	43.9	43.8	39.4	41.8	41.4	43.1	44.9	46.1
Knit	58.6	56.1	56.2	60.6	58.2	58.6	56.9	55.1	53.9

Source: United Nations Commodity Trade Statistics Database (UN Comtrade).

Note: Exports represented by imports reported by partner countries; apparel classified as Harmonized Commodity Description and Coding System (HS) 1992: Woven: HS62; Knit: HS61; growth rate reflects change from previous year.

products in total apparel exports also increased slightly, from 58.6 percent in 1995 to 60.6 percent in 2004.

The overall importance of the whole textile and apparel industry for Pakistan's economy did not change between the 1990s and the early 2000s—the industry accounted for around 60 percent of exports over the period 1990–2005. However, the significance of individual segments changed. Generally, Pakistan moved away from the export of unprocessed cotton and increased the local value added of its largely cotton-based textile and apparel complex. In particular, exports of made-up textiles, including towels and bed linen, as well as hosiery (mostly knitted under-garments and nightwear) expanded, as well as apparel exports (table 14.3 and figure 14.1).

This trajectory has to be assessed against the background of the chang-ing international trade regime, in particular the Multi-fibre Arrangement/Agreement on Textiles and Clothing (MFA/ATC) and temporary market access improvements granted by the United States and the EU. Pakistani exports were geared toward the quota-restricted markets, and exports were limited by quotas in its key products, including bed linen, towels, and woven trousers (Khan 2003). On aggregate, however, the quotas were less restrictive than those imposed on China and India by the EU and the United States (ILO 2005). Against the background of the "war on terror," Pakistan was granted improved market access for its textile and apparel products to the EU and the United States, which spurred exports during the first half of the 2000s, particularly apparel exports. For instance, Pakistani apparel exports to the EU increased by 25 percent in 2002 after tariffs were slashed for a variety of products and quotas increased under the Generalized System of Preferences (GSP) "special arrangement to combat drug production and trafficking" (EC Delegation to Pakistan 2004). In the case of the United States, only quota extensions were granted.

Besides these trade-related factors, the development of the industry was also driven by specific domestic policies, in particular the Textile Vision 2005. This strategy was jointly elaborated at the turn of the millennium by Pakistan's authorities and industry groups in anticipation of the MFA phaseout. It highlighted major weaknesses of the whole textile-apparel chain, including a narrow export base with a strong dependency on low-value yarns and fabrics as well as the lack of a trained workforce, and laid out a policy framework to meet these challenges (GoP 2000). A shift toward apparel and made-up textiles as well as increased attention to quality across the whole chain was promoted to prepare and reposition

Table 14.3 Pakistani Textile and Apparel Exports by HS Categories, 1995–2009

HS code	Description	Customs value ($, million)					Market share (%)				
		1995	2000	2005	2008	2009	1995	2000	2005	2008	2009
50–63	Total	5,241	6,021	8,866	10,510	9,649	12.5	19.4	25.6	29.2	29.6
63	Made-up textiles	657	1,168	2,267	3,067	2,858	14.3	16.4	17.5	18.4	17.7
61	Knitted apparel	749	985	1,555	1,930	1,712	10.1	12.4	12.6	15.0	15.4
62	Woven apparel	529	747	1,118	1,574	1,482					
5204–07	Cotton yarn	1,405	1,175	1,379	1,265	1,346	26.8	19.5	15.6	12.0	13.9
5208–12	Cotton fabric	953	852	1,260	1,387	1,265	18.2	14.2	14.2	13.2	13.1
54–55	MMF yarn, fabric	538	608	738	749	532	10.3	10.1	8.3	7.1	5.5
5201–03	Raw cotton	145	174	144	127	151	2.8	2.9	1.6	1.2	1.6
60	Knitted fabric	40	30	34	57	49	0.8	0.5	0.4	0.5	0.5

Source: United Nations Commodity Trade Statistics Database (UN Comtrade).

Note: Harmonized Commodity Description and Coding System (HS) 1992: Codes 50–63; exports represented by partner country imports; MMF = man-made fiber.

Figure 14.1   Pakistani Textile and Apparel Exports by HS Categories, 1995–2009

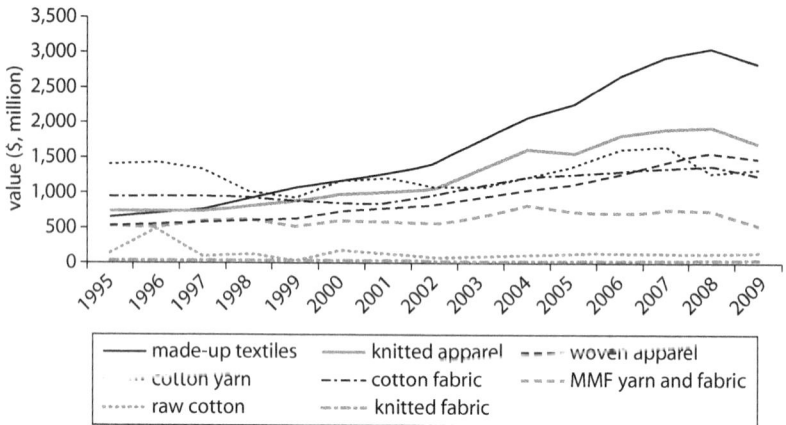

Source: United Nations Commodity Trade Statistics Database (UN comtrade).
Note: Harmonized Commodity Description and Coding System (HS) 1992: Codes 50–63; exports represented by partner country imports; MMF = man-made fiber.

the industry for the MFA phaseout. This focus implied technology upgrading at all stages of textile processing as well as workforce development and increased marketing efforts (Siegmann 2006). Further, tariffs on some inputs and machinery were reduced in the early 2000s for apparel exporters, and special schemes for duty-free imports of input materials were introduced (USITC 2004). However, the implementation of this comprehensive strategy occurred only selectively and focused on the textile sector (Nordås 2005; Siegmann 2006). Upgrading of the skill base and the development of nonmanufacturing capabilities that would allow exporting of higher-value products were lagging (ADB 2004; Siegmann 2006).

Expectations regarding the impact of the MFA phaseout on Pakistan's apparel exports were pessimistic, but it was assumed that textile exports would increase. However, textile as well as apparel exports increased during the first three years after the end of the MFA/ATC (Siegmann 2009). Export performance would have been even better had the EU not imposed an antidumping duty (13.1 percent) on bedwear (ILO 2005) and had the special market access to the EU not ended because of complaints at the World Trade Organization (WTO) by India. However, specific segments were affected differently by the MFA phaseout (figure 14.1). In particular, bed linen—a traditionally strong category—experienced reduced export values, while towels continued a slow but steady growth. The export of yarn and fabrics decreased, with higher shares of the local production feeding into exports of finished apparel items. Apparel exports continued to expand post-MFA. Only in 2005 did exports of knitted apparel decrease slightly, while woven apparel exports continued to expand continuously until 2008.

In the U.S. market, apparel exports from Pakistan increased in value terms post-MFA and extended their market share from 1.7 percent in 2004 to 2.1 percent in 2008 (table 14.4). However, average unit values of apparel exports in the U.S. market decreased considerably post-MFA. The drop was particularly pronounced in the more important knitwear segment, while woven apparel registered an increase in average unit values after the quota. In the EU-15 market, Pakistan's apparel exports decreased by 15 percent in value terms in 2005; in 2006, they increased again by 15 percent (table 14.5). Unit prices in the EU-15 remained relatively stable, with a slight decrease in knitted apparel and an increase in woven apparel similar to the United States. According to the government's own assessment, the Pakistani apparel industry was not able to take advantage of the quota-free environment, where other factors (for example, quality or fast turnaround) became more important in global sourcing. Instead, the industry has remained entrapped in a low-value, low-productivity vicious cycle in which low labor costs remain the focus of doing business (GoP 2008a).

To counter heightened competition post-MFA, the Pakistani government deployed several measures to stabilize the industry (IFPRI 2008). In particular, a 6 percent "Research & Development" cash subsidy was introduced in 2005 for apparel exporters that in the following years was extended to the textile industry. Its stated aims were to enhance

Table 14.4   U.S. Apparel Imports from Pakistan

	1996	1998	2001	2004	2005	2006	2007	2008	2009
Total value ($, million)	567	683	935	1,147	1,273	1,427	1,514	1,508	1,319
Annual growth rate (%)	—	9.5	0.6	12.1	11.0	12.1	6.0	−0.3	−12.6
Share of all U.S. apparel imports (%)	1.5	1.4	1.6	1.7	1.8	1.9	2.0	2.1	2.1
Woven and Knit Value ($, million)									
Woven	167	224	300	290	345	394	445	460	385
Knit	401	459	635	857	928	1,033	1,069	1,049	934
Woven and Knit Share of Total Import Value (%)									
Woven	29.4	32.8	32.1	25.3	27.1	27.6	29.4	30.5	29.2
Knit	70.6	67.2	67.9	74.7	72.9	72.4	70.6	69.5	70.8

Source: U.S. International Trade Commission (USITC).
Note: Apparel imports represented by Harmonized Commodity Description and Coding System (HS) Codes 61 and 62; General Customs Value; growth rate reflects change from previous year. — = not available.

Table 14.5   EU-15 Apparel Imports from Pakistan

	1995	1998	2001	2004	2005	2006	2007	2008	2009
Total value (€, million)	434	492	646	906	770	889	890	865	872
Total quantity (kg, million)	58	60	75	115	102	117	116	115	114
Share of all EU-15 apparel imports (%)	0.9	0.7	0.8	1.1	0.9	0.9	0.9	0.8	0.9
Annual growth rate (%) of									
Value	—	2.6	8.6	13.1	−15.0	15.4	0.2	−2.9	0.9
Quantity	—	1.2	10.3	12.0	−11.0	14.2	−0.8	−0.7	−1.2
Woven and knit value (€, million)									
Woven	226	264	392	466	447	502	503	505	530
Knit	208	228	253	440	323	387	387	360	343
Woven and knit share (%)									
Woven	52.1	53.7	60.8	51.4	58.1	56.4	56.6	58.4	60.7
Knit	47.9	46.3	39.2	48.6	41.9	43.6	43.4	41.6	39.3
Woven and knit quantity (kg, million)									
Woven	29	31	42	57	56	60	61	61	61
Knit	29	29	34	58	46	57	54	54	52

Source: Eurostat.

Note: Apparel imports represented by Harmonized Commodity Description and Coding System (HS) Codes 61 and 62; growth rate reflects change from previous year. kg = kilogram; — = not available. EU-15 = the 15 member states of the European Union (EU) as of December 31, 2003, before the new member states joined the EU: Austria, Belgium, Denmark, Finland, France, Germany, Greece, Ireland, Italy, Luxembourg, the Netherlands, Portugal, Spain, Sweden, and the United Kingdom.

operations through product development, innovation, human resource development, and technological upgradation. Roughly PRs 30 billion was spent under this scheme until 2008; however, it failed to "induce technological upgradation" (GoP 2008b). This failure can be related to a dramatic change in the domestic environment in 2007–08. In particular, the cost of financing increased significantly, with interest rates going up to 35 percent, cotton prices surging, and inflation rising. According to industry representatives, the government's support was vital to help the industry fulfill its export commitments against rising financing, utility, and raw material costs (*Just-style* 2008).

As in most apparel-exporting countries, Pakistani exports were also negatively affected by the slump in global demand in the context of the global economic crisis. Textile exports declined by 8.4 percent between 2008 and 2009; apparel exports, by 8.3 percent (tables 14.1 and 14.2). Despite this absolute loss in value terms, Pakistan slightly extended its share in world markets, to 3.6 percent in textiles and 1.1 percent in apparel, in 2009. Exports were hampered not only by deteriorating opportunities in traditional export markets in 2008–09 but also by rising input costs. World cotton prices have gone up since 2008, and China in particular has increasingly demanded cotton yarn from Pakistan. In this context, domestic cotton producers and yarn spinners have preferred to export their products rather than selling to domestic producers of fabric and apparel. Given the dependence on cotton as a major input, this situation has negatively affected Pakistani textile and apparel firms. To ensure availability of adequate inputs for textile and apparel exporters, the government allowed duty-free imports of cotton yarn. Along the same lines, export quotas on cotton yarn were introduced in 2009, and duty drawbacks as well as special export refinancing facilities were installed (*PTJ* 2010a).

Despite the harsh conditions for apparel exporters in 2010, Pakistan seems to be among the winners. Notwithstanding terrorist bombings, a catastrophic flood, and unreliable energy, the textile and apparel industries increased their exports in 2010. Textile mills and apparel fabrics kept supplies running to the ports during the August floods, and cotton supplies were not hit too badly (*Just-style* 2010a). A number of factors have contributed to this performance: a large supply of domestically grown raw cotton, vertically integrated textile and apparel capacities, low-cost labor, large investments in state-of-the-art machinery, a depreciating currency, and government incentives (Sekhar 2010).

Structure of the Apparel Industry

Types of Firms

Pakistan is one of the few countries (besides China, India, and Turkey) that have a significant raw material base and vertical manufacturing activities. Its textile and apparel complex remains strongly centered on the textile segment, although the apparel industry has increased in importance over the past decade. The textile and apparel industry has been modernized with the help of the government and, hence, it possesses modern spinning, weaving, and lately, finishing technologies. The country has 1,221 cotton ginning factories, mainly located in Pakistan's cotton-growing areas of Punjab and Sindh. Pakistan has a total number of 521 textile units with 11.3 million spindles and roughly 200,000 rotors, resulting in the third-largest spinning capacity in Asia. Around 50 percent of spindle capacity is less than seven years old (*Just-style* 2010b). In the weaving sector, Pakistan has around 360,000 small power looms operating around major cities like Faisalabad, Karachi, and Lahore (table 14.6).

Pakistan's apparel sector remains characterized by a significant share of cottage industry. Industry estimates state that around 70–80 percent

Table 14.6   Number of Firms and Capacities in the Pakistani Textile and Apparel Sector

Sector	Number of Units	Size
Ginning	1,221	5,488 saws
Spinning	521 (50 composite, 471 spinning)	11,266 million spindles 196,000 rotors
Weaving	150	27,900 shuttleless looms
	500	360,000 power looms
Finishing	750	4,600 million square meters
Apparel (woven)	800	160,000 industrial sewing machines
	5,000	450,000 domestic sewing machines
Terry Towels	800	700 shuttleless looms 10,000 conventional looms
Knitwear	1,200	18,000 knitting machines 10,000 flat knitting machines 12,000 circular knitting machines
Canvas	—	2,000 looms 300,000 Industrial looms

Source: Textile Commissioner's Organization.
Note: Figures under the column "Size" represent estimates. — = not available.

of production units consist of small units in workers' homes. The rest is largely made up of large, integrated firms that are generally involved in the knit segment (SMEDA 2002; cf. USITC 2004). The knitted segment is characterized by vertically integrated units that produce fabric primarily based on indigenous cotton yarns and process them into knitted apparels (GoP 2008a). In contrast, firms focused on woven apparel are small to medium firms, and many of them operate in the cottage industry, having between 50 and 300 machines each (*Just-style* 2010b). Most apparel firms are in or around the major cities Karachi, Lahore, and Faisalabad, as well as in Multan, Gujranwala, and Sialkot. According to industry sources, the knitwear sector is seen as the area with the best growth potential, with a projected growth rate of 12 percent a year over the next five years (*Just-style* 2010b).

FDI has not played an important role in Pakistan's textile and apparel industries thus far. This situation is in line with the generally low level of FDI in Pakistan, which only picked up in the mid-2000s, with most of it going to the financial and telecom services and natural resource sectors (Hamdani 2009). According to statistics of the State Bank of Pakistan, however, FDI inflows to the textile and apparel sectors increased until 2007; afterward they have decreased (table 14.7). Most of the FDI went

Table 14.7 FDI Inflows to Pakistani Textile and Apparel Industry

	2000–01	2001–02	2002–03	2003–04	2004–05	2005–06	2006–07	2007–08	2008–09	2009–10
Textiles and apparel ($, million)	4.6	18.5	26.1	35.4	39.3	47.0	59.4	30.1	36.9	27.8
Total FDI ($, million)	322.4	484.7	798.0	949.4	1,523.9	3,521.0	5,139.6	5,409.8	3,719.9	2,150.8
T&A share of total (%)	1.4	3.8	3.3	3.7	2.6	1.3	1.2	0.6	1.0	1.3

Source: Board of Investment, Government of Pakistan.

Note: FDI = foreign direct investment; T&A = textiles and apparel.

419

to the textile sector. The role of foreign investors in the apparel sector is estimated to be less than 2 percent (Hamdani 2009). In recent years, the government has adopted several measures to attract FDI to help modernize the economy. However, despite Pakistan having an overall liberal and friendly FDI regime, the insecurities, in particular related to the "war on terror," seem to outweigh the certified ease of doing business.[2] With regard to FDI in the textile and apparel sector, China has been particularly targeted for investments (*Just-style* 2010c).

Given its key role in the economy, the Pakistani textile and apparel sector has received considerable attention via various policy initiatives. Many of these policies were geared toward technologically upgrading the sector. In the context of the Textile Vision 2005 strategy devised in 1999–2000 and subsequent policy initiatives, Pakistan invested substantially in its textile and apparel industries (ADB 2004). According to the Textile Commissioner's Office, the cumulative investment over the 10-year period 1999–2009 amounted to roughly $7.5 billion, with the spinning sector receiving more than 50 percent of the total while apparel received a relatively small share of barely 7 percent (table 14.8).

End Markets

Pakistan's apparel exports are highly concentrated with regard to end markets. In 2009, 87 percent of apparel exports went to the United States and the EU-15, with 43.6 percent of exports going to the United States and 43.4 percent to the EU-15 (table 14.9). Canada, Turkey, and Poland ranked behind, with market shares of 2.3 percent, 1.5 percent, and 1.3 percent, respectively. The concentration toward the United States and the EU-15, however, has decreased; those two markets accounted for 92.6 percent in 2000. The importance of the United States decreased from 58.4 percent in 2000 to 43.6 percent in 2009, whereas the share of

Table 14.8   Total Cumulative Investment in Pakistani Textile and Apparel Sector, 1999–2009

Sector	Share of total investment (%)
Spinning	50.20
Weaving	15.23
Textile processing	17.08
Apparel (knitwear and garments)	7.02
Made-ups	4.71
Synthetic textiles	5.76

Source: Textile Commissioner's Organization; cf. PRGMEA 2010.

Table 14.9 Top Five Pakistani Apparel Export Markets, 1995, 2000, 2005, 2008, and 2009

Country/region	Customs value ($, million)					Market share (%)				
	1995	2000	2005	2008	2009	1995	2000	2005	2008	2009
World	**1,279**	**1,731**	**2,673**	**3,504**	**3,212**					
United States	598	1,010	1,377	1,609	1,402	46.8	58.4	51.5	45.9	43.6
EU-15	588	593	1,088	1,463	1,393	46.0	34.3	40.7	41.8	43.4
Canada	46	50	57	69	72	3.6	2.9	2.1	2.0	2.3
Turkey	n.a.	n.a.	n.a.	51	48	n.a.	n.a.	n.a.	1.5	1.5
Poland	n.a.	n.a.	n.a.	39	41	n.a.	n.a.	n.a.	1.1	1.3
United Arab Emirates	n.a.	n.a.	18	n.a.	n.a.	n.a.	n.a.	0.7	n.a.	n.a.
Saudi Arabia	13	10	14	n.a.	n.a.	1.0	0.6	0.5	n.a.	n.a.
Australia	n.a.	10	n.a.	n.a.	n.a.	n.a.	0.6	n.a.	n.a.	n.a.
Norway	5	n.a.	n.a.	n.a.	n.a.	0.4	n.a.	n.a.	n.a.	n.a.
Top five share	**1,250**	**1,674**	**2,553**	**3,232**	**2,956**	**97.8**	**96.7**	**95.5**	**92.2**	**92.0**

Source: United Nations Commodity Trade Statistics Database (UN Comtrade).

Note: Harmonized Commodity Description and Coding System (HS) 1992: Codes 61 and 62; exports represented by country imports from Pakistan; n.a. = not applicable (indicates country not in top 5 for given year). EU-15 = the 15 member states of the European Union (EU) as of December 31, 2003, before the new member states joined the EU: Austria, Belgium, Denmark, Finland, France, Germany, Greece, Ireland, Italy, Luxembourg, the Netherlands, Portugal, Spain, Sweden, and the United Kingdom.

the EU-15 increased from 34.3 percent to 43.4 percent in the same period. The rest of the world increased its share from 4.5 percent to 10.8 percent of total apparel exports (figure 14.2). Textile exports are less concentrated. In 2009, Pakistan's main textile export markets were also the EU-15 and the United States, which together accounted for 53.9 percent of total textile exports (table 14.10). China; Hong Kong SAR, China; and Turkey are also important export markets. While the market shares of traditional Asian export destinations, in particular Hong Kong SAR, China, and the Republic of Korea, have gone down, demand from China, and Turkey has increased since 2005 (figure 14.3).

Export Products

With regard to textile and apparel exports, made-up textiles constituted the majority of exports, accounting for 29.6 percent of total textile and apparel exports in 2009, followed by knitted apparel (17.7 percent), woven apparel (15.4 percent), cotton yarn (13.9 percent), and cotton fabric (13.1 percent) (table 14.3). With regard to apparel exports, knitted products accounted for roughly 54 percent of Pakistan's apparel exports in 2009. Its share peaked with 60.6 percent in 2004 and since then has

Figure 14.2   Top Four Pakistani Apparel Export Markets, 2000 and 2009
% market share

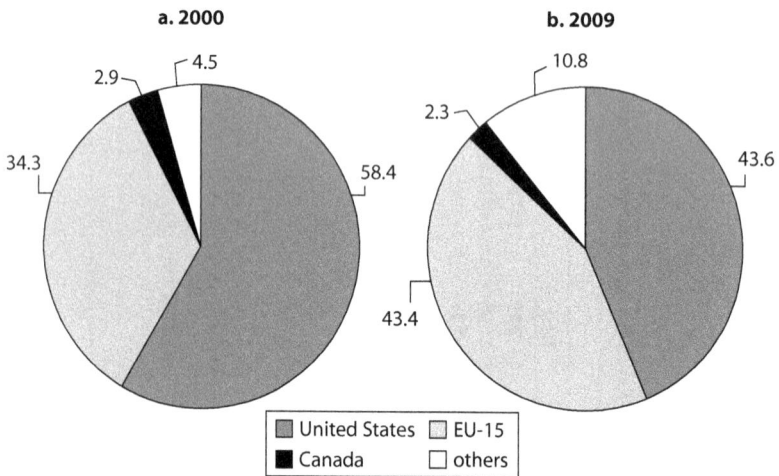

Source: United Nations Commodity Trade Statistics Database (UN Comtrade),
Note: Harmonized Commodity Description and Coding System (HS) 1992: Codes 61 and 62; exports represent partners' imports from Pakistan. EU-15 = the 15 member states of the European Union (EU) as of December 31, 2003, before the new member states joined the EU: Austria, Belgium, Denmark, Finland, France, Germany, Greece, Ireland, Italy, Luxembourg, the Netherlands, Portugal, Spain, Sweden, and the United Kingdom.

Table 14.10 Top 10 Pakistani Textile Export Markets, 1995, 2000, 2005, 2008, and 2009

Country/economy region	Customs value ($, million)					Market share (%)				
	1995	2000	2005	2008	2009	1995	2000	2005	2008	2009
World	**3,848**	**4,102**	**5,976**	**6,825**	**6,252**					
EU-15	1,039	1,013	1,545	2,189	1,939	27.0	24.7	25.9	32.1	31.0
United States	434	981	1,704	1,619	1,433	11.3	23.9	28.5	23.7	22.9
China	167	408	574	598	907	4.3	9.9	9.6	8.8	14.5
Turkey	145	56	261	371	367	3.8	1.4	4.4	5.4	5.9
Hong Kong SAR, China	559	489	492	338	273	14.5	11.9	8.2	5.0	4.4
Korea, Rep.	225	204	123	87	102	5.8	5.0	2.1	1.3	1.6
Sri Lanka	n.a.	n.a.	n.a.	102	95	n.a.	n.a.	n.a.	1.5	1.5
Canada	88	100	101	88	81	2.3	2.4	1.7	1.3	1.3
South Africa	n.a.	n.a.	n.a.	85	68	n.a.	n.a.	n.a.	1.2	1.1
Australia	80	83	n.a.	79	66	2.1	2.0	n.a.	1.2	1.1
Bangladesh	134	n.a.	87	n.a.	n.a.	3.5	n.a.	1.5	n.a.	n.a.
United Arab Emirates	n.a.	86	86	n.a.	n.a.	n.a.	2.1	1.4	n.a.	n.a.
Japan	472	152	75	n.a.	n.a.	12.3	3.7	1.3	n.a.	n.a.
Top 10 share	**3,343**	**3,572**	**5,048**	**5,555**	**5,332**	**86.9**	**87.1**	**84.5**	**81.4**	**85.3**

Source: United Nations Commodity Trade Statistics Database (UN Comtrade).

Note: Standard International Trade Classification Rev. 3; exports represented by countries' imports from Pakistan; n.a. = not applicable (indicates country not in top 10 in given year). EU-15 = the 15 member states of the European Union (EU) as of December 31, 2003, before the new member states joined the EU: Austria, Belgium, Denmark, Finland, France, Germany, Greece, Ireland, Italy, Luxembourg, the Netherlands, Portugal, Spain, Sweden, and the United Kingdom.

Figure 14.3   Top 10 Pakistani Textile Export Markets, 2000 and 2009
% market share

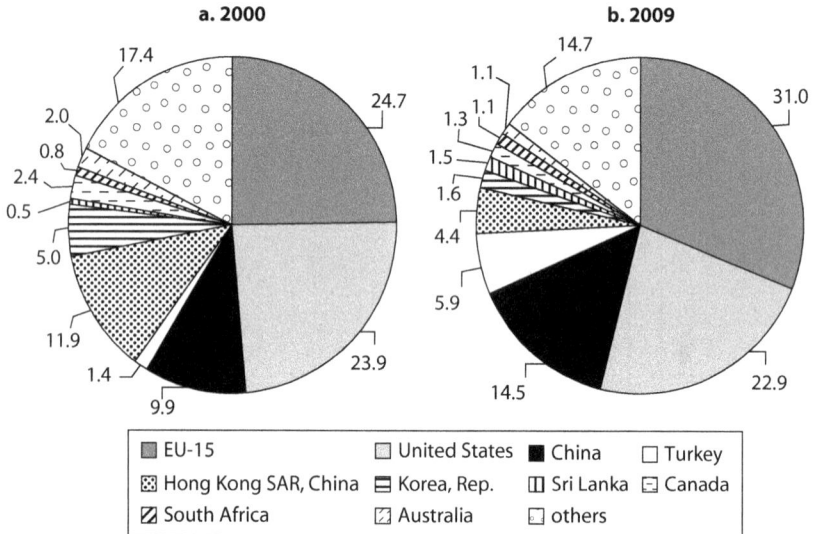

a. 2000

b. 2009

EU-15	United States	■ China	□ Turkey
Hong Kong SAR, China	Korea, Rep.	Sri Lanka	Canada
South Africa	Australia	others	

Source: United Nations Commodity Trade Statistics Database (UN comtrade).
Note: Standard International Trade Classification 65, Rev. 3; exports represented by partner country imports from Pakistan. Countries included are the top 10 textile export destinations in 2009. EU-15 = the 15 member states of the European Union (EU) as of December 31, 2003, before the new member states joined the EU: Austria, Belgium, Denmark, Finland, France, Germany, Greece, Ireland, Italy, Luxembourg, the Netherlands, Portugal, Spain, Sweden, and the United Kingdom.

decreased consistently. In value terms, knit and woven apparel have continued to expand after 2005. However, woven exports grew stronger and, hence, increased in relative importance (table 14.11). Pakistan's apparel exports, woven and knitted, are highly concentrated in a few products. The top 5 product categories accounted for 63 percent of total U.S. apparel exports in 2009 and for 60 percent in the EU-15 market; the top 10 product categories, for 83 percent and 71.5 percent, respectively (tables 14.11 and 14.12). Product concentration levels to the United States and the EU-15 have increased since 2000.

The top apparel export product categories to the United States and the EU-15 are overlapping—8 of the top 10 products appear in the U.S. and the EU-15 list. The most important products in both markets are trousers, sweaters and sweatshirts, T-shirts, shirts, and socks. In the U.S. market, knits account for 7 of the top 10 products, and in the EU-15 market, knits represent 8 of the top 10 imported products. However, despite the majority of categories representing knitted apparel, the two largest categories in the EU-15 market are actually woven. In the EU-15

Table 14.11 Top 10 U.S. Apparel Imports from Pakistan, 1996, 2000, 2005, 2008, and 2009

HS code	Product	Customs value ($, million)					Market share (%)				
		1996	2000	2005	2008	2009	1996	2000	2005	2008	2009
Total		**567**	**929**	**1,273**	**1,508**	**1,319**					
611020	Sweatshirts	98	284	322	245	225	17.3	30.6	25.3	16.2	17.1
620342	Trousers	22	71	114	221	167	3.9	7.6	8.9	14.7	12.6
610910	T-Shirts	25	35	76	170	152	4.3	3.7	6.0	11.3	11.5
610510	Shirts	211	172	192	200	148	37.2	18.6	15.1	13.2	11.2
611595a	Socks	n.a.	n.a.	76	138	140	n.a.	n.a.	6.0	9.2	10.6
620462	Trousers	9	17	64	104	94	1.5	1.9	5.0	6.9	7.2
610120	Jackets	n.a.	n.a.	51	83	84	n.a.	n.a.	4.0	5.5	6.4
621142	Garments	16	25	26	36	36	2.8	2.7	2.0	2.4	2.7
610342	Trousers	n.a.	n.a.	n.a.	n.a.	29	n.a.	n.a.	n.a.	n.a.	2.2
610462	Trousers	n.a.	n.a.	22	29	20	n.a.	n.a.	1.7	1.9	1.5
610220	Jackets	n.a.	n.a.	24	22	n.a.	n.a.	n.a.	1.9	1.4	n.a.
620520	Shirts	27	34	n.a.	n.a.	n.a.	4.7	3.7	n.a.	n.a.	n.a.
620343	Trousers	n.a.	20	n.a.	n.a.	n.a.	n.a.	2.2	n.a.	n.a.	n.a.
620891	Underwear	n.a.	18	n.a.	n.a.	n.a.	n.a.	1.9	n.a.	n.a.	n.a.
620192	Jackets	n.a.	15	n.a.	n.a.	n.a.	n.a.	1.6	n.a.	n.a.	n.a.
610610	Shirts	17	n.a.	n.a.	n.a.	n.a.	3.0	n.a.	n.a.	n.a.	n.a.
620630	Shirts	13	n.a.	n.a.	n.a.	n.a.	2.2	n.a.	n.a.	n.a.	n.a.
620442	Dresses	9	n.a.	n.a.	n.a.	n.a.	1.7	n.a.	n.a.	n.a.	n.a.
Top 10 share		**447**	**691**	**967**	**1,248**	**1,095**	**78.7**	**74.4**	**75.9**	**82.7**	**83.0**

Source: U.S. International Trade Commission (USITC).

Note: U.S. General Customs Value. Apparel classified as Harmonized Commodity Description and Coding System (HS) 1992: Woven: HS62; Knit: HS61. n.a. = not applicable (indicates product not in the top 10 in given year).

a. HS code changed from 611592 to 611595 in 2007.

Table 14.12 Top 10 EU-15 Apparel Imports from Pakistan, 1998, 2000, 2005, 2008, and 2009

HS code	Product	Customs value (€, million)					Market share (%)				
		1998	2000	2005	2008	2009	1998	2000	2005	2008	2009
Total		**492**	**595**	**770**	**865**	**872**					
620342	Trousers	102	130	177	265	286	20.8	21.9	22.9	30.7	32.8
620462	Trousers	41	68	114	94	106	8.4	11.4	14.8	10.9	12.1
611020	Sweatshirts	28	29	47	47	50	5.8	4.8	6.1	5.5	5.7
610910	T-Shirts	28	40	64	48	46	5.7	6.8	8.3	5.5	5.3
611595a	Socks NESOI	16	21	34	35	39	3.2	3.6	4.5	4.0	4.5
610510	Shirts	21	18	20	33	29	4.3	3.0	2.5	3.8	3.4
611610	Gloves	n.a.	n.a.	18	27	22	n.a.	n.a.	2.4	3.2	2.5
610462	Trousers	34	27	14	n.a.	16	6.8	4.6	1.8	n.a.	1.9
611030	Sweatshirts	n.a.	n.a.	n.a.	n.a.	16	n.a.	n.a.	n.a.	n.a.	1.8
610342	Trousers	n.a.	n.a.	n.a.	16	14	n.a.	n.a.	n.a.	1.9	1.6
611692	Gloves NESOI	17	19	12	16	n.a.	3.5	3.2	1.5	1.9	n.a.
620791	Undershirts and bathrobes	n.a.	n.a.	18	16	n.a.	n.a.	n.a.	2.3	1.9	n.a.
610831	Nightdresses and pajamas	17	15	n.a.	n.a.	n.a.	3.4	2.5	n.a.	n.a.	n.a.
620891	Undershirts and bathrobes	12	14	n.a.	n.a.	n.a.	2.4	2.3	n.a.	n.a.	n.a.
Top 10 share		**318**	**381**	**516**	**599**	**624**	**64.5**	**64.0**	**67.0**	**69.2**	**71.5**

Source: Eurostat.

Note: Apparel classified as Harmonized Commodity Description and Coding System (HS) 1992: Woven: HS62; Knit: HS61. NESOI = not elsewhere specified or indicated; n.a. = not applicable (indicates product not in the top 10 in given year). EU-15 = the 15 member states of the European Union (EU) as of December 31, 2003, before the new member states joined the EU: Austria, Belgium, Denmark, Finland, France, Germany, Greece, Ireland, Italy, Luxembourg, the Netherlands, Portugal, Spain, Sweden, and the United Kingdom.
a. HS code changed from 611592 to 611595 in 2007.

market, cotton woven trousers for men and women are particularly important, accounting for 44.9 percent of total exports in 2009 and representing the top two apparel export products. In the United States, men's woven trousers are significantly more important than women's, and sweaters and sweatshirts are the most important imported product by value. In the U.S. market, cotton products dominate; all of the top 10 imports are cotton. In the EU-15 market, the situation is slightly more diversified, with only 8 of the top 10 products made from cotton.

In terms of average unit price, Pakistan's apparel exports are among the cheapest, pointing to the dominance of low-value exports (PRGMEA 2010). An older ADB study (2004) suggests that Pakistan was specialized in the low-value segment of the industry. According to data from the Pakistan Readymade Garment Manufacturer and Exporter Association (PRGMEA), average unit values for woven apparel have increased since 2004, while average unit values of knitted apparel have experienced a decline. Table 14.13 shows that for the U.S. and EU-15 markets, unit prices of apparel exports have on average slightly decreased post-MFA.

Table 14.14 presents Pakistan's top textile export categories. In general, exports increased from 1995 through 2008 but decreased in 2009.

Table 14.13   Unit Values of Pakistani Apparel Exports to the EU-15 and the United States

	EU-15 unit values (€/kg)			U.S. unit values ($/dozen)		
Year	Knit	Woven	Total	Knit	Woven	Total
1996	7.40	7.90	7.70	48.10	33.90	42.80
1997	7.80	8.40	8.10	50.80	37.60	45.10
1998	7.80	8.60	8.20	48.90	38.60	44.90
1999	7.50	8.10	7.80	47.40	35.80	43.00
2000	7.90	9.40	8.70	43.90	34.00	40.00
2001	7.60	9.40	8.60	48.10	29.20	39.60
2002	7.90	8.40	8.20	41.90	29.70	37.30
2003	7.30	8.20	7.80	39.70	29.60	36.60
2004	7.60	8.10	7.90	38.30	31.50	36.30
2005	7.00	8.00	7.50	35.30	33.80	34.90
2006	6.80	8.40	7.60	31.60	36.80	33.00
2007	7.10	8.20	7.70	31.50	40.80	34.00
2008	6.60	8.30	7.50	29.80	41.10	32.90
2009	6.50	8.60	7.70	28.90	39.50	31.60

Sources: Eurostat, volumes reported in kilograms; U.S. International Trade Commission (USITC), only includes products in which the first unit of quantity is volumes reported in dozens.
Note: EU-15 = the 15 member states of the European Union (EU) as of December 31, 2003, before the new member states joined the EU: Austria, Belgium, Denmark, Finland, France, Germany, Greece, Ireland, Italy, Luxembourg, the Netherlands, Portugal, Spain, Sweden, and the United Kingdom.

Table 14.14 Top Three Pakistani Textile Export Products

Category and SITC code	Customs value ($, million)					Market share (%)				
	1995	2000	2005	2008	2009	1995	2000	2005	2008	2009
Total textiles: 65	3,848	4,102	5,976	6,825	6,252					
Cotton yarn: 651.3	1,428	1,174	1,373	1,263	1,345	37.1	28.6	23.0	18.5	21.5
Cotton woven fabric: 652	983	866	1,278	1,398	1,274	25.5	21.1	21.4	20.5	20.4
Household linens: 658.4	516	850	1,721	2,462	2,312	13.4	20.7	28.8	36.1	37.0
Top three share	**2,926**	**2,890**	**4,372**	**5,123**	**4,932**	**76.0**	**70.4**	**73.2**	**75.1**	**78.9**

Source: United Nations Commodity Trade Statistics Database (UN Comtrade).

Note: Standard International Trade Classification Rev. 3, codes 65, 651.3, 652, and 658.4; exports represent partners' imports from Pakistan.

The decline in 2009 appears to have largely come from a dip in exports of cotton woven fabric. Export growth has largely stemmed from home textile product exports and, to a lesser extent, from cotton woven fabrics. Cotton yarn exports have generally decreased or remained steady. Pakistan has had a major success story in denim fabric exports in recent years, and it was the only exporting country in the top 10 in 2009 that did not suffer because of the recession (increased by 54.1 percent). Over the 2005–09 time frame, Pakistan's denim fabric exports rose by an average of 24.4 percent per year, which is the highest growth rate among the top 10 exporters. During the 2005–09 time frame, two of the major export markets for denim with cotton content 85 percent or more were Turkey (33 percent) and Bangladesh (23 percent).

Pakistan's largest textile export category in 2009 was bed, bath, and kitchen (household) linens. This category has increased significantly over the past 15 years. In 1995, it represented only 13.4 percent of all textile exports, but the share increased to 37.0 percent in 2009. Figure 14.4 shows the top four items within this category. The most significant shift has been the increase in market share of woven cotton bed linens.

Backward Linkages

Pakistan has a significant raw material base and is one of the few countries worldwide that has a vertically integrated sector across all stages of cotton-textile-apparel production. Pakistan is the world's fourth-largest producer and third-largest consumer of cotton. Thus, backward linkages

Figure 14.4   Pakistani Made-up Textile Exports, 1995, 2000, 2005, and 2009
% market share

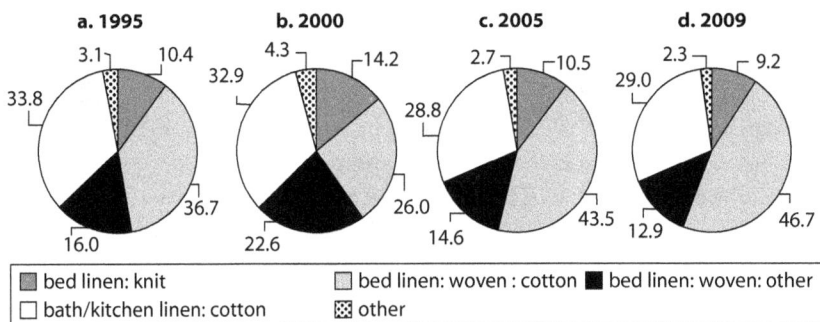

Source: United Nations Commodity Trade Statistics Database (UN Comtrade).
Note: Standard International Trade Classification Rev. 3, codes 65841, 65842, 65843, and 65847; exports represent partners' imports from Pakistan.

from the apparel sector to the textile and even fiber sector are well developed. In the textile sector there has been a trend toward modernization through the adoption of new technology and the installation of advanced production facilities. This trend can be seen in increased imports of machinery for woven fabric, knit fabric, and yarn production (Brocklehurst 2009). However, fiber and textile production is strongly dominated by cotton-based products, and the Pakistani apparel industry remains focused on locally produced cotton textiles. Pakistan's MMF manufacturing base is narrow, and the increasing demand for MMF is largely met via imported textiles. Furthermore, the quality of Pakistan's cotton is inferior, as it has a high share of waste. Given Pakistan's focus on short and medium cotton staples, it has to import long and extra-long staples, which are a key input for higher-value products (GoP 2008a).

Given the recent rise in cotton prices and increasing exports of cotton and cotton yarn, imports of cotton textiles have also increased, particularly from India. However, total textile imports are substantially smaller than textile exports—in 2009, textile exports accounted for $6,247 million and imports for $1,867 million. Historically, textile imports largely came from Asian countries. In 2009, China accounted for 57.5 percent, India for 23.1 percent, Afghanistan for 3.5 percent, Korea for 3.1 percent, and Thailand for 2.4 percent of total textile imports (table 14.15). While the prospects for regional integration within the South Asian Association for Regional Cooperation (SAARC) are uncertain, China's increasing role as a source for textile imports is remarkable. One reason is related to the strengthening of Pakistan-China relationships, including the conclusion of a free trade agreement (FTA) and increasing Chinese investment in Pakistan.

Employment

Given the importance of informal cottage production in Pakistan's textile and apparel industries, assessing employment levels is difficult. According to the PRMGEA, in 2009, around 2.5 million people worked in the textile and apparel sectors and around 2 million people worked in the apparel sector, making it the most important employment-generating sector in Pakistan (PRMGEA 2010).[3] Older studies from the mid-2000s report figures between 1.4 and 2.3 million workers for both the textile and apparel industries (Nordås 2005). The only more disaggregated data found are from 2000 and show total textile and apparel employment of more than 1.3 million with apparel accounting for 54 percent of the total (table 14.16).

Table 14.15   Top Five Textile Suppliers to Pakistan, 1995, 2000, 2005, 2008, and 2009

Country/ economy/ region	Customs value ($, million)					Market share (%)				
	1995	2000	2005	2008	2009	1995	2000	2005	2008	2009
World	142	188	772	1,444	1,867					
China	n.a.	21	426	854	1,073	n.a.	11.2	55.2	59.1	57.5
India	n.a.	n.a.	n.a.	129	431	n.a.	n.a.	n.a.	8.9	23.1
Afghanistan	n.a.	n.a.	n.a.	136	65	n.a.	n.a.	n.a.	9.4	3.5
Korea, Rep.	26	48	59	59	59	18.5	25.6	7.7	4.1	3.1
Thailand	n.a.	n.a.	51	37	45	n.a.	n.a.	6.6	2.6	2.4
EU-15	24	21	32	n.a.	n.a.	17.0	11.0	4.1	n.a.	n.a.
Indonesia	n.a.	n.a.	29	n.a.	n.a.	n.a.	n.a.	3.7	n.a.	n.a.
Japan	26	15	n.a.	n.a.	n.a.	18.5	7.7	n.a.	n.a.	n.a.
United Arab Emirates	n.a.	12	n.a.	n.a.	n.a.	n.a.	6.6	n.a.	n.a.	n.a.
Singapore	12	n.a.	n.a.	n.a.	n.a.	8.4	n.a.	n.a.	n.a.	n.a.
Hong Kong SAR, China	10	n.a.	n.a.	n.a.	n.a.	7.1	n.a.	n.a.	n.a.	n.a.
Top five share	**99**	**117**	**597**	**1,215**	**1,673**	**69.5**	**62.0**	**77.3**	**84.2**	**89.6**

Source: United Nations Commodity Trade Statistics Database (UN Comtrade).
Note: Standard International Trade Classification Rev. 3; imports represented by countries' exports to Pakistan; n.a. = not applicable (indicates country not in top five in given year). EU-15 = the 15 member states of the European Union (EU) as of December 31, 2003, before the new member states joined the EU: Austria, Belgium, Denmark, Finland, France, Germany, Greece, Ireland, Italy, Luxembourg, the Netherlands, Portugal, Spain, Sweden, and the United Kingdom.

Table 14.16   Employment in Pakistani Textile and Apparel Sector, 2000

	Employment	Share (%)
Apparel	734,805	54
Weaving	294,213	22
Spinning	201,152	15
Processing and finishing	61,206	5
Knitting	47,221	4
Ginning	10,000	1
Total	**1,348,597**	**100**

Source: GoP 2000.

In contrast to most other textile and apparel exporters, the share of females is relatively modest. According to the manufacturing census in 2005, the share of female workers in the textile and apparel sectors stood at 2.5 percent and 10.5 percent, respectively. However, since the census does not cover significant shares of the sector (see note 3), the actual share is likely to be higher. A 2008 survey commissioned by the United Nations Development Programme (UNDP) Pakistan analyzed female employment in the apparel sector and estimated that around 20 percent of the apparel workforce are women (UNDP 2008).[4] A recent survey by the Pakistan Institute of Labor Education and Research reports that around 30 percent of the apparel workforce are women (Sandhu 2011). The relatively low share of female workers can be explained by sociocultural constraints for women to join work in the apparel or any other industry. Main issues include lack of training opportunities, transportation, male-dominated house culture, poverty, and cultural constraints (Sandhu 2011). Despite this comparatively small share, the apparel sector is a crucial sector for women workers because it is one of the few opportunities for paid—but not necessarily formal—employment (Siegmann 2006; FBS 2009). The share of women working in the textile and apparel sectors has increased since the 1990s; this increase is related to the increasing role of apparel and home-textile exports, which are based on female employment. Siegmann (2009) suggests that female apparel workers have particularly increased post-MFA as a way to enhance the sector's competitiveness. At the same time, the author suggests that given the current gender and skill composition, industrial upgrading may imply a loss in unskilled jobs, which would—everything else being equal—imply a loss of female jobs (Siegmann 2009).

Absolute labor costs are comparatively low in Pakistan, and there is a large supply of workers. With regard to average labor costs per hour, Pakistan ranks third, with a rate of $0.37, after Bangladesh and Cambodia in a comparison with regional competitor countries in 2008. The minimum wage was increased to PRs 7,000 or $82 per month in 2010. Low wages are accompanied by relatively low levels of labor productivity. A critical reason for the relatively low productivity in Pakistan's apparel and textile sectors is lack of skilled workers and managers. With regard to workers, there is high demand for skilled sewing operators, but, because of limited supply, most firms hire unskilled workers and train them within the firm. Table 14.17 gives an estimate of losses due to skill-technology mismatches, underlining that the losses range between 23 and 30 percent. A key problem is the relatively high share in the cottage industry and the increasing use of contract workers (Amjad 2005).

However, the skill gap is more severe with regard to technical, design and fashion, and management skills. A comparison of competitor countries suggests that while operator skills are also poor in other countries, at

Table 14.17   Pakistani Losses Due to Skill-Technology Mismatch

Type of loss	Percent
Cut-to-shipment losses	2–3
Knitting losses	2
Dyeing and finishing losses	4–7
Cutting and stitching losses	15–18
Total	**23–30**

Sources: Textile Commissioner's Organization; cf. IFPRI 2008.

Table 14.18   Cross-country Evaluation of Apparel Human Resources

	Pakistan	India	China	Bangladesh	Sri Lanka
Industry weakness					
Operator skills	1–2	1–2	3	1	4
Market management and shop floor	1–2	2–3	3–4	2	4
Management organization	1–2	3	4	2–3	4
Education training					
Primary	1–2	3	1–2	1	2
Secondary	1–2	3	1–2	1–2	3
Operator-vocational training	1–2	2–3	2	1	2–3
Market management and shop floor	1–2	2–3	2–3	1	3
University/college	–	+	+	+	+

Sources: Textile Commissioner's Organization; cf. IFPRI 2008. Interview with a leading garment manufacture: International Textile Manufacturers Federation (ITMF). 1 = very poor, 2 = poor, 3 = average, 4 = good, 5 = very good, – = generally negative, + = generally positive.

the management level, skills are superior in other countries (table 14.18). Against this background, training institutes and special credit faculties were set up. Also, the establishment of a new fashion school was announced, and consultants for technology and brand development, social compliance, and other requirements of the international market can be paid from a technology upgradation fund, which includes PRs 3.47 billion (IFPRI 2008). The success of these programs is, however, still to be seen.

In the context of heightened competition post-MFA, the Pakistani government relaxed labor legislation to reduce labor costs. One measure was the extension of daily working hours from 8 to 12 (Siegmann 2006). Although the minimum wage was set to PRs 7,000 or $82 per month starting from July 2010, implementation has been limited, and most factories pay less than the minimum wage. Also, annual wage increments are often ignored (*Just-style* 2010b). Preliminary findings from research commissioned by the International Labour Organization (ILO) highlight that short-term or temporary contracts are widely used, particularly for women workers, to avoid additional costs for the employer (for example, maternity leave, transportation, and day care facilities) (ILO 2010). Although the Pakistani trade union movement has experienced some consolidation over the past years, it remains fragmented along ethnic, regional, and linguistic lines. Organizing efforts are limited, and the unions lack financial resources (Ghayur 2009).

Trade Regulations and Proactive Policies

Preferential Market Access

Pakistan enjoys preferential market access to the EU market via the EU's GSP scheme. In addition to the normal GSP status, Pakistan was granted special preferences under the "special arrangement to combat drug production and trafficking" against the background of the terrorist attacks in the United States of September 11, 2001 (EC Delegation to Pakistan 2004). Hence, between 2002 and 2005, Pakistan was granted duty-free access to the EU for 95 percent of the tariff lines under the scheme (Siegmann 2006). Further, Pakistan signed an agreement with the EU in 2001 for improved market access whereby the EU increased quotas for textiles and apparel by 15 percent (Nordås 2005). Against this background, exports, especially bed linens, fared very well. However, in March 2004, the EU imposed a 13.1 percent antidumping duty on bed linens, which impacted negatively on Pakistan's export performance (Fakhar 2005). Moreover, Pakistan lost its preferential status justified by the "special arrangement" in 2005 in light of pressures at the WTO level when India successfully challenged part of the EU's GSP system. Since then, Pakistan has received special preferences under the normal GSP, which grants duty-free access in 60 percent of tariff lines (CARIS 2008). The EU recognizes SAARC as a regional grouping for the purpose of determining eligibility for GSP treatment (Saheed 2009).This grouping permits a manufacturer to use textiles produced in one or more SAARC countries subject to certain conditions on value addition. This situation may present an opportunity for Pakistan to expand textile exports to nearby countries. Most recently, as a response to the massive floods in the summer of 2010, the EU proposed to temporarily suspend tariffs on key export products from Pakistan to help Pakistan overcome the natural disaster.

Pakistan is also included in the U.S. GSP system. However, most key export products from the textile and apparel sectors are excluded, so the effects are limited (Fakhar 2005). In 2004, the GSP coverage of textile and apparel products was only about 1 percent of total textile and apparel exports from Pakistan to the United States (Hufbauer and Burki 2006). Recent legislation was proposed to establish special economic zones—so-called Reconstruction Opportunity Zones (ROZs)—along the Pakistan-Afghanistan border, which should promote investment in manufacturing industries and thereby support economic development and social stability. The proposed legislation is modeled after the Qualified Industrial Zones established in the Arab Republic of Egypt, Israel, and Jordan, where goods processed in these zones enjoy duty-free access to the U.S. market. The proposal was criticized for its limited range of products (excluding Pakistani key export products such as cotton trousers and shorts and knit tops) and its geographic coverage (limited to remote tribal or border areas, which lack infrastructure and business stability) (Elliott 2010; USA-ITA 2010).

The most important agreement at the regional level for Pakistan is the South Asian Free Trade Agreement (SAFTA), which was signed in 2004 by all members of SAARC, except for Afghanistan. The signatories— Bangladesh, Bhutan, India, the Maldives, Nepal, Pakistan, and Sri Lanka— agreed to phase out tariffs on practically all products, with the exception of services, by the end of 2016 (CARIS 2008). However, so far there is little sign of progress in implementing SAFTA. In particular, long-standing political issues between India and Pakistan impede the potential gains derived from regional integration. Against this background, bilateral agreements (also between SAFTA countries) have become more important (Weerakoon 2010). Over the past years Pakistan has signed several FTAs, including one with Sri Lanka (2005), China (2006), and Malaysia (2007) (CARIS 2008). In particular, the FTA with China is seen as an important step to strengthen Sino-Pakistani economic relationships, which used to be largely centered on military cooperation (CFR 2010). For the textile and apparel sectors, the duty-free access of a variety of Pakistani products in the Chinese market could help to diversify export markets.

Proactive Policies

At the national level, institutions and policies at several levels have been crucial in the development of Pakistan's textile and apparel sectors. The most important national actors include the government and active industry associations such as PRGMEA and groups that represent the

Figure 14.5   Overview of Pakistani Textile and Apparel Economic Planning Process

Planning	Fiscal	Financing	Investment	Import	Export	Labor	Miscellaneous
Five-year plans	Import duty	Credit	Incentives	Import facilities price	Bilateral agreement	Education	R&D
Annual plans	Production	WB	Tax concessions	Price stabilization	WTO	Training	Quality control
Strategy	Income tax	ADB	Industrial zones	Antidumping	ATC	Skill development	Productivity
Targets	Misc. tax	Special credits	Infrastructure		Export promotion	Welfare	Standardization
Local demand	Exemptions	Foreign private loans	Location				Conflict resolution
Export demand	Sector specific	Suppliers credits repatriatable investment nonrepatriatable investment	Facilitation/ promotion development of support industry, machinery, synthetic raw material, services, packaging, trips, and trims		Cotton policy market development		Price control and price support

Sources: Textile Commissioner's Organization; cf. IFPRI 2008.
Note: WB = World Bank; ADB = Asian Development Bank; ATC = Agreement on Textiles and Clothing;
WTO = World Trade Organization; R&D = research and development.

spinning industry. The Pakistani government has its own textile ministry, which includes the Textile Commissioner's Organization (TCO). Figure 14.5 provides an overview of the various aspects of the policy-planning process in Pakistan's textile and apparel sectors. The key role is assumed by the TCO, which ensures the implementation of policies. But Pakistani policy making is quite complex, and implementation can be very slow.

In anticipation of the MFA phaseout, a comprehensive policy framework—Textile Vision 2005—was started in 1999–2000. To meet the challenges of the MFA phaseout and to boost competitiveness, a number of measures, including technology and skill upgrading, were proposed to shift toward higher-value textile and apparel products. However, general implementation was slow and selective, with an emphasis on textile investments in equipment and technology. In contrast, upgrading the human skill base and developing nonmanufacturing capabilities necessary to export higher-value products lagged. Hence, the expected targets set by the government and industry participants were not met.

In 2008, a new policy framework—Textile Policy 2009–14—was presented that includes the introduction of a technology upgradation scheme to further increase investment in textile machinery and technology as well as to establish training and research facilities. The policy offers 10-year tax holidays for foreign investors in textile machinery and cotton warehousing. According to industry sources, the policy specifically targets Chinese investment in industrial parks dedicated to textiles and apparel in Faisalabad, Karachi, and Lahore (*Just-style* 2010c). Further, a 6 percent research and development cash subsidy for the apparel industry was introduced and later extended to the textile industry (GoP 2008b, 2010).

The government of Pakistan also signed a Memorandum of Understanding (MOU) with Korea for the establishment of a Garment Technology Training Centre (GTTC) in Karachi. Under the MOU, the Korea International Co-operation Agency (KOICA) will provide $1.5 million to the government of Pakistan for the establishment of the GTTC, plus necessary equipment, machinery, expertise, and technical guidance. GTTC will provide vocational training in the five areas of garment technology, knitwear technology, apparel marketing, line supervisor, and sewing machine operators. The Federal Minister for Textile stated that skill development and capacity building were a vital component of the five-year Textile Policy 2009–14 (Abdullah 2009).

The Pakistani government also provided preferential short- and long-term financing, which became increasingly important when interest rates and inflation started to increase significantly in 2006–07.

Notes

1. The EU-15 is the 15 member states of the European Union (EU) as of December 31, 2003, before the new member states joined the EU: Austria, Belgium, Denmark, Finland, France, Germany, Greece, Ireland, Italy, Luxembourg, the Netherlands, Portugal, Spain, Sweden, and the United Kingdom.

2. According to the World Bank's *Doing Business* Report (2010). Pakistan is ranked number 83 out of 183 countries and praises itself as topping the list of countries in the South Asian region (Government of Pakistan, Board of Investment, http://investinpakistan.pk/EaseDB.htm).

3. Figures collected via the manufacturing census suggest lower employment levels. However, the census covers only larger units (more than 10 employees). In addition, the informal sector, which plays an important role in the Pakistan economy, is also not included. Along the same lines, the reliance on daily and contract labor also complicates collection of accurate data.

4. Female employment is very high in the cotton sector, particularly in cotton picking, where women and girls represent the large majority of the around 2 million workers (Siegmann 2009).

References

Abdullah, Ahmed. 2009. "Pakistan: South Korea Invests in Garment Technology Centre." *Just-style*, October 15.

ADB (Asian Development Bank). 2004. "Industrial Competitiveness. The Challenge for Pakistan." ADB Institute-Pakistan Resident Mission Seminar Paper, Islamabad.

Amjad, Rashid. 2005. "Skills and Competitiveness: Can Pakistan Break Out of the Low-Level Skills Trap?" *Pakistan Development Review* 44 (4): 387–409.

Brocklehurst, G. 2009. "Trends in U.S. Textile and Clothing Imports." *Textile Outlook International* 144: 122–97.

CARIS (Centre for the Analysis of Regional Integration at Sussex). 2008. "The Impact of Trade Policies on Pakistan's Preferential Access to the European Union." Report for the Economic Commission, Centre for the Analysis of Regional Integration at Sussex, Department of Economics, University of Sussex, U.K.

CFR (Council on Foreign Relations). 2010. "China-Pakistan Relations, Backgrounder." Council on Foreign Relations. http://www.cfr.org/china/china-pakistan-relations/p10070.

EC Delegation to Pakistan. 2004. "European Union–Pakistan Trade Relations." http://www.delpak.cec.eu.int/eupaktrade/New-EU-Pak-Trade-May-04.htm.

Elliott, Kimberly Ann. 2010. "Stimulating Pakistani Exports and Job Creation. Special Zones Won't Help Nearly as Much as Cutting Tariffs across the Board." Centre for Global Development, Washington, DC.

Fakhar, Huma. 2005. "The Political Economy of the EU GSP Scheme: Implications for Pakistan." In *South Asian Yearbook of Trade and Development 2005*, Centre for Trade and Development (Centad), 395–412. New Delhi: Centad.

FBS (Federal Bureau of Statistics). 2009. "Compendium on Gender Statistics in Pakistan 2009." Federal Bureau of Statistics, Islamabad.

Ghayur, Sabur. 2009. "Evolution of the Industrial Relations System in Pakistan." ILO Working Paper, International labour Organization, New Delhi.

GoP (Government of Pakistan). 2000. "Textile Vision 2005." Government of Pakistan, Islamabad.

———. 2008a. "Textiles and Clothing Trade 2002–07." Research, Development, and Advisory Cell, Ministry of Textiles, Government of Pakistan, Islamabad.

———. 2008b. "Investment in Imported Textile Machinery." Research, Development, and Advisory Cell, Ministry of Textiles, Government of Pakistan, Islamabad.

————. 2010. "Economic Survey—Chapter 3: Manufacturing." Government of Pakistan, Islamabad.

Hamdani, Khalil. 2009. "Foreign Direct Investment Prospects for Pakistan." Powerpoint presentation, Pakistan Institute of Development Economics, Islamabad.

Hisam, Zeenat. 2010. "Organising for Labour Rights. Women Workers in Textile/ Readymade Garments Sector in Pakistan and Bangladesh." Report published by Pakistan Institute of Labour Education and Research and South Asia Alliance for Poverty Eradication (SAAPE), Karachi.

Hufbauer, Gary Clyde, and Shahid Javed Burki. 2006. "Sustaining Reform with a US-Pakistan Free Trade Agreement." Peterson Institute for International Economics, Washington, DC.

IFPRI (International Food Policy Research Institute). 2008. "Cotton-Textile-Apparel Sectors of Pakistan, Situations and Challenges Faced." Discussion Paper 00800, IFPRI, Washington, DC.

ILO (International Labour Organization). 2005. "Promoting Fair Globalization in Textiles and Clothing in a Post-MFA Environment." Report for discussion at the Tripartite Meeting on Promoting Fair Globalization in Textiles and Clothing in a Post-MFA Environment, ILO, Geneva.

————. 2010."Women Continue to Face Discrimination in the World of Work." Press Release ILO Islamabad Office, December 6. http://www.ilo.org/islam abad/info/public/pr/lang--en/WCMS_150228/index.htm. Accessed February 21, 2011.

Just-style. 2008. "Pakistan: Extends R&D Subsidy for Apparel Exports." August 8.

————. 2010a. "Uncertainty the Latest Threat to Pakistan Makers." September 7.

————. 2010b. "Pakistan Snapshot: Apparel Trade Overview." August 20.

————. 2010c. "Construction to Begin at Karachi Garment City." July 14.

Khan, Zubair. 2003. "Impact of Post-ATC Environment on Pakistan's Textile Trade." United Nations Development Programme (UNDP) Asia Pacific Regional Initiative on Trade, Economic Governance and Human Development (Asia Trade Initiative), New York.

Nordås, Hildegunn. K. 2005. "Labour Implications of the Textiles and Clothing Quota Phase-out." Working Paper 224, January, International Labour Organization, Geneva.

PRGMEA (Pakistan Readymade Garment Manufacturer and Exporter Association). 2010. "Pakistan's Garment Sector. An Overview." PowerPoint presentation, Pakistan Readymade Garment Manufacturer and Exporter Association. http://www.prgmea.org.

PTJ (Pakistan Textile Journal). 2010a. "Pak-China Economic and Trade Relations." September.

————. 2010b. "Pakistan: The Third Largest Spinner Country in Asia." February.

Saheed, Hassen. 2009. "Prospects for the Textile and Garment Industry in Pakistan." *Textile Outlook International* 142: 55–102.

Sandhu, Kamran Yousef. 2011. "Challenges to Pakistan's Value Added Industry." Presentation made at the Third International Conference on Textile and Clothing, Institute of Textile and Industrial Science, Lahore.

Sekhar, Uday. 2010. "Denim Fabric: Global Trade and Leading Players." *Textile Outlook International* 146: 32–55.

Siegmann, Karin Astrid. 2006. "Pakistan's Textile Sector and the EU." *South Asian Journal* 13 (September).

————. 2009. "The Trade and Gender Interface: A Perspective from Pakistan." Sustainable Development Policy Institute, Islamabad.

SMEDA (Small and Medium Development Authority). 2002. "Apparel Sector Brief." Small and Medium Development Authority, Government of Pakistan, Lahore.

UNDP (United Nations Development Programme). 2008. "Current Status and Prospects of Female Employment in the Apparel Industry Pakistan." Baseline study submitted to the Gen-Prom Pakistan, United Nations Development Programme, New York.

USA-ITA (U.S. Association of Importers of Textiles and Apparel). 2010. White Paper on the Need for Meaningful Pakistan-Afghan ROZs." http://www.usaita.com/pdf/82_20100113120548.pdf.

USITC (U.S. International Trade Commission). 2004. "Textiles and Apparel: Assessment of the Competitiveness of Certain Foreign Supplier to the U.S. Market." Publication 3671, USITC, Washington, DC.

Weerakoon, Dushni. 2010. "SAFTA—Current Status and Prospects." In *Promoting Economic Cooperation in South Asia: Beyond SAFTA*, ed. Sadiq Ahmed, Saman Kelegama, and Ejaz Ghani, 71–88. Washington, DC: World Bank.

World Bank. 2010. *Doing Business 2010: Reforming through Difficult Times.* Washington, DC: World Bank.

CHAPTER 15

Sri Lanka

Overview

• The export-oriented apparel sector has been the main source of growth of exports and formal employment for the past three decades in Sri Lanka. The industry contributes about 40 percent of total industrial production and directly employs around 280,000 people, which accounts for around 14 percent of the industrial labor force and 20.8 percent of the manufacturing labor force. Indirectly, more than 1.2 million people are dependent on the apparel sector.

• The Multi-fibre Arrangement (MFA), liberal trade and investment policies, and government support were crucial in starting apparel exporting in the late 1970s. The start of the sector was driven by foreign direct investment (FDI), as Hong Kong SAR, China, and other East Asian manufacturers, motivated by MFA quota hopping and Sri Lanka's liberal trade and investment regime, began investing in and sourcing from Sri Lanka. Local entrepreneurs followed and established apparel firms motivated by markets guaranteed by quotas, low investment requirements, and initial technology and know-how transfer from foreign investors.

• Although expectations were gloomy for Sri Lanka's apparel exports after the MFA/phaseout, the sector increased export value after 2004. However, in the context of the global economic crisis and the phaseout of the China safeguards at the end of 2008, Sri Lanka's apparel exports declined in 2009.

• In the context of the MFA phaseout, Sri Lanka's apparel industry has experienced significant upgrading on various dimensions, including production processes, product composition, functions performed, and to a lesser extent supply chain upgrading. Competitive strengths include a comparatively long experience in the sector, visionary local entrepreneurs and a highly skilled workforce, broader capabilities in addition to cut-make-trim (CMT), increasing forward linkages to product development, design and marketing, concentration on higher-value export products (in particular lingerie), and strategic relationships with certain buyers. The collaborative institutional environment, in particular the formation of the Joint Apparel Association Forum (JAAF) and the five-year strategy, has been instrumental in achieving these upgrading processes. Main challenges include relatively high and increasing labor costs, labor shortages, long lead times, and limited backward linkages, as well as concentration with regard to the end market of the United States and the EU-15.[1]

Development of the Apparel Industry

Prior to 1977, a few locally owned firms produced simple low-end apparel for the domestic market, while textile was a state-controlled import substitution industry that provided fabric inputs for local apparel firms (Kelegama and Wijayasiri 2004; Kelegama 2009). In 1977, Sri Lanka was the first South Asian country that liberalized its economy. MFA quota hopping together with the liberal trade and investment regime attracted East Asian apparel exporters, in particular from Hong Kong SAR, China, who relocated apparel production to Sri Lanka. Besides East Asian manufacturers, who were the majority of foreign investors, European investors also came because of rising production costs in their home countries and because they were attracted by the liberal trade and investment regime (Kelegama and Wijayasiri 2004). Government support was also crucial in the development of the apparel export sector. The government was very supportive of the sector, in particular through the Board of Investors

(BOI),[2] and offered incentives for investors, including duty-free imports of inputs and capital goods, off-shore financing facilities, tax holidays and other tax concessions, freedom to repatriate profits, and a "one-stop shop." These support programs not only attracted foreign investment but were also supportive of the development of local apparel firms. Local entrepreneurs increasingly established apparel firms, motivated by markets guaranteed by quotas, low investment requirements, and initial technology and know-how transfer from foreign investors.

From the late 1970s until 2004, Sri Lanka's apparel exports increased significantly. Import data from Sri Lanka's trading partners show an increase from $1,680 million in 1995 to $2,973 million in 2004 (table 15.1). In the 1980s and 1990s, the industry recorded double-digit growth rates per year. However, in the late 1990s, export growth decelerated, and exports even declined in 2001 and 2002. This decline was related to lower demand in developed countries but more importantly to bomb attacks at the Colombo International Airport in July 2001, which triggered the imposition of war-risk insurance charges (Kelegama and Wijayasiri 2004). The reduction in orders and escalating insurance costs hit the industry severely, and as a result several small and medium enterprises (SMEs) closed in the early 2000s. The share of Sri Lanka in global apparel exports increased from 1.1 percent in 1995 to 1.2 percent in

Table 15.1   Sri Lankan Apparel Exports to the World

	1995	1998	2001	2004	2005	2006	2007	2008	2009
Total value ($, million)	1,680	2,172	2,442	2,973	3,082	3,364	3,595	3,809	3,532
Annual rowth rate (%)	—	6.3	−3.0	15.6	3.7	9.1	6.9	6.0	−7.3
Share of world exports (%)	1.1	1.2	1.2	1.2	1.1	1.2	1.1	1.1	1.2
Woven and knit value ($, million)									
Woven	1,213	1,491	1,587	1,826	1,782	1,796	1,813	1,893	1,761
Knit	467	680	855	1,147	1,300	1,567	1,782	1,916	1,771
Woven and knit share of total import value (%)									
Woven	72.2	68.7	65.0	61.4	57.8	53.4	50.4	49.7	49.8
Knit	27.8	31.3	35.0	38.6	42.2	46.6	49.6	50.3	50.2

Source: United Nations Commodity Trade Statistics Database (UN Comtrade).
Note: Imports reported by partner countries. Classification: Harmonized Commodity Description and Coding System (HS) 1992: Woven Apparel: HS62; Knitted Apparel: HS61. Growth rate reflects change from previous year.
— = not available.

2001 and remained steady at 1.2 percent in 2004. The overall export figures mask a change in the composition of Sri Lanka's apparel exports. In 1995, woven exports accounted for 72 percent of total apparel exports, but the share of woven decreased consistently, reaching 61 percent in 2004. Regarding the export market, there occurred a minor shift toward the EU-15 market from 2001 to 2004; however, the U.S. market still remained the foremost export destination, accounting for 55 percent of total exports in 2004 (figure 15.1).

The number of apparel firms increased from around 142 in 1990 to their highest level of above 1,000 in 2001 (table 15.2). From then on, the number of firms has declined, reaching around 830 in 2003. Employment grew from around 100,000 in 1990 to around 340,000 in 2003. Sri Lanka's apparel sector accounted for more than 33 percent (one-third) of manufacturing employment, over 50 percent of total exports, and over two-thirds of industrial exports in 2004.

Expectations on the impact of the MFA phaseout for Sri Lanka's apparel exports had been pessimistic. It was expected that exports would decrease by half and that 40 percent of firms would close in 2005 (Kelegama 2006, 2009). However, although exports developed quite badly in the first half of 2005, for the whole year 2005, apparel exports grew by 3.7 percent. For the period 2004 to 2008, apparel exports as a share of total exports remained above 40 percent, and the share of

Figure 15.1   Sri Lankan Apparel Exports to the EU-15 and the United States

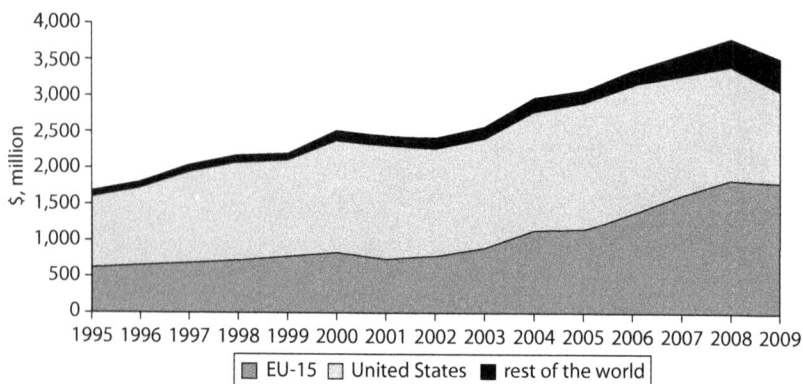

Source: United Nations Commodity Trade Statistics Database (UN Comtrade).
Note: Imports reported by partner countries. EU-15 = the 15 member states of the European Union (EU) as of December 31, 2003, before the new member states joined the EU: Austria, Belgium, Denmark, Finland, France, Germany, Greece, Ireland, Italy, Luxembourg, the Netherlands, Portugal, Spain, Sweden, and the United Kingdom.

**Table 15.2   Employment and Number of Factories
in Sri Lankan Apparel Sector, 1990–2009**

Year	Employment	Factories
1990	102,000	142
1995	250,000	678
1998	227,000	891
1999	280,000	891
2001	338,704	1,061
2003	340,367	830
2005	273,600	733
2007	290,000	—
2008	270,000	350
2009	280,000	300

Sources: Kelegama 2005a, 2005b, 2006, 2009; Tait 2008; *Just-style* 2009;
Saheed 2010.
Note: Employment values for 1990–98 reflect textiles and apparel.
— = not available.

Sri Lanka in global apparel exports remained quite stable at around
1.1–1.2 percent (table 15.1). Although export levels grew quite stably
after 2004, the composition of apparel exports has changed considerably
since the MFA. With regard to end markets, over the whole period 2004
to 2008, EU-15 exports increased in importance relative to U.S. exports
(tables 15.3 and 15.4). In 2004, the U.S. market was still more important,
accounting for around 55 percent of exports, and the European Union
(EU) market accounted for 39 percent (other markets for 6 percent). In
2008, the EU accounted for nearly 50 percent and the United States for
41 percent; other markets accounted for 9 percent. The importance of
the EU market increased because the EU granted Sri Lanka Generalized
System of Preferences (GSP) + status in 2005. An additional reason for
the shift to EU markets was that EU buyers generally demand more services and more involvement in the sourcing and design process, are more
prepared to pay higher prices for good quality, and are generally more
relationship driven in their sourcing policies (Gibbon 2003). These characteristics suited the apparel sector in Sri Lanka, in particular large firms
that upgraded their production processes and capabilities. With regard to
products, the export increase post-MFA was based on knit exports.

The impact of the global economic crisis that started in 2008 but
evolved particularly in 2009 has to be assessed together with the phaseout of the China safeguards at the end of 2008. In 2008, Sri Lanka's
apparel exports increased by 6.0 percent, but in 2009 they decreased by
7.3 percent. The decrease was based on U.S. exports, which decreased by

Table 15.3   U.S. Apparel Imports from Sri Lanka

	1996	1998	2001	2004	2005	2006	2007	2008	2009
Total value ($, million)	1,002	1,300	1,486	1,553	1,653	1,687	1,584	1,490	1,220
Growth rate (%)	—	8.5	2.0	8.5	6.4	2.0	−6.1	−5.9	−18.1
Share of all U.S. apparel imports (%)	2.6	2.6	2.5	2.3	2.3	2.3	2.1	2.0	1.9
Woven and knit value ($, million)									
Woven	769	992	1,070	1,102	1,063	974	878	816	692
Knit	233	308	416	451	590	713	706	674	529
Woven and knit share of total import value (%)									
Woven	76.8	76.3	72.0	70.9	64.3	57.8	55.4	54.8	56.7
Knit	23.2	23.7	28.0	29.1	35.7	42.2	44.6	45.2	43.3

Source: U.S. International Trade Commission (USITC).
Note: Apparel represented by Harmonized Commodity Description and Coding System (HS) Codes 61 and 62; General Customs Value; growth rate reflects change from previous year. — = not available.

Table 15.4   EU-15 Apparel Imports from Sri Lanka

	1995	1998	2001	2004	2005	2006	2007	2008	2009
Total value (€, million)	424	583	763	806	795	968	1,034	1,113	1,143
Total quantity (kg, million)	29	34	39	59	51	59	64	70	67
Share of all EU-15 apparel imports (%)	0.8	0.9	0.9	0.9	0.9	1.0	1.0	1.1	1.2
Annual growth rate (%)									
Value	—	9.0	−8.2	16.6	−1.4	21.7	6.9	7.7	2.7
Quantity	—	4.1	−5.6	19.7	−12.2	15.1	8.7	8.5	−4.0
Woven and knit value (€, million)									
Woven	260	310	383	387	382	462	465	500	511
Knit	164	273	380	419	412	506	569	613	632
Woven and knit share (%)									
Woven	61.4	53.2	50.2	48.0	48.1	47.7	45.0	44.9	44.7
Knit	38.6	46.8	49.8	52.0	51.9	52.3	55.0	55.1	55.3
Woven and knit quantity (kg, million)									
Woven	15	16	18	26	23	26	28	31	31
Knit	14	18	21	32	28	33	37	39	36

Source: Eurostat.
Note: Apparel represented by Harmonized Commodity Description and Coding System (HS) Codes 61 and 62; growth rate reflects change from previous year. kg = kilogram, EU-15 = the 15 member states of the European Union (EU) as of December 31, 2003, before the new member states joined the EU: Austria, Belgium, Denmark, Finland, France, Germany, Greece, Ireland, Italy, Luxembourg, the Netherlands, Portugal, Spain, Sweden, and the United Kingdom. — = not available.

18 percent in 2009 (and already by 6 percent in 2007 and 2008); EU-15 exports increased by 3 percent in 2009 (tables 15.3 and 15.4). In May 2010, the Joint Apparel Association Forum (JAAF) cut its export targets for the next five years up to 2015 by $1 billion (from $5 billion to $4 billion) due to the continuing poor export climate. JAAF data show that over the first three months of 2010, export earnings dropped by about 15 percent compared to 2009.

Given this trend, the industry is expecting 2010 export earnings to be lower than 2009 earnings (*Just-style* 2010a). Another urgent challenge is that the EU suspended GSP+ benefits for Sri Lanka in August 2010 due to significant shortcomings in the implementation of three UN human rights conventions, as the GSP+ requires fulfilling criteria with regard to sustainable development and good governance. The average duty on apparel imports to the EU is 12.5 percent, but Sri Lanka still qualifies for the 20 percent duty reduction provided by the general GSP scheme. Thus, the duty rate would increase to 9.6 percent due to the loss of GSP+ preference. Of the $1.8 billion apparel exports to the EU, around 75 percent qualify for GSP+, which accounts for around one-third of total apparel exports. Thus, as costs increased by roughly 10 percent, this share accounts for around $100 million. This rate has had an effect, in particular on the still remaining lower end of production, which is motivated by GSP+ preferences. As of November 2010, large manufacturers such as MAS and Brandix had not reported a decline in orders due to the resulting increase in duty rates. In a few cases of very price-sensitive products, firms report moving some production to Bangladesh operations (*Just-style* 2010d).

The composition of the sector also changed significantly post-MFA, with the number of small firms shrinking and a trend to consolidation within the largest firms. The total number of firms declined from around 830 in 2003 to 733 factories in 2005. The number of small firms decreased by half, from 282 to 140, between 2003 and 2005 (UNDP 2006; Kelegama 2009). This structural change has been accelerated in recent years, as in 2008 the number of exporting firms dropped to 350 but production capacity remained quite stable. The number of employees dropped from more than 340,000 in 2003 to around 273,600 in 2005, which reflects a decline of nearly 20 percent. Most displacement occurred in the SMEs, in which 130,000 workers were employed out of the total of 340,000 in 2003 (UNDP 2006). Smaller firms had depended particularly on MFA quotas, and many small and medium-scale players either shut down or were acquired by or merged with larger firms; some started

to work as subcontractors for large firms. Larger firms were generally better prepared for the MFA phaseout. In particular, the largest firms such
as MAS (today the largest apparel firm in Sri Lanka[3]) and Brandix (today
the second largest apparel firm in Sri Lanka[4]) had invested in new
technology and machinery, developed broader capabilities, and established
direct relationships with buyers to counter post-MFA challenges.

The resilience of Sri Lanka's apparel exports in the first years after the
MFA phaseout can be explained by several factors. The United States and
the EU established safeguard quotas against imports from China from
2005 until the end of 2008, which cushioned the impact of the MFA
phaseout. Nearly one-third of Sri Lanka's exports to the EU and one-fifth
to the United States involved categories that were placed under safeguards (Wijayasiri and Dissanayake 2008). However, the positive development cannot solely be explained by the China safeguards. Other
factors were important, in particular the GSP+, through which Sri Lanka
received duty-free access to the EU market in July 2005; important
upgrading processes with regard to production processes, products, and
capabilities that have taken place in Sri Lanka's apparel sector since the
1980s and 1990s, in particular in the largest firms; and proactive policies
of industry actors who came together in 2002 to develop a five-year
strategy with the objective of preparing the apparel industry in Sri Lanka
for the MFA phaseout. Further, Sri Lanka's quota dependence gradually
declined during the decade prior to the MFA phaseout, in particular
when quota-free entry to the EU was granted in March 2001. In the early
2000s, only around 55 percent of overall apparel exports were quota
dependent (Kelegama 2009). Developments in recent years, however,
draw a rather gloomy picture of Sri Lanka's apparel sector. The sector is
divided between large, very capable firms that dominate exports and
smaller, less capable firms. The largest three firms—MAS ($700 million
business volume per year), Brandix ($370 million business volume), and
Hirdaramani ($250 million business volume)[5]—account for a large share
of the total export industry, have direct relationships with buyers,
upgraded their capabilities, and fared well post-MFA.

Structure of the Apparel Industry

Types of Firms

FDI played a central role in establishing the apparel industry in Sri
Lanka—either through foreign ownership or through joint ventures,
which have been common among the largest local apparel manufacturers.

In particular, joint ventures brought crucial technology, know-how, and skills to Sri Lanka. However, the industry soon became dominated by local firms. Already by the early 1990s, local firms dominated the apparel industry in Sri Lanka; in 1999, around 80–85 percent of the factories were locally owned (Kelegama and Wijayasiri 2004). According to BOI data, FDI accounted for about 50 percent of total investment (cumulative) in the apparel sector—either wholly owned or jointly owned in the early 2000s (USITC 2004). Today, FDI plays a more limited role in the apparel sector, but FDI has recently increased in the textile sector.

Besides important variations within the industry, there has been significant functional upgrading in Sri Lanka's apparel sector. A central objective of the five-year strategy that was developed in the context of the MFA phaseout was the transformation of the industry from a contract manufacturer to a provider of fully integrated services. An important part of the apparel sector in Sri Lanka today provides full manufacturing services offering input sourcing and at least an understanding of product development and design. These efforts were driven by large manufacturers such as Brandix and MAS, which started in the early 1990s to increase their capabilities and develop broader services. They established their own design centers with in-house designers that work closely with the design teams of brand owners, interpreting their designs, making suggestions, and sometimes even giving ideas. MAS has even established design studios in the United Kingdom, the United States, and Hong Kong SAR, China, to offer design solutions to its main customers Victoria's Secret, Gap, and Speedo. Brandix has not opened design centers abroad but has marketing offices in New York and London to improve linkages with buyers (Wijayasiri and Dissanayake 2008).

Some large manufacturers have also established their own brands. For instance, MAS developed a range of intimate wear under the brand Amante in 2007. This is a significant innovation, as Sri Lanka's apparel industry until then did not possess any brands. Amante was first introduced in Bangalore, Chennai, and Hyderabad, but MAS aims to expand across India and to the rest of South Asia, with further potential in the Middle East. The brand caters to the middle- and upper-income consumers and competes with international brands such as La Senza, (Wijayasiri and Dissanayake 2008). Brandix has also developed its own brand. Large manufacturers also established plants abroad. Such investments enhance upgrading whereby firms in Sri Lanka take an intermediary role of managing and organizing regional and international production and sourcing networks. Sri Lankan apparel manufacturers have opened factories in

Jordan, Kenya, Madagascar, Maldives, Mauritius, and more recently in Bangladesh, India, and elsewhere in South Asia. For instance, Brandix and MAS have set up textile and apparel industrial parks in India.[6] Both manufacturers had already established plants in other countries, but their investments in India are at a much larger scale than previous initiatives, which were mainly driven by availability of quotas.

Technology levels of Sri Lanka's apparel sector vary. Large manufacturers have invested in the latest technology and in workforce development, while SMEs use simpler technology (JAAF 2002). JAAF launched the Productivity Improvement Program (PIP) in 2004 in the context of the five-year strategy to reduce waste, provide leaner organizations, and increase productivity in factories. The large manufacturers in Sri Lanka have been engaged in implementing lean manufacturing methods in their production processes to reduce wastage and lead times and to lower production costs. For instance, MAS started a lean manufacturing drive called MAS Operating System (MOS) based on the Toyota model. The largest manufacturers have also invested in supply chain–enabling technologies such as enterprise resource planning (ERP) systems, as the efficient management of supply chains has become increasingly important in the apparel sector (Wijayasiri and Dissanayake 2008).

More recently, the three largest manufacturers have started to invest in environmentally compliant facilities due to growing concerns regarding the environmental impact of industries and pressure from buyers to adhere to environment-friendly standards. Green manufacturing plants involve a method of manufacturing that minimizes waste and pollution, achieved through product and process design. MAS, Brandix, and Hirdaramani have invested in "green factories" that minimize environmental impacts, especially through the reduction of energy and water consumption.[7]

End Markets

Sri Lanka's apparel exports are highly concentrated with regard to export markets, as well as buyers. The EU-15 and the United States together comprise 87 percent of Sri Lanka's total apparel exports, with the EU-15 accounting for 51 percent and the United States for 36 percent in 2009 (table 15.5). Within the EU-15, exports are concentrated toward the United Kingdom (which accounts for nearly two-thirds of total EU-15 exports), Italy, Germany, and France. The only other important export markets are Turkey (1.8 percent), Canada (1.5 percent), and the United Arab Emirates (1.3 percent). The concentration toward the United States and the EU-15, however, has slightly decreased. There has been increased

Table 15.5   Top Five Sri Lankan Apparel Export Markets, 1995, 2000, 2005, 2008, and 2009

Country/ economy/ region	Value ($, million)					Market share (%)				
	1995	2000	2005	2008	2009	1995	2000	2005	2008	2009
World	**1,680**	**2,518**	**3,082**	**3,809**	**3,532**					
EU-15	619	834	1,159	1,859	1,814	36.9	33.1	37.6	48.8	51.4
United States	977	1,554	1,749	1,569	1,272	58.2	61.7	56.8	41.2	36.0
Turkey	n.a.	n.a.	n.a.	59	62	n.a.	n.a.	n.a.	1.5	1.8
Canada	31	44	46	54	51	1.9	1.8	1.5	1.4	1.5
United Arab Emirates	n.a.	n.a.	n.a.	n.a.	47	n.a.	n.a.	n.a.	n.a.	1.3
Russian Federation	n.a.	n.a.	n.a.	30	n.a.	n.a.	n.a.	n.a.	0.8	n.a.
Japan	17	15	16	n.a.	n.a.	1.0	0.6	0.5	n.a.	n.a.
Mexico	n.a.	n.a.	18	n.a.	n.a.	n.a.	n.a.	0.6	n.a.	n.a.
Hong Kong SAR, China	n.a.	11	n.a.	n.a.	n.a.	n.a.	0.4	n.a.	n.a.	n.a.
Korea, Rep.	10	n.a.	n.a.	n.a.	n.a.	0.6	n.a.	n.a.	n.a.	n.a.
Top five share	**1,655**	**2,458**	**2,988**	**3,571**	**3,247**	**98.5**	**97.6**	**96.9**	**93.7**	**91.9**

Source: United Nations Commodity Trade Statistics Database (UN Comtrade).
Note: Harmonized Commodity Description and Coding System (HS) 1992: Codes 61 and 62; exports represented by country imports from Sri Lanka; n.a. = not applicable (indicates country not in top five for given year). EU-15 = the 15 member states of the European Union (EU) as of December 31, 2003, before the new member states joined the EU: Austria, Belgium, Denmark, Finland, France, Germany, Greece, Ireland, Italy, Luxembourg, the Netherlands, Portugal, Spain, Sweden, and the United Kingdom.

concentration as well as diversification in export markets. The largest export market—the EU-15—increased its share from 33 percent in 2000 to 51 percent in 2009. This increase is related to preferential market access to the EU market and in particular GSP+, which was granted in July 2005. The United States, however, decreased its export share from 62 percent to 36 percent between 2000 and 2009. The rest of the world increased their export share from 5.2 percent in 2000 to 12.6 percent in 2009 (figure 15.2). JAAF has undertaken market development programs in France, Germany, and India to diversify export markets. Recently, JAAF called for trade negotiations with Brazil, China, Japan, and the Russian Federation and demanded from the government to expand existing trade concessions from India, in a bid to reduce its dependence on the EU-15 and the U.S. market. Intraregional trade in final apparel products remains marginal. Less than 1 percent of total apparel exports from South Asia are exported to other South Asian countries. In Sri Lanka,

Figure 15.2   Top Five Sri Lankan Apparel Export Markets, 2000 and 2009

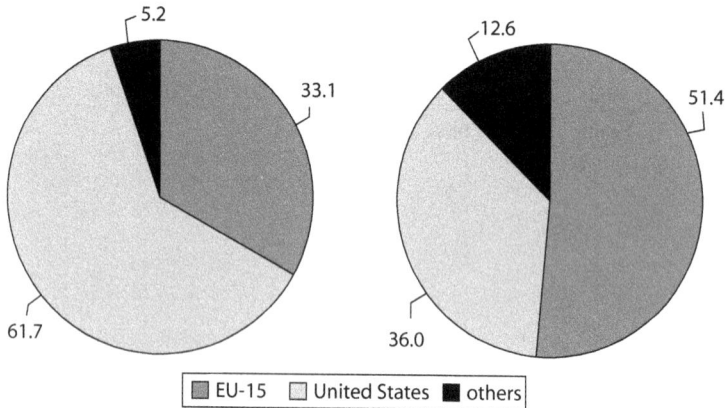

Source: United Nations Commodity Trade Statistics Database (UN Comtrade).
Note: Harmonized Commodity Description and Coding System (HS) 1992: Codes 61 and 62; exports represent country imports from Sri Lanka. EU-15 = the 15 member states of the European Union (EU) as of December 31, 2003, before the new member states joined the EU: Austria, Belgium, Denmark, Finland, France, Germany, Greece, Ireland, Italy, Luxembourg, the Netherlands, Portugal, Spain, Sweden, and the United Kingdom.

only 0.2 percent of total apparel exports went to the region in 2009, largely to India.

Export Products

Knit products have increased in importance throughout the 1990s and 2000s; today knit and woven account for an equal share of total apparel exports. Sri Lanka's apparel exports, woven and knit, are concentrated in relatively few products; however, Sri Lanka's product concentration is lower than in most Asian competitor countries. The top five product categories accounted for 41 percent of total EU-15 apparel exports in 2009 and for 48 percent in the U.S. market; the top 10 product categories, for 57.4 percent and 65.6 percent, respectively (tables 15.6 and 15.7). Product concentration levels have increased since 2000. Six products are in the top 10 list of the EU-15 and the United States. In the EU-15 and the U.S. market, cotton products dominate. Of the top 10 export products to the EU-15, 6 are cotton based, and of the U.S. top 10, 7 are cotton based. Knits constitute the majority of the top 10 products in the EU-15 (7) and the U.S. (6) markets. However, men's and women's cotton trousers constitute the top two products to the U.S. markets, accounting together for 31 percent of total U.S. exports in 2009. These two products are also important in the EU-15 market, where they rank third and fouth and together accounted for 27 percent of total apparel

Table 15.6 Top 10 U.S. Apparel Imports from Sri Lanka, 1996, 2000, 2005, 2008, and 2009

HS code	Product	Customs value ($, million)					Market share (%)				
		1996	2000	2005	2008	2009	1996	2000	2005	2008	2009
Total		**1,002**	**1,457**	**1,653**	**1,490**	**1,220**					
620462	Trousers	60	93	187	231	178	6.0	6.4	11.3	15.5	14.6
620342	Trousers	59	85	86	131	119	5.9	5.8	5.2	8.8	9.8
621210	Bras	32	71	110	102	112	3.2	4.8	6.7	6.9	9.2
611020	Sweaters	57	99	123	126	91	5.7	6.8	7.4	8.5	7.4
610821	Underwear	n.a.	n.a.	80	106	87	n.a.	n.a.	4.8	7.1	7.1
620520	Shirts	68	94	120	76	66	6.8	6.5	7.3	5.1	5.4
610462	Trousers	n.a.	n.a.	n.a.	48	45	n.a.	n.a.	n.a.	3.2	3.7
610822	Underwear	n.a.	n.a.	n.a.	40	37	n.a.	n.a.	n.a.	2.7	3.0
610510	Shirts	47	48	61	58	34	4.7	3.3	3.7	3.9	2.8
611241	Swimwear	n.a.	n.a.	n.a.	n.a.	33	n.a.	n.a.	n.a.	n.a.	2.7
611610	Gloves	n.a.	n.a.	n.a.	41	n.a.	n.a.	n.a.	n.a.	2.8	n.a.
620630	Shirts	52	88	74	n.a.	n.a.	5.2	6.0	4.5	n.a.	n.a.
620452	Skirts	n.a.	n.a.	46	n.a.	n.a.	n.a.	n.a.	2.8	n.a.	n.a.
620193	Jackets	62	84	45	n.a.	n.a.	6.2	5.8	2.7	n.a.	n.a.
611030	Sweaters	n.a.	56	n.a.	n.a.	n.a.	n.a.	3.8	n.a.	n.a.	n.a.
620293	Jackets	n.a.	45	n.a.	n.a.	n.a.	n.a.	3.1	n.a.	n.a.	n.a.
620444	Dresses	33	n.a.	n.a.	n.a.	n.a.	3.3	n.a.	n.a.	n.a.	n.a.
621142	Garments NESOI	33	n.a.	n.a.	n.a.	n.a.	3.3	n.a.	n.a.	n.a.	n.a.
Top 10 share							**50.3**	**52.4**	**56.4**	**64.4**	**65.6**

Source: U.S. International Trade Commission (USITC).

Note: Apparel classification: Harmonized Commodity Description and Coding System (HS) 1992: Woven: HS62; Knit: HS61. NESOI = not elsewhere specified or indicated; n.a. = not applicable (product not in top 10 in given year).

Table 15.7 Top 10 EU-15 Apparel Imports from Sri Lanka, 1996, 2000, 2005, 2008, and 2009

HS code	Product	Customs value (€, million)					Market share (%)				
		1996	2000	2005	2008	2009	1996	2000	2005	2008	2009
Total		**460**	**831**	**795**	**1,113**	**1,143**					
610910	T-Shirts	17	44	81	140	151	3.8	5.3	10.1	12.6	13.2
621210	Bras	n.a.	n.a.	54	113	125	n.a.	n.a.	6.8	10.1	10.9
620342	Trousers	24	51	52	69	74	5.3	6.2	6.5	6.2	6.5
620462	Trousers	n.a.	32	66	81	69	n.a.	3.8	8.2	7.2	6.1
610821	Underwear	n.a.	22	21	46	48	n.a.	2.6	2.7	4.2	4.2
610822	Underwear	n.a.	n.a.	n.a.	47	46	n.a.	n.a.	n.a.	4.2	4.0
610711	Underwear	n.a.	n.a.	n.a.	42	43	n.a.	n.a.	n.a.	3.8	3.7
611020	Sweaters	14	37	38	44	40	3.0	4.5	4.8	4.0	3.5
611610	Gloves	n.a.	25	39	42	31	n.a.	3.0	4.8	3.7	2.7
610990	T-Shirts	14	n.a.	n.a.	n.a.	30	3.0	n.a.	n.a.	n.a.	2.7
620463	Trousers	n.a.	n.a.	21	28	n.a.	n.a.	n.a.	2.7	2.5	n.a.
611030	Sweaters	26	90	36	n.a.	n.a.	5.7	10.8	4.5	n.a.	n.a.
620343	Trousers	n.a.	n.a.	23	n.a.	n.a.	n.a.	n.a.	2.9	n.a.	n.a.
620640	Shirts	48	43	n.a.	n.a.	n.a.	10.4	5.2	n.a.	n.a.	n.a.
620520	Shirts	24	28	n.a.	n.a.	n.a.	5.3	3.3	n.a.	n.a.	n.a.
610510	Shirts	13	21	n.a.	n.a.	n.a.	2.8	2.6	n.a.	n.a.	n.a.
620444	Dresses	16	n.a.	n.a.	n.a.	n.a.	3.6	n.a.	n.a.	n.a.	n.a.
620193	Jackets	13	n.a.	n.a.	n.a.	n.a.	2.8	n.a.	n.a.	n.a.	n.a.
Top 10 share							**45.7**	**47.3**	**54.0**	**58.6**	**57.4**

Source: Eurostat.

Note: Classification: Harmonized Commodity Description and Coding System (HS) 1992: Woven Apparel: HS62; Knitted Apparel: HS61. n.a. = not applicable (indicates product not in the top 10 in given year). EU-15 = the 15 member states of the European Union (EU) as of December 31, 2003, before the new member states joined the EU: Austria, Belgium, Denmark, Finland, France, Germany, Greece, Ireland, Italy, Luxembourg, the Netherlands, Portugal, Spain, Sweden, and the United Kingdom.

exports in 2009. An important feature of Sri Lanka's apparel exports is the high share of lingerie products, including underwear, bras, and swimwear, which accounted for nearly a quarter of total EU-15 and U.S. exports in 2009. In particular, the export of bras (with a complicated production process) is important in both markets, ranking second in the EU-15 and third in the United States and accounting for around 10 percent of total exports to the EU-15 and the United States.

Besides important variations within the industry, an important part of the apparel sector in Sri Lanka has upgraded to higher-value products. This change was based on a conscious effort by large manufacturers to upgrade to middle and high value-added or niche products, in particular lingerie and to a lesser extent activewear. Product upgrading efforts had started already in the late 1980s. At this time, firms such as MAS and Brandix established close relationships with buyers and started to produce more sophisticated products targeting the middle market segment. An important role in product upgrading was played by partnerships with buyers or sourcing agencies and technical experts. For instance, MAST, a large sourcing firm owned by The Limited (which also owns Victoria's Secret), began sourcing in Sri Lanka in 1979. MAST also invested in joint ventures with local entrepreneurs—beginning with Brandix in 1986. Another joint venture between MAS, MAST, and Triumph was instrumental in starting the lingerie business in Sri Lanka in the end of the 1980s and beginning of the 1990s.

Unit value analysis shows that Sri Lanka's apparel exports have generally higher unit values than those of other Asian apparel exporter countries. Unit values of apparel exports from Sri Lanka and India to the EU are the highest compared to Asian competitor countries, including Bangladesh, Cambodia, China, Pakistan, and Vietnam (Tewari 2008). Between 2004 and 2007, the average price of apparel exports to the United States fell from $64.50 to $52.20 per dozen, representing a decline of 19 percent over three years. Average unit prices for knit fell by 26 percent, but prices for woven increased by 4 percent in the same period. In the EU-15, the average price of apparel exports increased from €13.80 to €16.10 per kilogram, representing an increase of nearly 17 percent between 2004 and 2007. Average prices for knit increased by 19 percent and for woven nearly 15 percent (table 15.8). Between 2007 and 2009, the average price of apparel exports to the United States fell from $52.20 to $50.50 per dozen, representing a decline of 3 percent over two years. Average unit prices for knit fell by 12 percent but for woven prices increased by nearly 10 percent for the same period. In the EU-15, the average price of apparel exports

Table 15.8   Unit Values of Sri Lankan Exports to the EU-15 and the United States

	EU-15 unit values (€/kg)			U.S. unit values ($/dozen)		
Year	Knit	Woven	Total	Knit	Woven	Total
1995	11.60	17.30	14.60	—	—	—
1996	12.40	17.70	15.20	53.00	75.80	69.50
1997	14.00	19.10	16.60	58.60	80.60	74.60
1998	15.30	19.70	17.30	64.50	81.60	77.20
1999	16.30	18.20	17.20	59.00	76.30	71.50
2000	18.30	21.90	19.90	58.40	75.60	70.60
2001	17.90	21.10	19.40	55.50	75.00	68.80
2002	16.30	17.70	16.90	54.30	69.70	64.80
2003	13.30	15.10	14.10	52.00	71.60	65.00
2004	13.10	14.60	13.80	50.10	72.70	64.50
2005	14.60	16.50	15.50	39.40	70.40	55.40
2006	15.50	17.40	16.40	35.60	74.20	51.40
2007	15.50	16.80	16.10	36.90	75.80	52.20
2008	15.70	16.20	15.90	34.10	79.40	50.50
2009	17.40	16.70	17.10	32.40	83.30	50.50

Sources: Eurostat, volumes reported in kilograms; U.S. International Trade Commission (USITC) only includes products in which the first unit of quantity is volumes reported in dozens. Updated table and text regarding unit values to match the table: April 15, 2011.

Note: EU-15 = the 15 member states of the European Union (EU) as of December 31, 2003, before the new member states joined the EU: Austria, Belgium, Denmark, Finland, France, Germany, Greece, Ireland, Italy, Luxembourg, the Netherlands, Portugal, Spain, Sweden, and the United Kingdom. — = not available.

increased from €16.10 to €17.10 per kilogram, representing an increase of 6 percent between 2007 and 2009. Average prices for knit increased by 12 percent, but woven declined by 1 percent.

Backward Linkages

Despite the growth record of the apparel sector in Sri Lanka and government efforts to support a local textile sector, there are comparatively few local suppliers of yarn, fabrics, and accessories. On average, over 65 percent of material input (excluding labor) used in the industry are imported (Kelegama 2009). In the early 2000s, an estimated 80–90 percent of fabric and 70–90 percent of accessories were imported (Kelegama and Wijayasiri 2004). In 2005, the ratio of imported yarn and fabric to apparel exports was 60 percent, and yarn and fabric imports accounted for a fourth of overall imports to Sri Lanka (Tewari 2008). However, this situation has changed partly since then, and local sourcing of accessories and knit fabrics has increased. Based on data from JAAF, between 2003 and 2008, apparel exports increased by 38 percent, yarn imports by 63 percent, and fabric imports only by 3.3 percent, and nonfabric imports were reduced by 18 percent. Hence, there have been important developments with regard to local accessories and in particular knit fabric production. Sourcing of local accessories has increased significantly, and it is estimated that 40–50 percent of knit fabric is sourced locally but all woven fabric is still imported. There are no spinning mills in Sri Lanka, but there are four knit mills that import yarn and two woven mills that are only involved in dyeing and finishing of fabric imported in greige form.[8] There are also several accessories suppliers that produce thread, zippers, buttons, labels, and so forth and support service firms that conduct embroidery, printing, washing, and so on.

With regard to imports in 2009, the top textile importer economies are China, which accounted for 31.6 percent of total textile imports; India (20.1 percent); Hong Kong SAR, China (11.9 percent); the EU-15 (10.9 percent); and Pakistan (7.4 percent) (table 15.9).[9] The main EU export markets—France, Germany, Italy, and the United Kingdom—are also important textile suppliers, in particular Italy, which indicates that for the kind of lingerie, swimwear, and formal apparel imported by these countries, a good share of the base fabric that Sri Lankan exporters use is also supplied by its main EU buyers (Tewari 2008). Although most textile inputs are still sourced from East Asia, Sri Lanka has significantly increased regional input sourcing, being motivated by shorter lead times, more control over the supply chain, and the EU GSP scheme's regional cumulation provision. Regional textile imports accounted for 27.5 percent

Table 15.9   Top Five Textile Suppliers to Sri Lanka, 1995, 2000, 2005, 2008, and 2009

Country/ economy/ region	Customs value ($, million)					Market share (%)				
	1995	2000	2005	2008	2009	1995	2000	2005	2008	2009
World	930	1,075	1,404	1,640	1,417					
China	53	133	374	502	448	5.7	12.3	26.7	30.6	31.6
India	65	104	173	286	284	7.0	9.7	12.3	17.4	20.1
Hong Kong SAR, China	257	270	291	233	169	27.7	25.1	20.7	14.2	11.9
EU-15	93	93	147	191	155	10.0	8.6	10.5	11.7	10.9
Pakistan	n.a.	n.a.	99	124	105	n.a.	n.a.	7.0	7.6	7.4
Korea, Rep.	210	232	n.a.	n.a.	n.a.	22.6	21.6	n.a.	n.a.	n.a.
Top five share	679	832	1,084	1,336	1,161	73.0	77.4	77.3	81.5	81.9
SAARC	97	132	277	410	389	10.4	12.3	19.7	25.0	27.5

Source: United Nations Commodity Trade Statistics Database (UN comtrade).
Note: Standard International Trade Classification 65 Rev. 3; Sri Lanka's imports represented by country exports. SAARC = South Asian Association for Regional Cooperation; n.a. = not applicable (indicates country not in top 5 in given year). EU-15 = the 15 member states of the European Union (EU) as of December 31, 2003, before the new member states joined the EU: Austria, Belgium, Denmark, Finland, France, Germany, Greece, Ireland, Italy, Luxembourg, the Netherlands, Portugal, Spain, Sweden, and the United Kingdom.

of total textile imports in 2009, with the majority coming from India (20.1 percent) and Pakistan (7.4 percent). Textile imports from the region increased by 81 percent between 2004 and 2009, including an increase of 105 percent of Indian imports and of 45 percent of Pakistani imports.

Employment

Employment levels in Sri Lanka's apparel sector increased from 102,000 in 1990 to 340,367 in 2004. After 2004, employment declined, reaching 273,600 in 2005, but then increased again to 280,000 in 2009 (figure 15.3). With regard to the gender distribution of employment, it is widely stated that more than 90 percent of apparel workers in the 1980s and 1990s were women. However, the female employment share in the apparel sector has decreased since the 1990s and 2000s, falling below 80 percent in the second half of the 2000s. In 2009, the apparel sector accounted for roughly 14.0 percent of industrial sector employment and 20.8 percent of manufacturing employment (Central Bank of Sri Lanka 2009).

The labor force in Sri Lanka is better educated and skilled than in most other Asian countries. This can be explained by a good general education system that is free through the university level and specific education and training facilities for the apparel and textile sectors at different levels, including university degrees in technical capabilities and design. Thus, there are also workers available with technical as well as design capabilities. These skills and capabilities allow firms to offer more services to buyers. The high skills of Sri Lankan workers can be also seen in the fact

Figure 15.3   Employment in the Sri Lankan Apparel Sector, 1990–2009

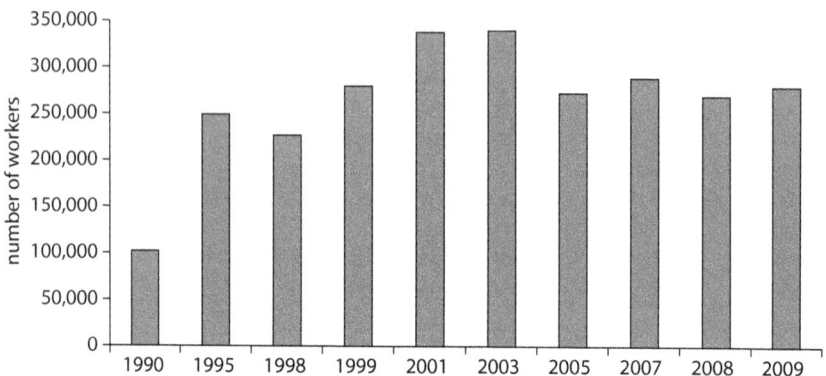

Sources: Kelegama 2005a, 2005b, 2006, 2009; Tait 2008; Just-style 2009; Saheed 2010.
Note: Employment values for 1990–98 reflect textiles and apparel.

that they work in the region as expatriates in supervisory or management positions.

Challenges with regard to labor involve comparatively high labor costs but more importantly availability of labor. Average labor costs were $0.43 per hour (including social charges) in 2008. This is twice as high as in Bangladesh and also higher than in Cambodia, Pakistan, and Vietnam but lower than in China and India. The labor shortage is related to the poor domestic image of the apparel industry due to perceived low wages and poor working conditions, as well as the reputation as a morally degrading industry because apparel workers are stigmatized as promiscuous and "bad girls." Estimates speak of around 150,000 vacancies in the industry across all skill groups (Wijayasiri and Dissanayake 2008). Around 150,000 apparel workers, mostly skilled workers, have sought employment in foreign countries, including Bangladesh, Kenya, the Maldives, Mauritius, and the Middle East, as they find higher wages and better economic and social opportunities abroad (Kelegama and Wijayasiri 2004). Besides low wages, issues such as the lack of appointment letters, long working hours, high work intensity, and in particular the lack of the right of association and collective bargaining (as many firms are reluctant to acknowledge trade unions) have been problematic in parts of the apparel sector, in particular (but not only) in smaller firms.

To improve working conditions and the international and local image of the apparel industry, JAAF established the Garment without Guilt initiative as part of the five-year strategy post-MFA. The international image-building campaign was launched in 2006 based on a buyers' survey that indicated that ethical compliance differentiates Sri Lanka from competitor countries. The campaign is a public-private partnership and is communicated through packing material and corporate communication media such as company letterheads, and there are plans to create a website to interact with buyers and consumers. A certification program is run by the industry that includes audits, and JAAF stated that more than 75 percent of firms are part of the initiative and the auditing. However, the number of certified firms has declined markedly in the past years, and in 2010, only 39 firms were listed as certified through this program (Goger 2010). Being the only country in Asia that is a signatory to 39 International Labour Organization conventions, Sri Lanka has an advantage in branding itself as a compliant supplier. The industry has also undertaken a local image-building campaign called Abhimani (pride) beginning in 2008 to improve the negative image of apparel workers in Sri Lanka, which has deterred women from joining the industry, resulting in labor shortage. Some large manufacturers have also started firm-based Corporate Social Responsibility (CSR) campaigns to address labor shortage and social compliance. Most large manufacturers provide benefits such as transportation to work; free meals; and medical care; as well as community benefits such as funding for the construction of houses, hospitals, and schools, and scholarships in the rural villages where factories are located. However, managers and CEOs do not seem to be convinced that their efforts to upgrade through Garment without Guilt (as well as the ecofactories) have paid off in terms of getting better price points, more orders, or more buyers. There is frustration among firms that they have not been rewarded for their efforts by the buyers (Goger 2010).

Trade Regulations and Proactive Policies

Preferential Market Access

Sri Lanka has enjoyed preferential market access to the EU under different GSP schemes since 2001. In March 2001, the EU granted Sri Lanka quota-free market access, but Sri Lanka still faced duties. In February 2004, the EU granted Sri Lanka a 20 percent duty concession for its compliance with international labor standards, which was in addition to an earlier 20 percent duty concession granted under the GSP General Agreement.[10] In July 2005, Sri Lanka qualified as the first South Asian country for the GSP+ scheme for vulnerable countries, permitting duty-free entry to the EU market. This development contributed to the strong growth of exports to the EU and made the EU the largest export destination of Sri Lankan apparel products. Preferential market access to the EU, however, requires the fulfillment of double transformation rules of origin (ROO), which cannot be fulfilled by all exports, in particular woven products. In 2004, Sri Lanka's utilization rate was only 28.0 percent (37.8 percent for knitted and 15.6 percent for woven apparel). The use of duty concessions could be maximized by increasing regional input sourcing based on the GSP's regional cumulation, as the EU allows for regional cumulation in the context of the South Asian Association for Regional Cooperation (SAARC). The most urgent challenge with regard to preferential market access is that the EU suspended GSP+ benefits for Sri Lanka in August 2010 due to significant shortcomings in the implementation of three United Nations human rights conventions.

At the regional level, there exists a multitude of regional cooperation and trade agreements under various stages of implementation in

South Asia, the most important one being SAARC.[11] However, despite these regional integration efforts, the potential for regional trade and investment in the apparel and textile sectors still remains largely unused. In India, Sri Lanka has benefited from duty-free market access since 2003 under the Indo-Sri Lanka bilateral free trade agreement (ILBFTA). Although textile and apparel products are under India's negative list, which includes products not eligible for tariff concessions, they are subjected to tariff rate quotas (TRQs). Thus, Sri Lanka can export 3 million pieces of apparel to India at zero duty per year under these quotas, without any entry-port or fabric restrictions. Another 5 million pieces, made of Indian fabrics, can enter India at zero duty or at a margin of preference of 75 percent—depending on the product category (*Just-style* 2010c). But Sri Lankan exporters have not used the whole quota. In 2009, only half of the quota was used, which is related to the existence of nontariff barriers, including high specific duties.

Proactive Policies

The government and the industry associations have generally been very active in supporting Sri Lanka's apparel sector, with most actions, however, being initiated by industry associations. In the context of the MFA phaseout, Sri Lanka was very active among main apparel-exporting countries and has initiated policies at different levels to secure its position in the global apparel sector post-MFA. Industry actors in Sri Lanka's apparel sector and the government came together in 2002 to develop the five-year strategy to face the MFA phaseout and associated heightened competition in the global apparel sector. An important aspect of this strategy was the establishment of the JAAF by the government and the five industry associations, including the Sri Lanka Apparel Exporters Association (SLAEA), the National Apparel Exporters Association, the Sri Lanka Chamber of Garment Exporters, the Free Trade Zone Manufacturers Association, and the Sri Lanka Garment Buying Office Association. The formation of JAAF consolidates the different associations under one roof and enabled an industrywide response to challenges in the context of the MFA phaseout. JAAF could be considered an innovation in organizational methods given that it fundamentally changed how firms interacted with one another and became the vehicle through which industry interests are promoted and through which challenges are addressed in a collaborative way (Wijayasiri and Dissanayake 2008).

Under the roof of JAAF, strengths and weaknesses of the industry were identified, and a comprehensive five-year strategy to lay the basis for post-MFA growth was developed (JAAF 2006). Nine committees were established to implement the strategic initiatives under the five-year strategy, including a secretariat to support the nine committees and oversee the implementation of the strategy. These committees (led by industry pioneers) focused on key areas such as backward integration, human resource and technology advancement, trade, SMEs, finance, logistics and infrastructure, and marketing and image building (OECD 2008; JAAF 2002; Kelegama 2005a, 2005b, 2009). The strategy had five main objectives:

- Increase the industry turnover from its 2001 level of $2.3 billion to $4.5 billion by 2007, which requires a growth rate of 12.0 percent between 2003 and 2007 (lower than the growth rate of 18.5 percent between 1989 and 2000).
- Transform the industry from a contract manufacturer to a provider of fully integrated services, including input sourcing, product development, and design, as buyers demand more functions from suppliers.
- Focus on high value-added apparel instead of low-cost apparel and penetrate premium market segments.
- Establish an international reputation as a superior manufacturer in four product areas: sportswear, casual wear, children's wear, and intimate apparel.
- Consolidate and strengthen the industry.

The strategy proposed initiatives at three levels to reach these objectives (Fonseka 2005). First, at the macro level the central issues were reduction in the costs of utilities, labor reforms, development of Electronic Data Interchange (EDI) facilities at the port and at customs, infrastructure development, and building of strong lobbies in Sri Lanka's main markets, such as Belgium, India, the United Kingdom, and the United States. Second, at the industry level the strategy realized the need for branding and promotion, research and development, market intelligence, greater market diversification, backward linkages, technological upgrading, building design, and product development skills, as well as the need to enhance productivity and reduce lead times. Third, at the firm level the central issues were reduction of manufacturing costs, upgrading of technology and human resources, and strong strategic alliances. Most large firms took steps to prepare for the MFA phaseout along these lines. They formed conglomerates, established factories overseas, introduced new technologies, established direct linkages with buyers, and increased the focus on specialized product lines (Arai 2006). For SMEs, however, it has been more difficult to pursue such strategies.

One of the main focuses of the five-year strategy was to shift the industry from a contract manufacturer to a fully integrated services supplier, including input sourcing and supply chain management, product development and design, and customer relationship management, besides strong manufacturing skills. The following steps were identified as key in functional upgrading:

- Encourage backward integration.
- Improve human resource capital and technology.
- Change labor laws and regulation.
- Promote Sri Lanka's image as a supplier with high labor standards.
- Cater to the needs of SMEs.
- Strengthen bilateral and multilateral linkages with key countries.
- Lobby the government for improved infrastructure.
- Mobilize funds to implement change.

The area of human resource development was seen as particularly important in the post-MFA environment (Kelegama 2009). JAAF's human resource development subcommittee had the objective of raising workers' productivity levels through the creation of a competent and skilled human resource pool beyond mere technological improvements. The government allocated SL 100 million to increase productivity in the apparel sector through the five-year strategy. The committee sought to implement the following six measures to reach its objective:

- Strengthen marketing capabilities.
- Create design capabilities.
- Improve productivity within firms.
- Develop technical competence.
- Enhance grassroots-level skills.
- Encourage a cohesive focus for apparel and textile education.

Five initiatives in the area of skill training have been implemented that built on already existing training facilities (Kelegama 2009):[12]

- To strengthen the design capabilities of the industry, JAAF (with the support of the Sri Lankan government) initiated a Fashion Design and Development program, which is a four-year degree course conducted at the Department of Textile and Clothing Technology at the University of Moratuwa in collaboration with the London College of Fashion (LCF). The Department of Textile and Clothing Technology was established in 1976 at the University of Moratuwa with support from the United Nations Educational, Scientific and Cultural Organization (UNESCO) and in collaboration with Leeds University for the textile part and with Manchester University for the apparel part. It offers the following textile and clothing degrees: a four-year bachelor of science in textile and apparel technology since 1993 with a specialization in either textile or apparel manufacturing; a part-time master of arts in textile studies, apparel studies, and textile and apparel management; and since 2002, the four-year bachelor degree in fashion design and product development in conjunction with the LCF. The program also has offered a variety of extension courses since 1991 for people employed in the textile and apparel sectors, including subjects such as production planning, quality control, pattern production, and merchandising.

- To strengthen the marketing competencies of the industry, JAAF in collaboration with the Chartered Institute of Marketing (CIM-UK) initiated an industry-specific professional marketing qualification. As a result, the industry has benefited from approximately 100 professionally qualified apparel marketers. The diploma is organized by the subcommittee in collaboration with CIM-UK, to strengthen linkages between local manufacturers and foreign buyers and to provide better marketing opportunities for local entrepreneurs. The postgraduate diploma course continues to be the only one of its kind in the world since its inception in July 2002 (Wijayasiri and Dissanayake 2008).

- To increase productivity, JAAF (with the support of the Sri Lankan government) initiated the Productivity Improvement Program (PIP), which started in 2004.[13] The objective of the program is to provide leaner and more effective organizations, which would result in higher productivity, lower costs, better quality, and on-time delivery (Wijayasiri and Dissanayake 2008). The PIP started at 200 selected apparel firms with the objective to increase productivity levels in these firms by 30 percent until 2007.

- To strengthen the technical capacity of the industry, JAAF entered into an agreement with the North Carolina State University (NCSU) College of Textiles in 2004 to deliver a NCSU-affiliated diploma in collaboration with the Clothing Industry Training Institute (CITI) and the Textile Training and Service Centre (TTSC). TTSC and CITI fall under the oversight of the Ministry of Industrial Development and were established in 1984 with technical assistance by the United Nations Development Programme (UNDP) and the United Nations Industrial Development Organization (UNIDO) and later the Japanese International Cooperation Agency. The two institutes were merged under the Sri Lanka Institute of Textile and Apparel. They built an alliance with NCSU to raise their training programs to world-class standards with a focus on technical competence, supply chain development, management, and industrial engineering. The Sri Lanka Institute of Textile and Apparel also organizes the Apparel Industry Suppliers Exhibition (AISEX)—a biannual exhibition for machinery suppliers to show new technology to support technology transfer in Sri Lanka; the Fabric and Accessory Sourcing Exhibition (FASE)—a fabric and accessories supplier exhibition showcasing new technology developments in the fabric and textiles around the world and improving the awareness of the local textiles manufacturers about global trends; a magazine (*Apparel Update*); and a conference (Apparel South Asia).

• Several grassroots skill training programs have been established in the context of the MFA phaseout, supported by donors. For instance, the United States Agency for International Development (USAID) created four model training centers within the 31 vocational training centers that provide training for the textile and apparel sectors (out of a total of 189 vocational training centers). The objectives are to upgrade infrastructure, equipment, and resource people at these four centers; to provide education in multiple disciplines with guaranteed employment upon completion of the program; and to empower rural youth with valuable skills and knowledge.

As part of the five-year strategy, two initiatives have been undertaken to improve the international and local image of the apparel industry—an international image-building campaign, Garments without Guilt, and a local image-building campaign, Abhimani (pride) (see preceding text).

Notes

1. The EU-15 are the 15 member states of the European Union (EU) as of December 31, 2003, before the new member states joined the EU: Austria, Belgium, Denmark, Finland, France, Germany, Greece, Ireland, Italy, Luxembourg, the Netherlands, Portugal, Spain, Sweden, and the United Kingdom.

2. At the time of the takeoff of apparel exports, the BOI was named Greater Colombo Economic Commission (GCEC); in 1992, it was renamed BOI.

3. MAS's apparel division started in 1987. Today it is a $700 million business, employs 44,000, and has over 20 production facilities in Sri Lanka and three plants in India. The intimate division accounts for $450 million and produces for buyers such as Victoria's Secret, Gap, Marks & Spencer, and Nike (the largest four buyers). The active division produces for buyers such as Adidas, Ann Taylor, Columbia, Nike, Speedo, and Reebok and involves mostly swimwear.

4. Brandix started in the 1970s. Today it is a $370 million business, employs 25,000, and has 25 production facilities in Sri Lanka and facilities in India. Brandix produces woven, knit, and lingerie apparel products to buyers such as Gap, Limited, Marks & Spencer, and Victoria's Secret.

5. A fourth large firm is Eam Maliban.

6. The Brandix India Apparel City (BIAC) located in Andra Pradesh covers 1,000 acres and was set up in 2006 with the backing of the state government. It is expected to generate a turnover of $1.2 billion and employ over 60,000 people. It aims to become India's largest vertically integrated textile and apparel venture, housing the total supply chain from fiber through spinning, knitting and weaving, trimming and accessories, apparel making and embellishment, to logistics and store services. MAS signed a Memorandum of Understanding (MOU) in 2006 to invest $200 million to set up a 750-acre park in Andra Pradesh (Wijayasiri and Dissanayake 2008).

7. The United Nations Industrial Development Organization (UNIDO) recommended Brandix's "green apparel factory" as a model of sustainable production to manufacturers around the world. The 130,000-square-foot Brandix Eco Centre is the Group's lead manufacturing plant for Marks & Spencer and has been rated Platinum under the Leadership in Energy and Environmental Design (LEED) Green Building Rating System of the U.S. Green Building Council (USGBC). Through this and other investments, Brandix aims to reduce its carbon footprint by 17 percent by December 2010, with a 30 percent cut targeted over the next two years (*Just-style* 2010b).

8. There is one weaving facility, but it only produces woven fabric for the domestic market.

9. Taiwan, China, is also an important textile supplier, but data on Taiwanese imports are not reported in the United Nations Commodity Trade Statistics Database (UN Comtrade).

10. The Republic of Moldova is the only other country that has succeeded in achieving GSP concessions for labor standards.

11. These agreements include the South Asian Association for Regional Cooperation (SAARC); the South Asian Preferential Trading Agreement

(SAPTA); the Bay of Bengal Initiative for Multi-Sectoral Economic Cooperation (BIMSTEC) involving Bangladesh, Bhutan, India, Myanmar, Nepal, Sri Lanka, and Thailand; and since 2004, the South Asian Free Trade Area (SAFTA).

12. In addition to these formal training programs, a variety of small-scale programs are run by nongovernmental organizations (NGOs) to train mostly women for employment in the industry, such as the American Center for International Labor Solidarity (ACILS), the Indian organization Community and Police (CAP), and the Italian Don Bosco. In addition, some courses running three to six months are offered by the government-run vocational training authority. Large firms such as Brandix and MAS have their own training institutes: Brandix College of Clothing Technology (BCCT, in collaboration with the Royal Melbourne Institute of Technology [RMIT], which used to be named Phoenix Clothing Training Institute before 2005, established in 1998); and MAS Institute of Management and Technology (MIMT).

13. Prior to this program, the ILO launched the Factory Improvement Program (FIP) in 2002 with funding from the U.S. Department of Labor and the Swiss Secretariat for Economic Affairs. FIP is a training program that aims to assist factories to increase their competitiveness, improve working conditions, and strengthen communication and collaboration between managers and workers. The Employers' Federation of Ceylon (EFC) together with the ILO has implemented the program with JAAF as a collaborating partner (Wijayasiri and Dissanayake 2008).

References

Arai, Etsuyo. 2006. "Readymade Garment Workers in Sri Lanka: Strategy to Survive in Competition." In *Employment in Readymade Garment Industry in Post-MFA Era: The Case of India, Bangladesh and Sri Lanka*, ed. Mayumi Murayama, 31–52. Chiba: Institute of Developing Economies. http://www.ide.go.jp/English/Publish/Jrp/pdf/jrp_140_02.pdf.

Central Bank of Sri Lanka. 2009. "Chapter 4: Prices, Wages, Employment, and Productivity." *Central Bank of Sri Lanka Annual Report*, 79–94. Colombo: Central Bank of Sri Lanka.

Fonseka, Tilak. 2005. "Survival Strategies for Sri Lanka's Garment Industry—post 2004." International conference on "After the Quota System: The Impact of the MFA Phase-Out on Growth and Employment in Asia," Colombo, April 26–27.

Gibbon, Peter. 2003. "The African Growth and Opportunity Act and the Global Commodity Chain for Clothing." *World Development* 31 (11): 1809–27.

Goger, Annelies. 2010. "Going beyond Monitoring: Ethical Regulation in the Sri Lankan Garment Industry." Unpublished working draft, Department of Geography, University of North Carolina at Chapel Hill.

JAAF (Joint Apparel Association Forum). 2002. "Sri Lanka Apparel Industry 5-Year Strategy." Joint Apparel Association Forum, Colombo.

———. 2006. "Strategy for the Apparel Industry of Sri Lanka (March Update)." Unpublished mimeograph, JAAF, Colombo.

Just-style. 2009. "Sri Lanka: Apparel Firms in Bullish Mood over GSP+." December 4.

———. 2010a. "Sri Lanka: Cuts Five-Year Export Targets by US$1bn." May 26.

———. 2010b. "Sri Lanka: Brandix 'Green' Apparel Plant Hailed as Global Model." June 16.

———. 2010c. "Sri Lanka: Apparel Industry Calls for New Trade Deals." July 20.

———. 2010d. "Sri Lankan Suppliers Shrug Off GSP+ Impact." November 19.

Kelegama, Saman. 2005a. "Ready-Made Garment Industry in Sri Lanka: Preparing to Face the Global Challenges." *Asia-Pacific Trade and Investment Review* 1 (1): 51–67.

———. 2005b. "Impact of the MFA Expiry on Sri Lanka." In *South Asia after the Quota System: Impact of the MFA Phase-out,* ed. Saman Kelegama. Colombo: Institute of Policy Studies of Sri Lanka in association with Friedrich Ebert Stiftung.

———. 2006. *Development under Stress: Sri Lankan Economy in Transition.* Sage Publications India, New Delhi.

———. 2009. "Ready-Made Garment Exports from Sri Lanka." *Journal of Contemporary Asia* 39 (4): 579–96.

Kelegama, Saman, and Janaka Wijayasiri. 2004. "Overview of the Garment Industry in Sri Lanka." In *Ready-Made Garment Industry in Sri Lanka: Facing the Global Challenge,* ed. Saman Kelegama. Colombo: Institute of Policy Studies.

OECD (Organisation for Economic Co-operation and Development). 2008. "Trade and Innovation Project. Case Study 3: The Ending of the Multi-Fibre Agreement and Innovation in Sri Lankan Textile and Clothing Industry." Trade Policy Working Paper 75, OECD, Paris.

Saheed, Hassen. 2010. "Prospects for the Textile and Clothing Industry in Sri Lanka." *Textile Outlook International* 147: 79–119.

Tait, Niki. 2008. "Textiles and Clothing in Sri Lanka: Profiles of Five Companies." *Textile Outlook International* 133: 59–81.

Tewari, Meenu. 2008. "Deepening Intraregional Trade and Investment in South Asia—The Case of the Textile and Clothing Industry." Working Paper 213, India Council for Research on International Economic Relations, New Delhi.

USITC (United States International Trade Commission). 2004. *Textile and Apparel: Assessment of the Competitiveness of Certain Foreign Suppliers to the U.S. Market*, vol. 1. Washington, DC: USITC.

UNDP (United Nations Development Programme). 2006. *Sewing Thoughts: How to Realise Human Development Gains in the Post-Quota World*, by Ratnakar Adhikari and Yumiko Yamamoto. Tracking report, UNDP, Colombo.

Wijayasiri, Janaka. 2007. "Utilization of Preferential Trade Arrangements: Sri Lanka's Experience with the EU and the U.S. GSP Schemes." Working Paper 2907, Asia-Pacific Research and Training Network on Trade (ARTNeT), an initiative of the United Nations Economic and Social Commission for Asia and the Pacific (UNESCAP) and the International Development Research Centre (IDRC), Canada.

Wijayasiri, Janaka, and Jagath Dissanayake. 2008. "Case Study 3: The Ending of the Multi-fiber Agreement and Innovation in Sri Lankan Textile and Clothing Industry, Trade and Innovation Project." Trade Policy Working Paper 75, Organisation for Economic Co-operation and Development (OECD), Paris.

CHAPTER 16

Vietnam

Overview

- Vietnam has only recently integrated into the world market and is a latecomer to apparel exporting. The adoption of the "doi-moi" reforms in 1986 marked the beginning of an export-led growth trajectory where the apparel sector has occupied a key role. Apparel exports were Vietnam's largest exports in the period 2005 to 2009 and accounted for 17 percent of Vietnam's total exports in 2009. The sector is the largest formal employer in Vietnam, providing jobs for more than 2 million people.

- Because of Vietnam's specific situation related to the Second Indochina War and the U.S. embargo (until 1994), its Council for Mutual Economic Assistance (CMEA) past and its socialist system, and its lack of membership in the World Trade Organization (WTO) (until 2007), Vietnam faced market access restrictions in the main markets of the European Union (EU) and in particular the United States. While apparel exports were initially driven by exports to Japan and the EU, since 2002, particularly, exports to the United States have fueled apparel export growth.

- As a non-WTO member, Vietnam was not directly affected by the Multi-fibre Arrangement (MFA) phaseout because it was not part of the Agreement on Textiles and Clothing (ATC). Quotas in the EU were, however, phased out in early 2005. Quotas in the United States remained until Vietnam's WTO accession in 2007. Exports still increased after the MFA phaseout and were resilient in the context of the global economic crisis.

- Vietnam's positive development after the MFA phaseout can be explained by its accession to the WTO in 2007, which improved market access and cost competitiveness. But Vietnam's apparel sector has also experienced important restructuring and upgrading with regard to production processes, capabilities, and backward linkages. The government initiated a comprehensive development strategy for the sector to cope with the post-MFA context. The main competitive advantages of Vietnam's apparel sector are low labor costs, backward linkages, and diversification toward new export markets and the domestic market. Main challenges are the skill gap, in particular with regard to technological, design and fashion, and management skills, and concentration on relatively simple low-value products.

Development of the Apparel Industry

The French laid the foundations for the textile and apparel industries in Vietnam in the late 19th century with the establishment of the Nam Dinh textile complex in the Red River Delta in Northern Vietnam. However, the sector only started to develop at a larger scale after the end of the First and Second Indochina Wars (1946–75) and in the context of the CMEA. During the 1980s, the sector evolved based on the cooperation program between Vietnam and the Soviet Union and Eastern European countries. Vietnam's role in this context was to assemble apparel products and some textiles such as embroidered products for exporting to the Soviet Union and Eastern European countries. All machines and inputs were supplied by foreign partners, and Vietnamese firms received an assembling fee for their production (cut-make-trim, CMT). However, this cooperation program did not last long due to the collapse of CMEA in the late 1980s, which had negative repercussions on Vietnam's apparel sector (Huy et al. 2001). Despite growing apparel production and exports in the 1980s, the scale of the apparel sector was relatively modest during the state socialist period, and the major phase of export-oriented development in the apparel sector started only in the early 1990s.

Against the background of internal weaknesses of the Vietnamese economy in the late 1970s and 1980s, a series of reforms was adopted starting in 1986 that gained momentum after the collapse of the Soviet bloc in 1989. The "doi-moi" (renovation) reforms were intended to transform Vietnam into a "socialist market economy under state guidance" and included the gradual liberalization of the domestic economy and the development of a private sector as well as the shift toward a more market-based system of foreign trade. A new era of export-led growth began alongside the attraction of foreign investment. State-owned enterprises (SOEs), however, still played a crucial role in the economy and the industrial development strategy. This reform process continued throughout the 1990s as Vietnam increasingly integrated into the global economy and exports increased, related to the gradual normalization of trade relations with the rest of the world.

The apparel sector played a key role in Vietnam's export-led development strategy. Other labor-intensive manufacturing industries such as footwear and electronics also became important export sectors during the 1990s, but apparel has remained the largest manufacturing sector and accounted for 16.5 percent of total export earnings in 2002. This export growth was based on SOEs that continued to play an important role in the sector, as well as on rising foreign investments, largely from other Asian countries. With regard to SOEs, reform continued throughout the 1990s, during which many of the vertical integrated textile and apparel SOEs modernized their equipment, drawing on preferential access to finance. Besides SOEs, foreign investors, in particular from Japan, the Republic of Korea, and Taiwan, China, invested in the apparel sector in the 1990s, motivated by access to low-cost labor. Thus, the share of firms with foreign participation in total output increased from 17 percent in 1995 to 30 percent in 1999 in textiles and from 18 percent to 25 percent in apparel (Huy et al. 2001).

In terms of end markets, Vietnam's main export markets differed substantially from those of other developing countries in the 1990s. Due to Vietnam's specific situation related to the Second Indochina War and the related U.S. embargo (until 1994), its CMEA past and socialist system, and its non-WTO membership (until 2007), Vietnam faced market access restrictions in the main markets of the EU-15[1] and in particular the United States. Thus, after the collapse of CMEA, the first alternative available for exporters was the Japanese market, which dominated apparel exports in the 1990s. In this context, triangular manufacturing relationships with investors from Japan, Korea, and Taiwan, China, were an important source of export growth (Huy et al. 2001). Since the early 2000s, however, the development in the Japanese market has been modest as compared to key final markets in the EU-15 and the United States.

From 1992 onward, exports to the EU also increased importantly due to the bilateral agreement concluded in 1992 and taking effect in January 1993, which secured improved market access for Vietnamese apparel exports in the EU. This agreement was widely perceived as an initial spark for the development of the sector (Huy et al. 2001; Nadvi et al. 2004b). According to the agreement, Vietnam was entitled to export to the EU market 151 categories, of which 46 were not subject to quota (Huy et al. 2001). The agreement was later followed by a broader cooperation agreement in which the EU granted most favored nation (MFN) status to Vietnam in 1995. More recently, Vietnam has also enjoyed preferential access under the EU's Generalized System of Preferences (GSP). Thus, EU imports from Vietnam are subject to a 9.6 percent average tariff, which, while better than the 12.0 percent MFN average tariff, is less advantageous than the tariff-free access for least developed countries (LDCs) such as Bangladesh and Cambodia.

Until the early 2000s, Vietnam was mostly excluded from the large U.S. market, which had played an important initial role in many other late industrializing countries. Although the United States terminated its embargo on exports from Vietnam in 1994, trade relations remained initially low (Martin 2010). Hence, in 1996, apparel exports to the United States only accounted for 2 percent of total apparel exports, while the EU accounted for 43 percent and Japan for 42 percent (Hill 1998). However, with the signing of a bilateral trade agreement in 2001, the United States granted Vietnam normal trading relations (MFN status). For apparel exports, the agreement reduced the average tariff rate from around 60.0 percent to MFN tariffs averaging at 11.5 percent and, unlike the EU preferential trade agreement, no quotas were initially foreseen. However, after significant export growth in 2002, the U.S. industry lobbied for quotas, and thus a bilateral quota agreement for selected apparel products was signed. The agreement placed quantity quotas on 38 categories of apparel imports from Vietnam from May 2003 onward.

Apparel exports have increased significantly since the early 1990s. Import data from Vietnam's trading partners show an increase from $831 million in 1995 to $4,408 million in 2004 (table 16.1). The share of Vietnam in global apparel exports increased from 0.5 percent in 1995 to 1.8 percent in 2004. Woven exports were higher than knit exports in

Table 16.1   Vietnamese Apparel Exports to the World

	1995	1998	2001	2004	2005	2006	2007	2008	2009
Total value ($, million)	831	1,263	1,522	4,408	4,737	5,931	7,694	9,541	9,395
Annual growth rate (%)	—	−0.8	−4.6	11.9	7.5	25.2	29.7	24.0	−1.5
Share of world exports (%)	0.5	0.7	0.8	1.8	1.8	2.1	2.4	2.8	3.2
Woven and knit value ($, million)									
Woven	641	996	1,232	2,848	3,068	3,738	4,532	5,358	5,051
Knit	190	267	290	1,559	1,669	2,193	3,162	4,183	4,344
Woven and knit share of total import value (%)									
Woven Share	77.2	78.9	80.9	64.6	64.8	63.0	58.9	56.2	53.8
Knit Share	22.8	21.1	19.1	35.4	35.2	37.0	41.1	43.8	46.2

Source: United Nations Commodity Trade Statistics Database (UN Comtrade).
Note: — = not available. Exports represent world imports from Vietnam; Apparel represented by Harmonized Commodity Description and Coding System (HS) 1992: Woven: HS62; Knit: HS61; growth rate reflects change from previous year.

the period 1995 to 2004 but declined in importance, accounting for 77.2 percent in 1995 and for 64.6 percent in 2004.

With regard to end markets, in the 1990s, Japan and the EU-15 were the only important end markets; up to 2002, exports did not go to the United States. In the early 2000s, Japan's share decreased and the United States emerged as an important export market, accounting for around $3,000 million or 60.7 percent of total exports in 2004 (figure 16.1).

The MFA phaseout affected Vietnam in different ways. As a non-WTO member it was not part of the ATC and, hence, it did not benefit from the abolishment of the quota regime at the end of 2004. However, it had negotiated a bilateral Market Access Agreement with the EU, which resulted in the lifting of quantitative restrictions on apparel exports in March 2005. This put Vietnam on a par with WTO members roughly two years ahead of Vietnam's WTO entry in 2007. In contrast, the U.S. bilateral textile agreement foresaw quotas for apparel exports until Vietnam's WTO accession in January 2007. But Vietnam was affected by the intensified competition and overcapacity in the global apparels sector after 2004.

Against the background of extended quotas in the U.S. market, Vietnam's performance post-MFA is particularly astonishing. According to import data by Vietnam's trading partners, total apparel exports increased to $4,737 million in 2005, which accounted for a 7.5 percent increase from 2004. Vietnam's share of global apparel exports remained

Figure 16.1   Vietnamese Apparel Exports to the EU-15, Japan, and the United States

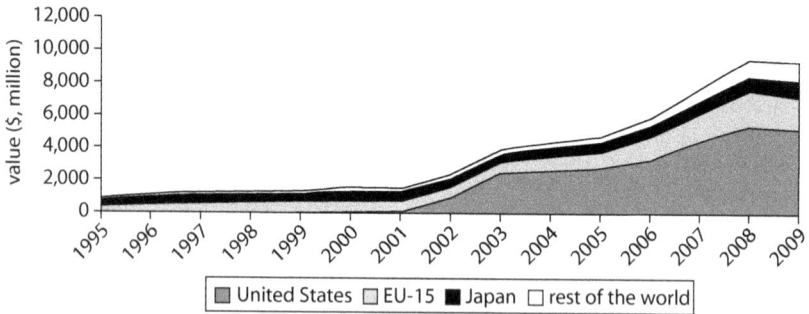

Source: United Nations Commodity Trade Statistics Database (UN Comtrade).
Note: Exports represented by imports reported by partner countries. EU-15 = the 15 member states of the
European Union (EU) as of December 31, 2003, before the new member states joined the EU: Austria, Belgium,
Denmark, Finland, France, Germany, Greece, Ireland, Italy, Luxembourg, the Netherlands, Portugal, Spain,
Sweden, and the United Kingdom.

Table 16.2   U.S. Apparel Imports from Vietnam

	1996	1998	2001	2004	2005	2006	2007	2008	2009
Total value (\$,million)	24	28	48	2,506	2,665	3,158	4,293	5,151	5,008
Annual growth rate (%)	—	9.6	1.2	7.1	6.4	18.5	35.9	20.0	−2.8
Share of all U.S. apparel imports (%)	0.1	0.1	0.1	3.7	3.8	4.3	5.7	7.0	7.8
Woven and knit value (\$ million)									
Woven	20	21	26	1,422	1,541	1,770	2,138	2,341	2,118
Knit	4	7	21	1,084	1,124	1,388	2,155	2,810	2,890
Woven and knit share of total import value (%)									
Woven	84.8	75.2	55.3	56.7	57.8	56.0	49.8	45.4	42.3
Knit	15.2	24.8	44.7	43.3	42.2	44.0	50.2	54.6	57.7

Source: United States International Trade Commission (USITC).
Note: Apparel imports represented by Harmonized Commodity Description and Coding System (HS) Codes 61
and 62; General Customs Value; growth rate reflects change from previous year. — = not available.

stable at 1.8 percent between 2004 and 2005, and increased to 2.1 percent in 2006 and 2.4 percent in 2007 (table 16.1). Viewed from its major
end markets, exports increased continuously with the exception of Japan.
In the United States, export growth was moderated by quotas until the
end of 2006. Nevertheless, Vietnam extended its market share in the U.S.
market from 3.7 percent in 2004 to 4.3 percent in 2006. In 2007, with
the elimination of quotas, exports grew by 35.9 percent, reaching
5.7 percent of total U.S. apparel imports. Exports to the EU-15 increased
by 9.0 percent in 2005 and 47.7 percent in 2006 (tables 16.2 and 16.3).

Table 16.3   EU-15 Apparel Imports from Vietnam

	1995	1998	2001	2004	2005	2006	2007	2008	2009
Total value (€, million)	271	517	738	610	664	981	1,072	1,201	1,163
Total quantity (kg, million)	15	26	40	43	50	71	92	96	79
Share of all EU-15 apparel emports (%)	0.5	0.8	0.9	0.7	0.7	1.0	1.0	1.2	1.2
Annual growth rate (%)									
Value	—	7.0	0.9	24.5	9.0	47.7	9.2	12.0	−3.1
Quantity	—	10.1	12.8	17.1	15.2	42.1	29.9	4.5	−17.6
Woven and knit value (€, million)									
Woven	240	444	621	478	504	701	778	860	846
Knit	31	72	117	132	161	280	294	341	317
Woven and knit share (%)									
Woven	88.5	86.0	84.1	78.4	75.8	71.5	72.6	71.6	72.7
Knit	11.5	14.0	15.9	21.6	24.2	28.5	27.4	28.4	27.3
Woven and knit quantity (kg, million)									
Woven	13	21	29	30	33	47	59	60	52
Knit	2	5	11	14	17	24	33	36	27

Source: Eurostat.
Note: Apparel represented by Harmonized Commodity Description and Coding System (HS) Codes 61 and 62; growth rate reflects change from previous year. kg = kilogram; — = not available. EU-15 = the 15 member states of the European Union (EU) as of December 31, 2003, before the new member states joined the EU: Austria, Belgium, Denmark, Finland, France, Germany, Greece, Ireland, Italy, Luxembourg, the Netherlands, Portugal, Spain, Sweden, and the United Kingdom.

The impact of the global economic crisis that started in 2008 but evolved particularly in 2009 has to be assessed together with the phase-out of the China safeguards at the end of 2008. Vietnam's apparel sector fared better than that of most competitor countries—with the exception of Bangladesh and China. Vietnam extended its global market share from 2.4 percent in 2007 to 2.8 percent in 2008 and to 3.2 percent in 2009 (table 16.1). Although apparel exports to its key markets—the United States and the EU-15—decreased by 2.8 percent and 3.1 percent, respectively, in 2009, this decline was relatively small compared to that of competitor countries. Hence, Vietnam extended its market share in the United States from 7.0 to 7.8 percent between 2008 and 2009 and retained a stable share of 1.2 percent in the EU-15 market. While apparel exports to the U.S. and EU-15 market fell in value terms, exports to Japan increased in 2009 as a result of the Vietnam-Japan Economic Partnership Agreement (EPA), which provided duty-free market access. Also, sales to the domestic market increased against the background of rising incomes. In particular, Vinatex (the largest SOE) increased its domestic sales by

26 percent in 2009. This expansion was fueled by the establishment of local retail channels, including 55 supermarkets and 22 fashion shops in 22 Vietnamese cities (EC 2010). However, Vietnamese producers supply only a minority share of the domestic market (30 percent), with Chinese imports supplying the majority (60 percent) (Saheed 2007).

Despite the relative resilience of apparel exports and a partial shift to production for the domestic market, the crisis had a large impact on Vietnam's apparels sector. Firms received fewer orders at prices 10–15 percent lower than the previous year. This decrease led to layoffs of 20,000 to 30,000 workers during that one-and-a-half-year period and partial closure of some plants (AFTEX 2010). In particular, smaller firms were affected as generally smaller and financially weaker firms closed during the crisis. Thus, the size of apparel firms has generally increased post-MFA.

Vietnam's positive development post-MFA can be explained by its entry to the WTO in 2007, which improved market access and eliminated quotas in the U.S. market. Further, relatively low labor costs spurred Vietnam's cost competitiveness. But Vietnam's apparel sector has also experienced important restructuring and upgrading with regard to production processes, capabilities, and backward linkages. The government initiated a comprehensive development strategy for the sector to cope with the post-MFA context that furthered competitiveness and upgrading.

Structure of the Apparel Industry

Types of Firms

According to the General Statistics Office of Vietnam, the number of apparel firms increased from 579 in 2000 to 3,174 in 2008; the number of textile firms from 408 to 1,577, respectively (table 16.4). Better Work Vietnam states that there were 3,719 textile and apparel firms in 2009, of which over 62 percent are located in the South and the Mekong Delta provinces (including Ho Chi Minh City and surrounding provinces), around 30 percent are located in the North (around the second largest city Hanoi), and 8 percent are located in the Central Areas of Vietnam. According to information from the Vietnam Textile and Apparel Association (VITAS), there existed 3,176 textile and apparel firms in 2009, of which 2,424 were apparel firms, 145 spinning mills, 401 weaving mills, 105 knitting mills, and 94 dyeing and finishing plants (table 16.5).

In terms of ownership, there are three types of firms in Vietnam—SOEs, locally owned private firms, and foreign-owned firms. With regard to

Table 16.4   Number of Firms in Vietnamese Textile and Apparel Sector

	2000	2001	2002	2003	2004	2005	2006	2007	2008
Textile	408	491	626	708	843	1,046	1,250	1,367	1,577
Apparel	579	763	996	1,211	1,567	1,745	1,958	2,352	3,174
Total	**987**	**1,254**	**1,622**	**1,919**	**2,410**	**2,791**	**3,208**	**3,719**	**4,751**

Source: General Statistics Office Vietnam, http://www.gso.gov.vn.

Table 16.5   Vietnamese Apparel Production Capacity, 2009

	Number of firms	Number of machines	Annual capacity
Spinning	145	3,789,000 spindles	350,000 tons
Weaving	401	21,800 units	1,000 mil sqm
Knitting	105	3,800 units	200,000 tons
Nonwoven	7	n.a	5,000 tons
Dyeing and finishing	94	1,109 units	700 mil sqm
Apparel	2,424	918,700 units	2,400 mil units

Source: Vietnam Textile and Apparel Association (VITAS).
Note: n.a. = not applicable; sqm = million square meters; mil = million.

apparel output, SOEs' share dropped from 32.0 percent in 2000 to 8.8 percent in 2009, while foreign firms increased their share from 25.0 to 47.0 percent in the same time period. In the textile sector, the role of foreign firms also increased, albeit not as strongly as in apparel. In 2009, 37 percent of textile output was accounted for by foreign firms compared to 26 percent in 2000, while the share of SOEs fell from 51 percent in 2000 to 24 percent in 2009 (Huy et al. 2001; table 16.6).

With regard to number of firms, SOEs account for roughly 2.0 percent of the 3,719 textile and apparel firms; co-ownership between state-owned and privately owned firms accounts for 76.0 percent; and the remaining 18.5 percent and 4.0 percent are foreign-owned firms and corporative alliances, respectively (Better Work Vietnam 2011). Although the number of SOEs has decreased, they still have a central role, and the largest SOE—Vinatex—accounted for more than 20 percent of total exports in 2009.[2]

SOEs tend to be large in size, often employing several thousands of workers. SOEs have had several advantages over private firms due to their direct access to the state system, including preferred status during quota assignments and access to investment funds (Huy et al. 2001; Nadvi et al. 2004b). The locally owned private firms are usually medium-size

Table 16.6   Vietnamese Textile and Apparel Sector Output, by Ownership

percent

	2005	2006	2007	2008	2009
Textiles					
State	39.0	34.0	28.0	25.0	24.0
Domestic private	16.0	20.0	27.0	28.0	26.0
Household sector	13.0	12.0	12.0	11.0	12.0
Collective	1.0	1.0	1.0	1.0	1.0
Foreign direct investment	31.0	33.0	32.0	35.0	37.0
Apparel					
State	25.0	20.6	13.4	10.3	8.8
Domestic private	21.9	25.5	30.0	31.1	29.8
Household sector	15.7	14.6	14.5	13.5	14.2
Collective	0.4	0.3	0.2	0.3	0.2
Foreign direct investment	37.0	39.0	41.9	44.8	47.0

Source: General Statistics Office Vietnam, http://www.gso.gov.vn.

owner-managed firms. The third category of firms is firms with foreign participation, which have increased since the late 1990s. In particular, investors from East Asia, including Korea and Taiwan, China, and to a lesser extent Japan, have entered joint ventures with SOEs and later increasingly set up 100 percent-owned subsidiaries that are focused almost exclusively on exports (Huy et al. 2001; Schaumburg-Müller 2009).

Based on 23 interviews, Goto (2007) concludes that an average apparel supplier in Vietnam produced 67 percent CMT and 33 percent free on board (FOB), based on total sales amount. However, as CMT is understated in value terms because FOB also includes the price of raw materials, data in volume terms are more adequate. In volume terms, Goto (2007) came up with 95 percent CMT and 5 percent FOB.[3] The three types of apparel firms discussed previously fulfill generally different functions in the global value chain (GVC). Domestic private firms tend to be locked into CMT positions, while the larger SOEs have more functional responsibility in the chain as mostly FOB producers. SOEs are generally in charge of input sourcing, also through their vertically integrated production units, and are less dependent on buyers with regard to production requirements (Nadvi et al. 2004a). SOEs can take larger orders, can manufacture a relatively wide product range, and are better able to meet global buyers' standards, in particular in terms of labor. They also aim to produce more up-market products and try to develop own-brand products for the international market (Schaumburg-Müller 2009). Foreign-owned subsidiaries tend to cater to the needs of their headquarters. There is limited room for functional upgrading of these plants as higher-value functions remain with the overseas headquarters. A recent survey carried out by the Central Institute for Economic Management (CIEM) focusing on 100 percent foreign-invested firms in the apparel industry in the Binh Duong, Dong Nai, Hai Duong, Hung Yen, and Vung Tau provinces revealed that these firms carry out relatively simple manufacturing activities with key business functions, including design, logistics, and retail, remaining overseas (CIEM 2010). Hence, besides FOB activities among SOEs and even some initiatives with regard to original equipment manufacturing (OEM) and original brand manufacturing (OBM) production, Vietnam's apparel sector is concentrated in CMT production.

A substantive number of Vietnamese firms produce own-brand products for the domestic market. Also, some large SOEs have their own retail outlets in major cities, but the items sold are often overproduced export items (Goto 2007). However, the focus on the domestic market seems to be increasing in the strategy of Vinatex and other locally owned firms. In particular, the mid-market is targeted by brands such as Foci, Ninomaxx, PT 2000, and Wow. Vietnamese firms also supply a number of high-quality brands to the domestic market, including Vee Sendy, Viettien, and TT-up. Inexpensive lady's and children's wear for the rural population appears to be a further promising segment (GTIA 2010).

At an aggregate level, investments during the 1990s and 2000s promoted significant productivity increases in Vietnam's apparel and textile sector (AFTEX 2010). But these productivity gains were unevenly distributed across the different types of firms. Foreign-owned firms generally use more modern production processes and machinery. Some SOEs, in particular Vinatex, have invested heavily to modernize equipment and production processes. Since 2005, Vinatex has invested $800 to $900 million in its modernization, including the renovation and improvement of obsolete facilities, resulting in productivity and quality levels that now meet regional and international standards; the establishment of a number of new vertically integrated spinning, weaving, knitting, and finishing factories; the establishment of local synthetic fiber plants; and the complete capitalization of all its former state-owned textile and apparel firms (AFTEX 2010).

End Markets

Vietnam's major apparel markets are concentrated with the EU-15, Japan, and the United States, accounting for 87.5 percent in 2009 (table 16.7). However, the composition of final markets has changed significantly. In particular, exports to the United States have come

Table 16.7 Top Five Vietnamese Apparel Export Markets, 1995, 2000, 2005, 2008, and 2009

Country/ economy-region	Customs value ($, million)					Market share (%)				
	1995	2000	2005	2008	2009	1995	2000	2005	2008	2009
World	**831**	**1,595**	**4,737**	**9,541**	**9,395**					
United States	18	53	2,832	5,417	5,225	2.2	3.3	59.8	56.8	55.6
EU-15	361	749	947	2,190	1,989	43.4	47.0	20.0	22.9	21.2
Japan	366	580	587	836	1,007	44.1	36.4	12.4	8.8	10.7
Canada	n.a.	23	87	215	239	n.a.	1.5	1.8	2.3	2.5
Korea, Rep.	22	35	41	n.a.	216	2.6	2.2	0.9	n.a.	2.3
Russian Federation	n.a.	n.a.	n.a.	132	n.a.	n.a.	n.a.	n.a.	1.4	n.a.
Singapore	11	n.a.	n.a.	n.a.	n.a.	1.3	n.a.	n.a.	n.a.	n.a.
Top five share	**778**	**1,440**	**4,494**	**8,789**	**8,675**	**93.5**	**90.3**	**94.9**	**92.1**	**92.3**

Source: United Nations Commodity Trade Statistics Database (UN Comtrade).

Note: Apparel represented by Harmonized Commodity Description and Coding System (HS) 1992: Codes 61 and 62); exports represented by partner country imports. n.a. = not applicable (indicates country not in top five in given year). EU-15 = the 15 member states of the European Union (EU) as of December 31, 2003, before the new member states joined the EU: Austria, Belgium, Denmark, Finland, France, Germany, Greece, Ireland, Italy, Luxembourg, the Netherlands, Portugal, Spain, Sweden, and the United Kingdom.

to dominate the apparel sector. In 2009, the U.S. market absorbed 55.6 percent of Vietnamese apparel exports, whereas in 2000, exports to the United States were almost nonexistent, with a 3.3 percent share (figure 16.2). In contrast, the shares of the EU-15 and Japan fell from 47.0 percent and 36.4 percent in 2000 to 21.2 percent and 10.7 percent in 2009, respectively. Two other, albeit less significant, end markets are Canada and Korea, which account for 2.5 percent and 2.3 percent of exports, respectively. Exports to Japan and Korea have increased since 2008 due to bilateral trade agreements with these countries. Firms are also increasingly looking to the domestic market and to nontraditional markets such as the Middle East (Thoburn 2009). Apparel exports to Association of South East Asian Nations (ASEAN) countries are very limited and have declined. They accounted for only 0.4 percent of total apparel exports in 2009, decreasing from 2.3 percent in 2000.

Export Products
Vietnam's apparel exports are almost equally divided between woven and knit apparel items, with 53.8 percent and 46.2 percent shares, respectively, in 2009. Until 2000, woven items dominated exports, accounting for

Figure 16.2   Top Five Vietnamese Apparel Export Markets, 2000 and 2009

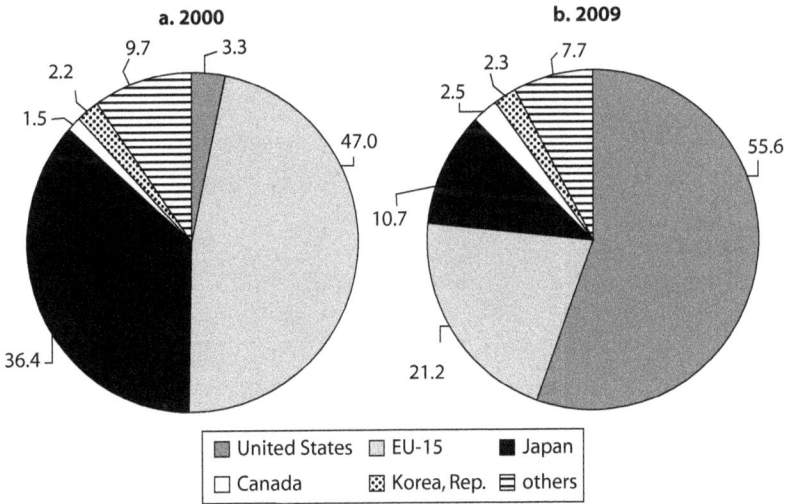

a. 2000
9.7   3.3
2.2
1.5
47.0
10.7
36.4
21.2

b. 2009
2.3   7.7
2.5
55.6
21.2

■ United States   ☐ EU-15   ■ Japan
☐ Canada   ⊠ Korea, Rep.   ☰ others

Source: United Nations Commodity Trade Statistics Database (UN Comtrade).
Note: Harmonized Commodity Description and Coding System (HS) 1992: Codes 61 and 62; exports represent partners' imports from Vietnam. EU-15 = the 15 member states of the European Union (EU) as of December 31, 2003, before the new member states joined the EU: Austria, Belgium, Denmark, Finland, France, Germany, Greece, Ireland, Italy, Luxembourg, the Netherlands, Portugal, Spain, Sweden, and the United Kingdom.

around 75–80 percent of total exports. Vietnam's apparel exports, woven and knit, are concentrated in a few products; however, the concentration is lower than in competitor countries such as Bangladesh and Cambodia. The top 5 product categories accounted for 39.5 percent of total U.S. apparel exports in 2009 and for 32.2 percent in the EU-15 market; the top 10 product categories, for 53.8 percent and 50.6 percent, respectively (tables 16.8 and 16.9). However, market product concentration levels have decreased in the 2000s for both the EU-15 and the U.S. market. The top export product categories to the United States and the EU-15 are overlapping—6 of the top 10 products appear in the U.S. and the EU-15 list. Among the top 10 products in the U.S. and the EU-15 market, knit and woven items are of different importance. In the U.S. market, knit products account for 6 out of the top 10 product categories. In contrast, in the EU-15, 8 out of the top 10 products were woven items in 2009. The most important products in both markets are trousers, sweaters and sweat-shirts, and shirts. Jackets are of greater importance in the EU-15 market, while T-shirts have greater significance in the U.S. market. Of the top 10 export products to the United States, 8 are cotton based and only 1 is based on man-made fiber (MMF) and 1 on synthetic fiber. In the EU-15 market, the situation is more diversified: the top 10 products include 4 cotton, 3 MMF, 2 synthetic, and 1 "plastic covered" product.

Unit values of Vietnam's apparel exports to the United States and the EU-15 generally declined or stagnated post-MFA. In the United States, average unit values decreased from $56.90 per dozen in 2004 to $45.00 in 2009. In the case of the EU-15, average unit values remained quite stable between 2004 and 2009, accounting for €14.20 and €R14.70 per kilogram, respectively (table 16.10).

Backward Linkages

Since the advent of the doi-moi reforms in 1986, Vietnam has success-fully modernized and reformed part of its SOEs. In the context of the textile sector, this reform has involved significant reduction of the work-force alongside rising textile output due to labor productivity increases. An important share of the remaining SOEs is vertically integrated—from spinning to weaving and knitting to apparel assembly. In contrast, the ris-ing numbers of locally owned private firms as well as many of the foreign-owned firms are not vertically integrated but focus on apparel assembly (Nadvi et al. 2004a). But foreign investments in the textile sector have increased, which can be seen by Korean and Taiwanese investments in cotton and synthetic fabrics. Some locally owned private firms have also

Table 16.8 Top 10 U.S. Apparel Imports from Vietnam, 2003, 2005, 2008, and 2009

HS code	Product	Customs value ($, million)				Market share (%)			
		2003	2005	2008	2009	2003	2005	2008	2009
Total		**2,340**	**2,665**	**5,151**	**5,008**				
611020	Sweatshirts	430	363	838	837	18.4	13.6	16.3	16.7
620462	Trousers	296	276	471	416	12.7	10.3	9.1	8.3
611030	Sweatshirts	74	73	246	293	3.2	2.7	4.8	5.8
620342	Trousers	237	136	254	246	10.1	5.1	4.9	4.9
610910	T-Shirts	n.a.	n.a.	198	193	n.a.	n.a.	3.8	3.8
610462	Trousers	78	n.a.	149	175	3.3	n.a.	2.9	3.5
610610	Shirts	74	81	172	143	3.2	3.1	3.3	2.8
620520	Shirts	62	110	n.a.	136	2.6	4.1	n.a.	2.7
620463	Trousers	n.a.	n.a.	151	135	n.a.	n.a.	2.9	2.7
610510	Shirts	98	101	139	121	4.2	3.8	2.7	2.4
620193	Jackets	128	167	164	n.a.	5.5	6.3	3.2	n.a.
620293	Jackets	73	97	n.a.	n.a.	3.1	3.6	n.a.	n.a.
620343	Trousers	n.a.	61	n.a.	n.a.	n.a.	2.3	n.a.	n.a.
Top 10 share		**1,550**	**1,464**	**2,782**	**2,693**	**66.2**	**54.9**	**54.0**	**53.8**

Source: U.S. International Trade Commission (USITC).

Note: U.S. Imports General Customs Value; Apparel represented by Harmonized Commodity Description and Coding System (HS) Codes 61 and 62; n.a. = not applicable (indicates product not in the top 10 in given year).

Table 16.9 Top 10 EU-15 Apparel Imports from Vietnam, 1998, 2000, 2005, 2008, and 2009

HS code	Product	Customs value (€, million)					Market share (%)				
		1998	2000	2005	2008	2009	1998	2000	2005	2008	2009
Total		**517**	**732**	**664**	**1,201**	**1,163**					
620520	Shirts	59	72	66	86	93	11.4	9.8	10.0	7.1	8.0
620193	Jackets	114	187	65	74	89	22.1	25.5	9.8	6.2	7.6
620463	Trousers	n.a.	n.a.	32	77	73	n.a.	n.a.	4.8	6.4	6.3
620293	Jackets	88	97	52	66	62	17.1	13.3	7.8	5.5	5.3
620343	Trousers	8	18	29	62	59	1.6	2.5	4.3	5.2	5.0
611030	Sweatshirts	13	17	30	64	52	2.6	2.4	4.5	5.4	4.5
620462	Trousers	n.a.	n.a.	n.a.	47	42	n.a.	n.a.	n.a.	3.9	3.6
620342	Trousers	17	19	32	57	41	3.3	2.6	4.8	4.7	3.5
621040	Garments	n.a.	n.a.	n.a.	n.a.	39	0.0	n.a.	n.a.	n.a.	3.3
611020	Sweatshirts	n.a.	n.a.	19	47	38	n.a.	n.a.	2.8	3.9	3.3
610910	T-Shirts	n.a.	n.a.	n.a.	43	n.a.	n.a.	n.a.	n.a.	3.6	n.a.
621210	Bras	n.a.	17	26	n.a.	n.a.	n.a.	2.3	3.9	n.a.	n.a.
620213	Overcoats	14	17	19	n.a.	n.a.	2.8	2.3	2.9	n.a.	n.a.
620192	Jackets	19	19	n.a.	n.a.	n.a.	3.7	2.6	n.a.	n.a.	n.a.
620113	Overcoats	16	16	n.a.	n.a.	n.a.	3.1	2.1	n.a.	n.a.	n.a.
621143	Garments NESOI	9	n.a.	n.a.	n.a.	n.a.	1.7	n.a.	n.a.	n.a.	n.a.
Top 10 share		**358**	**478**	**370**	**623**	**588**	**69.3**	**65.4**	**55.5**	**52.0**	**50.6**

Source: Eurostat.

Note: Apparel represented by Harmonized Commodity Description and Coding System (HS) Codes 61 and 62. NESOI = not elsewhere specified or indicated; n.a. = not applicable (indicates product not in the top 10 in given year). EU-15 = the 15 member states of the European Union (EU) as of December 31, 2003, before the new member states joined the EU: Austria, Belgium, Denmark, Finland, France, Germany, Greece, Ireland, Italy, Luxembourg, the Netherlands, Portugal, Spain, Sweden, and the United Kingdom.

Table 16.10   Unit Values of Vietnamese Apparel Exports to the EU-15 and the United States

	EU-15 unit values (€/kg)			U.S. unit values ($/dozen)		
Year	Knit	Woven	Total	Knit	Woven	Total
1995	12.80	18.50	17.60	—	—	—
1996	13.80	19.20	18.10	32.60	34.10	33.70
1997	15.60	21.40	20.30	26.00	37.80	34.00
1998	13.60	21.30	19.70	25.80	34.40	31.30
1999	13.40	20.10	18.70	30.20	33.10	32.00
2000	14.10	22.70	20.80	23.40	29.90	26.90
2001	10.60	21.70	18.60	24.00	30.20	26.80
2002	12.10	19.00	17.30	38.90	61.30	47.60
2003	6.70	16.70	13.30	39.50	61.20	48.60
2004	9.70	16.20	14.20	44.50	73.20	56.90
2005	9.70	15.20	13.40	45.90	73.00	58.10
2006	11.70	15.00	13.90	44.70	72.00	56.40
2007	8.90	13.30	11.70	44.40	69.00	53.70
2008	9.50	14.30	12.50	41.80	69.90	50.90
2009	11.80	16.20	14.70	36.70	66.50	45.00

Source: Eurostat, volumes reported in kilograms; U.S. International Trade Commission (USITC) only includes products in which the first unit of quantity is volumes reported in dozens.
Note: — = not available. EU-15 = the 15 member states of the European Union (EU) as of December 31, 2003, before the new member states joined the EU: Austria, Belgium, Denmark, Finland, France, Germany, Greece, Ireland, Italy, Luxembourg, the Netherlands, Portugal, Spain, Sweden, and the United Kingdom.

invested in the textiles sector, in particular in yarn spinning to be exported to Japan, Korea, Malaysia, and Turkey.

Despite the existence of a textile sector concentrated within SOEs, Vietnam's boom in apparel exports has relied to an important extent on imported textiles (Hill 2000; Huy et al. 2001; GTIA 2010). According to the government-sponsored "Vietnamese Competitiveness 2010" report, the sector imported 70–80 percent of its inputs in 2009 (CIEM 2010). However, Vinatex suggests that the local content ratio for exported apparel has increased steadily since 2000 and stood at 38 percent in 2009 (GTIA 2010). According to Vinatex, the domestic textile industry's annual production amounts to up to 10,000 tons of cotton fiber; 50,000 tons of man-made fiber; 260,000 tons of short-staple fiber and yarn; 15,000 tons of knitted fabric; and 680 million meters of woven fabric. Better Work Vietnam states that the industry's yearly total production capacity reaches 510,000 tons of material-processing products (cotton ginning, spinning); 300,000 tons of knitted wear; and 680 million meters of weaving fabric. Table 16.11 shows data from the *Statistical Yearbook of Vietnam* (General Statistics Office Vietnam 2010) on the output quantity of main textile and apparel products.

Table 16.11   Yearly Output Quantity of Vietnamese Textile and Apparel Products

Products	2005	2006	2007	2008	2009
Textile fibers (tons)	**259,245**	**268,582**	**384,924**	**392,915**	**396,845**
State	101,515	124,408	94,670	87,955	84,437
Nonstate	67,653	88,276	153,909	158,686	163,208
Foreign direct investment	90,078	55,898	136,345	146,274	149,200
Knitting wool (tons)	**2,983**	**2,421**	**4,828**	**6,011**	**6,766**
State	351	134	809	1,045	1,568
Nonstate	2,186	1,236	3,108	3,046	2,894
Foreign direct investment	446	1,051	911	1,920	2,304
Fabrics of all kinds (million square meters)	**560.8**	**570.3**	**700.4**	**1,076.4**	**1,087.2**
State	176.8	200.7	154.2	126.8	129.3
Nonstate	184.9	183.6	319.8	404.1	406.9
Foreign direct investment	199.1	186.0	226.4	545.5	551.0
Apparel (million pieces)	**1,010.8**	**1,155.5**	**1,936.1**	**2,045.0**	**2,290.0**
State	218.9	144.9	121.2	72.3	68.6
Nonstate	482.3	426.3	951.9	959.3	1,055.8
Foreign direct investment	309.6	584.3	863.0	1,013.4	1,165.6

Source: General Statistics Office Vietnam 2010.

In the textile sector, there has been a trend toward modernization through the adoption of new technology and the installation of advanced production facilities. Vietnam ranked fifth in 2009 with regard to shipments of shuttleless looms. Vietnam has also significantly increased purchases of machinery for knitted fabric production in recent years. In 2009, Vietnam ranked 5th in hand-knitting and semiautomatic flat knitting machinery, 8th in single jersey circular knitting machinery, and 11th in double jersey circular knitting machinery. With regard to the spinning industry, Vietnam was the third-largest purchaser of short-staple spindles in 2009 (behind China and India). The International Textile Manufacturers Federation (ITMF) estimated that in 1997–2006, firms invested in the installation of 840,132 new spindles; 19,784 pen-ended rooters; and 6,012 shuttleless looms.

Raw cotton production is quite limited; forecasts spoke of 3,000–4,000 tons in 2010, which only covers 1–2 percent of total demand for raw cotton by the domestic textile industry. Vietnam's government has launched a program aimed at boosting cotton cultivation in the country over the next decade (Adams 2010). Vietnam also lacks synthetic yarn and thread manufacturing facilities. In 2010, an initiative was started to increase the production of polyester fiber by investing in the Dinh Vu industrial zone polyester fiber mill. In 2008, the government also agreed to invest more in raw materials and accessories to reduce reliance on imports. The industry aims to produce around 490,000 tons of cotton, man-made fiber, and yarn by 2010; 750,000 tons by 2015; and 1.1 million tons by 2020 to help meet domestic production demands by 50 percent, 60 percent, and 70 percent in those respective periods (AFTEX 2010).

In 2009, 45.3 percent of textile imports came from China; 23.3 percent from Korea; 10.1 percent from Hong Kong SAR, China; 8.8 percent from Japan; and 3.4 percent from Thailand (table 16.12). Only 7.0 percent of total textile imports are sourced from the region, representing a considerable decrease from 15.5 percent in 2000. Most regional textile imports come from Thailand (3.4 percent), Indonesia (1.6 percent), Malaysia (1.6 percent), and Singapore (0.5 percent).

Employment

With more than 2 million people employed, the textile and apparel sector was the largest provider of formal employment in Vietnam in 2009 (Better Work Vietnam 2011). Alongside the growth in exports, jobs in the sector have increased significantly. Official statistics from Vietnam's General Statistics Office, however, report lower employment levels. Table 16.13 and figure 16.3 report total textile and apparel employment

Table 16.12   Top Five Textile Suppliers to Vietnam, 1995, 2000, 2005, 2008, and 2009

Country/ economy/ region	Customs value ($, million)					Market share (%)				
	1995	2000	2005	2008	2009	1995	2000	2005	2008	2009
World	735	1,060	2,543	4,755	4,913					
China	53	105	765	2,006	2,225	7.3	9.9	30.1	42.2	45.3
Korea, Rep.	338	407	736	1,168	1,145	46.0	38.4	28.9	24.6	23.3
Hong Kong SAR, China	66	69	333	509	495	9.0	6.6	13.1	10.7	10.1
Japan	98	222	311	418	431	13.4	21.0	12.2	8.8	8.8
Thailand	n.a.	n.a.	n.a.	n.a.	167	n.a.	n.a.	n.a.	n.a.	3.4
EU-15	n.a.	n.a.	90	157	n.a.	n.a.	n.a.	3.6	3.3	n.a.
Malaysia	44	67	n.a.	n.a.	n.a.	6.0	6.3	n.a.	n.a.	n.a.
Top five share	599	870	2,235	4,257	4,463	81.6	82.2	87.9	89.5	90.8
ASEAN share	120	165	234	360	346	16.4	15.5	9.2	7.6	7.0

Source: United Nations Commodity Trade Database (UN Comtrade).
Note: Textiles represented by Standard International Trade Classification (SITC) 65 Rev. 3. Imports represented by partner country exports to Vietnam. ASEAN = Association of South East Asian Nations; n.a. = not applicable (indicates country not in the top five in given year). EU-15 = the 15 member states of the European Union (EU) as of December 31, 2003, before the new member states joined the EU: Austria, Belgium, Denmark, Finland, France, Germany, Greece, Ireland, Italy, Luxembourg, the Netherlands, Portugal, Spain, Sweden, and the United Kingdom.

Table 16.13   Employment in Vietnamese Textile and Apparel Sectors

	2000	2001	2002	2003	2004	2005	2006	2007	2008
Textile	122,759	138,376	152,293	165,438	168,196	188,365	203,829	195,139	179,076
Apparel	231,948	253,613	356,395	436,342	498,226	511,278	585,414	706,093	758,274
Total	**354,707**	**391,989**	**508,688**	**601,780**	**666,422**	**699,643**	**789,243**	**901,232**	**937,350**

Source: General Statistics Office Vietnam, http://www.gso.gov.vn.

Figure 16.3   Employment in Vietnamese Textile and Apparel Sectors

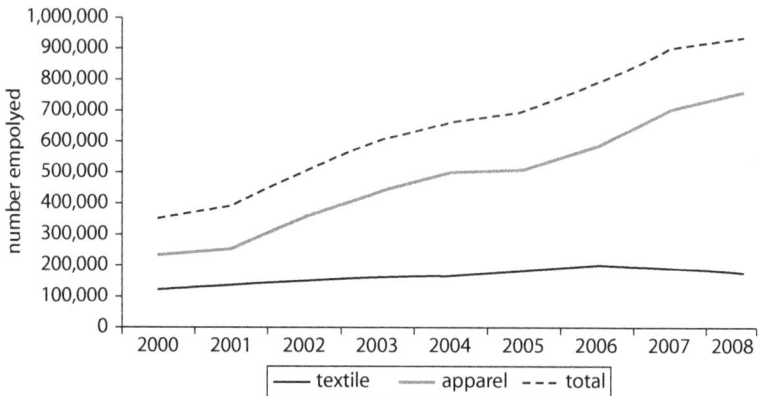

Source: General Statistics Office Vietnam, http://www.gso.gov.vn.

of 937,350 in 2008, nearly 80 percent of the total accounting for the apparel sector. This figure increased significantly from 354,707 in 2000.

Estimates indicate that the share of women working in the Vietnamese textile and apparel export sector is as high as 80 percent, while in the whole economy women account for about 44 percent of the workforce (ILO 2010). Official statistics from Vietnam's General Statistics Office report a female employment share of 83 percent for the years 2006–08 in the apparel sector, or 486,629 and 628,030 women in 2006 and 2008, respectively, and of between 64 percent and 69 percent for the same years in the textile sector, or 141,226 and 115,448 women in 2006 and 2008, respectively (table 16.14). Survey data suggest that women apparel workers tend to be young and single, with at least secondary education, and have recently migrated from the countryside (Kabeer and Anh 2006). For many of them, taking up apparel work is perceived as a step to save and take up self-employed work, hence, potentially increasing their economic independence. An earlier study found that women workers employed in SOEs and foreign-owned plants generally fared better than those working for domestic private firms and

**Table 16.14   Employment of Women and Men in Vietnamese
Textile and Apparel Sectors, 2006–08**

	2006	2007	2008
Textiles	203,829	195,139	179,076
Male	62,603	63,991	63,628
Female	141,226	131,148	115,448
Apparel	585,414	706,093	758,274
Male	98,785	118,804	130,244
Female	486,629	587,289	628,030

Source: General Statistics Office Vietnam, http://www.gso.gov.vn.

cooperatives (Kabeer and Anh 2003). There is a gender-based division of labor whereby the better-paid jobs with higher skill levels are by and large reserved for male workers and sewing jobs are largely reserved for women (Kabeer and Anh 2003).

Apparel labor costs are relatively low in Vietnam, at $0.38 per hour in 2008 (Jassin-O'Rourke Group 2008). However, they are higher than labor costs per hour in Bangladesh, Cambodia, and Pakistan—important competitor countries. Labor productivity also seems to be higher than in those countries. A study by Nathan Associates in 2007 concluded with regard to Cambodia that the difference in wages does not compensate for the higher productivity of labor in Vietnam. A critical determinant of labor productivity is the skills of workers and managers. Vietnam offers an abundant and quick-learning labor force at a relative competitive cost. However, there is a lack of skilled workers with experience in technology, marketing, and design and fashion and in important business functions such as middle management.

A key issue—not only in the textile and apparel sector but also more generally in the Vietnamese economy—is the lack of independent trade unions. Against this background, the first industrywide collective labor agreement in Vietnam, concluded between the Vietnam Textile and Apparel Trade Union and the Vietnam Textile and Apparel Association in the summer of 2010, is a positive step. The agreement came after a rise in "illegal" strikes (387 in 2006, 541 in 2007, and 773 in 2008). The agreement contains 14 articles that cover provisions on job assurance, minimum wage, and related allowances and bonuses. According to the agreement, workers' base salary for normal hours must be at least D 1.3 million ($68) to D 1.7 million ($90), depending on their region. In total, 69 firms employing more than 90,000 workers are to implement the agreement, with the majority being SOEs. Foreign Asian subsidiaries are said to fail in terms of compliance with labor standards as they tend to pay lower than minimum wages and often fail to pay social security contributions.

Better Work Vietnam was launched in 2009 by the International Labour Organization (ILO) and the International Finance Corporation (IFC). The program aims to improve compliance with labor standards and raise the competitiveness of the sector by assessing current workplace conditions and offering advisory services and training to factories. The initial focus of the program is Ho Chi Minh City and surrounding regions. Better Work Vietnam aims to improve conditions for roughly 150,000 workers in the first two years and for up to 700,000 workers over five years (Better Work Vietnam 2011). The first compliance synthesis reports provide an overview of labor conditions at 32 factories assessed by the program between December 2009 and June 2010. With respect to national labor law, the majority of findings relate to occupational safety and health, as well as working hours. In the area of compensation, assessments did not find issues with noncompliance of paying the minimum wage, though some findings did show improper payment of leave entitlements. Key findings in international labor standards are in the area of freedom of association and collective bargaining (Better Work Vietnam 2011).

Trade Regulations and Proactive Policies

Preferential Market Access

Vietnam's WTO accession in 2007 and earlier preferential market access to Japan, the EU since 1992, and the United States since 2001 have played a key role in promoting the sector. Currently, Vietnam faces preferential market access to Japan, where it has enjoyed duty-free market access since 2009 in the context of the Vietnam-Japan EPA, as well as to the EU, where Vietnam enjoys GSP status. However, in the U.S. market (Vietnam's most important export market), Vietnam's apparel exports face MFN tariffs. Vietnam's export development has also been influenced by the growth of regional trade arrangements. Vietnam's most important regional trade agreement is ASEAN, which it joined in 1995 (the same year that WTO accession talks formally began). Exports to ASEAN have been duty free since 2009. One of the principal objectives of tariff elimination within ASEAN is to stimulate the development of a regionally integrated industry, with individual countries differentiating in terms of product mix, design, and quality. As a member of ASEAN, Vietnam is part of the ASEAN-China Free Trade Agreement (ACFTA). ACFTA was signed in 2002 and is being implemented in stages. ASEAN also has a trade agreement with Korea.

Proactive Policies

Given Vietnam's socialist political system, the government has had a large role in the development of the apparel and textile sectors, together with the state-dominated industry association and trade union. The government established export processing zones (EPZs) and duty drawback regulations to allow for the duty-free import of inputs based on the condition that they are reexported as apparel products within 90–120 days. In the late 1990s, the government initiated a strategy for the development of the textile and apparel sector—the Speed-up Development Strategy for 2010. A key aim was to further vertical integration of the apparel sector, in particular by restructuring the domestic textile industry to improve the quality and availability of local textiles. In this way, the plan hoped to raise the share of local content in apparel exports from 25 percent in 2000 to 75 percent in 2010. The second important aim was to promote a shift from the dominant CMT role of Vietnamese suppliers toward FOB and later original design manufacturing (ODM) and OBM (Nadvi et al. 2004a; Goto 2007). In the context of this strategy, the government planned to invest around $3 billion in developing the textile and apparel sector during the run-up to 2010. It was envisaged that $180 million would be spent on projects to expand raw material supplies, $2.27 billion on textile and dyeing projects, $443 million on apparel projects, and $200 million on trade centers and personal training. VITAS planned to invest in (i) the manufacture of accessories (including thread, buttons, and interlining), (ii) the improvement of existing facilities, and (iii) the establishment of special industrial zones for textile and apparel manufacture. Vinatex planned to invest over $1 billion in 24 key expansion projects from 2006 to 2010. According to Vinatex, these projects aimed to develop production and distribution systems, fashion design, and infrastructure. One sector targeted for expansion is raw cotton production. To process the additional cotton produced, Vinatex planned to invest $26.7 million in the construction of five new cotton-processing mills in a bid to satisfy demand for raw materials from the country's textile producers (Saheed 2007).

To combat weaker global demand in the context of the global economic crisis, the government initiated several policies (ILO 2009):

• The Vietnamese Ministry of Industry and Trade is piloting an export credit insurance project to assist exporters.

- The Vietnamese government excluded private sector manufacturers from a recent minimum wage rise to avoid apparel industry layoffs.
- The Vietnamese government has developed a bank loan subsidy program to provide affordable working capital to businesses with fewer than 500 workers.
- The government encouraged firms to turn to the local market by initiating awareness-raising efforts to "buy Vietnamese" apparel.

More generally, the industry's strategy in 2010 reflects its attention to shifting markets, labor demographics, and the nature of business deals. The following points are seen as central (AFTEX 2010):

- Restructure production by moving textile manufacturing out of cities and into industrial parks with wastewater treatment plants to protect the environment and by moving apparel manufacturing to rural areas where labor is readily available and less expensive.
- Encourage large firms to establish and maintain long-term relationships with overseas importers and retailers.
- Add value to products by improving finishing segments and using fashion techniques (design, services, and branding) to increase customer, and thus retailer, loyalty.
- Pay proper attention to local markets regarding appropriate products, prices, and distribution channels.
- Improve the quality of life of workers through training to increase job loyalty and minimize labor disputes.
- Increase vertical integration in the apparel and textiles sector to reduce imported materials.

Notes

1. The EU-15 is the 15 member states of the European Union (EU) as of December 31, 2003, before the new member states joined the EU: Austria, Belgium, Denmark, Finland, France, Germany, Greece, Ireland, Italy, Luxembourg, the Netherlands, Portugal, Spain, Sweden, and the United Kingdom.
2. Vinatex was established in 1995 as a holding company for SOEs and comprises 90 companies today, of which 52 are joint stock companies and 38 joint venture operations. A total of 66 of these companies are actual manufacturers, while the remainder includes research institutes, educational and training facilities, commercial offices, spares suppliers, and distributors. Vinatex is involved in apparel (40 percent of total production) and textiles

(60 percent of production), and in 2009 it produced 100,000 tons of cotton and blended yarns; 3,000 tons of acrylic and wool-acrylic yarns; 1,500 tons of sewing and embroidery thread; 250 million square meters of woven and knitted fabrics; 150 million towels; 80 million pieces of woven apparel; and 50 million pieces of knitted apparel (Adams 2010). In June 2007, the Vietnamese government approved the privatization of Vinatex, which was initially expected to be completed in 2008 (Saheed 2007). However, according to the Vietnam competitiveness report, only smaller SOEs were privatized, while larger SOEs are still largely consolidated into state conglomerates and put under the direct oversight of the central government (CIEM 2010).

3. In the survey, however, there was a wide variation in how "FOB" was interpreted. FOB I (which refers to 94 percent of the cases) and FOB II (which accounts for 6 percent of the cases) are similar to what is more commonly referred to as OEM (original equipment manufacturing). In FOB III, the supplier firm develops its own designs and has changed its primary function from supplier to coordinator of its own value chain. This type of supplier is more broadly called ODM (original design manufacturing), which virtually does not exist in Vietnam.

References

Adams, Wilson. 2010. "Textiles and Clothing in Vietnam: Riding the Crest of a Wave." *Textile Outlook International* 146 (August).

AFTEX (ASEAN Federation of Textile Industries). 2010. "Vietnam's Garment and Textile Industry." http://sourceasean.com/.

Better Work Vietnam. 2011. Better Work Vietnam website. http://www.betterwork.org/sites/VietNam/English/Pages/index.aspx.

Business Monitor International. 2009. "Vietnam Textile & Clothing Report Q4 2009." Industry Report and Forecast Series, August.

CIEM (Central Institute for Economic Management, Vietnam). 2010. "Vietnam Competitiveness Report," by Christian Ketels, Nguyen Dinh Cung, Nguyen Thi Tue Anh, and Do Hong Hanh, CIEM, Hanoi. http://www.ciem.org.vn/home/en/.

EC (European Commission). 2010. "2010 Commercial Counselors Report on Vietnam." Delegation of the European Union to Vietnam, Hanoi.

General Statistics Office Vietnam. 2010. *Statistical Yearbook of Vietnam 2009.* Hanoi: Statistical Publishing House.

Goto, Kenta. 2007. "Industrial Upgrading of the Vietnamese Garment Industry: An Analysis from the Global Value Chains Perspective." Working Paper 07-1,

Ritsumeikan Center for Asia Pacific Studies Beppu, Japan. http://www
.apu.ac.jp/rcaps/?lang=english.

GTIA (Germany Trade and Investment Agency). 2010. *Vietnams Textil- und Bekleidungsbranche wächst weiter zweistellig*, by Stefanie Schmitt. Report for Germany Trade and Investment Agency, Berlin.

Hill, H. 1998. "Vietnam Textile and Garment Industry: Notable Achievements, Future Challenges." Appendix II of the Industrial Competitiveness Review, prepared for Ministry of Planning and Investment of Vietnam and United Nations Industrial Development Organization (UNIDO), Canberra.

———. 2000. "Export Success against the Odds: A Vietnamese Case Study." *World Development* 28 (2): 283–300.

ILO (International Labour Organization). 2009. "Sectoral Coverage of the Global Economic Crisis—Implications of the Global Financial and Economic Crisis on the Textile and Clothing Sector." International Labour Organization, Geneva.

———. 2010. "Labor and Social Trends in Viet Nam 2009/10." International Labour Organization, Hanoi.

Huy, Vu Quoc, Vi Tri Thanh, Nguyen Thang, Cu Chi Loi, Nguyen Thi Thanh Ha, and Nguyen Van Tien. 2001. "Trade Liberalisation and Competitiveness of Selected Industries in Vietnam Project: Analysis of Qualitative Factors Affecting Competitiveness of Textile and Garment Firms in Vietnam." Institute of Economics (Hanoi)/International Development Research Center (Canada), Hanoi.

Jassin-O'Rourke Group, L. 2008. "Global Apparel Manufacturing Labor Cost Analysis 2008, Textile and Apparel Manufacturers & Merchants." http://tammonline.com/files/GlobalApparelLaborCostSummary2008.pdf.

Kabeer, Naila, and Tran Thi Van Anh. 2003. "Global Production, Local Markets: Gender, Poverty and Export Manufacturing in Vietnam." Mimeograph, Institute of Development Studies, Brighton, U.K.

———. 2006. "Globalisation, Gender and Work in the Context of Transition: The Case of Vietnam." Working Paper 06-3, The Gender and Macro International Working Group (GEM-IWG), Salt Lake City, Utah.

Martin, Michael F. 2010. "U.S.-Vietnam Economic and Trade Relations: Issues for the 112th Congress." Congressional Research Service, Washington, DC.

Nadvi, K., J. Thoburn, T. T. Bui, T. T. H. Nguyen, T. H. Nguyen, H. L. Dao, and E. B. Armas. 2004a. "Vietnam in the Global Garment and Textile Value Chain: Impacts on Firms and Workers." *Journal of International Development* 16 (1): 111–23.

Nadvi, K., J. Thoburn, T. T. Bui, T. T. H. Nguyen, T. H. Nguyen, and H. L. Dao. 2004b. "Challenges to Vietnamese Firms in the World Garment and Textile

Value Chain, and the Implications for Alleviating Poverty." *Journal of the Asia Pacific Economy* 9 (2): 249–67.

Nathan Associates. 2007. "Factory-Level Value Chain Analysis of Cambodia's Apparel Industry." United States Agency for International Development, Washington, DC.

Saheed, Hassan. 2007. "Prospects for the Textile and Garment Industry in Vietnam." *Textile Outlook International* 129: 12–50.

Schaumburg-Müller, Henrik. 2009. "Garment Exports from Vietnam: Changes in Supplier Strategies." *Journal of the Asia Pacific Economy* 14 (2): 162–71.

Thoburn, John. 2009. "The Impact of World Recession on the Textile and Garment Industries of Asia." Working Paper 17/2009, United Nations Industrial Development Organization (UNIDO) Research and Statistics Branch, Vienna.

———. 2010. "Vietnam as a Role Model for Development." Research Paper 2009/30, United Nations University (UNU-WIDER), Helsinki, Finland.

Thomson, Lotte. 2007. "Accessing Global Value Chains? The Role of Business–State Relations in the Private Clothing Industry in Vietnam." *Journal of Economic Geography* 7: 753–76.

Vietnam Business News. 2010. "FDI Rushes into Vietnam." http://vietnambusiness .asia/fdi-rushes-into-vietnam%E2%80%99s-textile-and-garment-sector.

www.ingramcontent.com/pod-product-compliance
Lightning Source LLC
Chambersburg PA
CBHW060911220326
41599CB00020B/2922